D0860213

P 99 .593

Studies in Natural Language Processing

Survey of the state of the art in human language technology

Studies in
NATURAL
LANGUAGE
PROCESSING

LINGUISTICA
COMPUTAZIONALE
Volumes XII-XIII

Survey of the state of the art in human language technology

Managing Editors

GIOVANNI BATTISTA VARILE

ANTONIO ZAMPOLLI

Editorial Board

RONALD COLE, *Editor in Chief*

JOSEPH MARIANI

HANS USZKOREIT

ANNIE ZAENEN

VICTOR ZUE

CAMBRIDGE
UNIVERSITY PRESS

GIARDINI EDITORI
E STAMPATORI IN PISA

Published in Italy by Giardini Editori e Stampatori in Pisa

Published in the rest of the World by
THE PRESS SYNDICATE OF THE UNIVERSITY OF CAMBRIDGE
The Pitt Building, Trumpington Street, Cambridge CB2 1RP
40 West 20th Street, New York, NY 10011–4211, USA
10 Stamford Road, Oakleigh, Melbourne 3166, Australia

© Giardini Editori e Stampatori in Pisa 1997

This book is in copyright. Subject to statutory exception
and to the provisions of relevant collective licensing agreements,
no reproduction of any part may take place without
the written permission of Cambridge University Press
and Giardini Editori.

First Published 1997

Printed in Italy

Typeset in Computer Modern

A catalog record for this book is available from the British Library.

Library of Congress Cataloging-in-Publication Data available

Cambridge University Press ISBN 0-521-59277-1 Hardback

Giardini Editori ISBN 88-427-0018-5 Hardback

Contents

9   Multimodality   287

10   Transmission and Storage   323

11   Mathematical Methods   337

12 Language Resources   381

13 Evaluation   409

Forewords

Foreword by the Editor in Chief

The field of human language technology covers a broad range of activities with the eventual goal of enabling people to communicate with machines using natural communication skills. Research and development activities include the coding, recognition, interpretation, translation, and generation of language.

The study of human language technology is a multidisciplinary enterprise, requiring expertise in areas of linguistics, psychology, engineering and computer science. Creating machines that will interact with people in a graceful and natural way using language requires a deep understanding of the acoustic and symbolic structure of language (the domain of linguistics), and the mechanisms and strategies that people use to communicate with each other (the domain of psychology). Given the remarkable ability of people to converse under adverse conditions, such as noisy social gatherings or band-limited communication channels, advances in signal processing are essential to produce robust systems (the domain of electrical engineering). Advances in computer science are needed to create the architectures and platforms needed to represent and utilize all of this knowledge. Collaboration among researchers in each of these areas is needed to create multimodal and multimedia systems that combine speech, facial cues and gestures both to improve language understanding and to produce more natural and intelligible speech by animated characters.

Human language technologies play a key role in the age of information. Today, the benefits of information and services on computer networks are unavailable to those without access to computers or the skills to use them. As the importance of interactive networks increases in commerce and daily life, those who do not have access to computers or the skills to use them are further handicapped from becoming productive members of society.

Advances in human language technology offer the promise of nearly universal access to on-line information and services. Since almost everyone speaks and understands a language, the development of spoken language systems will allow the average person to interact with computers without special skills or training, using common devices such as the telephone. These systems will combine spoken language understanding and generation to allow people to interact with computers using speech to obtain information on virtually any topic, to conduct business and to communicate with each other more effectively.

Advances in the processing of speech, text and images are needed to make sense of the massive amounts of information now available via computer networks. A student's query: "Tell me about global warming," should set in motion a set of procedures that locate, organize and summarize all available information about global warming from books, periodicals, newscasts, satellite images and other sources. Translation of speech or text from one language to another is needed to access and interpret all available material and present it to the student in her native language.

This book surveys the state of the art of human language technology. The goal of the survey is to provide an interested reader with an overview of the field—the main areas of work, the capabilities and limitations of current technology, and the technical challenges that must be overcome to realize the vision of graceful human computer interaction using natural communication skills.

The book consists of thirteen chapters written by 97 different authors. In order to create a coherent and readable volume, a great deal of effort was expended to provide consistent structure and level of presentation within and across chapters. The editorial board met six times over a two-year period. During the first two meetings, the structure of the survey was defined, including topics, authors, and guidelines to authors. During each of the final four meetings (in four different countries), each author's contribution was carefully reviewed and revisions were requested, with the aim of making the survey as inclusive, up-to-date and internally consistent as possible.

This book is due to the efforts of many people. The survey was the brainchild of Oscar Garcia (then program director at the National Science Foundation in the United States), and Antonio Zampolli, professor at the University of Pisa, Italy. Oscar Garcia and Mark Liberman helped organize the survey and participated in the selection of topics and authors; their insights and contributions to the survey are gratefully acknowledged. I thank all of my colleagues on the editorial board, who dedicated remarkable amounts of time and effort to the survey. I am particularly grateful to Joseph Mariani for his diligence and support during the past two years, and to Victor Zue for his help and guidance throughout this project. I thank Hans Uszkoreit and Antonio Zampolli for their help in finding publishers. The survey owes much to the efforts of Vince Weatherill, the production editor, who worked with the editorial board and the authors to put the survey together, and to Don Colton, who indexed the book several times and copyedited much of it. Finally, on behalf of the editorial board, we thank the authors of this survey, whose talents and patience were responsible for the quality of this product.

The survey was supported by a grant from the National Science Foundation to Ron Cole, Victor Zue and Mark Liberman, and by the European Commission. Additional support was provided by the Center for Spoken Language Understanding at the Oregon Graduate Institute and the University of Pisa, Italy.

Ron Cole
Poipu Beach
Kauii, Hawaii, USA
January 31, 1996

Foreword by the Former Program Manager of the National Science Foundation

This book is the work of many different individuals whose common bond is the love for the understanding and use of spoken language between humans and with machines. I was fortunate enough to have been included in this community through the work of one of my students, Alan Goldschen, who brought to my attention almost a decade ago the intriguing problem of lipreading. Our unfinished quest for a machine which could recognize speech more robustly via acoustic and optical channels was my original motivation for entering the wide world of spoken language research so richly exemplified in this book.

I have been credited with producing the small spark which began this truly joint international work via a small National Science Foundation (NSF) award, and a parallel one abroad, while I was a rotating program officer in the Computer and Information Science and Engineering Directorate. We should remember that the International Division of NSF also contributed to the work of U.S. researchers, as did the European Commission for others in Europe. The spark occurred at a dinner meeting convened by George Doddington, then of ARPA, during the 1993 Human Language Technology Workshop at the Merril Lynch Conference Center in New Jersey. I made the casual remark to Antonio Zampolli that I thought it would be interesting and important to summarize, in a unifying piece of work, the most significant research taking place worldwide in this field. Mark Liberman, present at the dinner, was also very receptive to the concept. Zampolli heartily endorsed the idea and took it to Nino Varile of the European Commission's DG XIII. I did the same and presented it to my boss at the NSF, the very supportive Y. T. Chien, and we proceeded to recruit some likely suspects for the enormous job ahead. Both Nino and Y. T. were infected with the enthusiasm to see this work done. The rest is history, mostly punctuated by fascinating "editorial board" meetings and the gentle but unforgiving prodding of Ron Cole. Victor Zue was, on my side, a pillar of technical strength and a superb taskmaster. Among the European contributors who distinguished themselves most in the work, and there were several including Annie Zaenen and Hans Uszkoreit, from my perspective, it was Joseph Mariani with his group at the Human-Machine Communication at LIMSI/CNRS, who brought to my attention the tip of the enormous iceberg of research in Europe on speech and language, making it obvious to me that the state-of-the-art survey must be done.

From a broad perspective point of view it is not surprising that this daunting task has taken so much effort: witness the wide range of topics related to language research ranging from generation and perception to higher level cognitive functions. The thirteen chapters that have been produced are a testimony of the depth and width of research that is necessary to advance the field. I feel gratified by the contributions of people with such a variety of backgrounds and I feel particularly happy that Computer Scientists and Engineers are becoming more aware of this, making significant contributions. But in spite of the excellent work done in reporting, the real task ahead remains: the deployment of reliable and robust systems which are usable in a broad range of applications, or as I like to call it "the cosumerization of speech technology." I personally consider the spoken language challenge one of the most difficult problems among the scientific and engineering inquiries of our time, but one that has an enormous reward to be received. Gordon Bell, of computer architecture fame, once confided that he had looked at the problem, thought it inordinately difficult, and moved on to work in other areas. Perhaps this survey will motivate new Gordon Bells to dig deeper into research in human language technology.

Finally, I would like to encourage any young researcher reading this survey to plunge into the areas of most significance to them, but in an unconventional and brash manner, as I feel we did in our work in lipreading. Deep knowledge of the subject is, of course, necessary but the boundaries of the classical work should not be limiting. I feel strongly that there is need and room for new and unorthodox approaches to human-computer dialogue that will reap enormous rewards. With the advent of world-wide networked graphical interfaces there is no reason for not including the speech interactive modality in it, at great benefit and relatively low cost. These network interfaces may further erode the international barriers which travel and other means of communications have obviously started to tear down. Interfacing with computers sheds much light on how humans interact with each other, something that spoken language research has taught us.

The small NSF grant to Ron Cole, I feel, has paid magnified results. The resources of the original sponsors have been generously extended by those of the Center for Spoken Language Understanding at the Oregon Graduate Institute, and their personnel, as well as by the University of Pisa. From an ex-program officer's point of view in the IRIS Division at NSF this grant has paid great dividends to the scientific community. We owe an accolade to the principal investigator's Herculean efforts and to his cohorts at home and abroad.

Oscar N. Garcia
Wright State University
Dayton, Ohio

Foreword by the Managing Editors[1]

Language Technology and the Information Society

The information age is characterized by a fast growing amount of information being made available either in the public domain or commercially. This information is acquiring an increasingly important function for various aspects of peoples' professional, social and private life, posing a number of challenges for the development of the Information Society.

In particular, the classical notion of universal access needs to be extended beyond the guarantee for physical access to the information channels, and adapted to cover the rights for all citizens to benefit from the opportunity to easily access and effectively process information.

Furthermore, with the globalization of the economy, business competitiveness rests on the ability to effectively communicate and manage information in an international context.

Obviously, languages, communication and information are closely related. Indeed, language is the prime vehicle in which information is encoded, by which it is accessed and through which it is disseminated.

Language technology offers people the opportunity to better communicate, provides them with the possibility of accessing information in a more natural way, supports more effective ways of exchanging information and control its growing mass.

There is also an increasing need to provide easy access to multilingual information systems and to offer the possibility to handle the information they carry in a meaningful way. Languages for which no adequate computer processing is being developed, risk gradually losing their place in the global Information Society, or even disappearing, together with the cultures they embody, to the detriment of one of humanity's great assets: its cultural diversity.

What Can Language Technology Offer?

Looking back, we see that some simple functions provided by language technology have been available for some time—for instance spelling and grammar checking. Good progress has been achieved and a growing number of applications are maturing every day, bringing real benefits to citizens and business. Language technology is coming of age and its deployment allows us to cope with increasingly difficult tasks.

Every day new applications with more advanced functionality are being deployed—for instance voice access to information systems. As is the case for other information technologies, the evolution towards more complex language processing systems is rapidly accelerating, and the transfer of this technology to the market is taking place at an increasing pace.

---

[1] The ideas expressed herein are the authors' and do not reflect the policies of the European Commission and the Italian National Research Council.

More sophisticated applications will emerge over the next years and decades and find their way into our daily lives. The range of possibilities is almost unlimited. Which ones will be more successful will be determined by a number of factors, such as technological advances, market forces, and political will.

On the other hand, since sheer mass of information and high bandwidth networks are not sufficient to make information and communication systems meaningful and useful, the main issue is that of an effective use of new applications by people, which interact with information systems and communicate with each other.

Among the many issues to be addressed are difficult engineering problems and the challenge of accounting for the functioning of human languages—probably one of the most ambitious and difficult tasks.

Benefits that can be expected from deploying language technology are a more effective usability of systems (enabling the user) and enhanced capabilities for people (empowering the user). The economic and social impact will be in terms of efficiency and competitiveness for business, better educated citizens, and a more cohesive and sustainable society. A necessary precondition for all this, is that the enabling technology be available in a form ready to be integrated into applications.

The subject of the thirteen chapters of this Survey are the key language technologies required for the present applications and research issues that need to be addressed for future applications.

Aim and Structure of the Book

Given the achievements so far, the complexity of the problem, and the need to use and to integrate methods, knowledge and techniques provided by different disciplines, we felt that the time was ripe for a reasonably detailed map of the major results and open research issues in language technology. The Survey offers, as far as we know, the first comprehensive overview of the state of the art in spoken and written language technology in a single volume.

Our goal has been to present a clear overview of the key issues and their potential impact, to describe the current level of accomplishments in scientific and technical areas of language technology, and to assess the key research challenges and salient research opportunities within a five- to ten-year time frame, identifying the infrastructure needed to support this research. We have not tried to be encyclopedic; rather, we have striven to offer an assessment of the state of the art for the most important areas in language processing.

The organization of the Survey was inspired by three main principles:

- an accurate identification of the key work areas and sub-areas of each of the fields;

- a well-structured multi-layered organization of the work, to simplify the coordination between the many contributors and to provide a framework in which to carry out this international cooperation;

- a granularity and style that, given the variety of potential readers of the Survey, would make it accessible to non-specialist and at the same time to serve for specialists, as a reference for areas not directly of their own expertise.

Each of the thirteen chapters of the Survey consists of:

- an introductory overview providing the general framework for the area concerned, with the aim of facilitating the understanding and assessment of the technical contributions;

- a number of sections, each dealing with the state of the art, for a given sub-area, i.e., the major achievements, the methods and the techniques available, the unsolved problems, and the research challenges for the future.

For ease of reference, the reader may find it useful to refer to the analytical index given at the end of the book.

We hope the Survey will be a useful reference to both non-specialists and practitioners alike, and that the comments received from our readers will encourage us to edit updated and improved versions of this work.

Relevance of International Collaboration

This Survey is the result of international collaboration, which is especially important for the progress of language technology and the success of its applications, in particular those aiming at providing multilingual information or communication services. Multilingual applications require close coordination between the partners of different languages to ensure the interoperability of components and the availability of the necessary linguistic data—spoken and written corpora, lexica, terminologies, and grammars.

The major national and international funding agencies play a key role in organizing the international cooperation. They are currently sponsoring major research activities in language processing through programs that define the objectives and support the largest projects in the field. They have undertaken the definition of a concrete policy for international cooperation[2] that takes into account the specific needs and the strategic value of language technology.

Various initiatives have, in the past ten years, contributed to forming the cooperative framework in which this Survey has been organized. One such initiative was the workshop on 'Automating the Lexicon' held in Grosseto, Italy, in 1986, which involved North American and European specialists, and resulted in recommendations for an overall coordination in building reusable large scale resources.

Another one took place in Turin, Italy, in 1991, in the framework of international cooperation agreement between the NSF and the ESPRIT programme

---

[2]Several international cooperation agreements in science and technology are currently in force; more are being negotiated.

of the European Commission. The experts convened at that meeting called for cooperation in building reusable language resources, integration between spoken and written language technology—in particular the development of methods for combining rule-based and stochastic techniques—and an assessment of the state of the art.

A special event convening representatives of American, European and Japanese sponsoring agencies was organized at COLING 92 and has since become a permanent feature of this bi-annual conference. For this event, an overview[3] of some of the major American, European and Japanese projects in the field was compiled.

The present Survey is the most recent in a series of cooperative initiatives in language technology.

Acknowledgements

We wish to express our gratitude to all those who, in their different capacities, have made this Survey possible, but first of all the authors who, on a voluntary basis, have accepted our invitation, and have agreed to share their expert knowledge to provide an overview for their area of expertise.

Our warmest gratitude goes to Oscar Garcia, who co-inspired the initiative and was an invaluable colleague and friend during this project. Without his scientific competence, management capability, and dedicated efforts, this Survey would not have been realized. His successor, Gary Strong, competently and enthusiastically continued his task.

Thanks also to the commitment and dedication of the editorial board consisting of Joseph Mariani, Hans Uszkoreit, Annie Zaenen and Victor Zue. Our deep-felt thanks to Ron Cole, who coordinated the board's activities and came to serve as the volume's editor-in-chief.

Mark Liberman, of the University of Pennsylvania and initially member of the editorial board, was instrumental in having the idea of this Survey approved, and his contribution to the design of the overall content and structure was essential. Unfortunately, other important tasks called him in the course of this project.

Invaluable support to this initiative has been provided by Y.T. Chien, the director of the Computer and Information Science and Engineering Directorate of the National Science Foundation, Vincente Parajon-Collada, the deputy-director general of Directorate General XIII of the European Commission, and Roberto Cencioni head of Language Engineering sector of the Telematics Application Programme.

Vince Weatherill, of Oregon Graduate Institute, dedicated an extraordinary amount of time, care and energy to the preparation and editing of the Survey.

---

[3]Synopses of American, European and Japanese Projects Presented at the International Projects Day at COLING 1992. In: *Linguistica Computazionale*, volume VIII, Giovanni Battista Varile and Antonio Zampolli, editors, Giardini, Pisa. ISSN 0392-6907 (out of print). This volume was the direct antecedent of and the inspiration for the present survey.

Colin Brace carried out the final copyediting work within an extremely short time schedule.

The University of Pisa, Italy, the Oregon Graduate Institute, and the Institute of Computational Linguistics of the Italian National Research Council generously contributed financial and human resources.

Antonio Zampolli   **Giovanni Battista Varile**

Chapter 1

Spoken Language Input

1.1 Overview

Victor Zue[a] **& Ron Cole**[b]

[a] MIT Laboratory for Computer Science, Cambridge, Massachusetts, USA
[b] Oregon Graduate Institute of Science & Technology, Portland, Oregon, USA

Spoken language interfaces to computers is a topic that has lured and fascinated engineers and speech scientists alike for over five decades. For many, the ability to converse freely with a machine represents the ultimate challenge to our understanding of the production and perception processes involved in human speech communication. In addition to being a provocative topic, spoken language interfaces are fast becoming a necessity. In the near future, interactive networks will provide easy access to a wealth of information and services that will fundamentally affect how people work, play and conduct their daily affairs. Today, such networks are limited to people who can read and have access to computers—a relatively small part of the population, even in the most developed countries. Advances in human language technology are needed to enable the average citizen to communicate with networks using natural communication skills and everyday devices, such as telephones and televisions. Without fundamental advances in user-centered interfaces, a large portion of society will be prevented from participating in the age of information, resulting in further stratification of society and tragic loss of human potential.

The first chapter in this survey deals with spoken language *input* technologies. A speech interface, in a user's own language, is ideal because it is the most natural, flexible, efficient, and economical form of human communication. The following sections summarize spoken input technologies that will facilitate such an interface.

Spoken input to computers embodies many different technologies and applications, as illustrated in Figure 1.1. In some cases, as shown at the bottom of the figure, one is interested not in the underlying linguistic content but in the identity of the speaker or the language being spoken. Speaker recognition can involve *identifying* a specific speaker out of a known population, which has forensic implications, or *verifying* the claimed identity of a user, thus enabling controlled access to locales (e.g., a computer room) and services (e.g., voice banking). Speaker recognition technologies are addressed in section 1.7. Language identification also has important applications, and techniques applied to this area are summarized in section 8.7.

When one thinks about speaking to computers, the first image is usually speech recognition, the conversion of an acoustic signal to a stream of words. After many years of research, speech recognition technology is beginning to pass the threshold of practicality. The last decade has witnessed dramatic improvement in speech recognition technology, to the extent that high performance algorithms and systems are becoming available. In some cases, the transition from laboratory demonstration to commercial deployment has already begun. Speech input capabilities are emerging that can provide functions like voice dialing (e.g., *Call home*), call routing (e.g., *I would like to make a collect call*), simple data entry (e.g., entering a credit card number), and preparation of structured documents (e.g., a radiology report). The basic issues of speech recognition, together with a summary of the state of the art, is described in section 1.2. As these authors point out, speech recognition involves several component technologies. First, the digitized signal must be transformed into a set of measurements. This *signal representation* issue is elaborated in section 1.3. Section 1.4 discusses techniques that enable the system to achieve robustness in the presence of transducer and environmental variations, and techniques for adapting to these variations. Next, the various speech sounds must be modeled appropriately. The most widespread technique for acoustic modeling is called hidden Markov modeling (HMM), and is the subject of section 1.5. The search for the final answer involves the use of language constraints, which is covered in section 1.6.

Speech recognition is a very challenging problem in its own right, with a well defined set of applications. However, many tasks that lend themselves to spoken input—making travel arrangements or selecting a movie—are in fact exercises in interactive problem solving. The solution is often built up incrementally, with both the user and the computer playing active roles in the "conversation." Therefore, several language-based input and output technologies must be developed and integrated to reach this goal. Figure 1.1 shows the major components of a typical conversational system. The spoken input is first processed through the speech recognition component. The natural language component, working in concert with the recognizer, produces a meaning representation. The final section of this chapter on spoken language understanding technology, section 1.8, discusses the integration of speech recognition and natural language processing techniques.

For information retrieval applications illustrated in this figure, the meaning representation can be used to retrieve the appropriate information in the form of text, tables and graphics. If the information in the utterance is insufficient or ambiguous, the system may choose to query the user for clarification.

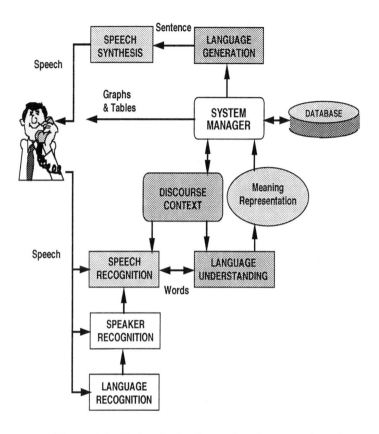

Figure 1.1: Technologies for spoken language interfaces.

Natural language generation and speech synthesis, covered in chapters 4 and 5 respectively, can be used to produce spoken responses that may serve to clarify the tabular information. Throughout the process, discourse information is maintained and fed back to the speech recognition and language understanding components, so that sentences can be properly understood in context.

1.2 Speech Recognition

Victor Zue,[a] Ron Cole,[b] & Wayne Ward[c]

[a] MIT Laboratory for Computer Science, Cambridge, Massachusetts, USA
[b] Oregon Graduate Institute of Science & Technology, Portland, Oregon, USA
[c] Carnegie Mellon University, Pittsburgh, Pennsylvania, USA

1.2.1   Defining the Problem

Speech recognition is the process of converting an acoustic signal, captured by a microphone or a telephone, to a set of words. The recognized words can be the final results, for such applications as commands & control, data entry, and document preparation. They can also serve as the input to further linguistic processing in order to achieve speech understanding, a subject covered in section 1.8.

   Speech recognition systems can be characterized by many parameters, some of the more important of which are shown in Figure 1.1. An isolated-word speech recognition system requires that the speaker pause briefly between words, whereas a continuous speech recognition system does not. Spontaneous, or extemporaneously generated, speech contains disfluencies and is much more difficult to recognize than speech read from script. Some systems require speaker enrollment—a user must provide samples of his or her speech before using them—whereas other systems are said to be speaker-independent, in that no enrollment is necessary. Some of the other parameters depend on the specific task. Recognition is generally more difficult when vocabularies are large or have many similar-sounding words. When speech is produced in a sequence of words, language models or artificial grammars are used to restrict the combination of words. The simplest language model can be specified as a finite-state network, where the permissible words following each word are explicitly given. More general language models approximating natural language are specified in terms of a context-sensitive grammar.

   One popular measure of the difficulty of the task, combining the vocabulary size and the language model, is *perplexity*, loosely defined as the geometric mean of the number of words that can follow a word after the language model has been applied (see section 1.6 for a discussion of language modeling in general and perplexity in particular). In addition, there are some external parameters that can affect speech recognition system performance, including the characteristics of the environmental noise and the type and the placement of the microphone.

Parameters	Range
Speaking Mode	Isolated words to continuous speech
Speaking Style	Read speech to spontaneous speech
Enrollment	Speaker-dependent to Speaker-independent
Vocabulary	Small (< 20 words) to large ($> 20,000$ words)
Language Model	Finite-state to context-sensitive
Perplexity	Small (< 10) to large (> 100)
SNR	High (> 30 dB) to low (< 10 dB)
Transducer	Voice-cancelling microphone to telephone

Table 1.1: Typical parameters used to characterize the capability of speech recognition systems

Speech recognition is a difficult problem, largely because of the many sources of variability associated with the signal. First, the acoustic realizations of phonemes, the smallest sound units of which words are composed, are highly dependent on the context in which they appear. These *phonetic variabilities* are exemplified by the acoustic differences of the phoneme[1] /t/ in *two, true,* and *butter* in American English. At word boundaries, contextual variations can be quite dramatic—making *gas shortage* sound like *gash shortage* in American English, and *devo andare* sound like *devandare* in Italian.

Second, *acoustic variabilities* can result from changes in the environment as well as in the position and characteristics of the transducer. Third, *within-speaker variabilities* can result from changes in the speaker's physical and emotional state, speaking rate, or voice quality. Finally, differences in sociolinguistic background, dialect, and vocal tract size and shape can contribute to *across-speaker variabilities*.

Figure 1.2 shows the major components of a typical speech recognition system. The digitized speech signal is first transformed into a set of useful measurements or features at a fixed rate, typically once every 10–20 msec (see sections 1.3 and 11.3 for signal representation and digital signal processing, respectively). These measurements are then used to search for the most likely word candidate, making use of constraints imposed by the acoustic, lexical, and language models. Throughout this process, training data are used to determine the values of the model parameters.

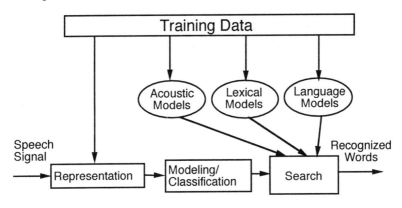

Figure 1.2: Components of a typical speech recognition system.

Speech recognition systems attempt to model the sources of variability described above in several ways. At the level of signal representation, researchers have developed representations that emphasize perceptually important speaker-independent features of the signal, and de-emphasize speaker-dependent characteristics (Hermansky, 1990). At the acoustic phonetic level, speaker variabil-

---

[1]Linguistic symbols presented between slashes, e.g., /p/, /t/, /k/, refer to *phonemes* [the minimal sound unit by changing it one changes the meaning of a word]. The acoustic realizations of phonemes in speech are referred to as *allophones, phones,* or *phonetic segments,* and are presented in brackets, e.g., [p], [t], [k].

ity is typically modeled using statistical techniques applied to large amounts of data. Speaker adaptation algorithms have also been developed that adapt speaker-independent acoustic models to those of the current speaker during system use (see section 1.4). Effects of linguistic context at the acoustic phonetic level are typically handled by training separate models for phonemes in different contexts; this is called context dependent acoustic modeling.

Word level variability can be handled by allowing alternate pronunciations of words in representations known as *pronunciation networks*. Common alternate pronunciations of words, as well as effects of dialect and accent are handled by allowing search algorithms to find alternate paths of phonemes through these networks. Statistical language models, based on estimates of the frequency of occurrence of word sequences, are often used to guide the search through the most probable sequence of words.

The dominant recognition paradigm in the past fifteen years is known as hidden Markov models (HMM). An HMM is a doubly stochastic model, in which the generation of the underlying phoneme string and the frame-by-frame, surface acoustic realizations, are *both* represented probabilistically as Markov processes, as discussed in sections 1.5, 1.6 and 11.2. Neural networks have also been used to estimate the frame based scores; these scores are then integrated into HMM-based system architectures, in what has become known as *hybrid systems*, as described in section 11.5.

An interesting feature of frame-based HMM systems is that speech segments are identified during the search process, rather than explicitly. An alternate approach is to first identify speech segments, then classify the segments and use the segment scores to recognize words. This approach has produced competitive recognition performance in several tasks (Zue, Glass, et al., 1990; Fanty, Barnard, et al., 1995).

1.2.2   State of the Art

Comments about the state-of-the-art need to be made in the context of specific applications which reflect the constraints on the task. Moreover, different technologies are sometimes appropriate for different tasks. For example, when the vocabulary is small, the entire word can be modeled as a single unit. Such an approach is not practical for large vocabularies, where word models must be built up from subword units.

Performance of speech recognition systems is typically described in terms of word error rate, E, defined as:

$$E = \frac{S + I + D}{N} 100$$

where N is the total number of words in the test set, and S, I, and D are, respectively, the total number of substitutions, insertions, and deletions.

The past decade has witnessed significant progress in speech recognition technology. Word error rates continue to drop by a factor of 2 every two years.

Substantial progress has been made in the basic technology, leading to the lowering of barriers to speaker independence, continuous speech, and large vocabularies. There are several factors that have contributed to this rapid progress. First, there is the coming of age of the HMM. HMM is powerful in that, with the availability of training data, the parameters of the model can be trained automatically to give optimal performance.

Second, much effort has gone into the development of large speech corpora for system development, training, and testing. Some of these corpora are designed for acoustic phonetic research, while others are highly task specific. Nowadays, it is not uncommon to have tens of thousands of sentences available for system training and testing. These corpora permit researchers to quantify the acoustic cues important for phonetic contrasts and to determine parameters of the recognizers in a statistically meaningful way. While many of these corpora (e.g., TIMIT, RM, ATIS, and WSJ; see section 12.3) were originally collected under the sponsorship of the U.S. Defense Department's Advanced Research Projects Agency (ARPA), to spur human language technology development among its contractors, they have nevertheless gained world-wide acceptance (e.g., in Canada, France, Germany, Japan, and the U.K.) as standards on which to evaluate speech recognition.

Third, progress has been brought about by the establishment of standards for performance evaluation. Only a decade ago, researchers trained and tested their systems using locally collected data, and had not been very careful in delineating training and testing sets. As a result, it was very difficult to compare performance across systems, and a system's performance typically degraded when it was presented with previously unseen data. The recent availability of a large body of data in the public domain, coupled with the specification of evaluation standards, has resulted in uniform documentation of test results, thus contributing to greater reliability in monitoring progress (corpus development activities and evaluation methodologies are summarized in chapters 12 and 13 respectively).

Finally, advances in computer technology have also indirectly influenced our progress. The availability of fast computers with inexpensive mass storage capabilities has enabled researchers to run many large scale experiments in a short amount of time. This means that the elapsed time between an idea and its implementation and evaluation is greatly reduced. In fact, speech recognition systems with reasonable performance can now run in real time using high-end workstations without additional hardware—a feat unimaginable only a few years ago.

One of the most popular and potentially most useful tasks with low perplexity ($PP = 11$) is the recognition of digits. For American English, speaker-independent recognition of digit strings, spoken continuously and restricted to telephone bandwidth, can achieve an error rate of 0.3% when the string length is known.

One of the best known moderate-perplexity tasks is the 1,000-word so-called Resource Management (RM) task, in which inquiries can be made concerning various naval vessels in the Pacific Ocean. The best speaker-independent per-

formance on the RM task is less than 4%, using a word-pair language model
that constrains the possible words following a given word ($PP = 60$). More recently, researchers have begun to address the issue of recognizing spontaneously
generated speech. For example, in the Air Travel Information Service (ATIS)
domain, word error rates of less than 3% has been reported for a vocabulary of
nearly 2,000 words and a bigram language model with a perplexity of around
15.

High perplexity tasks with a vocabulary of thousands of words are intended
primarily for the dictation application. After working on isolated-word, speaker-
dependent systems for many years, since 1992 the community has moved towards
very-large-vocabulary (20,000 words and more), high-perplexity ($PP \approx 200$),
speaker-independent, continuous speech recognition. The best system in 1994
achieved an error rate of 7.2% on read sentences drawn from North American
business news (Pallett, Fiscus, et al., 1994).

With the steady improvements in speech recognition performance, systems
are now being deployed within telephone and cellular networks in many countries. Within the next few years, speech recognition will be pervasive in telephone networks around the world. There are tremendous forces driving the
development of the technology; in many countries, touch tone penetration is
low, and voice is the only option for controlling automated services. In voice
dialing, for example, users can dial 10–20 telephone numbers by voice (e.g., *Call
Home*) after having enrolled their voices by saying the words associated with
telephone numbers. AT&T, on the other hand, has installed a call routing system using speaker-*independent* word-spotting technology that can detect a few
key phrases (e.g., *person to person, calling card*) in sentences such as: *I want to
charge it to my calling card.*

At present, several very large vocabulary dictation systems are available
for document generation. These systems generally require speakers to pause
between words. Their performance can be further enhanced if one can apply
constraints of the specific domain such as dictating medical reports.

Even though much progress is being made, machines are a long way from
recognizing conversational speech. Word recognition rates on telephone conversations in the *Switchboard* corpus are around 50% (Cohen, Gish, et al., 1994).
It will be many years before unlimited vocabulary, speaker-independent, continuous dictation capability is realized.

1.2.3   Future Directions

In 1992, the U.S. National Science Foundation sponsored a workshop to identify
the key research challenges in the area of human language technology and the
infrastructure needed to support the work. The key research challenges are
summarized in Cole, Hirschman, et al. (1992). Research in the following areas
of speech recognition were identified:

Robustness: In a robust system, performance degrades gracefully (rather
than catastrophically) as conditions become more different from those under

which it was trained. Differences in channel characteristics and acoustic environment should receive particular attention.

Portability: Portability refers to the goal of rapidly designing, developing and deploying systems for new applications. At present, systems tend to suffer significant degradation when moved to a new task. In order to return to peak performance, they must be trained on examples specific to the new task, which is time consuming and expensive.

Adaptation: How can systems continuously adapt to changing conditions (new speakers, microphone, task, etc.) and improve through use? Such adaptation can occur at many levels in systems, subword models, word pronunciations, language models, etc.

Language Modeling: Current systems use statistical language models to help reduce the search space and resolve acoustic ambiguity. As vocabulary size grows and other constraints are relaxed to create more habitable systems, it will be increasingly important to get as much constraint as possible from language models; perhaps incorporating syntactic and semantic constraints that cannot be captured by purely statistical models.

Confidence Measures: Most speech recognition systems assign scores to hypotheses for the purpose of rank ordering them. These scores do not provide a good indication of whether a hypothesis is correct or not, just that it is better than the other hypotheses. As we move to tasks that require actions, we need better methods to evaluate the absolute correctness of hypotheses.

Out-of-Vocabulary Words: Systems are designed for use with a particular set of words but system users may not know exactly which words are in the system vocabulary. This leads to a certain percentage of out-of-vocabulary words in natural conditions. Systems must have some method of detecting such out-of-vocabulary words, or they will end up mapping a word from the vocabulary onto the unknown word, causing an error.

Spontaneous Speech: Systems that are deployed for real use must deal with a variety of spontaneous speech phenomena, such as filled pauses, false starts, hesitations, ungrammatical constructions and other common behaviors not found in read speech. Development on the ATIS task has resulted in progress in this area, but much work remains to be done.

Prosody: Prosody refers to acoustic structure that extends over several segments or words. Stress, intonation, and rhythm convey important information for word recognition and the user's intentions (e.g., sarcasm, anger). Current systems do not capture prosodic structure. How to integrate prosodic information into the recognition architecture is a critical question that has yet to be answered.

Modeling Dynamics: Systems assume a sequence of input frames which are treated as if they were independent. But it is known that perceptual cues for words and phonemes require the integration of features that reflect the movements of the articulators, which are dynamic in nature. How to model dynamics and incorporate this information into recognition systems is an unsolved problem.

1.3   Signal Representation

Melvyn J. Hunt
Dragon Systems UK Ltd., Cheltenham, UK

In statistically based automatic speech recognition, the speech waveform is sampled at a rate between 6.6 kHz and 20 kHz and processed to produce a new representation as a sequence of vectors containing values that are generally called *parameters*. The vectors ($y(t)$ in the notation used in section 1.5) typically comprise between 10 and 20 parameters, and are usually computed every 10 or 20 msec. These parameter values are then used in succeeding stages in the estimation of the probability that the portion of waveform just analyzed corresponds to a particular phonetic event in the phone-sized or whole-word reference unit being hypothesized. In practice, the representation and the probability estimation interact strongly: what one person sees as part of the representation, another may see as part of the probability estimation process. For most systems, though, we can apply the criterion that if a process is applied to all speech, it is part of the representation, while if its application is contingent on the phonetic hypothesis being tested, it is part of the later matching stage.

Representations aim to preserve the information needed to determine the phonetic identity of a portion of speech while being as impervious as possible to factors such as speaker differences, effects introduced by communications channels, and paralinguistic factors such as the emotional state of the speaker. They also aim to be as compact as possible.

Representations used in current speech recognizers (see Figure 1.3), concentrate primarily on properties of the speech signal attributable to the shape of the vocal tract rather than to the excitation, whether generated by a vocal-tract constriction or by the larynx. Representations are sensitive to whether the vocal folds are vibrating or not (the voiced/unvoiced distinction), but try to ignore effects due to variations in their frequency of vibration (F_0).

Representations are almost always derived from the short-term power spectrum; that is, the short-term phase structure is ignored. This is primarily because our ears are largely insensitive to phase effects. Consequently, speech communication and recording equipment often does not preserve the phase structure

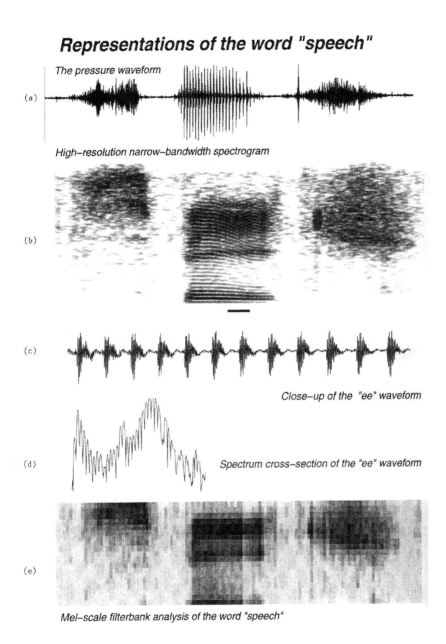

Figure 1.3: Examples of representations used in current speech recognizers: (a) Time varying waveform of the word *speech*, showing changes in amplitude (y axis) over time (x axis); (b) Speech spectrogram of (a), in terms of frequency (y axis), time (x axis) and amplitude (darkness of the pattern); (c) Expanded waveform of the vowel *ee* (underlined in b); (d) Spectrum of the vowel *ee*, in terms of amplitude (y axis) and frequency (x axis); (e) Mel-scale spectrogram.

of the original waveform, and such equipment, as well as factors such as room acoustics, can alter the phase spectrum in ways that would disturb a phase-sensitive speech recognizer, even though a human listener would not notice them.

The power spectrum is, moreover, almost always represented on a log scale. When the gain applied to a signal varies, the shape of the log power spectrum is preserved; the spectrum is simply shifted up or down. More complicated linear filtering caused, for example, by room acoustics or by variations between telephone lines, which appear as convolutional effects on the waveform and as multiplicative effects on the *linear* power spectrum, become simply additive constants on the log power spectrum. Indeed, a voiced speech waveform amounts to the convolution of a quasi-periodic excitation signal and a time-varying filter determined largely by the configuration of the vocal tract. These two components are easier to separate in the log-power domain, where they are additive. Finally, the statistical distributions of log power spectra for speech have properties convenient for statistically based speech recognition that are not, for example, shared by linear power spectra. Because the log of zero is infinite, there is a problem in representing very low energy parts of the spectrum. The log function therefore needs a lower bound, both to limit the numerical range and to prevent excessive sensitivity to the low-energy, noise-dominated parts of the spectrum.

Before computing short-term power spectra, the waveform is usually processed by a simple *pre-emphasis* filter, giving a 6 dB/octave increase in gain over most of its range to make the average speech spectrum roughly flat.

The short-term spectra are often derived by taking successive overlapping portions of the pre-emphasized waveform, typically 25 msec long, tapering at both ends with a bell-shaped window function, and applying a Fourier transform. The resulting power spectrum has undesirable harmonic fine structure at multiples of F_0. This can be reduced by grouping neighboring sets of components together to form about 20 frequency bands before converting to log power. These bands are often made successively broader with increasing frequency above 1 kHz, usually according to the *technical mel* frequency scale (Davis & Mermelstein, 1980), reflecting the frequency resolution of the human ear. A less common alternative to the process just described is to compute the energy in the bands, directly using a bank of digital filters. The results are similar.

Since the shape of the spectrum imposed by the vocal tract is smooth, energy levels in adjacent bands tend to be correlated. Removing the correlation allows the number of parameters to be reduced while preserving the useful information. It also makes it easier to compute reasonably accurate probability estimates in a subsequent statistical matching process. The *cosine transform* (a version of the Fourier transform using only cosine basis functions) converts the set of log energies to a set of *cepstral coefficients*, which turn out to be largely uncorrelated. Compared with the number of bands, typically only about half as many of these cepstral coefficients need be kept. The first cepstral coefficient (C_0) described the shape of the log spectrum independent of its overall level:

C_1 measures the balance between the upper and lower halves of the spectrum, and the higher order coefficients are concerned with increasingly finer features in the spectrum.

To the extent that the vocal tract can be regarded as a lossless, unbranched acoustic tube with plane-wave sound propagation along it, its effect on the excitation signal is that of a series of resonances; that is, the vocal tract can be modeled as an *all-pole* filter. For many speech sounds in favorable acoustic conditions, this is a good approximation. A technique known as linear predictive coding (LPC) (Markel & Gray, 1976) or *autoregressive modeling* in effect fits the parameters of an all-pole filter to the speech spectrum, though the spectrum itself need never be computed explicitly. This provides a popular alternative method of deriving cepstral coefficients.

LPC has problems with certain signal degradations and is not so convenient for producing mel-scale cepstral coefficients. Perceptual Linear Prediction (PLP) combines the LPC and filter-bank approaches by fitting an all-pole model to the set of energies (or, strictly, loudness levels) produced by a perceptually motivated filter bank, and then computing the cepstrum from the model parameters (Hermansky, 1990).

Many systems augment information on the short-term power spectrum with information on its rate of change over time. The simplest way to obtain this dynamic information would be to take the difference between consecutive frames. However, this turns out to be too sensitive to random interframe variations. Consequently, linear trends are estimated over sequences of typically five or seven frames (Furui, 1986b).

Some systems go further and estimate acceleration features as well as linear rates of change. These second-order dynamic features need even longer sequences of frames for reliable estimation (Applebaum & Hanson, 1989).

Steady factors affecting the shape or overall level of the spectrum (such as the characteristics of a particular telephone link) appear as constant offsets in the log spectrum and cepstrum. In a technique called *blind deconvolution* (Stockham, Connon, et al., 1975), cepstrum is computed, and this average is subtracted from the individual frames. This method is largely confined to non-real-time experimental systems. Since they are based on differences, however, dynamic features are intrinsically immune to such constant effects. Consequently, while C_0 is usually cast aside, its dynamic equivalent, δC_0, depending only on relative rather than absolute energy levels, is widely used.

If first-order dynamic parameters are passed through a *leaky* integrator, something close to the original static parameters are recovered with the exception that constant and very slowly varying features are reduced to zero, thus giving independence from constant or slowly varying channel characteristics. This technique, sometimes referred to as *RASTA*, amounts to band-pass filtering of sequences of log power spectra, is better suited than blind deconvolution to real-time systems (Hermansky, Morgan, et al., 1993). A similar technique, applied to sequences of power spectra before logs are taken, is capable of reducing the effect of steady or slowly varying additive noise (Hirsch, Meyer, et al., 1991).

Because cepstral coefficients are largely uncorrelated, a computationally efficient method of obtaining reasonably good probability estimates in the subsequent matching process consists of calculating Euclidean distances from reference model vectors after suitably weighting the coefficients. Various weighting schemes have been used. One empirical scheme that works well derives the weights for the first 16 coefficients from the positive half cycle of a sine wave (Juang, Rabiner, et al., 1986). For PLP cepstral coefficients, weighting each coefficient by its index (root power sum (RPS) weighting) giving C_0 a weight of zero, etc., has proved effective. Statistically based methods weight coefficients by the inverse of their standard deviations computed about their overall means, or preferably computed about the means for the corresponding speech sound and then averaged over all speech sounds (so-called *grand-variance weighting*) (Lippmann, Martin, et al., 1987).

While cepstral coefficients are substantially uncorrelated, a technique called principal components analysis (PCA) can provide a transformation that can completely remove linear dependencies between sets of variables. This method can be used to de-correlate not just sets of energy levels across a spectrum but also combinations of parameter sets such as dynamic and static features, PLP and non-PLP parameters. A double application of PCA with a weighting operation, known as linear discriminant analysis (LDA), can take into account the discriminative information needed to distinguish between speech sounds to generate a set of parameters, sometimes called IMELDA coefficients, suitably weighted for Euclidean-distance calculations. Good performance has been reported with a much reduced set of IMELDA coefficients, and there is evidence that incorporating degraded signals in the analysis can improve robustness to the degradations while not harming performance on undegraded data (Hunt & Lefèbvre, 1989).

Future Directions

The vast majority of major commercial and experimental systems use representations akin to those described here. However, in striving to develop better representations, wavelet transforms (Daubechies, 1990) are being explored, and neural network methods are being used to provide non-linear operations on log spectral representations. Work continues on representations more closely reflecting auditory properties (Greenberg, 1988) and on representations reconstructing articulatory gestures from the speech signal (Schroeter & Sondhi, 1994). This latter work is challenging because there is a one-to-many mapping between the speech spectrum and the articulatory settings that could produce it. It is attractive because it holds out the promise of a small set of smoothly varying parameters that could deal in a simple and principled way with the interactions that occur between neighboring phonemes and with the effects of differences in speaking rate and of carefulness of enunciation.

As we noted earlier, current representations concentrate on the spectrum envelope and ignore fundamental frequency; yet we know that even in isolated-word recognition fundamental frequency contours are an important cue to lexical identity not only in tonal languages such as Chinese but also in languages such as English where they correlate with lexical stress. In continuous speech recognition fundamental frequency contours can potentially contribute valuable information on syntactic structure and on the intentions of the speaker (e.g., *No, I said 2* **5** *7*). The challenges here lie not in deriving fundamental frequency but in knowing how to separate out the various kinds of information that it encodes (speaker identity, speaker state, syntactic structure, lexical stress, speaker intention, etc.) and how to integrate this information into decisions otherwise based on identifying sequences of phonetic events.

The ultimate challenge is to match the superior performance of human listeners over automatic recognizers. This superiority is especially marked when there is limited material to allow adaptation to the voice of the current speaker, and when the acoustic conditions are difficult. The fact that it persists even when nonsense words are used shows that it exists at least partly at the acoustic/phonetic level and cannot be explained purely by superior language modeling in the brain. It confirms that there is still much to be done in developing better representations of the speech signal. For additional references, see Rabiner and Schafer (1978) and Hunt (1993).

1.4 Robust Speech Recognition

Richard M. Stern

Carnegie Mellon University, Pittsburgh, Pennsylvania, USA

Robustness in speech recognition refers to the need to maintain good recognition accuracy even when the quality of the input speech is degraded, or when the acoustical, articulatory, or phonetic characteristics of speech in the training and testing environments differ. Obstacles to robust recognition include acoustical degradations produced by additive noise, the effects of linear filtering, nonlinearities in transduction or transmission, as well as impulsive interfering sources, and diminished accuracy caused by changes in articulation produced by the presence of high-intensity noise sources. Some of these sources of variability are illustrated in Figure 1.4. Speaker-to-speaker differences impose a different type of variability, producing variations in speech rate, co-articulation, context, and dialect. Even systems that are designed to be speaker-independent exhibit dramatic degradations in recognition accuracy when training and testing conditions differ (Cole, Hirschman, et al., 1992; Juang, 1991).

Speech recognition systems have become much more robust in recent years with respect to both speaker variability and acoustical variability. In addition to achieving speaker-independence, many current systems can also automatically compensate for modest amounts of acoustical degradation caused by the effects of unknown noise and unknown linear filtering.

As speech recognition and spoken language technologies are being transferred to real applications, the need for greater robustness in recognition technology is becoming increasingly apparent. Nevertheless, the performance of even the best

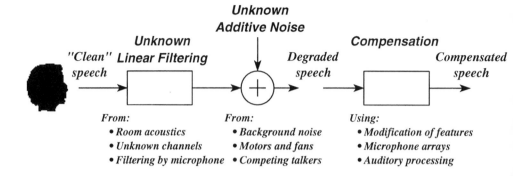

Figure 1.4: Schematic representation of some of the sources of variability that can degrade speech recognition accuracy, along with compensation procedures that improve environmental robustness.

state-of-the art systems tends to deteriorate when speech is transmitted over telephone lines, when the signal-to-noise ratio (SNR) is extremely low (particularly when the unwanted noise consists of speech from other talkers), and when the speaker's native language is not the one with which the system was trained.

Substantial progress has also been made over the last decade in the dynamic adaptation of speech recognition systems to new speakers, with techniques that modify or warp the systems' phonetic representations to reflect the acoustical characteristics of individual speakers (Gauvain & Lee, 1991; Huang & Lee, 1993; Schwartz, Chow, et al., 1987). Speech recognition systems have also become more robust in recent years, particularly with regard to slowly-varying acoustical sources of degradation.

In this section we focus on approaches to environmental robustness. We begin with a discussion of dynamic adaptation techniques for unknown acoustical environments and speakers. We then discuss two popular alternative approaches to robustness: the use of multiple microphones and the use of signal processing based on models of auditory physiology and perception.

1.4.1   Dynamic Parameter Adaptation

Dynamic adaptation of either the features that are input to the recognition system, or of the system's internally stored representations of possible utterances, is the most direct approach to environmental and speaker adaptation. Three different approaches to speaker and environmental adaptation are discussed: (1) the use of optimal estimation procedures to obtain new parameter values in the testing conditions; (2) the development of compensation procedures based on empirical comparisons of speech in the training and testing environments; and (3) the use of high-pass filtering of parameter values to improve robustness.

Optimal Parameter Estimation: Many successful robustness techniques are based on a formal statistical model that characterizes the differences between speech used to train and test the system. Parameter values of these models are estimated from samples of speech in the testing environments, and either the features of the incoming speech or the internally-stored representations of speech in the system are modified. Typical structural models for adaptation to acoustical variability assume that speech is corrupted either by additive noise with an unknown power spectrum (Porter & Boll, 1984; Ephraim, 1992; Erell & Weintraub, 1990; Gales & Young, 1992; Lockwood, Boudy, et al., 1992; Bellegarda, de Souza, et al., 1992), or by a combination of additive noise and linear filtering (Acero & Stern, 1990). Much of the early work in robust recognition involved a re-implementation of techniques developed to remove additive noise for the purpose of speech enhancement, as reviewed in section 10.3. The fact that such approaches were able to substantially reduce error rates in machine recognition of speech, even though they were largely ineffective in improving human speech intelligibility (when measured objectively) (Lim & Oppenheim, 1979), is one indication of the limited capabilities of automatic speech recognition systems, compared to human speech perception.

Approaches to speaker adaptation are similar in principle except that the models are more commonly general statistical models of feature variability (Gauvain & Lee, 1991; Huang & Lee, 1993) rather than models of the sources of speaker-to-speaker variability. Solution of the estimation problems frequently requires either analytical or numerical approximations or the use of iterative estimation techniques, such as the estimate-maximize (EM) algorithm (Dempster, Laird, et al., 1977). These approaches have all been successful in applications where the assumptions of the models are reasonably valid, but they are limited in some cases by computational complexity.

Another popular approach is to use knowledge of background noise drawn from examples to transform the means and variances of phonetic models that had been developed for *clean* speech to enable these models to characterize speech in background noise (Varga & Moore, 1990; Gales & Young, 1992). The technique known as parallel model combination(Gales & Young, 1992) extends this approach, providing an analytical model of the degradation that accounts for both additive and convolutional noise. These methods work reasonably well, but they are computationally costly at present and they rely on accurate estimates of the background noise.

Empirical Feature Comparison: Empirical comparisons of features derived from high-quality speech with features of speech that is simultaneously recorded under degraded conditions can be used (instead of a structural model) to compensate for mismatches between training and testing conditions. In these algorithms, the combined effects of environmental and speaker variability are typically characterized as additive perturbations to the features. Several successful empirically-based robustness algorithms have been described that either apply additive correction vectors to the features derived from incoming speech waveforms (Neumeyer & Weintraub, 1994; Liu, Stern, et al., 1994) or apply additive correction vectors to the statistical parameters characterizing the internal representations of these features in the recognition system (e.g., Anastasakos, Makhoul, et al. (1994); Liu, Stern, et al. (1994)). (In the latter, case, the variances of the templates may also be modified.) Recognition accuracy can be substantially improved by allowing the correction vectors to depend on SNR, specific location in parameter space within a given SNR, or presumed phoneme identity (Neumeyer & Weintraub, 1994; Liu, Stern, et al., 1994). For example, the numerical difference between cepstral coefficients derived on a frame-by-frame basis from high-quality speech and simultaneously recorded speech that is degraded by both noise and filtering primarily reflects the degradations introduced by the filtering at high SNRs, and the effects of the noise at low SNRs. This general approach can be extended to cases when the testing environment is unknown *a priori*, by developing ensembles of correction vectors in parallel for a number of different testing conditions, and by subsequently applying the set of correction vectors (or acoustic models) from the condition that is deemed to be most likely to have produced the incoming speech. In cases where the test condition is not one of those used to train correction vectors, recognition accuracy can be further improved by interpolating the correction vectors or statistics representing the best candidate conditions.

Empirically-derived compensation procedures are extremely simple, and they are quite effective in cases when the testing conditions are reasonably similar to one of the conditions used to develop correction vectors. For example, in a recent evaluation using speech from a number of unknown microphones in a 5000-word continuous dictation task, the use of adaptation techniques based on empirical comparisons of feature values reduced the error rate by 40% relative to a baseline system with only cepstral mean normalization (described below). Nevertheless, empirical approaches have the disadvantage of requiring *stereo* databases of speech that are simultaneously recorded in the training environment and the testing environment.

Cepstral High-pass Filtering: The third major adaptation technique is cepstral high-pass filtering, which provides a remarkable amount of robustness at almost zero computational cost (Hermansky, Morgan, et al., 1991; Hirsch, Meyer, et al., 1991). In the well-known RASTA method (Hermansky, Morgan, et al., 1991), a high-pass (or band-pass) filter is applied to a log-spectral representation of speech such as the cepstral coefficients. In cepstral mean normalization (CMN), high-pass filtering is accomplished by subtracting the short-term average of cepstral vectors from the incoming cepstral coefficients.

The original motivation for the RASTA and CMN algorithms is discussed in section 1.3. These algorithms compensate directly for the effects of unknown linear filtering because they force the average values of cepstral coefficients to be zero in both the training and testing domains, and hence equal to each other. An extension to the RASTA algorithm, known as J-RASTA (Koehler, Morgan, et al., 1994), can also compensate for noise at low SNRs. In an evaluation using

13 isolated digits over telephone lines, it was shown (Koehler, Morgan, et al., 1994) that the J-RASTA method reduced error rates by as much as 55 % relative to RASTA when both noise and filtering effects are present. Cepstral high-pass filtering is so inexpensive and effective that it is currently embedded in some form in virtually all systems that are required to perform robust recognition.

1.4.2 Use of Multiple Microphones

Further improvements in recognition accuracy can be obtained at lower SNRs by the use of multiple microphones. As noted in the discussion on speech enhancement in section 10.3, microphone arrays can, in principle, produce directionally sensitive gain patterns that can be adjusted to increase sensitivity to the speaker and reduce sensitivity in the direction of competing sound sources. In fact, results of recent pilot experiments in office environments (Che, Lin, et al., 1994; Sullivan & Stern, 1993) confirm that the use of delay-and-sum beamformers, in combination with a post-processing algorithm that compensates for the spectral coloration introduced by the array itself, can reduce recognition error rates by as much as 61%.

Array processors that make use of the more general minimum mean square error (MMSE)-based classical adaptive filtering techniques can work well when signal degradation is dominated by additive-independent noise, but they do not perform well in reverberant environments when the distortion is at least in part a delayed version of the desired speech signal (Peterson, 1989; Alvarado & Silverman, 1990). (This problem can be avoided by only adapting during non-speech segments: Van Compernolle, 1990.)

A third approach to microphone array processing is the use of cross-correlation-based algorithms, which have the ability to reinforce the components of a sound field arriving from a particular azimuth angle. These algorithms are appealing because they are similar to the processing performed by the human binaural system, but thus far they have demonstrated only a modest superiority over the simpler delay-and-sum approaches (Sullivan & Stern, 1993).

1.4.3 Use of Physiologically Motivated Signal Processing

A number of signal processing schemes have been developed for speech recognition systems that mimic various aspects of human auditory physiology and perception (e.g., Cohen, 1989; Ghitza, 1988; Lyon, 1982; Seneff, 1988; Hermansky, 1990; Patterson, Robinson, et al., 1991). Such *auditory models* typically consist of a bank of bandpass filters (representing auditory frequency selectivity) followed by nonlinear interactions within and across channels (representing hair-cell transduction, lateral suppression, and other effects). The nonlinear processing is (in some cases) followed by a mechanism to extract detailed timing information as a function of frequency (Seneff, 1988; Duda, Lyon, et al., 1990).

Recent evaluations indicate that auditory models can indeed provide better recognition accuracy than traditional cepstral representations when the quality of the incoming speech degrades, or when training and testing conditions differ (Hunt & Lefèbvre, 1989; Meng & Zue, 1990). Nevertheless, auditory models have not yet been able to demonstrate better recognition accuracy than the most effective dynamic adaptation algorithms, and conventional adaptation techniques are far less computationally costly (Ohshima, 1993). It is possible that the success of auditory models has been limited thus far because most of the evaluations were performed using hidden Markov model classifiers, which are not well matched to the statistical properties of features produced by auditory models. Other researchers suggest that we have not yet identified the features of the models' outputs that will ultimately provide superior performance. The approach of auditory modeling continues to merit further attention, particularly with the goal of resolving these issues.

1.4.4   Future Directions

Despite its importance, robust speech recognition has become a vital area of research only recently. To date, major successes in environmental adaptation have been limited either to relatively benign domains (typically with limited amounts of quasi-stationary additive noise and/or linear filtering, or to domains in which a great deal of environment-specific training data are available). Speaker adaptation algorithms have been successful in providing improved recognition for native speakers other than the one with which a system is trained, but recognition accuracy obtained using non-native speakers remains substantially worse, even with speaker adaptation (e.g., Pallett, Fiscus, et al. (1995)).

At present, it is fair to say that hardly any of the major limitations to robust recognition cited in section 1.1 have been satisfactorily resolved. Success in the following key problem areas is likely to accelerate the development and deployment of practical speech-based applications.

Speech over Telephone Lines: Recognition of telephone speech is difficult because each telephone channel has its own unique SNR and frequency response. Speech over telephone lines can be further corrupted by transient interference and nonlinear distortion. Telephone-based applications must be able to adapt to new channels on the basis of a very small amount of channel-specific data.

Low-SNR Environments: Even with state-of-the art compensation techniques, recognition accuracy degrades when the channel SNR decreases below about 15 dB, despite the fact that humans can obtain excellent recognition accuracy at lower SNRs.

Co-channel Speech Interference: Interference by other talkers poses a much more difficult challenge to robust recognition than interference from broadband noise sources. So far, efforts to exploit speech-specific information to reduce the effects of co-channel interference from other talkers have been largely unsuccessful.

Rapid Adaptation for Non-native Speakers: In today's pluralistic and highly mobile society, successful spoken-language applications must be able to cope with the speech of non-native as well as native speakers. Continued development of non-intrusive rapid adaptation to the accents of non-native speakers will be needed to ensure commercial success.

Common Speech Corpora with Realistic Degradations: Continued rapid progress in robust recognition will depend on the formulation, collection, transcription, and dissemination of speech corpora that contain realistic examples of the degradations encountered in practical environments. The selection of appropriate tasks and domains for shared database resources is best accomplished through the collaboration of technology developers, applications developers, and end users. The contents of these databases should be realistic enough to be useful as an impetus for solutions to actual problems, even in cases for which it may be difficult to *calibrate* the degradation for the purpose of evaluation.

1.5 HMM Methods in Speech Recognition

Renato De Mori[a] & Fabio Brugnara[b]

[a] McGill University, Montréal, Québéc, Canada
[b] Istituto per la Ricerca Scientifica e Tecnologica, Trento, Italy

Modern architectures for Automatic Speech Recognition (ASR) are mostly software architectures which generate a sequence of word hypotheses from an acoustic signal. The most popular algorithms implemented in these architectures are based on statistical methods. Other approaches can be found in Waibel and Lee (1990), where a collection of papers describes a variety of systems with historical reviews and mathematical foundations.

A vector y_t of acoustic features is computed every 10 to 30 msec. Details of this component can be found in section 1.3. Various possible choices of vectors, together with their impact on recognition performance, are discussed in Haeb-Umbach, Geller, et al. (1993).

Sequences of vectors of acoustic parameters are treated as observations of acoustic word models used to compute $p(y_1^T|W)$,[2] the probability of observing a sequence y_1^T of vectors when a word sequence W is pronounced. Given a sequence y_1^T, a word sequence $\widehat{W}$ is generated by the ASR system with a search process based on the rule:

$$\widehat{W} = \arg\max_W \ p(y_1^T|W) \, p(W)$$

$\widehat{W}$ corresponds to the candidate having maximum a-posteriori probability (MAP). $p(y_1^T|W)$ is computed by Acoustic Models (AM), while $p(W)$ is computed by Language Models (LM).

---

[2]Here, and in the following, the notation y_h^k stands for the sequence $[y_h, y_{h+1}, \ldots, y_k]$.

For large vocabularies, search is performed in two steps. The first generates a word lattice of the *n-best* word sequences with simple models to compute approximate likelihoods in real-time. In the second step, more accurate likelihoods are compared with a limited number of hypotheses. Some systems generate a single word sequence hypothesis with a single step. The search produces an hypothesized word sequence if the task is dictation. If the task is understanding, then a conceptual structure is obtained with a process that may involve more than two steps. Ways of automatically learning and extracting these structures are described in Kuhn, De Mori, et al. (1994).

1.5.1   Acoustic Models

In a statistical framework, an inventory of elementary probabilistic models of basic linguistic units (e.g., phonemes) is used to build word representations. A sequence of acoustic parameters, extracted from a spoken utterance, is seen as a realization of a concatenation of elementary processes described by hidden Markov models (HMMs). An HMM is a composition of two stochastic processes, a *hidden* Markov chain, which accounts for *temporal* variability, and an observable process, which accounts for *spectral* variability. This combination has proven to be powerful enough to cope with the most important sources of speech ambiguity, and flexible enough to allow the realization of recognition systems with dictionaries of tens of thousands of words.

Structure of a Hidden Markov Model

A hidden Markov model is defined as a pair of stochastic processes (X, Y). The X process is a first order Markov chain, and is not directly observable, while the Y process is a sequence of random variables taking values in the space of acoustic parameters, or *observations*.

Two formal assumptions characterize HMMs as used in speech recognition. The *first-order Markov hypothesis* states that history has no influence on the chain's future evolution if the present is specified, while the *output independence hypothesis* states that neither chain evolution nor past observations influence the present observation if the last chain transition is specified.

Letting $y \in \mathcal{Y}$ be a variable representing observations and $i, j \in \mathcal{X}$ be variables representing model states, the model can be represented by the following parameters:

$$
\begin{aligned}
A &\equiv \{a_{i,j} | i, j \in \mathcal{X}\} \quad \text{transition probabilities} \\
B &\equiv \{b_{i,j} | i, j \in \mathcal{X}\} \quad \text{output distributions} \\
\Pi &\equiv \{\pi_i | i \in \mathcal{X}\} \quad\quad \text{initial probabilities}
\end{aligned}
$$

with the following definitions:

$$
\begin{aligned}
a_{i,j} &\equiv p(X_t = j | X_{t-1} = i) \\
b_{i,j}(y) &\equiv p(Y_t = y | X_{t-1} = i, X_t = j) \\
\pi_i &\equiv p(X_0 = i)
\end{aligned}
$$

A useful tutorial on this topic can be found in Rabiner (1989).

Types of Hidden Markov Models

HMMs can be classified according to the nature of the elements of the B matrix, which are distribution functions.

Distributions are defined on finite spaces in the so called *discrete HMMs*. In this case, observations are vectors of symbols in a finite alphabet of N different elements. For each one of the Q vector components, a discrete density $\{w(k)|k = 1, \ldots, N\}$ is defined, and the distribution is obtained by multiplying the probabilities of each component. Notice that this definition assumes that the different components are independent. Figure 1.5 shows an example of a discrete HMM with one-dimensional observations. Distributions are associated with model transitions.

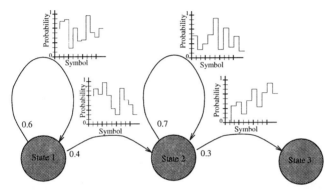

Figure 1.5: Example of a discrete HMM. A transition probability and an output distribution on the symbol set is associated with every transition.

Another possibility is to define distributions as probability densities on continuous observation spaces. In this case, strong restrictions have to be imposed on the functional form of the distributions, in order to have a manageable number of statistical parameters to estimate. The most popular approach is to characterize the model transitions with mixtures of base densities g of a family G having a simple parametric form. The base densities $g \in G$ are usually Gaussian or Laplacian, and can be parameterized by the mean vector and the covariance matrix. HMMs with these kinds of distributions are usually referred to as *continuous HMMs*. In order to model complex distributions in this way, a rather large number of base densities has to be used in every mixture. This may require a very large training corpus of data for the estimation of the distribution parameters. Problems arising when the available corpus is not large enough can be alleviated by sharing distributions among transitions of different models. In *semi-continuous HMMs* Huang, Ariki, et al. (1990), for example, all mixtures are expressed in terms of a common set of base densities. Different mixtures are characterized only by different weights.

A common generalization of semi-continuous modeling consists of interpreting the input vector y as composed of several components $y[1], \ldots, y[Q]$, each of which is associated with a different set of base distributions. The components are assumed to be statistically independent, hence the distributions associated with model transitions are products of the component density functions.

Computation of probabilities with discrete models is faster than with continuous models, but it is nevertheless possible to speed up the mixture densities computation by applying vector quantization (VQ) on the gaussians of the mixtures (Bocchieri, 1993).

Parameters of statistical models are estimated by iterative learning algorithms (Rabiner, 1989) in which the likelihood of a set of training data is guaranteed to increase at each step.

Bengio, DeMori, et al. (1992) propose a method for extracting additional acoustic parameters and performing transformations of all the extracted parameters using a Neural Network (NN) architecture, whose weights are obtained by an algorithm that, at the same time, estimates the coefficients of the distributions of the acoustic models. Estimation is driven by an optimization criterion that tries to minimize the overall recognition error.

1.5.2   Word and Unit Models

Words are usually represented by networks of phonemes. Each path in a word network represents a pronunciation of the word.

The same phoneme can have different acoustic distributions of observations if pronounced in different contexts. *Allophone* models of a phoneme are models of that phoneme in different contexts. The decision as to how many allophones should be considered for a given phoneme may depend on many factors, e.g., the availability of enough training data to infer the model parameters.

A conceptually interesting approach is that of *polyphones* (Shukat-Talamazzini, Niemann, et al., 1992). In principle, an allophone should be considered for every different word in which a phoneme appears. If the vocabulary is large, it is unlikely that there is enough data to train all these allophone models, so models for allophones of phonemes are considered at a different level of detail (word, syllable, triphone, diphone, context independent phoneme). Probability distributions for an allophone having a certain degree of generality can be obtained by mixing the distributions of more detailed allophone models. The loss in specificity is compensated by a more robust estimation of the statistical parameters, due to an increase in the ratio between training data and free parameters.

Another approach consists of choosing allophones by *clustering* possible contexts. This choice can be made automatically with Classification and Regression Trees (CART). A CART is a binary tree having a phoneme at the root and, associated with each node n_i, a question Q_i about the context. Questions Q_i are of the type, "Is the previous phoneme a nasal consonant?" For each possible answer (*YES* or *NO*) there is a link to another node with which other questions are associated. There are algorithms for growing and pruning CARTs based on automatically assigning questions to a node from a manually determined pool of questions. The leaves of the tree may be simply labeled by an allophone symbol. Papers by Bahl, de Souza, et al. (1991) and Hon and Lee (1991) provide examples of the application of this concept and references to the description of a formalism for training and using CARTs.

Each allophone model is an HMM made of states, transitions and probability distributions. In order to improve the estimation of the statistical parameters of these models, some distributions can be the same or tied. For example, the distributions for the central portion of the allophones of a given phoneme can be tied reflecting the fact that they represent the stable (context-independent) physical realization of the central part of the phoneme, uttered with a stationary configuration of the vocal tract.

In general, all the models can be built by sharing distributions taken from a pool of, say, a few thousand cluster distributions, called *senones*. Details on this approach can be found in Hwang and Huang (1993).

Word models or allophone models can also be built by concatenation of basic structures made by states, transitions and distributions. These units, called *fenones*, were introduced by Bahl, Brown, et al. (1993). Richer models of the same type but using more sophisticated building blocks, called *multones*, are described in Bahl, Bellegarda, et al. (1993).

Another approach consists of having clusters of distributions characterized by the same set of Gaussian probability density functions. Allophone distributions are built by considering mixtures with the same components but with different weights (Digalakis & Murveit, 1994).

1.5.3 Language Models

The probability $p(W)$ of a sequence of words $W = w_1, \ldots, w_L$ is computed by a Language Model (LM). In general $p(W)$ can be expressed as follows:

$$p(W) = p(w_1, .., w_n) = \prod_{i=1}^{n} p(w_i | w_0, .., w_{i-1})$$

Motivations for this approach and methods for computing these probabilities are described in the following section.

1.5.4 Generation of Word Hypotheses

Generation of word hypotheses can result in a single sequence of words, in a collection of the *n-best* word sequences, or in a lattice of partially overlapping word hypotheses.

This generation is a search process in which a sequence of vectors of acoustic features is compared with word models. In this section, some distinctive characteristics of the computations involved in speech recognition algorithms will be described, first focusing on the case of a single-word utterance and then considering the extension to continuous speech recognition.

In general, the speech signal and its transformations do not exhibit clear indication of word boundaries, so word boundary detection is part of the hypothesization process carried out as a search. In this process, all the word models are compared with a sequence of acoustic features. In the probabilistic framework, "comparison" between an acoustic sequence and a model involves the computation of the probability that the model assigns to the given sequence. This is the key ingredient of the recognition process. In this computation, the following quantities are used:

$\alpha_t(\boldsymbol{y}_1^T, i)$: probability of having observed the partial sequence $\boldsymbol{y}_1^t$ and being in state i at time t

$$\alpha_t(\boldsymbol{y}_1^T, i) \equiv \begin{cases} p(X_0 = i), & t = 0 \\ p(X_t = i, \boldsymbol{Y}_1^t = \boldsymbol{y}_1^t), & t > 0 \end{cases}$$

$\beta_t(\boldsymbol{y}_1^T, i)$: probability of observing the partial sequence $\boldsymbol{y}_{t+1}^T$ given that the model is in state i at time t

$$\beta_t(\boldsymbol{y}_1^T, i) \equiv \begin{cases} p\left(\boldsymbol{Y}_{t+1}^T = \boldsymbol{y}_{t+1}^T | X_t = i\right), & t < T \\ 1, & t = T \end{cases}$$

$\psi_t(\boldsymbol{y}_1^T, i)$: probability of having observed the partial sequence $\boldsymbol{y}_1^t$ along the best path ending in state i at time t:

$$\psi_t(\boldsymbol{y}_1^T, i) \equiv \begin{cases} p(X_0 = i), & t = 0 \\ \max_{i_0^{t-1}} p\left(\boldsymbol{X}_0^{t-1} = i_0^{t-1}, X_t = i, \boldsymbol{Y}_1^t = \boldsymbol{y}_1^t\right) & t > 0 \end{cases}$$

α and β can be used to compute the total emission probability $p(\boldsymbol{y}_1^T | W)$ as

$$p(\boldsymbol{Y}_1^T = \boldsymbol{y}_1^T) = \sum_i \alpha_T(\boldsymbol{y}_1^T, i) \tag{1.1}$$

$$= \sum_i \pi_i \beta_0(\boldsymbol{y}_1^T, i) \tag{1.2}$$

An approximation for computing this probability consists of following only the path of maximum probability. This can be done with the ψ quantity:

$$\text{Pr}^*[\boldsymbol{Y}_1^T = \boldsymbol{y}_1^T] = \max_i \psi_T(\boldsymbol{y}_1^T, i) \tag{1.3}$$

The computations of all the above probabilities share a common framework, employing a matrix called a *trellis*, depicted in Figure 1.6. For the sake of simplicity, we can assume that the HMM in Figure 1.6 represents a word and that the input signal corresponds to the pronunciation of an isolated word.

Every trellis column holds the values of one of the just introduced probabilities for a partial sequence ending at different time instants, and every interval between two columns corresponds to an input frame. The arrows in the trellis represent model transitions composing possible paths in the model from the initial time instant to the final one. The computation proceeds in a column-wise

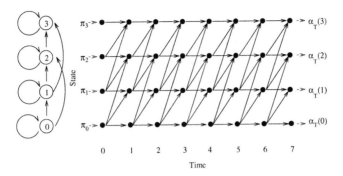

Figure 1.6: A state-time trellis.

manner, at every time frame updating the scores of the nodes in a column by means of recursion formulas which involve the values of an adjacent column, the transition probabilities of the models, and the values of the output distributions for the corresponding frame. For α and ψ coefficients, the computation starts at the leftmost column, whose values are initialized with the values of π_i, and ends at the opposite side, computing the final value with (1.1) or (1.3). For the β coefficients, the computation goes from right to left.

The algorithm for computing ψ coefficients, known as the *Viterbi algorithm*, can be seen as an application of dynamic programing for finding a maximum probability path in a graph with weighted arcs. The recursion formula for its computation is the following:

$$\psi_t(\boldsymbol{y}_1^T, i) = \begin{cases} \pi_i, & t = 0 \\ \max_j \psi_{t-1}(\boldsymbol{y}_1^T, j)a_{j,i}b_{j,i}(y_t), & t > 0 \end{cases}$$

By keeping track of the state j giving the maximum value in the above recursion formula, it is possible, at the end of the input sequence, to retrieve the states visited by the best path, thus performing a sort of time-alignment of input frames with models' states.

All these algorithms have a time complexity $O(MT)$, where M is the number of transitions with non-zero probability and T is the length of the input sequence. M can be at most equal to S^2, where S is the number of states in the model, but is usually much lower, since the transition probability matrix is generally sparse. In fact, a common choice in speech recognition is to impose severe constraints on the allowed state sequences, for example $a_{i,j} = 0$ for $j < i, j > i + 2$, as is the case of the model in Figure 1.6.

In general, recognition is based on a search process which takes into account all the possible segmentations of the input sequence into words and the *a priori* probabilities that the LM assigns to sequences of words.

Good results can be obtained with simple LMs based on bigram or trigram probabilities. As an example, let us consider a bigram language model. This model can be conveniently incorporated into a finite state automaton as shown in Figure 1.7, where dashed arcs correspond to transitions between words with probabilities of the LM.

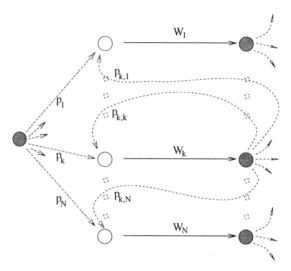

Figure 1.7: Bigram LM represented as a weighted word graph. $p_{h,k}$ stands for $p(W_k|W_h)$, p_h stands for $p(W_h)$. The leftmost node is the starting node, rightmost ones are finals.

After substitution of the word-labeled arcs with the corresponding HMMs, the resulting automaton becomes a large HMM itself, on which a Viterbi search for the most probable path, given an observation sequence, can be carried out. The dashed arcs are to be treated as *empty transitions*, i.e., transitions without an associated output distribution. This requires some generalization of the Viterbi algorithm. During the execution of the Viterbi algorithm, a minimum of backtracking information is kept to allow the reconstruction of the best path in terms of word labels. Note that the solution provided by this search is *suboptimal* in the sense that it gives the probability of a single state sequence of the composite model and not the total emission probability of the best word model sequence. In practice, however, it has been observed that the path probabilities computed with the above mentioned algorithms exhibit a dominance property, consisting of a single state sequence accounting for most of the total probability (Merhav & Ephraim, 1991).

The composite model grows with the vocabulary and can lead to large search spaces. Nevertheless, the uneven distribution of probabilities among different paths can help; when the number of states is large, at every time instant, a large portion of states have an accumulated likelihood which is much less than the highest one. It is therefore very unlikely that a path passing through one of these states would become the best path at the end of the utterance. This consideration leads to a complexity reduction technique called *beam search* (Ney, Mergel, et al., 1992), consisting of neglecting states whose accumulated score is lower than the best one minus a given threshold. In this way, computation needed to expand *bad* nodes is avoided. It is clear from the naivety of the pruning criterion that this reduction technique has the undesirable property of being *not admissible*, possibly causing the loss of the best path. In practice, good tuning of the beam threshold results in a gain in speed by an order of magnitude, while introducing a negligible amount of search errors.

When the dictionary is of the order of tens of thousands of words, the network becomes too big and other methods have to be considered.

At present, different techniques exist for dealing with very large vocabularies. Most of them use multi-pass algorithms. Each pass prepares information for the next one, reducing the size of the search space. Details of these methods can be found in Alleva, Huang, et al. (1993); Aubert, Dugast, et al. (1994); Murveit, Butzberger, et al. (1993); Kubala, Anastasakos, et al. (1994).

In a first phase, a set of candidate interpretations is represented in an object called *word lattice*, whose structure varies in different systems: it may contain only hypotheses on the location of words, or it may carry a record of acoustic scores as well. The construction of the word lattice may involve only the execution of a Viterbi beam search with memorization of word scoring and localization, as in Aubert, Dugast, et al. (1994), or may itself require multiple steps, as in Alleva, Huang, et al. (1993); Murveit, Butzberger, et al. (1993); Kubala, Anastasakos, et al. (1994). Since the word lattice is only an intermediate result, to be inspected by other detailed methods, its generation is performed with a bigram language model, and often with simplified acoustic models.

The word hypotheses in the lattice are scored with a more accurate language model, and sometimes with more detailed acoustic models. Lattice rescoring may require new calculations of HMM probabilities (Murveit, Butzberger, et al., 1993), may proceed on the basis of precomputed probabilities only (Aubert, Dugast, et al., 1994; Alleva, Huang, et al., 1993), or even exploit acoustic models which are not HMMs (Kubala, Anastasakos, et al., 1994). In Alleva, Huang, et al. (1993), the last step is based on an A^* search (Nilsson, 1971) on the word lattice, allowing the application of a *long distance language model*, i.e., a model where the probability of a word may not only depend on its immediate predecessor. In Aubert, Dugast, et al. (1994), a dynamic programming algorithm, using trigram probabilities, is performed.

A method which does not make use of the word lattice is presented in Paul (1994). Inspired by one of the first methods proposed for continuous speech recognition (CSR) (Jelinek, 1969), it combines both powerful language modeling and detailed acoustic modeling in a single step, performing an A^* based search.

1.5.5 Future Directions

Interesting software architectures for ASR have been recently developed. They provide acceptable recognition performance almost in real time for dictation of large vocabularies (more than 10,000 words). Pure software solutions require, at the moment, a considerable amount of central memory. Special boards make it possible to run interesting applications on PCs.

There are aspects of the best current systems that still need improvement. The best systems do not perform equally well with different speakers and different speaking environments. Two important aspects, namely recognition in noise and speaker adaptation, are discussed in section 1.4. They have difficulty in handling out-of-vocabulary words, hesitations, false starts, and other phenomena typical of spontaneous speech. Rudimentary understanding capabilities are available for speech understanding in limited domains. Key research challenges for the future are acoustic robustness, use of better acoustic features and models, use of multiple word pronunciations and efficient constraints for the access of a very large lexicon, sophisticated and multiple language models capable of representing various types of contexts, rich methods for extracting conceptual representations from word hypotheses and automatic learning methods for extracting various types of knowledge from corpora.

1.6   Language Representation

Salim Roukos

IBM T. J. Watson Research Center, Yorktown Heights, New York, USA

A speech recognizer converts the observed acoustic signal into the corresponding orthographic representation of the spoken sentence. The recognizer chooses its guess from a finite vocabulary of *words* that can be recognized. For simplicity, we assume that a word is uniquely identified by its spelling.[3]

Dramatic progress has been demonstrated in solving the speech recognition problem via the use of a statistical model of the joint distribution $p(W, O)$ of the sequence of spoken words W and the corresponding observed sequence of acoustic information O. This approach, pioneered by the IBM Continuous Speech Recognition group, is called the *source-channel model*. In this approach, the speech recognizer determines an estimate $\hat{W}$ of the identity of the spoken word sequence from the observed acoustic evidence O by using the *a posteriori* distribution $p(W|O)$. To minimize its error rate, the recognizer chooses the word sequence that maximizes the *a posteriori* distribution:

$$\hat{W} = \arg\max_W p(W|O) = \arg\max_W \frac{p(W)p(O|W)}{p(O)}$$

where $p(W)$ is the probability of the sequence of n-words W and $p(O|W)$ is the probability of observing the acoustic evidence O when the sequence W is spoken. The *a priori* distribution $p(W)$ of what words might be spoken (the source) is referred to as a language model (LM). The observation probability model $p(O|W)$ (the channel) is called the acoustic model. In this section, we discuss various approaches and issues for building the language model.

---

[3]For example, we treat as the same word the present and past participle of the verb read (*I read* vs. *I have read*) in the LM while the acoustic model will have different models corresponding to the different pronunciations.

The source-channel model has also been used in optical character recognition (OCR) where the observation sequence is the image of the printed characters, in handwriting recognition where the observation is the sequence of strokes on a tablet, or in machine translation (MT) where the observation is a sequence of words in one language and W represents the desired translation in another language. For all these applications, a language model is key. Therefore, the work on language modeling has a wide spectrum of applications.

1.6.1   Trigram Language Model

For a given word sequence $W = \{w_1, .., w_n\}$ of n words, we rewrite the LM probability as:

$$p(W) = p(w_1, .., w_n) = \prod_{i=1}^{n} p(w_i | w_0, .., w_{i-1})$$

where w_0 is chosen appropriately to handle the initial condition. The probability of the next word w_i depends on the history h_i of words that have been spoken so far. With this factorization the complexity of the model grows exponentially with the length of the history. To have a more practical and parsimonious model, only some aspects of the history are used to affect the probability of the next word. One way[4] to achieve this is to use a mapping $\phi(\ )$ that divides the space of histories into K equivalence classes. Then we can use as a model:

$$p(w_i | h_i) \approx p(w_i | \phi(h_i)).$$

Some of the most successful models of the past two decades are the simple *n-gram* models, particularly the trigram model ($n = 3$) where only the most recent two words of the history are used to condition the probability of the next word. The probability of a word sequence becomes:

$$p(W) \approx \prod_{i=1}^{n} p(w_i | w_{i-2}, w_{i-1}).$$

To estimate the trigram probabilities, one can use a large corpus of text, called the *training corpus*, to estimate trigram frequencies:

$$f_3(w_3 | w_1, w_2) = \frac{c_{123}}{c_{12}}$$

where c_{123} is the number of times the sequence of words $\{w_1, w_2, w_3\}$ is observed and c_{12} is the number of times the sequence $\{w_1, w_2\}$ is observed. For a vocabulary size V there are V^3 possible trigrams, which for 20,000 words

---

[4]Instead of having a single partition of the space of histories, one can use the exponential family to define a set of features that are used for computing the probability of an event. See the discussion on Maximum Entropy in Lau, Rosenfeld, et al. (1993); Darroch and Ratcliff (1972); Berger, Della Pietra, et al. (1994) for more details.

translates to 8 trillion trigrams. Many of these trigrams will not be seen in the training corpus. So these unseen trigrams will have zero probability using the trigram frequency as an estimate of the trigram probability. To solve this problem one needs a smooth estimate of the probability of unseen events. This can be done by linear interpolation of trigram, bigram, and unigram frequencies and a uniform distribution on the vocabulary:

$$p(w_3|w_1, w_2) = \lambda_3 f_3(w_3|w_1, w_2) + \lambda_2 f_2(w_3|w_2) + \lambda_1 f_1(w_3) + \lambda_0 \frac{1}{V}$$

where $f_2(\ )$ and $f_1(\ )$ are estimated by the ratio of the appropriate bigram and unigram counts. The weights of the linear interpolation are estimated by maximizing the probability of new *held-out* data different from the data used to estimate the *n-gram* frequencies. The forward-backward algorithm can be used to perform this maximum likelihood estimation problem.

In general, one uses more than one λ vector; one may want to rely more on the trigram frequencies for those histories that have a high count as compared to those histories that have a low count in the training data. To achieve this, one can use a bucketing scheme on the bigram and unigram counts of the history $b(c_{12}, c_2)$ to determine the interpolation weight vector $\lambda_{b(c_{12}, c_2)}$. Typically, 100 to 1,000 buckets are used. This method of smoothing is called *deleted interpolation* (Bahl, Jelinek, et al., 1983). Other smoothing schemes have been proposed such as backing-off, co-occurrence smoothing, and count re-estimation. In the work on language modeling, corpora varying in size from about a million to 500 million words have been used to build trigram models. Vocabulary sizes varying from 1,000 to 267,000 words have also been used. We discuss in the following section the perplexity measure for evaluating a language model.

1.6.2   Perplexity

Given two language models, one needs to compare them. One way is to use them in a recognizer and find the one that leads to the lower recognition error rate. This remains the best way of evaluating a language model. But to avoid this expensive approach one can use the information theory quantity of entropy to get an estimate of how good a LM might be. The basic idea is to average the log probability on a per word basis for a piece of new text not used in building the language model.

Denote by p the true distribution, that is unknown to us, of a segment of new text x of k words. Then the entropy on a per word basis is defined

$$H = \lim_{n \to \infty} -\frac{1}{k} \sum_{x} p(x) \log_2 p(x)$$

If every word in a vocabulary of size $|V|$ is equally likely then the entropy would be $\log_2 |V|$; for other distributions of the words $H \leq \log_2 |V|$.

To determine the probability of this segment of text we will use our language model denoted by $\tilde{p}$ which is different from the true unknown distribution p of

Domain	Perplexity
Radiology	20
Emergency medicine	60
Journalism	105
General English	247

Table 1.2: Perplexity of trigram models for different domains.

the new text. We can compute the average *logprob* on a per word basis defined as:

$$lp_k = -\frac{1}{k} \sum_{i=1}^{k} \log_2 \tilde{p}(w_i|h_i)$$

One can show that $\lim_{k->\inf} lp_k = lp \geq H$; i.e., the average *logprob* is no lower than the entropy of the test text. Obviously our goal is to find that LM which has an average *logprob* that is as close as possible to the entropy of the text.

A related measure to the average *logprob* called *perplexity* is used to evaluate a LM. Perplexity is defined as 2^{lp}. Perplexity is, crudely speaking, a measure of the size of the set of words from which the next word is chosen given that we observe the history of spoken words. The perplexity of a LM depends on the domain of discourse. For radiology reports, one expects less variation in the sentences than in general English. Table 1.2 shows the perplexity of several domains for large vocabulary (20,000 to 30,000 words) dictation systems. The lowest perplexity that has been published on the standard Brown Corpus of 1 million words of American English is about 247, corresponding to an entropy of 1.75 bits/character.

1.6.3 Vocabulary Size

The error rate of a speech recognizer is no less than the percentage of spoken words that are not in its vocabulary V. So a major part of building a language model is to select a vocabulary that will have maximal coverage on new text spoken to the recognizer. This remains a human intensive effort. A corpus of text is used in conjunction with dictionaries to determine appropriate vocabularies. A tokenizer[5] (a system that segments text into words) is needed. Then a unigram count for all of the spellings that occur in a corpus is determined. Those words that also occur in the dictionary are included. In addition a human screens the most frequent subset of new spellings to determine if they are words.

---

[5]Tokenizing English is fairly straightforward since white space separates words and simple rules can capture much of the punctuation. Special care has to be taken for abbreviations. For oriental languages such as Japanese and Chinese, word segmentation is a more complicated problem since space is not used between words.

Vocabulary Size	Static Coverage
20,000	94.1%
64,000	98.7%
100,000	99.3%
200,000	99.4%

Table 1.3: Static coverage of unseen text as a function of vocabulary size.

Number of added words	Text size	Static Coverage	Dynamic Coverage
100	1,800	93.4%	94.5%
400	12,800	94.8%	97.5%
3,100	81,600	94.8%	98.1%
6,400	211,000	94.4%	98.9%

Table 1.4: Dynamic coverage of unseen text as a function of vocabulary size and amount of new text.

Table 1.3 shows the coverage of new text using a fixed vocabulary of a given size for English. For more inflectional languages such as French or German, larger vocabulary sizes are required to achieve coverage similar to that of English. For a user of a speech recognition system, a more personalized vocabulary can be much more effective than a general fixed vocabulary. Table 1.4 shows the coverage as new words are added to a starting vocabulary of 20,000 words as more text is observed. In addition, Table 1.4 indicates the size of text recognized to add that many words. For many users, the dynamic coverage will be much better than the results shown in Table 1.4, with coverage ranging from 98.4% to 99.6% after 800 words are added.

1.6.4   Improved Language Models

A number of improvements have been proposed for the trigram LM. We give a brief overview of these models.

Class Models: Instead of using the actual words, one can use a set of word classes (which may be overlapping, i.e., a word may belong to many classes). Classes based on the part of speech tags, the morphological analysis of words, or semantic information have been tried. Also, automatically derived classes based on some statistical models of co-occurrence have been tried (see Brown,

Della Pietra, et al., 1990). The general class model is:

$$p(W) = \sum_{c_1^n} \prod_{i=1}^{n} p(w_i|c_i)p(c_i|c_{i-2}, c_{i-1})$$

If the classes are non-overlapping, then c(w) is unique and the probability is:

$$p(W) = \prod_{i=1}^{n} p(w_i|c_i)p(c_i|c_{i-2}, c_{i-1})$$

These tri-class models have had higher perplexities that the corresponding trigram model. However, they have led to a reduction in perplexity when linearly combined with the trigram model.

Dynamic Models: Another idea introduced in DeMori and Kuhn (1990) is to take into account the document-long history to capture the burstiness of words. For example, in this section the probability that the word *model* will occur is much higher than its average frequency in general text. Using a cache of the recently observed words one can build a more dynamic LM using either the class model (DeMori & Kuhn, 1990) or the trigram model (Jelinek, Merialdo, et al., 1991). Expanding on this idea, one can can also affect the probability of related words called triggered words (see Lau, Rosenfeld, et al., 1993).

Mixture Models: Another approach is based on clustering corpora into several clusters. The linear combination of cluster-specific trigram models is used for modeling new text:

$$p(W) = \prod_{i=1}^{n} \sum_{j=1}^{k} \lambda_j p_j(w_n|w_{n-2}, w_{n-1})$$

where $p_j()$ is estimated from the j-th cluster of text. Another type of mixture is to use a sentence level mixture as in Iyer, Ostendorf, et al. (1994).

Structure-based Models: Instead of using the identity of most recent words to define the equivalence class of a history, the state of a parser has been used to define the conditioning event (Goddeau & Zue, 1992). Also, the use of link grammar to capture long distance bigrams has recently been proposed (Lafferty, Sleator, et al., 1992).

1.6.5 Future Directions

There are several areas of research that can be pursued for improved language modeling.

- **Vocabulary Selection:** How to determine a vocabulary for a new domain, particularly to personalize the vocabulary to a user while maximizing the coverage for a user's text. This is a problem that may be more severe for highly inflected languages and for oriental languages where the notion of a word is not clearly defined for native speakers of the language.

- **Domain Adaptation:** How to estimate an effective language model for domains which may not have large online corpora of representative text. Another related problem is topic spotting where the topic-specific language model can be used to model the incoming text from a collection of domain-specific language models.

- **Incorporating Structure:** The current state of the art in language modeling has not been able to improve on performance by the use of the structure (whether surface parse trees or deep structure such as predicate argument structure) that is present in language. A concerted research effort to explore structure-based language models may be the key to significant progress in language modeling. This will become more possible as annotated (parsed) data becomes available. Current research using probabilistic LR grammars, or probabilistic Context-Free grammars (including link grammars) is still in its infancy and would benefit from the increased availability of parsed data.

1.7   Speaker Recognition

Sadaoki Furui

NTT Human Interface Laboratories, Tokyo, Japan

1.7.1   Principles of Speaker Recognition

Speaker recognition, which can be classified into identification and verification, is the process of automatically recognizing who is speaking on the basis of individual information included in speech waves. This technique makes it possible to use the speaker's voice to verify their identity and control access to services such as voice dialing, banking by telephone, telephone shopping, database access services, information services, voice mail, security control for confidential information areas, and remote access to computers. AT&T and TI (with Sprint) have started field tests and actual application of speaker recognition technology; Sprint's Voice Phone Card is already being used by many customers. In this way, speaker recognition technology is expected to create new services that will make our daily lives more convenient. Another important application of speaker recognition technology is for forensic purposes.

Figure 1.8 shows the basic structures of speaker identification and verification systems. Speaker identification is the process of determining which registered speaker provides a given utterance. Speaker verification, on the other hand, is the process of accepting or rejecting the identity claim of a speaker. Most applications in which a voice is used as the key to confirm the identity of a speaker are classified as speaker verification.

There is also the case called *open set* identification, in which a reference model for an unknown speaker may not exist. This is usually the case in forensic applications. In this situation, an additional decision alternative, *the unknown*

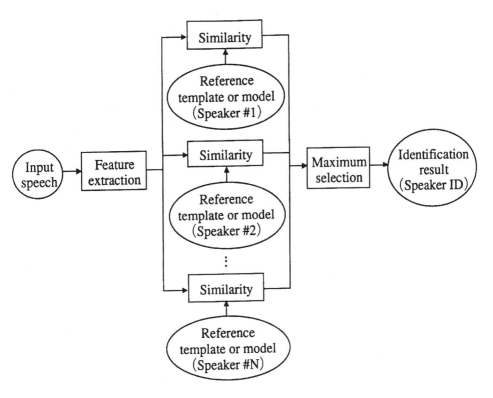

(a) Speaker identification

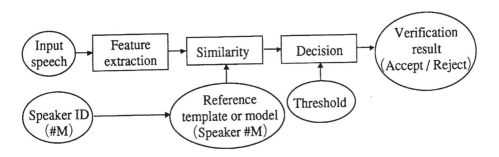

(b) Speaker verification

Figure 1.8: Basic structures of speaker recognition systems.

does not match any of the models, is required. In both verification and identification processes, an additional threshold test can be used to determine if the match is close enough to accept the decision or if more speech data needed.

Speaker recognition methods can also be divided into text-dependent and text-independent methods. The former require the speaker to say key words or sentences having the same text for both training and recognition trials, whereas the latter do not rely on a specific text being spoken.

Both text-dependent and independent methods share a problem however. These systems can be easily deceived because someone who plays back the recorded voice of a registered speaker saying the key words or sentences can be accepted as the registered speaker. To cope with this problem, there are methods in which a small set of words, such as digits, are used as key words and each user is prompted to utter a given sequence of key words that is randomly chosen every time the system is used. Yet even this method is not completely reliable, since it can be deceived with advanced electronic recording equipment that can reproduce key words in a requested order. Therefore, a text-prompted (machine-driven-text-dependent) speaker recognition method has recently been proposed by Matsui and Furui (1993b).

1.7.2 Feature Parameters

Speaker identity is correlated with the physiological and behavioral characteristics of the speaker. These characteristics exist both in the spectral envelope (vocal tract characteristics) and in the supra-segmental features (voice source characteristics and dynamic features spanning several segments).

The most common short-term spectral measurements currently used are Linear Predictive Coding (LPC)-derived cepstral coefficients and their regression coefficients. A spectral envelope reconstructed from a truncated set of cepstral coefficients is much smoother than one reconstructed from LPC coefficients. Therefore it provides a stabler representation from one repetition to another of a particular speaker's utterances. As for the regression coefficients, typically the first- and second-order coefficients are extracted at every frame period to represent the spectral dynamics. These coefficients are derivatives of the time functions of the cepstral coefficients and are respectively called the delta- and delta-delta-cepstral coefficients.

1.7.3 Normalization Techniques

The most significant factor affecting automatic speaker recognition performance is variation in the signal characteristics from trial to trial (intersession variability and variability over time). Variations arise from the speakers themselves, from differences in recording and transmission conditions, and from background noise. Speakers cannot repeat an utterance precisely the same way from trial to trial. It is well known that samples of the same utterance recorded in one session are much more highly correlated than samples recorded in separate sessions. There are also long-term changes in voices.

It is important for speaker recognition systems to accommodate these variations. Two types of normalization techniques have been tried; one in the parameter domain, the other in the distance/similarity domain.

Parameter-Domain Normalization

Spectral equalization, the so-called *blind equalization* method, is a typical normalization technique in the parameter domain that has been confirmed to be effective in reducing linear channel effects and long-term spectral variation (Atal, 1974; Furui, 1981). This method is especially effective for text-dependent speaker recognition applications that use sufficiently long utterances. Cepstral coefficients are averaged over the duration of an entire utterance and the averaged values subtracted from the cepstral coefficients of each frame. Additive variation in the log spectral domain can be compensated for fairly well by this method. However, it unavoidably removes some text-dependent and speaker specific features; therefore it is inappropriate for short utterances in speaker recognition applications.

Distance/Similarity-Domain Normalization

A normalization method for distance (similarity, likelihood) values using a likelihood ratio has been proposed by Higgins, Bahler, et al. (1991). The likelihood ratio is defined as the ratio of two conditional probabilities of the observed measurements of the utterance: the first probability is the likelihood of the acoustic data given the claimed identity of the speaker, and the second is the likelihood given that the speaker is an imposter. The likelihood ratio normalization approximates optimal scoring in the Bayes sense.

A normalization method based on *a posteriori* probability has also been proposed by Matsui and Furui (1994a). The difference between the normalization method based on the likelihood ratio and the method based on *a posteriori* probability is whether or not the claimed speaker is included in the speaker set for normalization; the speaker set used in the method based on the likelihood ratio does not include the claimed speaker, whereas the normalization term for the method based on *a posteriori* probability is calculated by using all the reference speakers, including the claimed speaker.

Experimental results indicate that the two normalization methods are almost equally effective (Matsui & Furui, 1994a). They both improve speaker separability and reduce the need for speaker-dependent or text-dependent thresholding, as compared with scoring using only a model of the claimed speaker.

A new method has recently been proposed in which the normalization term is approximated by the likelihood of a single mixture model representing the parameter distribution for all the reference speakers. An advantage of this method is that the computational cost of calculating the normalization term is very small, and this method has been confirmed to give much better results than either of the above-mentioned normalization methods (Matsui & Furui, 1994a). 1994].

1.7.4   Text-Dependent Speaker Recognition Methods

Text-dependent methods are usually based on template-matching techniques. In this approach, the input utterance is represented by a sequence of feature vectors, generally short-term spectral feature vectors. The time axes of the input utterance and each reference template or reference model of the registered speakers are aligned using a dynamic time warping (DTW) algorithm, and the degree of similarity between them, accumulated from the beginning to the end of the utterance, is calculated.

The hidden Markov model (HMM) can efficiently model statistical variation in spectral features. Therefore, HMM-based methods were introduced as extensions of the DTW-based methods, and have achieved significantly better recognition accuracies (Naik, Netsch, et al., 1989).

1.7.5   Text-Independent Speaker Recognition Methods

One of the most successful text-independent recognition methods is based on vector quantization (VQ). In this method, VQ codebooks consisting of a small number of representative feature vectors are used as an efficient means of characterizing speaker-specific features. A speaker-specific codebook is generated by clustering the training feature vectors of each speaker. In the recognition stage, an input utterance is vector-quantized using the codebook of each reference speaker and the VQ distortion accumulated over the entire input utterance is used to make the recognition decision.

Temporal variation in speech signal parameters over the long term can be represented by stochastic Markovian transitions between states. Therefore, methods using an ergodic HMM, where all possible transitions between states are allowed, have been proposed. Speech segments are classified into one of the broad phonetic categories corresponding to the HMM states. After the classification, appropriate features are selected.

In the training phase, reference templates are generated and verification thresholds are computed for each phonetic category. In the verification phase, after the phonetic categorization, a comparison with the reference template for each particular category provides a verification score for that category. The final verification score is a weighted linear combination of the scores from each category.

This method was extended to the richer class of mixture autoregressive (AR) HMMs. In these models, the states are described as a linear combination (mixture) of AR sources. It can be shown that mixture models are equivalent to a larger HMM with simple states, with additional constraints on the possible transitions between states.

It has been shown that a continuous ergodic HMM method is far superior to a discrete ergodic HMM method and that a continuous ergodic HMM method is as robust as a VQ-based method when enough training data is available. However, when little data are available, the VQ-based method is more robust than a continuous HMM method (Matsui & Furui, 1993a).

A method using statistical dynamic features has recently been proposed. In this method, a multivariate auto-regression (MAR) model is applied to the time series of cepstral vectors and used to characterize speakers. It was reported that identification and verification rates were almost the same as obtained by an HMM-based method (Griffin, Matsui, et al., 1994).

1.7.6 Text-Prompted Speaker Recognition Method

In the text-prompted speaker recognition method, the recognition system prompts each user with a new key sentence every time the system is used and accepts the input utterance only when it decides that it was the registered speaker who repeated the prompted sentence. The sentence can be displayed as characters or spoken by a synthesized voice. Because the vocabulary is unlimited, prospective impostors cannot know in advance what sentence will be requested. Not only can this method accurately recognize speakers, but it can also reject utterances whose text differs from the prompted text, even if it is spoken by the registered speaker. A recorded voice can thus be correctly rejected.

This method is facilitated by using speaker-specific phoneme models as basic acoustic units. One of the major issues in applying this method is how to properly create these speaker-specific phoneme models from training utterances of a limited size. The phoneme models are represented by Gaussian-mixture continuous HMMs or tied-mixture HMMs, and they are made by adapting speaker-independent phoneme models to each speaker's voice. In order to properly adapt the models of phonemes that are not included in the training utterances, a new adaptation method based on tied-mixture HMMs was recently proposed by Matsui and Furui (1994b).

In the recognition stage, the system concatenates the phoneme models of each registered speaker to create a sentence HMM, according to the prompted text. Then, the likelihood of the input speech matching the sentence model is calculated and used for the speaker recognition decision. If the likelihood is high enough, the speaker is accepted as the claimed speaker.

1.7.7 Future Directions

Although many recent advances and successes in speaker recognition have been achieved, there are still many problems for which good solutions remain to be found. Most of these problems arise from variability, including speaker-generated variability and variability in channel and recording conditions. It is very important to investigate feature parameters that are stable over time, insensitive to the variation of speaking manner, including the speaking rate and level, and robust against variations in voice quality due to causes such as voice disguise or colds. It is also important to develop a method to cope with the problem of distortion due to telephone sets and channels, and background and channel noises.

From the human-interface point of view, it is important to consider how the users should be prompted, and how recognition errors should be handled.

Studies on ways to automatically extract the speech periods of each person separately from a dialogue involving more than two people have recently appeared as an extension of speaker recognition technology.

This section was not intended to be a comprehensive review of speaker recognition technology. Rather, it was intended to give an overview of recent advances and the problems which must be solved in the future. The reader is referred to the following papers for more general reviews: Furui, 1986a; Furui, 1989; Furui, 1991; Furui, 1994; O'Shaughnessy, 1986; Rosenberg & Soong, 1991.

1.8   Spoken Language Understanding[6]

Patti Price

SRI International, Menlo Park, California, USA

1.8.1   Overview

Spoken language understanding involves two primary component technologies (each covered elsewhere in this volume): speech recognition (SR), and natural language (NL) understanding. The integration of speech and natural language has great advantages: To NL, SR can bring prosodic information (information important for syntax and semantics but not well represented in text); NL can bring to SR additional knowledge sources (e.g., syntax and semantics). For both, integration affords the possibility of many more applications than could otherwise be envisioned, and the acquisition of new techniques and knowledge bases not previously represented. The integration of these technologies presents technical challenges, and challenges related to the quite different cultures, techniques and beliefs of the people representing the component technologies.

In large part, NL research has grown from symbolic systems approaches in computer science and linguistics departments. The desire to model language understanding is often motivated by a desire to understand cognitive processes and, therefore, the underlying theories tend to be from linguistics and psychology. Practical applications have been less important than increasing intuitions about human processes. Therefore, coverage of phenomena of theoretical interest—usually the more rare phenomena—has traditionally been more important than broad coverage.

Speech recognition research, on the other hand, has largely been practiced in engineering departments. The desire to model speech is often motivated by a desire to produce practical applications. Techniques motivated by knowledge of human processes have therefore been less important than techniques that can be automatically developed or tuned, and broad coverage of a representative sample is more important than coverage of any particular phenomenon.

---

[6]I am grateful to Victor Zue for many very helpful suggestions.

There are certainly technical challenges to the integration of SR and NL. However, progress toward meeting these challenges has been slowed by the differences outlined above. Collaboration can be inhibited by differences in motivation, interests, theoretical underpinnings, techniques, tools, and criteria for success. However, both groups have much to gain from collaboration. For the SR engineers, human language understanding provides an existence proof, and needs to be taken into account, since most applications involve interaction with at least one human. For the AI NL researchers, statistical and other engineering techniques can be important tools for their inquiries.

A survey of the papers on SR and NL in the last five to ten years indicates that there is growing interest in the use of engineering techniques in NL investigations. Although the use of linguistic knowledge and techniques in engineering seems to have lagged, there are signs of growth as engineers tackle the more abstract linguistic units. These units are more rare, and therefore more difficult to model by standard, data-hungry engineering techniques.

1.8.2 State of the Art

Evaluation of spoken language understanding systems (see chapter 13) is required to estimate the state of the art objectively. However, evaluation itself has been one of the challenges of spoken language understanding. A brief survey of spoken language understanding work in Europe, Japan and the U.S. is surveyed briefly below, and evaluation will be discussed in the following section.

Several sites in Canada, Europe and Japan have been researching spoken language understanding systems, including INRS in Canada, LIMSI in France, KTH in Sweden, the Center for Language Technology in Denmark, SRI International and DRA in the UK, Toshiba in Japan. The five year ESPRIT SUNDIAL project, which concluded in August 1993, involved several sites and the development of prototypes for train timetable queries in German and Italian and flight queries in English and French. All these systems are described in articles in Eurospeech (1993). The special issue of Speech Communication on Spoken Dialogue (Shirai & Furui, 1994), also includes several system descriptions, including those from NTT, MIT, Toshiba, and Canon.

In the ARPA program, the air travel planning domain has been chosen to support evaluation of spoken language systems (Pallett, 1991; Pallett, 1992; Pallett, Dahlgren, et al., 1992; Pallett, Fisher, et al., 1990; Pallett, Fiscus, et al., 1993; Pallett, Fiscus, et al., 1994; Pallett, Fiscus, et al., 1995). Vocabularies for these systems are usually about 2000 words. The speech and language are spontaneous, though fairly planned (since people are typically talking to a machine rather than to a person, and often use a push-to-talk button). The speech recognition utterance error rates in the December 1994 benchmarks was about 13% to 25%. The utterance understanding error rates range from 6% to 41%, although about 25% of the utterances are considered *unevaluable* in the testing paradigm, so these figures do not consider the same set (Pallett, 1991; Pallett, 1992; Pallett, Dahlgren, et al., 1992; Pallett, Fisher, et al., 1990; Pallett, Fiscus, et al., 1993; Pallett, Fiscus, et al., 1994; Pallett, Fiscus, et al., 1995).

For limited domains, these error rates may be acceptable for many potential applications. Since conversational repairs in human-human dialogue can often be in the ranges observed for these systems, the bounding factor in applications may not be the error rates so much as the ability of the system to manage and recover from errors.

1.8.3   Evaluation of Spoken Language Understanding Systems

The benchmarks for spoken language understanding involve spontaneous speech input usually involving a real system, and sometimes with a human in the loop. The systems are scored in terms of the correctness of the response from the common database of information, including flight and fare information. Performing this evaluation automatically requires human annotation to select the correct answer, define the minimal and maximal answers accepted, and to decide whether the query is ambiguous and/or answerable. The following sites participated in the most recent benchmarks for spoken language understanding: AT&T Bell Laboratories, Bolt Beranek and Newman, Carnegie Mellon University, Massachusetts Institute of Technology, MITRE, SRI International, and Unisys. Descriptions of these systems appear in ARPA (1995b).

There is a need to reduce the costs of evaluation, and to improve the quality of evaluations. One limitation of the current methodology is that the evaluated systems must be rather passive, since the procedure does not generally allow for responses that are not a database response. This means that the benchmarks do not assess an important component of any real system: its ability to guide the user and to provide useful information in the face of limitations of the user or of the system itself. This aspect of the evaluation also forces the elimination of a significant portion of the data (about 25% in the most recent benchmark). Details on evaluation mechanisms are included in chapter 13. Despite the imperfections of these benchmarks, the sharing of ideas and the motivational aspects of the common benchmarks have yielded a great deal of technology transfer and communication.

1.8.4   Challenges

The integration of SR and NL in applications is faced with many of the same challenges that each of the components face: accuracy, robustness, portability, speed, and size, for example. However, the integration also gives rise to some new challenges as well, including: integration strategies, coordination of understanding components with system outputs, the effective use in NL of a new source of information from SR (prosody, in particular), and the handling of spontaneous speech effects (since people do not speak the way they write). Each of these areas will be described briefly below.

Integration

Several mechanisms for the communication among components have been explored. There is much evidence that human speech understanding involves the integration of a great variety of knowledge sources, including knowledge of the world or context, knowledge of the speaker and/or topic, lexical frequency, previous uses of a word or a semantically related topic, facial expressions, and prosody, in addition to the acoustic attributes of the words. In SR, tighter integration of components has consistently led to improved performance, and tight integration of SR and NL has been a rather consistent goal. However, as grammatical coverage increases, standard NL techniques can become computationally difficult. Further, with increased coverage, NL tends to provide less constraint for SR.

The simplest approach of integration is simply to concatenate an existing speech recognition system and an existing NL system. However, this is suboptimal for several reasons. First, it is a very fragile interface and any errors that might be in the speech recognition system are propagated to the NL system. Second, the speech system does not then have a chance to take advantage of the more detailed syntactic, semantic and other higher level knowledge sources in deciding on what the words are. It is well known that people rely heavily on these sources in deciding what someone has said.

Perhaps the most important reason for the sub-optimality of a simple concatenation is the fact that the writing mode differs greatly from the speaking mode. In the written form, people can create more complex sentences than in the spoken form because they have more time to think and plan. Readers have more time than do listeners to think and review, and they have visual cues to help ascertain the structure. Further, most instances of written text are not created in an interactive mode. Therefore, written communications tend to be more verbose than verbal communications. In non-interactive communications, the writer (or speaker in a non-interactive monologue) tries to foresee what questions a reader (or listener) may have. In an interactive dialogue, a speaker can usually rely on the other participant to ask questions when clarification is necessary, and therefore it is possible to be less verbose.

Another important difference between the written and spoken mode is that the spoken mode is strictly linear. A writer can pause for days or months before continuing a thought, can correct typos, can rearrange grammatical constructions and revise the organization of the material presented without leaving a trace in the result the reader sees. In spoken language interactions, every pause, restart, revision and hesitation has a consequence available to the listener. These effects are outlined further in the section on spontaneous speech below.

The differences between speaking and writing are compounded by the fact that most NL work has focussed on the written form, and if spoken language has been considered, except for rare examples such as Hindle (1983), it has largely been based on intuitions about the spoken language that would have occurred if not for the *noise* of spontaneous speech effects. As indicated in the overview, coverage of *interesting* linguistic phenomena has been a more important goal than testing coverage on occurring samples, written or spoken. More attention has been paid to correct analyses of complete sentences than to methods for recovery of interpretations when parses are incomplete, with the exceptions of some *robust* parsing techniques which still require a great deal more effort before they can be relied on in spoken language understanding systems (see section 3.7).

Because of the differences between speaking and writing, statistical models based on written materials will not match spoken language very well. With NL analyses based predominantly on complete parsing of *grammatically correct* sentences (based on intuitions of grammaticality of written text), traditional NL analyses often do very poorly when faced with transcribed spontaneous speech. Further, very little work has considered spontaneous effects. In sum, simple concatenation of existing modules does not, in general, tend to work very well.

To combat the mismatch between existing SR and NL modules, two trends have been observed. The first is an increased use of *semantic*, as opposed to *syntactic grammars* (see section 3.6). Such grammars rely on finding an interpretation without requiring *grammatical* input (where *grammatical* may be interpreted either in terms of traditional text-book grammaticality, or in terms of a particular grammar constructed for the task). Because semantic grammars focus on meaning in terms of the particular application, they can be more robust to grammatical deviations (see section 3.6). The second observed trend is the *n-best* interface. In the face of cultural and technical difficulties related to a tight integration, *n-best* integration has become popular. In this approach, the connection between SR and NL can be strictly serial: one component performs its computation, sends it to another component, and that result is sent to yet another module. The inherent fragility of the strictly serial approach is mitigated by the fact that SR sends NL not just the best hypothesis from speech recognition, but the *n-best* (where N may be on the order of 10 to 100 sentence hypotheses). The NL component can then score hypotheses for grammaticality and/or use other knowledge sources to determine the best-scoring hypothesis. Frequently, the more costly knowledge sources are saved for this rescoring. More generally, there are several passes, a *progressive search* in which the search space is gradually narrowed and more knowledge sources are brought to bear. This approach is computationally tractable and accommodates great modularity of design. The (D)ARPA, ESCA Eurospeech and ICSLP proceedings over the past several years contain several examples of the *n-best* approach and ways of bringing higher level knowledge sources to bear in SR (DARPA, 1990; DARPA, 1991a; DARPA, 1992a; ARPA, 1993a; ARPA, 1994; ARPA, 1995a; Eurospeech, 1989; Eurospeech, 1991; Eurospeech, 1993; ICSLP, 1990; ICSLP, 1992; ICSLP, 1994). In addition, the special issue of Speech Communication on Spoken Dialogue (Shirai & Furui, 1994) contains several contributions investigating the integration of SR and NL.

Coordination of Understanding Components with System Outputs

With few exceptions, current research in spoken language systems has focused on the input side; i.e., the understanding of spoken input. However, many if not most potential applications involve a collaboration between the human and the computer. In many cases, spoken language output is an appropriate means of communication that may or may not be taken advantage of. Telephone-based applications are particularly important, since their use in spoken language understanding systems can make access to crucial data as convenient as the nearest phone, and since voice is the natural and (except for the as yet rare video-phones) usually the only modality available. Spoken outputs are also crucial in speech translation. The use of spoken output technologies, covered in more detail in chapter 5, is an important challenge to spoken language systems. In particular, we need reliable techniques to:

- decide when it is appropriate to provide a spoken output in conjunction with some other (e.g., screen-based) output and/or to instigate a clarification dialogue in order to recover from a potential misunderstanding,

- generate the content of spoken output given the data representation, context and dialogue state, and coordinate it with other outputs when present,

- synthesize a natural, easily interpreted and appropriate spoken version of the response taking advantage of the context and dialogue state to emphasize certain information or to express urgency, for example, and

- coordinate spoken outputs to guide the user toward usage better adapted to system capabilities.

Since people tend to be very cooperative in conversation, a system should not output structures it is not capable of understanding. By coordinating inputs and outputs, the system can guide the user toward usage better adapted to the particular system. Not doing so can be very frustrating for the user.

Prosody

Prosody can be defined as the suprasegmental information in speech; that is, information that cannot be localized to a specific sound segment, or information that does not change the segmental identity of speech segments. For example, patterns of variation in fundamental frequency, duration, amplitude or intensity, pauses, and speaking rate have been shown to carry information about such prosodic elements as lexical stress, phrase breaks, and declarative or interrogative sentence form. Prosody consists of a phonological aspect (characterized by discrete, abstract units) and a phonetic aspect (characterized by continuously varying acoustic correlates).

Prosodic information is a source of information not available in text-based systems, except insofar as punctuation may indicate some prosodic information. Prosody can provide information about syntactic structure, it can convey discourse information, and it can also relay information about emotion and attitude. Surveys of how this can be done appear in Price and Ostendorf (1995); Shirai and Furui (1994); ESCA (1993).

Functionally, in languages of the world, prosody is used to indicate segmentation and saliency. The segmentation (or grouping) function of prosody may be related more to syntax (with some relation to semantics), while the saliency or prominence function may play a larger role in semantics than in syntax. To make maximum use of the potential of prosody will require tight integration, since the acoustic evidence needs to inform abstract units in syntax, semantics, discourse, and pragmatics.

Spontaneous Speech

The same acoustic attributes that indicate much of the prosodic structure (pitch and duration patterns) are also very common in aspects of spontaneous speech that seem to be more related to the speech planning process than to the structure of the utterance. For example, an extra long syllable followed by a pause can indicate either a large boundary that may be correlated with a syntactic boundary, or that the speaker is trying to plan the next part of the utterance. Similarly, a prominent syllable may mean that the syllable is new or important information, or that it replaces something previously said in error.

Disfluencies (e.g., *um*, repeated words, and repairs or false starts) are common in normal speech. It is possible that these phenomena can be isolated, e.g., by means of a posited *edit signal*, by joint modeling of intonation and duration, and/or by models that take into account syntactic patterns. However, modeling of speech disfluencies is only beginning to be modeled in spoken language systems. Two recent Ph.D. theses survey this topic (Lickley, 1994; Shriberg, 1994).

Disfluencies in human-human conversation are quite frequent, and a normal part of human communication. Their distribution is not random, and, in fact, may be a part of the communication itself. Disfluencies tend to be less frequent in human-computer interactions than in human-human interactions. However, the reduction in occurrences of disfluencies may be due to the fact that people are as yet not comfortable talking to computers. They may also be less frequent because there is more of an opportunity for the speaker to plan, and less of a potential for interruption. As people become increasingly comfortable with human-computer interactions and concentrate more on the task at hand than on monitoring their speech, disfluencies can be expected to increase. Speech disfluencies are a challenge to the integration of SR and NL since the evidence for disfluencies is distributed throughout all linguistic levels, from phonetic to at least the syntactic and semantic levels.

1.8.5   Future Directions

Although there have been significant recent gains in spoken language understanding, current technology is far from human-like: only systems in limited domains can be envisioned in the near term, and the portability of existing techniques is still rather limited. On the near horizon, application areas that appear to be a good match to technology include those that are naturally limited, for example database access (probably the most popular task across languages). With the rise in cellular phone use, and as rapid access to information becomes an increasingly important economic factor, telephone access to data and telephone transactions will no doubt rise dramatically. Mergers of telecommunications companies with video and computing companies will also no doubt add to the potential for automatic speech understanding.

While such short-term applications possibilities are exciting, if we can successfully meet the challenges outlined in previous sections, we can envision an information revolution on par with the development of writing systems. Spoken language is still the means of communication used first and foremost by humans, and only a small percentage of human communication is written. Automatic spoken language understanding can add many advantages normally associated only with text: random access, sorting, and access at different times and places. Making this vision a reality will require significant advances in the integration of SR and NL, and, in particular, the ability to better model prosody and disfluencies.

1.9　Chapter References

Acero, A. and Stern, R. M. (1990). Environmental robustness in automatic speech recognition. In *Proceedings of the 1990 International Conference on Acoustics, Speech, and Signal Processing*, pages 849–852, Albuquerque, New Mexico. Institute of Electrical and Electronic Engineers.

Alleva, F., Huang, X., and Hwang, M. Y. (1993). An improved search algorithm using incremental knowledge for continuous speech recognition. In *Proceedings of the 1993 International Conference on Acoustics, Speech, and Signal Processing*, volume 2, pages 307–310, Minneapolis, Minnesota. Institute of Electrical and Electronic Engineers.

Alvarado, V. M. and Silverman, H. F. (1990). Experimental results showing the effects of optimal spacing between elements of a linear microphone array. In *Proceedings of the 1990 International Conference on Acoustics, Speech, and Signal Processing*, pages 837–840, Albuquerque, New Mexico. Institute of Electrical and Electronic Engineers.

Anastasakos, T., Makhoul, J., and Schwartz, R. (1994). Adaptation to new microphones using tied-mixture normalization. In *Proceedings of the 1994 International Conference on Acoustics, Speech, and Signal Processing*, volume 1, pages 433–436, Adelaide, Australia. Institute of Electrical and Electronic Engineers.

Applebaum, T. H. and Hanson, B. A. (1989). Regression features for recognition of speech in quiet and in noise. In *Proceedings of the 1989 International*

Conference on Acoustics, Speech, and Signal Processing, pages 985–988, Glasgow, Scotland. Institute of Electrical and Electronic Engineers.

ARPA (1993). *Proceedings of the 1993 ARPA Human Language Technology Workshop*, Princeton, New Jersey. Advanced Research Projects Agency, Morgan Kaufmann.

ARPA (1994). *Proceedings of the 1994 ARPA Human Language Technology Workshop*, Princeton, New Jersey. Advanced Research Projects Agency, Morgan Kaufmann.

ARPA (1995a). *Proceedings of the 1995 ARPA Human Language Technology Workshop*. Advanced Research Projects Agency, Morgan Kaufmann.

ARPA (1995b). *Proceedings of the ARPA Spoken Language Systems Technology Workshop*. Advanced Research Projects Agency, Morgan Kaufmann.

Atal, B. S. (1974). Effectiveness of linear prediction characteristics of the speech wave for automatic speaker identification and verification. *Journal of the Acoustical Society of America*, 55(6):1304–1312.

Aubert, X., Dugast, C., Ney, H., and Steinbiss, V. (1994). Large vocabulary continuous speech recognition of wall street journal data. In *Proceedings of the 1994 International Conference on Acoustics, Speech, and Signal Processing*, volume 2, pages 129–132, Adelaide, Australia. Institute of Electrical and Electronic Engineers.

Bahl, L. R., Bellegarda, J. R., de Souza, P. V., Gopalakrishnan, P. S., Nahamoo, D., and Picheny, M. A. (1993). Multonic Markov word models for large vocabulary continuous speech recognition. *IEEE Transactions on Speech and Audio Processing*, 1(3):334–344.

Bahl, L. R., Brown, P. F., de Souza, P. V., Mercer, R. L., and Picheny, M. A. (1993). A method for the construction of acoustic Markov models for words. *IEEE Transactions on Speech and Audio Processing*, 1(4):443–452.

Bahl, L. R., de Souza, P. V., Gopalakrishnan, P. S., Nahamoo, D., and Picheny, M. A. (1991). Decision trees for phonological rules in continuous speech. In *Proceedings of the 1991 International Conference on Acoustics, Speech, and Signal Processing*, volume 1, pages 185–188, Toronto. Institute of Electrical and Electronic Engineers.

Bahl, L. R., Jelinek, F., and Mercer, R. L. (1983). A maximum likelihood approach to continuous speech recognition. *IEEE Transactions on Pattern Analysis and Machine Intelligence*, 5(2):179–190.

Bellegarda, J. R., de Souza, P. V., Nadas, A. J., Nahamoo, D., Picheny, M. A., and Bahl, L. (1992). Robust speaker adaptation using a piecewise linear acoustic mapping. In *Proceedings of the 1992 International Conference on Acoustics, Speech, and Signal Processing*, volume 1, pages 445–448, San Francisco. Institute of Electrical and Electronic Engineers.

Bengio, Y., DeMori, R., Flammia, G., and Kompe, R. (1992). Global optimization of a neural network—hidden Markov model hybrid. *IEEE Transactions on Neural Networks*, 3(2):252–259.

Berger, A., Della Pietra, S., and Della Pietra, V. (1994). Maximum entropy methods in machine translation. Technical report, IBM Research Report.

Bocchieri, E. L. (1993). Vector quantization for the efficient computation of continuous density likelihoods. In *Proceedings of the 1993 International Conference on Acoustics, Speech, and Signal Processing*, volume 2, pages 692–694, Minneapolis, Minnesota. Institute of Electrical and Electronic Engineers.

Brown, P. F., Della Pietra, V. J., de Souza, P. V., Lai, J. C., and Mercer, R. L. (1990). Class-based *n*-gram models of natural language. In *Proceedings of the IBM Natural Language ITL*, Paris, France.

Che, C., Lin, J., Pearson, J., de Vries, B., and Flanagan, J. (1994). Microphones arrays and neural networks for robust speech recognition. In *Proceedings of the 1994 ARPA Human Language Technology Workshop*, Princeton, New Jersey. Advanced Research Projects Agency, Morgan Kaufmann.

Cohen, J., Gish, H., and Flanagan, J. (1994). Switchboard—the second year. Technical Report /pub/caipworks2 at ftp.rutgers.edu, CAIP Summer Workshop in Speech Recognition: Frontiers in Speech Processing II.

Cohen, J. R. (1989). Application of an auditory model to speech recognition. *Journal of the Acoustical Society of America*, 85(6):2623–2629.

Cole, R. A., Hirschman, L., et al. (1992). Workshop on spoken language understanding. Technical Report CSE 92-014, Oregon Graduate Institute of Science & Technology, P.O.Box 91000, Portland, OR 97291-1000 USA.

DARPA (1990). *Proceedings of the Third DARPA Speech and Natural Language Workshop*, Hidden Valley, Pennsylvania. Defense Advanced Research Projects Agency, Morgan Kaufmann.

DARPA (1991). *Proceedings of the Fourth DARPA Speech and Natural Language Workshop*, Pacific Grove, California. Defense Advanced Research Projects Agency, Morgan Kaufmann.

DARPA (1992). *Proceedings of the Fifth DARPA Speech and Natural Language Workshop*. Defense Advanced Research Projects Agency, Morgan Kaufmann.

Darroch, J. N. and Ratcliff, D. (1972). Generalized iterative scaling for log-linear models. *The Annals of Mathematical Statistics*, 43:1470–1480.

Daubechies, I. (1990). The wavelet transform, time-frequency localization and signal analysis. *IEEE Transactions on Acoustics, Speech and Signal Processing*, ASSP-36(5):961–1005.

Davis, S. B. and Mermelstein, P. (1980). Comparison of parametric representations for monosyllabic word recognition in continuously spoken sentences. *IEEE Transactions on Acoustics, Speech and Signal Processing*, ASSP-28:357–366.

DeMori, R. and Kuhn, R. (1990). A cache-based natural language model for speech recognition. *IEEE Transactions on Pattern Analysis and Machine Intelligence*, PAMI-12(6):570–583.

Dempster, A. P., Laird, N. M., and Rubin, D. B. (1977). Maximum-likelihood from incompete data via the EM algorithm. *Journal of the Royal Statistical Society, Ser. B.*, 39:1–38.

Digalakis, V. and Murveit, H. (1994). Genones: Optimizing the degree of mixture tying in a large vocabulary hidden Markov model based speech recognizer. In *Proceedings of the 1994 International Conference on Acoustics, Speech, and Signal Processing*, volume 1, pages 537–540, Adelaide, Australia. Institute of Electrical and Electronic Engineers.

Duda, R. O., Lyon, R. F., and Slaney, M. (1990). Correlograms and the separation of sounds. In *Proceedings of the 24th Asilomar Conference on Signals, Systems and Computers*, volume 1, pages 7457–7461.

Ephraim, Y. (1992). Gain-adapted hidden Markov models for recognition of clean and noisy speech. *IEEE Transactions on Acoustics, Speech and Signal Processing*, 40:1303–1316.

Erell, A. and Weintraub, M. (1990). Recognition of noisy speech: Using minimum-mean log-spectral distance estimation. In *Proceedings of the Third DARPA Speech and Natural Language Workshop*, pages 341–345, Hidden Valley, Pennsylvania. Defense Advanced Research Projects Agency, Morgan Kaufmann.

ESCA (1993). Proceedings of the ESCA workshop on prosody. Technical Report Working Papers 41, Lund University Department of Linguistics.

Eurospeech (1989). *Eurospeech '89, Proceedings of the First European Conference on Speech Communication and Technology*, Paris. European Speech Communication Association, European Speech Communication Association.

Eurospeech (1991). *Eurospeech '91, Proceedings of the Second European Conference on Speech Communication and Technology*, Genova, Italy. European Speech Communication Association.

Eurospeech (1993). *Eurospeech '93, Proceedings of the Third European Conference on Speech Communication and Technology*, Berlin. European Speech Communication Association.

Fanty, M., Barnard, E., and Cole, R. A. (1995). Alphabet recognition. In *Handbook of Neural Computation*. Publisher Unknown. In press.

Furui, S. (1981). Cepstral analysis technique for automatic speaker verification. *IEEE Transactions on Acoustics, Speech and Signal Processing*, 29(2):254–272.

Furui, S. (1986a). Research on individuality features in speech waves and automatic speaker recognition techniques. *Speech Communication*, 5(2):183–197.

Furui, S. (1986b). Speaker-independent isolated word recognition using dynamic features of the speech spectrum. *IEEE Transactions on Acoustics, Speech and Signal Processing*, 29(1):59–59.

Furui, S. (1989). *Digital Speech Processing, Synthesis, and Recognition*. Marcel Dekker, New York.

Furui, S. (1991). Speaker-dependent-feature extraction, recognition and processing techniques. *Speech Communication*, 10(5-6):505–520.

Furui, S. (1994). An overview of speaker recognition technology. In *Proceedings of the ESCA Workshop on Automatic Speaker Recognition, Identification and Verification*, pages 1–9.

Gales, M. J. F. and Young, S. J. (1992). An improved approach to the hidden Markov model decomposition of speech and noise. In *Proceedings of the 1992 International Conference on Acoustics, Speech, and Signal Processing*, volume 1, pages 233–236, San Francisco. Institute of Electrical and Electronic Engineers.

Gauvain, J.-L. and Lee, C.-H. (1991). Bayesian learning for hidden markov model with gaussian mixture state observation densities. In *Eurospeech '91, Proceedings of the Second European Conference on Speech Communication and Technology*, pages 939–942, Genova, Italy. European Speech Communication Association.

Ghitza, O. (1988). Temporal non-place information in the auditory-nerve firing patterns as a front end for speech recognition in a noisy environment. *Journal of Phonetics*, 16(1):109–124.

Goddeau, D. and Zue, V. (1992). Integrating probabilistic LR parsing into speech understanding systems. In *Proceedings of the 1992 International Conference on Acoustics, Speech, and Signal Processing*, volume 1, pages 181–184, San Francisco. Institute of Electrical and Electronic Engineers.

Greenberg, S. (1988). Theme issue: Representation of speech in the auditory periphery. *Journal of Phonetics*, 16(1).

Griffin, C., Matsui, T., and Furui, S. (1994). Distance measures for text-independent speaker recognition based on MAR model. In *Proceedings of the 1994 International Conference on Acoustics, Speech, and Signal Processing*, volume 1, pages 309–312, Adelaide, Australia. Institute of Electrical and Electronic Engineers.

Haeb-Umbach, R., Geller, D., and Ney, H. (1993). Improvements in connected digit recognition using linear discriminant analysis and mixture densities. In *Proceedings of the 1993 International Conference on Acoustics, Speech, and Signal Processing*, volume 2, pages 239–242, Minneapolis, Minnesota. Institute of Electrical and Electronic Engineers.

Hermansky, H. (1990). Perceptual linear predictive (PLP) analysis for speech. *Journal of the Acoustical Society of America*, 87(4):1738–1752.

Hermansky, H., Morgan, N., Bayya, A., and Kohn, P. (1991). Compensation for the effects of the communication channel in auditory-like analysis of speech. In *Eurospeech '91, Proceedings of the Second European Conference on Speech Communication and Technology*, pages 1367–1370, Genova, Italy. European Speech Communication Association.

Hermansky, H., Morgan, N., and Hirsch, H. G. (1993). Recognition of speech in additive and convolutional noise based on RASTA spectral processing. In *Proceedings of the 1993 International Conference on Acoustics, Speech, and Signal Processing*, volume 2, pages 83–86, Minneapolis, Minnesota. Institute of Electrical and Electronic Engineers.

Higgins, A. L., Bahler, L., and Porter, J. (1991). Speaker verification using randomized phrase prompting. *Digital Signal Processing*, 1:89–106.

Hindle, D. (1983). Deterministic parsing of syntactic nonfluencies. In *Proceedings of the 21st Annual Meeting of the Association for Computational Linguistics*, pages 123–128, Cambridge, Massachusetts. Association for Computational Linguistics.

Hirsch, H. G., Meyer, P., and Ruehl, H. W. (1991). Improved speech recognition using high-pass filtering of subband envelopes. In *Eurospeech '91, Proceedings of the Second European Conference on Speech Communication and Technology*, pages 413–416, Genova, Italy. European Speech Communication Association.

Hon, H.-W. and Lee, K.-F. (1991). CMU robust vocabulary-independent speech recognition system. In *Proceedings of the 1991 International Conference on Acoustics, Speech, and Signal Processing*, volume 2, pages 889–892, Toronto. Institute of Electrical and Electronic Engineers.

Huang, X. D., Ariki, Y., and Jack, M. (1990). *Hidden Markov Models for Speech Recognition*. Edinburgh University Press.

Huang, X. D. and Lee, K. F. (1993). On speaker-independent, speaker-dependent, and speaker-adaptive speech recognition. *IEEE Transactions on Speech and Audio Processing*, 1(2):150–157.

Hunt, M. J. (1993). Signal processing for speech. In Asher, R. E., editor, *The Encyclopedia of Language and Linguistics*. Pergamon Press.

Hunt, M. J. and Lefèbvre, C. (1989). A comparison of several acoustic representations for speech recognition with degraded and undegraded speech. In *Proceedings of the 1989 International Conference on Acoustics, Speech, and Signal Processing*, pages 262–265, Glasgow, Scotland. Institute of Electrical and Electronic Engineers.

Hwang, M. Y. and Huang, X. (1993). Shared-distribution hidden Markov models for speech recognition. *IEEE Transactions on Speech and Audio Processing*, 1(4):414–420.

ICASSP (1987). *Proceedings of the 1987 International Conference on Acoustics, Speech, and Signal Processing*, Dallas. Institute of Electrical and Electronic Engineers.

ICASSP (1989). *Proceedings of the 1989 International Conference on Acoustics, Speech, and Signal Processing*, Glasgow, Scotland. Institute of Electrical and Electronic Engineers.

ICASSP (1990). *Proceedings of the 1990 International Conference on Acoustics, Speech, and Signal Processing*, Albuquerque, New Mexico. Institute of Electrical and Electronic Engineers.

ICASSP (1991). *Proceedings of the 1991 International Conference on Acoustics, Speech, and Signal Processing*, Toronto. Institute of Electrical and Electronic Engineers.

ICASSP (1992). *Proceedings of the 1992 International Conference on Acoustics, Speech, and Signal Processing*, San Francisco. Institute of Electrical and Electronic Engineers.

ICASSP (1993). *Proceedings of the 1993 International Conference on Acoustics, Speech, and Signal Processing*, Minneapolis, Minnesota. Institute of Electrical and Electronic Engineers.

ICASSP (1994). *Proceedings of the 1994 International Conference on Acoustics, Speech, and Signal Processing*, Adelaide, Australia. Institute of Electrical and Electronic Engineers.

ICSLP (1990). *Proceedings of the 1990 International Conference on Spoken Language Processing*, Kobe, Japan.

ICSLP (1992). *Proceedings of the 1992 International Conference on Spoken Language Processing*, Banff, Alberta, Canada. University of Alberta.

ICSLP (1994). *Proceedings of the 1994 International Conference on Spoken Language Processing*, Yokohama, Japan.

Iyer, R., Ostendorf, M., and Rohlicek, R. (1994). An improved language model using a mixture of Markov components. In *Proceedings of the 1994 ARPA Human Language Technology Workshop*, Princeton, New Jersey. Advanced Research Projects Agency, Morgan Kaufmann.

Jelinek, F. (1969). A fast sequential decoding algorithm using a stack. *IBM journal of Research and Development*, 13.

Jelinek, F., Merialdo, B., Roukos, S., and Strauss, M. (1991). A dynamic language model for speech recognition. In *Proceedings of the Fourth DARPA Speech and Natural Language Workshop*, pages 293–295, Pacific Grove, California. Defense Advanced Research Projects Agency, Morgan Kaufmann.

Juang, B. H. (1991). Speech recognition in adverse environments. *Computer Speech and Language*, pages 275–294.

Juang, B. H., Rabiner, L. R., and Wilpon, J. G. (1986). On the use of bandpass liftering in speech recognition. In *Proceedings of the 1986 International Conference on Acoustics, Speech, and Signal Processing*, pages 765–768, Tokyo. Institute of Electrical and Electronic Engineers.

Koehler, J., Morgan, N., Hermansky, H., Hirsch, H. G., and Tong, G. (1994). Integrating RASTA-PLP into speech recognition. In *Proceedings of the 1994 International Conference on Acoustics, Speech, and Signal Processing*, volume 1, pages 421–424, Adelaide, Australia. Institute of Electrical and Electronic Engineers.

Kubala, F., Anastasakos, A., Makhoul, J., Nguyen, L., Schwartz, R., and Zavaliagkos, G. (1994). Comparative experiments on large vocabulary speech recognition. In *Proceedings of the 1994 International Conference on Acoustics, Speech, and Signal Processing*, volume 1, pages 561–564, Adelaide, Australia. Institute of Electrical and Electronic Engineers.

Kuhn, R., De Mori, R., and Millien, E. (1994). Learning consistent semantics from training data. In *Proceedings of the 1994 International Conference on Acoustics, Speech, and Signal Processing*, volume 2, pages 37–40, Adelaide, Australia. Institute of Electrical and Electronic Engineers.

Lafferty, J., Sleator, D., and Temperley, D. (1992). Grammatical trigrams: A probabilistic model of link grammar. In *Proceedings of the AAAI Fall Symposium on Probabilistic Approaches to Natural Language*.

Lau, R., Rosenfeld, R., and Roukos, S. (1993). Trigger-based language models: A maximum entropy approach. In *Proceedings of the 1993 International Conference on Acoustics, Speech, and Signal Processing*, volume 2, pages 45–48, Minneapolis, Minnesota. Institute of Electrical and Electronic Engineers.

Lickley, R. J. (1994). *Detecting Disfluency in Spontaneous Speech*. PhD thesis, University of Edinburgh, Scotland.

Lim, J. and Oppenheim, A. (1979). Enhancement and bandwidth compression of noisy speech. *Proceedings of the IEEE*, 67:1586–1604.

Lippmann, R. P., Martin, F. A., and Paul, D. B. (1987). Multi-style training for robust isolated-word speech recognition. In *Proceedings of the 1987 International Conference on Acoustics, Speech, and Signal Processing*, pages 709–712, Dallas. Institute of Electrical and Electronic Engineers.

Liu, F.-H., Stern, R. M., Acero, A., and Moreno, P. (1994). Environment normalization for robust speech recognition using direct cepstral comparison. In *Proceedings of the 1994 International Conference on Acoustics, Speech, and Signal Processing*, volume 2, pages 61–64, Adelaide, Australia. Institute of Electrical and Electronic Engineers.

Lockwood, P., Boudy, J., and Blanchet, M. (1992). Non-linear spectral subtraction (NSS) and hidden Markov models for robust speech recognition in car noise environments. In *Proceedings of the 1992 International Conference on Acoustics, Speech, and Signal Processing*, volume 1, pages 265–268, San Francisco. Institute of Electrical and Electronic Engineers.

Lyon, R. F. (1982). A computational model of filtering, detection, and compression in the cochlea. In *Proceedings of the 1982 International Conference on Acoustics, Speech, and Signal Processing*, pages 1282–1285. Institute of Electrical and Electronic Engineers.

Markel, J. D. and Gray, Jr., A. H. (1976). *Linear Prediction of Speech*. Springer-Verlag, Berlin.

Matsui, T. and Furui, S. (1993a). Comparison of text-independent speaker recognition methods using VQ-distortion and discrete/continuous HMMs. In *Proceedings of the 1993 International Conference on Acoustics, Speech, and Signal Processing*, volume 2, pages 157–160, Minneapolis, Minnesota. Institute of Electrical and Electronic Engineers.

Matsui, T. and Furui, S. (1993b). Concatenated phoneme models for text-variable speaker recognition. In *Proceedings of the 1993 International Conference on Acoustics, Speech, and Signal Processing*, volume 2, pages 391–394, Minneapolis, Minnesota. Institute of Electrical and Electronic Engineers.

Matsui, T. and Furui, S. (1994a). Similarity normalization method for speaker verification based on a posteriori probability. In *Proceedings of the ESCA Workshop on Automatic Speaker Recognition, Identification and Verification*, pages 59–62.

Matsui, T. and Furui, S. (1994b). Speaker adaptation of tied-mixture-based phoneme models for text-prompted speaker recognition. In *Proceedings of the 1994 International Conference on Acoustics, Speech, and Signal Processing*, volume 1, pages 125–128, Adelaide, Australia. Institute of Electrical and Electronic Engineers.

Meng, H. M. and Zue, V. W. (1990). A comparative study of acoustic representations of speech for vowel classification using multi-layer perceptrons. In *Proceedings of the 1990 International Conference on Spoken Language Processing*, volume 2, pages 1053–1056, Kobe, Japan.

Merhav, N. and Ephraim, Y. (1991). Maximum likelihood hidden markov modeling using a dominant state sequence of states. *IEEE Transactions on Signal Processing*, 39(9):2111–2114.

Murveit, H., Butzberger, J., Digilakis, V., and Weintraub, M. (1993). Large-vocabulary dictation using SRI's DECIPHER speech recognition system: Progressive search techniques. In *Proceedings of the 1993 International Conference on Acoustics, Speech, and Signal Processing*, volume 2, pages 319–322, Minneapolis, Minnesota. Institute of Electrical and Electronic Engineers.

Naik, J. M., Netsch, L. P., and Doddington, G. R. (1989). Speaker verification over long distance telephone lines. In *Proceedings of the 1989 International Conference on Acoustics, Speech, and Signal Processing*, pages 524–527, Glasgow, Scotland. Institute of Electrical and Electronic Engineers.

Neumeyer, L. and Weintraub, M. (1994). Probabilistic optimum filtering for robust speech recognition. In *Proceedings of the 1994 International Conference on Acoustics, Speech, and Signal Processing*, volume 1, pages 417–420, Adelaide, Australia. Institute of Electrical and Electronic Engineers.

Ney, H., Mergel, D., Noll, A., and Paesler, A. (1992). Data driven search organization for continuous speech recognition. *IEEE Transactions on Signal Processing*, 40(2):272–281.

Nilsson, N. J. (1971). *Problem-Solving Methods in Artificial Intelligence*. McGraw-Hill, New York.

Ohshima, Y. (1993). *Robustness in Speech Recognition using Physiologically-Motivated Signal Processing*. PhD thesis, CMU.

O'Shaughnessy, D. (1986). Speaker recognition. *IEEE Acoustics, Speech and Signal Processing Magazine*, 3(4):4–17.

Pallett, D. (1991). DARPA resource management and ATIS benchmark test poster session. In *Proceedings of the Fourth DARPA Speech and Natural Language Workshop*, pages 49–58, Pacific Grove, California. Defense Advanced Research Projects Agency, Morgan Kaufmann.

Pallett, D. (1992). ATIS benchmarks. In *Proceedings of the Fifth DARPA Speech and Natural Language Workshop*. Defense Advanced Research Projects Agency, Morgan Kaufmann.

Pallett, D., Dahlgren, N., Fiscus, J., Fisher, W., Garofolo, J., and Tjaden, B. (1992). DARPA February 1992 ATIS benchmark test results. In *Proceedings of the Fifth DARPA Speech and Natural Language Workshop*, pages 15–27. Defense Advanced Research Projects Agency, Morgan Kaufmann.

Pallett, D., Fiscus, J., Fisher, W., and Garofolo, J. (1993). Benchmark tests for the DARPA spoken language program. In *Proceedings of the 1993 ARPA Human Language Technology Workshop*, pages 7–18, Princeton, New Jersey. Advanced Research Projects Agency, Morgan Kaufmann.

Pallett, D., Fiscus, J., Fisher, W., Garofolo, J., Lund, B., and Prysbocki, M. (1994). 1993 benchmark tests for the ARPA spoken language program. In *Proceedings of the 1994 ARPA Human Language Technology Workshop*, pages 49–74, Princeton, New Jersey. Advanced Research Projects Agency, Morgan Kaufmann.

Pallett, D., Fisher, W., Fiscus, J., and Garofolo, J. (1990). DARPA ATIS test results. In *Proceedings of the Third DARPA Speech and Natural Language Workshop*, pages 114–121, Hidden Valley, Pennsylvania. Defense Advanced Research Projects Agency, Morgan Kaufmann.

Pallett, D. S., Fiscus, J. G., Fisher, W. M., Garofolo, J. S., Lund, B. A., Martin, A., and Przybocki, M. A. (1995). 1994 benchmark tests for the ARPA spoken language program. In *Proceedings of the 1995 ARPA Human Language Technology Workshop*, pages 5–36. Advanced Research Projects Agency, Morgan Kaufmann.

Patterson, R. D., Robinson, K., Holdsworth, J., McKeown, D., Zhang, C., and Allerhand, M. (1991). Complex sounds and auditory images. In *Auditory Physiology and Perception*, pages 429–446. Pergamon Press.

Paul, D. B. (1994). The Lincoln large-vocabulary stack-decoder based HMM CSR. In *Proceedings of the 1994 ARPA Human Language Technology Workshop*, pages 374–379, Princeton, New Jersey. Advanced Research Projects Agency, Morgan Kaufmann.

Peterson, P. M. (1989). Adaptive array processing for multiple microphone hearing aids. Technical Report 541, Research Laboratory of Electronics, MIT, Cambridge, Massachusetts.

Porter, J. E. and Boll, S. F. (1984). Optimal estimators for spectral restoration of noisy speech. In *Proceedings of the 1984 International Conference on Acoustics, Speech, and Signal Processing*, pages 18.A.2.1–4. Institute of Electrical and Electronic Engineers.

Price, P. and Ostendorf, M. (1995). Combining linguistic with statistical methods in modeling prosody. In Morgan, J. L. and Demuth, K., editors, *Signal to syntax: Bootstrapping from speech to grammar in early acquisition*. Lawrence Erlbaum Associates, Hillsdale, New Jersey.

Rabiner, L. R. (1989). A tutorial on hidden Markov models and selected applications in speech recognition. *Proceedings of the IEEE*, 77(2):257–286.

Rabiner, L. R. and Schafer, R. W. (1978). *Digital Processing of Speech Signals*. Signal Processing. Prentice-Hall, Englewood Cliffs, New Jersey.

Rosenberg, A. E. and Soong, F. K. (1991). Recent research in automatic speaker recognition. In Furui, S. and Sondhi, M. M., editors, *Advances in Speech Signal Processing*, pages 701–737. Marcel Dekker, New York.

Schroeter, J. and Sondhi, M. M. (1994). Techniques for estimating vocal tract shapes from the speech signal. *IEEE Transactions on Speech and Audio Processing*, 2(1):133–150.

Schwartz, R., Chow, Y., and Kubala, F. (1987). Rapid speaker adaption using a probabalistic spectral mapping. In *Proceedings of the 1987 International Conference on Acoustics, Speech, and Signal Processing*, pages 633–636, Dallas. Institute of Electrical and Electronic Engineers.

Seneff, S. (1988). A joint synchrony/mean-rate model of auditory speech processing. *Journal of Phonetics*, 16(1):55–76.

Shirai, K. and Furui, S. (1994). Special issue on spoken dialogue. *Speech Communication*, 15(3-4).

Shriberg, E. E. (1994). *Preliminaries to a Theory of Speech Disfluencies*. PhD thesis, Stanford University.

Shukat-Talamazzini, E. G., Niemann, H., Eckert, W., Kuhn, T., and Rieck, S. (1992). Acoustic modeling of sub-word units in the ISADORA speech recognizer. In *Proceedings of the 1992 International Conference on Acoustics, Speech, and Signal Processing*, volume 2, pages 577–580, San Francisco. Institute of Electrical and Electronic Engineers.

Stockham, T. G., J., Connon, T. M., and Ingebretsen, R. B. (1975). Blind deconvolution through digital signal processing. *Proceedings of the IEEE*, 63(4):678–692.

Sullivan, T. M. and Stern, R. M. (1993). Multi-microphone correlation-based processing for robust speech recognition. In *Proceedings of the 1993 International Conference on Acoustics, Speech, and Signal Processing*, volume 2, pages 91–94, Minneapolis, Minnesota. Institute of Electrical and Electronic Engineers.

Van Compernolle, D. (1990). Switching adaptive filters for enhancing noisy and reverberant speech from microphone array recordings. In *Proceedings of the 1990 International Conference on Acoustics, Speech, and Signal Processing*, pages 833–836, Albuquerque, New Mexico. Institute of Electrical and Electronic Engineers.

Varga, A. P. and Moore, R. K. (1990). Hidden Markov model decomposition of speech and noise. In *Proceedings of the 1990 International Conference on Acoustics, Speech, and Signal Processing*, pages 845–848, Albuquerque, New Mexico. Institute of Electrical and Electronic Engineers.

Waibel, A. and Lee, K. F. (1990). *Readings in Speech Recognition*. Morgan Kaufmann.

Zue, V., Glass, J., Phillips, M., and Seneff, S. (1990). The MIT SUMMIT speech recognition system: A progress report. In *Proceedings of the Third DARPA Speech and Natural Language Workshop*, Hidden Valley, Pennsylvania. Defense Advanced Research Projects Agency, Morgan Kaufmann.

Chapter 2

Written Language Input

2.1 Overview

Sargur N. Srihari & Rohini K. Srihari

State University of New York at Buffalo, New York, USA

The written form of language is contained in printed documents, such as newspapers, magazines and books, and in handwritten matter, such as found in notebooks and personal letters. Given the importance of written language in human transactions, its automatic recognition has practical significance. This overview describes the nature of written language, how written language is transduced into electronic data and the nature of written language recognition algorithms.

2.1.1 Written Language

Fundamental characteristics of writing are:

1. it consists of artificial graphical marks on a surface;

2. its purpose is to communicate something;

3. this purpose is achieved by virtue of the mark's conventional relation to language (Coulmas, 1989).

Although speech is a sign system that is more natural than writing to humans, writing is considered to have made possible much of culture and civilization.

   Different writing systems, or scripts, represent linguistic units, words, syllables and phonemes, at different structural levels. In alphabetic writing systems, principal examples of which are the Latin, Greek and Russian scripts, alphabets are the primitive elements, or characters, which are used to represent words. Several languages such as English, Dutch, French, etc, share the Latin script. The Devanagari script, which represents syllables as well as alphabets, is used by several Indian languages, including Hindi. The Chinese script, which consists of ideograms, is an alternative to alphabets. The Japanese script consists of the Chinese ideograms (Kanji) and syllables (Kana). There are roughly two dozen different scripts in use today (ignoring minor differences in orthography, as between English and French).

Each script has its own set of icons, known as characters or letters, that have certain basic shapes. Each script has its rules for combining the letters to represent the shapes of higher level linguistic units. For example, there are rules for combining the shapes of individual letters so as to form cursively written words in the Latin alphabet.

In addition to linguistic symbols, each script has a representation for numerals, such as the Arabic-Indic digits used in conjunction with the Latin alphabet. In addition, there are icons for special symbols found on keyboards.

2.1.2   Transducers

Since the invention of the printing press in the fifteenth century by Johannes Gutenberg (an invention whose principal elements included the movable type, an alloy for letter faces, printing mechanism and oil-based ink), most of archived written language has been in the form of printed paper documents. In such documents, text is presented as a visual image on a high contrast background, where the shapes of characters belong to families of type fonts.

Paper documents, which are an inherently analog medium, can be converted into digital form by a process of scanning and digitization. This process yields a digital image. For instance, a typical 8.5 × 11 inch page is scanned at a resolution of 300 dots per inch (dpi) to create a gray-scale image of 8.4 megabytes. The resolution is dependent on the smallest font size that needs reliable recognition, as well as the bandwidth needed for transmission and storage of the image. A typical fax image of a page is a binary image scanned at a resolution of 200 dpi along the scan line and 100 dpi along the paper feed direction.

More recently, it has become possible to store and view electronically prepared documents as formatted pages on a computer graphics screen, where the scanning and recognition process is eliminated. However, the elimination of printed paper documents is hardly likely, due to the convenience and high-contrast they offer in comparison with the bulky computer screens of today.

Written language is also encountered in the form of handwriting inscribed on paper or registered on an electronically sensitive surface. Handwriting data is converted to digital form either by scanning the writing on paper or by writing with a special pen on an electronic surface such as a Liquid Crystal Display (LCD). The two approaches are distinguished as *off-line* and *on-line* handwriting. In the on-line case, the two-dimensional coordinates of successive points of the writing are stored in order— thus the order of strokes made by the writer are readily available. In the off-line case, only the completed writing is available as an image. The on-line case deals with a one-dimensional representation of the input, whereas the off-line case involves analysis of the two-dimensional image. The raw data storage requirements are widely different, e.g., the data requirements for an average cursively written word are: 230 bytes in the on-line case (sampling at 100 samples/sec), and 80 Kb in the off-line case (sampling at 300 dpi). The recognition rates reported are also much higher for the on-line case in comparison with the off-line case.

2.1.3 Recognition

Written language recognition is the task of transforming language represented in its spatial form of graphical marks into its symbolic representation. For English orthography, this symbolic representation is typically the ASCII representation of text. The characters of most written languages of the world are representable today in the form of the Unicode (Unicode Consortium, The, 1990).

We discuss here many of the issues in the recognition of English orthography, for printed text as well as handwriting. The central tasks are character recognition and word recognition. A necessary preprocessing step for recognizing written language is the spatial issue of locating and registering the appropriate text when there are complex two-dimensional spatial layouts employed. The latter task is referred to as document image analysis.

Character Recognition

The basic problem is to assign the digitized character into its symbolic class. In the case of a print image, this is referred to as Optical Character Recognition (OCR) (Srihari & Hull, 1992). In the case of handprint, it is referred to as Intelligent Character Recognition (ICR).

The typical classes are the upper- and lower-case characters, the ten digits, and special symbols such as the period, exclamation mark, brackets, dollar and pound signs, etc. A pattern recognition algorithm is used to extract shape features and assign the observed character into the appropriate class. Artificial neural networks have emerged as fast methods for implementing classifiers for OCR. Algorithms based on nearest-neighbor methods have higher accuracy, but are slower.

Recognition of characters from a single font family on a well-printed paper document can be done very accurately. Difficulties arise when there are decorative fonts, many fonts to be handled, , or when the document is of poor quality. Some examples of poor quality machine-printed and handwritten characters are shown in Figure 2.1. In the difficult cases, it becomes necessary to use models to constrain the choices at the character and word levels. Such models are essential in handwriting recognition due to the wide variability of handprinting and cursive script.

A word recognition algorithm attempts to associate the word image to choices in a lexicon. Typically, a ranking is produced. This is done either by the *analytical* approach of recognizing the individual characters or by the *holistic* approach of dealing with the entire word image. The latter approach is useful in the case of touching printed characters and handwriting. A higher level of performance is observed by combining the results of both approaches.

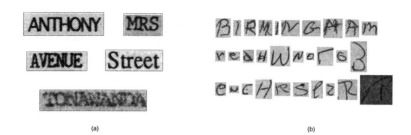

(a)   (b)

Figure 2.1: Examples of low-quality machine-printed characters involving segmentation difficulties (a) and handwritten characters (b).

In the off-line unconstrained handwritten word recognition problem, recognition rates of 95%, 85% and 78% have been reported for the top choice for lexicon sizes of 10, 100 and 1,000 respectively (Govindaraju, Shekhawat, et al., 1993).

In the on-line case, larger lexicons are possible for the same accuracy; a top choice recognition rate of 80% with pure cursive words and a 21,000 word lexicon has been reported (Seni & Srihari, 1994).

Language Models

Language models are useful in recovering strings of words after they have been passed through a noisy channel, such as handwriting or print degradation. The most important model for written language recognition is the lexicon of words. The lexicon, in turn, is determined by linguistic constraints, e.g., in recognizing running text, the lexicon for each word is constrained by the syntax, semantics and pragmatics of the sentence.

The performance of a recognition system can be improved by incorporating statistical information at the word sequence level. The performance improvement derives from selection of lower-rank words from the word recognition output when the surrounding context indicates such selection makes the entire sentence more probable. Lexical techniques such as collocational analysis can be used to modify word neighborhoods generated by a word recognizer. Modification includes re-ranking, deleting or proposing new word candidates. Collocations are word patterns that occur frequently in language; intuitively, if word A is present, there is a high probability that word B is also present.

Methods to apply linguistic knowledge include: n-gram word models, n-gram class (e.g., part-of-speech) models, context-free grammars, and stochastic context-free grammars. An example of a handwritten sentence together with recognition choices produced by a word recognizer and grammatically determined correct paths are shown in Figure 2.2. An increase in top choice word recognition rate from 80% to 95% is possible with the use of language models (Srihari & Baltus, 1993).

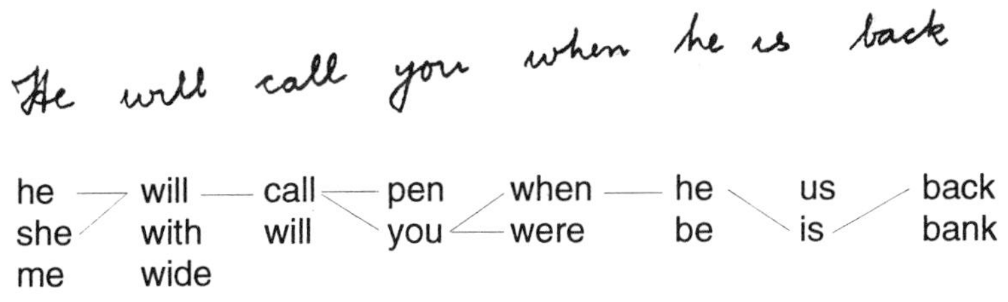

he — will — call — pen	when — he	us	back
she	with	will	you — were	be	is	bank
me	wide			

Figure 2.2: Handwritten Sentence Recognition. The path through top word choices is determined using part-of-speech tags.

Document Image Analysis

Interaction with written language recognition is the task of document image analysis. It involves determining the physical (spatial) and logical structure of document content. There is wide variability in the structure of documents, as in the case of newspapers, magazines, books, forms, letters and handwritten notes. In the case of a newspaper page, the objective of document analysis is to:

1. determine spatial extent of document segments and to associate appropriate labels with them, e.g., half-tone photographs, text, graphics, separating lines, etc.,

2. group image parts into meaningful units, e.g., figure and caption, heading, subheading, etc.,

3. determine reading order of blocks of text.

Document image analysis involves traditional image processing operations to printed text, such as enhancement, gray-scale image binarization, texture analysis, segmentation, etc. Additional difficult problems in the case of handwriting are: separation of lines of text, separation of words within a line and the separation of touching characters.

2.1.4   Future Directions

Research on automated written language recognition dates back several decades. Today, cleanly printed text in documents with simple layouts can be recognized reliably by off-the-shelf OCR software. There is also some success with handwriting recognition, particularly for isolated handprinted characters and words, e.g., in the on-line case, the recently introduced personal digital assistants have practical value. Most of the off-line successes have come in constrained domains such as postal addresses (Cohen, Hull, et al., 1991), bank checks, and census forms. The analysis of documents with complex layouts, recognition of degraded printed text, and the recognition of running handwriting, continue to remain largely in the research arena. Some of the major research challenges in recognizing handwriting are in: word and line separation, segmentation of words into characters, recognition of words when lexicons are large and use of language models in aiding preprocessing and recognition.

2.2   Document Image Analysis

Richard G. Casey
IBM Almaden Research Center, San Jose, California, USA

Document analysis, or more precisely, document image analysis, is the process that performs the overall interpretation of document images. This process is the answer to the question, "How is everything that is known about language, document formatting, image processing and character recognition combined in order to deal with a particular application?" Thus, document analysis is concerned with the global issues involved in recognition of written language in images. It adds to OCR a superstructure that establishes the organization of the document and applies outside knowledge in interpreting it.

The process of determining document structure may be viewed as guided by a model, explicit or implicit, of the class of documents of interest. The model describes the physical appearance and the relationships between the entities that make up the document. OCR is often at the final level of this process, i.e., it provides a final encoding of the symbols contained in a logical entity such as *paragraph* or *table*, once the latter has been isolated by other stages. However, it is important to realize that OCR can also participate in determining document layout. For example, as part of the process of extracting a newspaper article, the system may have to recognize the character string, *continued on page 5*, at the bottom of a page image, in order to locate the entire text.

In practice then, a document analysis system performs the basic tasks of image segmentation, layout understanding, symbol recognition and application of contextual rules, in an integrated manner (Wong, Casey, et al., 1982; Nagy, Seth, et al., 1985). Current work in this area can be summarized under four main classes of applications.

2.2.1   Text Documents

The ultimate goal for text systems can be termed *inverse formatting* or completion of the *Gutenberg loop*, meaning that a scanned printed document is translated back into a document description language from which it could be accurately reprinted if desired. At the research level, this has been pursued in domains such as technical papers, business letters and chemical structure diagrams (Tsujimoto & Asada, 1992; Schürmann et al., 1992; Nagy, Seth, et al., 1985). Some commercial OCR systems provide limited inverse formatting, producing codes for elementary structures such as paragraphs, columns, and tables (Bokser, 1992). Current OCR systems will detect, but not encode, halftones and line drawings.

In certain applications, less than total interpretation of the document is required. A system for indexing and retrieving text documents may perform only a partial recognition. For example, a commercially available retrieval system for technical articles contains a model of various journal styles, assisting it to locate and recognize the title, author, and abstract of each article, and to extract keywords. Users conduct searches using the encoded material, but retrieve the scanned image of desired articles for reading.

2.2.2 Forms

Forms are the printed counterparts of relations in a data base. A typical form consists of an n-tuple of data items, each of which can be represented as an ordered pair (item name, item value). OCR is used to recognize the item value; more general document analysis operations may be needed in order to identify the item name (Casey et al., 1992).

The capability for locating items on a form, establishing their name class, and encoding the accompanying data values has many applications in business and government. Form documents within a single enterprise and single application are highly repetitive in structure from one example to the next. In such a case the model for the document can consist largely of physical parameters whose values are estimated from sample documents. Such systems for gathering form data are commercially available. The Internal Revenue Service of the U.S. has recently granted a large contract to automate processing of scanned income tax forms. This will require extraction of data from a large variety of forms, as well as adaptation to perturbations of a single form resulting from different printing systems.

2.2.3 Postal Addresses and Check Reading

These applications are characterized by a well-defined logical format (but a highly variable physical layout), and a high degree of contextual constraint on the symbolic data (Srihari, 1992). The latter is potentially very useful in the attainment of high accuracy. Contextual rules can modify OCR results to force agreement of city names and postal codes, for example, or to reconcile numeric dollar amounts on checks with the written entry in the legal amount field. Contextual constraints can also assist in the detection of misrecognized documents, so that these can be handled by manual or other processes. While pieces of mail and checks are actually a subclass of form documents, the large amount of effort invested in these problems justifies listing them separately.

Current equipment in use for these applications make limited use of contextual information, and is limited to reading postal codes in the case of handwritten addresses, or numeric amounts for checks. Postal machines now in development will read the complete address field and obtain greater accuracy by applying contextual constraints. At the same time they will provide a higher granularity in the sorting of mail. In the U.S., for example, new machines are planned to arrange pieces of mail into delivery order for the route of individual postmen.

2.2.4   Line Drawings

Much of the activity in this area centers on entry of engineering drawings to Computer-Assisted Design / Computer-Assisted Manufacture (CADCAM) systems (Kasturi, Sira, et al., 1990; Vaxiviere & Tombre, 1992). A project for input of integrated circuit diagrams has reported cost-efficient conversion of drawings compared with conventional manual input. This project offers evidence that new circuits can most efficiently be created on paper and then encoded by recognition processes. The claim is that this is better than direct input at a terminal, due to the small screen sizes on present-day equipment. A commercial version of such a system is available. Other research in progress aims at obtaining 3-D models for multiple views in drawings of manufactured parts. Research progress has also been reported in conversion of land-use maps.

2.2.5   Future Directions

One source of motivation for work in document analysis has been the great increase in image systems for business and government. These systems provide fast storage, recall and distribution of documents in workflow processing and other applications. Document analysis can help with the indexing for storage and recall, and can partition the image into subregions of interest for convenient access by users.

In the near future, such capabilities will be extended to the creation of electronic libraries which will likewise benefit from automatic indexing and formatting services. In the longer range, efforts will increase to interpret more of the information represented in the stored images, in order to provide more flexible retrieval and manipulation facilities (Dengel et al., 1992).

How will document analysis capabilities have to improve to meet future needs? There is a strong need to incorporate context, particularly language context, into the models that govern document analysis systems. Over 35 years of research and development have still not been able to produce OCR based on shape that has the accuracy of human vision. Contextual knowledge must be invoked in order both to minimize errors and to reject documents that can not be interpreted automatically. An important research issue here is how to define such constraints in a generic way, such that they can easily be redefined for different applications. Beyond this, how are such rules to be converted to software that integrates with recognition processes, in order to optimize performance?

Linguistic analysis may not simply be a postprocessing stage in future document analysis systems. Modern recognition processes often perform trial segmentation of character images and choose the best segmentation from a set of alternatives using recognition confidence as a guide. Such an operation might be performed most reliably if it were implemented as a sequential process, with contextual rules governing the choice of the sequence.

In order to facilitate future progress in document analysis, there is a need for a number of scanned document data bases, each representative of a different class of documents: text, engineering drawings, addresses, forms, handwritten manuscripts, etc. Currently such collections are limited to text-oriented documents. With access to common research material, different researchers will be able to compare results and gain greater benefit from each other's efforts.

2.3 OCR: Print

Abdel Belaïd
CRIN/CNRS & INRIA, Nancy, Lorraine, France

Currently, there is considerable motivation to provide computerized document analysis systems. Giant steps have been made in the last decade, both in terms of technological supports and in software products. Character recognition (OCR) contributes to this progress by providing techniques to convert large volumes of data automatically. There are so many papers and patents advertising recognition rates as high as 99.99%; this gives the impression that automation problems seem to have been solved. However, the failure of some real applications show that performance problems subsist on composite and degraded documents (i.e., noisy characters, tilt, mixing of fonts, etc.) and that there is still room for progress. Various methods have been proposed to increase the accuracy of optical character recognizers. In fact, at various research laboratories, the challenge is to develop robust methods that remove as much as possible the typographical and noise restrictions, while maintaining rates similar to those provided by limited-font commercial machines.

There is a parallel analogy between the various stages of evolution of OCR systems and those of pattern recognition. To overcome the recognition deficiency, the classical approach focusing on isolated characters has been replaced with more contextual techniques. The opening of OCR domain to document recognition leads to combination of many strategies such as document layout handling, dictionary checking, font identification, word recognition, integration of several recognition approaches with consensual voting, etc.

The rest of this section is devoted to a summary of the state of the art in the domain of printed OCR (similar to the presentations in Impedovo, Ottaviano, et al., 1991; Govindan & Shivaprasad, 1990; Nadler, 1984; Mantas, 1986), by focussing attention essentially on the new orientations of OCR in the document recognition area.

2.3.1 Document Image Analysis Aspects

Characters are arranged in document lines following some typesetting conventions which we can use to locate characters and find their style. Typesetting rules can help in distinguishing such characters as *s* from *5*, *h* from *n*, and *g* from *9*, which often can be confused in multifont context (Kahan, Pavlidis, et al., 1987). They can also limit the search area according to characters' relative positions and heights with respect to the baseline (Luca & Gisotti, 1991a; Luca & Gisotti, 1991b; Kanai, 1990). The role of typesetting cues to aid document understanding is discussed by Holstege, Inn, et al. (1991).

Layout Segmentation

Location of characters in a document is always preceded by a layout analysis of the document image. The layout analysis involves several operations such as determining the skew, separating picture from text, and partitioning the text into columns, lines, words, and connected components. The portioning of text is effected through a process known as segmentation. A survey of segmentation techniques is given in Nadler (1984).

Character Building

In building character images, one is often confronted with touching or broken characters that occur in degraded documents (such as fax, photocopy, etc.). It is still challenging to develop techniques for properly segmentating words into their characters. Kahan, Pavlidis, et al. (1987) detected touching characters by evaluation of vertical pixel projection. They executed a branch-and-bound search of alternative splittings and merges of symbols, pruned by word-confidence scores derived from symbol confidence. Tsujimoto and Asada (1991) used a decision tree for resolving ambiguities. Casey and Nagy (1982) proposed a recursive segmentation algorithm. Liang, Ahmadi, et al. (1993) added contextual information and a spelling checker to this algorithm to correct errors caused by incorrect segmentation. Bayer (1987) proposed a hypothesis approach for merging and splitting characters. The hypotheses are tested by several experts to see whether they represent a valid character. The search is controlled by the A* algorithm resolving backtracking processing. The experts comprise the character classifier and a set of algorithms for context processing.

Font Consideration

A document reader must cope with many sources of variations, notably that of font and size of the text. In commercial devices, the multifont aspect was for a long time neglected for the benefit of speed and accuracy, and substitution solutions were proposed. At first, to cater for some institutions, the solution was to work on customized fonts (such as OCR-A and OCR-B) or on a selected font from a trained library to minimize the confusion between similar looking characters. The accuracy was quite good, even on degraded images, provided the font is carefully selected. However, recognition scores drop rapidly when fonts or sizes are changed. This is due to the fact that the limitation to one font naturally promotes the use of simple and sensitive pattern recognition algorithms, such as template matching (Duda & Hart, 1973).

In parallel with commercial investigations, the literature proposed multifont recognition systems that are based on typographical features. Font information is inherent in the constituent characters (Rubinstein, 1988) and feature-based methods are less font sensitive (Srihari, 1984; Ullman, 1973; Kahan, Pavlidis, et al., 1987). Two research paths were taken with multifont machines. One gears towards the office environment. This introduced systems which can be trained by the user to read any given font (Schurmann, 1978; Shlien, 1988; Belaïd &

Anigbogu, 1991; Anigbogu & Belaïd, 1991a; Anigbogu & Belaïd, 1991b). The system is only able to recognize a font from among those learned. The others try to be font independent. The training is based on pattern differentiation, rather than on font differentiation (Lam & Baird, 1987; Baird, Kahan, et al., 1986; Baird & Fossey, 1991).

2.3.2 Character Recognition

Feature Extraction

This step is crucial in the context of document analysis, where several variations may be caused by a number of different sources: geometric transformation because of low data quality, slant and stroke width variation because of font changing, etc. It seems reasonable to look for features which are invariant and which capture the characteristics of the character by filtering out all attributes which make the same character assume different appearances. The classifier could store a single prototype per character. Schurmann, Bartneck, et al. (1992) applies normalizing transformations to reduce certain well-defined variations as far as possible. The inevitably remaining variations are left for learning by statistical adaptation of the classifier.

Character Learning

The keys of printed character learning are essentially training set and classification adaptation to new characters and new fonts. The training set can be given either by user or extracted directly from document samples. In the first case, the user selects the fonts and the samples to represent each character in each font and then guides the system to create models as in Anigbogu and Belaïd (1991b). Here, the user must use sufficient number of samples in each font according to the difficulty of its recognition. However, it is difficult in an omnifont context to collect a training set of characters having the expected distribution of noise and pitch size. Baird (1990) suggested parameterized models for imaging defects, based on a variety of theoretical arguments and empirical evidence. In the second case, the idea is to generate the training set directly from document images chosen from a wide variety of fonts and image quality and to reflect the variability expected by the system (Bokser, 1992). The problem here is that one is not sure that all valid characters are present.

Contextual Processing

Contextual processing attempts to overcome the shortcoming of decisions made on the basis of local properties and to extend the perception on relationships between characters into word. Most of the techniques try to combine geometric information, as well as linguistic information. See Srihari and Hull (1985) for an overview of these techniques. Anigbogu and Belaïd (1991a); Anigbogu and Belaïd (1991b); Belaïd and Anigbogu (1991) used hidden Markov models for character and word modeling. Characters are merged into groups which are matched against words in a dictionary using the Ratcliff/Obershelp pattern matching method. In a situation where no acceptable words are found, the list of confused characters is passed through a Viterbi net and the output is taken as the most likely word. The bigram and character position-dependent probabilities used for this purpose were constructed from a French dictionary of some 190,000 words. The word-level recognition stands at over 98%.

2.3.3   Commercial Products

Commercial OCR machines came in practically at the beginning of 1950s and have evolved in parallel with research investigations. The first series of products heavily relied on customized fonts, good printing quality and very restricted document layout. Nowadays, we can find a vast range of products, more powerful than the previous ones. Among these are certain hand-held scanners, page readers, and integrated flat-bed and document readers. The tendency is to use the fax machine as an image sensor. Instead of printing the fax message on paper, it is taken directly as input to an OCR system. It is to be noted that the obtained images are of a poor quality. The challenge in this area is the development of high performing tools to treat degraded text that give results as good as those of classical OCRs.

OCR is used in three main domains: the banking environment for data entry and checking, office automation for text entry, and the post office for mail sorting. We can find many surveys on commercial products in Mori, Suen, et al. (1992); Mantas (1986); Bokser (1992); Nagy (1992). Recently, the Information Science Research Institute had the charge to test technologies for OCR from machine printed documents. A complete review has been published (Nartker, Rice, et al., 1994) giving a benchmark of different products in use in the U.S. market.

2.3.4   Future Directions

We have attempted to show that OCR is an essential part of the document analysis domain. Character recognition cannot be achieved without typesetting cues to help the segmentation in a multifont environment. We have also shown the unavoidable recourse to linguistic context; the analysis must be extended to this domain. The training still remains the weak side of OCR for now, as it is difficult to generate a training set of characters which includes all the variability the system will be expected to handle. Finally, real-world OCR requires the combination of a variety of different techniques to yield high recognition scores (Anigbogu & Belaïd, 1991b; Ho, 1992). For this reason, the tendency is to combine the results of many OCR systems in order to obtain the best possible performance.

2.4 OCR: Handwriting

Claudie Faure & Eric Lecolinet

Télécom Paris, Paris, France

2.4.1 The Domain

For more than thirty years, researchers have been working on handwriting recognition. As in the case of speech processing, they have aimed at designing systems able to understand personal encoding of natural language.

Over the last few years, the number of academic laboratories and companies involved in research on handwriting recognition has continually increased. Simultaneously, commercial products have become available. This new stage in the evolution of handwriting processing results from a combination of several elements: improvements in recognition rates, the use of complex systems integrating several kinds of information, the choice of relevant application domains, and new technologies such as high quality high speed scanners and inexpensive, powerful CPUs. A selection of recent publications on this topic include: Impedovo (1994); IWFHR (1993); Plamondon (1993); Pavlidis and Mori (1992); Impedovo and Simon (1992); Wang (1991).

Methods and recognition rates depend on the level of constraints on handwriting. The constraints are mainly characterized by the types of handwriting, the number of scriptors, the size of the vocabulary and the spatial layout. Obviously, recognition becomes more difficult when the constraints decrease. Considering the types of Roman script (roughly classified as hand printed, discrete script and cursive script), the difficulty is lower for handwriting produced as a sequence of separate characters than for cursive script, which has much in common with continuous speech recognition. For other writing systems, character recognition is hard to achieve, as in the case of Kanji which is characterized by complex shapes and a huge number of symbols.

The characteristics which constrain handwriting may be combined in order to define handwriting categories for which the results of automatic processing are satisfactory. The trade-off between constraints and error rates give rise to applications in several domains. The resulting commercial products have proved that handwriting processing can be integrated into working environments. Most efforts have been devoted to mail sorting, bank check reading, forms processing in administration and insurance. These applications are of great economic interest, each of them concerning millions of documents.

Mail sorting is a good illustration of the evolution in the domain. In this case, the number of writers is unconstrained. In the early stages, only ZIP code was recognized. Then, cities (and states such as in the U.S.) were processed, implying the recognition of several types of handwriting: hand printed, cursive, or a mixture of both. The use of the redundancy between the ZIP code and the city name, as well as redundancy between numeral and literal amounts in bank checks, shows that combining several sources of information improves the recognition rates. Today, the goal is to read the full address, down to the level of the information used by the individual carrier. This necessitates precisely extracting the writing lines, manipulating a very large vocabulary and using contextual knowledge as the syntax of addresses (such as in the case of reading the literal amount of checks, the use of syntactic rules improves the recognition). These new challenges bring the ongoing studies closer to unconstrained handwritten language processing, the ultimate aim. The reading of all of the handwritten and printed information present on a document is necessary to process it automatically, to use content dependent criteria to store, access and transmit it and to check its content. Automatic handwritten language processing will also allow one to convert and to handle manuscripts produced over several centuries within a computer environment.

2.4.2   Methods and Strategies

Recognition strategies heavily depend on the nature of the data to be recognized. In the cursive case, the problem is made complex by the fact that the writing is fundamentally ambiguous, because the letters in the word may be linked together, poorly written, or even missing. On the contrary, hand printed word recognition is more related to printed word recognition, the individual letters composing the word being usually much easier to isolate and to identify. As a consequence of this, methods working on a letter basis (i.e., based on character segmentation and recognition) are well suited to hand printed word recognition, while cursive scripts require more specific and/or sophisticated techniques. Inherent ambiguity must then be compensated for by the use of contextual information.

Intense activity was devoted to the character recognition problem during the seventies and the eighties and pretty good results have been achieved (Mori, Suen, et al., 1992). Current research is instead focusing on large character sets like Kanji and on the recognition of handwritten Roman words. The recognition of handwritten characters being much related to printed character recognition, we will mainly focus on cursive word recognition.

Character Recognition

Character Recognition techniques can be classified according to two criteria: the way preprocessing is performed on the data and the type of the decision algorithm.

Preprocessing techniques include three main categories: the use of global transforms (correlation, Fourier descriptors, etc.), local comparison (local densities, intersections with straight lines, variable masks, characteristic loci, etc.) and geometrical or topological characteristics (strokes, loops, openings, diacritical marks, skeleton, etc.).

Depending on the type of preprocessing stage, various kinds of decision methods have been used, including statistical methods, neural networks, structural matchings (on trees, chains, etc.) and stochastic processing (Markov chains, etc.). Many recent methods mix several techniques together in order to obtain improved reliability, despite great variation in handwriting.

Handwritten Word Recognition

As pointed out in the chapter overview, two main types of strategies have been applied to this problem since the beginning of research in this field: the holistic approach and the analytical approach (Lecolinet & Baret, 1994; Lorette & Lecourtier, 1993; Hull, Ho, et al., 1992; Simon, Baret, et al., 1994). In the first case recognition is globally performed on the whole representation of words and there is no attempt to identify characters individually.

The main advantage of holistic methods is that they avoid word segmentation (Rocha & Pavlidis, 1993). Their main drawback is that they are related to a fixed lexicon of word descriptions: as these methods do not rely on letters, words are directly described by means of features and adding new words to the lexicon requires human training or the automatic generation of word descriptions from ASCII words. These methods are generally based on dynamic programming (DP) (edit distance, DP-matching, etc.) or model-discriminant hidden Markov models.

Analytical strategies deal with several levels of representation, corresponding to increasing levels of abstraction (usually the feature level, the grapheme or pseudo-letter level and the word level). Words are not considered as a whole but as sequences of smaller size units, which must be easily related to characters in order to make recognition independent from a specific vocabulary.

These methods are themselves subclassed into two categories: analytical methods with explicit (or *external*) segmentation, where grapheme or pseudo-letter segmentation takes place before recognition (Lecolinet & Crettez, 1991) and analytical methods with implicit (or *internal*) segmentation (Burges, Matan, et al., 1992; Chen, Kundu, et al., 1992) which perform segmentation and recognition simultaneously (segmentation is then a *by-product* of recognition). In both cases, lexical knowledge is heavily used to help recognition. This lexical knowledge can either be described by means of a lexicon of ASCII words (which is often represented by means of a lexical tree) or by statistical information on letter co-occurrence (n-grams, transitional probabilities, etc.). The advantage of letter-based recognition methods is that the vocabulary can be dynamically defined and modified without the need for word training.

Many techniques initially designed for character recognition (like neural networks, Burges, Matan, et al., 1992) have been incorporated to analytical methods for recognizing tentative letters or graphemes. The contextual phase is generally based on dynamic programming and/or Markov chains (edit distance, Viterbi algorithm, etc.). Fruitful research has been realized in recent years in the field of analytic recognition with implicit segmentation using various kinds of hidden Markov models (Chen, Kundu, et al., 1992).

2.4.3   Future Directions

Exploitable results can already be obtained when the data is sufficiently constrained. Commercial products are already available for hand printed character
recognition in forms and recent research projects have shown that cursive word
recognition is feasible for small lexicons and/or when strong sentence syntax is
provided. For instance, recognition rates of 95% (respectively 90%) or more have
been obtained for lexicons of American city names whose size varies between 10
and 100 (respectively 1000) words (Kimura, Shridhar, et al., 1993).

Recent studies show the emergence of two promising tendencies:

1. hybrid systems that combine several recognition techniques

2. the use of contextual analysis at word, sentence or text level to predict or
   confirm word recognition.

This is already the direction that several major research teams have decided to
follow (Hull, 1994) and there is no doubt that contextual analysis will be a field
of intense research and achievements in the next few years.

2.5   Handwriting as Computer Interface

Isabelle Guyon & Colin Warwick

AT&T Bell Laboratories, Holmdel, New Jersey, USA

2.5.1   Pen Computers: Dream and Reality

Pen computers (Forman & Zahorjan, 1994) offer an interesting alternative to
paper. One can write directly on a Liquid Crystal Display (LCD) screen with
a stylus or *pen*. The screen has an invisible sensitive matrix which records
the position of the pen on the surface. The trajectory of the pen appears
almost instantaneously on the screen giving the illusion of ink (electronic ink).
Handwriting recognition allows text and computer commands to be entered.

While nothing opposes the idea of a computer that would use multiple input modalities, including speech, keyboard and pen, some applications call for
a pen-only computer interface: in a social environment, speech does not provide enough privacy; for small hand-held devices and for large alphabet (e.g.,
Chinese), the keyboard is cumbersome. Applications are numerous: personal
organizer, personal communicator, notebook, data acquisition device for order
entries, inspections, inventories, surveys, etc.

The dream is to have a computer that looks like paper, feels like paper but is
better than paper. Currently, paper is the most popular medium for sketching,
note taking and form filling, because it offers a unique combination of features:
light, cheap, reliable, available almost everywhere any time, easy to use, flexible,
foldable, pleasing to the eye and to the touch, silent. But paper also has its
drawbacks: in large quantities it is no longer light and cheap, it is hard to reuse
and recycle, difficult to edit, expensive to copy and to mail, and inefficient to

transform into computer files. With rapid technology progress, electronic ink could become cheaper and more convenient than paper, if only handwriting recognition worked.

As of today, the mediocre quality of handwriting recognition has been a major obstacle to the success of pen computers. Users report that it is "too inaccurate, too slow and too demanding for user attention" (Chang & Scott MacKenzie, 1994). The entire pen computing industry is turning its back on handwriting and reverting to *popup keyboards*. On small surfaces, keypad tapping is difficult and slow: 10–21 words per minute, compared to 15–18 wpm for handprint and 20–32 wpm for a full touch screen keyboard. However, it remains the preferred entry mode because of its low error rate: less than 1% for the speed quoted, compared to 5–6% with a state-of-the-art recognizer (CIC) (MacQueen, Scott MacKenzie, et al., 1994; Chang & Scott MacKenzie, 1994). In one of our recent studies, we discovered that a good typist tolerates only up to 1% error using a special keyboard that introduced random typing errors at a software-controllable rate; 0.5% error is unnoticeable; 2% error is intolerable! (Warwick, 1995) Human subjects make 4–8% error for isolated letters read in the absence of context and 1.5% error with the context of the neighboring letters (Wilkinson, Geist, et al., 1992; Geist et al., 1994). Therefore, the task of designing usable handwriting recognizers for pen computing applications is tremendously hard. Human recognition rates must be reached and even outperformed.

2.5.2 The State of the Art in On-line Handwriting Recognition

The problem of recognizing handwriting recorded with a digitizer as a time sequence of pen coordinates is known as *on-line handwriting recognition*. In contrast, *off-line handwriting recognition* refers to the recognition of handwritten paper documents which are optically scanned.

The difficulty of recognition varies with a number of factors:

- Restrictions on the number of writers.

- Constraints on the writer: entering characters in boxes or in combs, lifting the pen between characters, observing a certain stroke order, entering strokes with a specific shape.

- Constraints on the language: limiting the number of symbols to be recognized, limiting the size of the vocabulary, limiting the syntax and/or the semantics.

Until the beginning of the nineties, on-line handwriting recognition research was mainly academic and most results were reported in the open literature (Tappert, Suen, et al., 1990). The situation has changed in the past few years with the rapid growth of the pen computing industry. Because of the very harsh competition, many companies no longer publish in peer-reviewed literature and no recent general survey is available.

In the last few years, academic research has focussed on cursive script recognition (Plamondon, 1995c; Lecolinet & Baret, 1994). Performances are reported on different databases and are difficult to compare. It can be said, with caution, that the state of the art for writer independent recognition of isolated English cursive words, with an alphabet of 26 letters and a vocabulary of 5,000–10,000 words, is between 5% and 10% character error rate and between 15% and 20% word error rate.

Most commercial recognizers perform writer independent recognition and can recognize characters, words or sentences, with either characters written in boxes or combs, or in run-on mode with pen-lifts between characters (e.g., CIC, AT&T-EO, Grid, IBM, Microsoft, Nestor). In addition, those systems recognize a set of gestures and can be trained with handwriting samples provided by the user. Some companies provide recognizers for both Latin and Kanji alphabets (e.g., CIC). Companies like Paragraph International and Lexicus offer cursive recognition. Palm Computing recently introduced a recognizer for a simplified alphabet (similarly as Goldberg & Richardson, 1993). It presumably reaches below 1% error, but a controlled benchmark has yet to be performed.

AT&T-GIS anonymously tested seven Latin alphabet recognizers, including five commercial recognizers, using an alphabet of 68 symbols (uppercase, lowercase, digits and six punctuation symbols) on two different tasks (Allen, Hunter, et al., 1994):

- The recognition of isolated characters written in boxes;

- The recognition of American addresses written in run-on mode on a baseline, without the help of boxes or combs, but with pen-lifts between characters. The vocabulary list was not disclosed.

The first task imposes constraints on the writer, but not on the language. Without any contextual information given by neighboring characters which are part of a same word or sentence, it is impossible to distinguish between the digit "0," the letter "O," and the letter "o." Even humans make errors in such cases, which we call *legitimate* errors. If all errors are counted, including the legitimate errors, the best recognizer has a 19% error rate. This error-rate is reduced by more than half if legitimate errors are removed. On such a data set, humans still make approximately half as many errors. Much higher recognition rates are obtained on subsets of the characters set which do not contain intrinsic ambiguities. For instance, less than 2% error can be obtained on digits only, which is close to the human performance on the same task.

The second task imposes less constraints on the writer, thus characters are harder to segment. However, the recognizers can use neighboring letters to determine relative character positions and relative sizes, which is helpful to discriminate between uppercase and lowercase letters. Using only such limited contextual information, the best recognizer has a 30% character error rate (including insertions, substitutions and deletions). Use can also be made of a model of language to help correcting recognition mistakes. The performance of the best recognizer using an English lexicon and a letter trigram model was

20% character error. Humans perform considerably better than machines on this task and make only a small percentage of errors.

2.5.3 A Brief Review of On-line Handwriting Recognition Techniques

Considerably more effort has been put into developing algorithms for Optical Character Recognition (OCR) and speech recognition than for on-line handwriting recognition. Consequently, on-line handwriting recognition, which bears similarity to both, has been borrowing a lot of techniques from these.

There is a natural temptation to convert pen trajectory data to pixel images and process them with an OCR recognizer. But, the on-line handwriting recognition problem has a number of distinguishing features which must be exploited to get best results:

- **Preprocessing** operations such as smoothing, deslanting, deskewing, and dehooking and **feature extraction** operations such as the detection of line orientations, corners, loops and cusps are easier and faster with the pen trajectory data than on pixel images.

- **Discrimination** between optically ambiguous characters (for example, "j" and ";") may be facilitated with the pen trajectory information.

- **Segmentation** operations are facilitated by using the pen-lift information, particularly for handprinted characters.

- **Immediate feed-back** is given by the writer, whose corrections can be used to further train the recognizer.

Another temptation is to use the pen trajectory as a temporal signal and process it with a speech recognizer. Other problems arise:

- **Stroke reordering** is usually necessary, to get rid of stroke order variability and of the problem of delayed strokes.

- **Data unfolding** in a purely one-dimensional representation may result in losing direct reference to the two-dimensional structure of the data.

Classically, on-line recognizers consist of a preprocessor, a classifier which provides estimates of probabilities for the different categories of characters (or other subword units) and a dynamic programming postprocessor (often a hidden Markov model), which eventually incorporates a language model (ICDAR, 1993; Hanson, Cowan, et al., 1993; ICASSP, 1994). The system has usually adjustable parameters whose values are determined during a training session. The Expectation Maximization (EM) algorithm (or its *K-means* approximation) is used to globally optimize all parameters.

While all postprocessors are very similar, a wide variety of classifiers have been used, including statistical classifiers, Bayesian classifiers, decision trees, neural networks and fuzzy systems. They present different speed/accuracy/memory trade-offs but none of them significantly outperforms all others in every respect. On-line systems also differ from one another in data representations, ranging from 2-dimensional maps of pixels or features to temporal sequences of features, and from local low level features to the encoding of entire strokes.

2.5.4   Future Directions

Only a few years ago, cursive handwriting recognition seemed out of reach. Today the dream has become reality. Yet, recognizers currently available are still disappointing to users. There is a wide margin for improvement which should challenge researchers and developers.

Because of the lack of success of the first generation of pen computers, the industry is currently focusing on two kinds of products:

- Data acquisition devices for form filling applications requiring only a limited alphabet and allowing very constrained grammars or language models. Users such as commercial agents would be willing to print characters in boxes or combs.

- Personal Digital Assistants combining agenda, address book and telecommunications facilities (phone, fax and mail). Users would want to use natural unconstrained handwriting, cursive or handprinted.

In the short term, to meet the accuracy requirements of industry applications, it is important to focus on simplified recognition tasks such as limited vocabulary handprinted character recognition. In the long term, however, research should be challenged by harder tasks, such as large vocabulary cursive recognition.

Hardware constraints presently limit commercial recognizers but the rapid evolution of computer hardware ensures that within two to three years discrepancies between the processing power of portable units and today's workstations will disappear. Therefore, it seems reasonable to use as a metric the processing power of today's workstations and concentrate most of the research effort on improving recognition accuracy rather than optimizing algorithms to fulfill today's speed and memory requirements.

To be able to read cursive writing, humans make use of sources of information that are still seldom taken into account in today's systems:

- elaborate language models;

- writing style models.

The success of incorporating both kind of models in speech recognition systems is an encouragement for handwriting recognition researchers to pursue in that direction.

Finally, there is often a large discrepancy between the error rate obtained in laboratory experiments and those obtained in the field. Recognizers should be tested, as far as possible, in realistic conditions of utilization, or at least on realistic test data. With projects such as UNIPEN (Guyon, Schomaker, et al., 1994), it will be possible to exchange a wide variety of data and organize public competitions.

2.6 Handwriting Analysis

Rejean Plamondon

Ecole Polytechnique de Montréal, Montréal, Québéc, Canada

2.6.1 Problem Statement

As in many well-mastered tasks, human subjects generally work at the highest and most efficient level of abstraction possible when reading a handwritten document. When difficulties are encountered in deciphering a part of the message using one level of interpretation, they often switch to a lower level of representation to resolve ambiguities. In this perspective, the lower levels of knowledge, although generally used in the background, constitute a cornerstone on which a large part of the higher and more abstract process levels relies. For example, according to motor theories of perception, it is assumed that motor processes enter into genesis of percepts and that handwriting generation and perception tasks interact and share sensorimotor information. Cursive script recognition or signature verfication tasks therefore require, directly or indirectly, an understanding of the handwriting generation processes.

Consistent with these hypotheses, some design methodologies incorporate this theoretical framework in the development of automatic handwriting processing systems. So far, numerous models have been proposed to study and analyze handwriting (Plamondon & Maarse, 1989; Plamondon, Suen, et al., 1989; Galen & Stelmach, 1993; Faure, Lorette, et al., 1994). Depending on the emphasis placed on the symbolic information or on the connectionist architecture, two complementary approaches have been followed: top-down and bottom-up. The top-down approach has been developed mainly by those researchers interested in the study and application of the various aspects of the high-level motor processes: fundamental unit of movement coding, command sequencing and retrieval, movement control and learning, task complexity, etc. The bottom-up approach has been used by those interested in the analysis and synthesis of the low-level neuromuscular processes. For this latter approach to be of interest in the study of the perceptivomotor strategies involved in the generation and perception of handwriting, two criteria must be met. On the one hand, a model should be realistic enough to reproduce specific pentip trajectories almost perfectly and, on the other, its descriptive power should be such that it provides consistent explanations of the basic properties of single strokes (asymmetric bell-shaped velocity profiles, speed accuracy trade-offs, etc.). In other words, the most interesting bottom-up models should allow the link to be made between the symbolic and connectionist approaches.

2.6.2   A Model of the Handwriting Generation System

A serious candidate model for a basic theory of human movement generation, in the sense that it addresses some of the key problems related to handwriting generation and perception, is based on two basic assumptions. First, it supposes that fast handwriting, like any other highly skilled motor process, is partially planned in advance (Lashley, 1987; van der Gon & Thuring, 1965), with no extra control during the execution of a continuous trace of handwritten text, hereafter called a string (Plamondon, 1989b). Second, it assumes some form of rotation invariance in movement representation and uses differential geometry to describe a handwritten string by its change of line curvature as a function of the curvilinear abscissa (Plamondon, 1989a).

In this context, a string can be described by a sequence of virtual targets that have to be reached within a certain spatial precision to guarantee the message legibility. Each individual stroke can be seen as a way to map these targets together in a specific two-dimensional space. To produce a continuous and fluent movement, it is necessary to superimpose these discrete movement units in time; that is, to start a new stroke, described by its own set of parameters, before the end of the previous one. This superimposition process is done vectorially in a 2D space. A complex velocity pattern, representing a word, thus emerges from the vectorial addition of curvilinear strokes.

A general way to look at the impulse response of a specific controller, say the module controller, is to consider the overall sets of neural and muscle networks involved in the production of a single stroke as a synergetic linear system, producing a curvilinear velocity profile from an impulse command of amplitude D occurring at t_0 (Plamondon, 1992). The curvilinear velocity profile thus directly reflects the impulse response H_{t-t_0} of neuromuscular synergy.

The mathematical description of this impulse response can be specified by considering each controller as composed of two systems that represent the sets of neural and muscular networks involved in the generation of the agonist and antagonist activities resulting in a specific movement (Plamondon, 1995b). Although various forms of interaction and coupling between these two systems probably exist throughout the process, we assume that their global effect can be taken into account at the very end of the process by subtracting the two outputs. If so, each of the systems constituting a controller can be considered as a linear time-invariant system and the output of a controller as the difference between the impulse responses of the agonist and antagonist systems, weighed by the respective amplitude of their input commands. The mathematical description of an agonist or antagonist impulse response can be specified if the sequential aspects of the various processing steps occurring within a system are taken into account. Indeed, as soon as an activation command is given, a sequence of processes goes into action. The activation command is propagated and a series of neuromuscular networks react appropriately to it. Due to the internal coupling between each of the subprocesses, one stage is activated before the activation of the previous one is completed. Within one synergy, the coupling between the various subprocesses can thus be taken into account by linking the time delays of each subprocess.

Using a specific coupling function and making an analogy between this function and the predictions of the central-limit theorem, as applied to the convolution of a large number of positive functions, it is predicted that the impulse response of a system under the coupling hypothesis will converge toward a log-normal curve (Plamondon, 1995b), provided that the individual impulse response of each subsystem meets some very general conditions (real, normalized and non-negative, with a finite third moment and scaled dispersion). So, under these conditions, the output of the module or the direction controller will be described by the weighted difference of two lognormals, hereafter called a delta lognormal equation (Plamondon, 1995b).

In this context, the control of the velocity module can now be seen as resulting from the simultaneous activation (at $t = t_0$) of a controller made up of two antagonistic neuromuscular systems, with a command of amplitude D_1 and D_2 respectively. Both systems react to their specific commands with an impulse response described by a lognormal function, whose parameters characterize the time delay and the response time of each process (Plamondon, 1995b).

One of the most stringent conclusions of this model, apart from its consistency with the major psychophysical phenomena regularly reported in studies dealing with speed/accuracy trade-offs, is that the angular component of the velocity vector just emerges from this superimposition process and is not controlled independently by a specific delta lognormal generator (Plamondon, 1995a). Each string is thus made up of a combination of curvilinear strokes, that is, curvilinear displacements characterized by delta-lognormal velocity profiles. Strokes can be described in terms of nine different parameters: t_0, the time occurrence of a synchronous pair of input commands; D_1 and D_2, the amplitude of agonist and antagonist commands respectively; μ_1, μ_2 and σ_1, σ_2, the logtime delays and the logresponse times of the agonist and the antagonist systems; θ_0 and C_0, the initial postural conditions, that is, stroke orientation and curvature. In this general context, a curvilinear stroke is thus defined as a portion of the pentip trajectory that corresponds to the curvilinear displacement resulting from the production of a delta-lognormal velocity profile, produced by a specific generator in response to a specific pair of impulse commands fed into it. These strokes are assumed to be the fundamental units of human handwriting movement and serve as the coding elements of the motor plan used in trajectory generation.

2.6.3 Testing the Model

Several comparative studies have been conducted to test and validate this model (Plamondon, Alimi, et al., 1993; Alimi & Plamondon, 1994; Alimi & Plamondon, 1993). Without entering into the details of each study, let us simply point out that it was concluded that the delta equation was the most powerful in reconstructing curvilinear velocity profiles and that its parameters were consistent with the hierarchical organization of the movement generation system. Computer simulations have also demonstrated that the delta lognormal model predicts the majority of phenomena consistently reported by many research groups studying the velocity profiles of simple movements (Plamondon, 1995b).

2.6.4   Conclusion

Further, the delta lognormal model provides a realistic and meaningful way to analyze and describe handwriting generation and provides information that can be used, in a perceptivomotor context to tackle recognition problems. Its first practical application has been the development of a model-based segmentation framework for the partitioning of handwriting (Plamondon, 1992) and its use in the development of an automatic signature verification system (Plamondon, 1994b). Based on this model, a multilevel signature verification system was developed (Plamondon, 1994a), which uses three types of representations based on global parameters and two other based on functions. The overall verification is performed using a step wise process at three distinct levels, using personalized decision thresholds.

2.6.5   Future Directions

As long as we partially succeed in processing handwriting automatically by computer, we will see on-line tools designed to help children learn to write appearing on the market, as well as intelligent electronic notebooks, signature verification, and recognition systems, not to mention the many automated off-line systems for processing written documents.

In order to see these newest inventions (all of which are dedicated to the popularization of handwriting) take shape, become a reality, and not be relegated to the status of laboratory curios, a great deal of research will be required, and numerous theoretical and technological breakthroughs must occur. Specifically, much more time and money must be spent on careful research and development, but with less of the fervor that currently prevails. False advertising must be avoided at all costs when technological breakthroughs are made, when development is still far from complete and any undue optimism arising from too many premature expectations risks compromising the scientific achievement.

In this perspective, multidisciplinarity will play a key role in future developments. Handwriting is a very complex human task that involves emotional, rational, linguistic and neuromuscular functions. Implementing any pen-based system requires us to take a few of these aspects into account. To do so, we have to understand how we control movements and how we perceive line images. Any breakthrough in the field will come from a better modeling of these underlying processes at different levels with various points of view. The intelligent integration of these models into functional systems will require the cooperation of scientists from numerous complementary disciplines. It is a real challenge for patient theoreticians.

2.7 Chapter References

Alimi, A. and Plamondon, R. (1993). Performance analysis of handwritten strokes generation models. In *Proceedings of the Third International Workshop on Frontiers in Handwriting Recognition*, pages 272–283, Buffalo, New York.

Alimi, A. and Plamondon, R. (1994). Analysis of the parameter dependence of handwriting generation models on movements characteristics. In Faure, C., Lorette, G., Vinter, A., and Keuss, P., editors, *Advances in Handwriting and Drawing: A multidisciplinary Approach*, Paris. Presse de l'Ecole Nationale Superieure de Telecommunication.

Allen, T., Hunter, W., Jacobson, M., and Miller, M. (1994). Comparing several discrete handwriting recognition algorithms. Technical report, AT&T GIS, Human Interface Technology Center, New User Interface Group.

Anigbogu, J. C. and Belaïd, A. (1991a). Application of hidden Markov models to multifont text recognition. In *Proceedings of the First International Conference on Document Analysis and Recognition*, volume 2, pages 785–793, St. Malo, France. AIPR-IEEE, IAPR.

Anigbogu, J. C. and Belaïd, A. (1991b). Recognition of Multifont Text Using Markov Models. In 7th *Scandinavian Conference on Image Analysis*, volume 1, pages 469–476.

Baird, H. S. (1990). Document Image Defect Models. In *Proceedings of the Workshop on Syntactical and Structural Pattern Recognition*, pages 38–47.

Baird, H. S. and Fossey, R. (1991). A 100-font classifier. In *Proceedings of the First International Conference on Document Analysis and Recognition*, volume 1, pages 332–340, St. Malo, France. AIPR-IEEE, IAPR.

Baird, H. S., Kahan, S., and Pavlidis, T. (1986). Components of a Omnifont Page Reader. In *Proceedings of the 8th International Conference on Pattern Recognition*, pages 344–348, Paris.

Bayer, T. (1987). Segmentation of Merged Character Patterns with Artificial Intelligence Techniques. In *Scandinavian Conference on Image Analysis*, pages 49–55, Stockholm.

Belaïd, A. and Anigbogu, J. C. (1991). Text recognition using stochastic models. In Gutiérrez, R. and Valderrama, M. J., editors, 5th *International Symposium on ASMDA*, pages 87–98. World Scientific.

Bokser, M. (1992). Omnidocument Technologies. *Proceedings of the IEEE*, 80(7):1066–1078.

Burges, C. J. C., Matan, O., Le Cun, Y., Denker, J. S., Jackel, L. D., Stenard, C. E., Nohl, C. R., and Ben, J. I. (1992). Shortest path segmentation: A method for training a neural network to recognize character strings. In *Proceedings of the 1992 International Joint Conference on Neural Networks*, volume 3, page 165, Baltimore, Maryland.

Casey, R. G. et al. (1992). Intelligent forms processing system. *Machine Vision Applications*, 5:143–155.

Casey, R. G. and Nagy, G. (1982). Recursive Segmentation and Classification of Composite Patterns. In *Proceedings of the 6th International Conference on Pattern Recognition*, pages 1023–1026.

Chang, L. and Scott MacKenzie, I. (1994). A comparison of two handwriting recognizers for pen-based computers. In *Proceedings of CANSON'94*, Canada.

Chen, M. Y., Kundu, A., Zhou, J., and Srihari, S. N. (1992). Off-line handwritten word recognition using hidden Markov model. In *Proceedings of the USPS Advanced Technology Conference*, page 563.

Cohen, E., Hull, J. J., and Srihari, S. N. (1991). Understanding handwritten text in a structured environment: determining zip codes from addresses. *International Journal of Pattern Recognition and Artificial Intelligence*, 5(1-2):221–264.

Coulmas, F. C. (1989). *The Writing Systems of the World*. Blackwell, New York.

Dengel, A. et al. (1992). From paper to office document standard representation. *IEEE Computer*, 25(7):63–67.

Duda, R. O. and Hart, P. E. (1973). *Pattern Recognition and Scene Analysis*. John Wiley, New York.

Faure, C., Lorette, G., Vinter, A., and Keuss, P. (1994). *Advances in Handwriting and Drawing: A Multidisciplinary Approach*. Europia, Paris.

Forman, G. and Zahorjan, J. (1994). The challenges of mobile computing. *IEEE Computer*, pages 38–47.

Galen, V. and Stelmach, G. E. (1993). Handwriting, issue of psychomotor control and cognitive models. *Acta Psychologica*, 82(1-3).

Geist, J. et al. (1994). The second census optical character recognition systems conference. Technical Report NISTIR-5452, National Institute of Standards and Technology, U.S. Department of Commerce.

Goldberg, D. and Richardson, D. (1993). Touch-typing with a stylus. In *INTERCHI'93 conference on Human factors in computer systems*, New York. ACM.

Govindan, V. K. and Shivaprasad, A. P. (1990). Character recognition—a review. *Pattern Recognition*, 23(7):671–683.

Govindaraju, V., Shekhawat, A., and Srihari, S. N. (1993). Interpretation of handwritten addresses in U.S. mail stream. In *Proceedings of the Second International Conference on Document Analysis and Recognition*, Tsukuba Science City, Japan. AIPR-IEEE, IAPR.

Guyon, I., Schomaker, L., Plamondon, R., Liberman, M., and Janet, S. (1994). UNIPEN project of on-line data exchange and recognizer benchmarks. In *Proceedings of the 12th International Conference on Pattern Recognition*, Jerusalem.

Hanson, S. J., Cowan, J. D., and Giles, C. L., editors (1993). *Advances in Neural Information Processing Systems 5*. Morgan Kaufmann.

Ho, T. K. (1992). *A Theory of Multiple Classifier Systems and Its Application to Visual Word Recognition*. PhD thesis, State University of New York at Buffalo. Also technical report number 92-12.

Holstege, M., Inn, Y. J., and Tokuda, L. (1991). Visual Parsing: An Aid to Text Understanding. In *Recherche d'Informations Assistée par Ordinateur 1991*, pages 175–193, France. RIAO.

Hull, J. (1994). Language-level syntactic and semantic constraints applied to visual word recognition. In Impedovo, S., editor, *Fundamentals in Handwriting Recognition*, NATO-Advanced Study Institute Series F, page 289. Springer-Verlag.

Hull, J., Ho, T. K., Favata, J., Govindaraju, V., and Srihari, S. (1992). Combination of segmentation-based and wholistic handwritten word recognition algorithms. In Impedovo, S. and Simon, J. C., editors, *From Pixels to Features III*, page 261. Elsevier Science, Amsterdam.

ICASSP (1994). *Proceedings of the 1994 International Conference on Acoustics, Speech, and Signal Processing*, Adelaide, Australia. Institute of Electrical and Electronic Engineers.

ICDAR (1991). *Proceedings of the First International Conference on Document Analysis and Recognition*, St. Malo, France. AIPR-IEEE, IAPR.

ICDAR (1993). *Proceedings of the Second International Conference on Document Analysis and Recognition*, Tsukuba Science City, Japan. AIPR-IEEE, IAPR.

Impedovo, S., editor (1994). *Fundamentals in Handwriting Recognition*. NATO-Advanced Study Institute Series F. Springer-Verlag.

Impedovo, S., Ottaviano, L., and Occhinegro, S. (1991). Optical Character Recognition—A Survey. *International Journal on Pattern Recognition and Artificial Intelligence*, 5(1-2):1–24.

Impedovo, S. and Simon, J. C., editors (1992). *From Pixels to Features III.* Elsevier Science, Amsterdam.

IWFHR (1993). *Proceedings of the Third International Workshop on Frontiers in Handwriting Recognition*, Buffalo, New York.

Kahan, S., Pavlidis, T., and Baird, H. S. (1987). On the Recognition of Printed Characters of Any Font and Size. *IEEE Transactions on Pattern Analysis and Machine Intelligence*, 9(2):274–288.

Kanai, J. (1990). Text Line Extraction and Baseline Detection. In *Recherche d'Informations Assistée par Ordinateur 1990*, pages 194–209, France. RIAO.

Kasturi, R., Sira, S., and O'Gorman, L. (1990). Techniques for line drawing interpretation: an overview. In *IAPR International Workshop on Machine Vision Applications*, pages 151–160, Tokyo.

Kimura, F., Shridhar, M., and Chen, Z. (1993). Improvements of a lexicon-directed algorithm for recognition off unconstrained handwritten words. In *Proceedings of the Second International Conference on Document Analysis and Recognition*, page 18, Tsukuba Science City, Japan. AIPR-IEEE, IAPR.

Lam, S. W. and Baird, H. S. (1987). Performance Testing of Mixed-font Variable-size Character Recognizers. In *Scandinavian Conference on Image Analysis*, pages 563–570, Stockholm.

Lashley, K. S. (1987). The accuracy of movements in the absence of excitation from the moving organ. *American journal of Physiology*, 20:169.

Lecolinet, E. and Baret, O. (1994). Cursive word recognition: Methods and strategies (survey on CSR). In Impedovo, S., editor, *Fundamentals in Handwriting Recognition*, volume 124 of *NATO-Advanced Study Institute Series F*. Springer-Verlag.

Lecolinet, E. and Crettez, J.-P. (1991). A grapheme-based segmentation technique for cursive script recognition. In *Proceedings of the First International Conference on Document Analysis and Recognition*, page 740, St. Malo, France. AIPR-IEEE, IAPR.

Liang, S., Ahmadi, M., and Shridhar, M. (1993). Segmentation of Touching Characters in Printed Document Recognition. In *Proceedings of the Second International Conference on Document Analysis and Recognition*, pages 569–572, Tsukuba Science City, Japan. AIPR-IEEE, IAPR.

Lorette, G. and Lecourtier, Y. (1993). Is recognition and interpretation of handwritten text a scene analysis problem? In *Proceedings of the Third International Workshop on Frontiers in Handwriting Recognition*, page 184.

Luca, P. G. and Gisotti, A. (1991a). How to Take Advantage of Word Structure in Printed Character Recognition. In *Recherche d'Informations Assistée par Ordinateur 1991*, pages 148–159, France. RIAO.

Luca, P. G. and Gisotti, A. (1991b). Printed Character Preclassification Based on Word Structure. *Pattern Recognition*, 24(7):609–615.

MacQueen, C., Scott MacKenzie, I., Nonnecke, B., Riddesma, S., and Meltz, M. (1994). A comparison of four methods of numeric entry on pen-based computers. In *Proceedings of Graphics Interface'94*, Toronto. Canadian Information Processing Society.

Mantas, J. (1986). An Overview of Character Recognition Methodologies. *Pattern Recognition*, 19(6):425–430.

Mori, S., Suen, C. Y., and Yamamoto, K. (1992). Historical review of OCR research and development. *Proceedings of the IEEE*, 80(7):1029–1058. Special Issue on Optical Character Recognition.

Nadler, M. (1984). A Survey of Document Segmentation and Coding Techniques. *Computer Vision and Image Processing*, 28:240–262.

Nagy, G. (1992). At the frontiers of OCR. *Proceedings of the IEEE*, 80(7):1093–1100.

Nagy, G., Seth, S., and Stoddard, S. (1985). Document analysis with an expert system. In *Proceedings of Pattern Recognition in Practice*, volume 2, Amsterdam.

Nartker, T. A., Rice, S. V., and Kanai, J. (1994). OCR Accuracy: UNLV's Second Annual Test. *Technical journal INFORM of the University of Nevada Las Vegas*.

Pavlidis, T. and Mori, S. (1992). Special issue on optical character recognition. *Proceedings of the IEEE*, 80(7).

Plamondon, R. (1989a). Handwriting control, a functional model. In Cotterill, R., editor, *Models of Brain Function*, pages 563–574. Academic Press, Cambridge, New York, Port Chester, Melbourne, Sydney.

Plamondon, R. (1989b). A handwriting model based on differential geometry,. In Plamondon, R., Suen, C. Y., and Simner, M., editors, *Computer Recognition and Human Production of Handwriting*, pages 179–192. World Scientific, Signapore, New Jersey, London, Hong Kong.

Plamondon, R. (1992). A model based segmentation framework for computer processing of handwriting. In *Proceedings of the 11th International Conference on Pattern Recognition*, pages 303–307.

Plamondon, R. (1993). Handwriting processing and recognition. *Pattern Recognition*, 26(3).

Plamondon, R. (1994a). The design of an on-line signature verification system: From theory to practice. In *Progress in Automatic Signature Verification*, volume 13 of *Machine Perception and Artificial Intelligence*, pages 795–811. World Scientific.

Plamondon, R. (1994b). A model-based dynamic signature verification system. In Impedovo, S., editor, *Fundamentals in Handwriting Recognition*, NATO-Advanced Study Institute Series F. Springer-Verlag.

Plamondon, R. (1995a). A delta-lognormal model for handwriting generation. In *Proceedings of the Seventh Biennal Conference of the International Graphonomics Society*, pages 126–127, London, Ontario.

Plamondon, R. (1995b). A kinematic theory of rapid human movements. *Biological Cybernetics*, 72:I:295–307 and II:309–320.

Plamondon, R. (1995c). Special issue on cursive script recognition. *Machine Vision and Applications*. In press.

Plamondon, R., Alimi, A., Yergeau, P., and Leclerc, F. (1993). Modelling velocity profiles of rapid movements: A comparative study. *Biological Cybernetics*, 69(2):119–128.

Plamondon, R. and Maarse, F. J. (1989). An evaluation of motor models of handwriting. *IEEE Trans. on Syst. Man Cybernetic*, 19(5):1060–1072.

Plamondon, R., Suen, C. Y., and Simner, M., editors (1989). *Computer Recognition and Human Production of Handwriting*. World Scientific.

RIAO (1991). *Recherche d'Informations Assistée par Ordinateur 1991*, France. RIAO.

Rocha, J. and Pavlidis, T. (1993). New method for word recognition without segmentation. In *Proceedings of SPIE*, volume 1906, page 76.

Rubinstein, R. (1988). *Digital Typography: An Introduction to Type and Composition for Computer System Design*. Addison-Wesley.

Schurmann, J. (1978). A Multifont Word Recognition System for Postal Address Reading. *IEEE Transactions on computers*, C-27(8):721–732.

Schurmann, J., Bartneck, N., Bayer, T., Franke, J., Mandler, E., and Oberlander, M. (1992). Document Analysis—From Pixels to Contents. *Proceedings of the IEEE*, 80(7):1101–1119.

Schürmann, J. et al. (1992). Document analysis—from pixels to contents. *Proceedings of the IEEE*, 80(7):1101–1119.

Seni, G. and Srihari, R. K. (1994). Hierarchical approach to on-line script recognition using a large vocabulary. In *Proceedings of the Fourth International Workshop on Frontiers in Handwriting Recognition*, Taipei, Taiwan.

Shlien, S. (1988). Multifont Character Recognition For Typeset Documents. *International journal of Pattern Recognition and Artificial Intelligence*, 2(4):603–620.

Simon, J. C., Baret, O., and Gorski, N. (1994). A system for the recognition of handwritten literal amounts of checks. In *Proceedings of DAS*, page 135, Kaiserslautern, Germany.

Srihari, R. and Baltus, C. M. (1993). Incorporating syntactic constraints in recognizing handwritten sentences. In *Proceedings of the 13th International Joint Conference on Artificial Intelligence*, page 1262, Chambery, France.

Srihari, S. N. (1984). *Computer Text Recognition and Error Correction*. IEEE Computer Society Press, Silver Springs, Maryland.

Srihari, S. N. (1992). High-performance reading machines. *Proceedings of the IEEE*, 80(7):1120–1132.

Srihari, S. N. and Hull, J. J. (1985). Address Recognition Techniques in Mail Sorting: Research Directions. Technical Report 85-09, Department of Computer Science, SUNY at Buffalo.

Srihari, S. N. and Hull, J. J. (1992). Character recognition. In Shapiro, S. C., editor, *Encyclopedia of Artificial Intelligence, second edition*, pages 138–150. John Wiley.

Tappert, C. C., Suen, C. Y., and Wakahara, T. (1990). The state of the art in on-line handwriting recognition. *IEEE Transactions on Pattern Analysis and Machine Intelligence*, 12(8):787–808.

Tsujimoto, S. and Asada, H. (1992). Major components of a complete text reading system. *Proceedings of the IEEE*, 80(7):1133–1149.

Tsujimoto, Y. and Asada, H. (1991). Resolving Ambiguity in Segmenting Touching Characters. In *Proceedings of the First International Conference on Document Analysis and Recognition*, pages 701–709, St. Malo, France. AIPR-IEEE, IAPR.

Ullman, J. R. (1973). *Pattern Recognition Techniques*. Crane-Russak, New York.

Unicode Consortium, The (1990). *The Unicode Standard, Worldwide Character Encoding*. Addison-Wesley.

van der Gon, J. J. D. and Thuring, J. P. (1965). The guiding of human writing movements. *Kybernetik*, 4(2):145–148.

Vaxiviere, P. and Tombre, K. (1992). Celesstin: CAD conversion of mechanical drawings. *IEEE Computer*, 25(7):46–54.

Wang, P. S. P. (1991). Character and handwriting recognition: Expanding frontiers. *International journal of Pattern Recognition and Artificial Intelligence*, 5.

Warwick, C. (1995). Trends and limits in the talk time of personal communicators. *Proceedings of the IEEE*, 83(4). In press.

Wilkinson, R. A., Geist, J., Janet, S., Grother, P. J., Burges, C. J. C., Creecy, R., Hammond, B., Hull, J. J., Larsen, N. J., Vogl, T. P., and Wilson, C. L. (1992). The first census optical character recognition systems conference. Technical Report NISTIR-4912, National Institute of Standards and Technology, U.S. Department of Commerce.

Wong, K. Y., Casey, R. G., and Wahl, F. M. (1982). A document analysis system. *IBM journal of Research and Development*, 26(6):647–656.

Chapter 3

Language Analysis and Understanding

3.1 Overview

Annie Zaenen[a] **& Hans Uszkoreit**[b]

[a] Rank Xerox Research Centre, Grenoble, France
[b] Deutsches Forschungszentrum für Künstliche Intelligenz
and Universität des Saarlandes, Saarbrücken, Germany

We understand larger textual units by combining our understanding of smaller ones. The main aim of linguistic theory is to show how these larger units of meaning arise out of the combination of the smaller ones. This is modeled by means of a grammar. Computational linguistics then tries to implement this process in an efficient way. It is traditional to subdivide the task into syntax and semantics, where syntax describes how the different formal elements of a textual unit, most often the sentence, can be combined and semantics describes how the interpretation is calculated.

In most language technology applications the encoded linguistic knowledge, i.e., the grammar, is separated from the processing components. The grammar consists of a lexicon, and rules that syntactically and semantically combine words and phrases into larger phrases and sentences. A variety of representation languages have been developed for the encoding of linguistic knowledge. Some of these languages are more geared towards conformity with formal linguistic theories, others are designed to facilitate certain processing models or specialized applications.

Several language technology products on the market today employ annotated phrase-structure grammars, grammars with several hundreds or thousands of rules describing different phrase types. Each of these rules is annotated by features, and sometimes also by expressions, in a programming language. When such grammars reach a certain size they become difficult to maintain, to extend, and to reuse. The resulting systems might be sufficiently efficient for some applications but they lack the speed of processing needed for interactive systems (such as applications involving spoken input) or systems that have to process large volumes of texts (as in machine translation).

In current research, a certain polarization has taken place. Very simple grammar models are employed, e.g., different kinds of finite-state grammars that support highly efficient processing. Some approaches do away with grammars altogether and use statistical methods to find basic linguistic patterns. These approaches are discussed in section 3.7. On the other end of the scale, we find a variety of powerful linguistically sophisticated representation formalisms that facilitate grammar engineering. An exhaustive description of the current work in that area would be well beyond the scope of this overview. The most prevalent family of grammar formalisms currently used in computational linguistics, constraint based formalisms, is described in short in section 3.3. Approaches to lexicon construction inspired by the same view are described in section 3.4.

Recent developments in the formalization of semantics are discussed in section 3.5.

The computational issues related to different types of sentence grammars are discussed in section 3.6. Section 3.7 evaluates how successful the different techniques are in providing robust parsing results, and section 3.2 addresses issues raised when units smaller than sentences need to be parsed.

3.2   Sub-Sentential Processing[1]

Fred Karlsson[a] & Lauri Karttunen[b]

[a] University of Helsinki, Finland
[b] Rank Xerox Research Centre, Meylan, France

3.2.1   Morphological Analysis

In the last ten to fifteen years, computational morphology has advanced further towards real-life applications than most other subfields of natural language processing. The quest for an efficient method for the analysis and generation of word-forms is no longer an academic research topic, although morphological analyzers still remain to be written for all but the commercially most important languages. This survey concentrates on the developments that have lead to large-scale practical analyzers, leaving aside many theoretically more interesting issues.

To build a syntactic representation of the input sentence, a parser must map each word in the text to some canonical representation and recognize its morphological properties. The combination of a surface form and its analysis as a canonical form and inflection is called a lemma.

---

[1]By *sub-sentential processing* we mean *morphological analysis, morphological disambiguation*, and *shallow* (light) *parsing*.

The main problems are:

1. morphological alternations: the same morpheme may be realized in different ways depending on the context.

2. morphotactics: stems, affixes, and parts of compounds do not combine freely, a morphological analyzer needs to know what arrangements are valid.

A popular approach to 1 is the cut-and-paste method. The canonical form is derived by removing and adding letters to the end of a string. The best known ancestor of these systems is MITalk's DECOMP, dating back to the 1960s (Allen, Hunnicutt, et al., 1987). The MORPHOGEN system (Petheroudakis, 1991) is a commercial toolkit for creating sophisticated cut-and-paste analyzers. In the MAGIC system (Schüller, Zierl, et al., 1993), cut-and-paste rules are applied in advance to produce the right allomorph for every allowed combination of a morpheme.

The use of finite-state technology for automatic recognition and generation of word forms was introduced in the early 1980s. It is based on the observation (Johnson, 1972; Kaplan & Kay, 1994) that rules for morphological alternations can be implemented by finite-state transducers. It was also widely recognized that possible combinations of stems and affixes can be encoded as a finite-state network.

The first practical system incorporating these ideas is the two-level model (Koskenniemi, 1983; Karttunen, 1993; Antworth, 1990; Karttunen & Beesley, 1992; Ritchie, Russell, et al., 1992; Sproat, 1992). It is based on a set of linked letter trees for the lexicon and parallel finite-state transducers that encode morphological alternations. A two-level recognizer maps the surface string to a sequence of branches in the letter trees using the transducers and computes the lemma from information provided at branch boundaries.

In a related development during the 1980s, it was noticed that large spellchecking wordlists can be compiled to surprisingly small finite-state automata (Appel & Jacobson, 1988; Lucchesi & Kowaltowski, 1993). An automaton containing inflected word forms can be upgraded to a morphological analyzer, for example, by adding a code to the end of the inflected form that triggers some predefined cut-and-paste operation to produce the lemma. The RELEX lexicon format, developed at the LADL institute in Paris in the late 1980s, is this kind of combination of finite-state and cut-and-paste methods (Revuz, 1991; Roche, 1993).

Instead of cutting and pasting it at runtime, the entire lemma can be computed in advance and stored as a finite-state transducer whose arcs are labeled by a pair of forms (Tzoukermann & Liberman, 1990). The transducer format has the advantage that it can be used for generation as well as analysis. The number of nodes in this type of network is small, but the number of arc-label pairs is very large as there is one symbol for each morpheme-allomorph pair.

A more optimal lexical transducer can be developed by constructing a finite-state network of lexical forms, augmented with inflectional tags, and composing it with a set of rule transducers (Karttunen & Beesley, 1992; Karttunen, 1993).

The arcs of the network are labeled by a pair of individual symbols rather than a pair of forms. Each path through the network represents a lemma.

Lexical transducers can be constructed from descriptions containing any number of levels. This facilitates the description of phenomena that are difficult to describe within the constraints of the two-level model.

Because lexical transducers are bidirectional, they are generally non-determinis in both directions. If a system is only to be used for analysis, a simple finite-state network derived just for that purpose may be faster to operate.

3.2.2   Morphological Disambiguation

Word-forms are often ambiguous. Alternate analyses occur because of categorial homonymy, accidental clashes created by morphological alternations, multiple functions of affixes, or uncertainty about suffix and word boundaries. The sentential context normally decides which analysis is appropriate. This is called disambiguation.

There are two basic approaches to disambiguation: rule-based and probabilistic. Rule-based taggers Greene and Rubin (1971); Karlsson, Voutilainen, et al. (1994) typically leave some of the ambiguities unresolved but make very few errors; statistical taggers generally provide a fully disambiguated output but they have a higher error rate.

Probabilistic (stochastic) methods for morphological disambiguation have been dominant since the early 1980s. One of the earliest is Constituent-Likelihood Automatic Word-tagging System (CLAWS), developed for tagging the Lancaster-Oslo/Bergen Corpus of British English in 1978–1983 (Marshall, 1983).

CLAWS uses statistical optimization over n-gram probabilities to assign to each word one of 133 part-of-speech tags. The success rate of CLAWS2 (an early version) is 96–97% (Garside, Leech, et al., 1987). An improved version, CLAWS4, is used for tagging the 100-million-word British National Corpus (Leech, Garside, et al., 1994). It is based on a tagset of 61 tags. Similar success rates as for CLAWS, i.e., 95–99%, have been reported for English in many studies, e.g., Church (1988); De Rose (1988).

Most of the stochastic systems derive the probabilities from a handtagged training corpus. Probabilistic taggers based on a hidden Markov model can also be trained on an untagged corpus with a reported success rate of around 96% for English (Kupiec, 1992; Cutting, Kupiec, et al., 1992; Elworthy, 1993).

The accuracy of probabilistic taggers for English has remained relatively constant for the past ten years under all of the various methods. This level has recently been surpassed by a rule-based disambiguator (Karlsson, Voutilainen, et al., 1994; Voutilainen, 1994). The system consists of some 1,100 disambiguation rules written in Karlsson's Constraint Grammar formalism. The accuracy in running text is 99.7% if 2–6% of the words are left with the most recalcitrant morphological ambiguities pending. Standard statistical methods can be applied to provide a fully disambiguated output.

3.2.3 Shallow Parsing

We use the term *shallow syntax* as a generic term for analyses that are less complete than the output from a conventional parser. The output from a shallow analysis is not a phrase-structure tree. A shallow analyzer may identify some phrasal constituents, such as noun phrases, without indicating their internal structure and their function in the sentence. Another type of shallow analysis identifies the functional role of some of the words, such as the main verb, and its direct arguments.

Systems for shallow parsing normally work on top of morphological analysis and disambiguation. The basic purpose is to infer as much syntactic structure as possible from the lemmata, morphological information, and word order configuration at hand. Typically, shallow parsing aims at detecting phrases and basic head/modifier relations. A shared concern of many shallow parsers is the application to large text corpora. Frequently partial analyses are allowed if the parser is not potent enough to resolve all problems.

Church (1988) has designed a stochastic program for locating simple noun phrases which are identified by inserting appropriate brackets, [...]. Thus, a phrase such as *a former top aide* would be bracketed as a noun phrase on the basis of the information available in separately coded morphological tags, in the following example: AT (article), AP (attributive adjective), and NN (common singular noun): [a/AT former/AP top/NN aide/NN]. Hindle's parser *Fidditch* (Hindle, 1989) provides an annotated surface structure, especially phrase structure trees. It has been applied to millions of words.

The IBM/Lancaster approach to syntax is based on probabilistic parsing methods which are tested and refined using as reference corpus a manually bracketed set of sentences (Black, Garside, et al., 1993). These sentences are partly *skeleton parsed*, i.e., clear constituents are bracketed but difficult problems may be left open.

The PEG (PLNLP English Grammar) is a broad-coverage system for lexical, morphological, and syntactic analysis of running English text (Jensen & Heidorn, 1993). It provides approximate parses if all requisite information is not available. Rules are available for ranking alternative parses. For many sentences, PEG provides thorough syntactic analyses.

The TOSCA parser for English created in Nijmegen (Oostdijk, 1991) is representative of shallow parsing in the sense that rule formulation is based on extensive corpus study.

Constraint Grammar syntax stamps each word in the input sentence with a surface syntactic tag. 85–90 English words out of 100 get a unique syntactic tag, 2% are erroneous. The system was used for the morphosyntactic tagging of the 200-million-word Bank of English corpus (Järvinen, 1994).

Koskenniemi (1990) has designed a surface syntactic parser where the syntactic constraints are applied in parallel and implemented as finite-state automata. One central idea is to have most of the morphological disambiguation done by the syntactic constraints proper.

3.2.4 Future Directions

There is a need for automatic or semi-automatic discovery procedures that infer rules and rule sets for morphological analyzers from large corpora. Such procedures would make it possible to partially automate the construction of morphological analyzers.

Much work remains to be done on interfacing morphological descriptions with lexicon, syntax, and semantics in a maximally informative way. This presupposes a global view of how the various processing components relate to one another. One current line of research concerns the integration of shallow syntactic parsers with *deeper* syntactic approaches. A shallow parser used as a kind of preprocessor paves the way for a parser addressing the most recalcitrant syntactic structures such as coordination and ellipsis, thus making the task of *deeper* parsers more manageable, e.g., by reducing the number of ambiguities.

Work remains to be done on a general theory for combining rule-based approaches and stochastic approaches in a principled way. Both are needed in the task of tagging (parsing) unrestricted running text. Their respective reasonable tasks and order of application are not yet clearly understood.

Much work is currently being done on refining the methodology for testing candidate rules on various types of corpora. The importance of having flexible methods available for corpus testing is growing.

3.3　Grammar Formalisms

Hans Uszkoreit[a] & Annie Zaenen[b]

[a] Deutsches Forschungzentrum für Künstliche Intelligenz, Saarbrücken, Germany and Universität des Saarlandes, Saarbrücken, Germany
[b] Rank Xerox Research Centre, Grenoble, France

A very advanced and wide-spread class of linguistic formalisms are the so-called constraint-based grammar formalisms which are also often subsumed under the term unification grammars. They go beyond many earlier representation languages in that they have a clean denotational semantics that permits the encoding of grammatical knowledge independent from any specific processing algorithm. Since these formalisms are currently used in a large number of systems, we will a provide a brief overview of their main characteristics.

Among the most used, constraint-based grammar models are Functional Unification Grammar (FUG), (Kay, 1984) Head-Driven Phrase-Structure Grammar (HPSG), (Pollard & Sag, 1994) Lexical Functional Grammar (LFG), (Bresnan, 1982), Categorial Unification Grammar (CUG), (Haddock, Klein, et al., 1987; Karttunen, 1989; Uszkoreit, 1986), and Tree Adjunction Grammar (TAG) (Joshi & Schabes, 1992). For these or similar grammar models, powerful formalisms have been designed and implemented that are usually employed for both grammar development and linguistic processing, e.g, LFG (Bresnan, 1982), PATR (Shieber, Uszkoreit, et al., 1983), ALE (Carpenter, 1992), STUF (Bouma,

Koenig, et al., 1988), ALEP (Alshawi, Arnold, et al., 1991), CLE (Alshawi, 1992) TDL (Krieger & Schaefer, 1994) TFS (Emele & Zajac, 1990).

One essential ingredient of all these formalisms is complex formal descriptions of grammatical units (words, phrases, sentences) by means of sets of attribute-value pairs, so called feature terms. These feature terms can be nested, i.e., values can be atomic symbols or feature terms. Feature terms can be underspecified. They may contain equality statements expressed by variables or co-reference markers. The formalisms share a uniform operation for the merging and checking of grammatical information, which is commonly referred to as unification.

The formalisms differ in other aspects. Some of them are restricted to feature terms with simple unification (PATR). Others employ more powerful data types such as disjunctive terms, functional constraints, or sets. Most formalisms combine phrase-structure rules or other mechanisms for building trees with the feature-term component of the language (LFG, TAG, TDL). A few formalisms incorporate the phrase-structure information into the feature terms (HPSG, TFS).

Some frameworks use inheritance type systems (HPSG, TFS, TDL, ALE). Classes of feature terms belong to types. The types are partially ordered in a tree or in a (semi) lattice. For every type, the type hierarchy determines which other types attributes and values are inherited, which attributes are allowed and needed for a well-formed feature term of the type, which types of values these attributes need, and with which other types the type can be conjoined by means of unification.

If the feature system allows complex features (attribute-value pairs in which values may again be feature-terms), this recursion can be constrained by recursive type definitions. In fact, all of grammatical recursion can be elegantly captured by such recursive types. In the extreme, the entire linguistic derivation (parsing, generation) can be construed as type deduction (HPSG, TFS).

The strength of unification grammar formalisms lies in the advantages they offer for grammar engineering. Experience has proven that large grammars can be specified, but that their development is extremely labour-extensive. Currently, no methods exist for efficient distributed grammar engineering. This constitutes a serious bottleneck in the development of language technology products. The hope is that the new class of declarative formalisms will greatly facilitate linguistic engineering and thus speed up the entire development cycle. There are indications that seem to support this expectation. For some sizable grammars written in unification grammar formalisms, the development time was four years or less (TUG, CLE, TDL), whereas the development of large annotated phrase structure grammars had taken eight to twelve years.

Another important issue in grammar engineering is the reusability of grammars. The more a grammar is committed to a certain processing model, the less are the chances that it can be adapted to other processing models or new application areas. Although scientists are still far from converging on a uniform representation format, the declarative formulation of grammar greatly facilitates porting of such grammars from one formalism to the other. Recent experiments in grammar porting seem to bear out these expectations.

It is mainly because of their expected advantages for grammar engineering that several unification formalisms have been developed or are currently used in industrial laboratories. Almost all ongoing European Union-funded language technology projects involving grammar development have adopted unification grammar formalisms.

3.4　Lexicons for Constraint-Based Grammars

Antonio Sanfilippo

Sharp Industries of Europe, Oxford, UK

The intelligent processing of natural language for real world applications requires lexicons which provide rich information about morphological, syntactic and semantic properties of words, are well structured and can be efficiently implemented (Briscoe, 1992). These objectives can be achieved by developing tools which facilitate the acquisition of lexical information from machine readable dictionaries and text corpora, as well as database technologies and theories of word knowledge offering an encoding of the information acquired which is desirable for NLP purposes. In the last decade, there has been a growing tendency to use unification-based grammar formalisms (Kay, 1979; Kaplan & Bresnan, 1982; Pollard & Sag, 1987; Pollard & Sag, 1994; Zeevat, Klein, et al., 1987) to carry out the task of building such lexicons. These grammar formalisms encode lexical descriptions as feature structures, with inheritance and unification as the two basic operations relating these structures to one another. The use of inheritance and unification is appealing from both engineering and linguistic points of view as these operations can be formalized in terms of lattice-theoretic notions (Carpenter, 1992) which are amenable to efficient implementation and are suitable to express the hierarchical nature of lexical structure. Likewise, feature structures have a clear mathematical and computational interpretation and provide an ideal data structure to encode complex word knowledge information.

Informally, a feature structure is a set of attribute-value pairs, where values can be atomic or feature structures themselves, providing a partial specification of words, affixes and phrases. Inheritance makes it possible to arrange feature structures into a subsumption hierarchy so that information which is repeated across sets of word entries needs only specifying once (Flickinger, 1987; Pollard & Sag, 1987; Sanfilippo, 1993). For example, properties which are common to all verbs (e.g., part of speech, presence of a subject) or subsets of the verb class (presence of a direct object for verbs such as *amuse* and *put*; presence of an indirect object for verbs such as *go* and *put*) can be defined as templates. Unification provides the means for integrating inherent and inherited specifications of feature structure descriptions.

In general, unification is monotonic: all information, whether inherently specified or inherited, is preserved. Consequently, a valid lexical entry can never contain conflicting values. Unification thus provides a way to perform a consistency check on lexical descriptions. For example, the danger of inadvertently assigning distinct orthographies or parts of speech to the same word entry is easily avoided as the unification of incompatible information leads to failure. An even more stringent regime of grammar checking has recently been made available through the introduction of *typed* feature structures (Carpenter, 1992). Through typing, feature structures can be arranged into a closed hierarchy so that two feature structures unify only if their types have a common subtype. Typing is also used to specify exactly which attributes are appropriate for a given feature structure so that arbitrary extensions of feature structures are easily eschewed.

A relaxation of monotonicity, however, is sometimes useful in order to capture regularities across the lexicon. For example, most irregular verbs in English follow the same inflectional patterns as regular verbs with respect to present and gerundive forms, while differing in the simple past and/or past participle. It would therefore be convenient to state that all verbs inherit the same regular morphological paradigm by default and then let the idiosyncratic specifications of irregular verbs override inherited information which is incompatible.

Default inheritance in the lexicon is desirable to achieve compactness and simplicity in expressing generalizations about various aspects of word knowledge (Flickinger, 1987; Gazdar, 1987), but it can be problematic if used in an unconstrained manner. For example, it is well known that multiple default inheritance can lead to situations which can only be solved *ad hoc* or nondeterministically when conflicting values are inherited from the parent nodes (Touretzsky, Horty, et al., 1987). Although a number of proposals have been made to solve these problems, a general solution is still not available so that the use of default inheritance must be tailored to specific applications.

Another difficult task in lexicon implementation, perhaps the most important with regard to grammar processing, concerns the treatment of lexical ambiguity. Lexical ambiguity can be largely related to our ability to generate appropriate uses of words in context by manipulation of semantic and/or syntactic properties of words. For example, *accord* is synonymous with either *agree* or *give/grant*, depending on its valency, *move* can also be interpreted as a psychological predicate when used transitively with a sentient direct object, and *enjoy* can take either a noun or verb phrase complement when used in the *experience* sense:

a Senator David Lock's bill does not accord State benefits to illegal aliens
  They accorded him a warm welcome

b The two alibis do not accord
  Your alibi does not accord with his

c Her sadness moves him

d John enjoys $\left\{ \begin{array}{l} \text{the book} \\ \text{reading the book} \end{array} \right\}$

Although the precise mechanisms which govern lexical knowledge are still largely unknown, there is strong evidence that word sense extensibility is not arbitrary (Atkins & Levin, 1992; Pustejovsky, 1991; Pustejovsky, 1994; Ostler & Atkins, 1992). For example, the amenability of a verb such as *move* to yield either

a movement or psychological interpretation can be generalized to most predicates of caused motion (e.g., *agitate, crash, cross, lift, strike, sweep, unwind*).
Moreover, the metonymical and metaphoric processes which are responsible for
polysemy appear to be subject to crosslinguistic variation. For example, the
"meat vs. animal" alternation that is found in English—viz. *feed the lamb* vs.
eat lamb—is absent in Eskimo (Nunberg & Zaenen, 1992) and is less productive in Dutch where nominal compounding is often used instead, e.g., *lam* vs.
lamsvlees.

Examples of this sort show that our ability to extend word use in context
is often systematic or conventionalized. Traditional approaches to lexical representation assume that word use extensibility can be modeled by exhaustively
describing the meaning of a word through closed enumeration of its senses.
Word sense enumeration provides highly specialized lexical entries, but:

- it fails to make explicit regularities about word sense extensibility which
  are necessary in promoting compactness in lexical description,

- it is at odds with our ability to create new word uses in novel contexts,
  and

- it generates massive lexical ambiguity.

Consequently, several attempts have been made to develop a more dynamic approach to lexical specification which provides a principled treatment of polysemy
and can be used to model creative aspects of word use. For example, Pustejovsky
(1991); Pustejovsky (1994) and Pustejovsky and Boguraev (1993) propose an integrated multilayered representation of word meaning which incorporates salient
aspects of world knowledge, e.g., purpose, origin, form and constituency properties are specified for object-denoting nominals. This makes it possible to conflate
different uses of the same word into a single *meta-entry* which can be extended
to achieve contextual congruity using lexical rules (Copestake & Briscoe, 1992).
Equivalent results can be obtained using abductive reasoning to generate different word senses from polysemic lexical representations (Hobbs, Stickel, et al.,
1993). The use of lexical rules or abductive reasoning provide a principled alternative to word sense enumeration in the treatment of polysemy and can be
made to cater for novel uses of words. However, it is not clear whether these
practices can address the question of lexical ambiguity efficiently as there is
no known general control regime on lexical rules or abductive reasoning which
would deterministically restricts polysemic expansion without preempting the
generation of possible word uses. A promising alternative is to use contextual information to guide sense extension. For example Sanfilippo, Benkerimi,
et al. (1994); Sanfilippo (1995) propose that polysemy be expressed as lexical polymorphism within a Typed Feature Structure formalism by assigning to
an ambiguous word entry a lexical type with subtype extensions describing all
admissible uses of the word. Lexical ambiguities can then be solved deterministically by using syntactic and semantic contextual information during language
processing to ground underspecified word entries.

3.4.1 Future Directions

Needless to say, the computational lexicon of the future is hard to detail with sufficient confidence given the speed at which language technology is evolving. A determining factor will certainly be the availability of better tools for lexical aquisition from text corpora, since manual creation of lexical resources is expensive and too easily affected by the human error. As long as portability and wide coverage will be regarded as necessary presuppositions to commercially viable language technology, it is reasonable to expect that advancements in the treatment of default inheritance and polysemy will be instrumental in shaping future developments in this area. Efficient ways of handling defaults with an acceptable degree of precision, while allowing the inheritance of conflicting information, greatly enhances compactness and simplicity in lexical representation. At the same time, a better understanding of how to characterize word senses and describe word usage extensibility is crucial in addressing the question of lexical ambiguity in language processing. Therefore, progress in both areas is necessary to satisfy the storage and processing requirements of NLP applications running on personal computers capable of dealing with unrestricted text.

3.5 Semantics[2]

Stephen G. Pulman

SRI International, Cambridge, UK
and University of Cambridge Computer Laboratory, Cambridge, UK

3.5.1 Basic Notions of Semantics

A perennial problem in semantics is the delineation of its subject matter. The term *meaning* can be used in a variety of ways, and only some of these correspond to the usual understanding of the scope of linguistic or computational semantics. We shall take the scope of semantics to be restricted to the literal interpretations of sentences in a context, ignoring phenomena like irony, metaphor, or *conversational implicature* (Grice, 1975; Levinson, 1983).

A standard assumption in computationally oriented semantics is that knowledge of the meaning of a sentence can be equated with knowledge of its truth conditions: that is, knowledge of what the world would be like if the sentence were true. This is not the same as knowing whether a sentence is true, which is (usually) an empirical matter, but knowledge of truth conditions is a prerequisite for such verification to be possible. *Meaning as truth conditions* needs to be generalized somewhat for the case of imperatives or questions, but is a common ground among all contemporary theories, in one form or another, and has an extensive philosophical justification, e.g., Davidson (1969); Davidson (1973).

---

[2]This survey draws in part on material prepared for the European Commission LRE Project 62-051, *FraCaS: A Framework for Computational Semantics.* I am grateful to the other members of the project for their comments and contributions.

A semantic description of a language is some finitely stated mechanism that allows us to say, for each sentence of the language, what its truth conditions are. Just as for grammatical description, a semantic theory will characterize complex and novel sentences on the basis of their constituents: their meanings, and the manner in which they are put together. The basic constituents will ultimately be the meanings of words and morphemes. The modes of combination of constituents are largely determined by the syntactic structure of the language. In general, to each syntactic rule combining some sequence of child constituents into a parent constituent, there will correspond some semantic operation combining the meanings of the children to produce the meaning of the parent.

A corollary of knowledge of the truth conditions of a sentence is knowledge of what inferences can be legitimately drawn from it. Valid inference is traditionally within the province of logic (as is truth) and mathematical logic has provided the basic tools for the development of semantic theories. One particular logical system, first order predicate calculus (FOPC), has played a special role in semantics (as it has in many areas of computer science and artificial intelligence). FOPC can be seen as a small model of how to develop a rigorous semantic treatment for a language, in this case an artificial one developed for the unambiguous expression of some aspects of mathematics. The set of sentences or well formed formulae of FOPC are specified by a grammar, and a rule of semantic interpretation is associated with each syntactic construct permitted by this grammar. The interpretations of constituents are given by associating them with set-theoretic constructions (their *denotation*) from a set of basic elements in some universe of discourse. Thus, for any of the infinitely large set of FOPC sentences we can give a precise description of its truth conditions, with respect to that universe of discourse. Furthermore, we can give a precise account of the set of valid inferences to be drawn from some sentence or set of sentences, given these truth conditions, or (equivalently, in the case of FOPC) given a set of rules of inference for the logic.

3.5.2   Practical Applications of Semantics

Some natural language processing tasks (e.g., message routing, textual information retrieval, translation) can be carried out quite well using statistical or pattern matching techniques that do not involve semantics in the sense assumed above. However, performance on some of these tasks improves if semantic processing is involved. (Not enough progress has been made to see whether this is true for all of the tasks).

Some tasks, however, cannot be carried out at all without semantic processing of some form. One important example application is that of database query, of the type chosen for the Air Travel Information Service (ATIS) task (DARPA, 1989). For example, if a user asks, *"Does every flight from London to San Francisco stop over in Reykjavik?"* then the system needs to be able to deal with some simple semantic facts. Relational databases do not store propositions of the form *every X has property P* and so a logical inference from the meaning of the sentence is required. In this case, *every X has property P* is equivalent to *there is no X that does not have property P* and a system that knows this will also therefore know that the answer to the question is *no* if a non-stopping flight is found and *yes* otherwise.

Any kind of generation of natural language output (e.g., summaries of financial data, traces of KBS system operations) usually requires semantic processing. Generation requires the construction of an appropriate meaning representation, and then the production of a sentence or sequence of sentences which express the same content in a way that is natural for a reader to comprehend, e.g., McKeown, Kukich, et al. (1994). To illustrate, if a database lists a 10 a.m. flight from London to Warsaw on the 1st–14th, and 16th–30th of November, then it is more helpful to answer the question *What days does that flight go?* by *Every day except the 15th* instead of a list of 30 days of the month. But to do this the system needs to know that the semantic representations of the two propositions are equivalent.

3.5.3 Development of Semantic Theory

It is instructive, though not historically accurate, to see the development of contemporary semantic theories as motivated by the deficiencies that are uncovered when one tries to take the FOPC example further as a model for how to do natural language semantics. For example, the technique of associating set theoretic denotations directly with syntactic units is clear and straightforward for the artificial FOPC example. But when a similar programme is attempted for a natural language like English, whose syntax is vastly more complicated, the statement of the interpretation clauses becomes in practice extremely baroque and unwieldy, especially so when sentences that are semantically but not syntactically ambiguous are considered (Cooper, 1983). For this reason, in most semantic theories, and in all computer implementations, the interpretation of sentences is given indirectly. A syntactically disambiguated sentence is first translated into an expression of some artificial logical language, where this expression in its turn is given an interpretation by rules analogous to the interpretation rules of FOPC. This process factors out the two sources of complexity whose product makes direct interpretation cumbersome: reducing syntactic variation to a set of common semantic constructs; and building the appropriate set-theoretical objects to serve as interpretations.

The first large scale semantic description of this type was developed by Montague (1973). Montague made a further departure from the model provided by FOPC in using a more powerful logic (*intensional logic*) as an intermediate representation language. All later approaches to semantics follow Montague in using more powerful logical languages: while FOPC captures an important range of inferences (involving, among others, words like *every*, and *some* as in the example above), the range of valid inference patterns in natural languages is far wider. Some of the constructs that motivate the use of richer logics are sentences involving concepts like *necessity* or *possibility* and *propositional attitude* verbs like *believe* or *know*, as well as the inference patterns associated with other English quantifying expressions like *most* or *more than half*, which cannot be fully captured within FOPC (Barwise & Cooper, 1981).

For Montague, and others working in frameworks descended from that tradition (among others, Partee, e.g., Partee, 1986, Krifka, e.g., Krifka, 1989, and Groenendijk and Stokhof, e.g., Groenendijk & Stokhof, 1984; Groenendijk & Stokhof, 1991a) the intermediate logical language was merely a matter of convenience which could, in principle, always be dispensed with provided the *principle of compositionality* was observed. (I.e., *The meaning of a sentence is a function of the meanings of its constituents*, attributed to Frege, (Frege, 1892)). For other approaches, (e.g., Discourse Representation Theory, Kamp, 1981) an intermediate level of representation is a necessary component of the theory, justified on psychological grounds, or in terms of the necessity for explicit reference to representations in order to capture the meanings of, for example, pronouns or other referentially dependent items, elliptical sentences or sentences ascribing mental states (beliefs, hopes, intentions). In the case of computational implementations, of course, the issue of the dispensability of representations does not arise: for practical purposes, some kind of meaning representation is a *sine qua non* for any kind of computing.

3.5.4   Discourse Representation Theory

Discourse Representation Theory (DRT) (Kamp, 1981; Kamp & Reyle, 1993), as the name implies, has taken the notion of an intermediate representation as an indispensable theoretical construct, and, as also implied, sees the main unit of description as being a discourse rather than sentences in isolation. One of the things that makes a sequence of sentences constitute a discourse is their connectivity with each other, as expressed through the use of pronouns and ellipsis or similar devices. This connectivity is mediated through the intermediate representation, however, and cannot be expressed without it. The kind of example that is typically used to illustrate this is the following:

   A computer developed a fault.

A simplified first order representation of the meaning of this sentence might be:

   exists(X,computer(X) and develop_a_fault(X))

   There is a computer X and X developed a fault. This is logically equivalent to:

   not(forall(X,not(computer(X) and develop_a_fault(X))))

   It isn't the case that every computer didn't develop a fault. However, whereas the first sentence can be continued thus:

   A computer developed a fault.

   It was quickly repaired.

—its logically equivalent one cannot be:

   It isn't the case that every computer didn't develop a fault.

   It was quickly repaired.

Thus, the form of the representation has linguistic consequences. DRT has developed an extensive formal description of a variety of phenomena such as this, while also paying careful attention to the logical and computational interpretation of the intermediate representations proposed. Kamp and Reyle (1993) contains detailed analyses of aspects of noun phrase reference, propositional attitudes, tense and aspect, and many other phenomena.

3.5.5 Dynamic Semantics

Dynamic semantics (e.g., Groenendijk & Stokhof, 1991a; Groenendijk & Stokhof, 1991b) takes the view that the standard truth-conditional view of sentence meaning deriving from the paradigm of FOPC does not do sufficient justice to the fact that uttering a sentence changes the context it was uttered in. Deriving inspiration in part from work on the semantics of programming languages, dynamic semantic theories have developed several variations on the idea that the meaning of a sentence is to be equated with the changes it makes to a context.

Update semantics (e.g., Veltman, 1985; van Eijck & de Vries, 1992) approaches have been developed to model the effect of asserting a sequence of sentences in a particular context. In general, the order of such a sequence has its own significance. A sequence like:

Someone's at the door. Perhaps it's John. It's Mary!

is coherent, but not all permutations of it would be:

Someone's at the door. It's Mary. Perhaps it's John.

Recent strands of this work make connections with the artificial intelligence literature on truth maintenance and belief revision (e.g Gärdenfors, 1990).

Dynamic predicate logic (Groenendijk & Stokhof, 1991a; Groenendijk & Stokhof, 1990) extends the interpretation clauses for FOPC (or richer logics) by allowing assignments of denotations to subexpressions to carry over from one sentence to its successors in a sequence. This means that dependencies that are difficult to capture in FOPC or other non-dynamic logics, such as that between *someone* and *it* in:

Someone's at the door. It's Mary.

can be correctly modeled, without sacrificing any of the other advantages that traditional logics offer.

3.5.6 Situation Semantics and Property Theory

One of the assumptions of most semantic theories descended from Montague is that information is total, in the sense that in every situation, a proposition is either true or it is not. This enables propositions to be identified with the set of situations (or *possible worlds*) in which they are true. This has many technical conveniences, but is descriptively incorrect, for it means that any proposition conjoined with a tautology (a logical truth) will remain the same proposition according to the technical definition. But this is clearly wrong: *all cats are cats* is a tautology, but *The computer crashed*, and *The computer crashed and all cats are cats* are clearly different propositions (reporting the first is not the same as reporting the second, for example).

Situation theory (Barwise & Perry, 1983) has attempted to rework the whole logical foundation underlying the more traditional semantic theories in order to arrive at a satisfactory formulation of the notion of a *partial state of the world* or situation, and in turn, a more satisfactory notion of proposition. This reformulation has also attempted to generalize the logical underpinnings away from previously accepted restrictions (for example, restrictions prohibiting sets containing themselves, and other apparently paradoxical notions) in order to be able to explore the ability of language to refer to itself in ways that have previously resisted a coherent formal description (Barwise & Etchemendy, 1987).

Property theory (Turner, 1988; Turner, 1992) has also been concerned to rework the logical foundations presupposed by semantic theory, motivated by similar phenomena.

In general, it is fair to say that, with a few exceptions, the contribution of dynamic semantics, situation theory, and property theory has so far been less in the analysis of new semantic phenomena than in the exploration of more cognitively and computationally plausible ways of expressing insights originating within Montague-derived approaches. However, these new frameworks are now making it possible to address data that resisted any formal account by more traditional theories.

3.5.7 Implementations

Whereas there are beginning to be quite a number of systems displaying wide syntactic coverage, there are very few that are able to provide corresponding semantic coverage. Almost all current large scale implementations of systems with a semantic component are inspired to a greater or lesser extent by the work of Montague (e.g., Bates, Bobrow, et al., 1994; Allen, Schubert, et al., 1995; Alshawi, 1992). This reflects the fact that the majority of descriptive work by linguists is expressed within some form of this framework, and also the fact that its computational properties are better understood.

However, Montague's own work gave only a cursory treatment of a few context-dependent phenomena like pronouns, and none at all of phenomena like ellipsis. In real applications, such constructs are very common and all contemporary systems supplement the representations made available by the base logic with constructs for representing the meaning of these context-dependent constructions. It is computationally important to be able to carry out at least some types of processing directly with these *underspecified representations*: i.e., representations in which the contextual contribution to meaning has not yet been made explicit, in order to avoid a combinatorial explosion of potential ambiguities. One striking motivation for underspecification is the case of quantifying noun phrases, for these can give rise to a high degree of ambiguity if treated in Montague's fashion. For example, *every keyboard is connected to a computer* is interpretable as involving either a single computer or a possibly different one for each keyboard, in the absence of a context to determine which is the plausible reading: sentences do not need to be much more complex for a large number of possibilities to arise.

One of the most highly developed of the implemented approaches addressing these issues is the *quasi-logical form* developed in the Core Language Engine (CLE) (Alshawi, 1990; Alshawi, 1992) a representation which allows for meanings to be of varying degrees of independence of a context. This makes it possible for the same representation to be used in applications like translation, which can often be carried out without reference to context, as well as in database query, where the context-dependent elements must be resolved in order to know exactly which query to submit to the database. The ability to operate with underspecified representations of this type is essential for computational tractability, since the task of spelling out all of the possible alternative fully specified interpretations for a sentence and then selecting between them would be computationally intensive even if it were always possible in practice.

3.5.8   Future Directions

Currently, the most pressing needs for semantic theory are to find ways of achieving wider and more robust coverage of real data. This will involve progress in several directions: (i) Further exploration of the use of underspecified representations so that some level of semantic processing can be achieved even where complete meaning representations cannot be constructed (either because of lack of coverage or inability to carry out contextual resolution). (ii) Closer cooperation with work in lexicon construction. The tradition in semantics has been to assume that word meanings can by and large simply be *plugged in* to semantic structures. This is a convenient and largely correct assumption when dealing with structures like *every X is P*, but becomes less tenable as more complex phenomena are examined. However, the relevant semantic properties of individual words or groups of words are seldom to be found in conventional dictionaries and closer cooperation between semanticists and computationally aware lexicographers is required. (iii) More integration between sentence or utterance level semantics and theories of text or dialogue structure. Recent work in semantics has shifted emphasis away from the purely sentence-based approach, but the extent to which the interpretations of individual sentences can depend on dialogue or text settings, or on the goals of speakers, is much greater than had been suspected.

3.6   Sentence Modeling and Parsing

Fernando Pereira

AT&T Bell Labs, Murray Hill, New Jersey, USA

The complex hidden structure of natural-language sentences is manifested in two different ways: *predictively*, in that not every constituent (for example, word) is equally likely in every context, and *evidentially*, in that the information carried by a sentence depends on the relationships among the constituents of the sentence. Depending on the application, one or the other of those two facets may play a dominant role. For instance, in *language modeling* for large-vocabulary connected speech recognition, it is crucial to distinguish the relative likelihoods of possible continuations of a sentence prefix, since the acoustic component of the recognizer may be unable to distinguish reliably between those possibilities just from acoustic evidence. On the other hand, in applications such as machine translation or text summarization, relationships between sentence constituents, such as that a certain noun phrase is the direct object of a certain verb occurrence, are crucial evidence in determining the correct translation or summary. *Parsing* is the process of discovering *analyses* of sentences, that is, consistent sets of relationships between constituents that are judged to hold in a given sentence, and, concurrently, what the constituents are, since constituents are typically defined inductively in terms of the relationships that hold between their parts.

It would not be possible to model or parse sentences without mechanisms to compute the properties of larger constituents from the properties of their parts, appropriately defined, since the properties of new sentences, which are unlikely to have been seen before, can only be inferred from knowledge of how their parts participate in the sentences we have observed previously. While this point may seem obvious, it has deep consequences both in language modeling and parsing. Any language model or parser must include a generative mechanism or *grammar* that specifies how sentences are built from their parts, and how the information associated to the sentence derives from the information associated to its parts. Furthermore, to be able to cope with previously unseen sentences, any such system must involve *generalization* with respect to the data from which the language model or parser was developed.

3.6.1   Grammars and Derivations

It is useful to think of the grammar in a language model or parser as the specification of a configuration space in which the configurations represent stages of constituent combination, and transitions between configurations describe how constituents are combined in deriving larger constituents. For instance, the configurations may be the states of a finite-state machine and the transitions represent how words may be appended to the end of a sentence prefix. In the more complex case of phrase-structure grammars, configurations represent sequences of phrases (*sentential forms*), and transitions the possible combinations of adjacent phrases into larger phrases. A *derivation* of a sentence according to the grammar is a path in the configuration space of the grammar, from an initial configuration to a final configuration, in which all the elementary constituents are consumed. (We will call such elementary constituents *words* in what follows, although the informal notion of word may not correspond to the appropriate technical definition, especially in languages with complex morphology.)

Even with respect to procedural parsers and language models which are not normally described as containing a grammar, such as certain deterministic (Marcus, 1980; Hindle, 1993) and probabilistic parsers (Black, Jelinek, et al., 1993; Magerman & Marcus, 1991), it is useful to identify the implicit grammar defined by the possible derivation moves which the parser can use under the control of its control automaton. For instance, in a parser based on a pushdown automaton such as a shift-reduce parser (Shieber, 1983; Pereira, 1985), the grammar corresponds to the possible transitions between stack and input configurations, while the automaton's finite-state control determines which transitions are actually used in a derivation.

3.6.2 Precision versus Coverage

The choice of a grammar for a particular parsing or language modeling application involves two conflicting requirements: *precision* and *coverage*. By precision, we mean how well the grammar encodes constraints on possible sentences and possible meaningful relationships carried by those sentences. By coverage, we mean what proportion of actual sentences have a reasonable derivation in the grammar. We are interested in precision because a more precise grammar is better able to rule out bad sentence hypotheses in predictive tasks and bad meaningful relationship hypotheses in evidential tasks. We are interested in coverage so that our systems will handle appropriately a wide range of actual spoken or written language. However, as we increase precision by encoding more constraints in the grammar, we tend to lose coverage of those actual sentences that violate some of the constraints while still being acceptable to language users. The reason for the problem is that the most powerful constraints are idealizations of the actual performance of language users. The tension between precision and coverage is central to the design trade-offs we will now survey.

3.6.3 Search Space and Search Procedure

We therefore see a sentence parser or language model as consisting of a grammar and a *search procedure* which, given an input sentence, will apply transitions specified by the grammar to construct derivations of the sentence and associated analyses. In cases where the input sentence is uncertain, such as speech recognition, we may further generalize the above picture to a simultaneous search of the configuration space for the grammar and of a space of *sentence hypotheses*, represented for instance as a *word lattice* (Murveit, Butzberger, et al., 1993).

The computational properties of parsers and language models depend on two main factors: the *structure* of the search space induced by the grammar, and the *exhaustiveness* of the search procedure.

Search Space Structure

Under the above definition of grammar, transitions from a configuration may have to take into account the whole configuration. However, most useful grammar classes have some degree of *locality* in that transitions involve only a bounded portion of a configuration. In that case, derivations can be factored into sub-derivations concerning independent parts of configurations, allowing independent sub-derivations to be shared among derivations, for potentially exponential reductions in the size of the search space. The search algorithm can then tabulate each sub-derivation and reuse it in building any derivation that shares that sub-derivation.[3] Such *tabular* algorithms are widely used in parsing and language modeling with appropriate kinds of grammars (Younger, 1967; Kay, 1986; Earley, 1970; Lang, 1974; Graham, Harrison, et al., 1980; Tomita, 1987), because they support exhaustive search algorithms with polynomial space and time with respect to sentence length. Furthermore, tabular algorithms can be readily extended to *dynamic programming* algorithms to search for optimal derivations with respect to appropriate evaluation functions on derivations, as we will see below.

Finite-state grammars have a straightforward tabular algorithm in which table entries consist of a state and an input position (such a table is called a *trellis* in the speech recognition literature). Context-free grammars are the standard example of a phrase structure grammar class whose derivations can be tabulated. In a bottom-up (from words to sentences) derivation for a context-free grammar, the portion of the derivation that corresponds to the recognition of a constituent labeled by a given nonterminal can be simply represented by a table entry, giving the nonterminal as a possible label of a substring of the input (Younger, 1967). Although this information leaves out the sequence of steps of the actual derivation, all derivations of that phrase can be easily reconstructed from the set of all table entries derivable for a given input string (Pointers can also be used to keep track of what table entries are used in deriving other entries.) (Younger, 1967; Earley, 1968).

Other grammar classes, such as the mildly-context-sensitive grammars (Joshi, Vijay-Shanker, et al., 1991) and some constraint-based grammars, are also suitable for tabular procedures (Shieber, 1992).

Search Exhaustiveness

Even if the grammar allows tabular search, it may not be computationally feasible to explore the entire search space because of the effect of grammar size on search space size. For example, the simple finite-state language models used in large-vocabulary speech recognition may have millions of states and transitions. Since each state is potentially considered at each input position, the computation per word recognized is too large for real-time performance. Many techniques have been explored in speech recognition to deal with this problem (Bahl, Jelinek, et al., 1983; Kenny, Hollan, et al., 1993; Paul, 1992; Murveit, Butzberger, et al., 1993; Nguyen, Schwartz, et al., 1993).

In general, the techniques to avoid exploring the entire grammar search space fall into two main classes, *pruning* and *admissible search*. In pruning, an *evaluation function* applied to configurations determines whether they will be expanded further. Since the evaluation function cannot predict the future (to do so accurately it would have to explore the entire search space), pruning may in fact block the correct derivation. The choice of evaluation function is

---

[3]The required properties are analogous to the cut-elimination property that underlies the connection between sequent and natural-deduction presentations of logics (Prawitz, 1965).

thus a trade-off between reduced search space (and thus reduced runtime and memory requirements) and the risk of missing the correct analysis (or even every analysis). Currently there is no theory of pruning trade-offs relating bounds on risk of error to the form of the evaluation function, so the design of evaluation functions is an empirical art.

Although pruning away the correct derivation is a problem in practical applications, in psycholinguistic modeling it may in fact correspond to failures of human sentence processing, for instance garden paths. *Deterministic parsers* (Marcus, 1980; Hindle, 1993) take pruning to an extreme in using elaborate evaluation functions to select exactly one course of derivation. Dead ends are then supposed to model the situations in which human subjects are forced to recover from parsing failures. Other models, particularly those based on neuronal notions of activation and lateral inhibition, may allow a local *race* between alternative expansions of a configuration but inhibit all but one of the alternatives within a bounded number of steps (Stevenson, 1993; McRoy & Hirst, 1990; Pritchett, 1988).

Admissible search procedures do not block potential derivations. Instead, they order sub-derivations, so that the ones that are more likely to be expanded to the best complete derivations will be considered before less promising ones. The difficulty is of course to define ordering criteria with high probability of reaching the best derivations before exploring a large set of useless configurations. Of particular interest here are A*-type algorithms (Nilsson, 1980) which expand the configuration with the lowest *cost estimate*, where the estimate is required to be a lower bound of the true cost (under a cost model appropriate for the task, see below) and identical to the true cost for complete derivations. The first complete derivation reached by an A* algorithm is then guaranteed to have the lowest cost. However, since it is difficult to choose cost estimates that narrow the search sufficiently, more aggressive estimates that may overshoot the true cost are often used, with the result that the first complete derivation may not be the best one.

Clearly, the selection of evaluation functions for pruning or admissible search is closely tied to the precision-coverage trade-off.

3.6.4 Grammar Classes

A wide range of grammar classes have been investigated in parsing and language modeling, depending on the nature of the application and on particular insights on language structure and sentence distribution. Grammar classes have been characterized along many different theoretical dimensions. What is known in those areas about certain important grammar classes is described elsewhere in this document 3.6.1.

Here, we consider a more informal and empirical dimension of variation that has great impact in the development of parsers and language models: how much of the required predictive and evidential power belongs to the grammar itself and how much resides in the search procedure controlling the use of the grammar. Choices along this dimension often involve philosophical disagreements on whether language is fundamentally governed by an innate system of rules (the rationalist position most closely identified with Chomsky) or rather a system of statistical regularities, associations and constructions derived by learning (the empiricist position informing much work in statistical language modeling). However, they also relate to different choices with respect to the coverage/precision trade-off.

At one end of the spectrum, which is often associated with empiricist work, extremely unconstraining grammars are controlled by search evaluation functions automatically learned from language data. An extreme example is finite-state *n-gram* grammars, in which states encode information on the last $n - 1$ observed words, have been used with practical success in speech recognition (Jelinek, Mercer, et al., 1992). In these grammars every sequence of words is considered a possible sentence, but probabilities are assigned to state transitions to model the relative likelihoods of different strings. As we will see, the association of probabilities to transitions is a useful technique in a wide range of grammatical settings.

While n-gram grammars have proven very useful for language modeling, derivation steps do not correspond in any direct way to possible meaningful relations in the sentence, for instance, those between a main verb and its arguments. Parsing requires more complex grammars, in which derivation steps are associated to possible relations of interest. Even in language modeling, distributional regularities associated with meaningful relationships may be an important source of additional predictive power (Hindle, 1990; Hindle & Rooth, 1991; Dagan, Markus, et al., 1993; Lafferty, Sleator, et al., 1992).

Grammatical representations of meaningful relationships may be usefully classified into three main classes: *linguistic grammars, task-oriented grammars* and *data-oriented grammars*. Linguistic grammars and task-oriented grammars have been in use since the beginning of computational linguistics. Data-oriented grammars, in their finite-state form, as discussed above, go back to the beginning of statistical studies of language by Markov, but investigations into data-oriented grammars capable of representing meaningful relationships have only recently begun.

Linguistic Grammars

Most formal linguistic theories have been used at some time or other as the basis for computational grammars. The main issues in applying linguistic theory to the development of computational grammars are: *coverage, predictive power* and *computational requirements.*

Coverage: Linguistic theories are typically developed to explain puzzling aspects of linguistic competence, such as the relationships between active and passive sentences, the constraints on use of anaphoric elements, or the possible scopes of quantifying elements such as determiners and adverbs. However, actual language involves a wide range of other phenomena and constructions, such as idioms, coordination, ellipsis, apposition and extraposition, which may not be germane to the issues addressed by a particular linguistic theory or which may offer unresolved challenges to the theory. Therefore, a practical grammar will have to go far beyond the proposals of any given theory to cover a substantial proportion of observed language. Even then, coverage gaps are relatively frequent and difficult to fill, as they involve laborious design of new grammar rules and representations.

Predictive Power: Linguistic grammars, being oriented towards the description of linguistic competence, are not intended to model *distributional* regularities arising from pragmatics, discourse and conventional use that manifest themselves in word and construction choice. Yet those are the regularities that appear to contribute most to the estimation of relative likelihoods of sentences or analyses. The encoding of distributional predictions must therefore be left to the search procedure, in the form of an appropriate evaluation function. However, the configurations generated by a grammar may not carry the most useful information in evaluating them. For example, whether a particular prepositional phrase modifies a direct object noun phrase or the main verb depends heavily on the actual verb, noun, preposition and prepositional object (Hindle & Rooth, 1991), but a traditional phrase-structure grammar does not make that information available in the syntactic categories of noun phrase, verb phrase and prepositional phrase. Therefore, in a phrase-structure setting whole derivations rather than individual configurations would have to be evaluated. But this would preclude the factorization of derivations that leads to tractable search as noted above. These considerations explain in part the recent growing interest in *lexicalized* grammatical frameworks such as dependency grammar (Mel'čuk, 1988; Hudson, 1990; Sleator & Temperley, 1991), slot grammar (McCord, 1980; McCord, 1989), categorial grammar (Lambek, 1958; Ades & Steedman, 1982; Moortgat, 1988), Head-Driven Phrase-Structure Grammar (HPSG) (Pollard & Sag, 1987) and lexicalized tree-adjoining grammar (Schabes, 1990), all of which lead to configurations made up of lexical items and direct relationships between them.

Computational Requirements: The best formal explanation of a particular aspect of linguistic competence has no necessary correlation with computational efficiency. For instance, modern versions of transformational grammar based on the theory of government and binding, or its more recent developments, involve either very complex search procedures or very complex compilation procedures into formalisms with better search properties (Stabler, 1992; Fong, 1992; Johnson, 1992). Similar problems have been noted with respect to HPSG and certain varieties of categorial grammar.

While direct use of formalized linguistic theories for parsing and language modeling seems computationally problematic, much progress has been made in the development of tractable grammatical formalisms capable of encoding important aspects of linguistic theory. The class of mildly context-sensitive formalisms (Joshi, Vijay-Shanker, et al., 1991), of which tree-adjoining grammars

(Joshi, Levy, et al., 1975; Joshi, 1985) and combinatory categorial grammar (Ades & Steedman, 1982) are two notable instances, has polynomial-time and space parsing algorithms, and can encode important aspects of transformational and categorial linguistic analysis. Constraint-based grammar formalisms can be intractable or even undecidable in general (Carpenter, 1992), but special cases of interest are often efficiently parsable (Alshawi, 1992). For instance, lexical-functional grammar combines a context-free skeleton with constraints describing non-constituent syntactic properties. Although the combination is intractable in general, a carefully designed constraint-application schedule can make it possible to parse with linguistically-plausible grammars in such a way that the intractability does not arise (Maxwell & Kaplan, 1989).

However, even polynomial-time algorithms may not be sufficiently fast for practical applications, given the effect of grammar size on parsing time. Search reduction techniques like those described in section 3.6.3 would then be needed to keep performance within reasonable bounds, at the risk of worse coverage.

Task-Oriented Grammars

For most current applications in text summarization, information retrieval and speech understanding, the predictive and evidential power of a general-purpose grammar and a general control mechanism are insufficient for reasonable performance in the task. Furthermore, even when parameters of the grammar and control mechanism can be learned automatically from training corpora, the required corpora do not exist or are too small for proper training. The alternative is then to devise grammars that specify directly how relationships relevant to the task may be expressed in natural language. For instance, one may use a phrase-structure grammar in which nonterminals stand for task concepts and relationships (for example, *flight* or *leave* in an airline reservation task) and rules specify possible expressions of those concepts and relationships (Seneff, 1992; Ward, 1991b). Such *semantic grammars* have often been used for database access tasks. More generally, a knowledge-representation language (for instance, a frame language) can be used to specify the possible relationships between concepts, and relatively low-power grammatical descriptions (often finite-state) describe natural-language expressions that give strong evidence for concepts and relationships (Jacobs & Rau, 1993; Hobbs, Appelt, et al., 1993).

Task-oriented grammars provide very strong guidance to a parser, but that guidance is bought at the expense of generality and coverage, since the detailed specifications they rely on may often fail to fit naturally-occurring language. Therefore, parsing algorithms for task-oriented grammars are usually allowed to *relax* the grammar by ignoring portions of the input that do not fit the given grammar (Ward, 1991a; Jackson, Appelt, et al., 1991). This can increase coverage usefully in applications such as limited-domain speech understanding and text-summarization, where there are very strong expectations of what are the relevant inputs, but the increase of coverage is in general at the expense of precision.

Data-Oriented Grammars

In so far as linguistic grammars and task-oriented grammars provide strong constraints for modeling and parsing, they risk low coverage because the constraints limit the transitions between configurations, and thus the availability of derivations for strings. As we have seen, this problem can be alleviated in a task-oriented setting, but as far as we know relaxation is a sensible policy only for highly-constrained tasks. An alternative way of increasing coverage is to start with less constraining grammars, and rely on an evaluation function to select the most likely derivations in the more densely connected search space that results from the less constraining grammar. However, this requires finding an appropriate evaluation function. In a data-oriented framework, a *learning* or *training* procedure tries to determine the evaluation function that produces best results on an appropriate training corpus. For example, an n-gram grammar allows any word sequence, but transitions are given probabilities derived from how often states were reached and transitions crossed running the grammar over a training corpus (Jelinek, Mercer, et al., 1992). As another example, frequencies of rule and nonterminal use can be used to estimate rule probabilities for an underconstrained context-free grammar (Baker, 1979; Lari & Young, 1990; Pereira & Schabes, 1992).

Although there have been some successes in training evaluation functions for previously-designed grammars (Fujisaki, Jelinek, et al., 1989; Black, Lafferty, et al., 1992), training with respect to a fixed grammar has the problem that either the grammar allows many transitions that are never observed in reality, forcing the evaluation function to be more complex to rule them out effectively, or it is too restrictive and does not allow transitions that actually occur. That difficulty has motivated the investigation of grammatical frameworks and learning algorithms that will concurrently learn a grammar and an appropriate evaluation function (Sampson, Haigh, et al., 1989; Bod, 1993; Hindle, 1992; Stolcke & Omohundro, 1993). One particular class of such procedures constructs a dictionary of commonly observed substrings or sub-analyses that can be combined by a small set of rules to yield the observed sentences or analyses, with the evaluation function discriminating between alternatives ways of reconstructing a sentence or analysis from the fragments in the dictionary (Bod, 1993; Hindle, 1992). A variety of predictive power and grammar size criteria (for example, Bayesian, minimum-description length) may then be used to find good trade-offs between grammar (dictionary) size, prediction of the training set, and generalization to new material.

3.6.5 Evaluating Derivations

In the overall view of parsing and language modeling given above, a parser or language model searches the configuration space defined by a grammar for possible derivations of the sentence(s) under analysis. Since the grammar by itself is unlikely to encode all the semantic, pragmatic and discourse information relevant to distinguishing plausible analyses from implausible ones, the search needs to be guided by an evaluation function that assigns plausibility scores to derivations. An especially important case is that of *probabilistic grammars*, which associate with each transition the conditional probability of taking that transition from a configuration given that the configuration was reached. Such grammars are based on a *Markovian* or *conditional independence* assumption that the probability of a (partial) derivation depends just on its penultimate configuration and the transition taken from it. Then the probability of a derivation is simply the product of the probability of its initial configuration by the product of the probabilities of the transitions in the derivation.

When transitions are directly associated with observable events (for example, extension of a partial sentence by one word in a finite-state model), transition probabilities can be estimated by simply counting the number of times the transition is taken for all possible derivations of all sentences in a training corpus. In general, however, the transition probabilities are not associated to directly observable events. In that case, iterative procedures may be used to find the transition probabilities that maximize the probability that the training corpus was observed (Dempster, Laird, et al., 1977; Baum & Petrie, 1966; Baker, 1979). For language modeling, the training corpus may just be a set of sentences, while for parsing a set of sentences tagged with constraints on possible grammatical relationships (for example, phrase boundaries) is often preferable (Black, Lafferty, et al., 1992; Pereira & Schabes, 1992).

While probabilistic evaluation functions dominate in language modeling, where they are used to estimate the likelihood that a certain word sequence was uttered, other types of evaluation function are often used in parsing, especially those based on the degree of agreement of the best scoring analyses and analyses in a training corpus (Alshawi & Carter, 1994).

Computationally, the critical property of an evaluation function is whether it is compatible with tabular algorithms for searching the derivation space, in the sense that the score of a derivation is determined by the scores of the sub-derivations into which the derivation is factored by tabulation. For probabilistic functions, this amounts to a strengthened Markovian condition for derivations, which, for instance, is satisfied by stochastic context-free grammars (Booth & Thompson, 1973; Baker, 1979), certain kinds of parsers for constraint-based grammars (Briscoe & Carroll, 1993) and stochastic tree-adjoining grammars (Schabes, 1992). In such cases, the tabular search algorithms can be converted into dynamic programming algorithms (Teitelbaum, 1973; Baker, 1979; Lang, 1989; Jelinek, Lafferty, et al., 1990; Lafferty, Sleator, et al., 1992; Schabes, 1992) to search efficiently for best-scoring derivations.

3.6.6   Future Directions

The issue that dominates current work in parsing and language modeling is to design parsers and evaluation functions with high coverage and precision with respect to naturally occurring linguistic material (for example, news stories, spontaneous speech interactions). Simple high-coverage methods such as n-gram models miss the higher-order regularities required for better prediction and for reliable identification of meaningful relationships, while complex hand-built grammars often lack coverage of the *tail* of individually rare but collectively frequent sentence structures (cf. Zipf's law). Automated methods for grammar and evaluation function acquisition appear to be the only practical way to create accurate parsers with much better coverage. The challenge is to discover how to use linguistic knowledge to constrain that acquisition process.

3.7 Robust Parsing

Ted Briscoe
Computer Laboratory, Cambridge University, Cambridge, UK

Despite over three decades of research effort, no practical domain-independent parser of unrestricted text has been developed. Such a parser should return the correct or a useful *close* analysis for 90% or more of input sentences. It would need to solve at least the following three problems, which create severe difficulties for conventional parsers utilizing standard parsing algorithms with a generative grammar:

1. *chunking*, that is, appropriate segmentation of text into syntactically parsable units;

2. *disambiguation*, that is, selecting the unique semantically and pragmatically correct analysis from the potentially large number of syntactically legitimate ones returned; and

3. *undergeneration*, or dealing with cases of input outside the systems' lexical or syntactic coverage.

Conventional parsers typically fail to return any useful information when faced with problems of undergeneration or chunking and rely on domain-specific detailed semantic information for disambiguation.

The problem of chunking is best exemplified by text sentences (beginning with a capital letter and ending with a period) which—and this sentence is an example—contain text adjuncts delimited by dashes, brackets or commas which may not always stand in a *syntactic* relation with surrounding material. There has been very limited work on this issue—Hindle (1983) describes a system which copes with related problems, such as false starts and *restarts* in transcribed spontaneous speech, whilst Jones (1994) describes a parser which makes limited use of punctuation to constrain syntactic interpretation. Nevertheless, an analysis of the 150K word balanced Susanne Corpus (Sampson, 1994) reveals that over 60% of sentences contain internal punctuation marks and of these around 30% contain text-medial adjuncts. Thus the problem is significant, and further research is required building on linguistic accounts of punctuation (Nunberg, 1990).

Disambiguation using knowledge-based techniques requires the specification of too much detailed semantic information to yield a robust domain-independent parser. Yet analysis of the Susanne Corpus with a crude parser suggests that over 80% of sentences are structurally ambiguous. Several parsers yielding a single *canonical parse* have been developed (Marcus, 1980; Hindle, 1983; de Marcken, 1990). These are often applied to a (partially) disambiguated sequence of lexical syntactic categories. Simplifying the input to the parser in this way circumvents many problems of lexical coverage suffered by systems which require rich sets of syntactic subcategories encoding, for example, valency of verbs (Jensen, 1991) as well as capitalizing on the relative success and practicality of lexical category disambiguation. Canonical parsers often represent many ambiguities implicitly (Marcus, Hindle, et al., 1983), rather than enumerating possible analyses, and use heuristic disambiguation rules (Hindle, 1989). Such techniques have yielded useful parsers for limited domains but their development is labour intensive and few general principles for their construction have emerged. In recent attempts to manually construct large *treebanks* of parsed texts, canonical parsing has been used as a first but small step of disputed merit (Marcus, Hindle, et al., 1983; Leech & Garside, 1991).

The availability of treebanks and, more generally, large bodies of machine-readable textual data has provided impetus to statistical approaches to disambiguation. Some approaches use stochastic language modeling inspired by the success of HMM-based lexical category disambiguation. For example, probabilities for a probabilistic version of a context-free grammar (PCFG) can be (re-)estimated from treebanks or plain text (Fujisaki, Jelinek, et al., 1989; Sharman, Jelinek, et al., 1990) and used to efficiently rank analyses produced by minimally-modified tabular parsing algorithms. These techniques yielded promising results but have been largely supplanted by statistical parse decision techniques in which the probabilistic model is sensitive to details of parse context (Magerman & Weir, 1992; Briscoe & Carroll, 1993; Black, Lafferty, et al., 1992) and integrated more closely with the parsing algorithm than the grammar. These systems have yielded results of around 75% accuracy in assigning analyses to (unseen) test sentences from the same source as the unambiguous training material. The barrier to improvement of such results currently lies in the need to use more discriminating models of context, requiring more annotated training material to adequate estimate the parameters of such models. This approach may yield a robust automatic method for disambiguation of acceptable accuracy, but the grammars utilized still suffer from undergeneration, and are labour-intensive to develop.

Undergeneration is a significant problem. In one project, a grammar for sentences from computer manuals containing words drawn from a restricted vocabulary of 3000 words which was developed over three years still failed to analyze 4% of unseen examples (Black, Lafferty, et al., 1992). This probably represents an upper bound using manual development of generative grammars; most more general grammars have far higher failure rates in this type of test. Early work on undergeneration focussed on knowledge-based manual specification of *error* rules or rule relaxation strategies (Kwasny & Sonheimer, 1981; Jensen & Heidorn, 1983). This approach, similar to the canonical parse approach to ambiguity, is labour-intensive and suffers from the difficulty of predicting the types of error or extragrammaticality liable to occur. More recently, attempts have been made to use statistical induction to *learn* the correct grammar for a given corpus of data, using generalizations of HMM maximum-likelihood re-estimation techniques to PCFGs (Lari & Young, 1990). This extends the application of stochastic language modeling from disambiguation to undergeneration by assuming the *weakest* grammar for a given category set—that is, the one which contains all possible rules that can be formed for that category set—and using iterative re-estimation of the rule probabilities to converge on the subset of these rules most appropriate to the description of the training corpus.

There are several inherent problems with these statistical techniques which have been partially addressed by recent work. Re-estimation involves considering all possible analyses of each sentence of the training corpus given an (initially) weak grammar, the search space is large and the likelihood of convergence on a useful grammar is low. Pereira and Schabes (1992); Schabes, Roth, et al. (1993) show that constraining the analyses considered during re-estimation to those consistent with manual parses of a treebank reduces computational complexity and leads to a useful grammar. Briscoe and Waegner (1993); Briscoe (1994) demonstrate that similar results can be obtained by imposing general linguistic constraints on the initial grammar and biasing initial probabilities to favour linguistically motivated *core rules*, while still training on plain text. Nevertheless, such techniques are currently limited to simple grammars with category sets of a dozen or so non-terminals or to training on manually parsed data. The induced PCFG can also be used to rank parses and results of around 80% *fit* between correct and automatically-generated analyses have been obtained. It is not possible to directly compare these results with those from pure disambiguation experiments, but there is no doubt that although these systems are achieving 100% or very close grammatical coverage, the use of the resulting PCFG language model for disambiguation only yields fully correct analyses in around 30% of cases.

3.8   Chapter References

ACL (1983). *Proceedings of the 21st Annual Meeting of the Association for Computational Linguistics*, Cambridge, Massachusetts. Association for Computational Linguistics.

ACL (1990). *Proceedings of the 28th Annual Meeting of the Association for Computational Linguistics*, Pittsburgh, Pennsylvania. Association for Computational Linguistics.

ACL (1992). *Proceedings of the 30th Annual Meeting of the Association for Computational Linguistics*, University of Delaware. Association for Computational Linguistics.

ACL (1993). *Proceedings of the 31st Annual Meeting of the Association for Computational Linguistics*, Ohio State University. Association for Computational Linguistics.

Ades, A. E. and Steedman, M. J. (1982). On the order of words. *Linguistics and Philosophy*, 4(4):517–558.

Allen, J., Hunnicutt, M. S., and Klatt, D. (1987). *From text to speech—the MITalk system*. MIT Press, Cambridge, Massachusetts.

Allen, J. F., Schubert, L. K., Ferguson, G., Heeman, P., Hwang, C. H., Kato, T., Light, M., Martin, N., Miller, B., Poesio, M., and Traum, D. R. (1995). The TRAINS project: a case study in building a conversational planning agent. *Journal of Experimental and Theoretical AI*.

Alshawi, H. (1990). Resolving quasi logical form. *Computational Linguistics*, 16:133–144.

Alshawi, H., editor (1992). *The Core Language Engine*. MIT Press, Cambridge, Massachusetts.

Alshawi, H., Arnold, D. J., Backofen, R., Carter, D. M., Lindop, J., Netter, K., Pulman, S. G., and Tsujii, J.-I. (1991). Rule formalism and virutal machine design study. Technical Report ET6/1, CEC.

Alshawi, H. and Carter, D. (1994). Training and scaling preference functions for disambiguation. *Computational Linguistics*, 20:635–648.

ANLP (1994). *Proceedings of the Fourth Conference on Applied Natural Language Processing*, Stuttgart, Germany. ACL, Morgan Kaufmann.

Antworth, E. L. (1990). PC-KIMMO: a two-level processor for morphological analysis. Technical Report Occasional Publications in Academic Computing No. 16, Summer Institute of Linguistics, Dallas, Texas.

Appel, A. W. and Jacobson, G. J. (1988). The world's fastest scrabble program. *Communications of the ACM*, 31(5):572–578.

ARPA (1993). *Proceedings of the 1993 ARPA Human Language Technology Workshop*, Princeton, New Jersey. Advanced Research Projects Agency, Morgan Kaufmann.

Atkins, B. T. S. and Levin, B. (1992). Admitting impediments. In *Lexical Acquisition: Using On-Line Resources to Build a Lexicon*. Lawrence Earlbaum, Hillsdale, New Jersey.

Bahl, L. R., Jelinek, F., and Mercer, R. L. (1983). A maximum likelihood approach to continuous speech recognition. *IEEE Transactions on Pattern Analysis and Machine Intelligence*, 5(2):179–190.

Baker, J. K. (1979). Trainable grammars for speech recognition. In Wolf, J. J. and Klatt, D. H., editors, *Speech communication papers presented at the 97th Meeting of the Acoustical Society of America*, pages 547–550. Acoustical Society of America, MIT Press.

Barwise, J. and Cooper, R. (1981). Generalized quantifiers and natural language. *Linguistics and Philosophy*, 4:159–219.

Barwise, J. and Etchemendy, J. (1987). *The Liar.* Chicago University Press, Chicago.

Barwise, J. and Perry, J. (1983). *Situations and Attitudes.* MIT Press, Cambridge, Massachusetts.

Bates, M., Bobrow, R., Ingria, R., and Stallard, D. (1994). The delphi natural language understanding system. In *Proceedings of the Fourth Conference on Applied Natural Language Processing*, pages 132–137, Stuttgart, Germany. ACL, Morgan Kaufmann.

Baum, L. E. and Petrie, T. (1966). Statistical inference for probablistic functions of finite state Markov chains. *Annals of Mathematical Statistics*, 37:1554–1563.

Berwick, R. C., Abney, S. P., and Tenny, C., editors (1992). *Principle-Based Parsing: Computation and Psycholinguistics.* Kluwer, Dordrecht, The Netherlands.

Black, E., Garside, R., and Leech, G., editors (1993). *Statistically-Driven Computer Grammars of English: The IBM/Lancaster Approach.* Rodopi, Amsterdam, Atlanta.

Black, E., Jelinek, F., Lafferty, J., Magerman, D. M., Mercer, D., and Roukos, S. (1993). Towards history-based grammars: Using richer models for probabilistic parsing. In *Proceedings of the 31st Annual Meeting of the Association for Computational Linguistics*, pages 31–37, Ohio State University. Association for Computational Linguistics.

Black, E., Lafferty, J., and Roukos, S. (1992). Development and evaluation of a broad-coverage probablistic grammar of English-language computer manuals. In *Proceedings of the 30th Annual Meeting of the Association for Computational Linguistics*, pages 185–192, University of Delaware. Association for Computational Linguistics.

Bod, R. (1993). Using an annotated corpus as a stochastic parser. In *Proceedings of the Sixth Conference of the European Chapter of the Association for Computational Linguistics*, pages 37–44, Utrecht University, The Netherlands. European Chapter of the Association for Computational Linguistics.

Booth, T. L. and Thompson, R. A. (1973). Applying probability measures to abstract languages. *IEEE Transactions on Computers*, C-22(5):442–450.

Bouma, G., Koenig, E., and Uszkoreit, H. (1988). A flexible graph-unification formalism and its application to natural-language processing. *IBM Journal of Research and Development.*

Bresnan, J., editor (1982). *The Mental Representation of Grammatical Relations.* MIT Press, Cambridge, Massachusetts.

Briscoe, E. J. (1992). Lexical issues in natural language processing. In Klein, E. and Veltman, F., editors, *Natural Language and Speech*, pages 39–68. Springer-Verlag.

Briscoe, E. J. (1994). Prospects for practical parsing: robust statistical techniques. In de Haan, P. and Oostdijk, N., editors, *Corpus-based Research into Language: A Feschrift for Jan Aarts*, pages 67–95. Rodopi, Amsterdam.

Briscoe, E. J. and Carroll, J. (1993). Generalized probabilistic LR parsing of natural language (corpora) with unification-based grammars. *Computational Linguistics*, 19(1):25–59.

Briscoe, E. J. and Waegner, N. (1993). Undergeneration and robust parsing. In Meijs, W., editor, *Proceedings of the ICAME Conference*, Amsterdam. Rodopi.

Carpenter, B. (1992). ALE—the attribute logic engine user's guide. Technical report, Carnegie Mellon University, Carnegie Mellon University, Pittsburgh, Pennsylvania.

Carpenter, B. (1992). *The Logic of Typed Feature Structures*, volume 32 of *Cambridge Tracts in Theoretical Computer Science*. Cambridge University Press.

Church, K. (1988). A stochastic parts program and noun phrase parser for unrestricted text. In *Proceedings of the Second Conference on Applied Natural Language Processing*, pages 136–143, Austin, Texas. ACL.

COLING (1994). *Proceedings of the 15th International Conference on Computational Linguistics*, Kyoto, Japan.

Cooper, R. (1983). *Quantification and Syntactic Theory.* Reidel, Dordrecht.

Copestake, A. and Briscoe, E. J. (1992). Lexical operations in a unification based framework. In Pustejovsky, J. and Bergler, S., editors, *Lexical Semantics and Knowledge Representation.* Springer-Verlag, Berlin.

Cutting, D., Kupiec, J., Pedersen, J., and Sibun, P. (1992). A practical part of speech tagger. In *Proceedings of the 3rd Conference on Applied Language Processing*, pages 133–140, Trento, Italy.

Dagan, I., Markus, S., and Markovitch, S. (1993). Contextual word similarity and estimation from sparse data. In *Proceedings of the 31st Annual Meeting of the Association for Computational Linguistics*, pages 164–171, Ohio State University. Association for Computational Linguistics.

DARPA (1989). *Proceedings of the Second DARPA Speech and Natural Language Workshop*, Cape Cod, Massachusetts. Defense Advanced Research Projects Agency.

DARPA (1991). *Proceedings of the Fourth DARPA Speech and Natural Language Workshop*, Pacific Grove, California. Defense Advanced Research Projects Agency, Morgan Kaufmann.

Davidson, D. (1969). Truth and meaning. In Davis, J. W. et al., editors, *Philosophical*, pages 1–20. Hingham.

Davidson, D. (1973). In defense of Convention T. In Leblanc, H., editor, *Truth, Syntax and Modality*, pages 76–85. North Holland.

de Marcken, C. (1990). Parsing the LOB corpus. In *Proceedings of the 28th Annual Meeting of the Association for Computational Linguistics*, pages 243–251, Pittsburgh, Pennsylvania. Association for Computational Linguistics.

De Rose, S. J. (1988). Grammatical category disambiguation by statistical optimization. *Computational Linguistics*, 14(1):31–39.

Dempster, A. P., Laird, N. M., and Rubin, D. B. (1977). Maximum likelihood from incomplete data via the EM algorithm. *Journal of the Royal Statistical Society*, 39(1):1–38.

EACL (1993). *Proceedings of the Sixth Conference of the European Chapter of the Association for Computational Linguistics*, Utrecht University, The Netherlands. European Chapter of the Association for Computational Linguistics.

Earley, J. C. (1968). *An Efficient Context-Free Parsing Algorithm*. PhD thesis, Computer Science Department, Carnegie-Mellon University.

Earley, J. C. (1970). An efficient context-free parsing algorithm. *Communications of the ACM*, 13(2):94–102.

Elworthy, D. (1993). Part-of-speech tagging and phrasal tagging. Technical report, University of Cambridge Computer Laboratory, Cambridge, England.

Emele, M. and Zajac, R. (1990). Typed unification grammars. In *Proceedings of the 28th Annual Meeting of the Association for Computational Linguistics*, Pittsburgh, Pennsylvania. Association for Computational Linguistics.

Flickinger, D. (1987). *Lexical Rules in the Hierarchical Lexicon*. PhD thesis, Stanford University.

Fong, S. (1992). The computational implementation of principle-based parsers. In Berwick, R. C., Abney, S. P., and Tenny, C., editors, *Principle-Based Parsing: Computation and Psycholinguistics*, pages 65–82. Kluwer, Dordrecht, The Netherlands.

Frege, G. (1892). Über sinn und bedeutung (translated as 'on sense and reference'). In Geach and Black, editors, *Translations from the Philosophical Writings of Gottlob Frege.* Blackwell, Oxford. translation 1960.

Fujisaki, T., Jelinek, F., Cocke, J., Black, E., and Nishino, T. (1989). A probabilistic parsing method for sentence disambiguation. In *Proceedings of the International Workshop on Parsing Technologies*, Pittsburgh.

Gärdenfors, P. (1990). The dynamics of belief systems: Foundations vs. coherence theories. *Revue Internationale de Philosophie*, 172:24–46.

Garside, R., Leech, G., and Sampson, G. (1987). *Computational Analysis of English: A Corpus-based Approach.* Longman, London.

Gazdar, G. (1987). Linguistic applications of default inheritance mechanisms. In Whitelock, P. H., Somers, H., Bennet, P., Johnson, R., and Wood, M. M., editors, *Linguistic Theory and Computer Applications*, pages 37–68. Academic Press, London.

Graham, S. L., Harrison, M. A., and Ruzzo, W. L. (1980). An improved context-free recognizer. *ACM Transactions on Programming Languages and Systems*, 2(3):415–462.

Greene, B. B. and Rubin, G. M. (1971). Automatic grammatical tagging of English. Technical report, Brown University.

Grice, H. P. (1975). Logic and conversation. In Cole, P., editor, *Speech Acts, Syntax and Semantics, Vol III: Speech Acts.* Academic Press, New York.

Groenendijk, J. and Stokhof, M. (1984). On the semantics of questions and the pragmantics of answers. In Landman, F. and Veltman, F., editors, *Varieties of Formal Semantics*, pages 143–170. Foris, Dordrecht.

Groenendijk, J. and Stokhof, M. (1990). Dynamic montague grammar. In Kalman, L. and Polos, L., editors, *Papers from the Second Symposium on Logic and Language*, pages 3–48. Akademiai Kiadoo, Budapest.

Groenendijk, J. and Stokhof, M. (1991a). Dynamic predicate logic. *Linguistics and Philosophy*, 14:39–100.

Groenendijk, J. and Stokhof, M. (1991b). Two theories of dynamic semantics. In van Eijck, J., editor, *Logics in AI—European Workshop JELIA '90, Springer Lecture Notes in Artificial Intelligence*, pages 55–64. Springer-Verlag, Berlin.

Haddock, J. N., Klein, E., and Morrill, G. (1987). *Unification Categorial Grammar, Unification Grammar and Parsing.* University of Edinburgh.

Hindle, D. (1983). Deterministic parsing of syntactic nonfluencies. In *Proceedings of the 21st Annual Meeting of the Association for Computational Linguistics,* pages 123–128, Cambridge, Massachusetts. Association for Computational Linguistics.

Hindle, D. (1983). User manual for Fidditch, a deterministic parser. Technical Report Technical Memorandum 7590-142, Naval Research Laboratory.

Hindle, D. (1989). Acquiring disambiguation rules from text. In *Proceeds of the 27th Annual Meeting of the Association for Computational Linguistics,* pages 118–125, Vancouver, Canada.

Hindle, D. (1990). Noun classification from predicate-argument structures. In *Proceedings of the 28th Annual Meeting of the Association for Computational Linguistics,* pages 268–275, Pittsburgh, Pennsylvania. Association for Computational Linguistics.

Hindle, D. (1992). An analogical parser for restricted domains. In *Proceedings of the Fifth DARPA Speech and Natural Language Workshop,* pages 150–154. Defense Advanced Research Projects Agency, Morgan Kaufmann.

Hindle, D. (1993). A parser for text corpora. In Atkins, B. T. S. and Zampolli, A., editors, *Computational Approaches to the Lexicon.* Oxford University Press.

Hindle, D. and Rooth, M. (1991). Structural ambiguity and lexical relations. In *Proceedings of the 29th Annual Meeting of the Association for Computational Linguistics,* pages 229–236, Berkeley, California. Association for Computational Linguistics.

Hobbs, J. R., Appelt, D., Bear, J., Israel, D., Kameyama, M., and Tyson, M. (1993). FASTUS: a system for extracting information from text. In *Proceedings of the 1993 ARPA Human Language Technology Workshop,* pages 133–137, Princeton, New Jersey. Advanced Research Projects Agency, Morgan Kaufmann.

Hobbs, J. R., Stickel, M., Appelt, D., and Martin, P. (1993). Interpretation as abduction. *Artificial Intelligence,* 63(1-2):69–142.

Hudson, R. (1990). *English Word Grammar.* Blackwell, Oxford, England.

Jackson, E., Appelt, D., Bear, J., Moore, R., and Podlozny, A. (1991). A template matcher for robust natural-language interpretation. In *Proceedings of the Fourth DARPA Speech and Natural Language Workshop,* pages 190–194, Pacific Grove, California. Defense Advanced Research Projects Agency, Morgan Kaufmann.

Jacobs, P. S. and Rau, L. F. (1993). Innovations in text interpretation. *Artificial Intelligence*, 63(1-2):143–191.

Järvinen, T. (1994). Annotating 200 million words. In *Proceedings of the 15th International Conference on Computational Linguistics*, Kyoto, Japan.

Jelinek, F., Lafferty, J. D., and Mercer, R. L. (1990). Basic methods of probabilistic context free grammars. Technical Report RC 16374 (72684), IBM, Yorktown Heights, NY 10598.

Jelinek, F., Mercer, R. L., and Roukos, S. (1992). Principles of lexical language modeling for speech recognition. In Furui, S. and Sondhi, M. M., editors, *Advances in Speech Signal Processing*, pages 651–699. Marcel Dekker.

Jensen, K. (1991). A broad-coverage natural language analysis system. In Tomita, M., editor, *Current Issues in Parsing Technology*. Kluwer Academic Press, Dordrecht.

Jensen, K. and Heidorn, G. (1993). *Natural Langauage Processing: The PLNLP Approach*. Kluwer Academic, Boston, Dordrecht, London.

Jensen, K. and Heidorn, G. E. (1983). The fitted parse: 100% parsing capability in a syntactic grammar of English. In *Proceedings of the First Conference on Applied Natural Language Processing*, pages 3–98.

Johnson, C. D. (1972). *Formal Aspects of Phonological Description*. Mouton, The Hague.

Johnson, M. (1992). Deductive parsing: The use of knowledge of language. In Berwick, R. C., Abney, S. P., and Tenny, C., editors, *Principle-Based Parsing: Computation and Psycholinguistics*, pages 39–64. Kluwer, Dordrecht, The Netherlands.

Jones, B. (1994). Can punctuation help parsing? In *Proceedings of the 15th International Conference on Computational Linguistics*, Kyoto, Japan.

Joshi, A. K. (1985). How much context-sensitivity is necessary for characterizing structural descriptions—Tree adjoining grammars. In Dowty, D., Karttunen, L., and Zwicky, A., editors, *Natural Language Processing—Theoretical, Computational and Psychological Perspectives*. Cambridge University Press, New York.

Joshi, A. K., Levy, L. S., and Takahashi, M. (1975). Tree adjunct grammars. *Journal of Computer and System Sciences*, 10(1).

Joshi, A. K. and Schabes, Y. (1992). Tree-adjoining grammars and lexicalized grammers. In *Tree Automata and LGS*. Elsevier Science, Amsterdam.

Joshi, A. K., Vijay-Shanker, K., and Weir, D. J. (1991). The convergence of mildly context-sensitive grammatical formalisms. In Sells, P., Shieber, S., and Wasow, T., editors, *Foundational Issues in Natural Language Processing*. MIT Press.

Kamp, H. (1981). A theory of truth and semantic representation. In Groenendijk, J., Janssen, T., and Stokhof, M., editors, *Formal Methods in the Study of Language*. Mathematisch Centrum, Amsterdam.

Kamp, H. and Reyle, U. (1993). *From Discourse to Logic*. Kluwer, Dordrecht.

Kaplan, R. M. and Bresnan, J. (1982). Lexical-functional grammar: a formal system for grammatical representation. In Bresnan, J., editor, *The Mental Representation of Grammatical Relations*. MIT Press, Cambridge, Massachusetts.

Kaplan, R. M. and Kay, M. (1994). Regular models of phonological rule systems. *Computational Linguistics*, 20(3):331–378. written in 1980.

Karlgren, H., editor (1990). *Proceedings of the 13th International Conference on Computational Linguistics*, Helsinki. ACL.

Karlsson, F., Voutilainen, A., Heikkilä, J., and Anttila, A., editors (1994). *Constraint Grammar: A Language-Independent Formalism for Parsing Unrestricted Text*. Mouton de Gruyter, Berlin, New York.

Karttunen, L. (1989). Radical lexicalism. In Baltin, M. and Kroch, A., editors, *Alternative Conceptions of Phrase Structure*. The University of Chicago Press, Chicago.

Karttunen, L. (1993). Finite-state lexicon compiler. Technical Report ISTL-NLTT-1993-04-02, Xerox PARC, Palo Alto, California.

Karttunen, L. and Beesley, K. R. (1992). Two-level rule compiler. Technical Report ISTL-92-2, Xerox PARC, Palo Alto, California.

Kay, M. (1979). Functional grammar. In *Proceedings of the Fifth Annual Meeting of the Berkeley Linguistic Society*, pages 142–158.

Kay, M. (1984). Functional unification grammar: a formalism for machine translation. In *Proceedings of the 10th International Conference on Computational Linguistics*, Stanford University, California. ACL.

Kay, M. (1986). Algorithm schemata and data structures in syntactic processing. In Grosz, B. J., Sparck Jones, K., and Webber, B. L., editors, *Readings in Natural Language Processing*, chapter I. 4, pages 35–70. Morgan Kaufmann Publishers, Inc., Los Altos, California. Originally published as a Xerox PARC technical report, 1980.

Kenny, P., Hollan, R., Gupta, V. N., Lenning, M., Mermelstein, P., and O'Shaughnessy, D. (1993). A*-admissible heuristics for rapid lexical access. *IEEE Transactions on Speech and Audio Processing*, 1(1):49–57.

Koskenniemi, K. (1983). *Two-Level Morphology: a General Computational Model for Word-Form Recognition and Production*. PhD thesis, University of Helsinki. Publications of the Department of General Linguistics,University of Helsinki, No. 11. Helsinki.

Koskenniemi, K. (1990). Finite-state parsing and disambiguation. In Karlgren, H., editor, *Proceedings of the 13th International Conference on Computational Linguistics*, volume 2, pages 229–232, Helsinki. ACL.

Krieger, H.-U. and Schaefer, U. (1994). TDL—a type description language of HPSG. Technical report, Deutsches Forschungszentrum für Künstliche Intelligenz GmbH, Saarbrücken, Germany.

Krifka, M. (1989). Nominal reference, temporal constitution and quantification in event semantics. In Bartsch, R., van Benthem, J., and van Emde-Boas, P., editors, *Semantics and Contextual Expressions*, pages 75–115. Foris, Dordrecht.

Kupiec, J. (1992). Robust part-of-speech tagging using a hidden Markov model. *Computer Speech and Language*, 6.

Kwasny, S. and Sonheimer, N. (1981). Relaxation techniques for parsing ill-formed input. *American journal of Computational Linguistics*, 7(2):99–108.

Lafferty, J., Sleator, D., and Temperley, D. (1992). Grammatical trigrams: a probabilistic model of link grammar. In Goldman, R., editor, *AAAI Fall Symposium on Probabilistic Approaches to Natural Language Processing*, Cambridge, Massachusetts. AAAI Press.

Lambek, J. (1958). The mathematics of sentence structure. *American Mathematical Monthly*, 65:154–170.

Lang, B. (1974). Deterministic techniques for efficient non-deterministic parsers. In Loeckx, J., editor, *Proceedings of the 2nd Colloquium on Automata, Languages and Programming*, pages 255–269, Saarbrücken, Germany. Springer-Verlag.

Lang, B. (1989). A generative view of ill-formed input processing. In *ATR Symposium on Basic Research for Telephone Interpretation*, Kyoto, Japan.

Lari, K. and Young, S. J. (1990). The estimation of stochastic context-free grammars using the Inside-Outside algorithm. *Computer Speech and Language Processing*, 4:35–56.

Leech, G. and Garside, R. (1991). Running a grammar factory: the production of syntactically analysed corpora or 'treebanks'. In Johansson, S. and Stenstrom, A., editors, *English Computer Corpora: Selected Papers and Bibliography*. Mouton de Gruyter, Berlin.

Leech, G., Garside, R., and Bryant, M. (1994). The large-scale grammatical tagging of text. In Oostdijk, N. and de Haan, P., editors, *Corpus-Based Research into Language*, pages 47–63. Rodopi, Atlanta.

Levinson, S. C. (1983). *Pragmatics*. Cambridge University Press.

Lucchesi, C. L. and Kowaltowski, T. (1993). Applications of finite automata representing large vocabularies. *Software-Practice and Experience*, 23(1):15–30.

Magerman, D. M. and Marcus, M. P. (1991). Pearl: A probabilistic chart parser. In *Proceedings of the Fourth DARPA Speech and Natural Language Workshop*, Pacific Grove, California. Defense Advanced Research Projects Agency, Morgan Kaufmann.

Magerman, D. M. and Weir, C. (1992). Efficiency, robustness and accuracy in Picky chart parsing. In *Proceedings of the 30th Annual Meeting of the Association for Computational Linguistics*, University of Delaware. Association for Computational Linguistics.

Marcus, M., Hindle, D., and Fleck, M. (1983). D-theory: talking about talking about trees. In *Proceedings of the 21st Annual Meeting of the Association for Computational Linguistics*, pages 129–136, Cambridge, Massachusetts. Association for Computational Linguistics.

Marcus, M. P. (1980). *A Theory of Syntactic Recognition for Natural Language*. MIT Press, Cambridge, Massachusetts.

Marshall, I. (1983). Choice of grammatical word-class without global syntactic analysis: tagging words in the LOB corpus. *Computers in the Humanities*, 17:139–150.

Maxwell, John T., I. and Kaplan, R. M. (1989). An overview of disjunctive constraint satisfaction. In Tomita, M., editor, *Proceedings of the First International Workshop on Parsing Technology*, Pittsburgh, Pennsylvania. Carnegie-Mellon University.

McCord, M. C. (1980). Slot grammars. *American journal of Computational Linguistics*, 6(1):255–286.

McCord, M. C. (1989). Design of LMT: A Prolog-based machine translation system. *Computational Linguistics*, 15(1):33–52.

McKeown, K., Kukich, K., and Shaw, J. (1994). Practical issues in automatic documentation generation. In *Proceedings of the Fourth Conference on Applied Natural Language Processing*, pages 7–14, Stuttgart, Germany. ACL, Morgan Kaufmann.

McRoy, S. and Hirst, G. (1990). Race-based parsing and syntactic disambiguation. *Cognitive Science*, 14:313–353.

Mel'čuk, I. A. (1988). *Dependency Syntax: Theory and Practice*. State University of New York Press, Albany, New York.

Montague, R. (1973). The proper treatment of quantification in ordinary English. In Hintikka, J., editor, *Approaches to Natural Language*, pages 221–242. Reidel.

Moortgat, M. (1988). *Categorial Investigations: Logical and Linguistic Aspects of the Lambek Calculus*. PhD thesis, University of Amsterdam, The Netherlands.

Murveit, H., Butzberger, J., Digilakis, V., and Weintraub, M. (1993). Large-vocabulary dictation using SRI's DECIPHER speech recognition system: Progressive search techniques. In *Proceedings of the 1993 International Conference on Acoustics, Speech, and Signal Processing*, volume 2, pages 319–322, Minneapolis, Minnesota. Institute of Electrical and Electronic Engineers.

Nguyen, L., Schwartz, R., Kubala, F., and Placeway, P. (1993). Search algorithms for software-only real-time recognition with very large vocabularies. In *Proceedings of the 1993 ARPA Human Language Technology Workshop*, pages 91–95, Princeton, New Jersey. Advanced Research Projects Agency, Morgan Kaufmann.

Nilsson, N. J. (1980). *Principles of Artificial Intelligence*. Tioga Publishing Company, Palo Alto, California.

Nunberg, G. (1990). The linguistics of punctuation. Technical Report Lecture Notes 18, CSLI, Stanford, California.

Nunberg, G. and Zaenen, A. (1992). Systematic polisemy in lexicology and lexicography. In *Proceedings of Eurolex 92*, Tampere, Finland.

Oostdijk, N. (1991). *Corpus Linguistics and the Automatic Analysis of English*. Rodopi, Amsterdam, Atlanta.

Ostler, N. and Atkins, B. T. S. (1992). Predictable meaning shifts: Some linguistic properties of lexical implication rules.

Partee, B. (1986). Noun phrase interpretation and type shifting principles. In Groenendijk, J. et al., editors, *Studies in Discourse Representation Theory and the Theory of Generalised Quantifiers*, pages 115–144. Foris, Dordrecht.

Paul, D. B. (1992). An efficient A* stack decoder algorithm for continuous speech recognition with a stochastic language model. In *Proceedings of the 1992 International Conference on Acoustics, Speech, and Signal Processing*, volume 1, pages 25–28, San Francisco. Institute of Electrical and Electronic Engineers.

Pereira, F. C. N. (1985). A new characterization of attachment preferences. In Dowty, D. R., Karttunen, L., and Zwicky, A. M., editors, *Natural Language Parsing—Psychological, Computational and Theoretical perspectives*, pages 307–319. Cambridge University Press.

Pereira, F. C. N. and Schabes, Y. (1992). Inside-outside reestimation from partially bracketed corpora. In *Proceedings of the 30th Annual Meeting of the Association for Computational Linguistics*, pages 128–135, University of Delaware. Association for Computational Linguistics.

Petheroudakis, J. (1991). MORPHOGEN automatic generator of morphological information for base form reduction. Technical report, Executive Communication Systems ECS, Provo, Utah.

Pollard, C. and Sag, I. (1994). *Head-driven Phrase Structure Grammar*. Center for the Study of Language and Information (CSLI) Lecture Notes. Stanford University Press and University of Chicago Press.

Pollard, C. and Sag, I. A. (1987). *An Information-Based Approach to Syntax and Semantics: Fundamentals*. Number 13 in Center for the Study of Language and Information (CSLI) Lecture Notes. Stanford University Press and Chicago University Press.

Prawitz, D. (1965). *Natural Deduction: A Proof-Theoretical Study*. Almqvist and Wiksell, Uppsala, Sweden.

Pritchett, B. (1988). Garden path phenomena and the grammatical basis of language processing. *Language*, 64(3):539–576.

Pustejovsky, J. (1991). The generative lexicon. *Computational Linguistics*, 17(4).

Pustejovsky, J. (1994). Linguistic constraints on type coercion. In St. Dizier, P. and Viegas, E., editors, *Computational Lexical Semantics*. Cambridge University Press.

Pustejovsky, J. and Boguraev, B. (1993). Lexical knowledge representation and natural language processing. *Artificial Intelligence*, 63:193–223.

Revuz, D. (1991). *Dictionnaires et lexiques, méthodes et algorithmes*. PhD thesis, Université Paris, Paris.

Ritchie, G. D., Russell, G. J., Black, A. W., and Pulman, S. G. (1992). *Computational Morphology*. MIT Press, Cambridge, Massachusetts.

Roche, E. (1993). Dictionary compression experiments. Technical Report IGM 93-5, Université de Marne la Vallée, Noisy le Grand, France.

Sampson, G. (1994). Susanne: a doomsday book of English grammar. In Oostdijk, N. and de Haan, P., editors, *Corpus-based Linguistics: A Feschrift for Jan Aarts*, pages 169–188. Rodopi, Amsterdam.

Sampson, G., Haigh, R., and Atwell, E. (1989). Natural language analysis by stochastic optimization: a progress report on project APRIL. *Journal of Experimental and Theoretical Artificial Intelligence*, 1:271–287.

Sanfilippo, A. (1993). LKB encoding of lexical knowledge. In Briscoe, T., Copestake, A., and de Paiva, V., editors, *Default Inheritance within Unification-Based Approaches to the Lexicon*. Cambridge University Press.

Sanfilippo, A. (1995). Lexical polymorphism and word disambiguation. In *Working Notes of the AAAI Spring Symposium on Representation and Acquisition of Lexical Knowledge: Polysemy, Ambiguity and Generativity*. Stanford University.

Sanfilippo, A., Benkerimi, K., and Dwehus, D. (1994). Virtual polysemy. In *Proceedings of the 15th International Conference on Computational Linguistics*, Kyoto, Japan.

Schabes, Y. (1990). *Mathematical and Computational Aspects of Lexicalized Grammars*. PhD thesis, University of Pennsylvania, Philadelphia. Also technical report (MS-CIS-90-48, LINC LAB179) from the Department of Computer Science.

Schabes, Y. (1992). Stochastic lexicalized tree-adjoining grammars. In *Proceedings of the 14th International Conference on Computational Linguistics*, Nantes, France. ACL.

Schabes, Y., Roth, M., and Osborne, R. (1993). Parsing the Wall Street Journal with the inside-outside algorithm. In *Proceedings of the Sixth Conference of the European Chapter of the Association for Computational Linguistics*, Utrecht University, The Netherlands. European Chapter of the Association for Computational Linguistics.

Schüller, G., Zierl, M., and Hausser, R. (1993). MAGIC. A tutorial in computational morphology. Technical report, Friedrich-Alexander Universität, Erlangen, Germany.

Seneff, S. (1992). TINA: A natural language system for spoken language applications. *Computational Linguistics*, 18(1):61–86.

Sharman, R., Jelinek, F., and Mercer, R. L. (1990). Generating a grammar for statistical training. In *Proceedings of the Third DARPA Speech and Natural Language Workshop*, pages 267–274, Hidden Valley, Pennsylvania. Defense Advanced Research Projects Agency, Morgan Kaufmann.

Shieber, S. M. (1983). Sentence disambiguation by a shift-reduce parsing technique. In *Proceedings of the 21st Annual Meeting of the Association for Computational Linguistics*, pages 113–118, Cambridge, Massachusetts. Association for Computational Linguistics.

Shieber, S. M. (1992). *Constraint-Based Grammar Formalisms*. MIT Press, Cambridge, Massachusetts.

Shieber, S. M., Uszkoreit, H., Robinson, J., and Tyson, M. (1983). *The formalism and Implementation of PATR-II*. SRI International, Menlo Park, California.

Sleator, D. and Temperley, D. (1991). Parsing English with a link grammar. Technical report CMU-CS-91-196, Department of Computer Science, Carnegie Mellon University, Pittsburgh, Pennsylvania.

Sproat, R. (1992). *Morphology and Computation*. MIT Press, Cambridge, Massachusetts.

Stabler, Edward P., J. (1992). *The Logical Approach to Syntax: Foundations, Specifications and Implementations of Theories of Government and Binding*. MIT Press, Cambridge, Massachusetts.

Stevenson, S. (1993). A competition-based explanation of syntactic attachment preferences and garden path phenomena. In *Proceedings of the 31st Annual Meeting of the Association for Computational Linguistics*, pages 266–273, Ohio State University. Association for Computational Linguistics.

Stolcke, A. and Omohundro, S. (1993). Hidden Markov model induction by Bayesian model merging. In Hanson, S. J., Cowan, J. D., and Giles, C. L., editors, *Advances in Neural Information Processing Systems 5*, pages 11–18. Morgan Kaufmann.

Teitelbaum, R. (1973). Context-free error analysis by evaluation of algebraic power series. In *Proceedings of the Fifth Annual ACM Symposium on Theory of Computing*, pages 196–199, Austin, Texas.

Tomita, M. (1987). An efficient augmented context-free parsing algorithm. *Computational Linguistics*, 13(1):31–46.

Touretzsky, D. S., Horty, J. F., and Thomason, R. M. (1987). A clash of intuitions: the current state of nonmonotonic multiple inheritance systems. In *Proceedings of the 10th International Joint Conference on Artificial Intelligence*, pages 476–482, Milan, Italy. Morgan Kaufmann.

Turner, R. (1988). A theory of properties. *The journal of Symbolic Logic*, 54.

Turner, R. (1992). Properties, propositions and semantic theory. In Rosner, M. and Johnson, R., editors, *Computational Linguistics and Formal Semantics*. Cambridge University Press, Cambridge.

Tzoukermann, E. and Liberman, M. Y. (1990). A finite-state morphological processor for Spanish. In Karlgren, H., editor, *Proceedings of the 13th International Conference on Computational Linguistics*, volume 3, pages 277–286, Helsinki. ACL.

Uszkoreit, H. (1986). Categorial unification grammars. In *Proceedings of the 11th International Conference on Computational Linguistics*, Bonn. ACL.

van Eijck, J. and de Vries, F. J. (1992). A sound and complete calculus for update logic. In Dekker, P. and Stokhof, M., editors, *Proceedings of the Eighth Amsterdam Colloquium*, pages 133–152, Amsterdam. ILLC.

Veltman, F. (1985). *Logics for Conditionals*. PhD thesis, University of Amsterdam, Amsterdam.

Voutilainen, A. (1994). *Three Studies of Grammar-Based Surface Parsing of Unrestricted English Text*. PhD thesis, University of Helsinki, Department of General Linguistics, University of Helsinki.

Ward, W. (1991a). Evaluation of the CMU ATIS system. In *Proceedings of the Fourth DARPA Speech and Natural Language Workshop*, pages 101–105, Pacific Grove, California. Defense Advanced Research Projects Agency, Morgan Kaufmann.

Ward, W. (1991b). Understanding spontaneous speech: the Phoenix system. In *Proceedings of the 1991 International Conference on Acoustics, Speech, and Signal Processing*, volume 1, pages 365–367, Toronto. Institute of Electrical and Electronic Engineers.

Younger, D. H. (1967). Recognition and parsing of context-free languages in time n^3. *Information and Control*, 10(2):189–208.

Zeevat, H., Klein, E., and Calder, J. (1987). An introduction to unification categorial grammar. In Haddock, J. N., Klein, E., and Morrill, G., editors, *Edinburgh Working Papers in Cognitive Science, volume 1: Categorial Grammar, Unification Grammar, and Parsing*, volume 1 of *Working Papers in Cognitive Science*. Centre for Cognitive Science, University of Edinburgh.

Chapter 4

Language Generation

4.1 Overview

Eduard Hovy

University of Southern California, Marina del Rey, California, USA

The area of study called natural language generation (NLG) investigates how computer programs can be made to produce high-quality natural language text from computer-internal representations of information. Motivations for this study range from entirely theoretical (linguistic, psycholinguistic) to entirely practical (for the production of output systems for computer programs). Useful overviews of the research are Dale, Hovy, et al. (1992); Paris, Swartout, et al. (1990); Kempen (1987); Bateman and Hovy (1992); McKeown and Swartout (1987); Mann, Bates, et al. (1981). The stages of language generation for a given application, resulting in speech output, are shown in Figure 4.1. This section discusses the following:

- the overall state of the art in generation,

- significant gaps of knowledge, and

- new developments and infrastructure.

For more detail, it then turns to two major areas of generation theory and practice: single-sentence generation (also called realization or tactical generation) and multisentence generation (also called text planning or strategic generation).

4.1.1 State of the Art

No field of study can be described adequately using a single perspective. In order to understand NLG it is helpful to consider independently the *tasks* of generation and the *process* of generation. Every generator addresses one or more

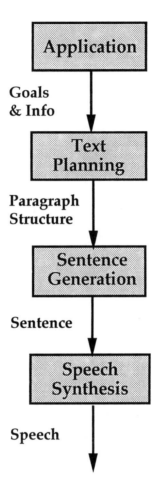

Figure 4.1: The stages of language generation.

tasks and embodies one (or sometimes two) types of process. One can identify three types of generator *task*: text planning, sentence planning, and surface realization. Text planners select from a knowledge pool which information to include in the output, and out of this create a text structure to ensure coherence. On a more local scale, sentence planners organize the content of each sentence, massaging and ordering its parts. Surface realizers convert sentence-sized chunks of representation into grammatically correct sentences. Generator *processes* can be classified into points on a range of sophistication and expressive power, starting with inflexible canned methods and ending with maximally flexible feature combination methods. For each point on this range, there may be various types of implemented algorithms.

The simplest approach, **canned text systems**, is used in the majority of software: the system simply prints a string of words without any change (error messages, warnings, letters, etc.). The approach can be used equally easily for single-sentence and for multi-sentence text generation. Trivial to create, the systems are very wasteful. **Template systems**, the next level of sophistication, are used as soon as a message must be produced several times with slight alterations. Form letters are a typical template application, in which a few open fields are filled in specified constrained ways. The template approach is used mainly for multisentence generation, particularly in applications whose texts are fairly regular in structure such as some business reports. The text planning components of the U.S. companies CoGenTex (Ithaca, NY) and Cognitive Systems Inc. (New Haven, CT) enjoy commercial use. On the research side, the early template-based generator ANA (Kukich, 1983) produced stock market reports from a news wire by filling appropriate values into a report template. More sophisticated, the multisentence component of TEXT (McKeown, 1985) could dynamically nest instances of four stereotypical paragraph templates called schemas to create paragraphs. TAILOR (Paris, 1993a) generalized TEXT by adding schemas and more sophisticated schema selection criteria.

Phrase-based systems employ what can be seen as generalized templates, whether at the sentence level (in which case the phrases resemble phrase structure grammar rules) or at the discourse level (in which case they are often called text plans). In such systems, a phrasal pattern is first selected to match the top level of the input (say, [SUBJECT VERB OBJECT]), and then each part of the pattern is expanded into a more specific phrasal pattern that matches some subportion of the input (say, [DETERMINER ADJECTIVES HEAD-NOUN MODIFIERS]), and so on; the cascading process stops when every phrasal pattern has been replaced by one or more words. Phrase-based systems can be powerful and robust, but are very hard to build beyond a certain size, because the phrasal interrelationships must be carefully specified to prevent inappropriate phrase expansions. The phrase-based approach has mostly been used for single-sentence generation (since linguists' grammars provide well-specified collections of phrase structure rules). A sophisticated example is MUMBLE (McDonald, 1980; Meteer, McDonald, et al., 1987), built at the University of Massachusetts, Amherst. Over the past five years, however, phrase-based multisentence text structure generation (often called text planning) has received considerable attention in the research community, with the development of the RST text structurer (Hovy, 1988), the EES text planner (Moore, 1989), and several similar systems (Dale, 1990; Cawsey, 1989; Suthers, 1993), in which each so-called text plan is a *phrasal* pattern that specifies the structure of some portion of the discourse, and each portion of the plan is successively refined by more specific plans until the single-clause level is reached. Given the lack of understanding of discourse structure and the paucity of the discourse plan libraries, however, such planning systems do not yet operate beyond the experimental level.

Feature-based systems represent, in a sense, the limit point of the generalization of phrases. In feature-based systems, each possible minimal alternative of expression is represented by a single feature; for example, a sentence is either POSITIVE or NEGATIVE, it is a QUESTION or an IMPERATIVE or a STATEMENT, its tense is PRESENT or PAST and so on. Each sentence is specified by a unique set of features. Generation proceeds by the incremental collection of features appropriate for each portion of the input (either by the traversal of a feature selection network or by unification), until the sentence is fully determined. Feature-based systems are among the most sophisticated generators built today. Their strength lies in the simplicity of their conception: any distinction in language is defined as a feature, analyzed, and added to the system. Their strength lies in the simplicity of their conception: any distinction in language can be added to the system as a feature. Their weakness lies in the difficulty of maintaining feature interrelationships and in the control of feature selection (the more features available, the more complex the input must be). No feature-based multisentence generators have been built to date. The most advanced single-sentence generators of this type include PENMAN (Matthiessen, 1983; Mann & Matthiessen, 1985) and its descendant KPML (Bateman, Maier, et al., 1991), the Systemic generators developed at USC/ISI and IPSI; COMMUNAL (Fawcett, 1992) a Systemic generator developed at Wales; the Functional Unification Grammar framework (FUF) (Elhadad, 1992) from Columbia University; SUTRA (Von Hahn, Höppner, et al., 1980) developed at the University of Hamburg; SEMTEX (Rösner, 1986) developed at the University of Stuttgart; and POPEL (Reithinger, 1991) developed at the University of the Saarland. The two generators most widely distributed, studied, and used are PENMAN/KPML and FUF. None of these systems are in commercial use.

4.1.2   Significant Gaps and Limitations

It is safe to say that at the present time one can fairly easily build a single-purpose generator for any specific application, or with some difficulty adapt an existing sentence generator to the application, with acceptable results. However, one cannot yet build a general-purpose sentence generator or a non-toy text planner. Several significant problems remain without sufficiently general solutions:

- lexical selection

- sentence planning

- discourse structure

- domain modeling

- generation choice criteria

Lexical Selection: Lexical selection is one of the most difficult problems in generation. At its simplest, this question involves selecting the most appropriate single word for a given unit of input. However, as soon as the semantic model approaches a realistic size, and as soon as the lexicon is large enough to permit alternative locutions, the problem becomes very complex. In some situation, one might have to choose among the phrases *John's car, John's sports car, his speedster, the automobile, the red vehicle, the red Mazda* for referring to a certain car. The decision depends on what has already been said, what is referentially available from context, what is most salient, what stylistic effect the speaker wishes to produce, and so on. A considerable amount of work has been devoted to this question, and solutions to various aspects of the problem have been suggested (see for example Goldman (1975); Elhadad and Robin (1992); McKeown, Robin, et al. (1993)). At this time no general methods exist to perform lexical selection. Most current generator systems simply finesse the problem by linking a single lexical item to each representation unit. *What is required:* Development of theories about and implementations of lexical selection algorithms, for reference to objects, event, states, etc., and tested with large lexica.

Discourse Structure: One of the most exciting recent research developments in generation is the automated planning of paragraph structure. The state of the art in discourse research is described in Chapter 6. So far, no text planner exists that can reliably plan texts of several paragraphs in general. *What is required:* Theories of the structural nature of discourse, of the development of theme and focus in discourse, and of coherence and cohesion; libraries of discourse relations, communicative goals, and text plans; implemented representational paradigms for characterizing stereotypical texts such as reports and business letters; implemented text planners that are tested in realistic non-toy domains.

Sentence Planning: Even assuming the text planning problem is solved, a number of tasks remain before well-structured multisentence text can be generated. These tasks, required for planning the structure and content of each sentence, include: pronoun specification, theme signaling, focus signaling, content aggregation to remove unnecessary redundancies, the ordering of prepositional phrases, adjectives, etc. An elegant system that addressed some of these tasks is described in (Appelt, 1985). While to the nonspecialist these tasks may seem relatively unimportant, they can have a significant effect and make the difference between a well-written and a poor text. *What is required:* Theories of pronoun use, theme and focus selection and signaling, and content aggregation; implemented sentence planners with rules that perform these operations; testing in realistic domains.

Domain Modeling: A significant shortcoming in generation research is the lack of large, well-motivated application domain models, or even the absence of clear principles by which to build such models. A traditional problem with generators is that the inputs are frequently hand-crafted, or are built by some other system that uses representation elements from a fairly small hand-crafted domain model, making the generator's inputs already highly oriented toward the final language desired. It is very difficult to link a generation system to a knowledge base or database that was originally developed for some non-linguistic purpose. The mismatches between the representation schemes demonstrate the need for clearly articulated principles of linguistically appropriate domain modeling and representational adequacy (see also Meteer, 1990). The use of high-level language-oriented concept taxonomies such as the Penman Upper Model (Bateman, Moore, et al., 1990) to act as a *bridge* between the domain application's concept organization and that required for generation is becoming a popular (though partial) solution to this problem. *What is required:* Implemented large-size (over 10,000 concepts) domain models that are useful both for some non-linguistic application and for generation; criteria for evaluating the internal consistency of such models; theories on and practical experience in the linking of generators to such models; lexicons of commensurate size.

Generation Choice Criteria: Probably the problem least addressed in generator systems today is the one that will take the longest to solve. This is the problem of guiding the generation process through its choices when multiple options exist to handle any given input. It is unfortunately the case that language, with its almost infinite flexibility, demands far more from the input to a generator than can be represented today. As long as generators remain fairly small in their expressive potential then this problem does not arise. However, when generators start having the power of saying *the same thing* in many ways, additional control must be exercised in order to ensure that appropriate text is produced. As shown in Hovy (1988) and Jameson (1987), different texts generated from the same input carry additional, non-semantic import; the stylistic variations serve to express significant interpersonal and situational meanings (text can be formal or informal, slanted or objective, colorful or dry, etc.). In order to ensure appropriate generation, the generator user has to specify not only the semantic content of the desired text, but also its pragmatic—interpersonal and situational—effects. Very little research has been performed on this question beyond a handful of small-scale pilot studies. *What is required:* Classifications of the types of reader characteristics and goals, the types of author goals, and the interpersonal and situational aspects that affect the form and content of language; theories of how these aspects affect the generation process; implemented rules and/or planning systems that guide generator systems' choices; criteria for evaluating appropriateness of generated text in specified communicative situations.

4.1.3   Future Directions

Infrastructure Requirements: The overarching challenge for generation is scaling up to the ability to handle real-world, complex domains. However, given the history of relatively little funding support, hardly any infrastructure required for generation research exists today.

The resources most needed to enable both high-quality research and large-scale generation include the following:

- Large well-structured lexicons of various languages. Without such lexicons, generator builders have to spend a great deal of redundant effort, collecting standard morphological and syntactic information to include in lexical items. As has been shown recently in the construction of the Penman English lexicon of 90,000+ items, it is possible to extract enough information from online dictionaries to create lexicons, or partial lexicons, automatically.

- Large well-structured knowledge bases. Paralleling the recent knowledge base construction efforts centered around WordNet (Miller, 1985) in the U.S., a large general-purpose knowledge base that acts as support for domain-specific application oriented knowledge bases would help to speed up and enhance generator porting and testing on new applications. An example is provided by the ontology construction program of the Pangloss machine translation effort (Hovy & Knight, 1993).

- Large grammars of various languages. The general availability of such grammars would free generator builders from onerous and often repetitive linguistic work, though different theories of language naturally result in very different grammars. However, a repository of grammars built according to various theories and of various languages would constitute a valuable infrastructure resource.

- Libraries of text plans. As discussed above, one of the major stumbling blocks in the ongoing investigation of text planning is the availability of a library of tested text plans. Since no consensus exists on the best form and content of such plans, it is advisable to pursue several different construction efforts.

Longer-term Research Projects: Naturally, the number and variety of promising long-term research projects is large. The following directions have all been addressed by various researchers for over a decade and represent important strands of ongoing investigation:

- stylistically appropriate generation

- psycholinguistically realistic generation

- reversible multilingual formalisms and algorithms

- continued development of grammars and generation methods

- generation of different genres/types of text

Near- and Medium-term Applications with Payoff Potential: Taking into account the current state of the art and gaps in knowledge and capability, the following applications (presented in order of increasing difficulty) provide potential for near-term and medium-term payoff:

- **Database Content Display:** The description of database contents in natural language is not a new problem, and some such generators already exist for specific databases. The general solution still poses problems, however, since even for relatively simple applications it still includes unsolved issues in sentence planning and text planning.

- **Expert System Explanation:** This is a related problem, often however requiring more interactive ability, since the user's queries may not only elicit more information from a (static, and hence well-structured) database, but may cause the expert system to perform further reasoning as well, and hence require the dynamic explanation of system behavior, expert system rules, etc. This application also includes issues in text planning, sentence planning, and lexical choice.

- **Speech Generation:** Simplistic text-to-speech synthesis systems have been available commercially for a number of years, but naturalistic speech generation involves unsolved issues in discourse and interpersonal pragmatics (for example, the intonation contour of an utterance can express dislike, questioning, etc.). Today, only the most advanced speech synthesizers compute syntactic form as well as intonation contour and pitch level.

- **Limited Report and Letter Writing:** As mentioned in the previous section, with increasingly general representations for text structure, generator systems will increasingly be able to produce standardized multiparagraph texts such as business letters or monthly reports. The problems faced here include text plan libraries, sentence planning, adequate lexicons, and robust sentence generators.

- **Presentation Planning in Multimedia Human-Computer Interaction:** By generalizing text plans, Hovy and Arens (1991) showed that it is possible also to control some forms of text formatting, and then argued that further generalization will permit the planning of certain aspects of multimedia presentations. Ongoing research in the WIP project at Saarbrücken (Wahlster, André, et al., 1991) and the COMET project at Columbia University (Feiner & McKeown, 1990) have developed impressive demonstration systems for multimedia presentations involving planning and language generation.

- **Automated Summarization:** A somewhat longer-term functionality that would make good use of language generation and discourse knowledge is the automated production of summaries. Naturally, the major problem to be solved first is the identification of the most relevant information.

During the past two decades, language generation technology has developed to the point where it offers general-purpose single-sentence generation capability and limited-purpose multisentence paragraph planning capability. The possibilities for the growth and development of useful applications are numerous and exciting. Focusing new research on specific applications and on infrastructure construction will help turn the promise of current text generator systems and theories into reality.

4.2 Syntactic Generation

Gertjan van Noord[a] & Günter Neumann[b]

[a] Alfa-informatica RUG, The Netherlands
[b] Deutsches Forschungzentrum für Künstliche Intelligenz, Saarbrücken, Germany

In a natural language generation module, we often distinguish two components. On the one hand it needs to be decided *what* should be said. This task is delegated to a *planning component*. Such a component might produce an expression representing the content of the proposed utterance. On the basis of this representation the syntactic generation component produces the actual output sentence(s). Although the distinction between planning and syntactic generation is not uncontroversial, we will nonetheless assume such an architecture here, in order to explain some of the issues that arise in syntactic generation.

A (natural language) grammar is a formal device that defines a relation between (natural language) utterances and their corresponding meanings. In practice, this usually means that a grammar defines a relation between strings and logical forms. During natural language understanding, the task is to arrive at a logical form that corresponds to the input string. Syntactic generation can be described as the problem of finding the corresponding string for an input logical form.

We are thus making a distinction between the grammar which *defines* this relation, and the procedure that *computes* the relation on the basis of such a grammar. In the current state of the art, unification-based (or more general: constraint-based) formalisms are used to express such grammars, e.g., Lexical Functional Grammar (LFG) (Bresnan, 1982), Head-Driven Phrase-Structure Grammar (HPSG) (Pollard & Sag, 1987) and constraint-based categorial frameworks (cf. Uszkoreit, 1986 and Zeevat, Klein, et al., 1987).

Almost all modern linguistic theories assume that a natural language grammar not only describes the correct sentences of a language, but that such a grammar also describes the corresponding semantic structures of the grammatical sentences. Given that a grammar specifies the relation between phonology and semantics it seems obvious that the generator is supposed to use this specification. For example, Generalized Phrase Structure Grammars (GPSG) (Gazdar, Klein, et al., 1985) provide a detailed description of the semantic interpretation of the sentences licensed by the grammar. Thus one might assume that a generator based on GPSG constructs a sentence for a given semantic structure, according to the semantic interpretation rules of GPSG. Alternatively, Busemann (1990) presents a generator, based on GPSG, which does not take as its input a logical form, but rather some kind of control expression which merely instructs the grammatical component which rules of the grammar to apply. Similarly, in the conception of Gardent and Plainfossé (1990), a generator is provided with some kind of *deep structure* which can be interpreted as a control expression instructing the grammar which rules to apply. These approaches to the generation problem clearly *solve* some of the problems encountered in generation—simply by pushing the problem into the conceptual component (i.e., the planning component). In this overview we focus on the more ambitious approach sketched above.

The success of the currently developed constraint-based theories is due to the fact that they are purely declarative. Hence, it is an interesting objective— theoretically and practically—to use one and the same grammar for natural language understanding and generation. In fact the potential for reversibility was a primary motivation for the introduction of Martin Kay's Functional Unification Grammar (FUG). In recent years interest in such a *reversible* architecture has led to a number of publications.[1]

4.2.1   State of the Art

The different approaches towards the syntactic generation problem can be classified according to a number of dimensions. It is helpful to distinguish between

- Definition of the search space

  - Left-right vs. Bidirectional processing
  - Top-down vs. Bottom-up processing

- Traversal of the search space

A generator proceeds from left to right if the elements of the right-hand-side of a rule are processed in a left-to-right order. This order is very common for parsing, but turns out to be unsuitable for generation. For example, Shieber (1988) presents an Earley-based generation algorithm that follows a left-to-right scheduling. It has been shown that such a strategy leads to a very inefficient behavior when applied for generation. The reason is that the important information that guides the generation process, namely the logical forms, is usually percolated in a different manner. Therefore, semantic-head-driven generation approaches have become popular, most notably the algorithm described in Shieber, Pereira, et al. (1990); VanNoord (1990); VanNoord (1993), but see also Calder, Reape, et al. (1989); Gerdemann and Hinrichs (1990); Gerdemann (1991); Neumann (1994). Such approaches aim at an order of processing in which an element of the right-hand-side of a rule is only processed once its corresponding logical form has been determined.

As in parsing theory, generation techniques can be classified according to the way they construct the derivation trees. Bottom-up and top-down traversals have been proposed as well as mixed strategies. For example, bottom-up generation strategies are described in Shieber (1988); VanNoord (1993), top-down approaches are described in Wedekind (1988); Dymetman, Isabelle, et al. (1990),

---

[1] See for example Strzalkowski, Carballo, et al. (1995); Strzalkowski (1994) a collection of papers based on the 1991 ACL workshop 'Reversible Grammars in Natural Language Processing'; some other references are Appelt (1987); Jacobs (1988); Dymetman and Isabelle (1988). However, it is currently a matter of debate, whether one and the same grammar should actually be employed at run-time by both processes without any change (e.g., Shieber, 1988; Shieber, Pereira, et al., 1990; VanNoord, 1993; Neumann, 1994) or whether two separate grammars should better be compiled out of a single source grammar (e.g., Block, 1994; Dymetman, Isabelle, et al., 1990; Strzalkowski, 1989.)

and mixed strategies are described in Shieber, Pereira, et al. (1990); Gerdemann (1991); Neumann (1994).

As in parsing, bottom-up approaches solve some non-termination problems that are encountered in certain top-down procedures.

The above mentioned two dimensions characterize the way in which derivation trees are constructed. A particular choice of these parameters defines a non-deterministic generation scheme, giving rise to a search space that is to be investigated by an actual generation algorithm. Hence, generation algorithms can be further classified with respect to the search strategy they employ. For example, a generation algorithm might propose a depth-first backtrack strategy. Potentially more efficient algorithms might use a *chart* to represent successfully branches of the search space, optionally combined with a breadth-first search (see for example, Gerdemann, 1991; Calder, Reape, et al., 1989). Moreover, there also exist chart-based agenda driven strategies which allow the modeling of preference-based *best-first* strategies (e.g., Den, 1994; Neumann, 1994).

4.2.2   Future Directions

Syntactic generation is one of the most elaborated and investigated fields in the area of natural language generation. In particular, due to the growing research in the Computational Linguistics area, syntactic generation has now achieved a methodological status comparable to that of natural language parsing. However, there are still strong limitations which weakens their general applicability for arbitrary application systems. Probably the most basic problems are:

- Lexical and grammatical coverage

- Re-usability

- Limited functional flexibility

None of the syntactic generators process grammars whose size and status would go beyond that of a *laboratory* one. The newly proposed approaches in Computational Linguistics are in principle capable of processing declaratively specified grammars, and hence are potentially open to grammars which can be incrementally extended. However, as long as the grammars do not achieve a critical mass, the usability of the approaches for very large grammars is purely speculative. The same is true for the status of the lexicons. Currently, generators only use small lexicons. Consequently most of the systems trivialize the problem of lexical choice as being a simple look-up method. However, if very large lexicons were to be used then the lexical choice problem would require more sophisticated strategies.

Of course, there exists some generators whose grammatical coverage is of interest, most notably those from the Systemic Linguistics camp (see section 4.1). However, these generation grammars have a less transparent declarative status, and hence are limited with respect to re-usability and adaptation to other systems.

All known syntactic generators have a limited degree of functionality. Although some approaches have been proposed for solving specific problems, such as generating ellipsis (e.g., Jameson & Wahlster, 1982); generation of paraphrases (e.g., Meteer & Shaked, 1988; Neumann, 1994); generation of referential expressions (Dale, 1990); or incremental generation (e.g., DeSmedt & Kempen, 1987), there exists currently no theoretical and practical framework, which could serve as a platform for combining all these specific operational issues.

Taking these limitations as a basis, important key research problems specific to syntactic generation are:

Large Grammars and Lexicons: These are needed for obtaining reasonable linguistic competence. As a prerequisite, grammatical knowledge must be specified declaratively in order to support the re-usability, not only for other systems, but also for integrating different specific generation performance methods.

Reversibility: If we want to obtain realistic generation systems then interleaving natural language generation and understanding will be important, e.g., for text revision. It is reasonable to assume that for the case of grammatical processing reversible grammars as well as uniform processing methods are needed. Such a uniform framework might also serve as a platform for integrating generation and understanding specific performance methods.

Incremental Processing: Rather than generating on the basis of a single complete logical form, some researchers have investigated the possibility of generating incrementally. In such a model small pieces of semantic information are provided to the tactical generator one at the time. Such a model might better explain certain psycholinguistic observations concerning human language production (cf. for example DeSmedt & Kempen, 1987).

Producing a non–Ambiguous Utterance: The generation procedures sketched above all come up with a possible utterance for a given meaning representation. However, given that natural language is very ambiguous the chances are that this proposed utterance itself is ambiguous, and therefore might lead to undesired *side-effects*. Some preliminary techniques to prevent the production of ambiguous utterances are discussed in Neumann and van Noord (1994); Neumann (1994).

Integration of Template- and Grammar-based Generation: This will be important in order to obtain efficient but flexible systems. This would allow competence grammar to be used in those cases where prototypical constructions (i.e., the templates) are not appropriate or even available.

Logical Equivalence: An important theoretical and practical problem for natural language generation is the problem of logical form equivalence. For a discussion of this problem, refer to Shieber (1993).

4.3 Deep Generation

John Bateman

GMD, IPSI, Darmstadt, Germany

Although crucial to the entire enterprise of automatic text generation, deep generation remains a collection of activities lacking a clear theoretical foundation at this time. The most widely accepted views on what constitutes deep generation are already exhausted by a small number of techniques, resources, and algorithms revealing as many problems as they can actually claim to solve. For these reasons, recent research work in text generation centers on aspects of deep generation and it is here that serious breakthroughs are most needed. Whereas the goal of deep generation is to produce specifications of sufficiently fine granularity and degree of linguistic abstraction to drive surface generators, how it is to do so, and from what starting point, remains unclear.

4.3.1 State of the Art

Although deep generation is most often seen as notionally involving two subtasks—selecting the content for a text and imposing an appropriate linear order on that content's expression—it is now usually accepted that this decomposition is problematic. The subtasks are sufficiently interdependent as to make such a decomposition questionable. Linear order is achieved by the intermediate step of constructing a recursive text structure, typically the province of *text planning*. The two standard methods for constructing text structure, *text schemata* (e.g., McKeown, 1985; McCoy, 1986; Rambox & Korelsky, 1992; Paris, 1993b) and *rhetorical structuring* (e.g., Mann & Thompson, 1987; Hovy, 1993; Moore & Paris, 1993), both combine content selection and textual organization.

Text schemata describe text on the model of constituency. A text is defined in terms of a *macro structure* with constituents given by *rhetorical predicates*, such as *Identification, Constituency*, and *Analogy*. Individual rhetorical predicates generally include both constraints on the information they express and particular surface realization constraints. Rhetorical predicates are combined in fixed configurations, the text schemata. The most commonly cited problems with text schemata are their rigidity and lack of intentional information (cf. Moore & Paris, 1993): i.e., if an *identification* predicate appears, there is no record as to why a speaker has selected this predicate. This is particularly problematic for dialogue situations where breakdowns can occur. Despite these problems, however, schemata are still sometimes selected on the basis of their simplicity and ease of definition (cf. Rambox & Korelsky, 1992).

In contrast to text schemata, rhetorical structures define the relational structure of a text. They show how a text can be recursively decomposed into smaller segments. These component segments are related to one another by means of a small set of *rhetorical relations*, such as *elaboration, solutionhood, volitional cause*, etc. Each such rhetorical relation is defined in terms of a distinctive set of constraints on the information presented in the segments related and in those segments' combination, on the speaker/hearer belief states, and on the effect that the speaker is attempting to achieve with the relation. It is generally assumed that imposing a rhetorical organization enables the information to be presented to be segmented into sufficiently small-scale chunks as to admit expression by surface generators. Rhetorical organization is typically constructed by using a top-down goal-oriented planning strategy with the rhetorical relation definitions as plan operators. However, while earlier rhetorical structure approaches tended to equate rhetorical relations with discourse intentions, this does not appear equally appropriate for all rhetorical relations. Those relations that are based on the informational content of the segments related undercon-strain possible discourse intentions; for example, a *circumstance* relation can be given for many distinct discourse purposes. The most well developed versions of rhetorical structure-based text planning thus separate out at least discourse intentions and rhetorical relations and allow a many-to-many relation between them, as defined by the system's planing operators.

An example of such a plan operator from the system of Moore and Paris (1993) is the following:

```
EFFECT: (PERSUADED ?hearer (DO ?hearer ?act))
CONSTRAINTS: (AND (STEP ?act ?goal)
                  (GOAL ?hearer ?goal)
                  (MOST-SPECIFIC ?goal)
                  (CURRENT-FOCUS ?act)
                  (SATELLITE))
NUCLEUS: (FORALL ?goal
                 (MOTIVATION ?act ?goal))
SATELLITES: nil
```

The successful application of this operator has the effect that a state of the hearer being *persuaded* (a discourse intention) to do some act is achieved. The operator may be applied when the specified constraints hold. When this is the case, a rhetorical structuring involving *motivation* is constructed. Information selection is thus achieved as a side-effect of binding variables in the operator's constraints. Further, such plan operators then decompose the rhetorical relation *motivation* until sequences of surface speech acts are reached. The Moore and Paris system contains approximately 150 such plan operators and is considered sufficiently stable for use in various application systems.

Particular text schemata are associated with specific communicative intentions (such as answering a specified user-question or constructing a specified text-type) directly. Rhetorical relations are included as the possible expansions of plan operators with communicative intentions as their effects. The intentions employed are typically defined by an application system or a research interest— for example, Suthers (1991) presents a useful set for generating pedagogically adequate explanations, others (McKeown, 1985; Reiter, Mellish, et al., 1992) adopt sets of possible responses to questions addressed to databases. The lack of clear definitions for what is to be accepted as an *intention* constitutes a substantial theoretical problem.

Whereas text schemata, which are now generally interpreted as pre-compiled plan sequences, and rhetorical structuring impose text structure on information, there are cases where it is argued that it is better for the information to be expressed imposes its structure more freely on text. Such *data-driven* approaches (cf. Hovy, 1988; Kittredge, Korelsky, et al., 1991; Suthers, 1991; Meteer, 1991; McDonald, 1992), allow an improved opportunistic response to the contingencies of particular generation situations. Data-driven critics can be combined with the top-down planning of rhetorical structures in order to improve structures according to *aggregation* rules (Hovy, 1993) or text heuristics (Scott & de Souza, 1990). A variation on data-driven content selection is offered by allowing transformation of the information itself, by means of logical inference rules defined over the knowledge base (e.g., Horacek, 1990).

Finally, a further active area of research is the addition of dynamic constraints on the construction of rhetorical structures. Two examples of such constraints are the use of *focus* (McCoy & Cheng, 1991) and *thematic development* (Hovy, Lavid, et al., 1992) to direct selection among alternative rhetorical organizations.

4.3.2 Limitations

Although an increasing number of systems find the use of rhetorical relations, augmented in the ways described above, an effective means of planning text, a lack of clarity in the definitions of rhetorical relations and weaknesses in their processing schemes result in some inherent limitations. These limitations are often hidden in specific contexts of use by hardwiring decisions and constraints that would most cases need to be explicitly represented as linguistic resources and decisions. Success in the particular case should therefore always be reconsidered in terms of the cost of re-use.

The selection of appropriate granularities for the presentation of information remains an unsolved problem. Information will be packaged into units depending on contingencies of that information's structure, on the text purpose, on the expected audience, on the writer's biases, etc. This general aggregation problem requires solutions that go beyond specific heuristics.

Also problematic is the assumption that a rhetorical structure can decompose a text down to the granularity of inputs required for surface generators. Current systems impose more or less *ad hoc* mappings from the smallest segments of the rhetorical structure to their realizations in clauses. Much fine-scaled text flexibility is thus sacrificed (cf. Meteer, 1991); this also reduces the multilingual effectiveness of such accounts.

Finally, algorithms for deep generation remain in a very early stage of development. It is clear that top-down planning is not sufficient. The interdependencies between many disparate kinds of information suggest the application of constraint-resolution techniques (Paris & Maier, 1991) (as shown in the example plan operator given above) , but this has not yet been carried out for substantial deep generation components. The kinds of inferences typically supported in deep generation components are also limited, and so more powerful inference techniques (e.g., abduction Lascarides & Oberlander, 1992; decompositional, causal-link planning Young, Moore, et al., 1994) may be appropriate.

4.3.3   Future Directions

Computational components responsible for deep generation are still most often shaped by their concrete contexts of use, rather than by established theoretical principles. The principal problem of deep generation is thus one of uncovering the nature of the necessary decisions underlying textual presentation and of organizing the space of such decisions appropriately. It is crucial that methodologies and theoretical principles be developed for this kind of linguistic description.

Furthermore, current work on more sophisticated inferencing capabilities need to be brought to bear on deep generation. Important here, however, is to ensure that this is done with respect to sufficiently complex sources of linguistic constraint. Approaches rooted in *mainstream* (computational) linguistics posit fewer linguistic constraints in favor of more powerful inferencing over common sense knowledge. Shieber (1993), for example, divides generation generally into the *generator* (i.e., surface generator: mapping semantics to syntax) and the *reasoner* (the rest: pragmatics), whereby inferences are allowed to blend into common sense reasoning. This leaves no theoretically well-specified space of linguistic decisions separate to general inferential capabilities. The consequences of this for generation are serious; it is essential that more structured sources of constraint are made available if generation is to succeed.

Very rich, but computationally underspecified, proposals in this area can be found in functional approaches to language and text (cf. Martin, 1992); results here suggest that the space of linguistic text organizational decisions is highly complex—similar to the kind of complexity found within grammars and lexicons. One methodology to improve the status of such accounts is then to use the control requirements of grammars and semantics as indications of the kinds of distinctions that are required at a deeper, more abstract level of organization (cf. Matthiessen, 1987; Bateman, 1991; McDonald, 1993). The richer the grammatical and semantic starting points taken here, the more detailed hypotheses concerning those deeper levels become. This then offers an important augmentation of the informationally weak approaches from structural linguistics. Sophisticated inferential capabilities *combined with* strong sources of theoretically motivated linguistic constraints appear to offer the most promising research direction. This is also perhaps the only way to obtain an appropriate balance between fine detail and generality in the linguistic knowledge proposed. New work in this area includes that of the ESPRIT Basic Research Action DANDE-LION (EP6665).

A further key problem is the availability of appropriately organized knowledge representations. Although in research the generation system and the application system are sometimes combined, this cannot be assumed to be the case in general. The information selected for presentation will therefore be drawn from a representational level which may or may not have some linguistically relevant structuring, depending on the application or generation system architecture involved. This information must then be construed in terms that can be related to some appropriate linguistic expression and, as McDonald (1994) points out with respect to application systems providing only raw numerical data, this latter step can be a difficult one in its own right. More general techniques for relating knowledge and generation intentions can only be provided if knowledge representation is guided more by the requirements of natural language. It is difficult for a knowledge engineer to appreciate just how inadequate a domain model that is constructed independently of natural language considerations—although possibly highly elegant and inferentially-adequate for some application—typically reveals itself when natural language generation is required (cf. Novak, 1991). If text generation is required, it is necessary for this to be considered at the outset in the design of any knowledge-based system; otherwise an expensive redesign or limited text generation capabilities will be unavoidable.

4.4 Chapter References

ANLP (1992). *Proceedings of the Third Conference on Applied Natural Language Processing*, Trento, Italy.

Appelt, D. E. (1985). *Planning English Sentences*. Cambridge University Press.

Appelt, D. E. (1987). Bidirectional grammars and the design of natural language generation systems. In Wilks, Y., editor, *Theoretical Issues in Natural Language Processing-3*, pages 185–191. Erlbaum, Hillsdale, New Jersey.

Bateman, J., Maier, E., Teich, E., and Wanner, L. (1991). Towards an architecture for situated text generation. In *Proceedings of the ICCICL*, Penang, Malaysia.

Bateman, J. A. (1991). Uncovering textual meanings: a case study involving systemic-functional resources for the generation of Japanese texts. In Paris, C. L., Swartout, W. R., and Mann, W. C., editors, *Natural Language Generation in Artificial Intelligence and Computational Linguistics*. Kluwer Academic.

Bateman, J. A. and Hovy, E. H. (1992). An overview of computational text generation. In Butler, C., editor, *Computers and Texts: An Applied Perspective*, pages 53–74. Basil Blackwell, Oxford, England.

Bateman, J. A., Moore, J. D., and Whitney, R. A. (1990). Upper modeling: A level of semantics for natural language processing. In IWNLG, editor, *Proceedings of the Fifth International Workshop on Natural Language Generation*, Pittsburgh, Pennsylvania. Springer-Verlag.

Block, H.-U. (1994). Compiling trace & unification grammar. In *Reversible Grammar in Natural Language Processing*, pages 155–174. Kluwer Academic Publishers.

Bresnan, J., editor (1982). *The Mental Representation of Grammatical Relations*. MIT Press, Cambridge, Massachusetts.

Busemann, S. (1990). *Generierung natürlicher Sprache mit Generalisierten Phrasenstruktur–Grammatiken.* PhD thesis, University of Saarland (Saarbrücken).

Calder, J., Reape, M., and Zeevat, H. (1989). An algorithm for generation in unification categorial grammar. In *Proceedings of the Fourth Conference of the European Chapter of the Association for Computational Linguistics*, pages 233–240, Manchester. European Chapter of the Association for Computational Linguistics.

Cawsey, A. (1989). *Generating Explanatory Discourse: A Plan-Based, Interactive Approach.* PhD thesis, University of Edinburgh.

COLING (1988). *Proceedings of the 12th International Conference on Computational Linguistics*, Budapest.

Dale, R. (1990). Generating receipes: An overview of epicure. In Dale, R., Mellish, C. S., and Zock, M., editors, *Current Research in Natural Language Generation*, pages 229–255. Academic Press, London.

Dale, R., Hovy, E. H., Rösner, D., and Stock, O., editors (1992). *Aspects of Automated Natural Language Generation*. Number 587 in Lecture Notes in AI. Springer-Verlag, Heidelberg.

Dale, R., Mellish, C. S., and Zock, M., editors (1990). *Current Research in Natural Language Generation*. Academic Press, London.

Den, Y. (1994). Generalized chart algorithm: An efficient procedure for cost-based abduction. In *Proceedings of the 32nd Annual Meeting of the Association for Computational Linguistics*, Las Cruces, New Mexico. Association for Computational Linguistics.

DeSmedt, K. and Kempen, G. (1987). Incremental sentence production, self-correction and coordination. In Kempen, G., editor, *Natural Language Generation*, pages 365–376. Martinus Nijhoff, Dordrecht.

Dymetman, M. and Isabelle, P. (1988). Reversible logic grammars for machine translation. In *Proceedings of the Second International Conference on Theoretical and Methodological issues in Machine Translation of Natural Languages*, Pittsburgh, Pennsylvania.

Dymetman, M., Isabelle, P., and Perrault, F. (1990). A symmetrical approach to parsing and generation. In Karlgren, H., editor, *Proceedings of the 13th International Conference on Computational Linguistics*, pages 90–96, Helsinki. ACL.

Elhadad, M. (1992). *Using Argumentation to Control Lexical Choice: A Functional Unification-Based Approach*. PhD thesis, Computer Science Department, Columbia University.

Elhadad, M. and Robin, J. (1992). Controlling content realization with functional unification grammars. In Dale, R., Hovy, E. H., Rösner, D., and Syock, O., editors, *Aspects of Automated Natural Language Generation*, pages 89–104. Springer, Heidelberg.

Fawcett, R. P. (1992). The state of the craft in computational linguistics: A generationist's viewpoint. Technical Report COMMUNAL Working Papers No. 2, Cardiff Computational Linguistics Unit, University of Wales.

Feiner, S. and McKeown, K. R. (1990). Coordinating text and graphics in explanation generation. In *Proceedings of the AAAI-90*, pages 442–449, Boston. American Association for Artificial Intelligence.

Gardent, C. and Plainfossé, A. (1990). Generating from a deep structure. In Karlgren, H., editor, *Proceedings of the 13th International Conference on Computational Linguistics*, pages 127–132, Helsinki. ACL.

Gazdar, G., Klein, E., Pullum, G., and Sag, I. (1985). *Generalized Phrase Structure Grammar*. Blackwell.

Gerdemann, D. and Hinrichs, E. W. (1990). Functor-driven generation with categorial-unification grammars. In Karlgren, H., editor, *Proceedings of the 13th International Conference on Computational Linguistics*, pages 145–150, Helsinki. ACL.

Gerdemann, D. D. (1991). *Parsing and Generation of Unification Grammars*. PhD thesis, University of Illinois. Also Cognitive Science Technical Report CS-91-06.

Goldman, N. (1975). Conceptual generation. In Schank, R., editor, *Conceptual Information Processing*. North-Holland, Amsterdam.

Horacek, H. (1990). The architecture of a generation component in a complete natural language dialogue system. In Dale, R., Mellish, C. S., and Zock, M., editors, *Current Research in Natural Language Generation*, pages 193–227. Academic Press, London.

Hovy, E., Lavid, J., Maier, E., Mittal, V., and Paris, C. (1992). Employing knowledge resources in a new text planner architecture. In *Aspects of automated natural language generation*, pages 57–72. Springer-Verlag, Berlin.

Hovy, E. H. (1988). *Generating Natural Language under Pragmatic Constraints.* Lawrence Erlbaum, Hillsdale, New Jersey.

Hovy, E. H. (1988). Planning coherent multisentential text. In *Proceedings of the 26th Annual Meeting of the Association for Computational Linguistics,* SUNY, Buffalo, New York. Association for Computational Linguistics.

Hovy, E. H. (1993). Automated discourse generation using discourse relations. *Artificial Intelligence,* 63:341–385.

Hovy, E. H. and Arens, Y. (1991). Automatic generation of formatted text. In *Proceedings of the 8th AAAI Conference,* Anaheim, California. American Association for Artificial Intelligence.

Hovy, E. H. and Knight, K. (1993). Motivation for shared ontologies: An example from the Pangloss collaboration. In *Proceedings of the Workshop on Knowledge Sharing and Information Interchange,* Chambery, France.

Jacobs, P. S. (1988). Achieving bidirectionality. In *Proceedings of the 12th International Conference on Computational Linguistics,* pages 267–274, Budapest.

Jameson, A. (1987). How to appear to be conforming to the 'maxims' even if you prefer to violate them. In Kempen, G., editor, *Natural Language Generation: Recent Advances in Artificial Intelligence, Psychology, and Linguistics,* pages 19–42. Kluwer Academic, Boston, Dordrecht.

Jameson, A. and Wahlster, W. (1982). User modelling in anaphora generation: Ellipsis and definite description. In *Proceedings of the 1982 European Conference on Artificial Intelligence,* pages 222–227, Orsay, France.

Karlgren, H., editor (1990). *Proceedings of the 13th International Conference on Computational Linguistics,* Helsinki. ACL.

Kempen, G., editor (1987). *Natural Language Generation: Recent Advances in Artificial Intelligence, Psychology, and Linguistics.* Kluwer Academic, Boston, Dordrecht.

Kittredge, R., Korelsky, T., and Rambow, O. (1991). On the need for domain communication knowledge. *Computational Intelligence,* 7(4):305–314.

Kukich, K. (1983). *Knowledge-Based Report Generation: A Knowledge-Engineering Approach.* PhD thesis, University of Pittsburgh.

Lascarides, A. and Oberlander, J. (1992). Abducing temporal discourse. In *Proceedings of the Sixth International Workshop on Natural Language Generation,* pages 167–182, Trento, Italy. Springer-Verlag. Also in Dale, Hovy, et al. (1992).

Mann, W. C., Bates, M., Grosz, B. J., McDonald, D. D., McKeown, K. R., and Swartout, W. R. (1981). Text generation: The state of the art and the literature. Technical Report RR-81-101, USC/Information Sciences Institute.

Mann, W. C. and Matthiessen, C. M. I. M. (1985). Nigel: A systemic grammar for text generation. In Benson, R. and Greaves, J., editors, *Systemic Perspectives on Discourse: Selected Papers from the Ninth International Systemics Workshop*. Ablex, London.

Mann, W. C. and Thompson, S. A. (1987). Rhetorical structure theory: description and construction of text structures. In Kempen, G., editor, *Natural Language Generation: Recent Advances in Artificial Intelligence, Psychology, and Linguistics*, pages 85–96. Kluwer Academic, Boston, Dordrecht.

Martin, J. R. (1992). *English text: systems and structure*. Benjamins, Amsterdam.

Matthiessen, C. M. I. M. (1983). Systemic grammar in computation: The Nigel case. In *Proceedings of the First Conference of the European Chapter of the Association for Computational Linguistics*, Pisa, Italy. European Chapter of the Association for Computational Linguistics.

Matthiessen, C. M. I. M. (1987). Notes on the organization of the environment of a text generation grammar. In Kempen, G., editor, *Natural Language Generation: Recent Advances in Artificial Intelligence, Psychology, and Linguistics*. Kluwer Academic, Boston, Dordrecht.

McCoy, K. F. (1986). The ROMPER system: Responding to object-related misconceptions using perspective. In *Proceedings of the 24th Annual Meeting of the Association for Computational Linguistics*, Columbia University, New York. Association for Computational Linguistics.

McCoy, K. F. and Cheng, J. (1991). Focus of attention: constraining what can be said next. In Paris, C. L., Swartout, W. R., and Mann, W. C., editors, *Natural Language Generation in Artificial Intelligence and Computational Linguistics*. Kluwer Academic.

McDonald, D. D. (1980). *Natural Language Production as a Process of Decision Making Under Constraint*. PhD thesis, Department of Computer Science and Electrical Engineering, Massachusetts Institute of Technology.

McDonald, D. D. (1992). Type-driven suppression of redundancy in the generation of inference-rich reports. In *Aspects of automated natural language generation*, pages 72–88. Springer-Verlag, Berlin.

McDonald, D. D. (1993). Issues in the choice of a source for natural language generation. *Computational Linguistics*, 19(1):191–197.

McDonald, D. D. (1994). Reversible NLP by linking the grammar to the knowledge base. In *Reversible Grammar in Natural Language Processing*, pages 257–292. Kluwer Academic Publishers.

McKeown, K. R. (1985). *Text Generation: Using Discourse Strategies and Focus Constraints to Generate Natural Language Text.* Studies in Natural Language Processing. Cambridge University Press.

McKeown, K. R., Robin, J., and Tanenblatt, M. (1993). Tailoring lexical choice to the user's vocabulary in multimedia explanation generation. In *Proceedings of the 31st Annual Meeting of the Association for Computational Linguistics*, pages 226–234, Ohio State University. Association for Computational Linguistics.

McKeown, K. R. and Swartout, W. R. (1987). Language generation and explanation. *Annual Reviews of Computer Science*, 2:401–449.

Meteer, M. (1990). *The "Generation Gap": The Problem of Expressibility in Text Planning.* PhD thesis, University of Massachusetts at Amherst.

Meteer, M., McDonald, D. D., Anderson, S., Foster, D., Gay, L., Huettner, A., and Sibun, P. (1987). Mumble-86: Design and implementation. Technical Report COINS-87-87, University of Massachusetts at Amherst.

Meteer, M. M. and Shaked, V. (1988). Strategies for effective paraphrasing. In *Proceedings of the 12th International Conference on Computational Linguistics*, Budapest.

Meteer, M. W. (1991). Bridging the generation gap between text planning and linguistic realization. *Computational Intelligence*, 7(4):296–304.

Miller, G. A. (1985). Wordnet: A dictionary browser. In *Information in Data: Proceedings of the 1st Conference of the UW Centre for the New Oxford Dictionary.* University of Waterloo, Canada.

Moore, J. D. (1989). *A Reactive Approach to Explanation in Expert and Advice-Giving Systems.* PhD thesis, University of California at Los Angeles.

Moore, J. D. and Paris, C. L. (1993). Planning texts for advisory dialogues: Capturing intentional and rhetorical information. *Computational Linguistics*, 19(4):651–694.

Neumann, G. (1994). *A Uniform Computational Model for Natural Language Parsing and Generation.* PhD thesis, Universität des Saarlandes, Germany.

Neumann, G. and van Noord, G. (1994). Reversibility and self-monitoring in natural language generation. In *Reversible Grammar in Natural Language Processing*, pages 59–96. Kluwer Academic Publishers.

Novak, H.-J. (1991). Integrating a generation component into a natural language understanding system. In Herzog, O. and Rollinger, C.-R., editors, *Text understanding in* LILOG: *integrating computational linguistics and artificial intelligence, Final report on the IBM Germany* LILOG-*Project*, pages 659–669. Springer-Verlag, Berlin, Heidelberg, New York. Lecture notes in artificial intelligence, 546.

Paris, C. L. (1993a). *The Use of Explicit Models in Text Generation*. Francis Pinter, London.

Paris, C. L. (1993b). *User modelling in text generation*. Francis Pinter, London.

Paris, C. L. and Maier, E. A. (1991). Knowledge sources of decisions? In *Proceedings of the IJCAI-91 Workshop on Decision Making Throughout the Generation Process*, pages 11–17, Sydney, Australia.

Paris, C. L., Swartout, W. R., and Mann, W. C., editors (1990). *Natural Language Generation in Artificial Intelligence and Computational Linguistics*. Kluwer Academic, Boston.

Paris, C. L., Swartout, W. R., and Mann, W. C., editors (1991). *Natural Language Generation in Artificial Intelligence and Computational Linguistics*. Kluwer Academic.

Pollard, C. and Sag, I. A. (1987). *An Information-Based Approach to Syntax and Semantics: Fundamentals*. Number 13 in Center for the Study of Language and Information (CSLI) Lecture Notes. Stanford University Press and Chicago University Press.

Rambox, O. and Korelsky, T. (1992). Applied text generation. In *Proceedings of the Third Conference on Applied Natural Language Processing*, pages 40–47, Trento, Italy.

Reiter, E., Mellish, C. S., and Levine, J. (1992). Automatic generation of on-line documentation in the IDAS project. In *Proceedings of the Third Conference on Applied Natural Language Processing*, pages 64–71, Trento, Italy.

Reithinger, N. (1991). *Eine Parallele Architektur zur Inkrementellen Generierung Multimodaler Dialogbeiträge*. PhD thesis, University of the Saarland.

Rösner, D. (1986). *Ein System zur Generierung von Deutschen Texten aus Semantischen Repräsentationen*. PhD thesis, University of Stuttgart.

Scott, D. and de Souza, C. S. (1990). Getting the message across in RST-based generation. In Dale, R., Mellish, C. S., and Zock, M., editors, *Current Research in Natural Language Generation*, pages 47–73. Academic Press, London.

Shieber, S. M. (1988). A uniform architecture for parsing and generation. In *Proceedings of the 12th International Conference on Computational Linguistics*, Budapest.

Shieber, S. M. (1993). The problem of logical-form equivalence. *Computational Linguistics*, 19(1):179–190.

Shieber, S. M., Pereira, F. C. N., van Noord, G., and Moore, R. C. (1990). Semantic-head-driven generation. *Computational Linguistics*, 16:30–42.

Strzalkowski, T. (1989). Automated inversion of a unification parser into a unification generator. Technical Report 465, Courant Institute of Mathematical Sciences, New York University.

Strzalkowski, T. (1994). *Reversible Grammar in Natural Language Processing*. Kluwer Academic Publishers.

Strzalkowski, T., Carballo, J. P., and Marinescu, M. (1995). Natural language information retrieval: TREC-3 report. In *National Institute of Standards and Technology Special Publication on the The Third Text REtrieval Conference (TREC-3)*, Washington, DC. National Institute of Standards and Technology, U.S. Department of Commerce, U.S. Government Printing Office.

Suthers, D. (1993). *An Analysis of Explanation and its Implications for the Design of Explanation Planners*. PhD thesis, University of Massachusetts at Amherst.

Suthers, D. D. (1991). Task-appropriate hybrid architectures for explanation. *Computational Intelligence*, 7(4):315–333.

Uszkoreit, H. (1986). Categorial unification grammars. In *Proceedings of the 11th International Conference on Computational Linguistics*, Bonn. ACL.

VanNoord, G. (1990). An overview of head-driven bottom-up generation. In Dale, R., Mellish, C. S., and Zock, M., editors, *Current Research in Natural Language Generation*, pages 141–165. Academic Press, London.

VanNoord, G. J. M. (1993). *Reversibility in Natural Language Processing*. PhD thesis, University of Utrecht, The Netherlands.

Von Hahn, W., Höppner, W., Jameson, A., and Wahlster, W. (1980). The anatomy of the natural language dialogue system HAM-RPM. In Bolc, L., editor, *Natural Language Based Computer Systems*. McMillan, Münich.

Wahlster, W., André, E., Graf, W., and Rist, T. (1991). Designing illustrated texts: How language production is influenced by graphics production. In *Proceedings of the Fifth Conference of the European Chapter of the Association for Computational Linguistics*, pages 8–14, Berlin. European Chapter of the Association for Computational Linguistics.

Wedekind, J. (1988). Generation as structure driven derivation. In *Proceedings of the 12th International Conference on Computational Linguistics*, Budapest.

Young, R. M., Moore, J. D., and Pollack, M. E. (1994). Towards a principled representation of discourse plans. In *Proceedings of the Sixteenth Conference of the Cognitive Science Society*, Atlanta.

Zeevat, H., Klein, E., and Calder, J. (1987). An introduction to unification categorial grammar. In Haddock, J. N., Klein, E., and Morrill, G., editors, *Edinburgh Working Papers in Cognitive Science, volume 1: Categorial Grammar, Unification Grammar, and Parsing*, volume 1 of *Working Papers in Cognitive Science*. Centre for Cognitive Science, University of Edinburgh.

Chapter 5

Spoken Output Technologies

5.1 Overview

Yoshinori Sagisaka

ATR Interpreting Telecommunications Research Laboratories, Tokyo, Japan

5.1.1 A Global View of Synthesis Research

Speech synthesis research predates other forms of speech technology by many years. In the early days of synthesis, research efforts were devoted mainly to simulating human speech production mechanisms, using basic articulatory models based on electro-acoustic theories. Though this modeling is still one of the ultimate goals of synthesis research, advances in computer science have widened the research field to include Text-to-Speech (TtS) processing in which not only human speech generation but also text processing is modeled (Allen, Hunnicutt, et al., 1987). As this modeling is generally done by a set of rules derived, e.g., from phonetic theories and acoustic analyses, the technology is typically referred to as speech synthesis by rule.

Figure 5.1 shows the configuration of a standard TtS system. In such systems, as represented by MITalk (Allen, Hunnicutt, et al., 1987), rule-based synthesis has attained highly intelligible speech quality and can already serve in many practical uses. Ceaseless efforts have improved the quality of rule-based synthetic speech, step by step, by alternating speech characteristics analysis with the development of control rules. However, most of this progress has been system dependent, and remains deeply embedded within system architectures in impenetrable meshes of detailed rules and finely tuned control parameters. As a consequence, the expert knowledge that has been incorporated is not available for sharing commonly and can be very hard to replicate in equivalent systems by other researchers.

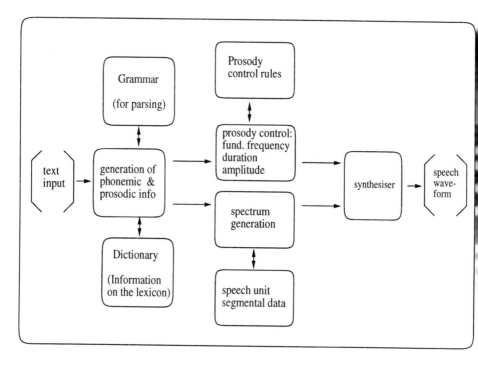

Figure 5.1: The configuration of a standard TtS system.

In contrast to this traditional rule-based approach, a corpus-based approach has also been pursued. In the corpus-based work, well-defined speech data sets have been annotated at various levels with information, such as acoustic-phonetic labels and syntactic bracketing, serving as the foundation for statistical modeling. Spectral and prosodic feature parameters of the speech data are analyzed in relation to the labeled information, and their control characteristics are quantitatively described. Based on the results of these analyses, a computational model is created and trained using the corpus. By subsequently applying the resulting model to unseen test data, its validity and any defects can be quantitatively shown. By feeding back results from such tests into the original model with extended training, further improvements can be attained in a cyclical process.

As can be easily seen, these formalized procedures characteristic of the corpus-based approach provide for a clear empirical formulation of the controls underlying speech and, with their specific training procedures and their objective evaluation results, can be easily replicated by other researchers with other databases of equivalently annotated speech. In the last decade, the corpus-based approach has been applied to both spectral and prosodic control for speech synthesis. In the following paragraphs, these speech synthesis research activities will be reviewed, with particular emphasis on the types of synthesis unit, on prosody control and on speaker charateristics. Other important topics, such as text processing for synthesis, and spectral parameters and synthesizers, will be detailed in later sections. Through this introduction to research activities, it will become clear that the corpus-based approach is the key to understanding current research directions in speech synthesis and to predicting the future outcome of synthesis technology.

5.1.2 Synthesis Segment Units

In TtS systems, speech units that are typically smaller than words are used to synthesize speech from arbitrary input text. Since there are over 10,000 different possible syllables in English, much smaller units such as phonemes and dyads (phoneme pairs) have typically been modeled. A speech segment's spectral characteristics vary with its phonetic context, as defined by neighboring phonemes, stress and positional differences, and recent studies have shown that speech quality can be greatly affected by these contextual differences (for example, see Olive, Greenwood, et al., 1993). However, in traditional rule-based synthesis, though these units have been carefully designed to take into account phonetic variations, no systematic studies have been carried out to determine how and where to best extract the acoustic parameters of units or what kind of speech corpus can be considered optimal.

To bring objective techniques into the generation of appropriate speech units, unit-selection synthesis has been proposed (Nakajima & Hamada, 1988; Takeda, Abe, et al., 1992; Sagisaka, Kaiki, et al., 1992). These speech units can be automatically determined through the analysis of a speech corpus using a measure of entropy on substrings of phone labels (Sagisaka, Kaiki, et al., 1992). In unit-selection synthesis, speech units are algorithmically extracted from a phonetically transcribed speech data set using objective measures based on acoustic and phonetic criteria. These measures indicate the contextual adequateness of units and the smoothness of the spectral transitions within and between units. Unlike traditional rule-based concatenation synthesis, speech segments are not limited to one token per type, and various types and sizes of units with different contextual variations are used. The phonetic environments of these units and their precise locations are automatically determined through the selection process. Optimal units to match an input phonetic string are then selected from the speech database to generate the target speech output.

The unit selection process involves a combinatorial search over the entire speech corpus, and consequently, fast search algorithms have been developed for this purpose as an integral part of current synthesis. This approach is in contrast to traditional rule-based synthesis where the design of the deterministic units required insights from the researcher's own knowledge and expertise. The incorporation of sophisticated but usually undescribed *knowledge* was the real bottleneck that prevented the automatic construction of synthesis systems.

Corpus-based methods provide for a specification of the speech segments required for concatenative synthesis in three factors:

1. the procedures of the unit selection algorithm;

2. the objective measures used in the selection criteria; and

3. the design of the speech corpus from which the units are extracted.

This modularization of system building is useful not only in reducing construction effort, but also in allowing precise mathematical specification of the problems and in defining ways to cope with them systematically, by improving the selection algorithms, criteria and data.

5.1.3   Prosody Control

For synthesis of natural-sounding speech, it is essential to control prosody, to ensure appropriate rhythm, tempo, accent, intonation and stress. Segmental duration control is needed to model temporal characteristics, just as fundamental frequency control is needed for tonal characteristics. In contrast to the relative sparsity of work on speech unit generation, many quantitative analyses have been carried out for prosody control. Specifically, quantitative analyses and modeling of segmental duration control have been carried out for many languages using massive annotated speech corpora (Carlson & Granström, 1986; Bartkova & Sorin, 1987; Klatt, 1987; Umeda, 1975).

Segmental duration is controlled by many language specific and universal factors. In early models, because these control factors were computed independently through the quantification of control rules, unexpected and serious errors were sometimes seen. These errors were often caused simply by the application of independently derived rules at the same time. To prevent this type of error and to assign more accurate durations, statistical optimization techniques that model the often complex interactions between all the contributing factors have more recently been used.

Traditional statistical techniques such as linear regressive analysis and tree regression analysis have been used for Japanese (Kaiki, Takeda, et al., 1992) and American English (Riley, 1992) respectively. To predict the interactions between syllable and segment level durations for British English a feed-forward neural network has been employed (Campbell, 1992). In this modeling, instead of attempting to predict the absolute duration of segments directly, their deviation from the average duration is employed to quantify the lengthening and shortening characteristics statistically. Moreover, hierarchical control has been included by splitting the calculation into the current syllable level and its constituent component levels.

While hierarchical control is desired to simulate human temporal organization mechanisms, it can be difficult to optimize such structural controls globally. Multiple split regression (MSR) uses error minimization at arbitrary hierarchical levels by defining a hierarchical error function (Iwahashi & Sagisaka, 1993). MSR incorporates both linear and tree regressions as special cases and interpolates between them by controlling the closeness of the control parameters.

Additive-multiplicative modeling, too, is also an extension of traditional linear analysis techniques, using bilinear expressions and statistical correlation analyses (Van Santen, 1992). These statistical models can optimize duration control without losing freedom of conditioned exception control.

To generate an appropriate fundamental frequency (F_0) contour when given only text as input, an intermediate prosodic structure needs to be specified. Text processing, as described in section 5.3, is needed to produce this intermediate prosodic structure. F_0 characteristics have been analyzed in relation to prosodic structure by many researchers (Maeda, 1976; Hakoda & Sato, 1980; Pierrehumbert, 1981; Liberman & Pierrehumbert, 1984; Fujisaki, 1992). As with duration control, in early models, F_0 control rules were made only by assembling independently analyzed F_0 characteristics. More recently however, statistical models have been employed to associate F_0 patterns with input linguistic information directly, without requiring estimates of the intermediate prosodic structure (Traber, 1992; Sagisaka, Kaiki, et al., 1992; Yamashita, Tanaka, et al., 1993). In these models, the same mathematical frameworks as used in duration control have been used, i.e., feed-forward neural networks, linear and tree regression models.

These computational models can be evaluated by comparing duration or F_0 values derived from the predictions of the models with actual values measured in the speech corpus for the same test input sentences. Perceptual studies have also been carried out to measure the effect of these acoustical differences on subjective evaluation scores by systematically manipulating the durations (Kato, Tsuzaki, et al., 1992). It is hoped that a systematic series of perceptual studies will reveal more about human sensitivities to the naturalness and intelligibility of synthesized speech scientifically and that time consuming subjective evaluation will no longer be needed.

5.1.4 Speaker Characteristics Control

Speech waveforms contain not only linguistic information but also speaker voice characteristics, as manifested in the glottal waveform of voice excitation and in the global spectral features representing vocal tract characteristics. The glottal waveform has been manipulated using a glottal source model (Fant, Liljencrants, et al., 1985) and female voices (more difficult to model) have been successfully synthesized. However, it is very difficult to fully automate such parameter extraction procedures and the establishment of an automatic analysis-synthesis scheme is longed for.

As for vocal tract characteristics, spectral conversion methods have been proposed that employ the speaker adaptation technology studied in speech recognition (Abe, Nakamura, et al., 1990; Matsumoto, Maruyama, et al., 1994; Moulines & Sagisaka, 1995). This technology is also a good example of the corpus-based approach. By deciding on a spectral mapping algorithm, a measure for spectral distance and a speech corpora for training of the mapping, non-parametric voice conversion is defined. The mapping accuracy can be measured using the spectral distortion measures commonly used in speech coding and recognition.

5.1.5   Future Directions

As indicated in the above paragraphs, speech synthesis will be studied continuously, aiming all the while at more natural and intelligible speech. It is quite certain that TtS technology will create new speech output applications associated with the improvement of speech quality. To accelerate this improvement, it is necessary to pursue research on speech synthesis in such a way that each step forward can be evaluated objectively and can be shared among researchers. To this end, a large amount of commonly available data is indispensable, and objective evaluation methods should be pursued in relation to perceptual studies. An important issue of concern to speech synthesis technology is the variability of output speech. As illustrated by recent advances in speaker characteristics control, the adaptation of vocal characteristics is one dimension of such variability. We also have to consider variabilities resulting from human factors, such as speaking purpose, utterance situation and the speaker's mental state. These paralinguistic factors cause changes in speaking styles reflected in a change of both voice quality and prosody. The investigation of these variations will contribute to elaborate synthetic speech quality and widen its application fields.

Such progress is not only restricted to TtS technology; future technologies related to the furtherance of human capabilities are also being developed. Human capabilities, such as the acquisition of spoken language, bear strong relations to the knowledge acquisition used in developing speech synthesis systems. Useful language training tools and educational devices can therefore be expected to come out of the pursuit and modeling of such knowledge acquisition processes. The corpus-based approach is well suited to this purpose, and inductive learning from speech corpora will give us hints on the directions this research must take. To pursue these new possibilities, it is essential for speech synthesis researchers to collaborate with researchers in other fields related to spoken language, and to freshly introduce the methodologies and knowledge acquired in those encounters.

5.2   Synthetic Speech Generation

Christophe d'Alessandro & Jean-Sylvain Liénard

LIMSI-CNRS, Orsay, France

Speech generation is the process which allows the transformation of a string of phonetic and prosodic symbols into a synthetic speech signal. The quality of the result is a function of the quality of the string, as well as of the quality of the generation process itself. For a review of speech generation in English, the reader is referred to Flanagan and Rabiner (1973) and Klatt (1987). Recent developments can be found in Bailly and Benoît (1992), and in Van Santen, Sproat, et al. (1995).

Let us examine first what is requested today from a text-to-speech (TtS) system. Usually, two quality criteria are proposed. The first one is intelligibility, which can be measured by taking into account several kinds of units (phonemes, syllables, words, phrases). The second one, more difficult to define, is often labeled as *pleasantness* or *naturalness*. Actually the concept of naturalness may be related to the concept of realism in the field of image synthesis: the goal is not to restitute the reality but to suggest it. Thus, listening to a synthetic voice must allow the listener to attribute this voice to some *pseudo-speaker* and to perceive some kind of expressivity as well as providing some indices characterizing the speaking style and the particular situation of elocution. For this purpose the corresponding extra-linguistic information must be supplied to the system (Granström & Nord, 1992).

Most of the present TtS systems produce an acceptable level of intelligibility, but the naturalness dimension, the ability to control expressivity, speech style and pseudo-speaker identity are still poorly mastered. Let us mention, however, that users demands vary to a large extent according to the field of application: general public applications such as telephonic information retrieval need maximal realism and naturalness, whereas some applications involving professionals (process or vehicle control) or highly motivated persons (visually impaired, applications in hostile environments) demand intelligibility with the highest priority.

5.2.1 Input to the Speech Generation Component

The input string to the speech generation component is basically a phonemic string resulting from the grapheme to phoneme converter. It is usually enriched with a series of prosodic marks denoting the accents and pauses. With few exceptions, the phoneme set of a given language is well defined; thus, the symbols are not ambiguous. However the transcript may represent either a sequence of abstract linguistic units (phonemes) or a sequence of acoustic-phonetic units (phones or transitional segments). In the former case (phonological or normative transcript), it may be necessary to apply some transformations to obtain the acoustical transcript. In order to make this distinction clearer, let us take a simple example in French. The word *médecin* (medical doctor) may appear in a pronunciation dictionary as: "mé–de–cin" /me–dœ–s$\tilde{\varepsilon}$/, which is perfectly correct. But when embedded in a sentence it is usually pronounced in a different way: "mèt–cin" /mɛt–s$\tilde{\varepsilon}$/. The tense vowel "é" /e/ is realized as its lax counterpart "è" /ɛ/, the "e" /œ/ disappears, the three syllables are replaced by only two, and the voicing of the plosive /d/ is neutralized by the presence of the unvoiced /s/ which follows. Without such rules, the output of the synthesizer may be intelligible, but it may be altered from the point of view of naturalness. Such transformations are not simple; they imply not only a set of phonological rules, but also some considerations on the speech style, as well as on the supposed socio-geographical origin of the pseudo-speaker and on the speech rate.

Analogously, the prosodic symbols must be processed differently according to their abstraction level. However, the problem is more difficult, because there is no general agreement in the phonetic community on a set of prosodic marks that would have a universal value, even within the framework of a given language. A noticeable exception is the ToBI system, for transcription of English (Pitrelli, Beckman, et al., 1994). Each synthesis system defines its own repertory of prosodic entities and symbols, that can be classified into three categories: phonemic durations, accents and pauses.

5.2.2   Prosody Generation

Usually only the accents and pauses, deduced from the text, are transcribed in the most abstract form of the prosodic string. But this abstract form has to be transformed into a flow of parameters in order to control the synthesizer. The parameters to be computed include the fundamental frequency (F_0), both the duration of each speech segment, and its intensity, and timber. A melodic (or intonational) model and a duration model are needed to implement the prosodic structure computed by the text processing component of the speech synthesizer.

F_0 evolution, often considered the main support of prosody, depends on phonetic, lexical, syntactic and pragmatic factors, as do phonemic durations . Depending on the language under study, the melodic model is built on different levels, generally the word level (word accent) and the sentence or phrase level (phrase accent). The aim of the melodic model is to compute F_0 curves. Three major types of melodic models are currently in use for F_0 generation. The first type of melodic model is production-oriented. It aims at representing the commands governing F_0 generation. This type of model associates melodic commands with word and phrase accents. The melodic command is either an impulse or a step signal. The F_0 contour is obtained as the response of a smoothing filter to these word and phrase commands (Fujisaki & Kawai, 1988). The second type of melodic model is rooted in perception research (Hart, Collier, et al., 1990). Synthetic F_0 contours are derived from stylized natural F_0 contours. At the synthesis stage, the F_0 curves are obtained by concatenation of melodic movements: F_0 rises, F_0 falls, and flat movements. Automatic procedures for pitch contour stylization have been developed (d'Alessandro & Mertens, 1995). In the last type of melodic model, F_0 curves are implemented as a set of target values, linked by interpolation functions (Pierrehumbert, 1981).

The phonemic durations result from multifold considerations. They are in part determined from the mechanical functioning of the synthesizer when the latter is of articulatory nature, or from the duration of the prerecorded segments in the case of concatenative synthesis. Another part is related to the accent. Another one, reflecting the linguistic function of the word in the sentence, is usually related to the syntactic structure. Finally, the last part is related to the situation and pseudo-speaker's characteristics (speech rate, dialect, stress, etc.).

Two or three levels of rules are generally present in durational models. The first level represents co-intrinsic duration variations (i.e., the modification of segment durations that are due to their neighbors). The second level is the phrase level: modification of durations that are due to prosodic phrasing. Some systems also take into account a third level, the syllabic level (Campbell & Isard, 1991).

The other prosodic parameters (intensity, timber) are usually implicitly fixed from the start. However, some research is devoted to voice quality characterization or differences between male and female voices (Klatt & Klatt, 1990).

One of the most difficult problems in speech to date is prosodic modeling. A large body of problems come from text analysis (see section 5.3), but there is also room for improvement in both melodic and durational models. In natural speech the prosodic parameters interact in a way that is still unknown, in order to supply the listener with prosodic information while keeping the feeling of fluency. Understanding the interplay of these parameters is one of the hottest topics for research on speech synthesis today. For prosodic generation, a move from rule-based modeling to statistical modeling is noticeable, as in many areas of speech and language technology (Van Santen, 1994).

5.2.3 Speech Signal Generation

The last step for speech output is synthesis of the waveform, according to the segmental and prosodic parameters defined at earlier stages of processing.

Speech signal generators (the *synthesizers*) can be classified into three categories:

1. articulatory synthesizers,

2. formant synthesizers, and

3. concatenative synthesizers.

Articulatory synthesizers are physical models based on the detailed description of the physiology of speech production and on the physics of sound generation in the vocal apparatus (Parthasarathy & Coker, 1992). Typical parameters are the position and kinematics of articulators. Then the sound radiated at the mouth is computed according to equations of physics. This type of synthesizer is rather far from applications and marketing because of its cost in terms of computation and the underlying theoretical and practical problems still unsolved.

Formant synthesis is a descriptive, acoustic-phonetic approach to synthesis (Allen, Hunnicutt, et al., 1987). Speech generation is not performed by solving equations of physics in the vocal apparatus, but by modeling the main acoustic features of the speech signal (Klatt, 1980; Stevens & Bickley, 1991). The basic acoustic model is the source/filter model. The filter, described by a small set of *formants*, represents *articulation* in speech. It models speech spectra that are representative of the position and movements of articulators. The source represents *phonation*. It models the glottal flow or noise excitation signals. Both source and filter are controlled by a set of phonetic rules (typically several hundred). High-quality, rule-based formant synthesizers, including multilingual systems, have been marketed for many years.

Concatenative synthesis is based on speech signal processing of natural speech databases. The segmental database is built to reflect the major phonological features of a language. For instance, its set of phonemes is described in terms of diphone units, representing the phoneme-to-phoneme junctures. Nonuniform units are also used (diphones, syllables, words, etc.). The synthesizer concatenates (coded) speech segments, and performs some signal processing to smooth unit transitions and to match predefined prosodic schemes. Direct pitch-synchronous waveform processing is one of the most simple and popular concatenation synthesis algorithms (Moulines & Charpentier, 1990). Other systems are based on multipulse linear prediction (Atal & Remde, 1982), or harmonic plus noise models (Laroche, Stylianou, et al., 1993; Dutoit & Leich, 1993; Richard & d'Alessandro, 1994). Several high-quality concatenative synthesizers, including multilingual systems, are marketed today.

5.2.4　Trends in Speech Generation

Perceptive assessment lies among the most important aspects of speech synthesis research (Van Bezooijen & Pols, 1990; Van Santen, 1993; Kraft & Portele, 1995). When one works on phonetic rule definition or segment concatenation, a robust and quick assessment methodology is absolutely necessary to improve the system. Besides, it is also necessary in order to compare the systems to each other. As far as speech naturalness is concerned, the problem is still almost untouched. Nobody knows what speech naturalness is or, more generally, what is expected from a synthesis system once its intelligibility is rated sufficiently highly. In order to explore this domain it will be mandatory to cooperate with psychologists and human factors specialists.

Although the recent developments of speech synthesis demonstrated the power of the concatenative approach, it seems that there is much room for improvement:

1. **Choice of Non-uniforms and Multi-scale Units** (see section 5.1.2): What are the best synthesis units? This question is rooted in psycholinguistics and is a challenging problem to phonology.

2. **Speech Signal Modification:** Signal representation for speech is still an open problem, particularly for manipulation of the excitation.

3. **Voice Conversion:** What are the parameters, phonetic description, and methods for characterization of a particular speaker, and conversion of the voice of a speaker into the voice of another speaker (Valbret, Moulines, et al., 1992)?

Accurate physical modeling of speech production is still not mature for technological applications. Nevertheless, as both basic knowledge on speech production and the power of computers increase, articulatory synthesis will help in improving formant-based methods, take advantage of computational physics (fluid dynamics equations for the vocal apparatus), and better mimic the physiology of human speech production.

Synthesis of human voice is not limited to speech synthesis. Since the beginning of speech synthesis research, many workers also paid some attention to the musical aspects of voice and to singing (Sundberg, 1987). Like TtS, synthesis of singing finds its motivations both in science and technology: on the one hand singing analysis and synthesis is a challenging field for scientific research, and on the other hand, it can serve for music production (contemporary music, film and disk industries, electronic music industry). As in speech synthesis, two major types of techniques are used for signal generation: descriptive-acoustic methods (rule-based formant synthesis) and signal processing methods (modification/concatenation of pre-recorded singing voices).

5.2.5   Future Directions

Prosodic modeling is probably the domain from which most of the improvements will come. In the long run, it may be argued that the main problems to be solved deal mainly with mastering the linguistic and extra-linguistic phenomena related to prosody, which reflect problems of another kind, related to oral person-to-person and person-to-machine interactions.

Concerning the phonetic-acoustic generation process, it may be foreseen that in the short run concatenative and articulatory syntheses will be boosted by the development of the microcomputer industry. By using off-the-shelf components, it is already possible to implement a system using a large number of speech segments, with several variants that take into account contextual and prosodic effects, even for several speakers. This tendency can only be reinforced by the apparently unlimited evolution of computer speed and memory capacity, as well as by the fact that the computer industry not only provides the tools but also the market: speech synthesis nowadays must be considered to be one of the most attractive aspects of virtual reality; it will benefit from the development of multimedia and information highways.

5.3   Text Interpretation for TtS Synthesis

Richard Sproat

AT&T Bell Labs, Murray Hill, New Jersey, USA

The problem of converting text into speech for some language can naturally be broken down into two subproblems. One subproblem involves the conversion of linguistic parameter specifications (e.g., phoneme sequences, accentual parameters) into parameters (e.g., formant parameters, concatenative unit indices, pitch time/value pairs) that can drive the actual synthesis of speech. The other subproblem involves the computation of these linguistic parameter specifications from input text, which for the present discussion we will assume to be written in the standard orthographic representation for the language in question, and electronically coded in a standard scheme such as ASCII, ISO, JIS, BIG5, GB, and the like, depending upon the language. It is this second problem that is the topic of this section.

In any language, orthography is an imperfect representation of the underlying linguistic form. To illustrate this point, and to introduce some of the issues that we will discuss in this section, consider an English sentence such as *Give me a ticket to Dallas or give me back my money*: see Figure 5.2.

Intonational Phrasing

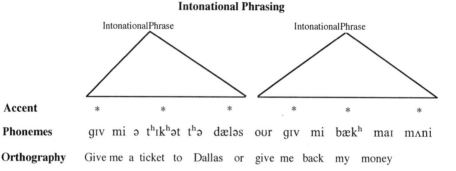

Figure 5.2: Some linguistic structures associated with the analysis of the sentence, "Give me a ticket to Dallas or give me back my money."

One of the first things that an English TtS system would need to do is tokenize the input into words: for English this is not generally difficult though it is more complicated for some other languages. A pronunciation then needs to be computed for each word; in English, given the irregularity of the orthography, this process involves a fair amount of lexical lookup though other processes are involved too. Some of the words in the sentence should be accented; in this particular case, a reasonable accentuation would involve accenting *content* words like *give, ticket, Dallas, back* and *money*, and leaving the other words unaccented. Then we might consider breaking the input into prosodic phrases: in this case, it would be reasonable to intone the sentence as if there were a comma between *Dallas* and *or*. Thus, various kinds of linguistic information need to be extracted from the text, but only in the case of word boundaries can this linguistic information be said to be represented directly in the orthography. In this survey, I will focus on the topics of tokenization into words; the pronunciation of those words; the assignment of phrasal accentuation; and the assignment of prosodic phrases. An important area about which I will say little, is what is often termed *text normalization*, comprising things like end-of-sentence detection, the expansion of abbreviations, and the treatment of acronyms and numbers.

5.3.1   Tokenization

As noted above, one of the first stages of analysis of the text input is the tokenization of the input into words. For many languages, including English, this problem is fairly easy in that one can, to a first approximation, assume that word boundaries coincide with whitespace or punctuation in the input text. In contrast, in many Asian languages the situation is not so simple, since spaces are never used in the orthographies of those languages to delimit words. In

Chinese for example, whitespace generally only occurs in running text at para-graph boundaries. The Chinese alphabet consists of several thousand distinct elements, usually termed *characters*. With few exceptions, characters are mono-syllabic. More controversially, one can also claim that most characters represent morphemes.

Just as words in English may consist of one or more morphemes, so Chinese words may also consist of one or more morphemes. In a TtS system there are various reasons why it is important to segment Chinese text into words (as op-posed to having the system read the input character-by-character). Probably the easiest of these to understand is that quite a few characters have more than one possible pronunciation, where the pronunciation chosen depends in many cases upon the particular word in which the character finds itself. A minimal re-quirement for word segmentation would appear to be an on-line dictionary that enumerates the word forms of the language. Indeed, virtually all Chinese seg-menters reported in the literature contain a reasonably large dictionary (Chen & Liu, 1992; Wu & Tseng, 1993; Lin, Chiang, et al., 1993; Sproat, Shih, et al., 1994). Given a dictionary, however, one is still faced with the problem of how to use the lexical information to segment an input sentence: it is often the case that a sentence has more than one possible segmentation, so some method has to be employed to decide on the best analysis. Both heuristic (e.g., a greedy algorithm that finds the longest word at any point) and statistical approaches (algorithms that find the most probable sequence of words according to some model) have been applied to this problem.

While a dictionary is certainly a necessity for doing Chinese segmentation, it is not sufficient, since in Chinese, as in English, any given text is likely to contain some words that are not found in the dictionary. Among these are words that are derived via morphologically productive processes, personal names and foreign names in transliteration. For morphologically complex forms, standard tech-niques for morphological analysis can be applied (Koskenniemi, 1983; Tzouk-ermann & Liberman, 1990; Karttunen, Kaplan, et al., 1992; Sproat, 1992), though some augmentation of these techniques is necessary in the case of statis-tical methods (Sproat, Shih, et al., 1994). Various statistical and non-statistical methods for handling personal and foreign names have been reported; see, for example, Chang, Chen, et al. (1992); Wang, Li, et al. (1992); Sproat, Shih, et al. (1994).

The period since the late 1980s has seen an explosion of work on the various problems of Chinese word segmentation, due in large measure to the increasing availability of large electronic corpora of Chinese text. There is still, however, much work left to be done in this area, both in improving algorithms, and in the development of reproducible evaluation criteria, the current lack of which makes fair comparisons of different approaches well-nigh impossible.

5.3.2   Word Pronunciation

Once the input is tokenized into words, the next obvious thing that must be done is to compute a pronunciation (or a set of possible pronunciations) for the words, given the orthographic representation of those words. The simplest approach is to have a set of *letter-to-sound rules* that simply map sequences of graphemes into sequences of phonemes, along with possible diacritic information, such as stress placement. This approach is naturally best suited to languages like Spanish or Finnish, where there is a relatively simple relation between orthography and phonology. For languages like English, however, it has generally been recognized that a highly accurate word pronunciation module must contain a pronouncing dictionary that at the very least records words whose pronunciation could not be predicted on the basis of general rules.[1]   Of course, the same problems of coverage that were noted in the Chinese segmentation problem also apply in the case of pronouncing dictionaries: many text words occur that are not to be found in the dictionary, the most important of these being morphological derivatives from known words, or previously unseen personal names.

For morphological derivatives, standard techniques for morphological analysis can be applied to achieve a morphological decomposition for a word; see Allen, Hunnicutt, et al. (1987). The pronunciation of the whole can then in general be computed from the (presumably known) pronunciation of the morphological parts, applying appropriate phonological rules of the language. Morphological analysis is of some use in the prediction of name pronunciation too, since some names are derived from others via fairly productive morphological processes (cf., *Robertson* and *Robert*). However, this is not always the case, and one must also rely on other methods. One such method involves computing the pronunciation of a new name by analogy with the pronunciation of a similar name (Coker, Church, et al., 1990; Golding, 1991) (and see also Dedina & Nusbaum, 1991 for a more general application of analogical reasoning to word pronunciation). For example, if we have the name *Califano* in our dictionary and know its pronunciation, then we can compute the pronunciation of a hypothetical name *Balifano* by noting that both names share the final substring *alifano*: *Balifano* can then be pronounced on analogy by removing the phoneme /k/, corresponding to the letter *C* in *Califano*, and replacing it with the phoneme /b/. Yet another approach to handling proper names involves computing the language of origin of a name, typically by means of n-gram models of letter sequences for the various languages; once the origin of the name is guessed, *language*-specific pronunciation rules can be invoked to pronounce the name (Church, 1985; Vitale, 1991).

In many languages, there are word forms that are inherently ambiguous in pronunciation, and for which a word pronunciation module as just described can only return a set of possible pronunciations, from which the most reasonable one must then be chosen. For example, the word *bass* rhymes with *lass* if it denotes a type of fish, and is homophonous with *base* if it denotes a musical range. An approach to this problem is discussed in Yarowsky (1994) (and see also Sproat,

---

[1]Some connectionist approaches to letter-to-sound conversion have attempted to replace traditional letter-to-sound rules with connectionist networks, and at the same time eschew the use of online dictionaries (for example, Sejnowski & Rosenberg, 1987). For English at least, these approaches would appear to have met with only limited success, however.

Hirschberg, et al., 1992). The method starts with a training corpus containing tagged examples in the context of each pronunciation of a homograph. Significant local evidence (e.g., *n*-grams containing the homograph in question that are strongly associated to one or another pronunciation) and wide-context evidence (i.e., words that occur anywhere in the same sentence that are strongly associated to one of the pronunciations) are collected into a decision list, wherein each piece of evidence is ordered according to its strength (log likelihood of each pronunciation given the evidence). A novel instance of the homograph is then disambiguated by finding the strongest piece of evidence in the context in which the novel instance occurs, and letting that piece of evidence decide the matter. It is clear that the above-described method can also be applied to other formally similar problems in TtS, such as abbreviation expansion: for example is *St.* to be expanded as *Saint* or *Street*?

5.3.3 Accentuation

In many languages, various words in a sentence are associated with *accents*, which are often manifested as upward or downward movements of fundamental frequency. Usually, not every word in the sentence bears an accent, however, and the decision of which words should be accented and which ones should not is one of the problems that must be addressed by a TtS system. More precisely, we will want to distinguish three levels of *prominence*, two being *accented* and *unaccented*, as just described, and the third being *cliticized*. Cliticized words are unaccented but additionally lack word stress, with the consequence that they tend to be durationally short.

A good first step in assigning accents is to make the accentual determination on the basis of broad lexical categories or parts of speech of words. Content words—nouns, verbs, adjectives and perhaps adverbs—tend, in general, to be accented; function words, including auxiliary verbs and prepositions, tend to be deaccented; short function words tend to be cliticized. Naturally this presumes some method for assigning parts of speech, and, in particular, for disambiguating words like *can* which can be either content words (in this case, a verb or a noun), or function words (in this case, an auxiliary); fortunately, somewhat robust methods for part-of-speech tagging exist (e.g., Church, 1988). Of course, a finer-grained part-of-speech classification also reveals a finer-grained structure to the accenting problem. For example, the distinction between prepositions (*up the spout*) and particles (*give up*) is important in English since prepositions are typically deaccented or cliticized while particles are typically accented (Hirschberg, 1993).

But accenting has a wider function than merely communicating lexical category distinctions between words. In English, one important set of constructions where accenting is more complicated than what might be inferred from the above discussion are complex noun phrases—basically, a noun preceded by one or more adjectival or nominal modifiers. In a *discourse-neutral* context, some constructions are accented on the final word (*Madison* **Avenue**), some on the penultimate (**Wall** *Street*, *kitchen* **towel** *rack*), and some on an even earlier word (**sump** *pump factory*). Accenting on nominals longer than two words is generally predictable given that one can compute the nominal's structure (itself a non-trivial problem), and given that one knows the accentuation pattern of the binary nominals embedded in the larger construction (Liberman & Prince, 1977; Liberman & Sproat, 1992; Sproat, 1994). Most linguistic work on nominal accent (e.g., Fudge, 1984; Liberman & Sproat, 1992, though see Ladd, 1984) has concluded that the primary determinants of accenting are semantic, but that within each semantic class there are lexically or semantically determined exceptions. For instance, right-hand accent is often found in cases where the left-hand element denotes a location or time for the second element (cf. *morning* **paper**), but there are numerous lexical exceptions (**morning** *sickness*). Recent computational models—e.g., Monaghan (1990); Sproat (1994)—have been partly successful at modeling the semantic and lexical generalizations; for example Sproat (1994) uses a combination of hand-built lexical and semantic rules, as well as a statistical model based on a corpus of nominals hand-tagged with accenting information.

Accenting is not only sensitive to syntactic structure and semantics, but also to properties of the discourse. One straightforward effect is *givenness*. In a case like *my son badly wants a <u>dog</u>, but I am* **allergic** *to <u>dogs</u>*, where the second occurrence of *dogs* would often be de-accented because of the previous mention of *dog*. (See Hirschberg (1993) for a discussion of how to model this and other discourse effects, as well as the syntactic and semantic effects previously mentioned, in a working TtS module.) While humanlike accenting capabilities are possible in many cases, there are still many unsolved problems, a point we return to in the concluding subsection.

5.3.4 Prosodic Phrasing

The final topic that we address is the problem of chunking a long sentence into prosodic phrases. In reading a long sentence, speakers will normally break the sentence up into several phrases, each of which can be said to *stand alone* as an intonational unit. If punctuation is used liberally, so that there are relatively few words between the commas, semicolons or periods, then a reasonable guess at an appropriate phrasing would be simply to break the sentence at the punctuation marks—though this is not always appropriate (O'Shaughnessy, 1989). The real problem comes when long stretches occur without punctuation; in such cases, human readers would normally break the string of words into phrases, and the problem then arises of where to place these breaks.

The simplest approach is to have a list of words, typically function words, that are likely indicators of good places to break (Klatt, 1987). One has to use some caution, however, since while a particular function word like *and* may coincide with a plausible phrase break in some cases, in other cases it might coincide with a particularly *poor* place to break: *I was forced to sit through a dog <u>and</u> pony show that lasted most of Wednesday afternoon.*

An obvious improvement would be to incorporate an accurate syntactic parser and then derive the prosodic phrasing from the syntactic groupings:

prosodic phrases usually do not coincide exactly with major syntactic phrases, but the two are typically not totally unrelated either. Prosodic phrasers that incorporate syntactic parsers are discussed in O'Shaughnessy (1989); Bachenko and Fitzpatrick (1990). O'Shaughnessy's system relies on a small lexicon of (mostly function) words that are reliable indicators of the beginnings of syntactic groups: articles such as *a* or *the* clearly indicate the beginnings of noun groups, for example. This lexicon is augmented by suffix-stripping rules that allow for part-of-speech assignment to words where this information can be predicted from the morphology. A bottom-up parser is then used to construct phrases based upon the syntactic-group-indicating words. Bachenko and Fitzpatrick employ a somewhat more sophisticated deterministic syntactic parser (FIDDITCH Hindle, 1983) to construct a syntactic analysis for a sentence; the syntactic phrases are then transduced into prosodic phrases using a set of heuristics.

But syntactic parsing *sensu stricto* may not be necessary in order to achieve reasonable predictions of prosodic phrase boundaries. Wang and Hirschberg (1992) report on a corpus-based statistical approach that uses CART (Breiman, Friedman, et al., 1984; Riley, 1989) to train a decision tree on transcribed speech data. In training, the dependent variable was the human prosodic phrase boundary decision, and the independent variables were generally properties that were computable automatically from the text, including: part of speech sequence around the boundary; the location of the edges of long noun phrases (as computable from automatic methods such as Church, 1988; Sproat, 1994); distance of the boundary from the edges of the sentence, and so forth.

5.3.5 Future Directions

This section has given an overview of a selected set of the problems that arise in the conversion of textual input into a linguistic representation suitable for input to a speech synthesizer, and has outlined a few solutions to these problems. As a result of these solutions, current *high-end* TtS systems produce speech output that is quite intelligible and, in many cases, quite natural. For example, in English it is possible to produce TtS output where the vast majority of words in a text are correctly pronounced, where words are mostly accented in a plausible fashion, and where prosodic phrase boundaries are chosen at mostly reasonable places. Nonetheless, even the best systems make mistakes on unrestricted text, and there is much room for improvement in the approaches taken to solving the various problems, though one can of course often improve performance marginally by tweaking existing approaches.

Perhaps the single most important unsolved issue that affects performance on many of the problems discussed in this section is that full machine *understanding* of unrestricted text is currently not possible, and so TtS systems can be fairly said to not know what they are talking about. This point comes up rather clearly in the treatment of accenting in English, though the point could equally well be made in other areas. As I noted above, previously mentioned items are often deaccented, and this would be appropriate for the second occurrence of *dog* in the sentence *my son badly wants a <u>dog</u>, but I am* **allergic** *to <u>dogs</u>*. But a moment's reflection will reveal that what is crucial is not the repetition of the word *dog*, but rather the repetition of the concept *dog*. That what is relevant is semantic or conceptual categories and not simply words becomes clear when one considers that one also would often de-accent a word if a conceptual supercategory of that word had been previously mentioned: *My son wants a <u>labrador</u>, but I'm* **allergic** *to <u>dogs</u>*. Various solutions involving semantic networks (such as WordNet) might be contemplated, but so far no promising results have been reported.

Note that *message*-to-speech systems have an advantage over *text*-to-speech systems specifically in that message-to-speech systems in some sense *know* what they are talking about because one can code as much semantic knowledge into the initial message as one desires. But TtS systems must compute everything from orthography which, as we have seen, is not very informative about a large number of linguistic properties of speech.

5.4   Spoken Language Generation

Kathleen R. McKeown[a] & Johanna D. Moore[b]

[a] Columbia University, New York, New York, USA
[b] University of Pittsburgh, Pittsburgh, Pennsylvania, USA

Interactive natural language capabilities are needed for a wide range of today's intelligent systems: expert systems must explain their results and reasoning, intelligent assistants must collaborate with users to perform tasks, tutoring systems must teach domain concepts and critique students' problem-solving strategies, and information delivery systems must help users find and make sense of the information they need. These applications require that a system be capable of generating coherent multisentential responses, and interpreting and responding to users' subsequent utterances in the context of the ongoing interaction.

Spoken language generation allows for provision of responses as part of an interactive human-machine dialogue, where speech is one medium for the response. This research topic draws from the fields of both natural language generation and speech synthesis. It differs from synthesis in that speech is generated from an abstract representation of concepts rather than from text. While a relatively under-emphasized research problem, the ability to generate spoken responses is clearly crucial for interactive situations, in particular when:

1. the user's hands and/or eyes are busy;

2. screen real estate is at a premium;

3. time is critical; or

4. system and user are communicating via a primarily audio channel such as the telephone.

Like written language generation, spoken language generation requires determining what concepts to include and how to realize them in words, but critically also requires determining intonational form. Several problems are particularly pertinent to the spoken context:

- The need to model and use knowledge about hearer goals, hearer background, and past discourse in determining content and form of a response. While the written context can include a general audience (e.g., for report generation), responses in an interactive dialogue are intended for a particular person and, to be useful, must take that person into account.

- What kind of language should be generated given a spoken context? Given the lack of visual memory that a text provides, the form required for speech is likely to be quite different from that found in text.

- In the process of determining the content and form of the response, how can a system provide information to control intonation, which is known to provide crucial clues as to intended meaning.

5.4.1 State of the Art

The field of spoken language generation is in its infancy, with very few researchers working on systems that deal with all aspects of producing spoken language responses, i.e., determining what to say, how to say it, and how to pronounce it. In fact, in spoken language systems, such as the ARPA Air Travel Information Service (ATIS), the focus has been on correctly interpreting the spoken request, relying on direct display of database search results and minimal response generation capabilities. However, much work on written response generation as part of interactive systems is directly applicable to spoken language generation; the same problems must be addressed in an interactive spoken dialogue system. Within speech synthesis, research on controlling intonation to signal meaning and discourse structure is relevant to the problem. This work has resulted in several concept to speech systems.

Interactive Systems

Research in natural language understanding has shown that coherent discourse has structure, and that recognizing the structure is a crucial component of comprehending the discourse (Grosz & Sidner, 1986; Hobbs, 1993; Moore & Pollack, 1992). Thus, generation systems participating in dialogue must be able to select and organize content as part of a larger discourse structure and convey this structure, as well as the content, to users. This has led to the development of several plan-based models of discourse, and to implemented systems that are capable of participating in a written, interactive dialogue with users (Cawsey, 1993; Maybury, 1992; Moore, 1995).

Two aspects of discourse structure are especially important for spoken language generation. First is *intentional structure*, which describes the roles that discourse actions play in the speaker's communicative plan to achieve desired effects on the hearer's mental state. Moore and Paris (1993) have shown that intentional structure is crucial for responding effectively to questions that address a previous utterance: without a record of what an utterance was intended to achieve, it is impossible to elaborate or clarify that utterance. In addition, information about speaker intentions has been shown to be an important factor in selecting appropriate lexical items, including discourse cues (e.g., *because, when, although*; Moser & Moore, 1995a; Moser & Moore, 1995b) and scalar terms (e.g., *difficult, easy*; Elhadad, 1992).

Second is *attentional structure* (Carberry, 1983; Grosz, 1977; Grosz & Sidner, 1986; Gordon, Grosz, et al., 1993; Sidner, 1979), which contains information about the objects, properties, relations, and discourse intentions that are most salient at any given point in the discourse. In natural discourse, humans *focus* or *center* their attention on a small set of entities and attention shifts to new entities in predictable ways. Many generation systems track focus of attention as the discourse progresses as well as during the construction of its individual responses (McCoy & Cheng, 1990; McKeown, 1985; Sibun, 1992). Focus has been used to determine when to pronimalize, to make choices in syntactic form (e.g., active vs. passive), and to appropriately mark changes in topic, e.g., the introduction of a new topic or return to a previous topic (Cawsey, 1993). Once tracked, such information would be available for use in speech synthesis, as described below.

Another important factor for response generation in interactive systems is the ability to tailor responses based on a model of the intended hearer. Researchers have developed systems capable of tailoring their responses to the user's background (Cohen, Jones, et al., 1989), level of expertise (Paris, 1988), goals (McKeown, 1988), preferences (Chu-Carroll & Carberry, 1994), or misconceptions (McCoy, 1986). In addition, generating responses that the user will understand requires that the system use terminology that is familiar to the user (McKeown, Robin, et al., 1993).

Controlling Intonation to Signal Meaning in Speech Generation

Many studies have shown that intonational information is crucial for conveying intended meaning in spoken language (Butterworth, 1975; Hirschberg & Pierrehumbert, 1986; Silverman, 1987). For example, Pierrehumbert and Hirschberg (1990) identify how pitch accents indicate the information status of an item (e.g., given/new) in discourse, how variations in intermediate phrasing can convey structural relations among elements of a phrase, and how variation in pitch range can indicate topic changes. In later work, Hirschberg and Litman (1993) show that pitch accent and prosodic phrasing distinguish between discourse and sentential uses of cue phrases (e.g., *now* and *well*), providing a model for selecting appropriate intonational features when generating these cue phrases in synthetic speech. There have been only a few interactive spoken language systems that exploit intonation to convey meaning. Those that do, generate speech from an abstract representation of content that allows tracking focus, given/new information, topic switches, and discourse segmentation (for one exception, see the Telephone Enquiry System (TES) (Witten & Madams, 1977) where text was augmented by hand to include a coded intonation scheme). The Speech Synthesis from Concept (SSC) system, developed by Young and Fallside (1979), showed how syntactic structure could be used to aid in decisions about accenting and phrasing. Davis and Hirschberg (1988) developed a *message-to-speech* system that uses structural, semantic, and discourse information to control assignment of pitch range, accent placement, phrasing and pause. The result is a system that generates spoken directions with appropriate intonational features given start and end coordinates on a map. The generation of contrastive intonation is being explored in a medical information system, where full answers to yes-no questions are generated (Prevost & Steedman, 1994; Prevost, 1995). It is only in this last system that language generation techniques (e.g., a generation grammar) are fully explored. Other recent approaches to concept to speech generation can also be found (Horne & Filipsson, 1994; House & Youd, 1990).

5.4.2 Future Directions

Spoken language generation is a field in which more remains to be done than has been done to date. Although response generation is a critical component of interactive spoken language systems, and of any human computer interface, many current systems assume that once a spoken utterance is interpreted, the response can be made using the underlying system application (e.g., the results of a database search) and commercial speech synthesizers. If we are to produce effective spoken language human computer interfaces, then a concerted effort on spoken language generation must be pursued. Such interfaces would be clearly useful in applications such as task-assisted instruction-giving (e.g., equipment repair), telephone information services, medical information services (e.g., updates during surgery), commentary on animated information (e.g., animated algorithms), spoken translation, or summarization of phone transcripts.

Interaction Between Generation and Synthesis

To date, research on the interaction between discourse features and intonation has been carried out primarily by speech synthesis groups. While language generation systems often track the required discourse features, there have been few attempts to integrate language generation and speech synthesis. This would require the generation system to provide synthesis with the parameters needed to control intonation. By providing more information than is available to a TtS synthesis system and by requiring language generation to refine representations of discourse features for intonation, research in both fields will advance.

Generating Language Appropriate to Spoken Situations

Selecting the words and syntactic structure of a generated response has been explored primarily from the point of view of written language (see Hovy, this

volume). If a response is to be spoken, however, it will have different characteristics than those of written language. For example, it is unlikely that long
complex sentences will be appropriate without the visual, written context. Research is needed that incorporates the results of work in psycholinguistics on
constraints on spoken language form (Levelt, 1989) into generation systems, that
identifies further constraints on variability in surface form, and that develops
both grammars and lexical choosers that produce the form of language required
in a spoken context. While there has been some work on the development of
incremental, real-time processes for generation of spoken language (De Smedt,
1990; McDonald, 1983), more work is needed on constraints.

Influence of Discourse History

When generation takes place as part of an interactive dialogue system, responses
must be sensitive to what has already been said in the current session and to the
individual user. This influences the content of the response; the system should
relate new information to recently conveyed material and avoid repeating old
material that would distract the user from what is new. The discourse history
also influences the form of the response; the system must select vocabulary that
the user can understand. Furthermore, knowledge about what information is
new, or not previously mentioned, and what information is given, or available
from previous discourse, influences the use of anaphoric expressions as well as
word ordering. There has been some work on generating referring expressions
appropriate to context, e.g., pronouns and definite descriptions (McDonald,
1980, pp. 218–220; Dale, 1989; Granville, 1984). In addition, there has been
some work on producing responses to follow-up questions (Moore & Paris, 1993),
on generating alternative explanations when a first attempt is not understood
(Moore, 1989), and on issues related to managing the initiative in a dialogue
(Haller, 1994; McRoy, 1995). However, much remains to be done, particularly in
dialogues involving collaborative problem solving or in cases where the dialogue
involves mixed initiative.

Coordination with Other Media

When response generation is part of a larger interactive setting, including speech,
graphics, animation, as well as written language, a generator must coordinate
its tasks with other components. For example, which information in the selected
content should appear in language and which in graphics? If speech and animation are used, how are they to be coordinated temporally (e.g., how much can be
said during a given scene)? What parameters, used during response generation
tasks, should be made available to a speech component? These are issues that
have only recently surfaced within the research community.

Evaluating Spoken Language Generation

There has been very little work on how to measure whether a generation system
is successful. Possibilities include evaluating how well a user can complete a

task which requires interaction with a system that generates responses, asking users to indicate satisfaction with system responses, performing a preference analysis between different types of text, degrading a response generation system and testing user satisfaction, and evaluating system generation against a target case. Each one of these has potential problems. For example, task completion measures definitely interact with the front end interface: that is, how easy is it for a user to request the information needed? Thus, it would be helpful to have interaction between the computer scientists who build the systems and psychologists, who are better trained in creating valid evaluation techniques to produce better ways for understanding how well a generation system works.

5.5 Chapter References

Abe, M., Nakamura, S., Shikano, K., and Kuwabara, H. (1990). Voice conversion through vector quantization. *Journal of the Acoustical Society of Japan*, E-11:71–76.

ACL (1986). *Proceedings of the 24th Annual Meeting of the Association for Computational Linguistics*, Columbia University, New York. Association for Computational Linguistics.

Allen, J., Hunnicutt, M. S., and Klatt, D. (1987). *From text to speech—the MITalk system*. MIT Press, Cambridge, Massachusetts.

Atal, B. S. and Remde, J. R. (1982). A new model of LPC excitation for producing natural-sounding speech at low bit rates. In *Proceedings of the 1982 International Conference on Acoustics, Speech, and Signal Processing*, volume 1, pages 614–617. Institute of Electrical and Electronic Engineers.

Bachenko, J. and Fitzpatrick, E. (1990). A computational grammar of discourse-neutral prosodic phrasing in English. *Computational Linguistics*, 16:155–170.

Bailly, G. and Benoît, C., editors (1990). *Proceedings of the First ESCA Workshop on Speech Synthesis*, Autrans, France. European Speech Communication Association.

Bailly, G. and Benoît, C., editors (1992). *Talking Machines: Theories, Models, and Designs*. Elsevier Science.

Bartkova, K. and Sorin, C. (1987). A model of segmental duration for speech synthesis in French. *Speech Communication*, 6:245–260.

Breiman, L., Friedman, J. H., Olshen, R. A., and Stone, C. J. (1984). *Classification and Regression Trees*. Wadsworth & Brooks, Pacific Grove, California.

Butterworth, B. (1975). Hesitation and semantic planning in speech. *Journal of Psycholinguistic Research*, 4:75–87.

Campbell, W. N. (1992). Syllable-based segmental duration. In Bailly, G. and Benoît, C., editors, *Talking Machines: Theories, Models, and Designs*, pages 211–224. Elsevier Science.

Campbell, W. N. and Isard, S. D. (1991). Segment durations in a syllable frame. *Journal of Phonetics Computation Speech and Language*, 19:37–47.

Carberry, S. (1983). Tracking user goals in an information-seeking environment. In *Proceedings of the Third National Conference on Artificial Intelligence*, pages 59–63, Washington, DC.

Carlson, R. and Granström, B. (1986). A search for durational rules in a real-speech data base. *Phonetica*, 43:140–154.

Cawsey, A. (1993). *Explanation and Interaction: The Computer Generation of Explanatory Dialogues*. MIT Press.

Chang, J.-S., Chen, S.-D., Zheng, Y., Liu, X.-Z., and Ke, S.-J. (1992). Large-corpus-based methods for Chinese personal name recognition. *Journal of Chinese Information Processing*, 6(3):7–15.

Chen, K.-J. and Liu, S.-H. (1992). Word identification for Mandarin Chinese sentences. In *Proceedings of the 14th International Conference on Computational Linguistics*, pages 101–107, Nantes, France. ACL.

Chu-Carroll, J. and Carberry, S. (1994). A plan-based model for response generation in collaborative task-oriented dialogues. In *Proceedings of the National Conference on Artificial Intelligence*, pages 799–805, Menlo Park, California. AAAI Press.

Church, K. (1985). Stress assignment in letter to sound rules for speech synthesis. In *Proceedings of the 23rd Annual Meeting of the Association for Computational Linguistics*, pages 246–253, University of Chicago. Association for Computational Linguistics.

Church, K. (1988). A stochastic parts program and noun phrase parser for unrestricted text. In *Proceedings of the Second Conference on Applied Natural Language Processing*, pages 136–143, Austin, Texas. ACL.

Cohen, R., Jones, M., Sanmugasunderam, A., Spencer, B., and Dent, L. (1989). Providing responses specific to a user's goals and background. *International Journal of Expert Systems*, 2(2):135–162.

Coker, C., Church, K., and Liberman, M. (1990). Morphology and rhyming: Two powerful alternatives to letter-to-sound rules for speech synthesis. In Bailly, G. and Benoît, C., editors, *Proceedings of the First ESCA Workshop on Speech Synthesis*, pages 83–86, Autrans, France. European Speech Communication Association.

COLING (1992). *Proceedings of the 14th International Conference on Computational Linguistics*, Nantes, France. ACL.

Dale, R. (1989). Cooking up referring expressions. In *Proceedings of the 27th Annual Meeting of the Association for Computational Linguistics*, pages 68–75, Vancouver, British Columbia. Association for Computational Linguistics.

d'Alessandro, C. and Mertens, P. (1995). Automatic pitch contour stylization using a model of tonal perception. *Computer Speech and Language*, 9:257–288.

Davis, J. R. and Hirschberg, J. (1988). Assigning intonational features in synthesized spoken directions. In *Proceedings of the 26th Annual Meeting of the Association for Computational Linguistics*, pages 187–193, SUNY, Buffalo, New York. Association for Computational Linguistics.

De Smedt, K. J. M. J. (1990). IPF: an incremental parallel formulator. In Dale, R., Mellish, C. S., and Zock, M., editors, *Current Research in Natural Language Generation*. Academic Press, London.

Dedina, M. and Nusbaum, H. (1991). PRONOUNCE: a program for pronunciation by analogy. *Computer Speech and Language*, 5:55–64.

Dutoit, T. and Leich, H. (1993). MBR-PSOLA: Text-to-speech synthesis based on an MBEre-synthesis of the segments database. *Speech Communication*, 13:432–440.

Elhadad, M. (1992). *Using Argumentation to Control Lexical Choice: A Functional Unification-Based Approach*. PhD thesis, Computer Science Department, Columbia University.

ESCA (1994). *Proceedings of the Second ESCA/IEEE Workshop on Speech Synthesis*, New Paltz, New York. European Speech Communication Association.

Fant, G., Liljencrants, J., and Lin, Q. (1985). A four parameter model of glottal flow. *Speech Transactions Laboratory Quarterly and Status Report*, 1985(4):1–13.

Flanagan, J. L. and Rabiner, L. R., editors (1973). *Speech Synthesis*. Dowden, Hutchinson & Ross.

Fudge, E. (1984). *English Word-Stress*. Allen and Unwin, London.

Fujisaki, H. (1992). Modeling the process of fundamental frequency contour generation. In *Speech perception, production and linguistic structure*, pages 313–326. Ohmsha IOS Press.

Fujisaki, T. and Kawai, H. (1988). Realization of linguistic information in the voice fundamental frequency contour of the spoken Japanese. In *Proceedings of the 1988 International Conference on Acoustics, Speech, and Signal Processing*, pages 663–666, New York.

Golding, A. (1991). *Pronouncing Names by a Combination of Case-Based and Rule-Based Reasoning*. PhD thesis, Stanford University.

Gordon, P. C., Grosz, B. J., and Gilliom, L. A. (1993). Prounouns, names and the centering of attention in discourse. *Cognitive Science*, 17(3):311–348.

Granström, B. and Nord, L. (1992). Neglected dimensions in speech synthesis. *Speech Communication*, 11:459–462.

Granville, R. (1984). Controlling lexical substitution in computer text generation. In *Proceedings of the 10th International Conference on Computational Linguistics*, pages 381–384, Stanford University, California. ACL.

Grosz, B. J. (1977). The representation and use of focus in dialogue understanding. Technical Report 151, SRI International, Menlo Park, California.

Grosz, B. J. and Sidner, C. L. (1986). Attention, intention, and the structure of discourse. *Computational Linguistics*, 12(3):175–204.

Hakoda, K. and Sato, H. (1980). Prosodic rules in connected speech synthesis. *Trans. IECE*, pages 715–722.

Haller, S. M. (1994). Recognizing digressive questions using a model for interactive generation. In *Proceedings of the 7th International Workshop on Natural Language Generation*, pages 181–188, Kinnebunkport, Maine.

Hart, J., Collier, R., and Cohen, A., editors (1990). *A perceptual study of intonation*. Cambridge University Press, Cambridge, England.

Hindle, D. (1983). User manual for Fidditch, a deterministic parser. Technical Report Technical Memorandum 7590-142, Naval Research Laboratory.

Hirschberg, J. (1993). Pitch accent in context: Predicting intonational prominence from text. *Artificial Intelligence*, 63:305–340.

Hirschberg, J. and Litman, D. (1993). Empirical studies on the disambiguation of cue phrases. *Computational Linguistics*, 19(3):501–530.

Hirschberg, J. and Pierrehumbert, J. (1986). The intonational structuring of discourse. In *Proceedings of the 24th Annual Meeting of the Association for Computational Linguistics*, pages 136–144, Columbia University, New York. Association for Computational Linguistics.

Hobbs, J. R. (1993). Intention, information, and structure in discourse. In *Proceedings of the NATO Advanced Research Workshop on Burning Issues in Discourse*, pages 41–66, Maratea, Italy.

Horne, M. and Filipsson, M. (1994). Computational extraction of lexico-grammatical information for generation of Swedish intonation. In *Proceedings of the Second ESCA/IEEE Workshop on Speech Synthesis*, pages 220–223, New Paltz, New York. European Speech Communication Association.

House, J. and Youd, N. (1990). Contextually appropriate intonation in speech synthesis. In Bailly, G. and Benoît, C., editors, *Proceedings of the First ESCA Workshop on Speech Synthesis*, pages 185–188, Autrans, France. European Speech Communication Association.

ICSLP (1992). *Proceedings of the 1992 International Conference on Spoken Language Processing*, Banff, Alberta, Canada. University of Alberta.

Iwahashi, N. and Sagisaka, Y. (1993). Duration modeling with multiple split regression. In *Eurospeech '93, Proceedings of the Third European Conference on Speech Communication and Technology*, volume 1, pages 329–332, Berlin. European Speech Communication Association.

Kaiki, N., Takeda, K., and Sagisaka, Y. (1992). Linguistic properties in the control of segmental duration for speech synthesis. In Bailly, G. and Benoît, C., editors, *Talking Machines: Theories, Models, and Designs*, pages 255–264. Elsevier Science.

Karttunen, L., Kaplan, R. M., and Zaenen, A. (1992). Two-level morphology with composition. In *Proceedings of the 14th International Conference on Computational Linguistics*, volume 1, pages 141–148, Nantes, France. ACL.

Kato, H., Tsuzaki, M., and Sagisaka, Y. (1992). Acceptability and discrimination threshold for distortion of duration in Japanese words. In *Proceedings of the 1992 International Conference on Spoken Language Processing*, volume 1, pages 507–510, Banff, Alberta, Canada. University of Alberta.

Klatt, D. H. (1980). Software for a cascade/parallel formant synthesizer. *Journal of the Acoustical Society of America*, 67:971–995.

Klatt, D. H. (1987). Review of text-to-speech conversion for English. *Journal of the Acoustical Society of America*, 82(3):737–793.

Klatt, D. H. and Klatt, L. C. (1990). Analysis, synthesis a, and perception of voice quality variations among female and male talkers. *Journal of the Acoustical Society of America*, 87:820–857.

Koskenniemi, K. (1983). *Two-Level Morphology: a General Computational Model for Word-Form Recognition and Production*. PhD thesis, University of Helsinki. Publications of the Department of General Linguistics,University of Helsinki, No. 11. Helsinki.

Kraft, V. and Portele, T. (1995). Quality evaluation of five German speech synthesis systems. *Acta Acustica*, 3:351–365.

Ladd, D. R. (1984). English compound stress. In Gibbon, D. and Richter, H., editors, *Intonation, Accent and Rhythm*, pages 253–266. W. de Gruyter, Berlin.

Laroche, J., Stylianou, Y., and Moulines, E. (1993). HNS: Speech modification based on a harmonic + noise model. In *Proceedings of the 1993 International Conference on Acoustics, Speech, and Signal Processing*, pages 550–553.

Levelt, W. (1989). *Speaking: from intention to articulation*. MIT Press, Cambridge, Massachusetts.

Liberman, M. and Pierrehumbert, J. B. (1984). Intonational invariance under changes in pitch range and length. In *Language Sound Structure*, pages 157–233. MIT Press.

Liberman, M. and Prince, A. (1977). On stress and linguistic rhythm. *Linguistic Inquiry*, 8:249–336.

Liberman, M. and Sproat, R. (1992). The stress and structure of modified noun phrases in English. In Szabolcsi, A. and Sag, I., editors, *Lexical Matters*. CSLI (University of Chicago Press).

Lin, M.-Y., Chiang, T.-H., and Su, K.-Y. (1993). A preliminary study on unknown word problem in Chinese word segmentation. In *ROCLING 6*, pages 119–141. ROCLING.

Maeda, S. (1976). *A characterization of American English intonation*. PhD thesis, MIT.

Matsumoto, H., Maruyama, Y., and Inoue, H. (1994). Voice quality conversion based on supervised spectral mapping. *Journal of the Acoustical Society of Japan*, E. In press.

Maybury, M. T. (1992). Communicative acts for explanation generation. *International Journal of Man-Machine Studies*, 37(2):135–172.

McCoy, K. F. (1986). The ROMPER system: Responding to object-related misconceptions using perspective. In *Proceedings of the 24th Annual Meeting of the Association for Computational Linguistics*, Columbia University, New York. Association for Computational Linguistics.

McCoy, K. F. and Cheng, J. (1990). Focus of attention: Constraining what can be said next. In Paris, C. L., Swartout, W. R., and Mann, W. C., editors, *Natural Language Generation in Artificial Intelligence and Computational Linguistics*, pages 103–124. Kluwer Academic, Boston.

McDonald, D. D. (1980). *Natural Language Production as a Process of Decision Making Under Constraint*. PhD thesis, Department of Computer Science and Electrical Engineering, Massachusetts Institute of Technology.

McDonald, D. D. (1983). Description directed control: its implications for natural language generation. In Grosz, B. J., Sparck Jones, K., and Webber, B. L., editors, *Readings in Natural Language Processing*. Morgan Kaufmann Publishers, Inc.

McKeown, K. R. (1985). *Text Generation: Using Discourse Strategies and Focus Constraints to Generate Natural Language Text*. Studies in Natural Language Processing. Cambridge University Press.

McKeown, K. R. (1988). Generating goal-oriented explanations. *International Journal of Expert Systems*, 1(4):377–395.

McKeown, K. R., Robin, J., and Tanenblatt, M. (1993). Tailoring lexical choice to the user's vocabulary in multimedia explanation generation. In *Proceedings of the 31st Annual Meeting of the Association for Computational Linguistics*, pages 226–234, Ohio State University. Association for Computational Linguistics.

McRoy, S. (1995). The repair of speech act misunderstandings by abductive inference. *Computational Linguistics*. In press.

Monaghan, A. (1990). Rhythm and stress in speech synthesis. *Computer Speech and Language*, 4:71–78.

Moore, J. D. (1989). Responding to "Huh?": Answering vaguely articulated follow-up questions. In *Proceedings of the Conference on Human Factors in Computing Systems*, pages 91–96, Austin, Texas.

Moore, J. D. (1995). *Participating in Explanatory Dialogues: Interpreting and Responding to Questions in Context*. MIT Press.

Moore, J. D. and Paris, C. L. (1993). Planning texts for advisory dialogues: Capturing intentional and rhetorical information. *Computational Linguistics*, 19(4):651–694.

Moore, J. D. and Pollack, M. E. (1992). A problem for RST: The need for multi-level discourse analysis. *Computational Linguistics*, 18(4):537–544.

Moser, M. and Moore, J. D. (1995a). Investigating cue selection and placement in tutorial discourse. In *Proceedings of the 33rd Annual Meeting of the Association for Computational Linguistics*, MIT. Association for Computational Linguistics.

Moser, M. and Moore, J. D. (1995b). Using discourse analysis and automatic text generation to study discourse cue usage. In *Proceedings of the AAAI Spring Symposium on Empirical Methods in Discourse Interpretation and Generation*.

Moulines, E. and Charpentier, F. (1990). Pitch-synchronous waveform processing techniques for text-to-speech synthesis using diphones. *Speech Communication*, 9:453–468.

Moulines, E. and Sagisaka, Y. (1995). Voice conversion: State of the art and perspectives. *Speech Communication*, 16(2). Guest editors.

Nakajima, S. and Hamada, H. (1988). Automatic generation of synthesis units based on context oriented clustering. In *Proceedings of the 1988 International Conference on Acoustics, Speech, and Signal Processing*, pages 659–662, New York. Institute of Electrical and Electronic Engineers.

Olive, J. P., Greenwood, A., and Coleman, J. (1993). *Acoustics of American English Speech, A Dynamic Approach*. Springer-Verlag.

O'Shaughnessy, D. (1989). Parsing with a small dictionary for applications such as text to speech. *Computational Linguistics*, 15:97–108.

Paris, C. L. (1988). Tailoring object descriptions to the user's level of expertise. *Computational Linguistics*, 14(3):64–78.

Parthasarathy, S. and Coker, C. H. (1992). Automatic estimation of articulatory parameters. *Computer Speech and Language*, 6:37–75.

Pierrehumbert, J. (1981). Synthesizing intonation. *Journal of the Acoustical Society of America*, 70:985–995.

Pierrehumbert, J. and Hirschberg, J. (1990). The meaning of intonational contours in interpretation of discourse. In Cohen, P. R., Morgan, J., and Pollack, M. E., editors, *Intentions in Communication*, pages 271–311. MIT Press, Cambridge, Massachusetts.

Pitrelli, J., Beckman, M., and Hirschberg, J. (1994). Evaluation of prosodic transcription labelling in the ToBI framework. In *Proceedings of the 1994 International Conference on Spoken Language Processing*, pages 123–126, Yokohama, Japan.

Prevost, S. A. (expected 1995). *Intonation, Context and Contrastiveness in Spoken Language Generation*. PhD thesis, University of Pennsylvania, Philadelphia, Pa.

Prevost, S. A. and Steedman, M. J. (1994). Specifying intonation from context for speech synthesis. *Speech Communication*, 15(1-2).

Richard, G. and d'Alessandro, C. (1994). Time-domain analysis-synthesis of the aperiodic component of speech signals. In *Proceedings of the ESCA Workshop on Speech Synthesis*, pages 5–8.

Riley, M. (1989). Some applications of tree-based modelling to speech and language. In *Proceedings of the Second DARPA Speech and Natural Language Workshop*, Cape Cod, Massachusetts. Defense Advanced Research Projects Agency.

Riley, M. D. (1992). Tree-based modeling of segmental durations. In Bailly, G. and Benoît, C., editors, *Talking Machines: Theories, Models, and Designs*, pages 265–273. Elsevier Science.

Sagisaka, Y., Kaiki, N., Iwahashi, N., and Mimura, K. (1992). ATR ν-Talk speech synthesis system. In *Proceedings of the 1992 International Conference on Spoken Language Processing*, volume 1, pages 483–486, Banff, Alberta, Canada. University of Alberta.

Sejnowski, T. and Rosenberg, C. (1987). Parallel networks that learn to pronounce English text. *Complex Systems*, 1.

Sibun, P. (1992). Generating text without trees. *Computational Intelligence*, 8(1):102–122.

Sidner, C. L. (1979). *Toward a Computational Theory of Definite Anaphora Comprehension in English Discourse*. PhD thesis, Massachusetts Institute of Technology, Cambridge, Mass.

Silverman, K. (1987). *The structure and processing of fundamental frequency contours*. PhD thesis, Cambridge University, Cambridge, England.

Sproat, R. (1992). *Morphology and Computation*. MIT Press, Cambridge, Massachusetts.

Sproat, R. (1994). English noun-phrase accent prediction for text-to-speech. *Computer Speech and Language*, 8:79–94.

Sproat, R., Hirschberg, J., and Yarowsky, D. (1992). A corpus-based synthesizer. In *Proceedings of the 1992 International Conference on Spoken Language Processing*, volume 1, pages 563–566, Banff, Alberta, Canada. University of Alberta.

Sproat, R., Shih, C., Gale, W., and Chang, N. (1994). A stochastic finite-state word-segmentation algorithm for Chinese. In *Proceedings of the 32nd Annual Meeting of the Association for Computational Linguistics*, pages 66–73, Las Cruces, New Mexico. Association for Computational Linguistics.

Stevens, K. N. and Bickley, C. (1991). Constraints among parameters simplify control of Klatt formant synthesizer. *Phonetics*, 19:161–174.

Sundberg, J. (1987). *The science of the singing voice*. Northern Illinois University Press, Dekalb, Illinois.

Takeda, K., Abe, K., and Sagisaka, Y. (1992). On the basic scheme and algorithms in non-uniform unit speech synthesis. In Bailly, G. and Benoît, C., editors, *Talking Machines: Theories, Models, and Designs*, pages 93–105. Elsevier Science.

Traber, C. (1992). F0 generation with a database of natural F0 pattern and with a neural network. In Bailly, G. and Benoît, C., editors, *Talking Machines: Theories, Models, and Designs*, pages 287–304. Elsevier Science.

Tzoukermann, E. and Liberman, M. Y. (1990). A finite-state morphological processor for Spanish. In Karlgren, H., editor, *Proceedings of the 13th International Conference on Computational Linguistics*, volume 3, pages 277–286, Helsinki. ACL.

Umeda, N. (1975). Vowel duration in American English. *Journal of the Acoustical Society of America*, 58(2):434–445.

Valbret, H., Moulines, E., and Tubach, J. (1992). Voice transformation using PSOLA. *Speech Communication*, 11:175–187.

Van Bezooijen, R. and Pols, L. (1990). Evaluation of text-to-speech systems: some methodological aspects. *Speech Communication*, 9:263–270.

Van Santen, J., Sproat, R., Olive, J., and Hirshberg, J., editors (1995). *Progress in Speech Synthesis*. Springer Verlag, New York.

Van Santen, J. P. H. (1992). Contextual effects on vowel duration. *Speech Communication*, 11:513–546.

Van Santen, J. P. H. (1993). Perceptual experiment for diagnostic testing of text-to-speech systems. *Computer Speech and Language*, 7:49–100.

Van Santen, J. P. H. (1994). Assignment of segmental duration in text-to-speech synthesis. *Computer Speech and Language*, 8:95–128.

Vitale, T. (1991). An algorithm for high accuracy name pronunciation by parametric speech synthesizer. *Computational Linguistics*, 17:257–276.

Wang, L.-J., Li, W.-C., and Chang, C.-H. (1992). Recognizing unregistered names for Mandarin word identification. In *Proceedings of the 14th International Conference on Computational Linguistics*, pages 1239–1243, Nantes, France. ACL.

Wang, M. Q. and Hirschberg, J. (1992). Automatic classification of intonational phrase boundaries. *Computer Speech and Language*, 6:175–196.

Witten, L. and Madams, P. (1977). The telephone inquiry service: a man-machine system using synthetic speech. *International Journal of Man-Machine Studies*, 9:449–464.

Wu, Z. and Tseng, G. (1993). Chinese text segmentation for text retrieval: Achievements and problems. *Journal of the American Society for Information Science*, 44(9):532–542.

Yamashita, Y., Tanaka, M., Amako, Y., Nomura, Y., Ohta, Y., Kitoh, A., Kakusho, O., and Mizoguchi, R. (1993). Tree-based approaches to automatic generation of speech synthesis rules for prosodic parameters. *Trans. IEICE*, E76-A(11):1934–1941.

Yarowsky, D. (1994). Homograph disambiguation in speech synthesis. In *Proceedings of the Second ESCA/IEEE Workshop on Speech Synthesis*, pages 244–247, New Paltz, New York. European Speech Communication Association.

Young, S. J. and Fallside, F. (1979). Speech synthesis from concept: a method for speech output from information systems. *Journal of the Acoustic Society of America*, 66(3):685–695.

Chapter 6

Discourse and Dialogue

6.1 Overview

Barbara Grosz

Harvard University, Cambridge, Massachusetts, USA

The problems addressed in discourse research aim to answer two general kinds of questions:

1. What information is contained in extended sequences of utterances that goes beyond the meaning of the individual utterances themselves?

2. How does the context in which an utterance is used affect the meaning of the individual utterances, or parts of them?

Computational work in discourse has focused on two different types of discourse: extended texts and dialogues, both spoken and written. Although there are clear overlaps between these—dialogues contain text-like sequences spoken by a single individual and texts may contain dialogues—the current state of the art leads research to focus on different questions for each. In addition, application opportunities and needs are different. Work on text is of direct relevance to document analysis and retrieval applications, whereas work on dialogue is of import for human-computer interfaces regardless of the modality of interaction. A good sense of the current state of research in text interpretation can be gained from reading the papers on text interpretation published in a recent special issue of *Artificial Intelligence* (hereafter, *AIJ-SI*), (Hobbs, Stickel, et al., 1994; Jacobs & Rau, 1994; Palmer, Passonneau, et al., 1994).

Text and dialogue have, however, two significant commonalities. First, a major result of early work in discourse was the determination that discourses divide into *discourse segments*, much like sentences divide into phrases. Utterances group into segments, with the meaning of a segment encompassing more than the meaning of the individual parts. Different theories vary on the factors they consider central to explaining this segmentation; a review of the alternatives can be found in a previous survey (Grosz, Pollack, et al., 1989) (hereafter, *Discourse Survey*).[1] However, many of the implications for language processing are shared. For example, segment boundaries need to be detected; recent work suggests there are intonational indicators of these boundaries in spoken language (e.g., Grosz & Hirschberg, 1992 and the references cited in this paper) and can be used to improve speech synthesis (e.g., Davis & Hirschberg, 1988).

Second, discourse research on the interpretation of referring expressions, including pronouns and definite descriptions (e.g., *le petit chat, das grüne Buch*), and the event reference aspect of verb phrase interpretation (e.g., the relationship between the buying and arriving events in the sequence *John went to Mary's house; he had bought flowers at her favorite florist's* is also relevant to both text and dialogue. Work on these problems before 1990 is described in *Discourse Survey*.

6.1.1   Beyond Sentence Interpretation

The major lines of research on determining what information a discourse carries, beyond what is literally expressed in the individual sentences the discourse comprises, fall into two categories which, following Hobbs, we will refer to as *informational* and *intentional*. There are currently efforts to combine these two approaches (e.g., Kehler, 1994; Kehler, 1995; Moore & Pollack, 1992); this is an important area of research.

According to the informational approaches, the coherence of discourse follows from semantic relationships between the information conveyed by successive utterances. As a result, the major computational tools used here are inference and abduction on representations of the propositional content of utterances. *Discourse Survey* describes work in this area under *inference-based approaches*; more recent work in this area is presented in *AIJ-SI*.

According to the intentional approaches the coherence of discourse derives from the intentions of speakers and writers, and understanding depends on recognition of those intentions. Thus, these approaches follow Grice (1969); early work in this area drew on speech act theory (Searle, 1969). A major insight of work in this area was to recognize the usefulness of applying AI planning techniques; this work is described in *Discourse Survey*. Recently, various limitations of this approach have been recognized. In particular, as originally argued by Searle (1990) and Grosz and Sidner (1990), models of individual plans are not adequate for understanding discourse; models of collaborative plans or joint intentions are required. A variety of approaches to developing such models are currently underway (Grosz & Kraus, 1993; Sonenberg, Tidhar, et al., 1994; Cohen & Levesque, 1990) and used for dialogue (Lochbaum, 1993; Lochbaum, 1994; Lochbaum, 1995).

---

[1] Many of the papers cited in this survey may be found in the collection *Readings in Natural Language Processing* (Grosz, Sparck Jones, et al., 1986).

6.1.2 Interpretation and Generation in Context

Research in this area also splits into two approaches, those that examine the interaction of choice or interpretation of expression with focus of attention, and those that are coherence-based.

Focus of attention interacts with the interpretation and generation of pronouns and definite descriptions (Grosz & Sidner, 1986). The coherence-based approaches have been taken with the informational approaches described above. The main new issues in this area concern how to combine these approaches, as it is clear that both kinds of consideration play roles both in determining which expressions to use and how to interpret expressions in context. The focus-based approaches have been applied cross-linguistically;

because this is a cognitively-oriented approach, it should have application to multi-media interfaces even when natural language is not being used, or when only a restricted subset can be handled.

6.2 Discourse Modeling

Donia Scott[a] & Hans Kamp[b]

[a] University of Brighton, UK
[b] University of Stuttgart, Germany

6.2.1 Overview: Discourse and Dialogue

A central problem which the development of dialogue systems encounters is one that it has inherited directly from contemporary linguistics, where one is still struggling to achieve a genuine integration of semantics and pragmatics. A satisfactory analysis of dialogue requires in general both semantic representation, i.e. representation of the content of what the different participants are saying, and pragmatic information, i.e., what kinds of speech acts they are performing (are they asking a question, answering a question that has just been asked, asking a question for clarification of what was just said, making a proposal, etc.?), what information is available to each of the participants and what information does she want; and, more generally, what is the purpose behind their various utterances or even behind their entering upon the dialogue in the first place. Determining the semantic representation of an utterance and its pragmatic features must in general proceed in tandem: to determine the pragmatic properties of the utterance it is often necessary to have a representation of its content; conversely, it is—especially for the highly elliptical utterances that are common in spoken dialogue—often hardly possible to identify content without an independent assessment of the pragmatic role the utterance is meant to play. A dialogue system identifying the relevant semantic and pragmatic information will thus have to be based on a theory in which semantics and pragmatics are: (i) both developed with the formal precision that is a prerequisite for implementation and (ii) suitably attuned to each other and intertwined.

Current approaches to discourse and dialogue from the field of artificial intelligence and computational linguistics are based on four predominant theories of discourse which emerged in the mid- to late-eighties:

Hobbs (1985): A theory of discourse coherence-based on a small, limited set of coherence relations, applied recursively to discourse segments. This is part of a larger, still-developing theory of the relations between text interpretation and belief systems.

Grosz and Sidner (1986): A tripartite organization of discourse structure according to the focus of attention of the speaker (the attentional state), the structure of the speaker's purposes (the intentional structure) and the structure of sequences of utterances (the linguistic structure); each of these three constituents deal with different aspects of the discourse.

Mann and Thompson (1987): A hierarchical organization of text spans, where each span is either the nucleus (central) or satellite (support) of one of a set of discourse relations. This approach is commonly known as Rhetorical Structure Theory (RST).

McKeown (1985): A hierarchical organization of discourse around fixed schema which guarantee coherence and which drive content selection in generation.

No theory is complete, and some (or aspects of some) lend themselves more readily to implementation than others. In addition, no single theory is suitable for use on both sides of the natural language processing coin: the approaches advocated by Grosz and Sidner, and by Hobbs are geared towards natural language understanding , whereas those of Mann and Thompson, and of McKeown are more appropriate for natural language generation. With the burgeoning of research on natural language generation since the late-eighties has come an expansion of the emphasis of computational approaches of discourse towards discourse production and, concomitantly, dialogue.

One important aspect of dialogues is that the successive utterances of which it consists are often interconnected by cross references of various sorts. For instance, one utterance will use a pronoun (or a deictic temporal phrase such as *the day after*, etc.) to refer to something mentioned in the utterance preceding it. Therefore the semantic theory underlying sophisticated dialogue systems must be in a position to compute and represent such cross references. Traditional theories and frameworks of formal semantics are sentence based and therefore not suited for discourse semantics without considerable extensions.

6.2.2 Discourse Representation Theory

Discourse Representation Theory (DRT) (cf. Kamp, 1981; Kamp & Reyle, 1993), a semantic theory developed for the express purpose of representing and computing trans-sentential anaphora and other forms of text cohesion, thus offers itself as a natural semantic framework for the design of sophisticated dialogue systems. DRT has already been used in the design of a number of question-answering systems, some of them of considerable sophistication.

Currently, DRT is being used as the semantic representation formalism in VERBMOBIL (Wahlster, 1993), a project to develop a machine translation system for face-to-face spoken dialogue funded by the German Department of Science and Technology. Here, the aim is to integrate DRT-like semantics with the various kinds of pragmatic information that are needed for translation purposes.

6.2.3 Future Directions

Among the key outstanding issues for computational theories of discourse are:

Nature of Discourse Relations: Relations are variously viewed as textual, rhetorical, intentional, or informational. Although each type of relation can be expected to have a different impact on a text, current discourse theories generally fail to distinguish between them.

Number of Discourse Relations: Depending on the chosen theoretical approach, these can range from anywhere between two and twenty-five. Altogether, there are over 350 relations available for use (see Hovy, 1990).

Level of Abstraction at which Discourse is Described: In general, approaches advocating fewer discourse relations tend to address higher levels of abstraction.

Nature of Discourse Segments: A key question here is whether discourse segments have psychological reality or whether they are abstract linguistic units akin to phonemes. Recently, there have been attempts to identify the boundary features of discourse segments (Hirschberg & Grosz, 1992; Litman & Passoneau, 1993).

Role of Intentions in Discourse: It is well-recognized that intentions play an important role in discourse. However, of the four predominant computational theories, only that of Grosz and Sidner provides an explicit treatment of intentionality.

Mechanisms for Handling Key Linguistic Phenomena: Of the predominant theories, only RST fails to address the issues of discourse focus, reference resolution and cue phrases. Existing treatments of focus, however, suffer from the sort of terminological confusion between notions of focus, theme and topic that is also rife in the text linguistics literature.

Mechanisms for Reasoning about Discourse: Cue phrases and certain syntactic forms are useful signals of prevailing discourse functions (e.g., discourse relations, discourse focus and topic) but do not occur with predictable regularity in texts. Reasoning mechanisms for retrieving and/or generating these discourse functions are thus required.

Recent advances have not involved the development of new theories but have been rather through the extension and integration of existing theories. Notable among them are:

- discourse as collaborative activity (e.g., Grosz & Sidner, 1990; Grosz & Kraus, 1993)

- the use of abduction as a mechanism for reasoning about discourse understanding and generation (e.g., Hobbs, Stickel, et al., 1993; Lascarides & Oberlander, 1992)

- integration of RST with AI approaches to planning (e.g., Hovy, 1991; Moore & Paris, 1993)

- introduction of intentions in computational approaches based on Hobbs' theory and on RST (e.g., Hobbs, 1993; Moore & Pollack, 1992)

- application of the theories to multimedia discourses (e.g., Wahlster, André, et al., 1993)

- application and extension of existing theories in the automatic generation of pragmatically-congruent multilingual texts (Delin, Scott, et al., 1993; Delin, Hartley, et al., 1994; Paris & Scott, 1994).

- extension of theories of monologic discourse to the treatment of dialogue (e.g., Cawsey, 1992; Moore & Paris, 1993; Green & Carberry, 1994; Traum & Allen, 1994

- identification of acoustic (suprasegmental) markers of discourse segments (Hirschberg & Grosz, 1992)

There are many implemented systems for discourse understanding and generation. Most involve hybrid approaches, selectively exploiting the power of existing theories. Available systems for handling dialogue tend either to have sophisticated discourse generation coupled to a crude discourse understanding systems or vice versa; attempts at full dialogue systems are only now beginning to appear.

6.3 Dialogue Modeling

Phil Cohen
Oregon Graduate Institute of Science & Technology, Portland, Oregon, USA

6.3.1 Research Goals

Two related, but at times conflicting, research goals are often adopted by researchers of dialogue. First, is the goal of developing a theory of dialogue, including, at least, a theory of cooperative task-oriented dialogue, in which the participants are communicating in service of the accomplishment of some goal-directed task. The often unstated objectives of such theorizing have generally been to determine:

- what properties of collections of utterances and acts characterize a dialogue of the genre being studied,

- what assumptions about the participants' mental states and the context need to be made in order to sanction the observed behavior as a rational cooperative dialogue, and

- what would be rational and cooperative dialogue *extensions* to the currently observed behavior

A second research goal is to develop algorithms and procedures to support a computer's participation in a cooperative dialogue. Often, the dialogue behavior being supported may only bear a passing resemblance to human dialogue. For example, database question-answering (ARPA, 1993) and *frame-filling* dialogues (Bilange, 1991; Bilange, Guyomard, et al., 1990; Bobrow & PARC Understander Group, 1977) are simplifications of human dialogue behavior in that the former consists primarily of the user asking questions, and the system providing answers, whereas the latter involve the system prompting the user for information (e.g., a flight departure time). Human-human dialogues exhibit much more varied behavior, including clarifications, confirmations, other communicative actions, etc. Some researchers have argued that because humans interact differently with computers than they do with people (Dahlbäck & Jönsson, 1992; Fraser & Gilbert, 1991), the goal of developing a system that emulates *real* human dialogue behavior is neither an appropriate, nor attainable target (Dahlbäck & Jönsson, 1992; Shneiderman, 1980). On the contrary, others have argued that the usability of current natural language systems, especially voice-interactive systems in a telecommunications setting, could benefit greatly from techniques that allow the human to engage in behavior found in their typical spoken conversations (Karis & Dobroth, 1991). In general, no consensus exists on the appropriate research goals, methodologies, and evaluation procedures for modeling dialogue.

Three approaches to modeling dialogue—dialogue grammars, plan-based models of dialogue, and joint action theories of dialogue—will be discussed, both from theoretical and practical perspectives.

6.3.2 Dialogue Grammars

One approach with a relatively long history has been that of developing a dialogue grammar (Polanyi & Scha, 1984; Reichman, 1981; Sinclair & Coulthard, 1975). This approach is based on the observation that there exist a number of sequencing regularities in dialogue, termed *adjacency pairs* (Sacks, Schegloff, et al., 1978), describing such facts as that questions are generally followed by answers, proposals by acceptances, etc. Theorists have proposed that dialogues are a collection of such act sequences, with embedded sequences for digressions and repairs (Jefferson, 1972). For some theorists, the importance of these sequences derives from the expectations that arise in the conversants for the occurrence of the remainder of the sequence, given the observation of an initial portion. For instance, on hearing a question, one expects to hear an answer. People can be seen to react to behavior that violates these expectations.

Based on these observations about conversations, theorists have proposed using phrase-structure grammar rules, following the Chomsky hierarchy, or equivalently, various kinds of state machines. The rules state sequential and hierarchical constraints on acceptable dialogues, just as syntactic grammar rules state constraints on grammatically acceptable strings. The terminal elements of these rules are typically illocutionary act names (Austin, 1962; Searle, 1969), such as request, reply, offer, question, answer, propose, accept, reject, etc. The nonterminals describe various stages of the specific type of dialogue being modeled (Sinclair & Coulthard, 1975), such as initiating, reacting, and evaluating. For example, the SUNDIAL system (Andry, Bilange, et al., 1990; Andry, 1992; Bilange, 1991; Bilange, Guyomard, et al., 1990; Guyomard & Siroux, 1988) uses a 4-level dialogue grammar to engage in spoken dialogues about travel reservations. Just as syntactic grammar rules can be used in parsing sentences, it is often thought that dialogue grammar rules can be used in *parsing* the structure of dialogues. With a bottom-up parser and top-down prediction, it is expected that such dialogue grammar rules can predict the set of possible next elements in the sequence, given a prior sequence (Gilbert, Wooffitt, et al., 1990). Moreover, if the grammar is context-free, parsing can be accomplished in polynomial time.

From the perspective of a state machine, the speech act become the state transition labels. When the state machine variant of a dialogue grammar is used as a control mechanism for a dialogue system, the system first recognizes the user's speech act from the utterance, makes the appropriate transition, and then chooses one of the outgoing arcs to determine the appropriate response to supply. When the system performs an action, it makes the relevant transition and uses the outgoing arcs from the resulting state to predict the type of response to expect from the user (Dahlbäck & Jönsson, 1992).

Arguments against the use of dialogue grammars as a general theory of dialogue have been raised before, notably by Levinson (1981).

First, dialogue grammars require that the communicative action(s) being performed by the speaker in issuing an utterance be identified. In the past, this has been a difficult problem for people and machines, for which prior solutions have required plan recognition (Allen & Perrault, 1980; Carberry, 1990; Kautz, 1990; Perrault & Allen, 1980). Second, the model typically assumes that only one state results from a transition. However, utterances are multifunctional. An utterance can be, for example, both a rejection and an assertion, and a speaker may expect the response to address more than one interpretation. The dialogue grammar subsystem would thus need to be in multiple states simultaneously, a property typically not allowed. Dialogues also contain many instances of speakers' using multiple utterances to perform a single illocutionary act (e.g., a request). To analyze and respond to such dialogue contributions using a dialogue grammar, a calculus of speech acts needs to be developed that can determine when two speech acts combine to constitute another. Currently, no such calculus exists. Finally, and most importantly, the model does not say how systems should choose amongst the next moves, i.e., the states currently reachable, in order for it to play its role as a cooperative conversant. Some analogue of planning is thus required.

In summary, dialogue grammars are a potentially useful computational tool to express simple regularities of dialogue behavior. However, they need to function in concert with more powerful plan-based approaches (described below) in order to provide the input data, and to choose a cooperative system response. As a theory, dialogue grammars are unsatisfying as they provide no explanation of the behavior they describe, i.e., why the actions occur where they do, why they fit together into a unit, etc.

6.3.3 Plan-based Models of Dialogue

Plan-based models are founded on the observation that utterances are not simply strings of words, but are rather the observable performance of communicative actions, or speech acts (Searle, 1969), such as requesting, informing, warning, suggesting, and confirming. Moreover, humans do not just perform actions randomly, but rather they plan their actions to achieve various goals, and, in the case of communicative actions, those goals include changes to the mental states of listeners. For example, speakers' requests are planned to alter the intentions of their addressees. Plan-based theories of communicative action and dialogue (Allen & Perrault, 1980; Appelt, 1985; Carberry, 1990; Cohen & Levesque, 1990; Cohen & Perrault, 1979; Perrault & Allen, 1980; Sadek, 1991; Sidner & Israel, 1981) assume that the speaker's speech acts are part of a plan, and the listener's job is to uncover and respond appropriately to the underlying plan, rather than just to the utterance. For example, in response to a customer's question of *Where are the steaks you advertised?*, a butcher's reply of *How many do you want?* is appropriate because the butcher has discovered that the customer's plan of getting steaks himself is going to fail. Being cooperative, he attempts to execute a plan to achieve the customer's higher-level goal of having steaks. Current research on this model is attempting to incorporate more complex dialogue phenomena, such as clarifications (Litman & Allen, 1990; Yamaoka & Iida, 1991; Litman & Allen, 1987), and to model dialogue more as a *joint* enterprise, something the participants are doing together (Clark & Wilkes-Gibbs, 1986; Cohen & Levesque, 1991b; Grosz & Sidner, 1990; Grosz & Kraus, 1993).

The major accomplishment of plan-based theories of dialogue is to offer a generalization in which dialogue can be treated as a special case of other rational noncommunicative behavior. The primary elements are accounts of planning and plan-recognition, which employ various inference rules, action definitions, models of the mental states of the participants, and expectations of likely goals and actions in the context. The set of actions may include speech acts, whose execution affects the beliefs, goals, commitments, and intentions, of the conversants. Importantly, this model of cooperative dialogue solves problems of indirect speech acts as a side-effect (Perrault & Allen, 1980). Namely, when inferring the purpose of an utterance, it may be determined that not only are the speaker's intentions those indicated by the form of the utterance, but there may be other intentions the speaker wants to convey. For example, in responding to the utterance *There is a little yellow piece of rubber,* the addressee's plan recognition process should determine that not only does the speaker want the addressee to believe such an object exists, the speaker wants the addressee to find the object and pick it up. Thus, the utterance could be analyzed by the same plan-recognition process as an informative utterance, as well as both a request to find it and to pick it up.

Drawbacks of the Plan-based Approach

A number of theoretical and practical limitations have been identified for this class of models.

Illocutionary Act Recognition is Redundant: Plan-based theories and algorithms have been tied tightly to illocutionary act recognition. In order to infer the speaker's plan, and determine a cooperative response, the listener (or system) had to recognize what *single* illocutionary act was being performed with each utterance (Perrault & Allen, 1980), even for indirect utterances. However, illocutionary act recognition in the Allen and Perrault model (Allen & Perrault, 1980; Perrault & Allen, 1980) was shown to be redundant (Cohen & Levesque, 1980); other inferences in the scheme provided the same results. Instead, it was argued that illocutionary acts could more properly be handled as complex action expressions, defined over patterns of utterance events and properties of the context, including the mental states of the participants (Cohen & Levesque, 1990). Importantly, using this analysis, a theorist can show how multiple acts were being performed by a given utterance, or how multiple utterances together constituted the performance of a given type of illocutionary act. Conversational participants, however, are not required to make these classifications. Rather, they need only infer what the speaker's intentions are.

Discourse versus Domain Plans: Although the model is capable of solving problems of utterance interpretation using nonlinguistic methods (e.g., plan-recognition), it does so at the expense of distinctions between task-related speech acts and those used to control the dialogue, such as clarifications (Grosz & Sidner, 1986; Litman & Allen, 1987; Litman & Allen, 1990). To handle these prevalent features of dialogue, *multilevel* plan structures have been proposed, in which a new class of discourse plans is posited, which take task-level (or other discourse-level) plans as arguments (Litman & Allen, 1987; Litman & Allen, 1990; Yamaoka & Iida, 1991). These are not higher level plans in an inclusion hierarchy, but rather are *meta*plans, which capture the set of ways in which a single plan structure can be manipulated. Rather than infer directly how utterances further various task plans, as single-level algorithms do, various multilevel algorithms first map utterances to a discourse plan, and determine how the discourse plan operates on an existing or new task plan. Just as with dialogue grammars, multi-level plan recognizers can be used to generate expectations for future actions and utterances, thereby assisting the interpretation of utterance fragments (Allen, 1979; Allen & Perrault, 1980; Carberry, 1985; Carberry, 1990; Sidner, 1985), and even providing constraints to speech recognizers (Andry, 1992; Yamaoka & Iida, 1991; Young, Hauptmann, et al., 1989).

Complexity of Inference: The processes of plan-recognition and planning are combinatorially intractable in the worst case, and in some cases, are undecidable (Bylander, 1991; Chapman, 1987; Kautz, 1990). The complexity arises in the evaluation of conditions, and in chaining from preconditions to actions they enable. Restricted planning problems in appropriate settings may still be reasonably well-behaved, but practical systems cannot be based entirely on the kind of first-principles reasoning typical of general-purpose planning and plan-recognition systems.

Lack of a Theoretical Base: Although the plan-based approach has much to recommend it as a computational model, and certainly has stimulated much informative research in dialogue understanding, it still lacks a crisp theoretical base. For example, it is difficult to express precisely what the various constructs (plans, goals, intentions, etc.) are, what the consequences are of those ascribing those theoretical constructs to be the user's mental state, and what kinds of dialogue phenomena and properties the framework can handle. Because of the procedural nature of the model, it is difficult to determine what analysis will be given, and whether it is correct, as there is no independently stated notion of correctness. In other words, what is missing is a *specification* of what the system should do. Section 6.4 will discuss such an approach.

6.3.4   Future Directions

Plan-based approaches that model dialogue simply as a product of the interaction of plan generators and recognizers working in synchrony and harmony, do not explain why addressees ask clarification questions, why they confirm, or even why they do not simply walk away during a conversation. A new theory of conversation is emerging in which dialogue is regarded as a joint activity, something that agents do *together* (Clark & Wilkes-Gibbs, 1986; Cohen & Levesque, 1991b; Grosz & Sidner, 1990; Grosz & Kraus, 1993; Lochbaum, 1994; Schegloff, 1981; Suchman, 1987). The joint action model claims that *both* parties to a dialogue are responsible for sustaining it. Participating in a dialogue requires the conversants to have at least a joint commitment to understand one another, and these commitments motivate the clarifications and confirmations so frequent in ordinary conversation.

Typical areas in which such models are distinguished from individual plan-based models are dealing with reference and confirmations. Clark and colleagues (Clark & Wilkes-Gibbs, 1986; Clark, 1989) have argued that actual referring behavior cannot be adequately modeled by the simple notion that speakers simply provide noun phrases and listeners identify the referents. Rather, both parties offer noun phrases, refine previous ones, correct mis-identifications, etc. They claim that people appear to be following the strategy of minimizing the joint effort involved in successfully referring. Computer models of referring based on this analysis are beginning to be developed (Heeman & Hirst, 1992; Edmonds, 1993). Theoretical models of joint action (Cohen & Levesque, 1991b; Cohen & Levesque, 1991a) have been shown to minimize the overall team effort in dynamic, uncertain worlds (Jennings & Mamdani, 1992). Thus, if a more general theory of joint action can be applied to dialogue as a special case, an explanation for numerous dialogue phenomena (such as collaboration on reference, confirmations, etc.) will be derivable. Furthermore, such a theory offers the possibility for providing a specification of what dialogue participants should do, which could be used to guide and evaluate dialogue management components for spoken language systems. Finally, future work in this area can also form the basis for protocols for communication among intelligent software agents.

6.4   Spoken Language Dialogue

Egidio Giachin

CSELT, Torino, Italy

The development of machines that are able to sustain a conversation with a human being has long been a challenging goal. Only recently, however, substantial improvements in the technology of speech recognition and understanding have enabled the implementation of experimental spoken dialogue systems, acting within specific semantic domains. The renewed interest in this area is represented by the numerous papers which appeared in conferences such as ESCA Eurospeech, ICSLP, and ICASSP, as well as by events such as the 1993 International Symposium on Spoken Dialogue and the 1995 ESCA Workshop on Spoken Dialogue Systems.

The need for a dialogue component in a system for human-machine interaction arises for several reasons. Often the user does not express his requirement with a single sentence, because that would be impractical; assistance is then expected from the system, so that the interaction may naturally flow in the course of several dialogue turns. Moreover, a dialogue manager should take care of identifying, and recovering from, speech recognition and understanding errors.

The studies on human-machine dialogue have historically followed two main theoretical guidelines traced by research on human-human dialogue. *Discourse analysis*, developed from studies on speech acts (Searle, 1976), views dialogue as a rational cooperation and assumes that the speakers' utterances be well-formed sentences. *Conversational analysis*, on the other hand, studies dialogue as a social interaction in which phenomena such as disfluencies, abrupt shift of focus, etc., have to be considered (Levinson, 1983). Both theories have contributed to the design of human-machine dialogue systems; in practice, freedom of design has to be constrained so as to find an adequate match with the other technologies the system rests on. For example, dialogue strategies for speech systems should recover from word recognition errors.

Experimental dialogue systems have been developed mainly as evolutions of speech understanding projects, which provided satisfactory recognition accuracy for speaker independent continuous speech tasks with lexicons of the order of 1000 words. The development of robust parsing methods for natural language was also an important step. After some recent experiences at individual sites (Siroux, 1989; Young & Proctor, 1989; Mast, Kompe, et al., 1992), one of the most representative projects in Europe that fostered the development of dialogue systems is the CEC SUNDIAL project (Peckham, 1993). The ARPA funded ATIS project in the United States also spurred a flow of research on spoken dialogue in some sites (Seneff, Hirschman, et al., 1991).

6.4.1 Functional Characteristics

The dialogue manager is the core of a spoken dialogue system. It relies on two main components, the *interaction history* and the *interaction model*. The interaction history is used to interpret sentences, such as those including anaphora and ellipsis, that cannot be understood by themselves, but only according to some existing context. The context (or, more technically, *active focus*) may change as the dialogue proceeds and the user shifts its focus. This requires the system to keep an updated history for which efficient representations (e.g., tree hierarchies) have been devised.

The interaction model defines the strategy that drives the dialogue. The dialogue strategy may lie between two extremes: the user is granted complete freedom of initiative, or the dialogue is driven by the dialogue manager. The former choice supports naturalness on the user's side but increases the risk of misunderstandings, while the latter provides easier recognition conditions, though the resulting dialogues can be long and unfriendly.

The *right* strategy depends on the application scenario and on the robustness of the speech recognition techniques involved. The design of a suitable strategy is a crucial issue, because the success of the interaction will depend mainly on that. A good strategy is flexible and lets the user take the initiative as long as no problem arises, but assumes control of the dialogue when things become messy; the dialogue manager then requires the user to reformulate his or her sentence or even use different interaction modalities, such as isolated words, spelling, or yes/no confirmations. The effectiveness of a dialogue strategy can be assessed only through extensive experimentation.

Several approaches have been employed to implement an interaction model. A simple one represents dialogue as a network of states with which actions are associated. The between-state transitions are regulated by suitable conditions. This implementation, used e.g., in Gerbino and Danieli (1993), enhances readability and ease of maintenance, while preserving efficiency at runtime through a suitable compilation. Architectures of higher complexity have been investigated. In the CEC SUNDIAL project, for example (see Peckham, 1993 and the references cited there), a dialogue manager based on the theory of speech acts was developed. A modular architecture was designed so as to insure portability to different tasks and favor the separation of different pieces of knowledge, with limited run time speed reduction.

6.4.2   Development of a Spoken Dialogue System

The development of an effective system requires extensive experimentation with real users. Human-human dialogue, though providing some useful insight, is of limited utility because a human behaves much differently when he or she is talking to a machine rather than to another human. The Wizard of Oz (WOZ) technique (Fraser & Gilbert, 1989) enables dialogue examples to be collected in the initial phase of system development: the machine is emulated by a human expert, and the user is led to believe that he or she is actually talking to a computer. This technique has been effective in helping researchers test ideas, however, since it is difficult to realistically mimic the actual behavior of recognition and dialogue systems, it may be affected by an overly optimistic estimation of performance, which may lead to a dialogue strategy that is not robust enough. A different approach suggests that experimentation with real users be performed in several steps, starting with a complete, though rough, bootstrap system and cyclically upgrading it. This technique was used for the system in Seneff, Hirschman, et al. (1991). The advantage of this method is that it enables the system to be developed in a close match with the collected database.

The above methodologies are not mutually exclusive, and in practical implementations they have been jointly employed. In every case, extensive corpora of (real or simulated) human-machine interaction are playing an essential role for development and testing.

6.4.3   Evaluation Criteria

The difficulty of satisfactorily evaluating the performance of voice processing systems increases from speech recognition dialogue, where the very nature of what should be measured is complex and ill-defined. Recent projects nevertheless favored the establishing of some ideas. Evaluation parameters can be classified as *objective* and *subjective*. The former category includes the total time of the utterance, the number of user/machine dialogue turns, the rate of correction/repair turns, etc. The *transaction success* is also an objective measure, though the precise meaning of *success* still lacks a standard definition. As a general rule, an interaction is declared successful if the user was able to solve his or her problem without being overwhelmed by unnecessary information from the system, in the spirit of what has been done in the ARPA community for the ATIS speech understanding task.

Objective measures are not sufficient to evaluate the overall system quality as seen from the user's viewpoint. The subjective measures, aimed at assessing the users' opinions on the system, are obtained through direct interview by questionnaire filling. Questions include such issues as ease of usage, naturalness, clarity, friendliness, robustness regarding misunderstandings, subjective length of the transaction, etc. Subjective measures have to be properly processed (e.g., through factorial analysis) in order to suggest specific upgrading actions. These measures may depart from what could be expected by analyzing objective data. Since user satisfaction is the ultimate evaluation criterion, subjective measures are helpful for focusing on weak points that might get overlooked and neglect issues that are of lesser practical importance.

Evaluation of state-of-the-art spoken dialogue technology indicates that a careful dialogue manager design permits high transaction success to be achieved in spite of the still numerous recognition or understanding errors (see e.g., Gerbino & Danieli, 1993. Robustness to spontaneous speech is obtained at the expense of speed and friendliness, and novices experience more trouble than expert users. Moreover, ease and naturalness of system usage are perceived differently according to user age and education. However, the challenge to bring this technology into real services is open.

6.4.4   Future Directions

The issues for future investigation can be specified only according to the purpose for which the spoken dialogue system is intended. If the goal is to make the system work *in the field*, then robust performance and real-time operation become the key factors, and the dialogue manager should drive the user to speak in a constrained way. Under these circumstances, the interaction model will be simple and the techniques developed so far are likely to be adequate. If, on the other hand, immediate applicability is not the main concern, there are several topics into which a deeper insight must still be gained. These include the design of strategies to better cope with troublesome speakers, to achieve better trade-offs between flexibility and robustness, and to increase portability to different tasks/languages.

The performance of the recognition/understanding modules can be improved when they are properly integrated in a dialogue system. The knowledge of the dialogue status, in fact, generates expectations on what the user is about to say, and hence can be used to restrict the dictionary or the linguistic constraints of the speech understanding module, thereby increasing their accuracy. These *predictions* have been shown to yield practical improvements (see e.g., Andry, 1992), though they remain a subject for research. Since recognition errors will never be completely ruled out, it is important that the user can detect and recover from wrong system answers in the shortest possible time. The influence of the dialogue strategy on error recovery speed was studied in Hirschman and Pao (1993). It is hoped that the growing collaboration between the speech and natural language communities may provide progress in these areas.

6.5   Chapter References

ACL (1994). *Proceedings of the 32nd Annual Meeting of the Association for Computational Linguistics*, Las Cruces, New Mexico. Association for Computational Linguistics.

Allen, J. F. (1979). A plan-based approach to speech act recognition. Technical Report 131, Department of Computer Science, University of Toronto, Toronto, Canada.

Allen, J. F. and Perrault, C. R. (1980). Analyzing intention in dialogues. *Artificial Intelligence*, 15(3):143–178.

Andry, F. (1992). Static and dynamic predictions: a method to improve speech understanding in cooperative dialogues. In *Proceedings of the 1992 International Conference on Spoken Language Processing*, volume 1, pages 639–642, Banff, Alberta, Canada. University of Alberta.

Andry, F., Bilange, E., Charpentier, F., Choukri, K., Ponamalé, M., and Soudoplatoff, S. (1990). Computerised simulation tools for the design of an oral dialogue system. In *Selected Publications, 1988-1990, SUNDIAL Project (Esprit P2218)*. Commission of the European Communities.

Appelt, D. E. (1985). *Planning English Sentences*. Cambridge University Press.

ARPA (1993). *Proceedings of the 1993 ARPA Spoken Language Systems Technology Workshop*. Advanced Research Projects Agency, MIT.

Austin, J. L. (1962). *How to do things with words*. Oxford University Press, London.

Bilange, E. (1991). A task independent oral dialogue model. In *Proceedings of the Fifth Conference of the European Chapter of the Association for Computational Linguistics*, Berlin. European Chapter of the Association for Computational Linguistics.

Bilange, E., Guyomard, M., and Siroux, J. (1990). Separating dialogue knowledge and task knowledge from oral dialogue management. In *COGNITIVA '90*, Madrid.

Bobrow, D. and PARC Understander Group, T. (1977). GUS-1, a frame driven dialog system. *Artificial Intelligence*, 8(2):155–173.

Bylander, E. (1991). Complexity results for planning. In *Proceedings of the 12th International Joint Conference on Artificial Intelligence*, pages 274–279, Sydney, Australia.

Carberry, S. (1985). A pragmatics-based approach to understanding intersen-
tential ellipses. In *Proceedings of the 23rd Annual Meeting of the Association for Computational Linguistics*, pages 188–197, University of Chicago.
Association for Computational Linguistics.

Carberry, S. (1990). *Plan recognition in natural language dialogue*. ACL-MIT
Press Series in Natural Language Processing. Bradford Books, MIT Press,
Cambridge, Massachusetts.

Cawsey, A. (1992). *Explanation and Interaction: The Computer Generation of
Explanatory Dialogues*. ACL-MIT Press.

Chapman, D. (1987). Planning for conjunctive goals. *Artificial Intelligence*,
32(3):333–377.

Clark, H. H. (1989). Contributing to discourse. *Cognitive Science*, 13:259–294.

Clark, H. H. and Wilkes-Gibbs, D. (1986). Referring as a collaborative process.
Cognition, 22:1–39. Reprinted in Cohen, Morgan, et al. (1990).

Cohen, P. R. and Levesque, H. J. (1980). Speech acts and the recognition
of shared plans. In *Proceedings of the Third Biennial Conference*, pages
263–271, Victoria, British Columbia. Canadian Society for Computational
Studies of Intelligence.

Cohen, P. R. and Levesque, H. J. (1990). Rational interaction as the basis for
communication. In Cohen, P. R., Morgan, J., and Pollack, M. E., editors,
Intentions in Communication. MIT Press, Cambridge, Massachusetts.

Cohen, P. R. and Levesque, H. J. (1991a). Confirmations and joint action. In
*Proceedings of the 12th International Joint Conference on Artificial Intel-
ligence*, pages 951–957, Sydney, Australia.

Cohen, P. R. and Levesque, H. J. (1991b). Teamwork. *Noûs*, 25(4):487–512.
Also Technical Note 504, Artificial Intelligence Center, SRI International,
Menlo Park, California, 1991.

Cohen, P. R., Morgan, J., and Pollack, M. E., editors (1990). *Intentions in
Communication*. MIT Press, Cambridge, Massachusetts.

Cohen, P. R. and Perrault, C. R. (1979). Elements of a plan-based theory of
speech acts. *Cognitive Science*, 3(3):177–212.

Dahlbäck, N. and Jönsson, A. (1992). An empirically based computationally
tractable dialogue model. In *Proceedings of the 14th Annual Conference of
the Cognitive Science Society (COGSCI-92)*, Bloomington, Indiana.

Dale, R., Hovy, E. H., Rösner, D., and Stock, O., editors (1992). *Aspects of
Automated Natural Language Generation*. Number 587 in Lecture Notes in
AI. Springer-Verlag, Heidelberg.

Davis, J. R. and Hirschberg, J. (1988). Assigning intonational features in synthesized spoken directions. In *Proceedings of the 26th Annual Meeting of the Association for Computational Linguistics*, pages 187–193, SUNY, Buffalo, New York. Association for Computational Linguistics.

Delin, J., Hartley, A., Paris, C., Scott, D., and Vander Linden, K. (1994). Expressing procedural relationships in multilingual instructions. In *Proceedings of the Seventh International Workshop on Natural Language Generation*, pages 61–70, Kennebunkport, Maine. Springer-Verlag, Berlin.

Delin, J., Scott, D., and Hartley, A. (1993). Knowledge, intention, rhetoric: Levels of variation in multilingual instructions. In *Proceedings of the Workshop on Intentionality and Structure in Discourse Relations*, Columbus, Ohio. Association for Computational Linguistics.

Edmonds, P. G. (1993). A computational model of collaboration on reference in direction-giving dialogues. Master's thesis, Computer Systems Research Institute, Department of Computer Science, University of Toronto.

Eurospeech (1993). *Eurospeech '93, Proceedings of the Third European Conference on Speech Communication and Technology*, Berlin. European Speech Communication Association.

Fraser, N. and Gilbert, N. (1989). Simulating speech systems. *Computer, Speech, and Language*, 3.

Fraser, N. M. and Gilbert, G. N. (1991). Simulating speech systems. *Computer Speech and Language*, 5(1):81–99.

Gerbino, E. and Danieli, M. (1993). Managing dialogue in a continuous speech understanding system. In *Eurospeech '93, Proceedings of the Third European Conference on Speech Communication and Technology*, volume 3, pages 1661–1664, Berlin. European Speech Communication Association.

Gilbert, N., Wooffitt, R., and Fraser, N. (1990). Organising computer talk. In Luff, P., Gilbert, N., and Frohlich, D., editors, *Computers and Conversation*, chapter 11, pages 235–258. Academic Press, New York.

Green, N. and Carberry, S. (1994). A hybrid reasoning model for indirect answers. In *Proceedings of the 32nd Annual Meeting of the Association for Computational Linguistics*, Las Cruces, New Mexico. Association for Computational Linguistics.

Grice, H. P. (1969). Utterer's meaning and intentions. *Philosophical Review*, 68(2):147–177.

Grosz, B. and Hirschberg, J. (1992). Some intonational characteristics of discourse structure. In *Proceedings of the 1992 International Conference on Spoken Language Processing*, volume 1, pages 429–432, Banff, Alberta, Canada. University of Alberta.

Grosz, B. and Kraus, S. (1993). Collaborative plans for group activities. In *Proceedings of IJCAI-93*, volume 1, pages 367–373, Chambery, France.

Grosz, B., Pollack, M., and Sidner, C. (1989). Discourse. In Posner, M., editor, *Foundations of Cognitive Science*. MIT Press.

Grosz, B. J. and Sidner, C. L. (1986). Attention, intention, and the structure of discourse. *Computational Linguistics*, 12(3):175–204.

Grosz, B. J. and Sidner, C. L. (1990). Plans for discourse. In Cohen, P. R., Morgan, J., and Pollack, M. E., editors, *Intentions in Communication*, pages 417–444. MIT Press, Cambridge, Massachusetts.

Grosz, B. J., Sparck Jones, K., and Webber, B. L., editors (1986). *Readings in Natural Language Processing*. Morgan Kaufmann Publishers, Inc.

Guyomard, M. and Siroux, J. (1988). Experimentation in the specification of an oral dialogue. In Niemann, H., Lang, M., and Sagerer, G., editors, *Recent Advances in Speech Understanding and Dialog Systems*, volume 46. Springer Verlag, Berlin. NATO ASI Series.

Heeman, P. A. and Hirst, G. (1992). Collaborating on referring expressions. Technical Report 435, Department of Computer Science, University of Rochester, Rochester, New York.

Hirschberg, J. and Grosz, B. J. (1992). Intonational features of local and global discourse structure. In *Proceedings of the Fifth DARPA Speech and Natural Language Workshop*. Defense Advanced Research Projects Agency, Morgan Kaufmann.

Hirschman, L. and Pao, C. (1993). The cost of errors in a spoken language system. In *Eurospeech '93, Proceedings of the Third European Conference on Speech Communication and Technology*, volume 2, pages 1419–1422, Berlin. European Speech Communication Association.

Hobbs, J. R. (1985). On the coherence and structure of discourse. Technical Report CSLI-85-37, Center for the Study of Language and Information, Stanford University.

Hobbs, J. R. (1993). Intention, information, and structure in discourse. In *Proceedings of the NATO Advanced Research Workshop on Burning Issues in Discourse*, pages 41–66, Maratea, Italy.

Hobbs, J. R., Stickel, M., Appelt, D., and Martin, P. (1993). Interpretation as abduction. *Artificial Intelligence*, 63(1-2):69–142.

Hobbs, J. R., Stickel, M. E., Appelt, D. E., and Martin, P. (1994). Interpretation as abduction. In Pereira, F. C. N. and Grosz, B. J., editors, *Natural Language Processing*. MIT Press, Cambridge, Massachusetts.

Hovy, E. H. (1990). Parsimonious and profligate approaches to the question of discourse structure relations. In IWNLG, editor, *Proceedings of the Fifth International Workshop on Natural Language Generation*, Pittsburgh, Pennsylvania. Springer-Verlag.

Hovy, E. H. (1991). Approaches to the planning of coherent text. In Paris, C. L., Swartout, W. R., and Mann, W. C., editors, *Natural Language Generation in Artificial Intelligence and Computational Linguistics*. Kluwer Academic.

ICSLP (1992). *Proceedings of the 1992 International Conference on Spoken Language Processing*, Banff, Alberta, Canada. University of Alberta.

IJCAI (1991). *Proceedings of the 12th International Joint Conference on Artificial Intelligence*, Sydney, Australia.

IWNLG (1994). *Proceedings of the Seventh International Workshop on Natural Language Generation*, Kennebunkport, Maine. Springer-Verlag, Berlin.

Jacobs, P. S. and Rau, L. F. (1994). Innovations in text interpretation. In Pereira, F. C. N. and Grosz, B. J., editors, *Natural Language Processing*. MIT Press, Cambridge, Massachusetts.

Jefferson, G. (1972). Side sequences. In Sudnow, D., editor, *Studies in Social Interaction*. Free Press, New York.

Jennings, N. R. and Mamdani, E. H. (1992). Using joint responsibility to coordinate collaborative problem solving in dynamic environments. In *Proceedings of the Tenth National Conference on Artificial Intelligence*, pages 269–275, Menlo Park, California. American Association for Artificial Intelligence, AAAI Press/MIT Press.

Kamp, H. (1981). A theory of truth and semantic representation. In Groenendijk, J., Janssen, T., and Stokhof, M., editors, *Formal Methods in the Study of Language*. Mathematisch Centrum, Amsterdam.

Kamp, H. and Reyle, U. (1993). *From Discourse to Logic*. Kluwer, Dordrecht.

Karis, D. and Dobroth, K. M. (1991). Automating services with speech recognition over the public switched telephone network: Human factors considerations. *IEEE Journal of Selected Areas in Communications*, 9(4):574–585.

Kautz, H. (1990). A circumscriptive theory of plan recognition. In Cohen, P. R., Morgan, J., and Pollack, M. E., editors, *Intentions in Communication*. MIT Press, Cambridge, Massachusetts.

Kehler, A. (1994). Common topics and coherent situations: Interpreting ellipsis in the context of discourse inference. In *Proceedings of the 32nd Annual Meeting of the Association for Computational Linguistics*, Las Cruces, New Mexico. Association for Computational Linguistics.

Kehler, A. (1995). *Interpreting Cohesive Forms in the Context of Discourse Inference*. PhD thesis, Harvard University.

Lascarides, A. and Oberlander, J. (1992). Abducing temporal discourse. In *Proceedings of the Sixth International Workshop on Natural Language Generation*, pages 167–182, Trento, Italy. Springer-Verlag. Also in Dale, Hovy, et al. (1992).

Levinson, S. (1981). Some pre-observations on the modelling of dialogue. *Discourse Processes*, 4(1):93–116.

Levinson, S. C. (1983). *Pragmatics*. Cambridge University Press.

Litman, D. and Passoneau, R. (1993). Feasibility of automated discourse segmentation. In *Proceedings of the 31st Annual Meeting of the Association for Computational Linguistics*, Ohio State University. Association for Computational Linguistics.

Litman, D. J. and Allen, J. F. (1987). A plan recognition model for subdialogues in conversation. *Cognitive Science*, 11:163–200.

Litman, D. J. and Allen, J. F. (1990). Discourse processing and commonsense plans. In Cohen, P. R., Morgan, J., and Pollack, M. E., editors, *Intentions in Communication*, pages 365–388. MIT Press, Cambridge, Massachusetts.

Lochbaum, K. E. (1993). A collaborative planning approach to discourse understanding. Technical Report TR-20-93, Harvard University.

Lochbaum, K. E. (1994). *Using Collaborative Plans to Model the Intentional Structure of Discourse*. PhD thesis, Harvard University.

Lochbaum, K. E. (1995). The use of knowledge preconditions in language processing. In *Proceedings of the 1995 International Joint Conference on Artificial Intelligence*, Montreal, Canada. In press.

Mann, W. C. and Thompson, S. A. (1987). Rhetorical structure theory: A theory of text organization. Technical Report ISI/RS-87-190, Information Sciences Institute, University of Southern California.

Mast, M., Kompe, R., Kummert, F., and Niemann, H. (1992). The dialog module of the speech recognition and dialog system EVAR. In *Proceedings of the 1992 International Conference on Spoken Language Processing*, volume 2, pages 1573–1576, Banff, Alberta, Canada. University of Alberta.

McKeown, K. R. (1985). *Text Generation: Using Discourse Strategies and Focus Constraints to Generate Natural Language Text*. Studies in Natural Language Processing. Cambridge University Press.

Moore, J. D. and Paris, C. L. (1993). Planning texts for advisory dialogues: Capturing intentional and rhetorical information. *Computational Linguistics*, 19(4):651–694.

Moore, J. D. and Pollack, M. E. (1992). A problem for RST: The need for multi-level discourse analysis. *Computational Linguistics*, 18(4):537–544.

Palmer, M. S., Passonneau, R. J., Weir, C., and Finin, T. (1994). The kernel text understanding system. In Pereira, F. C. N. and Grosz, B. J., editors, *Natural Language Processing*. MIT Press, Cambridge, Massachusetts.

Paris, C. and Scott, D. (1994). Stylistic variation in multilingual instructions. In *Proceedings of the Seventh International Workshop on Natural Language Generation*, pages 45–52, Kennebunkport, Maine. Springer-Verlag, Berlin.

Peckham, J. (1993). A new generation of spoken language systems: recent results and lessons from the SUNDIAL project. In *Eurospeech '93, Proceedings of the Third European Conference on Speech Communication and Technology*, volume 1, pages 33–42, Berlin. European Speech Communication Association. Keynote address.

Pereira, F. C. N. and Grosz, B. J., editors (1994). *Natural Language Processing*. MIT Press, Cambridge, Massachusetts.

Perrault, C. R. and Allen, J. F. (1980). A plan-based analysis of indirect speech acts. *American Journal of Computational Linguistics*, 6(3):167–182.

Polanyi, R. and Scha, R. (1984). A syntactic approach to discourse semantics. In *Proceedings of the 10th International Conference on Computational Linguistics*, pages 413–419, Stanford University, California. ACL.

Reichman, R. (1981). *Plain-speaking: A theory and grammar of spontaneous discourse*. PhD thesis, Department of Computer Science, Harvard University, Cambridge, Massachusetts.

Sacks, H., Schegloff, E., and Jefferson, G. (1978). A simplest systematics for the organization of turn-taking in conversation. In Schenkein, J., editor, *Studies in the Organization of Conversational Interaction*. Academic Press, New York.

Sadek, D. (1991). Dialogue acts are rational plans. In *Proceedings of the ESCA/ETRW Workshop on the Structure of Multimodal Dialogue*, Maratea, Italy.

Schegloff, E. A. (1981). Discourse as an interactional achievement: Some uses of unh-huh and other things that come between sentences. In Tannen, D., editor, *Analyzing discourse: Text and talk*. Georgetown University Roundtable on Languages and Linguistics, Georgetown University Press, Washington, DC.

Searle, J. R. (1969). *Speech Acts: An essay in the philosophy of language*. Cambridge University Press.

Searle, J. R. (1976). The classification of illocutionary acts. *Language in Society*, 5.

Searle, J. R. (1990). Collective intentionality. In Cohen, P. R., Morgan, J., and Pollack, M. E., editors, *Intentions in Communication*. MIT Press, Cambridge, Massachusetts.

Seneff, S., Hirschman, L., and Zue, V. W. (1991). Interactive problem solving and dialogue in the ATIS domain. In *Proceedings of the Fourth DARPA Speech and Natural Language Workshop*, Pacific Grove, California. Defense Advanced Research Projects Agency, Morgan Kaufmann.

Shneiderman, B. (1980). Natural vs. precise concise languages for human operation of computers: Research issues and experimental approaches. In *Proceedings of the 18th Annual Meeting of the Association for Computational Linguistics*, pages 139–141, Philadelphia, Pennsylvania. Association for Computational Linguistics.

Sidner, C. and Israel, D. (1981). Recognizing intended meaning and speaker's plans. In *Proceedings of the 7th International Joint Conference on Artificial Intelligence*, pages 203–208, Vancouver, British Columbia.

Sidner, C. L. (1985). Plan parsing for intended response recognition in discourse. *Computational Intelligence*, 1(1):1–10.

Sinclair, J. M. and Coulthard, R. M. (1975). *Towards an analysis of discourse: The English used by teachers and pupils*. Oxford University Press, London.

Siroux, J. (1989). Pragmatics in a realization of a dialogue module. In Taylor, M. M., Néel, F., and Bouwhuis, D. G., editors, *The structure of multimodal dialogue*. Elsevier Science, Amsterdam.

Sonenberg, E., Tidhar, G., Werner, E., Kinny, D., Ljungberg, M., and Rao, A. (1994). Planned team activity. Technical Report 26, Australian Artificial Intelligence Institute.

Suchman, L. A. (1987). *Plans and situated actions: The problem of human/machine communication*. Cambridge University Press.

Traum, D. R. and Allen, J. F. (1994). Discourse obligations in dialogue processing. In *Proceedings of the 32nd Annual Meeting of the Association for Computational Linguistics*, Las Cruces, New Mexico. Association for Computational Linguistics.

Wahlster, W. (1993). Verbmobil, translation of face-to-face dialogs. In *Proceedings of the Fourth Machine Translation Summit*, pages 127–135, Kobe, Japan.

Wahlster, W., André, E., Finkler, W., Profitlich, H.-J., and Rist, T. (1993). Plan-based integration of natural language and graphics generation. *Artificial Intelligence*, pages 387–427.

Yamaoka, T. and Iida, H. (1991). Dialogue interpretation model and its application to next utterance prediction for spoken language processing. In *Eurospeech '91, Proceedings of the Second European Conference on Speech Communication and Technology*, pages 849–852, Genova, Italy. European Speech Communication Association.

Young, S. J. and Proctor, C. E. (1989). The design and implementation of dialogue control in voice operated database inquiry systems. *Computer, Speech, and Language*, 3.

Young, S. R., Hauptmann, A. G., Ward, W. H., Smith, E. T., and Werner, P. (1989). High level knowledge sources in usable speech recognition systems. *Communications of the ACM*, 32(2).

Chapter 7

Document Processing

7.1 Overview

Per-Kristian Halvorsen

Xerox-PARC, Palo Alto, California, USA

7.1.1 The Document

Work gets done through documents. When a negotiation draws to a close, a document is drawn up: an accord, a law, a contract, or an agreement. When a new organization is established, it is announced with a document. When research culminates, a document is created and published. And knowledge is transmitted through documents: research journals, text books, and newspapers. Documents are information organized and presented for human understanding. Documents are where information meets with people and their work. By bringing technology to the process of producing and using documents one has the opportunity to achieve significant productivity enhancements. This point is important in view of the fact that the derivation of productivity increases and economic value from technological innovation in information technologies has proven difficult. In the past decade, we have seen unsurpassed innovation in the area of information technology and in its deployment in the general office. Proven increases in the effectiveness of work have been much harder to come by (David, 1991; Brynjolfsson, 1993). By focusing on the work practices that surround the use of documents, we bring technology to bear on the pressure points for efficiency. While the prototypical document of the present may be printed, the document is a technology with millennia of technological change behind it.

An important change vector for the document concerns new types of content (speech and video in addition to text and pictures) and non-linear documents (hyper-media). Of equal importance is the array of new technologies for processing, analyzing and interpreting the content, in particular the natural language content, of the document. Language, whether spoken or written, provides the bulk of the information-carrying capacity of most work-oriented documents. The introduction of multi-media documents only extends the challenge for language technologies: analysis of spoken as well as written language will enhance the ability to navigate and retrieve multi-media documents.

7.1.2   Document Work Practices

The utility of information technology is amplified when its application reaches outside its native domain—the domain of the computer—and into the domain of everyday life. Files are the faint reflections in the computer domain of documents in the domain of everyday life. While files are created, deleted, renamed, backed up, and archived, our involvement with documents forms a much thicker fabric: Documents are read, understood, translated, plagiarized, forged, hated, loved and emasculated. The major phases of a document's life cycle are creation, storing, rendering (e.g., printing or other forms of presentation), distribution, acquisition, and retrieving (Figure 7.1). Each of these phases is now fundamen-

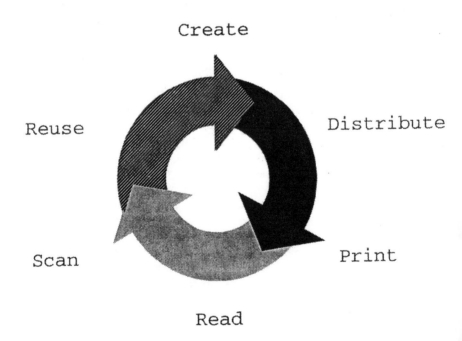

Figure 7.1: The life cycle of a document.

tally supported by digital technology: Word processors and publishing systems (for the professional publisher as well as for the desktop user) facilitate the creation phase, as do multi-media production environments.

Document (text) databases provide storage for the documents. Rendering is made more efficient through software for the conversion of documents to Page Description Languages (PDLs), and so-called imagers, which take PDL representations to a printable or projectable image. Distribution takes place through fax, networked and on-demand printing, Electronic Data Interchange (EDI), and electronic mail. Acquisition of documents in print form for the purpose of integration into the electronic domain takes place through the use of scanners, image processing software, optical character recognition (OCR), and document recognition or reconstruction. Access is accomplished through document databases. Natural language technologies can yield further improvements in these processes when combined with the fundamental technologies in each phase to facilitate the work that is to be done.

Creation: Authoring aids put computing to the task of assisting in the preparation of the content and linguistic expression in a document in the same way that word processors assist in giving the document form. This area holds tremendous potential. Even the most basic authoring aid—spelling checking—is far from ubiquitous in 1994: The capability and its utility has been proven in the context of English language applications, but the deployment in product settings for other languages is just beginning, and much descriptive linguistic work remains to be done. Grammar and style checking, while unproven with respect to their productivity enhancement, carry significant attraction as an obvious extension to spelling checking. The dependence on challenging linguistic descriptive work is even more compelling for this capability than for the spelling checking task. Authoring tools do not exhaust the range of language-based technologies which can help in the document creation process. Document creation is to a large extent document reuse. The information in one document often provides the basis for the formulation of another, whether through translation, excerpting, summarizing, or other forms of content-oriented transformation (as in the preparation of new legal contracts). Thus, what is often thought of as access technologies can play an important role in the creation phase.

Storage: Space, speed and ease of access are the most important parameters for document storage technologies. Linguistically based compression techniques (e.g., token-based encoding) can result in dramatically reduced space requirements in specialized application settings. Summarization techniques can come into play at the time of storage (filing) to prepare for easier access through the generation of compact but meaningful representatives of the documents. This is not a fail-safe arena for deployment, and robustness of the technology is essential for success in this application domain.

Distribution: With the geometric increase in electronically available information, the demand for automatic filtering and routing techniques has become universal. Current e-mail and work group support systems have rudimentary capabilities for filtering and routing. The document understanding and information extraction technologies described in this chapter could provide dramatic improvements on these functions by identifying significant elements in the content of the document available for the use of computational filtering and routing agents.

Acquisition: The difficulty of integrating the world of paper documents into the world of electronic document management is a proven productivity sink. The role of natural language models in improving optical character recognition and document reconstruction is highly underexploited and just now being reflected in commercial products.

Access: An organization's cost for accessing a document far dominates the cost of filing it in the first place. The integration of work flow systems with content-based document access systems promises to expand one of the fastest growing segments of the enterprise level software market (work flow) from the niche of highly structured and transaction oriented organizations (e.g., insurance claim processing), to the general office which traffics in *free text* documents, and not just forms. The access phase is a ripe area for the productivity enhancing injection of language processing technology. Access is a fail-safe area in that improvements are cumulative and 100% accuracy of the language analysis is not a prerequisite for measurably improved access. Multiple technologies (e.g., traditional retrieval techniques, summarization, information extraction) can be synergetically deployed to facilitate access.

7.2   Document Retrieval

Donna Harman,[a] Peter Schäuble,[b] & Alan Smeaton[c]

[a] NIST, Gaithersburg, Maryland, USA
[b] ETH Zurich, Switzerland
[c] Dublin City University, Ireland, UK

Document retrieval is defined as the matching of some stated user query against useful parts of free-text records. These records could be any type of mainly unstructured text, such as bibliographic records, newspaper articles, or paragraphs in a manual. User queries could range from multi-sentence full descriptions of an information need to a few words, and the vast majority of retrieval systems currently in use range from simple Boolean systems through to systems using statistical or natural language processing. Figure 7.2 illustrates the manner in which documents are retrieved from various sources.

Several events have recently occurred that are having a major effect on research in this area. First, computer hardware is more capable of running sophisticated search algorithms against massive amounts of data, with acceptable response times. Second, Internet access, such as World Wide Web (WWW), brings new search requirements from untrained users who demand user-friendly, effective text searching systems. These two events have contributed to creating

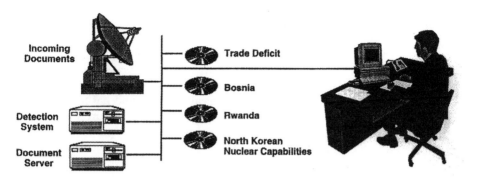

Figure 7.2: The document retrieval process.

an interest in accelerating research to produce more effective search methodologies, including more use of natural language processing techniques.

There has been considerable research in the area of document retrieval for more than thirty years (Belkin & Croft, 1987), dominated by the use of statistical methods to automatically match natural language user queries against records. For almost as long, there has been interest in using natural language processing to enhance single term matching by adding phrases (Fagan, 1989), yet to date natural language processing techniques have not significantly improved performance of document retrieval, although much effort has been expended in various attempts. The motivation and drive for using natural language processing (NLP) in document retrieval is mostly intuitive; users decide on the relevance of documents by reading and analyzing them and if we can automate document analysis this should help in the process of deciding on document relevance.

Some of the research into document retrieval has taken place in the ARPA-sponsored TIPSTER project. One of the TIPSTER groups, the University of Massachusetts at Amherst, experimented with expansion of their state-of-the-art INQUERY retrieval system so that it was able to handle the three gigabyte test collection. This included research in the use of query structures, document structures, and extensive experimentation in the use of phrases (Broglio, Callan, et al., 1993). These phrases (usually noun phrases) were found using a part-of-speech tagger and were used either to improve query performance or to expand the query. In general, the use of phrases, as opposed to single terms, for retrieval did not significantly improve performance, although the use of noun phrases to expand a query shows much more promise. This group has found phrases to be useful in retrieval for smaller collections, or for collections in a narrow domain.

A second TIPSTER group using natural language processing techniques was Syracuse University. A new system, the DR-LINK system, based on automatically finding conceptual structures for both documents and queries, was developed using extensive natural language processing techniques such as document structure discovery, discourse analysis, subject classification, and complex nominal encapsulation. This very complex system was barely finished by the end of phase I (Liddy & Myaeng, 1993), but represents the most complex natural language processing system ever developed for document retrieval .

The TIPSTER project has progressed to a second phase that will involve even more collaboration between NLP researchers and experts. The plan is to develop an architecture that will allow standardized communication between document retrieval modules (usually statistically based) and natural language processing modules (usually linguistically based). The architecture will then be used to build several projects that require the use of both types of techniques. In addition to this theme, the TIPSTER phase II project will investigate more thoroughly the specific contributions of natural language processing to enhanced retrieval performance. Two different groups, the University of Massachusetts at Amherst group combined with a natural language group at BBN Inc., and a group from New York University will perform many experiments that are likely to uncover further evidence of the usefulness of natural language processing in document retrieval.

The same collection used for testing in the TIPSTER project has been utilized by a much larger worldwide community of researchers in the series of Text REtrieval Conference (TREC) evaluation tasks. Research groups representing very diverse approaches to document retrieval have taken part in this annual event and many have used NLP resources like lexicons, dictionaries, thesauri, proper name recognizers and databases, etc. One of these groups, New York University, investigated the gains for using more intensive natural language processing on top of a traditional statistical retrieval system (Strzalkowski, Carballo, et al., 1995). This group did a complete parse of the two Gbyte texts to locate content-carrying terms, discover relationships between these terms, and then use these terms to expand or modify the queries. This entire process is completely automatic, and major effort has been put into the efficiency of the natural language processing part of the system. A second group using natural language processing was the group from General Electric Research and Development Center (Jacobs, 1994). They used natural language processing techniques to extract information from (mostly) the training texts. This information was then used to create manual filters for the routing task part of TREC. Another group using natural language processing techniques in TREC was CLARITECH (Evans & Lefferts, 1994). This group used only noun phrases for retrieval and built dynamic thesauri for query expansion for each topic using noun phrases found in highly ranked documents. A group from Dublin City University derived tree structures from texts based on syntactic analysis and incorporated syntactic ambiguities into the trees (Smeaton, O'Donnell, et al., 1995). In this case document retrieval used a tree-matching algorithm to rank documents. Finally, a group from Siemens used the WordNet lexical database as a basis for query expansion (Voorhees, Gupta, et al., 1995) with mixed results.

The situation in the U.S. as outlined above is very similar to the situation in Europe. The European Commission's Linguistic Research and Engineering (LRE) sub-programme funds projects like CRISTAL, which is developing a multilingual interface to a database of French newspaper stories using NLP techniques, and RENOS, which is doing similar work in the legal domain. The E.U.-funded SIMPR project also used morpho-syntactic analysis to identify indexing phrases for text. Other European work using NLP is reported in Hess (1992); Ruge (1992); Schwarz and Thurmair (1986); Chiaramella and Nie (1990) and summarized in Smeaton (1992).

Most researchers in the information retrieval community believe that retrieval effectiveness is easier to improve by means of statistical methods than by NLP-based approaches and this is borne out by results, although there are exceptions. The fact that only a fraction of information retrieval research is based on extensive natural language processing techniques indicates that NLP techniques do not dominate the current thrust of information retrieval research as does something like the Vector Space Model. Yet NLP resources used in extracting information from text as described by Paul Jacobs in section 7.3, resources like thesauri, lexicons, dictionaries, proper name databases, are used regularly in information retrieval research. It seems, therefore, that NLP *resources* rather than NLP techniques are having more of an impact on document retrieval effectiveness at present. Part of the reason for this is that natural language processing techniques are generally not designed to handle large amounts of text from many different domains. This is reminiscent of the situation with respect to information extraction which likewise is not currently successful in broad domains. But information retrieval systems do need to work on broad domains in order to be useful, and the way NLP techniques are being used in information retrieval research is to attempt to integrate them with the dominant statistically-based approaches, almost piggy-backing them together. There is, however, an inherent granularity mismatch between the statistical techniques used in information retrieval and the linguistic techniques used in natural language processing. The statistical techniques attempt to match the rough statistical approximation of a record to a query. Further refinement of this process using fine-grained natural language processing techniques often adds only noise to the matching process, or fails because of the vagaries of language use. The proper integration of these two techniques is very difficult and may be years in coming. What is needed is the development of NLP techniques specifically for document retrieval and, vice versa, the development of document retrieval techniques specifically for taking advantage of NLP techniques.

Future Directions

The recommendations for further research are therefore to continue to pursue this integration but paying more attention to how to adapt the output of current natural language methods to improving information retrieval techniques. In addition, NLP techniques could be used directly to produce tools for information retrieval, such as creating knowledge bases or simple thesauri using data mining.

7.3   Text Interpretation: Extracting Information

Paul Jacobs

SRA International, Arlington, Virginia, USA

The proliferation of on-line text motivates most current work in text interpretation. Although massive volumes of information are available at low cost in free text form, people cannot read and digest this information any faster than before; in fact, for the most part they can digest even less. Often, being able to make efficient use of information from text requires that the information be put in some sort of structured format, for example, in a relational database, or systematically indexed and linked. Currently, extracting the information required for a useful database or index is usually an expensive manual process; hence on-line text creates a need for automatic text processing methods to extract the information automatically (Figure 7.3).

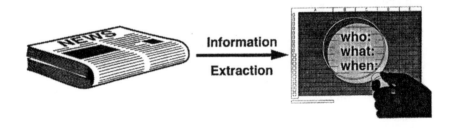

Figure 7.3: The problem of information extraction from text.

Current methods and systems can digest and analyze significant volumes of text at rates of a few thousand words per minute. Using *text skimming*, often driven by finite-state recognizers (discussed in chapters 3 and 11 of this volume), current methods generally start by identifying key artifacts in the text, such as proper names, dates, times, and locations, and then use a combination of linguistic constraints and domain knowledge to identify the important content of each relevant text. For example, in news stories about joint ventures, a system can usually identify joint venture partners by locating names of companies, finding linguistic relations between company names and words that describe business tie-ups, and using certain domain knowledge, such as understanding that ventures generally involve at least two partners and result in the formation of a new company. Other applications are illustrated in Ciravegna, Campia, et al. (1992); Mellish et al. (1995). Although there has been independent work in this area and there are a number of systems in commercial use, much of the recent progress in this area has come from U.S. government-sponsored programs and evaluation conferences, including the TIPSTER Text Program and the MUC and TREC evaluations described in chapter 13. In information extraction from text, the TIPSTER program, for example, fostered the development of systems that could extract many important details from news stories in English and Japanese. The scope of this task was much broader than in any previous project.

The current state of the art has produced rapid advances in the robustness and applicability of these methods. However, current systems are limited because they invariably rely, at least to some degree, on domain knowledge or other specialized models, which still demands time and effort (usually several person-months, even in limited domains). These problems are tempered somewhat by the availability of on-line resources, such as lexicons, corpora, lists of companies, gazetteers, and so forth, but the issue of how to develop a technology base that applies to many problems is still the major challenge.

In recent years, technology has progressed quite rapidly, from systems that could accurately process text in only very limited domains (for example, engine service reports) to programs that can perform useful information extraction from a very broad range of texts (for example, business news). The two main forces behind these advances are: (1) the development of robust text processing architectures, including finite state approximation and other shallow but effective sentence processing methods, and (2) the emergence of weak heuristic and statistical methods that help to overcome knowledge acquisition problems by making use of corpus and training data.

Finite-state approximation (Jacobs, Krupka, et al., 1993; Pereira, 1990) is a key element of current text interpretation methods. Finite-state recognizers generally admit a broader range of possible sentences than most parsers based on context-free grammars, and usually apply syntactic constraints in a weaker fashion. Although this means that finite-state recognizers will sometimes treat sentences as grammatical when they are not, the usual effect is that the finite state approximation is more efficient and fault tolerant than a context-free model.

The success of finite-state and other shallow recognizers, however, depends on the ability to express enough word knowledge and domain knowledge to control interpretation. While more powerful parsers tend to be controlled mainly by linguistic constraints, finite state recognizers usually depend on lexical constraints to select the best interpretation of an input. In limited domains, these constraints are part of the domain model; for example, when the phrase *unidentified assailant* appears in a sentence with *terrorist attack*, it is quite likely that the assailant is the perpetrator of the attack.

In broader domains, successful interpretation using shallow sentence processing requires lexical data rather than domain knowledge. Such data can often be obtained from a corpus using statistical methods (Church, Gale, et al., 1991). These statistical models have been of only limited help so far in information extraction systems, but they show promise for continuing to improve the coverage and accuracy of information extraction in the future.

Much of the key information in interpreting texts in these applications comes not from sentences but from larger discourse units, such as paragraphs and even complete documents. Interpreting words and phrases in the context of a complete discourse, and identifying the discourse structure of extended texts, are important components of text interpretation. At present, discourse models rely mostly on domain knowledge (Iwanska, Appelt, et al., 1991). Like the problem of controlling sentence parsing, obtaining more general discourse processing capabilities seems to depend on the ability to use discourse knowledge acquired from examples in place of detailed hand-crafted domain models.

Future Directions

We can expect that the future of information extraction will bring broader and more complete text interpretation capabilities; this will help systems to categorize, index, summarize, and generalize from texts from information sources such as newspapers and reference materials. Such progress depends now on the development of better architectures for handling information beyond the sentence level, and on continued progress in acquiring knowledge from corpus data.

7.4   Summarization

Karen Sparck Jones

University of Cambridge, Cambridge, UK

Automatic abstracting was first attempted in the 1950s, in the form of Luhn's auto-extracts, (cf. Paice, 1990); but since then there has been little work on, or progress made with, this manifestly very challenging task. However, the increasing volume of machine-readable text, and advances in natural language processing, have stimulated a new interest in automatic summarizing reflected in the 1993 Dagstuhl Seminar, *Summarizing text for intelligent communication* (Endres-Niggemeyer, Hobbs, et al., 1995). Summarizing techniques tested so far have been limited either to general, but shallow and weak approaches, or to deep but highly application-specific ones. There is a clear need for more powerful, i.e., general but adaptable, methods. But these must as far as possible be linguistic methods, not requiring extensive world knowledge and being able to deal with large-scale text structure as well as individual sentences.

7.4.1   Analytical Framework

Work done hitherto, relevant technologies, and required directions for new research are usefully characterized by reference to an analytical framework covering both factors affecting summarizing and the essential summarizing process. I shall concentrate on text, but the framework applies to discourse in general including dialogue.

A summary text is a derivative of a source text condensed by selection and/or generalization on important content. This is not an operational definition, but it emphasizes the crux of summarizing, reducing whole sources without requiring pre-specification of desired content, and allows content to cover both information and its expression. This broad definition subsumes a very wide range of specific variations. These stem from the *context factors* characterizing individual summarizing applications. Summarizing is conditioned by *input factors* categorizing source form and subject; by *purpose factors* referring to audience and function; and also, subject to input and purpose constraints, by *output factors* including summary format and style.

The global process model has two major phases: *interpretation* of the source text involving both local sentence analysis and integration of sentence analyses into an overall *source meaning representation*; and *generation* of the summary by formation of the *summary representation* using the source one and subsequent synthesis of the summary text. This logical model emphasizes the role of text representations and the central transformation stage. It thus focuses on what source representations should be like for summarizing, and on what condensation on important content requires. Previous approaches to summarizing can be categorized and assessed, and new ones designed, according to (a) the nature of their source representation, including its distance from the source text, its relative emphasis on *linguistic, communicative* or *domain information* and therefore the structural model it employs and the way this marks important content; and (b) the nature of its processing steps, including whether all the model stages are present and how independent they are.

7.4.2 Past Work

For instance, reviewing past work (see Paice, 1990; Sparck Jones, 1993), source text extraction using statistical cues to select key sentences to form summaries is taking both source and summary texts as their own linguistic representations and also essentially conflating the interpretation and generation steps. Approaches using cue words as a base for sentence selection are also directly exploiting only linguistic information for summarizing. When headings or other locational criteria are exploited, this involves a very shallow source text representation depending on primarily linguistic notions of text grammar, though Liddy et al. (1993) has a richer grammar for a specific text type.

Approaches using scripts or frames on the other hand (Young & Hayes, 1985; DeJong, 1979) involve deeper representations and ones of an explicitly domain-oriented kind motivated by properties of the world. DeJong's work illustrates the case where the source representation is deliberately designed for summarizing, so there is little transformation effort in deriving the summary template representation. In the approach of Rau (1988), however, the hierarchic domain-based representation allows generalization for summarizing.

There has also been research combining different information types in representation. Thus, Hahn (1990) combines linguistic theme and domain structure in source representations, and seeks salient concepts in these for summaries.

Overall in this work, source reduction is mainly done by selection: this may use general, application-independent criteria, but is more commonly domain-guided as in Marsh, Hamburger, et al. (1984), or relies on prior, inflexible specification of the kind of information sought, as with DeJong (1979), which may be as tightly constrained as in MUC. There is no significant condensation of input content taken as a whole: in some cases even little length reduction. There has been no systematic comparative study of different types of source representation for summarizing, or of context factor implications. Work hitherto has been extremely fragmentary and, except where it resembles indexing or is for very specific and restricted kinds of material, has not been very successful. The largest-scale automatic summarizing experiment done so far has been DeJong's, applying script-based techniques to news stories. There do not appear to be any operational summarizing systems.

7.4.3   Relevant Disciplines

The framework suggests there are many possibilities to explore. But given the nature and complexity of summarizing, it is evident that ideas and experience relevant to automatic summarizing must be sought in many areas. These include human summarizing, a trained professional skill that provides an iterative, processual view of summarizing often systematically exploiting surface cues; discourse and text linguistics supplying a range of theories of discourse structure and of text types bearing on summarizing in general, on different treatments suited to different source types, and on the relation between texts, as between source and summary texts; work on discourse comprehension, especially that involving or facilitating summarizing; library and information science studies of user activities exploiting abstracts e.g., to serve different kinds of information need; research on user modeling in text generation, for tailoring summaries; and NLP technology generally in supplying both workhorse sentence processing for interpretation and generation and methods for dealing with local coherence, as well as results from experiments with forms of large-scale text structure, if only for generation so far, not recognition. Some current work drawing on these inputs is reported in IPM (1995); it also illustrates a growing interest in generating summaries from non-text material.

7.4.4   Future Directions

The *full text revolution*, also affecting indexing, implies a pressing need for automatic summarizing, and current NLP technology provides the basic resource for this. There are thus complementary shorter and longer term lines of work to undertake, aimed at both practical systems and a scientific theory of summarizing, as follows:

1. Develop shallow-processing techniques that exploit robust parsing, and surface or statistical pointers to key topics and topic connections, for simple indexing-type information extracts and summaries.

2. Seek generalizations of deep, domain-based approaches using e.g., frames, to reduce tight application constraints and extend system scopes.

3. Carry out systematic experiments to assess the potentialities of alternative types of source representation both for any summarizing strategy and in relation to different context factor conditions.

4. Engage in user studies to establish roles and hence requirements for summaries as leading to or providing information, and to determine sound methods of evaluating summaries.

5. Explore dynamic, context-sensitive summarizing for interactive situations, in response to changing user needs as signaled by feedback and as affected by *ad hoc* assemblies of material.

7.5 Computer Assistance in Text Creation and Editing

Robert Dale
Microsoft Institute of Advanced Software Technology, Sydney, Australia

On almost every office desk there sits a PC, and on almost every PC there resides a word processing program. The business of text creation and editing represents a very large market, and a very natural one in which to ask how we might apply speech and natural language processing technologies. Below, we look at how language technologies are already being applied here, sketch some advances to be expected in the next five to ten years, and suggest where future research effort is needed.

Information technology solutions are generally of three types: accelerative, where an existing process is made faster; delegative, where the technology carries out a task previously the responsibility of a person; and augmentative, where the technology assists in an existing task. The major developments in the next five to ten years are likely to be of an augmentative nature, with increasingly sophisticated systems that have people and machines doing what they each do best. The key here is to add intelligence and sophistication to provide *language sensitivity*, enabling the software to see a text not just as a sequence of characters, but as words and sentences combined in particular structures for particular semantic and pragmatic effect.

7.5.1 Creation and Revision of Unconstrained Text: The Current Situation

Although language technologies can play a part in the process of text creation by providing intelligent access to informational resources, the more direct role is in the provision of devices for organizing text. The degree of organizational assistance that is possible depends very much on the extent to which regularity can be perceived or imposed on the text concerned. Document production systems which impose structure support text creation; the most useful offspring here has been the outliner, now a standard part of many word processing systems. In general, however, the model of documenthood these systems embody is too constrained for widespread use in text creation. While relatively structured documents are appropriate in some business contexts, other future markets will focus on home and leisure usage, where concerns other than structure may become relevant to the creation of text. In the following two subsections we focus on unconstrained text, whereas controlled languages are treated in section 7.6.

No existing tools in this area embody any real language sensitivity. Much of the initial exploratory work required here has reached computational linguistics via research in natural language generation; but we are still far away from being able to automatically *interpret* discourse structure in any sophisticated sense. Current models of discourse structure do not mirror the sophistication of our models of sentence structure, and so the scope for assistance in text creation will remain limited until significant research advances are made.

The story is very different for text revision. Here, language technology finds a wide range of possible applications. We already have the beginnings of language sensitivity in spelling correction technology: the techniques used here are now fairly stable, although without major advances (for example, taking explicit account of syntax and even semantics) we cannot expect much beyond current performance.

Grammar checking technology is really the current frontier of the state of the art. Commercial products in this area are still much influenced by the relatively superficial techniques used in the early Unix Writer's Workbench (WWB) system, but some current commercial systems (such as Grammatik and CorrecText) embody greater sophistication: these are the first products to use anything related to the parsing technologies developed in the research field. As machines become more powerful, and as broad-coverage grammars become more feasible, we can expect to see more of the CPU-hungry techniques developed in research labs finding their way into products; IBM's Critique system gives a flavor of what is to come.

Beyond grammar checking, the next important step is stylistic analysis. Anything more than the very simple string and pattern matching techniques first used in the Unix WWB system require the substrate of syntactic analysis, and, indeed, there are many aspects of style for which semantic and pragmatic analyses are required. Here, more than anywhere, the problem of different perceptions of the shape of the task rears its head: style is a term used to cover many things, from the form in which a date should be written to the overall feel of a text. Some of the simpler problems here are already being dealt with in products on the market, and this is where we can expect to see most developments in the next five years.

7.5.2   Future Directions

Medium-term Prospects

The key to medium-term developments in this area is the productization of parsing and grammar technologies. There are a number of shifts in research focus that are needed to accelerate this process.

1. Linguistic theories need to be assessed for their value in this working context: For example, are some theories more suited than others to the de-

velopment of a theory of syntactic error detection and correction? Do the standard linguistic distinctions between syntax, semantics and pragmatics stand up in this domain?

2. Parsing mechanisms need to be made far more robust than is usually taken to be necessary: no matter how broad coverage a grammar is, there will always be texts that do not conform. How does a system decide that it is faced with an ungrammatical sentence rather than a correct sentence for which it does not have a grammar rule? How is the handling of unknown words best integrated with the handling of grammatical errors?

3. How do we evaluate these systems? Corpora of errors are needed in order to determine which categories of errors are most frequent and where effort is best applied. A real problem here is knowing how to measure performance: the appropriate metrics have not yet been developed. Underlying these requirements is a need for a properly elaborated theory of textual error: what exactly counts as a spelling error as opposed to a syntactic error, for example?

4. How is the user to understand the basis of the system's proposed revisions? Because of the mismatch between the user's view of the problem and the language technologist's view, there is a need for better means of explaining errors to users in an acceptable way.

5. Finally, and most importantly, if we are to progress beyond rather trivial assistance in stylistic matters, we need a sizable effort directed at research on stylistic issues to build computational theories at that level.

Longer-term Prospects

We have already alluded above to the scope for incorporating sophisticated theories of discourse into the creation task in writing tools; similarly, the acceleration and delegation of language-centered tasks will become increasingly viable as advances are made in speech processing and natural language generation in the longer term.

Looking more broadly, we should be concerned not only with the words themselves, but also how they appear on the page or screen. The fact that, for example, we often have to make our texts fit word limits means that we have to take account of physical space. Systems should be able to reason about graphics as well as words, and systems should know about typographic devices.

Beyond these areas, there are new categories of assistance we might expect in the longer term. Modes of writing themselves are likely to adapt to accommodate the uneven profile of ability offered by existing systems, with currently unpredictable back and forwards effects on the tools that become required. We cannot easily foresee what new market possibilities for computer-based writing tools the information superhighway will lead to; but there is a strong possibility that the categories we have previously thought in will no longer be the most appropriate.

7.6   Controlled Languages in Industry

Richard H. Wojcik & James E. Hoard

Boeing Information & Support Services, Seattle, Washington, USA

7.6.1   The Reason Why

Natural language permits an enormous amount of expressive variation. Writers, especially technical writers, tend to develop special vocabularies (jargons), styles, and grammatical constructions. Technical language becomes opaque not just to ordinary readers, but to experts as well. The problem becomes particularly acute when such text is translated into another language, since the translator may not even be an expert in the technical domain. Controlled Languages (CL) have been developed to counter the tendency of writers to use unusual or overly-specialized, inconsistent language.

A CL is a form of language with special restrictions on grammar, style, and vocabulary usage. Typically, the restrictions are placed on technical documents, including instructions, procedures, descriptions, reports, and cautions. One might consider formal written English to be the ultimate Controlled Language: a form of English with restricted word and grammar usages, but a standard too broad and too variable for use in highly technical domains. Whereas formal written English applies to society as a whole, CLs apply to the specialized sublanguages of particular domains.

The objective of a CL is to improve the consistency, readability, translatability, and retrievability of information. Creators of CLs usually base their grammar restrictions on well-established writing principles. For example, AECMA Simplified English limits the length of instructional sentences to no more than 20 words. It forbids the omission of articles in noun phrases, and requires that sequential steps be expressed in separate sentences.

7.6.2   Results

By now, hundreds of companies have turned to CLs as a means of improving readability or facilitating translation to other languages. The original CL was Caterpillar Fundamental English (CFE), created by the Caterpillar Tractor Company (USA) in the 1960s. Perhaps the best known recent controlled language is AECMA Simplified English (AECMA, 1995), which is unique in that it has been adopted by an entire industry, namely, the aerospace industry. The standard was developed to facilitate the use of maintenance manuals by non-native speakers of English. Aerospace manufacturers are required to write aircraft maintenance documentation in Simplified English. Some other well-known CLs are Smart's Plain English Program (PEP), White's International Language for Serving and Maintenance (ILSAM), Perkins Approved Clear English (PACE), and COGRAM (see Adriaens & Schreuers, 1992, which refers to some of these systems). Many CL standards are considered proprietary by the companies that have developed them.

7.6.3 Prospects

The prospects for CLs are especially bright today. Many companies believe that using a CL can give them something of a competitive edge in helping their customers operate and service their products. With the tremendous growth in international trade that is occurring worldwide, more and more businesses are turning to CLs as a method for making their documents easier to read for non-native speakers of the source language or easier to translate into the languages of their customers.

One of the factors stimulating the use of CLs is the appearance of new language engineering tools to support their use. Because the style, grammar, and vocabulary restrictions of a CL standard are complex, it is nearly impossible to produce good, consistent documents that comply with any CL by manual writing and editing methods. The Boeing Company has had a Simplified English Checker in production use since 1990, and Boeing's maintenance manuals are now supplied in Simplified English (Hoard, Wojcik, et al., 1992; Wojcik, Harrison, et al., 1993; LIM, 1993). Since 1990, several new products have come onto the market to support CL checking. A number of others exist in varying prototype stages. The Commission of the European Union has authorized a recent program to fund the development of such tools to meet the needs of companies that do business in the multilingual EU.

7.6.4 Future Directions

There are two principal problems that need to be kept in focus in the language engineering area. The first is that any CL standard must be validated with real users to determine if its objectives are met. If some CL aims, say, to improve readability by such and such an amount, then materials that conform to the standard must be tested to ensure that the claim is valid. Otherwise, bearing the cost and expense of putting materials into the CL is not worth the effort. The second problem is to develop automated checkers that help writers conform to the standard easily and effectively. One cannot expect any checker to certify that a text conforms completely to some CL. The reason is that some rules of any CL require human judgments that are beyond the capability of any current natural language software and may, in fact, never be attainable. What checkers can do is remove nearly all of the mechanical errors that writers make in applying a CL standard, leaving the writer to make the important judgments about the organization and exposition of the information that are so crucial to effective descriptions and procedures. The role of a checker is to make the grammar, style, and vocabulary usages consistent across large amounts of material that is created by large numbers of writers. Checkers reduce tremendously the need for editing and harmonizing document sections. Over the next decade, the kinds of CL rules that can be checked automatically will expand. With current technology, it is possible to check for syntactic correctness. In the coming years, it will also be quite feasible to check a text for conformity with sanctioned word senses and other semantic constraints. This will increase the cost effectiveness of providing documents in a CL to levels that can only be guessed at now.

7.7   Chapter References

Adriaens, G. and Schreuers, D. (1992). From COGRAM to ALCOGRAM: Toward a controlled English grammar checker. In *Proceedings of the 14th International Conference on Computational Linguistics*, pages 595–601, Nantes, France. ACL.

AECMA (1995). *AECMA Simplified English: A Guide for the Preparation of Aircraft Maintenance Documentation in the International Aerosace Maintenance Language*. AECMA, Brussels.

Belkin, N. J. and Croft, W. B. (1987). Retrieval techniques. In Williams, M., editor, *Annual Review of Information Science and Technology*, volume 22, pages 109–145. Elsevier, New York.

Broglio, J., Callan, J., and Croft, W. (1993). The INQUERY system. In Merchant, R., editor, *Proceedings of the TIPSTER Text Program—Phase I*, San Mateo, California. Morgan Kaufmann.

Brynjolfsson, E. (1993). The productivity paradox of information technology. *Communications of the ACM*, 36(12).

Chiaramella, Y. and Nie, J. (1990). A retrieval model based on an extended modal logic and its applications to the RIME experimental approach. In Vidick, J.-L., editor, *Proceedings of the 13th International Conference on Research and Development in Information Retrieval*, pages 25–44, Brussels, Belgium. ACM.

Church, K., Gale, W., Hanks, P., and Hindle, D. (1991). Using statistics in lexical analysis. In Zernik, U., editor, *Lexical Acquisition: Using On-Line Resources To Build A Lexicon*. Lawrence Earlbaum, Hillsdale, New Jersey.

Ciravegna, F., Campia, P., and Colognese, A. (1992). Knowledge extraction by SINTESI. In *Proceedings of the 14th International Conference on Computational Linguistics*, pages 1244–1248, Nantes, France. ACL.

COLING (1992). *Proceedings of the 14th International Conference on Computational Linguistics*, Nantes, France. ACL.

David, P. A. (1991). *Technology and Productivity The Challenge for Economic Policy*, chapter Computer and Dynamo—The modern productivity paradox in a not-too-distant mirror. ODED, Paris.

DeJong, G. F. (1979). *Skimming stories in real time: an experiment in integrated understanding*. PhD thesis, Yale University.

Endres-Niggemeyer, B., Hobbs, J., and Sparck Jones, K. (1995). Summarizing text for intelligent communication. Technical Report Dagstuhl Seminar Report 79, 13.12-19.12.93 (9350), IBFI, Dagstuhl. http://www.bid.fh-hannover.de/SimSum/Abstract/ (Short and Full versions, the latter only available in electronic form).

Evans, D. and Lefferts, R. (1994). Design and evaluation of the CLARIT–
  TREC-2 system. In Harman, D., editor, *National Institute of Standards
  and Technology Special Publication No. 500-215 on the The Second Text
  REtrieval Conference (TREC-2)*, Washington, DC. National Institute of
  Standards and Technology, U.S. Department of Commerce, U.S. Govern-
  ment Printing Office.

Fagan, J. L. (1989). The effectiveness of a nonsyntactic approach to automatic
  phrase indexing for document retrieval. *Journal of the American Society
  for Information Science*, 40(2):115–132.

Hahn, U. (1990). Topic parsing: accounting for text macro structures in full-text
  analysis. *Information Processing and Management*, 26(1):135–170.

Harman, D., editor (1994). *National Institute of Standards and Technology Special Publication No. 500-215 on the The Second Text REtrieval Conference
  (TREC-2)*, Washington, DC. National Institute of Standards and Technology, U.S. Department of Commerce, U.S. Government Printing Office.

Hess, M. (1992). An incrementally extensible document retrieval system based
  on linguistic and logical principles. In *Proceedings of the 15th SIGIR Conference*, pages 190–197, Copenhagen, Denmarkp.

Hoard, J., Wojcik, R., and Holzhauser, K. (1992). An automated grammar and
  style checker for writers of simplified English. In Holt, P. and Williams, N.,
  editors, *Computers and Writing*. Kluwer Academic Publishers, Boston.

IPM (1995). Special issue on automatic summarizing. *Information Processing
  and Management*, 31(3).

Iwanska, L., Appelt, D., Ayuso, D., Dahlgren, K., Glover Stalls, B., Grishman,
  R., Krupka, G., Montgomery, C., and Riloff, E. (1991). Computational
  aspects of discourse in the context of MUC-3. In *Proceedings of the Third
  Message Understanding Conference*, San Diego, California. Morgan Kaufmann.

Jacobs, P. (1994). GE in TREC-2: Results of a Boolean approximation method
  for routing and retrieval. In Harman, D., editor, *National Institute of Standards and Technology Special Publication No. 500-215 on the The Second
  Text REtrieval Conference (TREC-2)*, Washington, DC. National Institute
  of Standards and Technology, U.S. Department of Commerce, U.S. Government Printing Office.

Jacobs, P., Krupka, G., Rau, L., Mauldin, M., Mitamura, T., Kitani, T., Sider,
  I., and Childs, L. (1993). The TIPSTER/SHOGUN project. In *Proceedings
  of the TIPSTER Phase I Final Meeting*, San Mateo, California. Morgan
  Kaufmann.

Liddy, E. D. et al. (1993). Development, implementation and testing of a discourse model for newspaper texts. In *Proceedings of the 1993 ARPA Human Language Technology Workshop*, pages 159–164, Princeton, New Jersey. Advanced Research Projects Agency, Morgan Kaufmann.

Liddy, E. D. and Myaeng, S. H. (1993). DR–LINK: A system update for TREC-2. In Merchant, R., editor, *Proceedings of the TIPSTER Text Program—Phase I*, San Mateo, California. Morgan Kaufmann.

LIM (1993). The boeing simplified English checker. *Language Industry Monitor*, (13).

Marsh, E., Hamburger, H., and Grishman, R. (1984). A production rule system for message summarization. In *Proceedings of the National Conference on Artificial Intelligence*, pages 243–246. American Association for Artificial Intelligence.

Mellish, C. S. et al. (1995). The TIC message analyser. *Computational Linguistics*.

Paice, C. D. (1990). Constructing literature abstracts by computer. *Information Processing and Management*, 26(1):171–186.

Pereira, F. (1990). Finite-state approximations of grammars. In *Proceedings of the Third DARPA Speech and Natural Language Workshop*, pages 20–25, Hidden Valley, Pennsylvania. Defense Advanced Research Projects Agency, Morgan Kaufmann.

Rau, L. F. (1988). Conceptual information extraction and information retrieval from natural language input. In *Proceedings of the Conference on User-Oriented, Content-Based, Text and Image Handling*, pages 424–437, Cambridge, Massachusetts.

Ruge (1992). Experiments in linguistically based term associations. *Information Processing and Management*, 28(3).

Schwarz and Thurmair, editors (1986). *Informationslinguistische texterschliessung*. Hildesheim: Georg Olms Verlag.

Smeaton, A. (1992). Progress in the application of natural language processing to information retrieval tasks. *The Computer Journal*, 35(3).

Smeaton, A. F., O'Donnell, R., and Kelledy, F. (1995). Indexing structures derived from syntax in TREC-3: System description. In *National Institute of Standards and Technology Special Publication on the The Third Text REtrieval Conference (TREC-3)*, Washington, DC. National Institute of Standards and Technology, U.S. Department of Commerce, U.S. Government Printing Office.

Sparck Jones, K. (1993). What might be in a summary? In Knorz, G., Krause, J., and Womser-Hacker, C., editors, *Information retrieval '93: von der modellierung zur anwendung*, pages 9–26. Konstanz, Universitatsverlag Konstanz.

Strzalkowski, T., Carballo, J. P., and Marinescu, M. (1995). Natural language information retrieval: TREC-3 report. In *National Institute of Standards and Technology Special Publication on the The Third Text REtrieval Conference (TREC-3)*, Washington, DC. National Institute of Standards and Technology, U.S. Department of Commerce, U.S. Government Printing Office.

TREC (1995). *National Institute of Standards and Technology Special Publication on the The Third Text REtrieval Conference (TREC-3)*, Washington, DC. National Institute of Standards and Technology, U.S. Department of Commerce, U.S. Government Printing Office.

Voorhees, E., Gupta, N. K., and Johnson-Laird, B. (1995). The collection fusion problem. In *National Institute of Standards and Technology Special Publication on the The Third Text REtrieval Conference (TREC-3)*, pages 95–104, Washington, DC. National Institute of Standards and Technology, U.S. Department of Commerce, U.S. Government Printing Office.

Wojcik, R., Harrison, P., and Bremer, J. (1993). Using bracketed parses to evaluate a grammar checking application. In *Proceedings of the 31st Annual Meeting of the Association for Computational Linguistics*, pages 38–45, Columbus, Ohio. ACL.

Young, S. R. and Hayes, P. J. (1985). Automatic classification and summarization of banking telexes. In *Proceedings of the Second Conference on Artificial Intelligence Applications*, pages 402–408.

Chapter 8

Multilinguality

8.1 Overview

Martin Kay

Xerox Palo Alto Research Center, Palo Alto, California, USA

Multilinguality is a characteristic of tasks that involve the use of more than one natural language. In the modern world, it is a characteristic of a rapidly increasing class of tasks. This fact is most apparent in an increased need for translations and a consequent interest in alternatives to the traditional ways of producing them. The principal alternatives that have been proposed include partially or fully automatic translation, machine aids for translators, and fully or partially automated production of original parallel texts in several languages. But multilinguality is more than just the preparation of parallel texts. Before anything nontrivial can be done with a text—before it can be filed, or sent to the appropriate person, or even responsibly destroyed—the language in which it is written must be identified. This so called *Language ID* problem is therefore a pressing one, and one on which technology has fruitfully been brought to bear. In working environments where more than one language is in use, the problem of storing and retrieving information acquires a multilingual dimension. These problems, as well as that of processing spoken material in a multilingual environment, will be reviewed in this chapter.

Where only one language is involved, a great deal of useful processing can be done on the basis of a model that sees texts essentially as sequences of characters. This is the view that most word processors embody. Words are recognized as having properties beyond the characters that make them up for the purposes of detecting and correcting spelling errors and in information retrieval. However, of the multilingual problems just identified, the only one that might possibly be treated with a character-oriented model is that of language identification. The remainder trade in an essential way on equivalences, or near equivalences, among words, sentences, and texts mediated through their meaning. Language processing of this kind is notoriously difficult and it behooves us to start by considering, however cursorily, why this is. We will do this in the context of translation, though what we say is true for the most part of the other tasks mentioned.

The question of why translation should have been so successful in resisting the most determined efforts to automate it for close to forty years is complex and sometimes quite technical. But it is not a mystery. The basic problems have long been known and, the most important thing that has been learnt about them recently is that they are more severe and more widespread than was first thought. Perhaps the most important problem concerns a distinction between meaning and interpretation. Another has to do with the more classical distinction between meaning and reference.

One example must suffice to give a sense of the problem concerning meaning and reference. The French sentence *Où voulez-vous que je me mette?* means, more or less literally, *Where do you want me to put myself?* Colloquially translated into English, however, it would have to be *Where do you want me to sit / stand / park / tie up (my boat) / sign my name, etc.* Information must be added which is not in the original to make the English sound natural. The sentence *Where do you want me to put myself?* means what the French means, but we claim a translator would deliberately choose a rendering that would change the meaning. In this case, it may also be possible to get the right effect by deleting information, as in *Where do you want me?* but this also changes the meaning. What remains invariant under translation is not the meaning, but the interpretation, that is, the response the text is intended to evoke in a reader. Interpretation depends on context, in there lies the principal source of the difficulty.

The distinction between meaning and interpretation, to the extent that it was recognized at all, has generally been thought too subtle to be of practical interest. The belief has been that, in sufficiently restricted or sufficiently technical domains of discourse, it essentially disappears. However, in the massive speech-to-speech translation project recently initiated by the German government (Kay, Gawron, et al., 1991), the universe of discourse is limited to discussions between a pair of individuals on the time and place of their next meeting. In one of the first simulated dialogues examined, the sentence *Geht es bei Ihnen?* occurs. There are two interpretations, which can be captured in English by *Is that alright with you?* and *Can we meet at your place?*. The domain of the discourse is already restricted to an extreme degree and it is clear that nothing but an analysis of the context will decide the interpretation. Restriction to a technical domain can help, but it can also hinder. When I order ice cream, I may be asked if I want two scoops or three—in French *Deux boules ou trois?* and, in German, *Zwei Kugeln oder drei?*. But *boule* and *Kugel* mean *ball*, not *scoop*. At first the problem seems easy to resolve. The words *scoop*, *boule* and *Kugel* are classifiers for ice cream in their respective languages, just as *loaf* is classifier for bread in English. But this fails utterly in a technical document, say a patent application, describing an ice cream scoop, the very point of which is that it delivers ice cream in different shaped pieces. To handle these words right in any context, one must understand the relationship of the scoop to the shape it imposes on the material it is used to manipulate. More importantly, one must understand from the context when the usual assumptions about this relationship no longer hold.

The question concerning meaning and reference has to do with a philosophical problem that is far beyond our present scope, namely the extent to which meaning is parasitic on reference. To many, it seems unlikely that a baby could learn a language in any useful sense without ever establishing an association between the words in it and objects in the environment. Essentially all computers lack anything that could reasonably be called a perceptual system—they have never seen, heard, felt, or smelt anything. Just how much processing of meaning and interpretation is possible for such a device is open to considerable doubt. Language processing is done, at worst, with characters and, at best, with meanings. Occasionally, programs have been written that manipulate toy blocks or the pieces on a chess board, and which talk about these objects using natural language, but these experiments have been too small to tell us anything about the importance of a genuine ability to refer to things. This will be taken up again in section 8.2.

Workers in artificial intelligence and computational linguistics are often at odds on the extent to which computer programs intended to mimic human performance for practical reasons need to use human methods. On the one hand, computers have quite different properties from humans; we usually do not know what methods humans use in any case; and airplanes do not flap their wings. On the other hand, divining the intended interpretation of a text requires second-guessing the intentions of its author in the given context, a task that seems essentially to require a human point of view.

There is an essentially *bottom-up* quality to the translation problem as usually seen by those that attempt to automate it. It starts with words, phrases, and sentences and rarely takes any account of larger structures. This adds greatly to its difficulty both for people and machines. The point is simply that the translator must attempt to reproduce the intention of the author, whatever it might be, in the large and in the small. To the extent that the translator can permit himself any assumptions about these matters, the problem assumes some *top-down* properties which make it, to however small an extent, more tractable. This is why the results reported in the recent ARPA Message Understanding Conferences (MUC) are so much more encouraging. The aim here was to extract information about terrorist incidents from newspaper material, ignoring all else, and attending only to certain facts about the incidents. For the same reason, some of the early experiments of Roger Shank and his students on translation also seemed encouraging, because they allowed themselves to make strong assumptions about the texts they were working with. They allowed themselves assumptions not only about the overall subject matter, but also about the structure of the texts themselves. For similar reasons, there is reason to hope for more positive results in multilingual information retrieval.

Three responses to the problems of context and interpretation suggest themselves. First, in the long run, there is no alternative to continuing to build more faithful models of human behavior. The second alternative is to design systems involving both people and machines, assigning to each those parts of the task to which they are best suited. The third is to seek ways of modifying the task so that the machine will naturally have greater control over the context. Section 8.4 explores the second of these alternatives. The third, we discuss briefly now.

The METEO machine-translation system translates Canadian meteorological bulletins between English and French. Realizing that METEO's spectacular success was due to the remarkably restricted nature of the texts it worked on, workers at the University of Montreal reflected on the possibility of eliminating the input text altogether in favor of data gathered directly from weather stations. This line of thought led to a system that produces parallel English and French marine weather bulletins for the Canadian eastern seaboard. The planning of what will be said and in which order is done once for both languages. It is only towards the end that the processes diverge (Chandioux, 1989). The same approach is being taken with reports based on Canadian labor statistics. The TECHDOC project at the University of Ulm aims to produce parallel technical documentation in multiple languages on the basis of a language-independent database (Rösner & Stede, 1994); and the Information Technology Research Institute at the University of Brighton has a group working on the automatic drafting of multilingual instructional technical texts in the context of GIST (Generating InStructional Text), part of the European Union's LRE program (Delin, Hartley, et al., 1994; Paris & Scott, 1994). These projects eliminate the problem of determining the intended interpretation of a piece of input text in differing degrees. In the second and third cases, there is still intentional material in the input but the idea in each case is to shift the emphasis from determining the intentions behind a given document to creating intentions for a new set of parallel documents.

8.2 Machine Translation: The Disappointing Past and Present

Martin Kay

Xerox Palo Alto Research Center, Palo Alto, California, USA

The field of machine translation has changed remarkably little since its earliest days in the fifties. The issues that divided researchers then remain the principal bones of contention today. The first of these concerns the distinction between the so-called interlingual and the transfer approach to the problem. The second concerns the relative importance of linguistic matters as opposed to common sense and general knowledge. The only major new lines of investigation that have emerged in recent years have involved the use of existing translations as a prime source of information for the production of new ones. One form that this takes is that of example-based machine translation (Furuse & Iida, 1992; Iida & Iida, 1991; Nagao, 1992; Sato, 1992) in which a system of otherwise fairly conventional design is able to refer to a collection of existing translations. A much more radical approach, championed by IBM (Brown, Cocke, et al., 1990), is the one in which virtually the entire body of knowledge that the system uses is acquired automatically from statistical properties of a very large body of existing translation.

In recent years, work on machine translation has been most vigorously pursued in Japan and it is also there that the greatest diversity of approaches is to be found. By and large, the Japanese share the general perception that the transfer approach offers the best chance for early success.

Two principal advantages have always been claimed for the interlingual approach. First, the method is taken as a move towards robustness and overall economy in that translation between all pairs of a set of languages in principle requires only translation to and from the interlingua for each member of the set. If there are n languages, n components are therefore required to be translated into the interlingua and n to translate from it, for a total of $2n$. To provide the same facilities, the transfer approach, according to which a major part of the translation system for a given pair of languages is specific to that pair, requires a separate device to translate in each direction for every pair of languages for a total of $n(n-1)$.

The PIVOT system of NEC (Okumura, Muraki, et al., 1991; Muraki, 1989) and ATLAS II of Fujitsu (Uchida, 1989) are commercial systems among a number of research systems based on the two-step method according to which texts are translated from the source language to an artificial interlingual representation and then into the target language. The Rosetta system at Philips (Landsbergen, 1987), and the DLT system at BSO (Witkam, 1988; Schubert, 1988) in the Netherlands also adopted this approach. In the latter, the interlingua is not a language especially designed for this purpose, but Esperanto.

According to the majority transfer view of machine translation, a certain amount of analysis of the source text is done in the context of the source language alone and a certain amount of work on the translated text is done in the context of the target language. But the bulk of the work relies on comparative information about the specific pair languages. This is argued for on the basis of the sheer difficulty of designing a single interlingua that can be all things for all languages and on the view that translation is, by its very nature, an exercise in comparative linguistics. The massive Eurotra system (Schutz, Thurmair, et al., 1991; Arnold & des Tombes, 1987; King & Perschke, 1987; Perschke, 1989), in which groups from all the countries of the European Union participated, was a transfer system, as is the current Verbmobil system sponsored by the German Federal Ministry for Research and Technology (BMFT).

A transfer system, in which the analysis and generation components are large relative to the transfer component and where transfer is therefore conducted in terms of quite abstract entities, takes on much of the flavor of an interlingual system, while not making the commitment to linguistic universality that many see as the hallmark of the interlingual approach. Such semantic transfer systems are attracting quite a lot of attention. Fujitsu's ATLAS I (Uchida, 1986) was an example, and Sharp's DUET system is another. The approach taken by SRI (Cambridge) with the Core Language Engine (Alshawi, Carter, et al., 1991) also falls in this category.

Just as these systems constitute something of an intermediate position between interlingua and transfer, they can also be seen to some extent as a compromise between the mainly linguistically based approaches we have been considering up to now and the so-called knowledge-based systems pursued most notably at Carnegie Mellon University (Nirenburg, Raskin, et al., 1986; Carbonell & Tomita, 1987), and at the Center for Research in Language at New Mexico State University (Farwell & Wilks, 1990). The view that informs these efforts, whose most forceful champion was Roger Shank, is that translation relies heavily on information and abilities that are not specifically linguistic. If it is their linguistic knowledge that we often think of as characterizing human translators, it is only because we take their common sense and knowledge of the everyday world for granted in a way we clearly cannot do for machines.

Few informed people still see the original ideal of fully automatic high-quality translation of arbitrary texts as a realistic goal for the foreseeable future. Many systems require texts to be pre-edited to put them in a form suitable for treatment by the system, and post-editing of the machine's output is generally taken for granted. The most successful systems have been those that have relied on their input being in a sublanguage (Kittredge, 1987), either naturally occurring, as in that case of weather reports, or deliberately controlled. The spectacular success of the METEO system (Chevalier, Dansereau, et al., 1978) working on Canadian weather reports encouraged the view that sublanguages might be designed for a number of different applications, but the principles on which such languages should be designed have failed to emerge and progress has been very limited.

Future Directions

Research in machine translation has developed traditional patterns which will clearly have to be broken if any real progress is to be made. The traditional view that the problem is principally a linguistic one is clearly not tenable, but the alternatives that require a translation system to have a substantial part of the general knowledge and common sense that humans have also seems to be unworkable. Compromises must presumably be found where knowledge of restricted domains can facilitate the translation of texts in those domains. The most obvious gains will come from giving up, at least for the time being, the idea of machine translation as a fully automatic batch process in favor of one in which the task is apportioned between people and machines. The proposal made in Kay (1980), according to which the translation machine would consult with a human speaker of the source language with detailed knowledge of the subject matter, has attracted more attention in recent times. A major objection to this approach, namely that the cost of operating such a system would come close to that of doing the whole job in the traditional way, will probably not hold up in the special, but widespread situation in which a single document has to be translated into a large number of languages.

8.3 (Human-Aided) Machine Translation: A Better Future?

Christian Boitet

Université Joseph Fourier, Grenoble, France

As the term *translation* covers many activities, it is useful to distinguish, at least, between:

- **re-creation**, e.g., the translation of poetry or publicity, which aims above all at transmitting the subjective aspect of a text, even if its objective meaning is somewhat altered;

- **localization**, practiced on a large scale nowadays on computer manuals for end users, where it is important to adapt certain parts of the content, and perhaps the style of the presentation, to a certain cultural and linguistic environment;

- **diffusion translation**, in particular the translation of technical documentation, where the objective content must be strictly rendered in another language, without addition and omission, even if the style *smells like translation*;

- **screening translation**, which covers translation of written material for gathering information as well as simultaneous interpretation of oral presentations.

8.3.1 Types of MAT Systems Available in 1994

It is impossible to envisage an automation of re-creation translation and of localization which would go beyond machine aids for human translators for many years to come. By contrast, the *translating function* may be automated in the case of diffusion-translation and screening-translation. To fix our vocabulary, we would like to take the term Machine-Assisted Translation (MAT) as covering all techniques for automating the translation activity. The term Human-Aided Machine Translation (HAMT) should be reserved for the techniques which rely on a real automation of the translating function, with some human intervention in pre-editing, post-editing, or interaction. The term Machine-Aided Human Translation (MAHT) concerns machine aids for translators or revisors and is the topic of section 8.4.

MT for Screening Purposes

Around 1949, MT projects were launched first in the US, and soon thereafter in the USSR. They were motivated by the growing needs for intelligence gathering. They gave rise to the first MT screening systems. The goal of such systems is to produce automatically, quickly and cheaply large volumes of *rough* translations.

The quality of the rough translations obtained is not essential. The output can be used to get an idea of the content. If the user wants a good translation of a part which looks interesting, he simply asks a human translator (who in general will judge the machine output to too bad to bother with revision).

What is essential is that in order to keep costs low, no professional translator or revisor should be used. Pre-editing should be reduced to confirming system proposals for separating figures, formulae, or sentences. Post-editing, if any, should consist only in formatting operations. The need for *screening* MT is still actual. However, civil uses (gathering technological, economical and financial information) are now predominant over military uses. Examples of working systems are SYSTRAN (Russian-English in the US and several language pairs at the EC), ATLAS-II (Japanese-English for the EC), and CAT from Bravice, used to access Japanese data bases in English (Sigurdson & Greatex, 1987).

Users can get access to these systems from terminals (even the French Minitel terminals), standard PCs, or Macintoshes connected to a network. In the last few years, stand-alone configurations have appeared on PCs and workstations. We will briefly describe the different access modes:

Access to a Server: In France, Systran SA commercializes an MT server via the Minitel network (six to seven million of these relatively dumb terminals are installed in French homes). This service gives access to several Systran *language pairs*. This system can meet user expectations if used for screening purposes (translation into the mother tongue). At the European Commission, Systran has also been used since the end of 1976. These translations are now distributed to interested readers *as is*, unrevised by human translators. With that change, the amount of texts going through MT has suddenly increased from 2,000 pages in 1988 to 40,000 in 1989 to 100,000 in 1993 (the total number of pages translated varying from 800,000 to 1,000,000 to 1,500,000). We should also mention the growing use of PCs connected to computer networks for getting access to rough MT translations of textual data bases (economical for NHK, scientific and technical at JICST, etc.), sometimes transcontinentally (Sigurdson & Greatex, 1987).

Integrated Stations: Hardware has become powerful and cheap enough to run some MT systems on a PC, possibly coupled with an OCR. These systems include very restricted systems for diffusion, such as METEO on PC, and some systems for screening, such as Translator by Catena on Macintosh. However, at this point, the size of the dictionaries and the sophistication (and associated computational cost) of the underlying tools make workstations mandatory for the majority of currently available commercial systems but this is bound to change soon.

MT for Diffusion Purposes

Work on diffusion MT or MT for the revisor began when the first interactive systems appeared. The aim is to automate the production of professional quality translations by letting the computer produce the *first draft*. Hence, MT systems must be designed to produce *raw* translations good enough so that professional revisors will agree to post-edit them, and that overall costs and delays are reduced. That is possible only if the system is specialized to texts of a certain style and domain ("suboptimization approach" in L. Bourbeau's terminology Bourbeau, Carcagno, et al., 1990; Lehrberger & Bourbeau, 1988). Political, scientific and industrial decision makers, as well as the public at large, often envisage that arrangement (pure MT followed by post-editing) as the only one possible.

About twenty systems are now commercially available. About fifteen of them are Japanese (AS-Transac by Toshiba, ATLAS-II by Fujitsu, PIVOT by NEC, HICAT by Hitachi, SHALT-J by IBM-Japan, PENSÉ by OKI, DUET by Sharp, MAJESTIC by JICST, etc.) and handle almost exclusively the language pairs Japanese / English. Other systems come from the U.S. (LOGOS, METAL, SPANAM), France (Ariane/aéro/F-E by SITE-B'VITAL, based on GETA's computer tools and linguistic methodology), or Germany (SUSY by IAI in Saarbrücken), and center on English, German or French, although mockups and prototypes exist for many other languages. Still others are large and operational, but not (yet?) commercially offered (JETS by IBM/Japan, LMT by IBM US/Europe, ALT/JE by NTT, etc.).

What can be expected from these systems? Essentially, to answer growing needs in technical translation. On average, a 250-word page is translated in 1 hour and revised in 20 min. Hence, 4 persons produce a finished translation at a rate of 3 pages per hour (p/h). Ideally, then, some translators could become revisors and 6 persons should produce 12 p/h. As it is, that is only an upper limit, and a more realistic figure is 8 p/h, if one counts a heavier revision rate of 30 min. per page (after adequate training). Several users report overall gains of 40 to 50%. An extreme case is the METEO system (Chandioux, 1989), which is so specialized that it can produce very high quality raw translations, needing only 3 text processor operations per 100 words translated. Another way of looking at the economics of MT is in terms of human effort: according to figures given by producers of MT systems (JEIDA, 1989), the creation of a new (operational) system from scratch costs between 200 and 300 man-years with highly specialized developers. Also, the cost to adapt an existing system to a new domain and a new typology of texts is in the order of 5 to 10 person-years, which makes it impractical for less than 10,000 pages to translate. All things counted, the break-even point lies between 9,000 and 10,000 pages, an already large amount.

This approach, then, is at present only conceivable for large flows of homogeneous and computerized texts, such as user or maintenance manuals. An essential condition of success is that the team in charge of developing and maintaining the lingware (dictionaries, grammars) be in constant touch with the revisors, and if possible with the authors of the documents to be translated. A good example in this respect are the Pan American Health Organization (PAHO) (Vasconcellos & Len, 1988) systems, ENGSPAN and SPANAM.

Users should consider this kind of MT systems in the same way they consider expert systems. Expert systems can be developed by third parties, but it is essential for users to master them in order to let them evolve satisfactorily and to use them best.

As the MT systems designed for diffusion purposes are computationally very heavy, they have been developed on mainframes. The situation is changing rapidly, however. Since powerful PCs are becoming widely available, they are now replacing terminals. Although many vendors offer specialized editors, on terminals or on PCs, there is a trend to let revisors work directly with their favorite text processor (such as Word, WordPerfect, WordStar, FrameMaker, Interleaf, Ventura, etc.) and to add specific functions as *tools* (such as Mercury/Termex or WinTool). But this technique is not yet able to offer all functions of specialized editors (such as showing corresponding source and target phrases in inverse video, or doing linguistic alignment, etc.). For example, the METAL system commercialized by Siemens runs on a LISP machine, while revision is done on a kind of PC. It seems also that the ATLAS II, PIVOT, and HICAT systems are still running on mainframes when used in-house for the translation of technical documentation, or externally by translation offices submitting possibly pre-edited material. In France, SITE-B'Vital has ported the Ariane-G5 MT system generator (not yet the development environment) on Unix-based workstations, but the current use is from a PC under Word accessing an MT server running on an IBM 9221 minicomputer. Finally, there is now a commercial offer for diffusion MT systems on workstations (Toshiba, Sharp, Fujitsu, Nec). About 3,000 machines in total had been sold in Japan by April 1992. Systems used for diffusion MT are characterized, of course, by their specialization for certain kinds of texts (grammatical heuristics, terminological lexicons), but also by the richness of the tools they offer for pre-editing, post-editing and stylistic system control (that is possible because intended users are bilingual specialists). They all include facilities to build terminological *user dictionaries*.

8.3.2   Four Main Situations in the Future

We anticipate that users of MT systems will increasingly be non-professionals, that is occasional translators or monolingual readers. According to the linguistic competence of the user and depending whether he works in a team or alone, we envisage four types of situations in the mid-term future, say, by the year 2000.

Individual Screening Translation Workstations: Servers should continue to coexist with integrated solutions on PCs or workstations. Servers would be appropriate for environments where the same information is likely to be required by many persons, and is already available in computer-readable form (textual data bases, short-lived messages such as weather bulletins and stock exchange notices, computerized libraries, etc.). Translation may be performed once, possibly in advance, and some amount of quick revision may even be performed. It is also possible to analyze the text typology and to use corresponding specialized versions of the MT system. Large-scale systems will no doubt be ported to the more powerful PCs which will soon be available.

In each case, we can expect environments to be generic. The only difference between the two solutions will be the required computer power. For accessing a server, basic PCs already suffice. But running MT systems requires more power, simply because small improvements in output quality and ergonomy will continue to require a lot of computational resources, and because the basic software tools are also continuously requiring more computer resources.

Occasional Translation: Current tools will no doubt be improved, in terms of speed, ergonomy, and functionality. As far as ergonomy is concerned, we envisage that the translator's aids will work in background and continuously offer help in windows associated with windows of the current application (text processor, spreadsheet, etc.). This is beginning to become possible, at least on the Apple Macintosh, where different applications can communicate.

New functionality should include more aids concerning the target language, in particular paraphrasing facilities and better tools for checking spelling, terminology, grammar, and style. They may even include some MT helps, not aiming at translating whole paragraphs or sentences, but rather at proposing translations for simple fragments, perhaps in several grammatical forms that seem possible in the context (case, number, person, time, etc.).

Individual Professional Translation: It can be envisaged that free-lance translators will make increasing use of communication facilities, to retrieve terminology, to communicate with authors, or to submit parts of their workload to some MT system. Perhaps they will even have computer tools to help them determine which MT system accessible over the network would be most suitable for the text currently at hand, if any. Current research in *example-based MT* will perhaps lead to much better tools for accessing previous translations of similar passages. As far as hardware is concerned, professional free-lance translators should increasingly equip themselves with comfortable, but not too expensive configurations, such as middle-range PCs with large screens, CD-ROMs, and lots of disk space.

Industrial Professional Translation: Industrial translation aims at a very high quality of fairly long documents. That is why the raw translation job (first draft) is usually divided among several translators, and why there is often more than one revision step. If MT is introduced, the revision job still has to be divided among several persons. There is a need for managing this collective effort. Hence, we can anticipate that this kind of translation will be organized around a local network, each translator/revisor working on a powerful PC, and accessing one or more MT servers, a terminology server, an example server (access to available parallel texts), etc., all being controlled by a senior translator using reserved managing facilities on his or her PC.

8.3.3   Future Directions

From the four types of users (screener, occasional translator, free lance translator, industrial translator), only the first and fourth can already use existing MT
technology in a cost-effective way. The third will probably also be able to use it
by the year 2000. But there is still a fifth possibility, which is now at the research
stage, that of MT for monolingual writers, or *personal MT*. See e.g., Boitet
(1986); Boitet and Blanchon (1993); Chandler, Holden, et al. (1987); Huang
(1990); Maruyama, Watanabe, et al. (1990); Sadler (1989); Somers, Tsujii, et al.
(1990); Tomita (1986); Wehrli (1992); Whitelock, Wood, et al. (1986); Wood
and Chandler (1988).

There is actually a growing need to translate masses of documents, notes,
letters, etc., in several languages, especially in the global market. People are
very conscious that they waste a lot of time and precision when they read or
write texts in another language, even if they master it quite well. To take
one language like English as the unique language of communication is not cost-
effective. There is a strong desire to use one's own language, while, of course,
trying to learn a few others for personal communication and cultural enrichment.

The idea behind this new kind of MT system is that users will accept to
spend a lot of time interacting with the machine to get their texts translated
into one or more languages, with a guaranteed high quality of the raw output.
Engineers or researchers accustomed to painfully (try to) translate their prose
into a foreign language (very often English, of course) would perhaps prefer to
spend about the same time in such interaction, that is 60 to 90 MN per page,
and get their text translated into all the languages of their correspondents.
The system would negotiate the text with the author, in order to normalize it
according to changeable parameters (style, terminology, etc.), and get a correct
abstract representation of it (a so-called *deep* or *intermediate* structure) by
asking questions to remove all ambiguities. Then, current technology could be
applied to produce quality texts, needing no revision as far as grammaticality is
concerned (the content is guaranteed to be correct because of the indirect pre-
editing performed by the author himself, but the form and style would certainly
be improvable).

This is, of course, another version of the old idea of interactive translation,
proposed time and again since the first experiments by Kay and Kaplan in the
sixties at the Rand Corporation (MIND system, Kay, 1973). We attribute the
relative failure of this approach to the fact that the user felt a *slave* of the machine, that the texts were supposed to be *sacred*, unchangeable, and that the
questions asked were at the same time very specialized and quite unsettling. We
hope that the time is now ripe for yet another attempt, using latest advances in
ergonomy, AI methods for designing intelligent dialogues, and improved linguistic technology. One of the most challenging aspects of that approach is actually
the need to express very sophisticated linguistic notions (such as modality, aspect, etc.) in a way understandable by users with no particular training in
linguistics or translation theory, and no knowledge of the target language(s).
Some computer firms are already working on that concept, and may propose

products well before the year 2000. But it will be a long time until it is possible to buy off-the-shelf multilingual systems of that kind, because of the tremendous amount of lexical and grammatical variety which is necessary if one does not want to restrict the domain and typology.

It will, of course, be possible to put a whole system of that kind on a very powerful PC. But an essential ingredient of success, we think, is that the user be never forced to wait, or to answer a question before being allowed to proceed with what he is doing. In other words, the system should simply tell (or better show) the user that there are some questions waiting to be answered before translation can proceed on some fragments of the text (or hypertext). Then, an attractive solution is to use a comparatively cheap PC as workstation, with a periodic connection to an MT server (exactly as is done nowadays by e-mail environments).

8.4 Machine-aided Human Translation

Christian Boitet

Université Joseph Fourier, Grenoble, France

Section 8.3 has covered Machine Translation (MT), where translation proper is performed by a computer, even if the human helps by pre-editing, post-editing, or answering questions to disambiguate the source text. In computer-aided translation, or more precisely Machine-Aided Human Translation (MAHT), by contrast, translation is performed by a human, and the computer offers supporting tools.

8.4.1 State of the Art

We can distinguish three types of MAHT systems, corresponding to three types of users, and offering different sets of functionality.

Specific Software Environments Designed for Professional Translators Working in Teams

Existing products now are those of Trados (MultiTerm), IBM (Translation Manager), and SITE-Eurolang (Eurolang Optimizer). They are available for Windows, OS/2, or Unix-based workstations.

The intended users are competent translators working in teams and linked through a local network. Each translator's workstation offers tools to:

- access a bilingual terminology.

- access a *translation memory.*

- submit parts to the text to an MT server.

These tools have to be completely integrated in the text processor. The software automatically analyzes the source text, and attaches keyboard shortcuts to the terms and sentences found in the terminology database and in the translation memory. One very important design decision is whether to offer a specific text processor, as in IBM's Translation Manager, or whether to use directly one or more text processors produced by third parties, as in Eurolang Optimizer.

The server supports tools to:

- manage the common multilingual lexical database (MLDB), often a multilingual terminological database (MTDB), and the common translation memory, where previous translations are recorded. Here, concurrent access and strict validation procedures are crucial.

- manage the translation tasks (not always offered).

Let us take the case of the most recent product, Eurolang Optimizer. On Sun workstations under Unix, the server uses a standard DBMS (database management system), such as Oracle or Sybase, to support the terminological database and the translation memory. The translator's workstations use Interleaf or Framemaker as text processors, while their database functions are degraded versions of those of the servers, and are implemented directly in C++. On the PC, the server runs under Windows NT, again with Oracle or Sybase, while the translator's workstations use Word 6 on PCs under Windows 3.1. Source languages currently include English, French, German, Italian and Spanish. There are seventeen target languages (almost all languages which use the Latin character set).

When a document has to be translated, it is pre-processed on the server, and sent to a translator's workstation with an associated *kit*, which contains the corresponding subsets of the dictionary and of the translation memory, as well as (optionally) translation proposals coming from a batch MT system. MAHT-related functionality are accessible through a supplementary menu (in the case of Word 6) and keyboard shortcuts dynamically associated with terms or full sentences. The translator may enrich the kit's lexicon. When translation is completed, the document is sent back to the server with its updated kit. On the server, the new translation pairs are added to the translation memory, and updates or additions to the dictionary are handled by the (human) manager of the MTDB. The overall productivity of the translators is said to be increased by up to 30% or 40%.

Environments for Independent Professional Translators

These environments are usually less powerful, significantly cheaper, and accessible from all, or at least many, commercial text and document processors. This is because free-lance translators are usually required to deliver their translations in the same formats as the source documents, and those vary from one customer to the next.

As far as dictionaries are concerned, the situation is different from the preceding case. There is no central MLDB to manage, but it is very important for independent translators to be able to easily create, access, modify, export and import terminological files.

Examples are MTX (Melby, 1982) by LinguaTech, a resident program for PCs, and WinTool (Winsoft, 1987), a desk accessory for Macintoshes. In 1992, MicroMATER, an SGML-based standard for PC-oriented terminological dictionaries, has been adopted in relation with ongoing efforts to devise standards for the encoding of more complex dictionary structures within the TEI initiative and in cooperation with InfoTerm (Vienna) and other organizations working on terminology.

Tools for Occasional Translators

An occasional translator may be competent in both languages, or only in the source language! As a matter of fact, there exist tools to help monolinguals produce parametrizable *canned* text in two languages. For example, Ambassador by Language Engineering Corp. runs on Macintoshes and PCs, is available in English-Japanese, English-French, English-Spanish and French-Japanese, and offers about 200 *templates* of letters and forms, and 450 textual *forms* (of sentence or paragraph size).

In the other context, the translator is at least bilingual, but is not a professional, and does not necessarily translate into his native tongue. Even if a translator does, he or she often may not know translations for specific terms they learned in the source language (take for example English-Malay or French-Arabic). Tools for bilinguals, such as SISKEP (Tong, 1987), are designed for such users. All are implemented on PCs.

These tools offer different functionality from those for professionals:

- There is no translation memory.

- The dictionaries must contain general terms, and there are usually three dictionary levels: personal and temporary terms, terminology, general vocabulary.

- There are aids concerning the target language (thesaurus, conjugator, style checker, etc.).

Again, it is possible to propose a specific editor, with filters to and from standard word processors, as is done in SISKEP, or to interface the tools directly with one or several word processors. That second course was impractical until a recent past, because developers had to obtain access to the source code of the text processors. This has changed since 1991, when Apple launched version 7 of Mac operating system, which offers the possibility of applications communicating through special *events*. Similar developments are afoot in the PC world.

8.4.2   Limitations in Current Technology

Serious problems in current technology concern the unavailability of truly multilingual support tools, the engineering of multilingual lexical data bases, the sacred character of the source text, and the limitation to handling only one language pair at a time.

Unavailability of Truly Multilingual Support Tools

MacOS 7.1, available since mid-1992, is still the only operating system supporting any number of writing systems at the same time. With a text processor based on Apple's Script Manager, such as WinText, it is possible to include English, Arabic, Chinese, Japanese, Thai, Russian, etc., in the same document, and to use the writing system as a distinctive feature in search-and-replace actions, or for checking the spelling or the grammar. But, in practice, the size of the operating system grows considerably, because it is necessary to include a variety of fonts and input methods. With the languages above, the latest version of the Macintosh operating system, version 7.1, requires four to five Mbytes of RAM. Input methods and fonts must also often be purchased from third parties.

For other environments, the situation is still very unsatisfactory. At best, it is possible to find localized versions, which handle one *exotic* writing system besides the English one.

Engineering of Multilingual Lexical Databases

The MLDBs found on MAHT servers are often nothing more than collections of bilingual dictionaries. In the case of terminology proper, MTDBs do exist, but are not yet integrated with MAHT environments. Such MTDBs include, for example, EuroDicautom at the EU (European Commission), Aquila by SITE-Sonovision, and MultiTerm by Trados. In the current state of Eurolang Optimizer, the MTDBs are planned to be monosource and multitarget, but are still bilingual, although the same company continues to market the fully multilingual Aquila on PC LANs.

As far as MLDBs are concerned, then, the problems concern more the management of the databases than their design. That is because the MTDBs have to evolve constantly, taking into account possibly contradictory or incomplete contributions by many translators. In the case of MLDBs of general terms, there are still many design problems, and available solutions, such as that of EDR in Tokyo, are still too heavy to be used in MAHT systems.

"Sacred" Character of the Source Text and Limitation to Handling One Language Pair at a Time

Very often, translation is more difficult than it should be because the source text is not well written. If translation has to be performed into several languages, which is often the case, for example for technical manuals, it would make sense to prepare the source text, possibly annotating or rewriting parts of it. That possibility is however not offered in current MAHT systems. The source texts are often considered *sacred*.

8.4.3 Future Directions

Current tools will no doubt be improved, in terms of speed, ergonomy and functionality. Key research issues concern ergonomy, progress in Example-Based MT (EBMT), and integration with Dialogue-Based MT (DBMT).

Ergonomy

It must be realized that accessing large MLDBs and translation memories are very computer intensive operations. To identify complex terms requires full morphological analysis and partial syntactic analysis. Matching a sentence against a large set of sentences and producing a meaningful set of exact or *near* matches is not feasible in real time. The current answer to that problem is to preprocess the documents on a server (or on the workstations, in the background), or, in the case of PC-oriented stand-alone tools for occasional translators, where real time behavior is required, to simplify the morphological analysis and to suppress the translation memory.

The increase of computing power and the object orientation of future operating systems should make it possible to drastically improve the ergonomy and power of MAHT tools, by searching the terminological database and the translation memory in the background, and dynamically updating MAHT suggestions for the current part of the document being translated, and possibly modified in the source form. These suggestions might appear in MAHT windows logically attached to the windows of the main applications (text processor, spreadsheet, etc.), or, if tighter integration is possible, in its application windows themselves. The main point here is that it would not be necessary to modify the code of the main applications.

Progress in EBMT

Example-Based MT (EBMT) goes one step further than the retrieval of identical or similar sentences. It aims at producing translation proposals by combining the translations of similar chunks of texts making up the sentence and previously identified as possible translation units in the translation memory. It is not yet clear whether the intensive efforts going into that direction will succeed to the point where EBMT could be included in MAHT tools in a cost-effective way.

8.5 Multilingual Information Retrieval

Christian Fluhr
CEA-INSTN, Saclay, France

8.5.1 State of the Art

The problem of multilingual access to text databases can be seen as an extension of the general information retrieval (IR) problem corresponding to paraphrase.

How does one retrieve documents containing expressions which do not exactly match those found in the query?

The most traditional approach to IR in general and to multilingual retrieval in particular, uses a controlled vocabulary for indexing and retrieval. In this approach, a documentalist (or a computer program) selects for each document a few descriptors taken from a closed list of authorized terms. Semantic relations (synonyms, related terms, narrower terms, broader terms) can be used to help choose the right descriptors, and solve the sense problems of synonyms and homographs. The list of authorized terms and semantic relations between them are contained in a thesaurus.

To implement multilingual querying using this approach, it is necessary to give the corresponding translation of each thesaural term for each new language recognized. This work is facilitated by the fact that each descriptor is not chosen randomly but in order to express a precise unambiguous concept. The CIENTEC term bank (Velho Lopes, 1989) is one of many multilingual projects adopting this approach.

A problem remains, however, since concepts expressed by one single term in one language sometime are expressed by distinct terms in another. For example, the common term *mouton* in French is represented by two different concepts in English, *mutton* and *sheep*. One solution to this problem, given that these distinctions are known between the languages implemented is to create pseudo-words such as *mouton (food)*—mutton, and *mouton (animal)*—sheep. These semantic domain tags (such as *animal* and *food*) as well as the choice of transfer terms depend on the final use of the multilingual thesaurus, and it is therefore sometimes easier to build a multilingual thesaurus from scratch rather than to adapt a monolingual one.

This controlled vocabulary approach gives acceptable results but prohibits precise queries that cannot be expressed with these authorized keywords. It is however a common approach in well-delimited fields for which multilingual thesauri already exist (legal domain, energy, etc.) as well as in multinational organizations or countries with several official languages, which contain lexico-graphical units familiar with problems of terminological translation.

Automation of such methods consists of deducing, during indexing, the key-words that would be supplied for a text from the terms contained in the full-text or summary. Links between full-text words and controlled descriptors can be constructed either manually or by an automatic learning process from previously indexed documents. During inquiry, the same process can deduce the key-words from the terms used in the query to produce a search request. If links between text words and key-words are pre-established using different languages, it is possible to analyze texts that are not in the same language as the query using the key-words as a pivot language. See figure 8.1.

Generally, the controlled vocabulary approach means that queries can only be as precise as the predefined key-words (i.e., concepts) present in the thesaurus, posing an upper limit on query precision.

A third approach to multilingual query is to use existing machine translation (MT) systems to automatically translate the queries, or even the entire textual

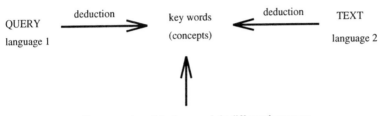

Figure 8.1: Multilingual query using interlingual pivot concepts.

database from one language to another. When only queries are translated from a source to target language, text can be searched in the target language and results can be dynamically translated back to the source language as they are displayed after the search.

This kind of method would be satisfactory if current MT systems did not make errors. A certain amount of syntactic mistakes are acceptable, but MT errors in translating concepts can prevent relevant documents, indexed on the missing concepts, from being found. For example, if the word *traitement* in French is translated by *processing* instead of *salary,* the retrieval process would yield incorrect results.

This drawback is limited in MT systems that use huge transfer lexicons of noun phrases like the RETRANS system developed by Belogonov, Khoroshilov, et al. (1993) in the VINITI, Moscow. But in any collection of text, ambiguous nouns will still appear as isolated noun phrases untouched by this approach.

A fourth approach to multilingual information retrieval is based on Salton's vector space model (Salton & McGill, 1983). This model represents documents in a n-dimensional space (n being the number of different words in the text database). If some documents are translated into a second language, these documents can be observed both in the subspace related to the first language and the subspace related to the second one. Using a query expressed in the second language, the most relevant documents in the translated subset are extracted (usually using a cosine measure of proximity). These relevant documents are in turn used to extract close untranslated documents in the subspace of the first language.

An improvement to this approach using existing translations of a part of the database has been investigated by a team in Bellcore (Landauer & Littman, 1990). Their information retrieval is based on latent semantic indexing. They approximate the full word-document matrix by a product of three lower dimensionality matrices of orthogonal factors derived from singular value decomposition. This transformation enables them to make a comparison not using individual words but taking into account sets of semantically related words. This approach uses implicit dependency links and co-occurrences that better approximate the notion of concept.

The method has been tested with some success on the English-French language pair using a sample of the Canadian Parliament bilingual corpus. 2482 paragraphs were selected. 900 were used for training, using both the English and French words in the documents to build the matrices. The 1582 remaining documents were added to the matrices in their French version only. The English versions of these 1582 documents were then used as queries using the 900 English documents of the training set to relate the French and English words in the latent semantic indexing. For 92% of the English text documents the closest document returned by the method was its correct French translation.

Such an approach presupposes that the sample used for training is really representative of the full database. Translation of the sample remains a huge undertaking that must be done for each new database.

Still another approach consists of combining machine translation methods with information retrieval methods. This approach has been developed by the European ESPRIT consortium (French, Belgian, German), EMIR (European Multilingual Information Retrieval) (EMIR, 1994). Experiments have been performed on French, English and German. This system uses 3 main tools:

- linguistic processors (morphological and syntactic analysis) which perform grammatical tagging, identify dependency relations (especially within noun phrases), and normalize the representation of uniterms and compounds;

- a statistical model which is used to weight the query-document intersection;

- a monolingual and multilingual reformulation system whose aim is to infer, from the original natural language query words, all possible expressions of the same concept that can occur in the document whatever the language.

The EMIR (1994) system uses large monolingual and bilingual dictionaries enabling it to process full-text databases in any domain. That means that all possible ambiguity in the language from both the syntactic and the semantic point of view are taken into account. A few additions are needed for unseen technical domains in the monolingual and bilingual dictionaries, especially in the bilingual dictionaries of multiterms.

Database texts are processed by linguistic processors which normalize single words and compounds. A weight is computed for all normalized words using a statistical model (Debili, Fluhr, et al., 1989). During the search, the text which is used as a query undergoes the same linguistic processing. The result of this processing is passed on to the reformulation process which infers new terms using monolingual reformulation rules (on source language and/or target language) and bilingual reformulation rules (transfer) (Fluhr, 1990). Compounds that are translated word for word are restructured by transformational rules. It can be seen that this approach differs significantly from the MT approach where only one translation of each query word is used. EMIR uses all possible translations in its database search.

In such an approach training for each database is not needed. Experiments on different databases have shown that, in most cases, the translation ambiguities (often more than 10 for each word) are solved by a comparison with the database lexicon and the co-occurrence with the translations of the other concepts of the query. Implicit semantic information contained in the database text is used as a semantic filter to find the right translation in cases where current MT systems would not succeed.

In the framework of EMIR, tests have been performed on the English CRANFIELD information retrieval testbed. First the original English language queries were translated into French by domain experts. Then two approaches were tested. Querying using the French-to-English SYSTRAN translation system followed by a monolingual search was compared to querying using the first bilingual EMIR prototype to access English text by expanding the French queries into English possibilities. The multilingual EMIR query was eight percent better than the one using SYSTRAN followed by monolingual query. On other hand, monolingual search using the original English queries with monolingual EMIR was twelve percent better than the bilingual search.

8.5.2   Future Directions

To continue research in the domain of multilingual information retrieval, it is necessary to develop tools and textual data resources whose construction will be costly. Apart from the need for tools that are required in all or most areas of natural language research, we see the need for the following:

- Large bilingual test corpora are urgently needed in order to evaluate and compare methods in an objective manner. Existing test databases are monolingual, mainly in English. Large-scale test databases which are truly multilingual (i.e., with texts which are strict translations of each other) are needed. It will then be necessary to elaborate a set of queries in the various languages tested as well as to find all the relevant documents for each query. This is a huge task. Such an undertaking for English textual databases has begun in the TREC (Text Retrieval Evaluation Conference) project (Harman, 1993). A similar process needs to be set in motion for multilingual test databases.

- Databases of lexical semantic relations as general as possible are needed in a variety of languages for monolingual reformulation using classical relations like synonyms, narrower terms, broader terms and also more precise relations like *part of, kind of, actor of the action, instrument of the action*, etc., like those being created for English in WordNet (Miller, 1990). Bilingual transfer dictionaries should also be as general as possible (general language as well as various specific domains).

- To accelerate the construction of such lexicons, tools are needed for extracting terminology and for automatic construction of the semantic relations from corpora of texts. If bilingual corpus of texts are available in a domain, tools for computer-aided building of transfer dictionaries should be developed. This extraction is specially needed for recognizing translations of compounds.

8.6   Multilingual Speech Processing

Alexander Waibel

Carnegie-Mellon University, Pittsburgh, Pennsylvania, USA
and Universität Karlsruhe, Germany

Multilinguality need not be textual only, but will take on spoken form, when information services are to extend beyond national boundaries, or across language groups. Database access by speech will need to handle multiple languages to service customers from different language groups within a country or travelers from abroad. Public service operators (emergency, police, department of transportation, telephone operators, and others) in the US, Japan and the EU frequently receive requests from foreigners unable to speak the national language (see also section 8.7.1).

Multilingual spoken language services is a growing industry, but so far these services rely exclusively on human operators. Telephone companies in the United States (e.g., AT&T Language Line), Europe and Japan now offer language translation services over the telephone, provided by human operators. Movies and foreign television broadcasts are routinely translated and delivered either by lipsynchronous speech (dubbing), subtitles or multilingual transcripts. The drive to automate information services, therefore, produces a growing need for automated multilingual speech processing.

The difficulties of speech processing are compounded with multilingual systems, and few, if any, commercial multilingual speech services exist to date. Yet intense research activity in areas of potential commercial interest are under way. These are aiming at:

- **Spoken Language Identification** By determining a speaker's language automatically, callers could be routed to human translation services. This is of particular interest to public services such as police, government offices (immigration service, drivers license offices, etc.) and experiments are underway in Japan and some regions of the US. The technical state of the art will be reviewed in the next section;

- **Multilingual Speech Recognition and Understanding** Future Spoken Language Services could be provided in multiple languages. Dictation systems and spoken language database access systems, for example, could operate in multiple languages, and deliver text or information in the language of the input speech.

- **Speech Translation** This ambitious possibility is still very much a research area, but could eventually lead to communication assistance in the form of portable voice activated dictionaries, phrase books or spoken language translators, telephone based speech translation services and/or automatic translation of foreign broadcasts and speeches. There is a wide spectrum of possibilities, but their full realization as commercial products still requires considerable research well into the next decade and beyond.

8.6.1 Multilingual Speech Recognition and Understanding

The last decade has seen much progress in the performance of speech recognition systems from cumbersome small-vocabulary isolated word systems to large-vocabulary continuous speech recognition (LV-CSR) over essentially unlimited vocabularies (50,000 words and more). Similarly, spoken language understanding systems now exist that process spontaneously spoken queries, although only in limited task domains under benign recording conditions (high quality, single speaker, no noise). A number of researchers have been encouraged by this state of affairs to extend these systems to other languages. They have studied similarities as well as differences across languages and improved the universality of current speech technologies.

Large-Vocabulary Continuous Speech Recognition (LV-CSR)

A number of LV-CSR systems developed originally for one language have now been extended to several languages, including systems developed by IBM (Cerf-Danon, DeGennaro, et al., 1991), Dragon Systems (Bamberg, Demedts, et al., 1991), Philips and Olivetti (Ney & Billi, 1991) and LIMSI. The extension of these systems to English, German, French, Italian, Spanish, Dutch and Greek illustrates that current speech technology can be generalized to different languages, provided sufficiently large transcribed speech databases are available. The research results show that similar modeling assumptions hold across languages with a few interesting exceptions. Differences in recognition performance are observed across languages, partially due to greater acoustic confusability (e.g., English), greater number of homonyms (e.g., French) and greater number of compound nouns and inflections (e.g., German). Such differences place a different burden on acoustic modeling vs. language modeling vs. the dictionary, or increase confusability, respectively. Also, a recognition vocabulary is not as easily defined as a unit for processing in languages such as Japanese and Korean, where pictographs, the absence of spaces, and large numbers of particles complicate matters.

Multilingual Spoken Language Systems

While LV-CSR systems tackle large vocabularies, but assume benign speaking styles (read speech), spoken language systems currently assume smaller domains and vocabularies, but require unrestricted speaking style. Spontaneous speech significantly degrades performance over read speech as it is more poorly articulated, grammatically ill-formed and garbled by noise. ARPA's Spoken Language projects have attacked this problem by focusing increasingly on the extraction of the semantic content of an utterance rather than accurate transcription. One such system, that has recently been extended to other languages is MIT's Voyager system (Glass, Goodine, et al., 1993). It was designed to handle information delivery tasks and can provide directions to nearby restaurants in Cambridge and also for airline travel information (ATIS). It has recently been extended to provide output in languages other than English. Researchers at LIMSI have developed a similar system for French (also airline travel information), thereby providing an extension to French on the input side as well. Availability of recognition capabilities in multiple languages have also recently led to interesting new language, speaker and gender identification strategies (Gauvain & Lamel, 1993). Transparent language identification could enhance the application of multilingual spoken language systems (see also section 8.7.1).

Despite the encouraging beginnings, multilingual spoken language systems still have to be improved before they can be deployed on a broad commercially feasible scale. Prototype systems have so far only been tested in benign recording situations, on very limited domains, with cooperative users, and without significant noise. Extending this technology to field situations will require increases in robustness as well as consideration of the human factors aspects of multilingual interface design.

8.6.2   Speech Translation Systems

There are no commercial speech translation systems in operation to date, but a number of industrial and government projects are exploring their feasibility. The feasibility of speech translation depends largely on the scope of the application, and ranges from applications that are well within range -such as voice activated dictionaries- to those that will remain impossible for the foreseeable future (e.g., unrestricted simultaneous translation.) Current research therefore aims at milestones between these extremes, namely limited domain speech translation. Such systems restrict the user in what he/she can talk about, and hence constrain the otherwise daunting task of modeling the world of discourse. Nevertheless such systems could be of practical and commercial interest, as they could be used to provide language assistance in common yet critical situations, such as registration for conferences, booking hotels, airlines, car rentals and theater tickets, ordering food, getting directions, scheduling meetings or in medical doctor-patient situations. If successful, it may also be possible to combine such domains to achieve translation in a class of domains (say, travel).

To be sure, spoken language translation—even in limited domains—still presents considerable challenges, which are the object of research in several large research undertakings around the world. Translation of spoken language (unlike text) is complicated by syntactically ill-formed speech, human (cough, laughter, etc.) and non-human (door-slams, telephone rings, etc.) noise, and has to contend with speech recognition errors. The spoken utterance does not provide unambiguous markers indicating the beginning or end of a sentence or phrase, and it frequently contains irrelevant information, that need not or should not be translated. Even simple concepts are expressed in quite different ways in different languages. A successful system must therefore interpret the speaker's intent -instead of translating his/her words- and deliver an appropriate message in the target language. For the speech processing components of a speech recognition system high accuracy is not the primary or only area of concern, but understanding, and understanding may be achieved by selectively extracting words of interest, and/or by occasionally prompting the user for important information. Researchers are now exploring solutions to the problem as a whole without expecting each separate part to function perfectly.

A speech translation system can likewise neither be solely categorized as "translation for assimilation" nor as "translation for dissemination", as textual translation systems are frequently described. It has some of the characteristics of both. Aiming at the interpretation of a speaker's intent, some research avenues in speech translation are attempting to extract (assimilate) the key information to interpret the gist of an utterance. Yet spoken language in many of the targeted application scenarios involves the interaction between two cooperative speakers, who can control to some extent the input to produce the desired result. This may allow for some limited domain systems to interact with the speaker of the source language until the correct interpretation can be transmitted (disseminated) in the target language(s).

A further complicating factor currently under investigation is that speech translation involves aspects of both human-human, as well as human-machine (the interpreting system) dialogues. This may require a system to distinguish between utterances and meta-level utterances, and to deal with code switching (change of language) in case of speakers with partial knowledge of each others' language or when referring to objects, names or items in the other language. Experiments over several speech databases in several languages indicate that human-to-human speech contains more disfluencies, more speaking rate variations and more co-articulation resulting in lower recognition rates (Levin, Suhm, et al., 1994) than human-machine interaction. These difficulties require further technological advances, a rethinking of common speech and language processing strategies, and a closer coupling between the acoustic and linguistic levels of processing.

Early Systems: Speech Translation research today is being developed against the background of early systems implemented in the eighties to demonstrate the feasibility of the concept. In addition to domain limitations, these early systems had also fixed speaking style, grammatical coverage and vocabulary size and were therefore too limited to be of practical value. Their system architecture is usually strictly sequential, involving speech recognition, language analysis and generation, and speech synthesis in the target language. Developed at industrial and academic institutions and consortia, they represented a modest but significant first step and proof of concept that multilingual communication by speech might be possible. Systems include research prototypes developed by NEC, AT&T, ATR, Carnegie Mellon University, Siemens AG, University of Karlsruhe, and SRI. Most have arisen or been made possible through international collaborations that provide the cross-linguistic expertise.

Among these international collaborations, the Consortium for Speech TrAnslation Research (C-STAR) was formed as a voluntary group of institutions committed to building speech translation systems. Its early members, ATR Interpreting Telephony Laboratories (now "Interpreting Telephony Laboratories") in Kyoto, Japan, Siemens AG in Munich, Germany, Carnegie Mellon University (CMU) in Pittsburgh, USA, and University of Karslruhe (UKA) in Karlsruhe, Germany, developed early systems, that accepted speech in each of the members' languages (i.e., English, German and Japanese) and produced output text in all the others (Morimoto, Takezawa, et al., 1993; Waibel, Jain, et al., 1991; Woszczyna, Aoki-Waibel, et al., 1994). The system modules allowed for continuous speaker-independent (or adaptive) input from a 500 word vocabulary in the domain of conference registration. The systems' modules operated strictly sequential, did not allow for feedback, and only accepted syntactically well formed utterances. After speech recognition, language analysis and generation, output text could then be transmitted to each of the partner sites for synthesis there. Translation was performed by an Interlingua approach in JANUS, the CMU/UKA system, while a transfer approach was used in ATR's ASURA and Siemens's systems. In early '93, they were shown to the public in a joint demonstration using video conferencing. Given the restrictions on speaking style and vocabulary, the systems performed well and provided good translation accuracy.

Early industrial speech-translation efforts are illustrated by AT&T's VEST (Roe, Pereira, et al., 1992) and NEC's Intertalker systems. VEST resulted from a collaboration between AT&T and Telefonica in Spain and translated English and Spanish utterances about currency exchange. It used a dictionary of 374 morphological entries and an augmented phrase structure grammar that is compiled into a finite state grammar used for both language modeling and translation. The system was demonstrated at EXPO'92 in Seville, Spain. NEC's Intertalker system also used finite state grammars to decode input sentences in terms of prescribed sentence patterns. The system ran on two separate tasks: reservation of concert tickets and travel information, and was successfully demonstrated at GlobCom'92. SRI in collaboration with Swedish Telecom recently reported on another system (Rayner et al., 1993), that is based on previously developed system components from SRI's air travel information system. The ATIS speech understanding component is interfaced with a generation component. The system's input language is English and it produces output in Swedish. It represents an early attempt at extending spontaneous multilingual human-machine dialogues to translation.

Translation of Spontaneous Speech: To develop more practical, usable speech translation, greater robustness in the face of spontaneous ill-formed speech has to be achieved. A number of research activities aiming at the translation of spontaneous speech have since been launched. Several industrial and academic institutions, as well as large national research efforts in Germany and in Japan are now working on this problem. Virtually all of these efforts aim at restricted domains, but now remove the limitation of a fixed vocabulary and size, and also no longer require the user to speak in syntactically well-formed sentences (an impossibility in practice, given stuttering, hesitations, false starts and other disfluencies found in spontaneous speech).

The C-STAR consortium was extended to translate spontaneous speech. In addition to the partners of the first phase, it includes presently ETRI (Korea), IRST (Italy), LIMSI (France), SRI (UK), IIT (India), Lincoln Labs (USA), MIT (USA), and AT&T (USA). Each C-STAR partner builds a complete system that at the very least accepts input in the language of this partner and produces output in one other language of the consortium. In a multinational consortium, building full systems thereby maximizes the technical exchange between the partners while minimizing costly software/hardware interfacing work. C-STAR continues to operate in a fairly loose and informal organizational style. Present activity has shifted toward a greater emphasis on interpretation of spoken language, i.e., the systems ability to extract the intent of a speaker's utterance. Several institutions involved in C-STAR therefore stress semantic parsers and an interlingual representation (CMU, UKA, MIT, AT&T, ETRI, IRST), more in line with message extraction than with traditional text translation. Other approaches under investigation include Example Based Translation (ATR), with its potential for improved portability and reduced development cost through the use of large parallel corpora. Robust Transfer Approaches (ATR, Siemens) are also explored, with robust and stochastic analysis to account for fragmentary input. System architectures under investigation are no longer strictly sequential, but begin to involve clarification or paraphrase in the speaker's language as first attempts at the machine's feedback of its understanding. At the time of this writing, such feedback is still very rudimentary and does not yet involve more elaborate confirmatory meta-level dialogues or repair mechanisms. Current research also begins to actively exploit discourse and domain knowledge, as well as prosodic information during turn taking, for more robust interpretation of ambiguous utterances.

Verbmobil is a large new research effort sponsored by the BMFT, the German Ministry for Science and Technology (Wahlster, 1993). Launched in 1993 the program sponsors over 30 German industrial and academic partners who work on different aspects of the speech translation problem and are delivering system components for a complete speech translation system. The system components (e.g., speech recognition components, analysis, generation, synthesis, etc.) are integrated into a research prototype, available to all. The initial task is appointment scheduling with possible extensions to other domains. Verbmobil is aimed at face-to-face negotiations, rather than telecommunication applications and assumes that two conversants have some passive knowledge of a common lan-

guage, English. It is to provide translation on demand for speakers of German
and Japanese, when they request assistance in an otherwise English conversation. Verbmobil is therefore concerned with code switching and the translation
of sentence fragments in a dialogue. Verbmobil is an eight-year project with an
initial four-year phase.

8.6.3   Future Directions

To meet the challenges in developing multilingual technology, an environment
and infrastructure must be developed. Contrary to research fostered and supported at the national level, multilingual research tends to involve collaborations across national boundaries. It is important to define and support efficient,
international consortia, that agree to jointly develop such mutually beneficial
technologies. An organizational style of cooperation with little or no overhead
is crucial, involving groups who are in a position to build complete speech translation systems for their own language. There is a need for common multilingual databases and data involving foreign accents. Moreover, better evaluation
methodology over common databases is needed to assess the performance of a
speech translation system in terms of accuracy and usability. Research in this
direction needs to be supported more aggressively across national boundaries.

Beyond improvements in component technologies (speech and language processing), innovations in language acquisition are badly needed to achieve greater
portability across domains. While acoustic models can be reused to a certain
extent (or at least adapted) across domains, most language work still requires
inordinate amounts of resources. Grammar development requires considerable
development work for each domain. Language models have to be retrained and
require large amounts of transcribed data within each domain. Continued research on language acquisition may provide better domain adaptation and/or
incrementally improving language models, grammars and dictionaries.

The limitation to restricted domains of discourse must be lifted, if broader
usage is to be guaranteed. Short of universal and reliable speech translation (as
could be needed for example, for automatically translated captions in movies, or
simultaneous translation), intermediate goals might be given by large domains
of discourse, that involve several subdomains. Integration of subdomains will
need to be studied.

Last, but not least, better human-computer interaction strategies have to be
developed, as multilingual spoken language translation becomes a tool to broker
an understanding between two humans rather than a black box that tries to
translate every utterance. A useful speech translation system should be able
to notice misunderstandings and negotiate alternatives. Such ability requires
better modeling of out-of-domain utterances, better generation of meta-level
dialogues and handling of interactive repair.

8.7 Automatic Language Identification[1]

Yeshwant K. Muthusamy[a] & A. Lawrence Spitz[b]

[a] Texas Instruments Incorporated, Dallas, Texas, USA
[b] Daimler Benz Research and Technology Center, Palo Alto, California, USA

8.7.1 Spoken Language

The importance of spoken language ID in the global community cannot be ignored. Telephone companies would like to quickly identify the language of foreign callers and route their calls to operators who can speak the language. A multilanguage translation system dealing with more than two or three languages needs a language identification front-end that will route the speech to the appropriate translation system. And, of course, governments around the world have long been interested in spoken language ID for monitoring purposes.

Despite twenty-odd years of research, the field of spoken language ID has suffered from the lack of (i) a common, public-domain multilingual speech corpus that could be used to evaluate different approaches to the problem, and (ii) basic research. The recent public availability of the OGI Multilanguage Telephone Speech Corpus (OGI_TS) (Muthusamy, Cole, et al., 1992), designed specifically for language ID, has led to renewed interest in the field and fueled a proliferation of different approaches to the problem. This corpus currently contains spontaneous and fixed vocabulary speech from 11 languages. The National Institute of Standards and Technology (NIST) conducts an annual common evaluation of spoken language ID algorithms using the OGI_TS corpus. At the time of writing, eight research sites from the U.S. and Europe participate in this evaluation. There are now papers on spoken language ID appearing in major conference proceedings (Berkling & Barnard, 1994; Dalsgaard & Andersen, 1994; Hazen & Zue, 1994; Kadambe & Hieronymus, 1994; Lamel & Gauvain, 1994; Li, 1994; Ramesh & Roe, 1994; Reyes, Seino, et al., 1994; Zissman & Singer, 1994). See Muthusamy, Barnard, et al. (1994) for a more detailed account of the recent studies in spoken language ID.

Many of the approaches to spoken language ID have adopted techniques used in current speaker-independent speech recognition systems. A popular approach to language ID consists of variants of the following two basic steps: (i) develop a phonemic/phonetic recognizer for each language, and (ii) combine the acoustic likelihood scores from the recognizers to determine the highest scoring language. Step (i) consists of an acoustic modeling phase and a language modeling phase. Trained acoustic models of phones in each language are used to estimate a stochastic grammar for each language. The models can be trained using either HMMs (Lamel & Gauvain, 1994; Zissman & Singer, 1994) or neural networks (Berkling & Barnard, 1994). The grammars used are usually bigram

---

[1]Automatic language identification (language ID for short) can be defined as the problem of identifying the language from a sample of speech or text. Researchers have been working on spoken and written language ID for the past two decades.

or trigram grammars. The likelihood scores for the phones resulting from step (i) incorporate both acoustic and phonotactic information. In step (ii), these scores are accumulated to determine the language with the largest likelihood. Zissman and Singer (1994) have achieved the best results to date on OGI_TS using a slight variant of this approach: They exploit the fact that a stochastic grammar for one language can be developed based on the acoustic models of a different language. This has the advantage that phonetic recognizers need not be developed for all the target languages. This system achieves 79% accuracy on the 11-language task using 50-second utterances and 70% accuracy using 10-second utterances.

Li (1994) has applied speaker recognition techniques to language ID with tremendous success. His basic idea is to classify an incoming utterance based on the similarity of the speaker of that utterance with the most similar speakers of the target languages. His similarity measure is based on spectral features extracted from experimentally determined syllabic nuclei within the utterances. His results on the 11-language task: 78% on 50-second utterances, and 63% on 10-second utterances.

The importance of prosodic information such as pitch and duration in recognizing speech or in discriminating between languages has long been acknowledged. However, this information has not yet been fully exploited in language ID systems. Muthusamy (1993) examined pitch variation within and across broad phonetic segments with marginal success. He found other prosodic information such as duration and syllabic rate to be more useful, as did Hazen and Zue (1994).

While the progress of language ID research in the last two years has been heartening, there is much to do. It is clear that there is no "preferred approach" as yet to spoken language ID; very different systems perform comparably on the 11-language task. Moreover, the level of performance is nowhere near acceptability in a real-world environment. Present systems perform much better on 50-second utterances than 10-second ones. The fact that human identification performance asymptotes for much shorter durations of speech (Muthusamy, Jain, et al., 1994) indicates that there are some important sources of information that are not being exploited in current systems.

8.7.2   Written Language

Written language identification has received less attention than spoken language recognition. House and Neuberg (1977) demonstrated the feasibility of written language ID using just broad phonetic information. They trained statistical (Markov) models on sequences of broad phonetic categories derived from phonetic transcriptions of text in eight languages. Perfect discrimination of the eight languages was obtained. Most methods rely on input in the form of character codes. Techniques then use information about short words (Kulikowski, 1991; Ingle, 1991); the independent probability of letters and the joint probability of various letter combinations (Rau, 1974 who used English and Spanish text, to devise an identification system for the two languages); n-grams of words

(Batchelder, 1992); n-grams of characters (Beesley, 1988; Cavner & Trenkle, 1994); diacritics and special characters (Newman, 1987); syllable characteristics (Mustonen, 1965), morphology and syntax (Ziegler, 1991).

More specifically, Heinrich (1989) evaluated two language ID approaches (one using statistics of letter combinations and the other using word rules) to help him convert French and English words to German in a German text-to-speech system. He found that the approach based on word-boundary rules, position independent rules (e.g., 'sch' does not occur in French) and exception word lists was more suited to the conversion task and performed better than the one based on statistics of letters, bigrams and trigrams. His experiments, however, did not use an independent test set.

Schmitt (1991) patented a trigram-based method of written language ID. He compared the successive trigrams derived from a body of text with a database of trigram sets generated for each language. The language for which the greatest number of trigram matches were obtained, and for which the frequencies of occurrence of the trigrams exceeded a language-specific threshold, was chosen the winner. No results were specified.

Ueda and Nakagawa (1990) evaluated multi-state ergodic (i.e., fully connected) HMMs, bigrams and trigrams to model letter sequences using text from six languages. Their experiments revealed that the HMMs had better entropy than bigrams but were comparable to the computationally expensive trigrams. A 7-state ergodic HMM, in which any state can be visited from any other state, provided 99.2% identification accuracy on a 50-letter test sequence.

Judging by the results, it appears that language ID from character codes is an easier problem than that from speech input. This makes intuitive sense: text does not exhibit the variability associated with speech (e.g., speech habits, speaker emotions, mispronunciations, dialects, channel differences, etc.) that contributes to the problems in speech recognition and spoken language ID.

More and more text is, however, only available as images, to be converted into possible character sequences by OCR. However, for OCR it is desirable to know the language of the document before trying the decoding. More recent techniques try to determine the language of the text before doing the conversions. The Fuji Xerox Palo Alto Laboratory (Spitz, 1993) developed a method of encoding characters into a small number of basic character shape codes (CSC), based largely on the number of connected components and their position with respect to the baseline and x-height. Thus characters with ascenders are represented differently from those with descenders and in turn from those which are entirely contained between the baseline and x-line. A total of 8 CSCs represent the 52 basic characters and their diacritic forms.

On the basis of different agglomerations of CSCs, a number of techniques for determining the language of a document have been developed. Early work used word shape tokens (WSTs) formed by one-to-one mappings of character positions within a word to character shape codes. Analysis of the most frequently occurring WSTs yields a highly reliable determination of which of twenty-three languages, all using the Latin character set, is present (Sibun & Spitz, 1994). More recent work uses the statistics of n-grams of CSCs (Nakayama, 1994).

8.7.3   Future Directions

A number of fundamental issues need to be addressed if progress is to be made in spoken language ID (Cole, Hirschman, et al., 1995). Despite the flattering results on OGI-TS, current studies have not yet addressed an important question: what are the fundamental acoustic, perceptual, and linguistic differences among languages? An investigation of these differences with a view to incorporating them into current systems is essential. Further, is it possible to define language-independent acoustic/phonetic models, perhaps in terms of an interlingual acoustic/phonetic feature set? An investigation of language-specific versus language-independent properties across languages might yield answers to that question. As for written language ID, languages using non-Latin and more general non-alphabetical scripts are the next challenge.

8.8   Chapter References

ACL (1991). *Proceedings of the 29th Annual Meeting of the Association for Computational Linguistics*, Berkeley, California. Association for Computational Linguistics.

Alshawi, H., Carter, D., et al. (1991). Translation by quasi logical form transfer. In *Proceedings of the 29th Annual Meeting of the Association for Computational Linguistics*, Berkeley, California. Association for Computational Linguistics.

ANLP (1994). *Proceedings of the Fourth Conference on Applied Natural Language Processing*, Stuttgart, Germany. ACL, Morgan Kaufmann.

Arnold, D. and des Tombes, L. (1987). Basic theory and methodology in EUROTRA. In Nirenburg, S., editor, *Machine Translation: Theoretical and Methodological Issues*, pages 114–135. Cambridge University Press.

ARPA (1993). *Proceedings of the 1993 ARPA Human Language Technology Workshop*, Princeton, New Jersey. Advanced Research Projects Agency, Morgan Kaufmann.

Bamberg, P., Demedts, A., Elder, J., Huang, C., Ingold, C., Mandel, M., Manganaro, L., and van Even, S. (1991). Phonem-based training for large-vocabulary recogntition in six european languages. In *Eurospeech '91, Proceedings of the Second European Conference on Speech Communication and Technology*, volume 1, pages 175–181, Genova, Italy. European Speech Communication Association.

Batchelder, E. O. (1992). A learning experience: Training an artificial neural network to discriminate languages. Technical Report.

Beesley, K. R. (1988). Language identifier: A computer program for automatic natural-language identification on on-line text. In *Proceedings of the 29th Annual Conference of the American Translators Association*, pages 47–54.

Belogonov, G., Khoroshilov, A., Khoroshilov, A., Kuznetsov, B., Novoselov, A., Pashchenko, N., and Zelenkov, Y. (1993). An interactive system of Russian-English and English-Russian machine translation of polythematic scientific and technical texts. Technical report, VINITI internal Report, Moscow.

Berkling, K. M. and Barnard, E. (1994). Language identification of six languages based on a common set of broad phonemes. In *Proceedings of the 1994 International Conference on Spoken Language Processing*, volume 4, pages 1891–1894, Yokohama, Japan.

Boitet, C. (1986). The French national MT-project: technical organization and translation results of CALLIOPE-AERO. *Computers and Translation*, 1:281.

Boitet, C. and Blanchon, H. (1993). Dialogue-based machine translation for monolingual authors and the LIDIA project. In Nomura, H., editor, *Proceedings of the 1993 Natural Language Processing Rim Symposium*, pages 208–222, Fukuoka. Kyushu Institute of Technology.

Bourbeau, L., Carcagno, D., Goldberg, E., Kittredge, R., and Polguere, A. (1990). Bilingual generation of wheather forecasts in an operations environment. In Karlgren, H., editor, *Proceedings of the 13th International Conference on Computational Linguistics*, volume 3, pages 318–320, Helsinki. ACL.

Brown, P., Cocke, J., Pietra, S. D., Pietra, V. J. D., Jelinek, F., Lafferty, J. D., Mercer, R. L., and Roossin, P. S. (1990). A statistical approach to machine translation. *Computational Linguistics*, 16(2):79–85.

Carbonell, J. G. and Tomita, M. (1987). Knowledge-based machine translation, the CMU approach. In Nirenburg, S., editor, *Machine Translation: Theoretical and Methodological Issues*, pages 68–89. Cambridge University Press.

Cavner, W. B. and Trenkle, J. M. (1994). N-gram based text categorization. In *Proceedings of the Third Annual Symposium on Document Analysis and Information Retrieval*, pages 261–169.

Cerf-Danon, H., DeGennaro, S., Ferreti, M., Gonzalez, J., and Keppel, E. (1991). Tangora—a large vocabulary speech recognition system for five languages. In *Eurospeech '91, Proceedings of the Second European Conference on Speech Communication and Technology*, volume 1, pages 183–192, Genova, Italy. European Speech Communication Association.

Chandioux, J. (1989). Meteo: 1000 million words later. In Hammond, D. L., editor, *American Translators Association Conference 1989: Coming of Age*, pages 449–453. Learned Information, Medford, New Jersey.

Chandler, B., Holden, N., Horsfall, H., Pollard, E., and McGee, M. W. (1987). N-tran final report, Alvey project. Technical Report 87/9, CCL/UMIST, Manchester.

Chevalier, M., Dansereau, J., et al. (1978). *TAUM-METEO: Description du Système.* Université de Montréal.

Cole, R. A., Hirschman, L., Atlas, L., Beckman, M., Bierman, A., Bush, M., Cohen, J., Garcia, O., Hanson, B., Hermansky, H., Levinson, S., McKeown, K., Morgan, N., Novick, D., Ostendorf, M., Oviatt, S., Price, P., Silverman, H., Spitz, J., Waibel, A., Weinstein, C., Zahorian, S., and Zue, V. (1995). The challenge of spoken language systems: Research directions for the nineties. *IEEE Transactions on Speech and Audio Processing*, 3(1):1–21.

COLING (1986). *Proceedings of the 11th International Conference on Computational Linguistics*, Bonn. ACL.

COLING (1988). *Proceedings of the 12th International Conference on Computational Linguistics*, Budapest.

COLING (1992). *Proceedings of the 14th International Conference on Computational Linguistics*, Nantes, France. ACL.

Dalsgaard, P. and Andersen, O. (1994). Application of inter-language phoneme similarities for language identification. In *Proceedings of the 1994 International Conference on Spoken Language Processing*, volume 4, pages 1903–1906, Yokohama, Japan.

Debili, F., Fluhr, C., and Radasao, P. (1989). About reformulation in full-text IRS. *Information Processing and Management*, 25:647–657.

Delin, J., Hartley, A., Paris, C., Scott, D., and Vander Linden, K. (1994). Expressing procedural relationships in multilingual instructions. In *Proceedings of the Seventh International Workshop on Natural Language Generation*, pages 61–70, Kennebunkport, Maine. Springer-Verlag, Berlin.

EMIR (1994). Final report of the EMIR project number 5312. Technical report, European Multilingual Information Retrieval Consortium For the Commission of the European Union, Brussels.

Eurospeech (1991). *Eurospeech '91, Proceedings of the Second European Conference on Speech Communication and Technology*, Genova, Italy. European Speech Communication Association.

Farwell, D. and Wilks, Y. (1990). *Ultra: A Multi-lingual Machine Translator.* New Mexico State University.

Fluhr, C. (1990). Multilingual information. In *AI and Large-Scale Information*, Nagoya.

Furuse, O. and Iida, H. (1992). Cooperation between transfer and analysis in example-based framework. In *Proceedings of the 14th International Conference on Computational Linguistics*, Nantes, France. ACL.

Gauvain, J.-L. and Lamel, L. F. (1993). Identification of non-linguistic speech features. In *Proceedings of the 1993 ARPA Human Language Technology Workshop*, page Session 6, Princeton, New Jersey. Advanced Research Projects Agency, Morgan Kaufmann.

Glass, J., Goodine, D., Phillips, M., Sakai, S., Seneff, S., and Zue, V. (1993). A bilingual voyager system. In *Proceedings of the 1993 ARPA Human Language Technology Workshop*, Princeton, New Jersey. Advanced Research Projects Agency, Morgan Kaufmann. Session 6.

Harman, D., editor (1993). *National Institute of Standards and Technology Special Publication No. 500-207 on the The First Text REtrieval Conference (TREC-1)*, Washington, DC. National Institute of Standards and Technology, U.S. Department of Commerce, U.S. Government Printing Office.

Hazen, T. J. and Zue, V. W. (1994). Recent improvements in an approach to segment-based automatic language identification. In *Proceedings of the 1994 International Conference on Spoken Language Processing*, volume 4, pages 1883–1886, Yokohama, Japan.

Heinrich, P. (1989). Language identification for automatic grapheme-to-phoneme conversion of foreign words in a german text-to-speech system. In *Speech-89*, pages 220–223.

House, A. S. and Neuberg, E. P. (1977). Toward automatic identification of the language of an utterance. I. Preliminary methodological considerations. *Journal of the Acoustical Society of America*, 62(3):708–713.

Huang, X. M. (1990). A machine translation system for the target language inexpert. In Karlgren, H., editor, *Proceedings of the 13th International Conference on Computational Linguistics*, volume 3, pages 364–367, Helsinki. ACL.

ICASSP (1994). *Proceedings of the 1994 International Conference on Acoustics, Speech, and Signal Processing*, Adelaide, Australia. Institute of Electrical and Electronic Engineers.

ICSLP (1994). *Proceedings of the 1994 International Conference on Spoken Language Processing*, Yokohama, Japan.

Iida, E. S. and Iida, H. (1991). Experiments and prospects of example-based machine translation. In *Proceedings of the 29th Annual Meeting of the Association for Computational Linguistics*, pages 185–192, Berkeley, California. Association for Computational Linguistics.

Ingle, N. C. (1991). A language identification table. *The Incorporated Linguist*, 15(4):98–101.

IWNLG (1994). *Proceedings of the Seventh International Workshop on Natural Language Generation*, Kennebunkport, Maine. Springer-Verlag, Berlin.

JEIDA (1989). A Japanese view of machine translation in light of the considerations and recommendations reported by ALPAC, USA. Technical report, Japanese Electronic Industry Development Association, Tokyo.

Kadambe, S. and Hieronymus, J. L. (1994). Spontaneous speech language identification with a knowledge of linguistics. In *Proceedings of the 1994 International Conference on Spoken Language Processing*, volume 4, pages 1879–1882, Yokohama, Japan.

Karlgren, H., editor (1990). *Proceedings of the 13th International Conference on Computational Linguistics*, Helsinki. ACL.

Kay, M. (1973). The MIND system. In Rustin, R., editor, *Courant Computer Science Symposium 8: Natural Language Processing*, pages 155–188. Algorithmics Press, New York.

Kay, M. (1980). *The Proper Place of Men and Machines in Language Translation*. Xerox Palo Alto Research Center, Palo Alto, California.

Kay, M., Gawron, J. M., and Norvig, P. (1991). Verbmobil: A translation system for face-to-face dialog. Technical report, Stanford University.

King, M. and Perschke, S. (1987). *Machine Translation Today: The State of the Art*. Edinburgh University Press. EUROTRA.

Kittredge, R. I. (1987). The significance of sublanguage for automatic translation. In Nirenburg, S., editor, *Machine Translation: Theoretical and Methodological Issues*, pages 59–67. Cambridge University Press.

Kulikowski, S. (1991). Using short words: a language identification algorithm. Unpublished technical report.

Lamel, L. F. and Gauvain, J.-L. S. (1994). Language identification using phone-based acoustic likelihoods. In *Proceedings of the 1994 International Conference on Acoustics, Speech, and Signal Processing*, volume 1, pages 293–296, Adelaide, Australia. Institute of Electrical and Electronic Engineers.

Landauer, T. K. and Littman, M. L. (1990). Fully automatic cross-language document retrieval using latent semantic indexing. In *Proceedings of the Sixth Annual Conference of the UW Centre for the New Oxford English Dictionary and Text Research*, UW Centre for the New OED and Text Research, Waterloo Ontario.

Landsbergen, J. (1987). Isomorphic grammars and their use in the ROSETTA translation system. In *Machine Translation Today: The State of the Art*. Edinburgh University Press, Edinburgh.

Lehrberger, J. and Bourbeau, L. (1988). *Machine translation: linguistic characteristics of MT systems and general methodology of evaluation*. John Benjamins, Amsterdam, Philadelphia.

Levin, L., Suhm, B., Coccaro, N., Carbonell, J., Horiguchi, K., Isotani, R., Lavie, A., Mayfield, L., Rose, C. P., Van Ess-Dykema, C., and Waibel, A. (1994). Speech–language integration in a multi-lingual speech translation system. In *Proceedings of the 1994 AAAI Conference*, Seattle. American Association for Artificial Intelligence.

Li, K.-P. (1994). Automatic language identification using syllabic features. In *Proceedings of the 1994 International Conference on Acoustics, Speech, and Signal Processing*, volume 1, pages 297–300, Adelaide, Australia. Institute of Electrical and Electronic Engineers.

Maruyama, H., Watanabe, H., and Ogino, S. (1990). An interactive Japanese parser for machine translation. In Karlgren, H., editor, *Proceedings of the 13th International Conference on Computational Linguistics*, volume 2, pages 257–262, Helsinki. ACL.

Melby, A. K. (1982). Multi-level translation aids in a distributed system. In *Proceedings of the 9th International Conference on Computational Linguistics*, volume 1 of *Ling. series 47*, pages 215–220, Prague. ACL.

Miller, G. (1990). Wordnet: An on-line lexical database. *International journal of Lexicography*, 3(4):235–312.

Morimoto, T., Takezawa, T., Yato, F., Sagayama, S., Tashiro, T., Nagata, M., and Kurematsu, A. (1993). ATR's speech translation system: ASURA. In *Proceedings of the Third Conference on Speech Communication and Technology*, pages 1295–1298, Berlin, Germany.

MTS (1989). *Proceedings of the Second Machine Translation Summit*, Tokyo. Omsha Ltd.

MTS (1991). *Proceedings of the Third Machine Translation Summit*, Carnegie Mellon University.

Muraki, K. (1989). PIVOT: Two-phase machine translation system. In *Proceedings of the Second Machine Translation Summit*, Tokyo. Omsha Ltd.

Mustonen, S. (1965). Multiple discriminant analysis in linguistic problems. In *Statistical Methods in Linguistics*. Skriptor Fack, Stockholm. Number 4.

Muthusamy, Y. K. (1993). *A Segmental Approach to Automatic Language Identification*. PhD thesis, Oregon Graduate Institute of Science & Technology, P.O.Box 91000, Portland, OR 97291-1000 USA.

Muthusamy, Y. K., Barnard, E., and Cole, R. A. (1994). Reviewing automatic language identification. *IEEE Signal Processing Magazine*, 11(4):33–41.

Muthusamy, Y. K., Cole, R. A., and Oshika, B. T. (1992). The OGI multi-language telephone speech corpus. In *Proceedings of the 1992 International Conference on Spoken Language Processing*, volume 2, pages 895–898, Banff, Alberta, Canada. University of Alberta.

Muthusamy, Y. K., Jain, N., and Cole, R. A. (1994). Perceptual benchmarks for automatic language identification. In *Proceedings of the 1994 International Conference on Acoustics, Speech, and Signal Processing*, volume 1, pages 333–336, Adelaide, Australia. Institute of Electrical and Electronic Engineers.

Nagao, M. (1992). Some rationales and methodologies for example-based approach. In *Fifth Generation Natural Language Processing*. Publisher Unknown.

Nakayama (1994). Modeling content identification from document images. In *Proceedings of the Fourth Conference on Applied Natural Language Processing*, pages 22–27, Stuttgart, Germany. ACL, Morgan Kaufmann.

Newman, P. (1987). Foreign language identification: First step in the translation process. In *Proceedings of the 28th Annual Conference of the American Translators Accociation*, pages 509–516.

Ney, H. and Billi, R. (1991). Prototype systems for large-vocabulary speech recognition: Polyglot and Spicos. In *Eurospeech '91, Proceedings of the Second European Conference on Speech Communication and Technology*, volume 1, pages 193–200, Genova, Italy. European Speech Communication Association.

Nirenburg, S., editor (1987). *Machine Translation: Theoretical and Methodological Issues*. Cambridge University Press.

Nirenburg, S., Raskin, V., et al. (1986). On knowledge-based machine translation. In *Proceedings of the 11th International Conference on Computational Linguistics*, Bonn. ACL.

Okumura, A., Muraki, K., and Akamine, S. (1991). Multi-lingual sentence generation from the PIVOT interlingua. In *Proceedings of the Third Machine Translation Summit*, Carnegie Mellon University.

Paris, C. and Scott, D. (1994). Stylistic variation in multilingual instructions. In *Proceedings of the Seventh International Workshop on Natural Language Generation*, pages 45–52, Kennebunkport, Maine. Springer-Verlag, Berlin.

Perschke, S. (1989). EUROTRA project. In *Proceedings of the Second Machine Translation Summit*, Tokyo. Omsha Ltd.

Ramesh, P. and Roe, D. B. (1994). Language identification with embedded word models. In *Proceedings of the 1994 International Conference on Spoken Language Processing*, volume 4, pages 1887–1890, Yokohama, Japan.

Rau, M. D. (1974). Language identification by statistical analysis. Master's thesis, Naval Postgraduate School.

Rayner, M. et al. (1993). A speech to speech translation system built from standard components. In *Proceedings of the 1993 ARPA Human Language Technology Workshop*, Princeton, New Jersey. Advanced Research Projects Agency, Morgan Kaufmann.

Reyes, A. A., Seino, T., and Nakagawa, S. (1994). Three language identification methods based on HMMs. In *Proceedings of the 1994 International Conference on Spoken Language Processing*, volume 4, pages 1895–1898, Yokohama, Japan.

Roe, D. B., Pereira, F. C., Sproat, R. W., and Riley, M. D. (1992). Efficient grammar processing for a spoken language translation system. In *Proceedings of the 1992 International Conference on Acoustics, Speech, and Signal Processing*, volume 1, pages 213–216, San Francisco. Institute of Electrical and Electronic Engineers.

Rösner, D. and Stede, M. (1994). Techdoc: Multilingual generation of online and offline instructional text. In *Proceedings of the Fourth Conference on Applied Natural Language Processing*, pages 209–210, Stuttgart, Germany. ACL, Morgan Kaufmann.

Sadler, V. (1989). Working with analogical semantics: Disambiguation technics in DLT. In Witkam, T., editor, *Distributed Language Translation (BSO/Research)*. Floris Publications, Dordrecht, Holland.

Salton, G. and McGill, M. (1983). *An Introduction to Modern Information Retrieval*. McGraw-Hill, New York.

Sato, S. (1992). CTM: An example-based translation aid system using the character-based best match retrieval method. In *Proceedings of the 14th International Conference on Computational Linguistics*, Nantes, France. ACL.

Schmitt, J. C. (1991). Trigram-based method of language identification. U.S. Patent number: 5062143.

Schubert, K. (1988). The architectre of DLT—interlingual or double direct. In *New Directions in Machine Translation*. Floris Publications, Dordrecht, Holland.

Schutz, J., Thurmair, G., et al. (1991). An architecture sketch of Eurotra-II. In *Proceedings of the Third Machine Translation Summit*, Carnegie Mellon University.

Sibun, P. and Spitz, L. A. (1994). Language determination: Natural language processing from scanned document images. In *Proceedings of the Fourth Conference on Applied Natural Language Processing*, pages 15–21, Stuttgart, Germany. ACL, Morgan Kaufmann.

Sigurdson, J. and Greatex, R. (1987). *Machine Translation of on-line searches in Japanese Data Bases*. RPI, Lund University.

Somers, H. L., Tsujii, J.-I., and Jones, D. (1990). Machine translation without a source text. In Karlgren, H., editor, *Proceedings of the 13th International Conference on Computational Linguistics*, volume 3, pages 271–276, Helsinki. ACL.

Spitz, L. A. (1993). Generalized line word and character finding. In *Proceedings of the International Conference on Image Analysis and Processing*, pages 686–690.

Tomita, M. (1986). Sentence disambiguation by asking. *Computers and Translation*, 1(1):39–51.

Tong, L. C. (1987). The engineering of a translator workstation. *Computers and Translation*, 2(4):263–273.

Uchida, H. (1986). Fujitsu machine translation system: ATLAS. In *Future Generations Computer Systems 2*, pages 95–100. Publisher Unknown.

Uchida, H. (1989). ATLAS-II: A machine translation system using conceptual structure as an interlingua. In *Proceedings of the Second Machine Translation Summit*, Tokyo. Publisher Unknown.

Ueda, Y. and Nakagawa, S. (1990). Prediction for phoneme/syllable/word-category and identification of language using HMM. In *Proceedings of the 1990 International Conference on Spoken Language Processing*, volume 2, pages 1209–1212, Kobe, Japan.

Vasconcellos, M. and Len, M. (1988). SPANAM and ENGSPAM: Machine translation at the Pan American Health Organization. In Slocum, J., editor, *Machine Translation systems*, pages 187–236. Cambridge University Press.

Velho Lopes, R. R. (1989). Automated access to multilingual information: a Brazilian case study. *Information Development*, 5(3).

Wahlster, W. (1993). Verbmobil, translation of face-to-face dialogs. In *Proceedings of the Fourth Machine Translation Summit*, pages 127–135, Kobe, Japan.

Waibel, A., Jain, A., McNair, A., Saito, H., Hauptmann, A., and Tebelskis, J. (1991). JANUS: a speech-to-speech translation system using connectionist and symbolic processing strategies. In *Proceedings of the 1991 International Conference on Acoustics, Speech, and Signal Processing*, volume 2, pages 793–796, Toronto. Institute of Electrical and Electronic Engineers.

Wehrli, E. (1992). The IPS system. In *Proceedings of the 14th International Conference on Computational Linguistics*, volume 3, pages 870–874, Nantes, France. ACL.

Whitelock, P. J., Wood, M. M., Chandler, B. J., Holden, N., and Horsfall, H. J. (1986). Strategies for interactive machine translation: The experience and implications of the UMIST Japanese project. In *Proceedings of the 11th International Conference on Computational Linguistics*, pages 25–29, Bonn. ACL.

Winsoft (1987). *Manuel d'utilisation de WinTool*. Winsoft Inc., Grenoble. Version 1.1.

Witkam, T. (1988). DLT—an industrial R&D project for multilingual machine translation. In *Proceedings of the 12th International Conference on Computational Linguistics*, Budapest.

Wood, M. M. and Chandler, B. (1988). Machine translation for monolinguals. In *Proceedings of the 12th International Conference on Computational Linguistics*, pages 760–763, Budapest.

Woszczyna, M., Aoki-Waibel, N., Buo, F. D., Coccaro, N., Horiguchi, K., Kemp, T., Lavie, A., McNair, A., Polzin, T., Rogina, I., Rose, C. P., Schultz, T., Suhm, B., Tomita, M., and Waibel, A. (1994). Towards spontaneous speech translation. In *Proceedings of the 1994 International Conference on Acoustics, Speech, and Signal Processing*, volume 1, pages 345–349, Adelaide, Australia. Institute of Electrical and Electronic Engineers.

Ziegler, D. V. (1991). *The automatic identification of languages using linguistic recognition signals*. PhD thesis, SUNY Buffalo.

Zissman, M. A. and Singer, E. (1994). Automatic language identification of telephone speech messages using phoneme recognition and n-gram modeling. In *Proceedings of the 1994 International Conference on Acoustics, Speech, and Signal Processing*, volume 1, pages 305–308, Adelaide, Australia. Institute of Electrical and Electronic Engineers.

Chapter 9

Multimodality

9.1 Overview

James L. Flanagan

Rutgers University, Piscataway, New Jersey, USA

9.1.1 Natural Communication with Machines

The human senses—evolved in primitive times primarily for survival—serve modern man as exquisitely-developed channels for communication and information exchange. Because the sensory modalities are highly learned and natural, we seek to endow machines with the ability to communicate in these terms. Complex machines can thereby be brought to serve human needs easier and more widely. Sensory realism, similar to face-to-face communication among humans, is the long-range objective.

Of the senses, sight and sound have been exploited to the greatest extent for human-machine communication. Technologies for image processing and voice interaction are being deploying rapidly. But, understanding of the touch modality is advancing, as tactile and manual interfaces develop. The dimensions of taste and smell are yet to be harnessed broadly. Advocates of Virtual Reality are sure to be at the forefront of research in this direction, as the search for sensory realism progresses.

The human is adept at integrating sensory inputs, and fusing data to meet needs of the moment. Machines, to date, are less able to emulate this ability. This issue is central to current research in multimedia information systems. But, the human ability to process information appears limited to rates that are small in comparison to the transport capacities of modern fiber optic networks.

Experiments (Keidel, 1968; Pierce, 1961; Cherry, 1957) place the human processing capacity for assimilating and reacting to sensory input at the order of 100 bits/sec., or less. But the human's ability to switch and allocate this processing power across modalities seems to reflect a refined mechanism for data fusion. Again, machines do not yet approach this ability.

In the domains of sight, sound, and touch, technologies have developed enough that experimental integration is now being studied. Because the constituent technologies are imperfect, task-specific applications domains represent the most prudent opportunities for realizing synergistic combinations of modalities. Because of performance limitations, careful systems design and human factors analyses are critical. Further, because advances in microelectronics are now providing vast and economical computation, the characteristics of human perception can to a greater extent be incorporated in the information processing, resulting in added economies of transmission and storage.

In discharging the duties of an overview, we propose to comment briefly on activities in image, voice and tactile interfaces for human-machine communication. Additionally, we point up issues in data networking, distributed databases, and synergistic integration of multiple modalities in information systems.

9.1.2   Image Compression and Spatially Realistic Displays

Image signals (in contrast to speech) can be of a great variety, ranging from the teeming crowd of a sports contest to a stationary pastoral country scene. Few constraints exist on the source, and most opportunities for efficient digital representation stem from limitations in the ability of the human eye to resolve detail both spatially and temporally. The eye's sensitivity to contrast is greatest for temporal frequencies of about 4 to 8 Hz, and for spatial frequencies of about 1 to 4 cycles/degree (Figure 9.1, adapted from Netravali & Haskel, 1988).

Decomposition of moving images by temporal and spatial filtering into subbands therefore offers the opportunity to trade on the eye's acuity in assigning digital representation bits, moment by moment (Podilchuk & Farvardin, 1991; Podilchuk, Jayant, et al., 1990). That is, available transmission capacity is used for those components representing the greatest acuity, hence maintaining the highest perceptual quality for a given transmission rate. Luminance dominates the transmission requirement with chrominance requiring little additional capacity.

Additionally, while video signals are not as *source-constrained* as speech, they nevertheless tend to be more low-pass in character (that is, the ratio of the frequency of the spectral centroid to the frequency of the upper band edge is typically smaller for video than for speech). As a consequence the signal is amenable to efficient coding by linear prediction, a simple form of which is differential pulse-code modulation (DPCM). Compression advantages over ordinary digital representation by PCM range in the order of 50:1 for television-grade images. It is thus possible, with economical processing, to transmit television grade video over about 1.5 Mbps capacity, or to store the signal efficiently on conventional CD-ROM.

For conferencing purposes, where image complexity typically involves only *head and shoulders*, the compression can be much larger, exceeding 100:1. Quality approximating that of VHS recording can be achieved and coded at less than

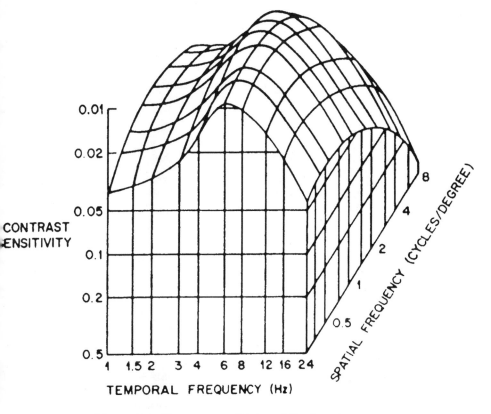

Figure 9.1: Contrast sensitivity of the human eye.

0.1 bit/pixel, which permits real-time video transmission over public switched-digital telephone service at 128 Kbps.

For high-quality color transmission of still images , sub-band coding permits good representation at about 0.5 bit/pixel, or 125 Kbits for an image frame of 500 x 500 pixels.

Spatial realism is frequently important in image display, particularly for interactive use with gesture, pointing or force feedback data gloves. Stereo display can be achieved by helmet fixtures for individual eye images, or by electronically-shuttered glasses that separately present left and right eye scenes. The ideal in spatial realism for image display might be color motion holography, but the understanding does not yet support this.

9.1.3 Speech Processing

The technologies of automatic speech recognition and speech synthesis from text have advanced to the point where rudimentary conversational interaction can be reliably accomplished for well-delimited tasks. For these cases, speech recognizers with vocabularies of a few hundred words can *understand* (in the task-specific sense) natural connected speech of a wide variety of users (speaker independent). A favored method for recognition uses cepstral features to describe the speech signal and hidden Markov model (HMM) classifiers for decisions about sound patterns. As long as the user stays within the bounds of the task (in terms of vocabulary, grammar and semantics), the machine performs usefully, and can generate intelligent and intelligible responses in its synthetic voice (Figure 9.2) (Flanagan, 1992).

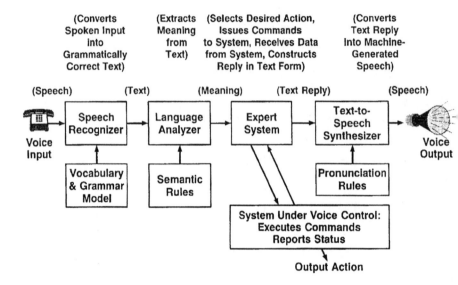

Figure 9.2: Task-specific speech recognition and synthesis in a dialogue system.

Systems of this nature are being deployed commercially to serve call routing in telecommunications, and to provide automated services for travel, ordering, and financial transactions.

The research frontier is in large vocabularies and language models that approach unconstrained natural speech. As vocabulary size increases, it becomes impractical to recognize acoustic patterns of whole words. The pattern recognizer design is driven to analysis of the distinctive sounds of the language, or phonemes (because there are fewer phonemes than words). Lexical information is programmed to estimate whole words. Systems are now in the research laboratory for vocabularies of several tens of thousand words.

A related technology is speaker recognition (to determine who is speaking, not what is said) (Furui, 1989). In particular, speaker verification, or authenticating a claimed identity from measurements of the voice signal, is of strong commercial interest for applications such as electronic funds transfer, access to privileged information, and credit validation.

Coding for efficient voice transmission and storage parallels the objectives of image compression. But, source constraints on the speech signal (i.e., the sounds of a given language produced by the human vocal tract) offer additional opportunities for compression. But, relatively, speech is a broader bandwidth signal than video (i.e., the ratio of centroid frequency to upper band edge is greater). Compression ratios over conventional PCM of the order of 10:1 are becoming possible with good quality. Representation with 1 bit/sample results in an 8 Kbps digital representation, and typically utilizes both source and auditory perceptual constraints.

Perceptual coding for wideband audio, such as compact disc quality, is possible through incorporating enough computation in the coder to calculate, moment by moment, auditory masking in frequency and time (Figure 9.3).

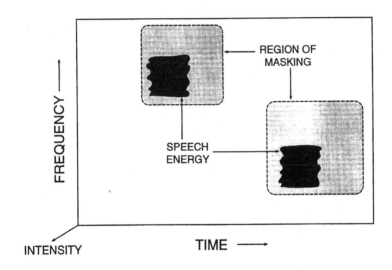

Figure 9.3: Illustration of the time-frequency region surrounding intense, punctuate signals where masking in both time and frequency is effective.

A major challenge in speech processing is automatic translation of spoken language. This possibility was demonstrated in concept at an early time by the C&C Laboratory of NEC.[1] More recently, systems have been produced in Japan by ATR for translating among Japanese/English/German, and by AT&T Bell Laboratories and Telefonica de España for English/Spanish (Roe, Moreno, et al., 1992).

In all systems to date, vocabularies are restricted to specific task domains, and language models span limited but usefully-large subsets of natural language.

---

[1]In a major display at Telecom 1983, Geneva, Switzerland, the NEC Corporation provided a concept demonstration of translating telephony. The application scenario was conversation between a railway stationmaster in Japan and a British tourist who had lost her luggage. Real-time connected speech, translated between Japanese and English, used a delimited vocabulary and *phrase book* grammar.

9.1.4   Tactile Interaction

So far, the sensory dimension of touch has not been applied in human-machine communication to the extent that sight and sound have. This is owing partly to the difficulty of designing tactile transducers capable of representing force and texture in all their subtleties. Nevertheless, systems related to manual input, touch and gesture are receiving active attention in a number of research laboratories (Brooks, Ouh-Young, et al., 1990; Burdea & Coiffet, 1994; Burdea & Zhuang, 1991; Blonder & Boie, 1992; Mariani, Teil, et al., 1992; ICP, 1993). Already, commercial systems for stylus-actuated sketch pad data entry are appearing, and automatic recognition of handwritten characters, substantially constrained, is advancing. Automatic recognition of unrestricted cursive script remains a significant research challenge.

One objective for tactile communication is to allow the human to interact in meaningful ways with computed objects in a virtual environment. Such interaction can be logically combined with speech recognition and synthesis for dialogue exchange (Figure 9.4; Burdea & Coiffet, 1994). A step in this direction at the CAIP Center is force feedback applied to a fiber-optic data glove (Figure 9.5; Burdea & Zhuang, 1991). Finger and joint deflections are detected by optical fibers that innervate the glove. Absolute position is sensed by a Polhemus coil on the back wrist. Additionally, single-axis pneumatic actuators can either apply or sense force at four of the finger tips. While primitive at present, the device allows the user to compute a hypothetical object, put a hand into the data glove and sense the relative position, shape and compliance of the computed object. Research collaboration with the university medical school includes training of endoscopic surgery and physical therapy for injured hands. In contrast, on the amusement side, equipped with glasses for a stereo display, the system offers a challenging game of handball (Figure 9.6). In this case, force feedback permits the user (player) to sense when the ball is grasped, and even to detect the compliance of the ball. More ambitious research looks to devise *smart skins* that can transduce texture in detail.

9.1.5   Data Networking and Distributed Databases

Human/machine communication implies connectivity. In the modern context, this means digital connectivity. And, the eternal challenge in data transport is speed. Fiber-optic networks, based upon packet-switched Asynchronous Transfer Mode (ATM) technology, are evolving with the aim of serving many simultaneous users with a great variety of information (video, audio, image, text, data). Within some limits, transport capacity can be traded for computation (to provide data compression). Effective data networking must therefore embrace user demands at the terminals, as well as information routing in the network. Particularly in real-time video/audio conferencing, it is important that network loading and traffic congestion be communicated to user terminals, moment by moment, so that compression algorithms can adjust to the available transport capacity without suffering signal interruption through overload.

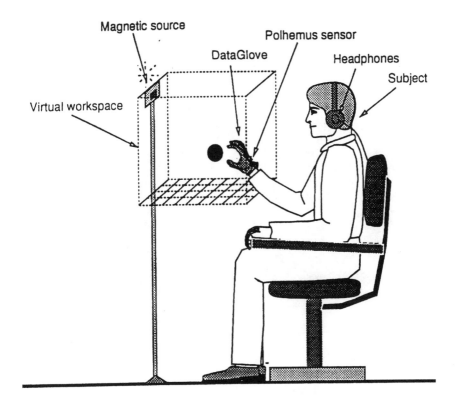

Figure 9.4: With a data glove capable of force feedback, the computer user can use the tactile dimension, as well as those for sight and sound, to interact with virtual objects. A Polhemus coil on the wrist provides hand position information to the computer.

Research in progress aims to establish protocols and standards for multipoint conferencing over ATM. One experimental system called XUNET (Xperimental University NETwork), spans the U.S. continent (Fraser, Kalmanek, et al., 1992). The network has nodes at several universities, AT&T Bell Laboratories, and several national laboratories (Figure 9.7; Fraser, Kalmanek, et al., 1992). Supported by AT&T Bell Laboratories, Bell Atlantic and the Advanced Research Projects Agency, the network runs presently at DS-3 capacity (45 Mbps), with several links already upgraded to 622 Mbps. It provides a working testbed for research on multipoint conferencing, shared distributed databases, switching algorithms and queuing strategies. Weekly transcontinental video conferences from laboratory workstations are presently identifying critical issues in network design.

At the same time, public-switched digital telephone transport is becoming pervasive, and is stimulating new work in compression algorithms for video, speech and image. Integrated Services Digital Network (ISDN) is the standard-

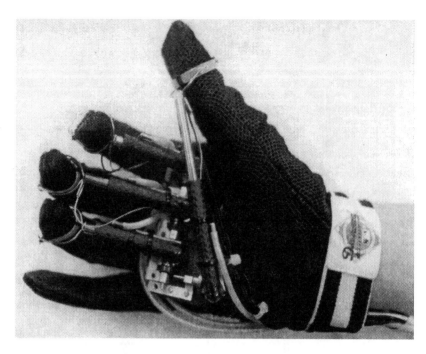

Figure 9.5: CAIP's force feedback transducers for a data glove are single-axis pneumatic thrusters, capable of sensing finger force or, conversely, of applying programmed force sequences to the hand. Joint motion is sensed by optical fibers in the glove, and hand position is measured magnetically by the Polhemus sensor.

ized embodiment, and in its basic-rate form provides two 64 Kbps channels (2B channels) and one 16 kbps signaling channel (1D channel).

9.1.6   Integration of Multiple Modalities

Although the technologies for human-machine communication by sight, sound, and touch are, as yet, imperfectly developed, they are, nevertheless, established firmly enough to warrant their use in combination—enabling experimentation on the synergies arising therefrom. Because of the performance limitations, careful design of the applications scenario is a prerequisite, as is human factors analysis to determine optimum information burdens for the different modalities in specific circumstances.

Among initial studies on integrating multiple modalities is the HuMaNet system of AT&T Bell Laboratories (Berkley & Flanagan, 1990). This system is designed to support multipoint conferencing over public-switched digital telephone capacity (basic-rate ISDN). System features include: hands-free sound pick up by auto directive microphone arrays; voice-control of call set up, data access and display by limited-vocabulary speech recognition; machine answer-

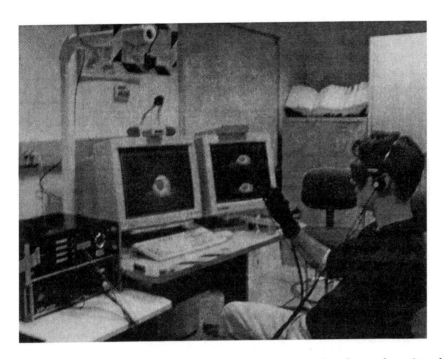

Figure 9.6: Using the force feedback data glove and simulated sound, a virtual handball game is played with the computer. The operator wears glasses to perceive the display in 3-dimensions. Under program control the resilience of the ball can be varied, as well as its dynamic properties. This same facility is being used in medical experiments aimed to train endoscopic surgery and joint palpation.

back and cueing by text-to-speech synthesis; remote data access with speaker verification for privileged data, high-quality color still image coding and display at 64 kbps; and wideband stereo voice coding and transmission at 64 kbps. The system uses a group of networked personal computers, each dedicated to mediate a specific function, resulting in an economical design. The applications scenario is multipoint audio conferencing, aided by image, text and numerical display accessed by voice control from remote databases. Sketch-pad complements, under experimentation, can provide a manual data feature.

Another experimental vehicle for integrating modalities of sight, sound, and touch is a video/audio conferencing system in the CAIP Center (Figure 9.8; Flanagan, 1994). The system uses a voice-controlled, near-life-size video display based on the Bell Communications Research video conferencing system. Hands-free sound pickup is accomplished by the same autodirective microphone system as in HuMaNet. The system is interfaced to the AT&T Bell Laboratories fiber-optic network XUNET. Current work centers on communication with HuMaNet. Tactile interaction, gesturing, and handwriting inputs are being examined as conferencing aids, along with automatic face recognition and speaker

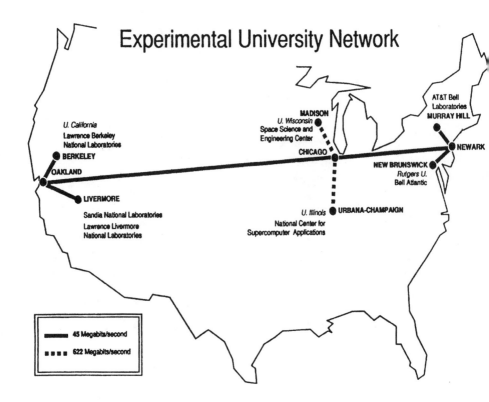

Figure 9.7: Nodes on the Xperimental University NETwork (XUNET).

verification for user authentication. An interesting possibility connected with face recognition includes automatic lip reading to complement speech recognition (Waibel, 1993).

Additionally, inexpensive computation and high-quality electret microphones suggest that major advances might be made in selective sound pick-up under the usually unfavorable acoustic conditions of conference rooms. This is particularly important when speech recognition and verification systems are to be incorporated into the system. Under the aegis of the National Science Foundation, the CAIP Center is examining possibilities for high-quality selective sound capture, bounded in three-dimensions, using large three-dimensional arrays of microphones. Signal processing to produce multiple beamforming (on the sound source and its major multipath images) leads to significant gains (Figures 9.9 and 9.10; Flanagan, Surendran, et al., 1993).

Equivalently, matched filtering applied to every sensor of the array provides spatial volume selectivity and mitigates reverberant distortion and interference by competing sound sources (Flanagan, Surendran, et al., 1993).

Figure 9.8: Experimental video/audio conferencing system in the CAIP Center.

9.1.7 Future Directions

For quite a few years in the past, algorithmic understanding in processing of human information signals, especially speech, outstripped economies in computing. This is much changed with the explosive progress in microelectronics. Device technologies in the 0.3 μ range, now evolving, promise commercially viable single chip computers capable of a billion operations/sec. This brings closer the possibilities for economical large-vocabulary speech recognition and high-definition image coding. Already, we have single chip implementations of low bit-rate speech coding (notably 8 kbps CELP coders for digital cellular telephone, and 16 kbps coders for voice mail coders) which achieve good communications quality. And, we have reliable speaker-independent speech recognizers capable of a few hundred words (Rabiner, 1989; Wilpon, Rabiner, et al., 1990). Even as we approach physical limits for serial processors, the opportunities for massively-parallel processing are opening.

This wealth of computation is an additional stimulant to new research in modeling human behavior in interactive communication with machines. To the extent that research can quantify communicative behavior, machines can be made much more helpful if they can understand the intent of the user and anticipate needs of the moment. Also through such quantification, the machine is enabled to make decisions about optimum sensory modes of information display, thereby matching its information delivery to the sensory capabilities of

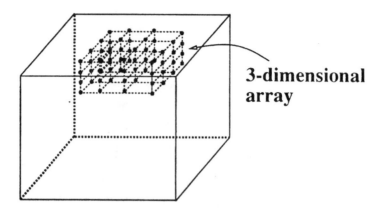

**3-dimensional
array**

Figure 9.9: Schematic of a cubic 3-dimensional array of microphones for use in conference rooms. The cluster of sensors, which typically is harmonically-nested in space, is positioned as a *chandelier* on the ceiling of the room. Digital processing provides multiple beam forming on the detected sound source and its major images, resulting in mitigation of multipath distortion and interference by noise sources.

the human. Automatic recognition of fluent conversational speech, for example, may advance to reliable performance only through good models of spontaneous discourse, with all its vagaries.

For the foreseeable future, success of multimodality systems will depend upon careful design of the applications scenario, taking detailed account of the foibles of the constituent technologies—for sight, sound and touch—and perhaps later taste and smell (Flanagan, 1994). In none of this research does limitation in computing power seem to be the dominant issue. Rather, the challenge is to quantify human behavior for multisensory inputs.

9.2   Representations of Space and Time

Gérard Ligozat

LIMSI-CNRS, Orsay, France

Asserting that most human activities requiring intelligence are grounded in space and time is commonplace. In the context of multimodal environments, spatial and temporal information has to be represented, exchanged, and processed between different components using various modes.

In particular, spatial and temporal knowledge may have to be extracted from natural language and further processed, or general knowledge involving spatial and temporal information may have to be expressed using natural language.

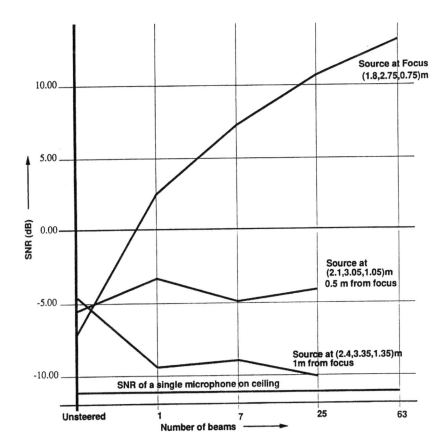

Figure 9.10: Improvements in signal-to-reverberant noise ratio from multiple beam forming on sound source and its major images using a three-dimensional array. The array is 7×7×7 sensors placed at the center of the ceiling of a 7×5×3m room. Comparison is made to the performance of a single microphone.

This makes apparent the fact that processing spatial and temporal knowledge in natural language draws upon two main domains:

1. Knowledge representation and reasoning about spatial and temporal knowledge, a branch of Artificial Intelligence, including such aspects as qualitative physics.

2. Theoretical and computational linguistics.

In the first domain, the main goal is to devise formalisms for representing and reasoning about spatial and temporal information in general.

In the second domain, which is of course closely related to the first, and often considered as a subdomain of application, the main focus is upon spatial and temporal information *in* natural language, understanding its content and meaning, and processing it.

Both aspects interact in many applications having to do at the same time with real world data and linguistic data: story understanding, scene description, route description.

In fact, despite the obvious interest and ultimate necessity of considering both spatial and temporal aspects jointly, the state of development of the branch of AI, computational linguistics or formal philosophy dealing with time is much more advanced than that of the corresponding branches which deal with space.

9.2.1   Time and Space in Natural Language

Understanding temporal and spatial information in natural language—or generating natural language to express temporal or spatial meanings, implies: (1) identifying the linguistic elements conveying this information (markers), (2) elucidating its semantic (and pragmatic) content, (3) devising suitable systems of representation to process this content, (4) implementing and using those representations.

Nature and Contents of the Markers for Time

The basic linguistic markers for temporal notions in many languages are verb *tenses* (e.g., preterite, pluperfect in English) and *temporal adverbials* (yesterday, tomorrow, two weeks from now).

However, tenses also express aspectual notions, which are important for understanding the implications of a given utterance: compare *He was crossing the street* and *He crossed the street*. Only the second sentence allows the inference *He reached the other side of the street*.

A basic property of temporal information in natural language is its deictic nature: an event in a past tense means it happened before the time of speech. Reichenbach introduced the time of speech S, time of reference R, and time of event E to explain the difference of meaning between the basic tenses in English.

Another important component is the fact that verbs behave in various ways according to their semantic class (Aktionsart). Variants or elaborations of Vendler's classification (states, activities, accomplishments and achievements) have been in common use.

Systems of Representation

The definition and study of modal tense logics by Prior has resulted in an important body of work in formal logic, with applications in philosophy (the original motivation of Prior's work), the semantics of natural language, and computer science. The simplest versions of tense logics use modal operators **F**, **G**, **P**, **H**. For instance, **F**p means that p *will be true at some future time*, and **G**p that p *will be true at all future times*; **P**p and **H**p have the corresponding interpretations in the past.

Hence, tense logic, in analogy to natural language, uses time as an implicit parameter: a formula has to get its temporal reference *from the outside*.

In Artificial Intelligence, both McDermott (1982) and Allen (1983) introduced reified logics for dealing with temporal information. Reification consists in incorporating part of the meta-language into the language: a formula in the object language becomes a propositional term in the new language. For example, p being true during time t might be written $HOLDS(p, t)$. This allows to make distinctions about different ways of *being true*, as well as quantification about propositional terms. A recent survey of temporal reasoning in AI is Vila (1994).

Processing Temporal Information

Typically, recent work on temporal information in natural language uses some or all of the preceding tools. A great deal of work is concerned with determining the temporal value of a given sentence. Good examples are Webber (1988) and Moens and Steedman (1988).

Nature and Contents of the Markers for Space

Primary linguistic markers of space are spatial prepositions (*in, on, under, below, behind, above*) and verbs of motion (*arrive, cross*). The seminal work by Herkovits (1986) showed that prepositions cannot be analyzed in purely geometric terms, and that their interpretation depends heavily on contextual factors. Following initial work by Vandeloise (1986), Vieu, Aurnague and Briffault developed general theories of spatial reference and interpretations of prepositions in French (see references in COSIT, 1993). It appears that spatial information also involves:

- Deictic aspects.

- Functional elements (e.g., the typical functions of objects, such as containment for a cup).

- The physical nature of objects (some objects can stick under a table for instance).

- Pragmatic considerations.

Developing systems for dealing with spatial information is best understood in the larger context of spatial reasoning in AI.

9.2.2 Implementation Issues

A general computational framework for expressing temporal information is in terms of binary constraint networks: Temporal information is represented by a network whose nodes are temporal entities (e.g., intervals), and information about binary relations between entities is represented by labels on the arcs.

In Allen's approach, such a qualitative network will represent a finite set of intervals, and labels on the arcs will be disjunctions of the thirteen basic relations (representing incomplete knowledge). Basic computational problems will be:

1. Determining whether a given network is coherent, i.e., describing at least one feasible scenario.

2. Finding all scenarios compatible with a given network.

3. For a given network, answering the previous questions in case new intervals or constraints are added.

The first two problems are NP-hard in the full algebra of intervals, whereas they are polynomial in the case of time points. Recent results of Nebel and Bürckert (1993) identify a maximal tractable subset.

Most algorithms in this framework are variants of the constraint propagation method first introduced in this context by Allen.

Binary constraint networks also are a suitable representation for representing quantitative constraints between time points. A case in point are *time maps* used by Dean and McDermott (see Vila, 1994).

9.2.3   Future Directions

A promising direction of research in the domain of temporal information in natural language is concerned with the integration of *the textual, or discourse level*. Two basic aspects are:

1. Temporal anaphora: in a given sentence, part of the indexes of reference (S, R, E) are determined by other sentences in the text.

2. Temporal structure: this has to do with determining general principles for the temporal structure of discourse. Nakhimovsky (1988) and Lascarides and Asher (1993) are recent examples.

In the spatial domain, two directions of interest are:

1. The development of an interdisciplinary, cognitively motivated field of research on spatial relations (Mark & Frank, 1991; Frank, Campari, et al., 1992; COSIT, 1993). This combines results from cognitive psychology on the perception and processing of spatial information, research in Artificial Intelligence on the representation of spatial information, as well as research on geographic information systems, which has to deal with spatial information both as numeric information (pixels) and symbolic information, e.g., maps, diagrams.

   Typical applications include the generation of route descriptions in natural language, the maintenance and querying of spatial databases, the interpretation and generation of maps describing spatio-temporal phenomena.

2. A trend towards the development of general formalisms for spatial reasoning, including:

- a critical examination of the parameters of existing proposals, such as the nature of the spatial objects considered (abstract regions, regions in 2-D space, points, vectors, rectangles; oriented or non-oriented objects), their physical properties, the dimension and nature of the ambient space, the presence of global orientations and frames of reference, and the types of relations considered (topological, alignment, directional) (Ligozat, 1993).

- importation of temporal techniques (understood as 1-D reasoning techniques) into the spatial domain;

- a development of logical tools (either predicate logics, or modal logics) and an investigation of their formal properties (Aurnague & Vieu, 1993; Cohn, 1993).

9.3   Text and Images

Wolfgang Wahlster

Deutsches Forschungszentrum für Künstliche Intelligenz, Saarbrücken, Germany

Text and images are ubiquitous in human communication and there are deep connections between the use of these two modalities. Whereas humans easily become experts for mapping from images to text (e.g., a radio reporter describing a soccer game) or from text to images (e.g., a cartoonist transforming a story into a comic strip), such complex transformations are a great challenge for computer systems. In multimodal communication humans utilize a combination of text and images (e.g., illustrated books, subtitles for animations) taking advantage of both the individual strength of each communication mode and the fact that both modes can be employed in parallel. Allowing the two modalities to refer to and depend upon each other is a key to the richness of multimodal communication. Recently, a new generation of intelligent multimodal human-computer interfaces has emerged with the ability to interpret some forms of multimodal input and to generate coordinated multimodal output.

9.3.1   From Images to Text

Over the past years, researchers have begun to explore how to translate visual information into natural language (McKevitt, 1994). Starting from a sequence of digitized video frames, a vision system constructs a geometrical representation of the observed scene, including the type and location of all visible objects on a discrete time scale. Then spatial relations between the recognized objects and motion events are extracted and condensed into hypothesized plans and plan interactions between the observed agents. These conceptual structures are finally mapped onto natural language constructs including spatial prepositions, motion verbs, temporal adverbs or conjunctions, and causal clauses. This means in terms of reference semantics, that explicit links between sensory data and natural language expressions are established by a bottom-up process.

While early systems like HAM-ANS (Wahlster, Marburger, et al., 1983), LandScan (Bajcsy, Joshi, et al., 1985), and NAOS (Neumann, 1989) generated retrospective natural language scene descriptions after the processing of the complete image sequence, current systems like VITRA (Wahlster, 1989) aim at an incremental analysis of the visual input to produce simultaneous narration. VITRA incrementally generates reports about real-world traffic scenes or short video clips of soccer matches. The most challenging open question in this research field is a tighter coordination of perception and language production by integrating the current bottom-up cascaded architectures with top-down and expectation-driven processing of images, such that text production can influence the low-level vision processing, e.g., by focusing on particular objects and by providing active control of the vision sensors.

A great practical advantage of natural language image description is the possibility of the application-specific selection of varying degrees of condensation of visual information. There are many promising applications in medical technology, remote sensing, traffic control and other surveillance tasks.

9.3.2   From Text to Images

Only a small number of researchers have dealt with the inverse direction, the generation of images from natural language text. The work in this area of natural language processing has shown how a physically based semantics of motion verbs and locative prepositions can be seen as conveying spatial, kinematic and temporal constraints, thereby enabling a system to create an animated graphical simulation of events described by natural language utterances.

The AnimNL project (Badler, Phillips, et al., 1993) aims to enable people to use natural language instructions as high-level specifications to guide animated human figures through a task. The system is able to interpret simple instructional texts in terms of intentions that the simulated agent should adopt, desired constraints on the agent's behavior and expectations about what will happen in the animation. In the ANTLIMA system (Schirra & Stopp, 1993) the generation of animations from text is based on the assumption that the descriptions always refer to the most typical case of a spatial relation or motion. Typicality potential fields are used to characterize the default distribution for the location and velocity of objects, the duration of events, and the temporal relation between events. In ANTLIMA and the SPRINT system (Yamada, Yamamoto, et al., 1992) all objects in the described scene are moved to a position with maximal typicality using a hill-climbing algorithm. If the location of an object is described by several spatial predications holding simultaneously, the algebraic average of the corresponding typicality distributions is used to compute the position of the object in the animation.

There is an expanding range of exciting applications for these methods like advanced simulation, entertainment, animation and Computer-Aided Design (CAD) systems.

9.3.3   Integrating Text and Images in Multimodal Systems

Whereas mapping images to text is a process of abstraction, mapping text to images is a process of concretion (Figure 9.11). However, in many situations the appropriate level of detail can only be achieved by a combination of text and images.

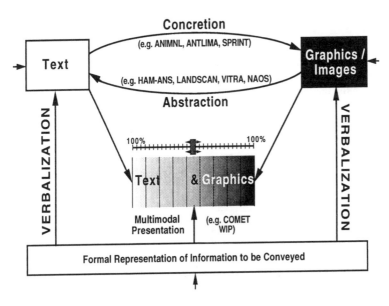

Figure 9.11: Generating and transforming presentations in different modes and media.

A new generation of intelligent multimodal systems (Maybury, 1993) goes beyond the standard canned text, predesigned graphics and prerecorded images and sounds typically found in commercial multimedia systems of today. A basic principle underlying these so-called *intellimedia* systems is that the various constituents of a multimodal communication should be generated on the fly from a common representation of what is to be conveyed without using any preplanned text or images. It is an important goal of such systems not simply to merge the verbalization and visualization results of a text generator and a graphics generator, but to carefully coordinate them in such a way that they generate a multiplicative improvement in communication capabilities. Such multimodal presentation systems are highly adaptive, since all presentation decisions are postponed until runtime. The quest for adaptation is based on the fact that it is impossible to anticipate the needs and requirements of each potential user in an infinite number of presentation situations.

The most advanced multimodal presentation systems, that generate text illustrated by 3-D graphics and animations, are COMET (Feiner & McKeown, 1993) and WIP (Wahlster, André, et al., 1993). COMET generates directions for maintenance and repair of a portable radio and WIP designs multimodal explanations in German and English on using an espresso-machine, assembling a lawn-mower, or installing a modem.

Intelligent multimodal presentation systems include a number of key processes: content planning (determining what information should be presented in a given situation), mode selection (apportioning the selected information to text and graphics), presentation design (determining how text and graphics can be used to communicate the selected information), and coordination (resolving conflicts and maintaining consistency between text and graphics).

Push the code switch S-4 to the right in order to set the modem for reception of data. Connect the telephone cable.

Turn the on/off switch to the right in order to switch on the modem. After switching on the modem, the LED L-11 lights up.

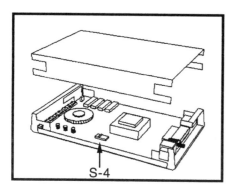
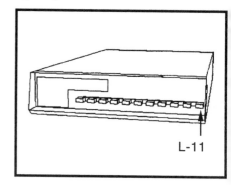

Figure 9.12: A text-picture combination generated by the WIP system.

An important synergistic use of multimodality in systems generating text-picture combinations is the disambiguation of referring expressions. An accompanying picture often makes clear what the intended object of a referring expression is. For example, a technical name for an object unknown to the user may be introduced by clearly singling out the intended object in the accompanying illustration (Figure 9.12). In addition, WIP and COMET can generate cross-modal expressions like, "The on/off switch is shown in the upper left part of the picture," to establish referential relationships of representations in one modality to representations in another modality.

The research so far has shown that it is possible to adapt many of the fundamental concepts developed to date in computational linguistics in such a way that they become useful for text-picture combinations as well. In particular, semantic and pragmatic concepts like communicative acts, coherence, focus, reference, discourse model, user model, implicature, anaphora, rhetorical relations and scope ambiguity take on an extended meaning in the context of multimodal communication.

9.3.4 Future Directions

Areas which require further investigation include the question how to reason about multiple modes so that the system becomes able to block false implicatures and to ensure that the generated text-picture combination is unambiguous, the role of layout as a rhetorical force, influencing the intentional and attential state of the viewer, the integration of facial animation and speech of the presentation agent, and the formalization of design knowledge for creating interactive presentations.

Key applications for intellimedia systems are multimodal helpware, information retrieval and analysis, authoring, training, monitoring, and decision support.

9.4 Modality Integration: Speech and Gesture

Yacine Bellik

LIMSI-CNRS, Orsay, France

Speech and gestures are the means of expression that are most commonly used in human communication. Learning their use begins with the first years of life. They are therefore the most obvious modality for us to communicate with computers (Hauptmann & McAvinney, 1993). Compared to speech, research that aims to integrate gesture as an expression mean (not only as an object manipulation mean) in Human-Computer Interaction (HCI) has recently begun. These works have been launched thanks to the appearance of new devices, in particular data gloves which allow us to know about the hand configuration (flexing angles of fingers) at any moment and to follow its position into the 3D space.

Multimodality aims not only at making several modalities cohabit in an interactive system, but especially at making them cooperate together (Coutaz, Nigay, et al., 1993; Salisbury, 1990) (for instance, if the user wants to move an object using a speech recognition system and a touch screen as in Figure 9.13, he just has to say *put that there* while pointing at the object and at its new position; Bolt, 1980).

In human communication, the use of speech and gestures is completely coordinated. Unfortunately, and at the opposite of human communication means, the devices used to interact with computers have not been designed at all to cooperate.

For instance, the difference between time responses of devices can be very large (a speech recognition system needs more time to recognize a word than a touch screen driver to compute the point coordinates relative to a pointing gesture). This implies that the system receives an information stream in an order which does not correspond to the real chronological order of user's actions (like a sentence in which words have been mixed up). Consequently, this can lead to bad interpretations of user statements.

Figure 9.13: Working with a multimodal interface including speech and gesture. The user speaks while pointing on the touch screen to manipulate the objects. The time correlation of pointing gestures and spoken utterances is important to determine the meaning of his action.

The fusion of information issued from speech and gesture constitutes a major problem. Which criteria should we use to decide the fusion of an information with another one, and at what abstraction level should this fusion be done? On the one hand, a fusion at a lexical level allows for designing generic multimodal interface tools, though fusion errors may occur. On the other hand, a fusion at a semantic level is more robust because it exploits many more criteria, but it is in general application-dependent. It is also important to handle possible semantic conflicts between speech and gesture and to exploit information redundancy when it occurs.

Time is an important factor in interfaces which integrate speech and gesture (Bellik, 1995). It is one of the basic criterion necessary (but not sufficient) for the fusion process and it allows for reconstituting the real chronological order of information. So it is necessary to assign dates (timestamps) to all messages (words, gestures, etc.) produced by the user.

It is also important to take into account the characteristics of each modality (Bernsen, 1993) and their technological constraints. For instance, operations which require high security should be assigned to the modalities which present lower error recognition risks, or should demand redundancy to reduce these risks. It may be necessary to define a multimodal grammar. In a perfect case, this grammar should also take into account other parameters such as the user state, current task, and environment (for instance, a high noise level will prohibit the use of speech).

Future Directions

The effectiveness of a multimodal interface depends to a large extent on the performance of each modality taken separately. If remarkable progress has been accomplished in speech processing, more efforts should be produced to improve gesture recognition systems, in particular for continuous gestures. Systems with touch feed-back and/or force feed-back which become more and more numerous will allow us to improve the comfort of gesture use, in particular for 3D applications, in the near future.

9.5 Modality Integration: Facial Movement & Speech Recognition

Alan J. Goldschen

Center of Innovative Technology, Herndon, Virginia, USA

9.5.1 Background

A machine should be capable of performing automatic speech recognition through the use of several knowledge sources, analogous, to a certain extent, to those sources that humans use (Erman & Lesser, 1990). Current speech recognizers use only acoustic information from the speaker, and in noisy environments often use secondary knowledge sources such as a grammar and prosody. One source of secondary information that has primarily been ignored is optical information (from the face and in particular the oral-cavity region of a speaker), that often has information redundant with the acoustic information, and is often not corrupted by the processes that cause the acoustical noise (Silsbee, 1993). In noisy environments, humans rely on a combination of speech (acoustical) and visual (optical) sources, and this combination improves the signal-to-noise ratio by a gain of 10 to 12 dB (Brooke, 1990). Analogously, machine recognition should improve when combining the acoustical source with an optical source that contains information from the facial region such as gestures, expressions, head-position, eyebrows, eyes, ears, mouth, teeth, tongue, cheeks, jaw, neck, and hair (Pelachaud, Badler, et al., 1994). Human facial expressions provide information about emotion (anger, surprise), truthfulness, temperament (hostility), and personality (shyness) (Ekman, Huang, et al., 1993). Furthermore, human speech production and facial expression are inherently linked by a synchrony phenomenon, where changes often occur simultaneously with speech and facial movements (Pelachaud, Badler, et al., 1994; Condon & Osgton, 1971). An eye blink movement may occur at the beginning or end of a word, while oral-cavity movements may cease at the end of a sentence.

In human speech perception experiments, the optical information is complementary to the acoustic information because many of the phones that are said to be close to each other acoustically are very distant from each other visually (Summerfield, 1987). Visually similar phones such as /p/, /b/, /m/ form a *viseme*, which is specific oral-cavity movements that corresponds to a phone (Fisher, 1968). It appears that the consonant phone-to-viseme mapping is many-to-one (Finn, 1986; Goldschen, 1993) and the vowel phone-to-viseme mapping is nearly one-to-one (Goldschen, 1993). For example, the phone /p/ appears visually similar to the phones /b/ and /m/ and at a signal-to-noise ratio of zero /p/ is acoustically similar to the phones /t/, /k/, /f/, /th/, and /s/ (Summerfield, 1987). Using both sources of information, humans (or machines) can determine the phone /p/. However, this fusion of acoustical and optical sources does sometimes cause humans to perceive a phone different from either the acoustically or optically presented phone, and is known as the *McGurk effect* (McGurk & MacDonald, 1976). In general, the perception of speech in noise improves greatly when presented with acoustical and optical sources because of the complementarity of the sources.

9.5.2   Systems

Some speech researchers are developing systems that use the complementary acoustical and optical sources of information to improve their acoustic recognizers, especially in noisy environments. These systems primarily focus on integrating optical information from the oral-cavity region of a speaker (automatic lipreading) with acoustic information. The acoustic source often consists of a sequence of vectors containing, or some variation of, linear predictive coefficients or filter bank coefficients (Rabiner & Schafer, 1978; Deller, Proakis, et al., 1993). The optical source consists of a sequence of vectors containing static oral-cavity features such as the area, perimeter, height, and width of the oral-cavity (Petajan, 1984; Petajan, Bischoff, et al., 1988), jaw opening (Stork, Wolff, et al., 1992), lip rounding and number of regions or blobs in the oral-cavity (Goldschen, 1993; Garcia, Goldschen, et al., 1992; Goldschen, Garcia, et al., 1994). Other researchers model the dynamic movements of the oral cavity using derivatives (Goldschen, 1993; Smith, 1989; Nishida, 1986), surface learning (Bregler, Omohundro, et al., 1994), deformable templates (Hennecke, Prasad, et al., 1994; Rao & Mersereau, 1994), or optical flow techniques (Pentland & Mase, 1989; Mase & Pentland, 1991).

There have been two basic approaches towards building a system that uses both acoustical and optical information. The first approach uses a *comparator* to merge the two independently recognized acoustical and optical events. This comparator may consist of a set of rules (e.g., if the top two phones from the acoustic recognizer is /t/ or /p/, then choose the one that has a higher ranking from the optical recognizer) (Petajan, Bischoff, et al., 1988) or a fuzzy logic integrator (e.g., provides linear weights associated with the acoustically and optically recognized phones) (Silsbee, 1993; Silsbee, 1994). The second approach performs recognition using a vector that includes both acoustical and optical information, such systems typically use neural networks to combine the optical information with the acoustic to improve the signal-to-noise ratio before phonemic recognition (Yuhas, Goldstein, et al., 1989; Bregler, Omohundro, et al., 1994; Bregler, Hild, et al., 1993; Stork, Wolff, et al., 1992; Silsbee, 1994).

Regardless of the signal-to-noise ratio, most systems perform better using both acoustical and optical sources of information than when using only one source of information (Bregler, Omohundro, et al., 1994; Bregler, Hild, et al., 1993; Mak & Allen, 1994; Petajan, 1984; Petajan, Bischoff, et al., 1988; Silsbee, 1994; Silsbee, 1993; Smith, 1989; Stork, Wolff, et al., 1992; Yuhas, Goldstein, et al., 1989). At a signal-to-noise ratio of zero with a 500-word task Silsbee (1993) achieves word accuracy recognition rates of 38%, 22%, and 58% respectively, using acoustical information, optical information, and both sources of information. Similarly, for a German alphabetical letter recognition task, Bregler, Hild, et al. (1993) achieve a recognition accuracy of 47%, 32%, and 77%, respectively, using acoustical information, optical information, and both sources of information.

9.5.3 Future Directions

In summary, most of the current systems use an optical source containing information from the oral-cavity region of speaker (lipreading) to improve the robustness of the information from the acoustic source. Future systems will likely improve this optical source and use additional features from the facial region.

9.6 Modality Integration: Facial Movement & Speech Synthesis

Christian Benoit,[a] Dominic W. Massaro,[b] & Michael M. Cohen[b]

[a] Université Stendhal, Grenoble, France
[b] University of California, Santa Cruz, California, USA

There is valuable and effective information provided by a view of the speaker's face in speech perception and recognition by humans. Visible speech is particularly effective when the auditory speech is degraded, because of noise, bandwidth filtering, or hearing-impairment (Sumby & Pollack, 1954; Erber, 1975; Summerfield, 1979; Massaro, 1987; Benoît, Mohamadi, et al., 1994)

The strong influence of visible speech is not limited to situations with degraded auditory input, however. A perceiver's recognition of an auditory-visual syllable reflects the contribution of both sound and sight. When an auditory syllable /ba/ is dubbed onto a videotape of a speaker saying /ga/, subjects perceive the speaker to be saying /da/ (McGurk & MacDonald, 1976).

There is thus an evidence that: (1) synthetic faces increase the intelligibility of synthetic speech, (2) but under the condition that facial gestures and speech sounds are coherent. To reach this goal, the articulatory parameters of the facial animation have to be controlled so that it looks and sounds like the auditory output is generated by the visual displacements of the articulators. Not only dissynchrony or incoherence between the two modalities don't increase speech intelligibility; they might even decrease it.

Most of the existing parametric models of the human face have been developed in the perspective of optimizing the visual rendering of facial expressions (Parke, 1974; Platt & Badler, 1981; Bergeron & Lachapelle, 1985; Waters, 1987; Magnenat-Thalmann, Primeau, et al., 1988; Viaud & Yahia, 1992). Few models have focused on the specific articulation of speech gestures: Saintourens, Tramus, et al. (1990); Benoît, Lallouache, et al. (1992); Henton and Litwinovitz (1994) prestored a limited set of facial images occurring in the natural production of speech in order to synchronize the processes of diphone concatenation and *visemes* display in a text-to-audio-visual speech synthesizer. Ultimately, the co-articulation effects and the transition smoothing are much more naturally simulated by means of parametric models specially controlled for visual speech animation, such as the 3-D lip model developed by Guiard-Marigny, Adjoudani, et al. (1994) or the 3-D model of the whole face adapted to speech control by Cohen and Massaro (1990). Those two models are displayed in Figure 9.14.

A significant gain in intelligibility due to a coherent animation of a synthetic face has obviously been obtained at the University of California in Santa Cruz by improving the Parke model (Cohen & Massaro, 1993) and then synchronizing it to the MITalk rule-based speech synthesizer (even though no quantitative measurements are yet available). In parallel, intelligibility tests have been carried out at the ICP-Grenoble in order to compare the benefit of seeing the natural face, a synthetic face, or synthetic lips while listening to natural speech under various conditions of acoustic degradation (Goff, Guiard-Marigny, et al., 1994).

Whatever the degradation level, the two thirds of the missing information are compensated by the vision of the entire speaker's face; half is compensated by the vision of a synthetic face controlled through six parameters directly measured on the original speaker's face; a third of the missing information is compensated by the vision of a 3-D model of the lips, controlled only through four of these command parameters (without seeing the teeth, the tongue or the jaw). All these findings support the evidence that technological spin-offs are expected in two main areas of application. On the one hand, even though the quality of some text-to-speech synthesizers is now such that simple messages are very intelligible when synthesized in clear acoustic conditions, it is no longer the case when the message is less predictable (proper names, numbers, complex sentences, etc.) or when the speech synthesizer is used in a natural environment (e.g., the telephone network or in public places with background noise.) Then, the display of a synthetic face coherently animated in synchrony with the synthetic speech makes the synthesizer sound more intelligible and look more pleasant and natural. On the other hand, the quality of computer graphics rendering is now such that human faces can be very naturally imitated. Today, the audience no longer accepts all those synthetic actors behaving as if their voice

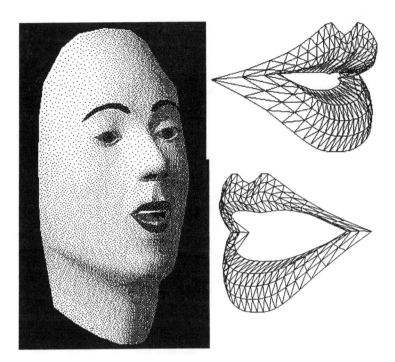

Figure 9.14: Left panel: gouraud shading of the face model originally developed by Parke (1974) and adapted to speech gestures by Cohen and Massaro (1993). A dozen parameters allow the synthetic face to be correctly controlled for speech. Right panel: wireframe structure of the 3-D model of the lips developed by Guiard-Marigny, Adjoudani, et al. (1994). The internal and external contours of the model can take all the possible shapes of natural lips speaking in a neutral expression.

was dubbed from another language. There is thus a strong pressure from the movie and entertainment industry to overcome the problem of automating the lip-synchronization process so that the actors facial gestures look natural.

Future Directions

To conclude, research in the area of visible speech is a fruitful paradigm for psychological inquiry (Massaro, 1987). Video analysis of human faces is a simple investigation technique which allows a better understanding of how speech is produced by humans (Abry & Lallouache, 1991). Face and lip modeling allows the experimenters to manipulate controlled stimuli and to evaluate hypotheses and descriptive parametrizations in terms of visual and bimodal intelligibility of speech. Finally, bimodal integration of facial animation and acoustic synthesis is a fascinating challenge for a better description and comprehension of each language in which this technology is developed. It is also a necessary and promising step towards the realization of autonomous agents in human-machine virtual interfaces.

9.7 Chapter References

Abry, C. and Lallouache, M. T. (1991). Audibility and stability of articulatory movements: Deciphering two experiments on anticipatory rounding in French. In *Proceedings of the 12th International Congress of Phonetic Sciences*, volume 1, pages 220–225, Aix-en-Provence, France.

Allen, J. (1983). Maintaining knowledge about temporal intervals. *Communications of the ACM*, 26(11):832–843.

Anger, F. D., Güsgen, H. W., and van Benthem, J., editors (1993). *Proceedings of the IJCAI-93 Workshop on Spatial and Temporal Reasoning (W17)*, Chambéry, France.

Asilomar (1994). *Proceedings of the 28th Asilomar Conference on Signals, Systems and Computers*. IEEE.

Aurnague, M. and Vieu, L. (1993). A logical framework for reasoning about space. In Anger, F. D., Güsgen, H. W., and van Benthem, J., editors, *Proceedings of the IJCAI-93 Workshop on Spatial and Temporal Reasoning (W17)*, pages 123–158, Chambéry, France.

Badler, N. I., Phillips, C. B., and Webber, B. L. (1993). *Simulating Humans: Computer Graphics Animation and Control*. Oxford University Press, New York.

Bajcsy, R., Joshi, A., Krotkov, E., and Zwarico, A. (1985). LandScan: A natural language and computer vision system for analyzing aerial images. In *Proceedings of the 9th International Joint Conference on Artificial Intelligence*, pages 919–921, Los Angeles.

Bellik, Y. (1995). *Interfaces Multimodales: Concepts, Modeles et Architectures*. PhD thesis, Universite d'Orsay, Paris.

Benoît, C., Lallouache, M. T., Mohamadi, T., and Abry, C. (1992). A set of French visemes for visual speech synthesis. In Bailly, G. and Benoît, C., editors, *Talking Machines: Theories, Models, and Designs*, pages 485–504. Elsevier Science.

Benoît, C., Mohamadi, T., and Kandel, S. (1994). Effects of phonetic context on audio-visual intelligibility of French. *Journal of Speech and Hearing Research*, 37:1195–1203.

Bergeron, P. and Lachapelle, P. (1985). Controlling facial expressions and body movements in the computer generated animated short 'tony de peltrie'. In *SigGraph '85 Tutorial Notes*.

Berkley, D. A. and Flanagan, J. L. (1990). HuMaNet: An experimental human/machine communication network based on ISDN. *AT&T Technical Journal*, 69:87–98.

Bernsen, N. O. (1993). Modality theory: Supporting multimodal interface design. In ERCIM, editor, *Proceedings of the Workshop ERCIM on Human-Computer Interaction*, Nancy.

Blonder, G. E. and Boie, R. A. (1992). Capacitive moments sensing for electronic paper. U.S. Patent 5 113 041.

Bolt, R. A. (1980). Put-that-there: Voice and gesture at the graphic interface. *Computer Graphics*, 14(3):262–270.

Bregler, C., Hild, H., Manke, S., and Waibel, A. (1993). Improving connected letter recognition by lipreading. In *Proceedings of the 1993 International Joint Conference on Speech and Signal Processing*, volume 1, pages 557–560. IEEE.

Bregler, C., Omohundro, S., and Konig, Y. (1994). A hybrid approach to bimodal speech recognition. In *Proceedings of the 28th Asilomar Conference on Signals, Systems and Computers*. IEEE.

Brooke, N. M. (1990). Visible speech signals: Investigating their analysis, synthesis and perception. In Taylor, M. M., Néel, F., and Bouwhuis, D. G., editors, *The Structure of Multimodal Dialogue*. Elsevier Science, Amsterdam.

Brooks, F., Ouh-Young, M., Batter, J., and Jerome, P. (1990). Project GROPE: Haytic displays for scientific visualization. *Computer Graphics*, 24(4):177–185.

Burdea, G. and Coiffet, P. (1994). *Virtual Reality Technology*. John Wiley, New York.

Burdea, G. and Zhuang, J. (1991). Dextrous telerobotics with force feedback. *Robotica*, 9(1 & 2):171–178; 291–298.

Cherry, C. (1957). *On Human Communication*. Wiley, New York.

Cohen, M. M. and Massaro, D. W. (1990). Synthesis of visible speech. *Behaviour Research Methods, Instruments & Computers*, 22(2):260–263.

Cohen, M. M. and Massaro, D. W. (1993). Modeling coarticulation in synthetic visual speech. In Thalmann, N. M. and Thalmann, D., editors, *Models and techniques in computer animation*, pages 139–156. Springer-Verlag, Tokyo.

Cohn, A. (1993). Modal and non-modal qualitative spatial logics. In Anger, F. D., Güsgen, H. W., and van Benthem, J., editors, *Proceedings of the IJCAI-93 Workshop on Spatial and Temporal Reasoning (W17)*, pages 87–92, Chambéry, France.

Condon, W. and Osgton, W. (1971). Speech and body motion synchrony of the speaker-hearer. In Horton, D. and Jenkins, J., editors, *The Perception of Language*, pages 150–184. Academic Press.

COSIT (1993). *Proceedings of the European Conference on Spatial Information Theory (COSIT'93)*, volume 716 of *Lecture Notes in Computer Science*. Springer-Verlag.

Coutaz, J., Nigay, L., and Salber, D. (1993). The MSM framework: A design space for multi-sensori-motor systems. In Bass, L., Gornostaev, J., and Under, C., editors, *Lecture Notes in Computer Science, Selected Papers, EWCHI'93, East-West Human Computer Interaction*, pages 231–241. Springer-Verlag, Moscow.

Deller, John R., J., Proakis, J. G., and Hansen, J. H. (1993). *Discrete-Time Processing of Speech Signals*. MacMillan.

Ekman, P., Huang, T., Sejnowski, T., and Hager, J. (1993). Final report to NSF of the planning workshop on facial expression understanding (July 30 to August 1, 1992). Technical report, University of California, San Francisco.

Erber, N. P. (1975). Auditory-visual perception of speech. *Journal of Speech and Hearing Disorders*, 40:481–492.

Erman, L. and Lesser, V. (1990). The Hearsay-II speech understanding system: A tutorial. In *Readings in Speech Recognition*, pages 235–245. Morgan Kaufmann.

ESCA (1994). *Proceedings of the Second ESCA/IEEE Workshop on Speech Synthesis*, New Paltz, New York. European Speech Communication Association.

Feiner, S. K. and McKeown, K. R. (1993). Automating the generation of coordinated multimedia explanations. In Maybury, M. T., editor, *Intelligent Multimedia Interfaces*, pages 117–138. AAAI Press, Menlo Park, California.

Finn, K. (1986). *An Investigation of Visible Lip Information to be use in Automatic Speech Recognition*. PhD thesis, Georgetown University.

Fisher, C. G. (1968). Confusions among visually perceived consonants. *Journal of Speech and Hearing Research*, 11:796–804.

Flanagan, J. L. (1992). Technologies for multimedia information systems. *Transactions, Institute of Electronics, Information and Communication Engineers*, 75(2):164–178.

Flanagan, J. L. (1994). Technologies for multimedia communications. *Proceedings of the IEEE*, 82(4):590–603.

Flanagan, J. L., Surendran, A. C., and Jan, E. E. (1993). Spatially selective sound capture for speech and audio processing. *Speech Communication*, 13:207–222.

Frank, A. U., Campari, I., and Formentini, U. (1992). Proceedings of the international conference GIS—from space to territory: Theories and methods of spatio-temporal reasoning. In *Proceedings of the International Conference GIS—From Space to Territory: Theories and Methods of Spatio-Temporal Reasoning*, number 639 in Springer Lecture Notes in Computer Science, Pisa, Italy. Springer-Verlag.

Fraser, A. G., Kalmanek, C. R., Kaplan, A. E., Marshall, W. T., and Restrick, R. C. (1992). XUNET 2: A nationwide testbed in high-speed networking. In *INFOCOM 92*, Florence, Italy.

Furui, S. (1989). *Digital Speech Processing, Synthesis, and Recognition.* Marcel Dekker, New York.

Garcia, O., Goldschen, A., and Petajan, E. (1992). Feature extraction for optical automatic speech recognition or automatic lipreading. Technical Report GWU-IIST-92-32, The George Washington University, Department of Electrical Engineering and Computer Science.

Goff, B. L., Guiard-Marigny, T., Cohen, M., and Benoît, C. (1994). Real-time analysis-synthesis and intelligibility of talking faces. In *Proceedings of the Second ESCA/IEEE Workshop on Speech Synthesis*, pages 53–56, New Paltz, New York. European Speech Communication Association.

Goldschen, A. (1993). *Continuous Automatic Speech Recognition by Lipreading.* PhD thesis, The George Washington University, Washington, DC.

Goldschen, A., Garcia, O., and Petajan, E. (1994). Continuous optical automatic speech recognition. In *Proceedings of the 28th Asilomar Conference on Signals, Systems and Computers.* IEEE.

Guiard-Marigny, T., Adjoudani, A., and Benoît, C. (1994). A 3-D model of the lips for visual speech synthesis. In *Proceedings of the Second ESCA/IEEE Workshop on Speech Synthesis*, pages 49–52, New Paltz, New York. European Speech Communication Association.

Hauptmann, A. G. and McAvinney, P. (1993). Gestures with speech for graphic manipulation. *International Journal of Man-Machine Studies*, 38(2):231–249.

Hennecke, M., Prasad, K., and Stork, D. (1994). Using deformable templates to infer visual speech dynamics. In *Proceedings of the 28th Asilomar Conference on Signals, Systems and Computers.* IEEE.

Henton, C. and Litwinovitz, P. (1994). Saying and seeing it with feeling: techniques for synthesizing visible, emotional speech. In *Proceedings of the Second ESCA/IEEE Workshop on Speech Synthesis*, pages 73–76, New Paltz, New York. European Speech Communication Association.

Herkovits, A. (1986). *Language and Cognition*. Cambridge University Press, New York.

ICP (1993). Bulletin de la communication parlée, 2. Université Stendhal, Grenoble, France.

Keidel, W. D. (1968). Information processing by sensory modalities in man. In *Cybernetic Problems in Bionics*, pages 277–300. Gordon and Breach.

Lascarides, A. and Asher, N. (1993). Maintaining knowledge about temporal intervals. *Linguistics and Philosophy*, 16(5):437–493.

Ligozat, G. (1993). Models for qualitative spatial reasoning. In Anger, F. D., Güsgen, H. W., and van Benthem, J., editors, *Proceedings of the IJCAI-93 Workshop on Spatial and Temporal Reasoning (W17)*, pages 35–45, Chambéry, France.

Magnenat-Thalmann, N., Primeau, E., and Thalmann, D. (1988). Abstract muscle action procedures for human face animation. *Visual Computer*, 3:290–297.

Mak, M. W. and Allen, W. G. (1994). Lip-motion analysis for speech segmentation in noise. *Speech Communication*, 14:279–296.

Mariani, J., Teil, D., and Silva, O. D. (1992). Gesture recognition. Technical Report LIMSI Report, Centre National de la Recherche Scientifique, Orsay, France.

Mark, D. M. and Frank, A. U., editors (1991). *Cognitive and Linguistic Aspects of Geographic Space*, Dordrecht. NATO Advanced Studies Institute, Kluwer.

Mase, K. and Pentland, A. (1991). Automatic lipreading by optical flow analysis. *Systems and Computer in Japan*, 22(6):67–76.

Massaro, D. W. (1987). *Speech perception by ear and eye: a paradigm for psychological inquiry*. Lawrence Earlbaum, Hillsdale, New Jersey.

Maybury, M. T., editor (1993). *Intelligent Multimedia Interfaces*. AAAI Press, Menlo Park, California.

McDermott, D. (1982). A temporal logic for reasoning about processes and plans. *Cognitive Science*, 6:101–155.

McGurk, H. and MacDonald, J. (1976). Hearing lips and seeing voices. *Nature*, 264:746–748.

McKevitt, P. (1994). The integration of natural language and vision processing. *Artificial Intelligence Review Journal*, 8:1–3. Special volume.

Moens, M. and Steedman, M. J. (1988). Temporal ontology and temporal reference. *Computational linguistics*, 14(2):15–28.

Nakhimovsky, A. (1988). Aspect, aspectual class, and the temporal structure of narrative. *Computational Linguistics*, 14(2):29–43.

Nebel, B. and Bürckert, H.-J. (1993). Reasoning about temporal relations: A maximal tractable subclass of Allen's interval algebra. Technical Report RR-93-11, DFKI, Saarbrücken, Germany.

Netravali, A. and Haskel, B. (1988). *Digital Pictures*. Plenum Press, New York.

Neumann, B. (1989). Natural language description of time-varying scenes. In Waltz, D., editor, *Semantic Structures*, pages 167–207. Lawrence Earlbaum, Hillsdale, New Jersey.

Nishida (1986). Speech recognition enhancement by lip information. *ACM SIGCHI Bulletin*, 17(4):198–204.

Parke, F. I. (1974). *A parametric model for human faces*. PhD thesis, University of Utah, Department of Computer Sciences.

Pelachaud, C., Badler, N., and Viaud, M.-L. (1994). Final report to NSF of the standards for facial animation workshop. Technical report, University of Pennsylvania, Philadelphia.

Pentland, A. and Mase, K. (1989). Lip reading: Automatic visual recognition of spoken words. Technical Report MIT Media Lab Vision Science Technical Report 117, Massachusetts Institute of Technology.

Petajan, E. (1984). *Automatic Lipreading to Enhance Speech Recognition*. PhD thesis, University of Illinois at Urbana-Champaign.

Petajan, E., Bischoff, B., Bodoff, D., and Brooke, N. M. (1988). An improved automatic lipreading system to enhance speech recognition. *CHI 88*, pages 19–25.

Pierce, J. R. (1961). *Symbols, Signals and Noise*. Harper and Row, New York.

Platt, S. M. and Badler, N. I. (1981). Animating facial expressions. *Computer Graphics*, 15(3):245–252.

Podilchuk, C. and Farvardin, N. (1991). Perceptually based low bit rate video coding. In *Proceedings of the 1991 International Conference on Acoustics, Speech, and Signal Processing*, volume 4, pages 2837–2840, Toronto. Institute of Electrical and Electronic Engineers.

Podilchuk, C., Jayant, N. S., and Noll, P. (1990). Sparse codebooks for the quantization of non-dominant sub-bands in image coding. In *Proceedings of the 1990 International Conference on Acoustics, Speech, and Signal Processing*, pages 2101–2104, Albuquerque, New Mexico. Institute of Electrical and Electronic Engineers.

Rabiner, L. R. (1989). A tutorial on hidden Markov models and selected applications in speech recognition. *Proceedings of the IEEE*, 77(2):257–286.

Rabiner, L. R. and Schafer, R. W. (1978). *Digital Processing of Speech Signals*. Signal Processing. Prentice-Hall, Englewood Cliffs, New Jersey.

Rao, R. and Mersereau, R. (1994). Lip modeling for visual speech recognition. In *Proceedings of the 28th Asilomar Conference on Signals, Systems and Computers*. IEEE.

Roe, D. B., Moreno, P. J., Sproat, R. W., Pereira, F. C. N., Riley, M. D., and Macarron, A. (1992). A spoken language translator for restricted-domain context-free languages. *Speech Communication*, 11:311–319. System demonstrated by AT&T Bell Labs and Telefonica de Espana, VEST, Worlds Fair Exposition, Barcelona, Spain.

Saintourens, M., Tramus, M. H., Huitric, H., and Nahas, M. (1990). Creation of a synthetic face speaking in real time with a synthetic voice. In Bailly, G. and Benoît, C., editors, *Proceedings of the First ESCA Workshop on Speech Synthesis*, pages 249–252, Autrans, France. European Speech Communication Association.

Salisbury, M. W. (1990). Talk and draw: Bundling speech and graphics. *IEEE Computer*, pages 59–65.

Schirra, J. and Stopp, E. (1993). ANTLIMA—a listener model with mental images. In *Proceedings of the 13th International Joint Conference on Artificial Intelligence*, pages 175–180, Chambery, France.

Silsbee, P. (1993). *Computer Lipreading for Improved Accuracy in Automatic Speech Recognition*. PhD thesis, The University of Texas at Austin.

Silsbee, P. (1994). Sensory integration in audiovisual automatic speech recognition. In *Proceedings of the 28th Asilomar Conference on Signals, Systems and Computers*. IEEE.

Smith, S. (1989). Computer lip reading to augment automatic speech recognition. *Speech Tech*, pages 175–181.

Stork, D., Wolff, G., and Levine, E. (1992). Neural network lipreading system for improved speech recognition. In *Proceedings of the 1992 International Joint Conference on Neural Networks*, Baltimore, Maryland.

Sumby, W. H. and Pollack, I. (1954). Visual contribution to speech intelligibility in noise. *Journal of the Acoustical Society of America*, 26:212–215.

Summerfield, Q. (1979). Use of visual information for phonetic perception. *Phonetica*, 36:314–331.

Summerfield, Q. (1987). Some preliminaries to a comprehensive account of audio-visual speech perception. In Dodd, B. and Campbell, R., editors, *Hearing by Eye: The Psychology of Lipreading*, pages 3–51. Lawrence Earlbaum, Hillsdale, New Jersey.

Vandeloise, C. (1986). *L'espace en français: sémantique des prépositions spatiales*. Seuil, Paris.

Viaud, M. L. and Yahia, H. (1992). Facial animation with wrinkles. In *Proceedings of the 3rd Workshop on Animation, Eurographic's 92*, Cambridge, England.

Vila, L. (1994). A survey on temporal reasoning in artificial intelligence. *AICOM*, 7(1):832–843.

Wahlster, W. (1989). One word says more than a thousand pictures. on the automatic verbalization of the results of image sequence analysis systems. *Computers and Artificial Intelligence*, 8:479–492.

Wahlster, W., André, E., Finkler, W., Profitlich, H.-J., and Rist, T. (1993). Plan-based integration of natural language and graphics generation. *Artificial Intelligence*, pages 387–427.

Wahlster, W., Marburger, H., Jameson, A., and Busemann, S. (1983). Overanswering yes-no questions: Extended responses in a NL interface to a vision system. In *Proceedings of the 8th International Joint Conference on Artificial Intelligence*, pages 643–646, Karlsruhe.

Waibel, A. (1993). Multimodal human-computer interaction. In *Eurospeech '93, Proceedings of the Third European Conference on Speech Communication and Technology*, volume Plenary, page 39, Berlin. European Speech Communication Association.

Waters, K. (1987). A muscle model for animating three-dimensional facial expression. In *Proceedings of Computer Graphics*, volume 21, pages 17–24.

Webber, B. L. (1988). Tense as discourse anaphor. *Computational linguistics*, 14(2):61–73.

Wilpon, J., Rabiner, L., Lee, C., and Goldman, E. (1990). Automatic recognition of key words in unconstrained speech using hidden markov models. *IEEE Transactions on Acoustics, Speech and Signal Processing*, 38(11):1870–1878.

Yamada, A., Yamamoto, T., Ikeda, H., Nishida, T., and Doshita, S. (1992). Reconstructing spatial images from natural language texts. In *Proceedings of the 14th International Conference on Computational Linguistics*, pages 1279–1283, Nantes, France. ACL.

Yuhas, B., Goldstein, M., and Sejnowski, T. (1989). Integration of acoustic and visual speech signals using neural networks. *IEEE Communications Magazine*, pages 65–71.

Chapter 10

Transmission and Storage

10.1   Overview

Isabel Trancoso

Instituto de Engenharia de Sistemas e Computadores, Lisbon, Portugal
and Instituto Superior Tecnico, Lisbon, Portugal

This chapter is devoted to two closely linked areas of speech processing: coding and enhancement. For many years, these have been active areas of research, motivated by the increasing need for speech compression for band-limited transmission and storage, and, on the other hand, the need to improve the intelligibility of speech contaminated by noise.

In an age where the word gigabit became common when talking about channel or disk capacity, the aim of compression is not clear to everyone and one needs to justify it by describing the myriad of new applications demanding fewer and fewer bits per second and the rapidly expanding corpora.

Until the late seventies, research in speech compression followed two different directions: *vocoders* (abbreviation of voice coders) and *waveform coders*. The two approaches substantially differ in their underlying principles and performance. Whereas the first explores our knowledge of speech production, attempting to represent the signal spectral envelope in terms of a small number of slowly varying parameters, the latter aims at a faithful reproduction of the signal either in the time or frequency domains. They also represent two opposite choices in terms of the interleaving of the four main dimensions of the performance of speech coding: bit rate, speech quality, algorithm complexity and communication delay. Vocoders achieve considerable bit rate savings at the cost of quality degradation, being aimed at bit rates below two to four Kbps (Tremain, 1982). For wave-form coders, on the other hand, the preservation of the quality of the synthesized speech is the prime goal, which demands bit rates well above sixteen Kbps (Jayant & Noll, 1984). For an excellent overview of the main speech coding activities at the end of that decade, see Flanagan et al. (1979).

The next decade saw an explosion of work on speech coding, although most of the new coders could hardly be classified according to the waveform-coder/vocoder distinction. This new generation of coders overcame the limitations of the dual-source excitation model typically adopted by vocoders. Complex prediction techniques were adopted, the masking properties of the human ear were exploited, and it became technologically feasible to quantize parameters in blocks (VQ—vector quantization) instead of individually, and use computationally complex analysis-by-synthesis procedures. CELP (Schroeder & Atal, 1985) multi-pulse (Atal & Remde, 1982) and regular-pulse (Kroon, Deprettere, et al., 1986) excitation methods are some of the most well-known *new generation* coders in the time domain, whereas in the frequency domain one should mention sinusoidal/harmonic (Almeida & Silva, 1984; McAulay & Quatieri, 1986) and multi-band excited coders (Griffin & Lim, 1988). Variants of these coders have been standardized for transmission at bit rates ranging from 13 down to 4.8 Kbps, and special standards have also been derived for low-delay applications (LD-CELP) (Chen, 1991). (See also Atal, Cuperman, et al., 1991 and Furui & Sondhi, 1991 for collections of extended papers on some of the most prominent coding methods of this decade.)

Nowadays, the standardization effort in the cellular radio domain that motivated this peak of coding activity is not so visible, and the research community is seeking new avenues. The type of quality that can be achieved with the so-called telephone bandwidth (3.2 kHz) is no longer enough for a wide range of new applications demanding wide-band speech or audio coding. At these bandwidths (5 to 20 kHz), waveform coding techniques of the sub-band and transform coding type have been traditionally adopted for high bit rate transmission. The need for eight to sixty-four Kbps coding is pushing the use of techniques such as linear prediction for these higher bandwidths, despite the fact that they are typical of telephone speech. The demand for lower bit rates for telephone bandwidth is, however, far from exhausted. New directions are being pursued to cope with the needs of the rapidly evolving digital telecommunication networks. Promising results have been obtained with approaches based, for instance, on articulatory representations, segmental time-frequency models, sophisticated auditory processing, models of the uncertainty in the estimation of speech parameters, etc. The current efforts to integrate source and channel coding are also worthy of mention.

Although the main use of speech coding so far has been transmission, speech encoding procedures based on Huffman coding of prediction residuals have lately become quite popular for the storage of large speech corpora.

The last part of this chapter covers an area closely related to coding and recognition, denoted as speech enhancement. The goal of speech enhancement is quality and/or intelligibility increase for a broad spectrum of applications, by (partly) removing the noise which overlaps the speech signal in both time and frequency. The first noise-suppression techniques using only one microphone adopted single-filter approaches, either of the spectral-subtraction type or based on MAP or MMSE estimators. In the last few years, several pattern matching techniques have been proposed, neural networks have become quite popular as well and a number of robust parameterization methods and better metrics have emerged to improve the recognition of noisy speech. Multiple-microphone approaches can also be adopted in several applications. For an extended overview of enhancement methods, see Lim and Oppenheim (1979) and Boll (1991).

10.2 Speech Coding

Bishnu S. Atal & Nikil S. Jayant

AT&T Bell Laboratories, Murray Hill, New Jersey, USA

Coding algorithms seek to minimize the bit rate in the digital representation of a signal without an objectionable loss of signal quality in the process. High quality is attained at low bit rates by exploiting signal redundancy as well as the knowledge that certain types of coding distortion are imperceptible because they are masked by the signal. Our models of signal redundancy and distortion masking are becoming increasingly more sophisticated, leading to continuing improvements in the quality of low bit rate signals. This section summarizes current capabilities in speech coding, and describes how the field has evolved to reach these capabilities. It also mentions new classes of applications that demand quantum improvements in speech compression, and comments on how we hope to achieve such results.

Vocoders and Waveform Coders

Speech coding techniques can be broadly divided into two classes: waveform coding that aims at reproducing the speech waveform as faithfully as possible and vocoders that preserve only the spectral properties of speech in the encoded signal. The waveform coders are able to produce high-quality speech at high enough bit rates; vocoders produce intelligible speech at much lower bit rates, but the level of speech quality—in terms of its naturalness and uniformity for different speakers—is also much lower. The applications of vocoders so far have been limited to low-bit-rate digital communication channels. The combination of the once-disparate principles of waveform coding and vocoding has led to significant new capabilities in recent compression technology. The main focus of this section is on speech coders that support application over digital channels with bit rates ranging from 4 to 64 Kbps.

10.2.1 The Continuing Need for Speech Compression

The capability of speech compression has been central to the technologies of robust long-distance communication, high-quality speech storage, and message encryption. Compression continues to be a key technology in communications in spite of the promise of optical transmission media of relatively unlimited bandwidth. This is because of our continued and, in fact, increasing need to use band-limited media such as radio and satellite links, and bit-rate-limited storage media such as CD-ROMs and silicon memories. Storage and archival of large volumes of spoken information makes speech compression essential even in the context of significant increases in the capacity of optical and solid-state memories.

Low bit-rate speech technology is a key factor in meeting the increasing demand for new digital wireless communication services. Impressive progress has been made during recent years in coding speech with high quality at low bit rates and at low cost. Only ten years ago, high quality speech could not be produced at bit rates below 24 Kbps. Today, we can offer high quality at 8 Kbps, making this the standard rate for the new digital cellular service in North America. Using new techniques for channel coding and equalization, it is possible to transmit the 8 Kbps speech in a robust fashion over the mobile radio channel, in spite of channel noise, signal fading and intersymbol interference. The present research is focussed on meeting the critical need for high quality speech transmission over digital cellular channels at 4 Kbps. Research on properly coordinated source and channel coding is needed to realize a good solution to this problem.

Wireless communication channels suffer from multipath interference producing error rates in excess of 10%. The challenge for speech research is to produce digital speech that can be transmitted with high quality over communication networks in the presence of up to 10% channel errors. A speech coder operating at 2 Kbps will provide enough bits for correcting such channel errors, assuming a total transmission rate on the order of 4 to 8 Kbps.

The bit rate of 2 Kbps has an attractive implication for voice storage as well. At this bit rate, more than 2 hours of continuous speech can be stored on a single 16 Mbit memory chip, allowing sophisticated voice messaging services on personal communication terminals, and extending significantly the capabilities of digital answering machines. Fundamental advances in our understanding of speech production and perception are needed to achieve high quality speech at 2 Kbps.

Applications of wideband speech coding include high quality audioconferencing with 7 kHz-bandwidth speech at bit rates on the order of 16 to 32 Kbps and high-quality stereoconferencing and dual-language programming over a basic ISDN link. Finally, the compression of a 20 kHz-bandwidth to rates on the order of 64 Kbps will create new opportunities in audio transmission and networking, electronic publishing, travel and guidance, teleteaching, multilocation games, multimedia memos, and database storage.

10.2.2   The Dimensions of Performance in Speech Compression

Speech coders attempt to minimize the bit rate for transmission or storage of the signal while maintaining required levels of speech quality, communication delay, and complexity of implementation (power consumption). We will now provide brief descriptions of the above parameters of performance, with particular reference to speech.

Speech Quality: Speech quality is usually evaluated on a five-point scale, known as the mean-opinion score (MOS) scale, in speech quality testing—an average over a large number of speech data, speakers, and listeners. The five points of quality are: *bad, poor, fair, good,* and *excellent.* Quality scores of 3.5 or higher generally imply high levels of intelligibility, speaker recognition and naturalness.

Bit Rate: The coding efficiency is expressed in bits per second (bps).

Communication Delay: Speech coders often process speech in blocks and such processing introduces communication delay. Depending on the application, the permissible total delay could be as low as 1 msec, as in network telephony, or as high as 500 msec, as in video telephony. Communication delay is irrelevant for one-way communication, such as in voice mail.

Complexity: The complexity of a coding algorithm is the processing effort required to implement the algorithm, and it is typically measured in terms of arithmetic capability and memory requirement, or equivalently in terms of cost. A large complexity can result in high power consumption in the hardware.

10.2.3 Current Capabilities in Speech Coding

Figure 10.1 shows the speech quality that is currently achievable at various bit rates from 2.4 to 64 Kbps for narrowband telephone (300–3400 Hz) speech. The intelligibility of coded speech is sufficiently high at these bit rates and is not an important issue. The speech quality is expressed on the five-point MOS scale along the ordinate in Figure 10.1.

PCM (pulse-code modulation) is the simplest coding system, a memoryless quantizer, and provides essentially transparent coding of telephone speech at 64 Kbps. With a simple adaptive predictor, adaptive differential PCM (ADPCM) provides high-quality speech at 32 Kbps. The speech quality is slightly inferior to that of 64 Kbps PCM, although the telephone handset receiver tends to minimize the difference. ADPCM at 32 Kbps is widely used for expanding the number of speech channels by a factor of two, particularly in private networks and international circuits. It is also the basis of low-complexity speech coding in several proposals for personal communication networks, including CT2 (Europe), UDPCS (USA) and Personal Handyphone (Japan).

For rates of 16 Kbps and lower, high speech quality is achieved by using more complex adaptive prediction, such as linear predictive coding (LPC) and pitch prediction, and by exploiting auditory masking and the underlying perceptual limitations of the ear. Important examples of such coders are multi-pulse excitation, regular-pulse excitation, and code-excited linear prediction (CELP)

Speech Quality

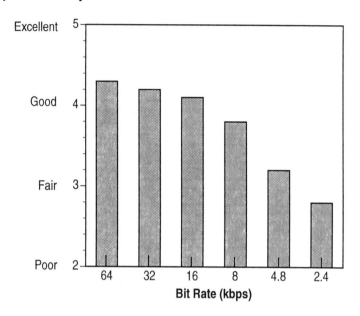

Figure 10.1: The speech quality mean opinion score for various bit rates.

coders. The CELP algorithm combines the high quality potential of waveform coding with the compression efficiency of model-based vocoders. At present, the CELP technique is the technology of choice for coding speech at bit rates of 16 Kbps and lower. At 16 Kbps, a low-delay CELP (LD-CELP) algorithm provides both high quality, close to PCM, and low communication delay and has been accepted as an international standard for transmission of speech over telephone networks.

At 8 Kbps, which is the bit rate chosen for first-generation digital cellular telephony in North America, speech quality is good, although significantly lower than that of the 64 Kbps PCM speech. Both North American and Japanese first generation digital standards are based on the CELP technique. The first European digital cellular standard is based on regular-pulse excitation algorithm at 13.2 Kbps.

The rate of 4.8 Kbps is an important data rate because it can be transmitted over most local telephone lines in the United States. A version of CELP operating at 4.8 Kbps has been chosen as a United States standard for secure voice communication. The other such standard uses an LPC vocoder operating at 2.4 Kbps. The LPC vocoder produces intelligible speech but the speech quality is not natural.

The present research is focussed on meeting the critical need for high quality speech transmission over digital cellular channels at 4 and 8 Kbps. Low bit rate speech coders are fairly complex, but the advances in VLSI and the availability of digital signal processors have made possible the implementation of both encoder and decoder on a single chip.

10.2.4   Technology Targets

Given that there is no rigorous mathematical formula for speech entropy, a natural target in speech coding is the achievement of high quality at bit rates that are at least a factor of two lower than the numbers that currently provide high quality: 4 Kbps for telephone speech, 8 Kbps for wideband speech and 24 Kbps for CD-quality speech. These numbers represent a bit rate of about 0.5 bit per sample in each case.

Another challenge is the realization of robust algorithms in the context of real-life imperfections such as input noise, transmission errors and packet losses.

Finally, an overarching set of challenges has to do with realizing the above objectives with low levels of implementation complexity.

In all of these pursuits, we are limited by our knowledge in several individual disciplines, and in the way these disciplines interact. Advances are needed in our understanding of *coding, communication and networking, speech production and hearing,* and *digital signal processing.*

In discussing directions of research, it is impossible to be exhaustive, and in predicting what the successful directions may be, we do not necessarily expect to be accurate. Nevertheless, it may be useful to define some broad research directions, with a range that covers the obvious as well as the speculative. The last part of this section is addressed to this task.

10.2.5   Future Directions

Coding, Communication, and Networking: In recent years, there has been significant progress in the fundamental building blocks of source coding: flexible methods of time-frequency analysis, adaptive vector quantization, and noiseless coding. Compelling applications of these techniques to speech coding are relatively less mature. Complementary advances in channel coding and networking include coded modulation for wireless channels and embedded transmission protocols for networking. Joint designs of source coding, channel coding, and networking will be especially critical in wireless communication of speech, especially in the context of multimedia applications.

Speech Production and Perception: Simple models of periodicity, and simple source models of the vocal tract need to be supplemented (or replaced) by models of articulation and excitation that provide a more direct and compact representation of the speech-generating process. Likewise, stylized models of distortion masking need to be replaced by models that maximize masking in the spectral and temporal domains. These models need to be based on better overall models of hearing, and also on experiments with real speech signals (rather than simplified stimuli such as tones and noise).

Digital Signal Processing: In current technology, a single general-purpose signal processor is capable of nearly 100 million arithmetic operations per second, and one square centimeter of silicon memory can store about 25 megabits of information. The memory and processing power available on a single chip are both expected to continue to increase significantly over the next several years. Processor efficiency as measured by mips-per-milliwatt of power consumption is also expected to improve by at least one order of magnitude. However, to accommodate coding algorithms of much higher complexity on these devices, we will need continued advances in the way we match processor architectures to complex algorithms, especially in configurations that permit graceful control of speech quality as a function of processor cost and power dissipation. The issues of power consumption and battery life are particularly critical for personal communication services and portable information terminals.

For further reading, we recommend Jayant and Noll (1984), Jayant, Johnston, et al. (1993), Lipoff (1994), Jayant (1992), Atal and Schroeder (1979), Atal (1982), Schroeder and Atal (1985), and Chen (1991).

10.3   Speech Enhancement

Dirk Van Compernolle

K.U. Leuven—ESAT, Heverlee, Belgium

Speech enhancement in the past decades has focused on the suppression of additive background noise. From a signal processing point of view additive noise is easier to deal with than convolutive noise or nonlinear disturbances. Moreover, due to the bursty nature of speech, it is possible to observe the noise by itself during speech pauses, which can be of great value.

Speech enhancement is a very special case of signal estimation as speech is nonstationary, and the human ear—the final judge—does not believe in a simple mathematical error criterion. Therefore subjective measurements of intelligibility and quality are required.

Thus the goal of speech enhancement is to find an *optimal estimate* (i.e., preferred by a human listener) $\hat{s}(t)$, given a noisy measurement $y(t) = s(t) + n(t)$. A number of overview papers can be found in Ephraim (1992) and Van Compernolle (1992).

10.3.1   Speech Enhancement by Spectral Magnitude Estimation

The relative unimportance of phase for speech quality has given rise to a family of speech enhancement algorithms based on spectral magnitude estimation. These are frequency-domain estimators in which an estimate of the clean-speech spectral magnitude is recombined with the noisy phase before resynthesis with a standard overlap-add procedure (Figure 10.2). The name *spectral subtraction* is loosely used for many of the algorithms falling into this class (Boll, 1979; Berouti, Schwartz, et al., 1979).

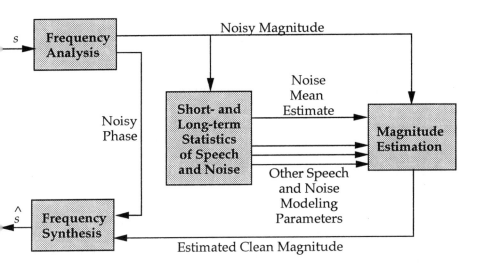

Figure 10.2: Speech enhancement by spectral magnitude estimation.

Power Spectral Subtraction: This is the simplest of all variants. It makes use of the fact that power spectra of additive independent signals are also additive and that this property is approximately true for short-time estimates as well. Hence, in the case of stationary noise, it suffices to subtract the mean noise power to obtain a least squares estimate of the power spectrum.

$$|\hat{S}(f)|^2 = |Y(f)|^2 - E[|N(f)|^2] \approx |Y(f)|^2 - |N(\bar{f})|^2 \qquad (10.1)$$
$$\hat{S}(f) = |\hat{S}(f)| \angle Y(f) \qquad (10.2)$$

The greatest asset of spectral subtraction lies in its simplicity and the fact that all that is required, is an estimate of the mean noise power and that the algorithm does not need any signal assumptions. At the same time the latter is its great weakness. Within this framework, occasional negative estimates of the power spectrum can occur. To make the estimates consistent, some artificial flooring is required, which yields a very characteristic *musical noise*, caused by the remaining isolated patches of energy in the time-frequency representation.

Much effort has been put into reducing this annoying musical noise. One effective way is smoothing over time of the short-time spectra. This has the contrary effect, however, of introducing echoes. While reducing the average level of the background noise substantially, plain spectral subtraction has been rather ineffective in improving intelligibility and quality for broadband background noise.

Minimum Mean Square Error Estimators: Power spectral subtraction is a minimum mean square estimator with little or no assumptions about the prior distributions for power spectral values of speech and noise. This is the underlying reason why *ad hoc* operations like clipping are necessary. Within the framework of spectral magnitude estimation two major improvements are: (i) modeling of realistic a priori statistical distributions of speech and noise spectral magnitude coefficients (Ephraim & Malah, 1984), (ii) minimizing the estimation error in a domain which is perceptually more relevant than the power spectral domain (e.g., log magnitude domain) (Porter & Boll, 1984; Ephraim & Malah, 1985; Van Compernolle, 1989).

Minimum mean square error estimators (MMSEEs) have been developed under various assumptions such as Gaussian sample distributions, lognormal distribution of spectral magnitudes, etc. While improving on quality, these estimators tend to be complex and computationally demanding.

Time Varying Speech Models and State-based Methods: In a first generation the MMSEEs used a single distribution modeling *all speech* and one modeling *all noise*. Significant improvement is still possible if one takes into account the nonstationarity of the speech signal (and the noise). The use of *local* speech models implies much smaller variances in the models and tighter estimates. There are two possible approaches: (i) the incoming speech is aligned with an ergodic (fully-connected) HMM in which a separate MMSEE is associated with each state (Ephraim, Malah, et al., 1989), (ii) the parameters in a simple parametric speech model can be continuously adapted on the basis of the observations (Xie & Van Compernolle, 1993). In the first approach a set of possible *states* has to be created during a training phase and this should be a complete set. In the second approach no explicit training is required, but a simpler model may be needed to make the continuous parameter updates feasible.

It is obvious that neither the state association nor the parameter updates will be trivial operations and that this adds another level of complexity to the spectral estimation problem. A side effect of these methods is that they require dynamic time alignment which is inherently noncausal. While at most a *few frames* extra delay is inserted, this may be a concern in some applications.

10.3.2   Wiener Filtering

The Wiener filter obtains a least squares estimate of $s(t)$ under stationarity assumptions of speech and noise. The construction of the Wiener filter requires an estimate of the power spectrum of the clean speech and the noise:

$$W(f) = \frac{\Phi_{ss}(f)}{\Phi_{ss}(f) + \Phi_{nn}(f)}$$

The previous discussion on global and local speech and noise models equally applies to Wiener filtering. Wiener filtering has the disadvantage, however, that the estimation criterion is fixed.

10.3.3   Microphone Arrays

Microphone arrays exploit the fact that a speech source is quite stationary and therefore, by using beamforming techniques, can suppress nonstationary interferences more effectively than any single sensor system. The simplest of all approaches is the delay and sum beamformer that phase aligns incoming wavefronts of the desired source before adding them together (Flanagan, 1985). This type of processing is robust and needs only limited computational hardware, but requires a large number of microphones to be effective. An easy way to achieve uniform improvement over the wide speech bandwidth is to use a subband approach together with a logarithmically spaced array. Different sets of microphones are selected to cover the different frequency ranges (Silverman, 1987). A much more complex alternative is the use of adaptive beamformers, in which case each incoming signal is adaptively filtered before being added together. These arrays are most powerful if the noise source itself is directional. While intrinsically much more powerful, the adaptive beamformer is prone to signal distortion in strong reverberation. A third class of beamformers is a mix of the previous schemes. A number of digital filters are predesigned for optimal wideband performance for a set of look directions. The adaptation now exists in selecting the optimal filter at any given moment using a proper tracking mechanism. Under *typical* reverberant conditions, this last approach may prove the best overall solution. It combines the robustness of a simple method with the power of digital filtering.

While potentially very powerful, microphone arrays bring about a significant hardware cost due to the number of microphones and/or required adaptive filters. As a final remark it should be said that apart from noise suppression alone, microphone arrays help to dereverberate the signals as well.

10.3.4   Future Directions

The most substantial progress in the past decade has come from the incorporation of a model of the nonstationary speech signal into the spectral subtraction and Wiener filtering frameworks. The models under consideration have mostly been quite simple. It may be expected that the use of more complex models, borrowed from speech recognition work, will take us even further (cf. section 1.4). This line of work is promising from a quality point of view but implies much greater computational complexity as well. At the same time these models may have problems in dealing with events that did not occur during the *training phase*. Therefore the truly successful approaches will be those who strike the optimal balance between sufficiently detailed modeling of the speech signal to have a high quality estimator and a sufficiently weak model to allow for plenty of uncertainties.

Microphone arrays are promising but are expensive and have to develop further. The combination of single-sensor and multiple-sensor noise suppression techniques remains a virtually unexplored field.

10.4   Chapter References

Almeida, L. and Silva, F. (1984). Variable-frequency synthesis: an improved harmonic coding scheme. In *Proceedings of the 1984 International Conference on Acoustics, Speech, and Signal Processing*, page 27.5. Institute of Electrical and Electronic Engineers.

Atal, B. S. (1982). Predictive coding of speech at low bit rates. *IEEE Transactions on Communication*, COM-30(4):600–614.

Atal, B. S., Cuperman, V., and Gersho, A., editors (1991). *Advances in Speech Coding*. Kluwer Academic, Boston.

Atal, B. S. and Remde, J. R. (1982). A new model of LPC excitation for producing natural-sounding speech at low bit rates. In *Proceedings of the 1982 International Conference on Acoustics, Speech, and Signal Processing*, volume 1, pages 614–617. Institute of Electrical and Electronic Engineers.

Atal, B. S. and Schroeder, M. R. (1979). Predictive coding of speech signals and subjective error criteria. *IEEE Transactions on Acoustics, Speech and Signal Processing*, pages 247–254.

Berouti, M., Schwartz, R., and Makhoul, J. (1979). Enhancement of speech corrupted by additive noise. In *Proceedings of the 1979 International Conference on Acoustics, Speech, and Signal Processing*, pages 208–211. Institute of Electrical and Electronic Engineers.

Boll, S. (1979). Suppression of acoustic noise in speech using spectral subtraction. *IEEE Transactions on Acoustics, Speech and Signal Processing*, ASSP-27(2):113–120.

Boll, S. (1991). Speech enhancement in the 1980s. In Furui, S. and Sondhi, M. M., editors, *Advances in Speech Signal Processing*. Marcel Dekker.

Chen, J.-H. (1991). A robust low delay CELP speech coder at 16 kb/s. In Atal, B. S., Cuperman, V., and Gersho, A., editors, *Advances in Speech Coding*, pages 25–35. Kluwer Academic, Boston.

Ephraim, Y. (1992). Statistical-model-based speech enhancement systems. *Proceedings of the IEEE*, 80(10):1526–1555.

Ephraim, Y. and Malah, D. (1984). Speech enhancement using a minimum mean-square error short-time spectral amplitude estimator. *IEEE Transactions on Acoustics Speech and Signal Processing*, ASSP-32(6):1109–1121.

Ephraim, Y. and Malah, D. (1985). Speech enhancement using a minimum mean-square log-spectral amplitude estimator. *IEEE Transactions on Acoustics Speech and Signal Processing*, ASSP-33(2):443–445.

Ephraim, Y., Malah, D., and Juang, B. H. (1989). Speech enhancement based upon hidden markov modeling. In *Proceedings of the 1989 International Conference on Acoustics, Speech, and Signal Processing*, pages 353–356, Glasgow, Scotland. Institute of Electrical and Electronic Engineers.

Flanagan, J. et al. (1979). Speech coding. *IEEE Transactions on Communications*, COM-27(4):710–737.

Flanagan, J. L. (1985). Use of acoustic filtering to control the beamwidth of steered microphone arrays. *Journal of the Acoustical Society of America*, 78(2):423–428.

Furui, S. and Sondhi, M. M., editors (1991). *Advances in Speech Signal Processing*. Marcel Dekker.

Griffin, D. and Lim, J. (1988). Multiband excitation vocoder. *IEEE Transactions on Acoustics, Speech and Signal Processing*, 36(8).

ICASSP (1984). *Proceedings of the 1984 International Conference on Acoustics, Speech, and Signal Processing*. Institute of Electrical and Electronic Engineers.

ICASSP (1989). *Proceedings of the 1989 International Conference on Acoustics, Speech, and Signal Processing*, Glasgow, Scotland. Institute of Electrical and Electronic Engineers.

Jayant, N., Johnston, J., and Safranek, R. (1993). Signal compression based on models of human perception. *Proceedings of the IEEE*, 81(10).

Jayant, N. S. (1992). Signal compression: Technology targets and research directions. *IEEE Jour. Select. Areas Comm.*, 10(5):796–818.

Jayant, N. S. and Noll, P. (1984). *Digital Coding of Waveforms: Principles and Applications to Speech and Video*. Prentice-Hall, Englewood Cliffs, New Jersey.

Kroon, P., Deprettere, E., and Sluyter, R. (1986). Regular-pulse excitation: a novel approach to effective and efficient multi-pulse coding of speech. *IEEE Transactions on Acoustics, Speech and Signal Processing*, ASSP-34:1054–1063.

Lim, J. and Oppenheim, A. (1979). Enhancement and bandwidth compression of noisy speech. *Proceedings of the IEEE*, 67:1586–1604.

Lipoff, S. J. (1994). Personal communication networks: Bridging the gap between cellular and cordless phones. *Proceedings of the IEEE*, pages 564–571.

McAulay, R. and Quatieri, T. (1986). Speech analysis-synthesis based on a sinusoidal representation. *IEEE Transactions on Acoustics, Speech and Signal Processing*, ASSP-34:744–754.

Porter, J. E. and Boll, S. F. (1984). Optimal estimators for spectral restoration of noisy speech. In *Proceedings of the 1984 International Conference on Acoustics, Speech, and Signal Processing*, pages 18.A.2.1–4. Institute of Electrical and Electronic Engineers.

Schroeder, M. R. and Atal, B. S. (1985). Code-excited linear prediction CELP: High quality speech at very low bit rates. In *Proceedings of the 1985 International Conference on Acoustics, Speech, and Signal Processing*, volume 1, pages 937–940, Tampa, Florida. Institute of Electrical and Electronic Engineers.

Silverman, H. (1987). Some analysis of microphone array for speech data acquisition. *IEEE Transactions on Acoustics Speech and Signal Processing*, 35(12):1699–1712.

Tremain, T. (1982). The government standard linear predictive coding algorithm: LPC-10. *Speech Technology Magazine*, pages 40–49.

Van Compernolle, D. (1989). Spectral estimation using a log-distance error criterion applied to speech recognition. In *Proceedings of the 1989 International Conference on Acoustics, Speech, and Signal Processing*, pages 258–261, Glasgow, Scotland. Institute of Electrical and Electronic Engineers.

Van Compernolle, D. (1992). DSP techniques for speech enhancement. In *Proceedings of the ESCA Workshop on Speech Processing in Adverse Conditions*, pages 21–30.

Xie, F. and Van Compernolle, D. (1993). Speech enhancement by nonlinear spectral estimation—a unifying approach. In *Eurospeech '93, Proceedings of the Third European Conference on Speech Communication and Technology*, volume 1, pages 617–620, Berlin. European Speech Communication Association.

Chapter 11

Mathematical Methods

11.1 Overview

Hans Uszkoreit

Deutsches Forschungzentrum für Künstliche Intelligenz, Saarbrücken, Germany
and Universität Saarlandes, Saarbrücken, Germany

Processing of written and spoken human language is computation. However, language processing is not a *single* type of computation. The different levels of information encoding in our language as well as the spectrum of applications for language technology pose a range of very distinct computational tasks. Therefore a wide variety of mathematical methods have been employed in human language technology. Some of them have led to specialized tools for a very restricted task, while others are part of the mathematical foundations of the technology. In this overview a very general map is drawn that groups the different approaches. Some particularly relevant classes of methods are highlighted in the remaining sections of the chapter.

In the early days of language processing, most if not all researchers underestimated the complexity of the problem. Many of them tried to bypass a mathematical characterization of their tasks and solve the problem simply by looking at the envisaged inputs and outputs of their systems. Purely procedural early approaches to machine translation fall in this category. These attempts failed very badly. However, there is one major difference between language processing and most other areas with highly complex calculation tasks, e.g., computational meteorology. One system exists that can handle human language quite decently, i.e., the human cognitive system. Moreover, there is a scientific discipline that strives for a formal description of the human language faculty. Very soon the great majority of researchers became convinced that one needed to utilize insights from linguistics—including phonetics and psycholinguistics—in order to make progress in modeling the human language user.

Modern linguistics tries to characterize the mapping between a spoken or written utterance and its meaning. Linguists do this in roughly the following way. They break up the complex mapping into suitable levels of representation, specify representations in dedicated formalisms, and they employ the same formalisms for specifying the implicit linguistic knowledge of a human language user. Traditionally their main data are collected or invented example sentences, judged and interpreted by introspection. Almost exclusively, discrete symbolic methods have been employed for representing different types of information in linguistics. (The only exception was phonetic signal processing, where Fourier transformations converted the two-dimensional acoustic signal into a three-dimensional spectrogram.)

11.1.1   High-level Linguistic Methods

The mathematical methods of syntax, morphology and phonology are suited for describing sets of strings, especially hierarchically structured strings. Most of these methods came from formal language theory. Most notable is the formal theory of languages and grammars emerging from the Chomsky hierarchy, an inclusion hierarchy of classes of languages. Each class of languages corresponds to a certain level of computational complexity. For these classes of languages, classes of grammars were found that generate the languages. Each class of languages also corresponds to a type of automaton that accepts strings of a language. Typical for this research was the close interaction between theoretical computer science and formal syntax with strong influences in both directions. Much investigation has gone into the question of the proper characterization of human language with respect to the Chomsky hierarchy.

The grammars and automata of formal language theory can rarely be applied to natural language processing without certain modifications. The grammar models developed in linguistics do not directly correspond to the ones from formal language theory. A variety of grammar models have been designed in linguistics and language technology. Some of these models are mentioned in section 3.3. For a comprehensive description you will have to resort to handbooks such as Jacobs, v. Stechow, et al. (1993). A long tradition of work was devoted to efficient parsing algorithms for many grammar models. This work is summarized in section 11.4.

The grammars of formal language theory are rewrite systems with atomic nonterminal symbols that stand for lexical and syntactic categories. However, in human language such categories have complex properties that influence their syntactic distribution. Therefore mathematical tools were developed for expressing linguistic entities as sets of complex features. A new class of logic, so-called feature logic evolved. This branch of research, often subsumed under the term unification grammar, had close links with similar developments in knowledge representation and programming languages. The specialized processing methods that were developed for unification grammars had strong connections with constraint logic programming. In this book, unification grammars are described in section 3.1. For a more detailed introduction, please refer to Shieber (1988).

The situation is somewhat different in semantics. Here representation languages are needed in which we can represent the meaning—or better informational content—of an utterance. In order to provide unambiguous representations of meaning that can serve as the basis for inferences, logic is employed. Many varieties of higher order predicate logic have been developed for this purpose. Special representation languages such as frame and script languages came from artificial intelligence (AI). In the last few years, many of them have received a logical foundation. General purpose and specialized inference techniques have been employed for interpreting the meaning representation in connection with knowledge about the linguistic context, situational context, and the world. Logical deduction is the inference technique mainly used, but there are also approaches that utilize abduction methods. For the use of some semantic formalisms in language technology, refer to section 3.5.

The last two decades witnessed a convergence of theoretical linguistics and language processing with respect to their mathematical methods. On the one hand, this movement proved very fruitful in many areas of language processing. On the other hand, it also lead to some disillusionment concerning the potentials of formal linguistic tools among practitioners of language technology.

Although the specification of linguistic knowledge improved quite a bit through the use of advanced representation techniques, the resulting systems still lacked coverage, robustness, and efficiency, the properties required for realistic applications. It even seemed that every increase in linguistic coverage was accompanied by a loss of efficiency since efficient processing methods for linguistic representation formalisms are still missing.

11.1.2 Statistical and Low-level Processing Methods

Encouraged by a breakthrough in the recognition of spoken words, many researchers turned to statistical data-driven methods for designing language technology applications. For most of them, the line of reasoning went as follows. Linguistic investigation of linguistic competence and cognitive modeling of human language processing have not yet achieved a sufficient understanding and formalization of the mapping from the language signal to the informational contents of the utterance or vice versa. However, only very few applications need the complete mapping anyway. Even if we had a formal model of the complete mapping, we do not have a model of the cognitive system that could support it, since AI has not come close to modeling human knowledge processing.

If one cannot get access to the human linguistic competence through standard methods of linguistic research, it may be possible to induce the knowledge necessary for a specific application indirectly by correlating linguistic data with the desired outputs of the machine. In case of a dictation system, this output is the appropriate written words. For a machine translation system, the output consists of the translated sentences. For an information access system, the output will be a query to a data base. After decades of expecting technological progress mainly from investigating the cognitive structures and processes of the human language user, attention moved back to the linguistic data produced by humans and to be processed by language technology.

The predominant approach is based on an information theoretic view of language processing as a noisy-channel information transmission. In this metaphor, it is assumed that a message is transmitted which we have to recover from observing the output of the noisy channel. It is described as the source-channel model in section 1.6. The approach requires a model that characterizes the transmission by giving for every message the probability of the observed output. The other component is the language model which gives the so-called a-priori distribution, the probability of a message in its context to be sent.

A special type of stochastic finite-state automata, hidden Markov models (HMMs), have been utilized for the recognition of spoken words, syllables or phonemes (section 1.5). Probabilistic derivatives of many grammar models have been proposed. Statistical methods are employed today for substituting or supporting discrete symbolic methods in almost every area of language processing. Examples of promising approaches are statistical part-of-speech tagging (section 3.2.2), probabilistic parsing (section 3.7), ambiguity resolution (section 3.7), lexical knowledge acquisition (Pustejovsky, 1992), and statistical machine translation (Brown, Cocke, et al., 1990).

A special area that has developed rapidly during the last few years, mainly in conjunction with the statistical methods, is the utilization of optimization techniques for spoken and written language processing. Optimization methods are used to find the best solution or solutions among a number of possible solutions applying some evaluation criterion. Since the number of possible solutions, e.g., word hypotheses for a whole utterance in speech recognition, can be rather large, the search needs to be highly efficient. Optimization techniques, especially from dynamic programming, are presented in section 11.7.

Connectionist methods constitute a different paradigm for statistical learning and probabilistic processing on the basis of an acquired language model. Neural nets have proven very useful in pattern recognition. In language technology, both self-trained and prestructured nets are explored for a variety of tasks. A major problem for syntactic and semantic processing is the limitations of connectionist methods concerning the modeling of recursion. A major problem for applying neural nets to speech processing that stems from the temporal nature of speech is time sequence matching. In section 11.5 connectionist methods for speech processing are summarized. A combination of connectionist methods with hidden Markov models is described.

Another major area of very promising new technology is the development of specialized low-level processing methods for natural language. Especially noteworthy is the renaissance of finite-state processing techniques. Finite state transducers were applied with great success to morphological processing. These approaches are described in section 11.6. Recently finite state parsers were constructed that out-perform their competition in coverage and performance. The finite-state technology for syntax is presented in section 3.2.2. Finite-state methods are also applied in semantics and in discourse modeling.

11.1.3 Future Directions

Challenges for future research concerning the individual mathematical methods are presented in the sections that describe them. We will conclude this section by addressing key research problems that extend over the multitude of approaches.

One major challenge is posed by the lack of good formal methods for concurrent symbolic processing. Although there have been various attempts to employ methods and programming languages for concurrent processing in language technology, the results are not yet convincing. The appropriate hardware and well-suited problems for parallel processing are there. What are missing are better formal concepts of concurrency in computation.

Badly needed for progress in language technology is a better general view linking the diverse formal approaches and characterizing their respective virtues and shortcomings. With respect to the employed mathematical methods, we currently witness the coexistence of three major research paradigms, shown in Figure 11.1. However, when we look at individual research systems and new

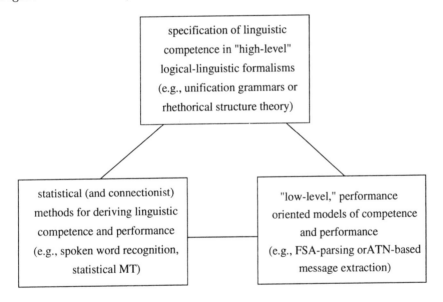

Figure 11.1: Major research paradigms.

applications, we rarely see a system that does not combine formal tools from more than one of the paradigms. In most cases the observed combinations of methods are rather *ad hoc*. There is no general methodology yet that tells us which mix of methods is most appropriate for a certain type of application.

A few examples from recent research may illustrate the relevant direction for future investigation:

Compilation methods may be used to relate high-level competence grammars and low-level performance methods (Alshawi, 1992; Kasper, Kiefer, et al., 1995). Alternatively, learning methods such as explanation-based learning can also be applied in order to derive low-level performance grammars from high-level linguistic specifications (Samuelsson, 1994).

The connections between statistical methods and general automata theory are addressed in Pereira, Riley, et al. (1994), where it is proposed that the concept of weighted finite-state automata (acceptors and transducers) may serve as the common formal foundation for language processing.

Statistical methods can be used for extending knowledge specified in high-level formalisms. An example is the learning of lexical valency information from corpora (Manning, 1993). Statistical methods can also be used for deriving control information that may speed up processing with high-level grammars. Specific linguistic generalizations could be merged or intersected with statistical language models in order to improve their robustness. Intersecting linguistic and statistical models, for instance, can improve precision in part-of-speech tagging.

We expect that extensive research on the theoretical and practical connections among the diverse methods will lead to a more unified mathematical foundation of human language processing.

11.2 Statistical Modeling and Classification

Steve Levinson

AT&T Bell Laboratories, Murray Hill, New Jersey, USA

The speech communication process is a very complicated one for which we have only an incomplete understanding. It has thus far proven to be best treated as a stochastic process which is well characterized by its statistical properties.

There are two fundamental assumptions which underlie the statistical model of speech. The first is that speech is literate. That is, it is well represented by a small set of abstract symbols which correspond to basic acoustic patterns. Second, the acoustic patterns are differentiated by their short duration amplitude spectra. Measurement of these spectra shows that they possess a high degree of variability even for the same symbol and thus are most accurately classified by means of statistical decision theory.

There is another property of speech that makes the application of statistical methods to it more difficult. Speech comprises several overlapping levels of linguistic structure including phonetic, phonological, phonotactic, prosodic, syntactic, semantic and pragmatic information. Thus, to be useful, a statistical characterization of the acoustic speech signal must include a principled means by which the statistics can be combined to satisfy all of the constraints composed by the aforementioned linguistic structure. This section describes briefly the most effective statistical methods currently in use to model the speech signal.

Although it is beyond the scope of this section to describe other uses of the statistical methodologies outlined below, it is worth noting that other important applications of the technology include machine translation (Alshawi et al., 1994), language identification (Kadambe & Hieronymus, 1994), and handwriting recognition (Wilfong, 1995).

11.2.1   Primitive Acoustic Features

We call the voltage analog of the sound pressure wave the speech signal. The signal is usually sampled at 0.1 msec. intervals to form a sequence of 16-bit integers. Because the signal is nonstationary, we divide it into short frames of, say, 10 to 30 msec. duration at 5 to 10 msec. intervals. Thus frames of around a hundred samples are considered to be stationary and a short duration spectrum is computed for each frame. Although many methods of spectral estimation have been advocated in the past, the method of linear prediction (Atal & Hanauer, 1971; Baker, 1979) is often used. Linear prediction provides an n-dimensional (where n is often twelve) parameterization of the spectrum usually in the form of cepstral coefficients (Juang et al., 1987). Thus the information bearing features of the speech signal are usually taken to be a sequence of twelve-dimensional cepstral vectors with one vector computed every 10 msec.

Due to the intrinsic variability of the speech signal and specific assumptions inherent in the linear prediction method, the sequence of cepstral vectors is a random process whose statistical properties can be estimated. The representation of speech signals is discussed in more detail in section 1.3 and section 11.3.

11.2.2   Quantization

Since we assume that speech is literate, the signal could also be represented as a sequence of symbols where each symbol corresponds to a phonetic unit of varying duration. Each phonetic unit corresponds to a region of the twelve-dimensional acoustic feature space. The regions are defined statistically by estimating the probability of each class conditioned on the vectors belonging to that class and then computing the pairwise decision boundaries between the classes as the locus of points in the feature space where both classes are equally probable.

If the decision boundaries are explicitly computed as described above, then an arbitrary feature vector can be classified as resulting from the utterance of one phonetic class simply by finding which region of the space it lies in. As a matter of practice, however, this computation is not performed explicitly. Rather, a statistical decision rule is used. The rule simply states that a feature vector belongs to that class whose probability is largest conditioned on the vector. The effect of this decision rule is to quantize the entire twelve-dimensional feature space into a small number of regions corresponding to the phonetic classes.

11.2.3   Maximum Likelihood and Related Rules

Although the above-described rule appears very intuitive, it is not easily implemented because there is no direct method for computing the probability of a phonetic unit given its acoustic features. If, however, a large set of acoustic vectors which have been phonetically labeled is available, then an indirect method, based on Bayes rule, can be devised. Bayes rule allows us to estimate the probability of a phonetic class given its features from the likelihood of the features given the class. This method leads to the maximum likelihood classifier which assigns an unknown vector to that class whose probability density function conditioned on the class has the maximum value. It is most important to understand that ALL statistical methods of speech recognition are based on this and related rules. The philosophy of maximum likelihood is now so much a part of speech recognition that citations of it in the literature are no longer given. However, the interested reader will find its origins recounted in any standard text on pattern recognition such as Duda and Hart (1973); Meisel (1972); Patrick (1972). Statistical methods in speech recognition are often called by different names such as minimum prediction residual method, minimum risk, minimum probability of error or nearest neighbor. These rules are all closely related as they derive from the same Bayesian argument.

11.2.4   Class Conditional Density Functions

From the previous section, it is clear that ALL statistical methods in speech recognition rest on the estimation of class conditional density functions for phonetic units or, as we shall see later, other linguistic constituents. Thus, the performance of a speech processing algorithm depends critically on the accuracy of the estimates of the class conditional density functions. These, in turn, depend on the existence of a sufficiently large, correctly labeled training set and well understood statistical estimation techniques. Regarding the former, there is little to be said of a practical nature except that the more data available, the better. There are some theoretical results, such as the Cramer-Rao (Patrick, 1972) bound relating variance of estimators to sample size. Obviously the larger the size, the lower the variance and hence the lower the error rate. However, it is quite difficult to relate estimator variance to error rate precisely, so the various rules of thumb which are often invoked to determine sample size needed for a specified performance level are unreliable.

There is one serious flaw to the above-described decision theory. It is predicated on the principle that if the class conditional density functions are known exactly, then no other decision rule based on the same training data can yield asymptotically better performance. Unfortunately, the assumption of exact knowledge of the class conditional density functions is never met in reality. The error may simply be in the parameter values of the densities or, worse, their form may be incorrect.

An elegant solution to this problem is to directly minimize the classification error. This may be done by Juang's method of Generalized Probabilistic Descent (GPD) (Juang, 1992) which has proven to be effective in very difficult speech recognition problems (Wilpon, 1994).

Another variant of the maximum likelihood methodology is clustering. In many classification problems, the items in a class differ amongst themselves in a systematic way. A simple example is the pronunciation of a word by speakers of different national or regional accents or dialects. In such cases the class conditional densities will be multi-modal with the modes and their shapes unknown. Such densities can be estimated by clustering techniques. The most effective such techniques are based on the Lloyd-Max optimum quantizer (Lloyd, 1982) which has come to be known as the k-means algorithm. These techniques have been applied to speech recognition by Levinson et al. (1979). As we shall see in the next section, clustering methods are implicitly used in the state-of-the-art recognition methods.

11.2.5 Hidden Markov Model Methodology

If speech were composed solely of isolated acoustic patterns then the classical statistical decision theory outlined above would be sufficient to perform speech recognition. Unfortunately, that is not the case. That is, the putative fundamental units of speech are combined according to a rich set of linguistic rules which are, themselves, so complicated that they are best captured statistically. The problem is that in order to accomplish speech recognition, one must capture all the subtlety of linguistic structure with a computationally tractable model. The lack of such a representation held back progress in speech recognition for many years.

In the early 1970s both Baker (1975) and Jelinek (1976) independently applied an existing mathematical technique based on the hidden Markov model (HMM) to speech recognition. As the name of the method implies, the original concepts were proposed by A. A. Markov himself (Markov, 1913). The modern form of the mathematics was developed by Baum and his colleagues (Baum & Eagon, 1967; Baum & Sell, 1968; Baum, 1972; Baum, Petrie, et al., 1970); the application of these methods to speech recognition is described in more detail in section 1.5.

11.2.6 Syntax

While the HMM has proven itself to be highly effective in representing several aspects of linguistic structure, other techniques are presently preferred for dealing with the cognitive aspects of language, syntax and semantics. Let us first consider syntax which refers to the relationship that words bear to each other in a sentence. Several aspects of this grammatical structure are well-captured using statistical methods.

The simplest useful way of thinking about syntax is to define it as word order constraint. That is, only certain words can follow certain other words. One way to quantify this is to make a list of allowable n-grams, sequences of n words, in a language. We can augment this list with n-gram probabilities, the probability of a word given its $n-1$ predecessors. This reduces syntax to a Markov n-chain, not to be confused with an HMM, and the desired probabilities can be estimated by counting relative frequencies in large text corpora. Once these numbers are available, an error-ridden lexical transcription of a spoken sentence can be corrected by finding the sequence of n-grams of maximum probability conditioned on the lexical transcription. A number of optimal search strategies are available to find the best sequence (Nilsson, 1971; Viterbi, 1967). For such practical cases, trigrams are typically used. A more detailed discussion of n-gram syntactic models is provided in section 1.6.

While the n-gram methods are useful, they do not constitute full syntactic analysis since syntax is more than word order constraint. In fact, the reason why syntax is considered to be part of cognition is that grammatical structure is a prerequisite to meaning. This aspect of syntax can also be exploited by statistical methods.

There are many ways to use full syntactic analysis, but the most intuitively appealing method is to use the linguist's notion of parts of speech. These syntactic constituents are categories which define the function of a word in a sentence. Associated with the parts of speech are rules of grammar which specify how parts of speech can be combined to form phrases which, in turn, can be combined to form sentences. Finally, using relative frequencies derived from text corpora, probabilities can be assigned to the grammatical rules. Using techniques from the theory of stochastic grammars (Fu, 1974), it is possible to find a sentence the joint probability of whose lexical transcription and syntactic structure, or parse, is maximized for a given corrupted transcription from a speech recognizer. In addition to these statistical parsing techniques, methods similar in spirit to HMM techniques have been studied by Baker (1979) and Jelinek (1990). In either case, syntax analysis both increases the accuracy of speech recognition and, as we shall see in the next section, provides information necessary for the extraction of meaning from a spoken utterance.

11.2.7 Semantics

The ultimate goal of speech recognition is to enable computers to understand the meaning of ordinary spoken discourse. Semantics is that aspect of linguistic structure relating words to meaning. Thus, the ultimate speech recognition machine will necessarily include a semantic analyzer. At present, there exists no general theory of the semantics of natural language. There are many proposed theories some of which are abstract and others of which are worked out for specific limited domains of discourse. All such theories rest on the idea that formal logical operations acting on lexical tokens and syntactic structures yield a formal symbolic representation of meaning. These theories have not yet been made statistical in any coherent way, although a new approach (Pieraccini, Levin, et al., 1993) based on the HMM seems promising.

There is, however, a statistical methodology which captures useful semantic information. It is called word sense disambiguation. A simple example is found in the word *bank* which has two meanings or senses. One sense is that of a financial institution and another refers to the shores of a river. Clearly, the words commonly associated with the two senses are quite different. If we know the words that are appropriate to each word sense, then we can use search techniques to maximize the joint probability of word sequences and word sense. This will result in higher lexical transcription accuracy.

The key to this line of reasoning is the precise measurement of the closeness of word associations. Church and Hanks (1990) proposed using the information theoretic measure of mutual information and has analyzed large text corpora to show that words clustered by large mutual information contents are indicative of a single word sense. It is thus possible to compile word sense statistics for large lexicons and apply them in statistical parsing techniques as described earlier.

11.2.8 Performance

It would be impossible in a short paper such as this is to completely and quantitatively characterize the performance of statistical speech recognizers. Instead, I will briefly mention three benchmarks established by systems based on the methodologies described above. They are moderate vocabulary speech understanding, large vocabulary speech recognition and small vocabulary recognition of telephony. Detailed summaries may be found in ARPA (1994); Wilpon (1994).

The most ambitious speech understanding experiment is presently ongoing under the sponsorship of ARPA. Several laboratories have built (ATIS) systems that provide airline travel information from spoken input. With a nominal vocabulary of 2000 words and spontaneous discourse from undesignated but cooperative speakers, approximately 95% of all queries are correctly answered.

Another highly ambitious project in speech recognition is also sponsored by ARPA. In this large vocabulary recognition task, the goal is lexical transcription only; so unlike the ATIS task, no semantic processing is used. The material is text read from North American business publications by undesignated speakers. The nominal vocabulary is 60,000 words. For this task, several laboratories have achieved word error rates of 11% or less. Unfortunately, such results are obtained by computer programs requiring hundreds of times real time.

Finally, the largest commercial use of speech recognition is in the AT&T telephone network for the placement of calls. In this case, customers are allowed to ask for one of five categories of service using any words they like so long as their utterance contains one of five key words. This system is currently processing about 1 billion calls per year. Calls are correctly processed more than 95% of the time without operator intervention.

11.2.9 Future Directions

Incremental improvements can be made to statistical models and classification methods in two distinct ways. First, existing models can be made more faithful. Second, existing models can be expanded to capture more linguistic structure. Making existing models more faithful reduces to the mathematical problem of lowering the variance of the statistical estimates of parameter values in the models. There are two ways to accomplish this. First, collect more data, more diverse data, more well-classified data, more data representing specific phenomena. The data needed is both text and speech. Second, improve estimation techniques by deriving estimators that have inherently lower variances. The statistical literature is replete with estimation techniques very few of which have been applied to large speech or text corpora. A related but different idea is to improve classification rules. One possibility would be to include a loss function reflecting the fact that some classification errors are more detrimental to transcription than others. The loss function could be estimated empirically and employed in a minimum risk decision rule rather than a maximum likelihood or minimum error probability rule. Existing models can also be made more general by making them represent known, well-understood linguistic structure. Two prime candidates are prosody and syntax. Speech synthesizers make extensive use of prosodic models yet none of that knowledge has found its way into speech recognition. Syntactic models tend to be of the n-gram variety and could capture much more structure if association statistics were collected on the basis of syntactic role rather than simple adjacency. Although semantics is much less well understood than either prosody or syntax, it is still amenable to more detailed statistical modeling than is presently done and the use of integrated syntactico-semantic models also seems worthy of further exploration. The above suggestions are indicative of the myriad possibilities for improvement of the speech technologies by building directly upon existing methods. However, the speech research community would do well to consider the possibility that no amount of incremental improvement will lead to a technology which displays human-like proficiency with language. The obvious and prudent policy for avoiding such an impasse is to encourage completely new concepts and models of speech processing and new generations of researchers to invent them.

11.3 DSP Techniques

John Makhoul

BBN Systems and Technologies, Cambridge, Massachusetts, USA

Digital Signal Processing (DSP) techniques have been at the heart of progress in speech processing during the last 25 years (Rabiner & Schafer, 1978). Simultaneously, speech processing has been an important catalyst for the development of DSP theory and practice. Today, DSP methods are used in speech analysis, synthesis, coding, recognition, and enhancement, as well as voice modification, speaker recognition, and language identification.

DSP techniques have also been very useful in written language recognition in all its forms (on-line, off-line, printed, handwritten). Some of the methods include preprocessing techniques for noise removal, normalizing transformations for line width and slant removal, global transforms (e.g., Fourier transform, correlation), and various feature extraction methods. Local features include the computation of slopes, local densities, variable masks, etc., while others deal with various geometrical characteristics of letters (e.g., strokes, loops). For summaries of various DSP techniques employed in written language recognition, the reader is referred to Impedovo, Ottaviano, et al. (1991); Tappert, Suen, et al. (1990), as well as the following edited special issues: Impedovo (1994); Pavlidis and Mori (1992); Impedovo and Simon (1992).

This section is a brief summary of DSP techniques that are in use today, or that may be useful in the future, especially in the speech recognition area. Many of these techniques are also useful in other areas of speech processing.

11.3.1 Feature Extraction

In theory, it should be possible to recognize speech directly from the digitized waveform. However, because of the large variability of the speech signal, it is a good idea to perform some form of feature extraction that would reduce that variability. In particular, computing the envelope of the short-term spectrum reduces the variability significantly by smoothing the detailed spectrum, thus eliminating various source information, such as whether the sound is voiced or fricated and, if voiced, it eliminates the effect of the periodicity or pitch. For nontonal languages, such as English, the loss of source information does not appear to affect recognition performance much because it turns out that the spectral envelope is highly correlated with the source information. However, for tonal languages, such as Mandarin Chinese, it is important to include an estimate of the fundamental frequency as an additional feature to aid in the recognition of tones (Hon, Yuan, et al., 1994).

To capture the dynamics of the vocal tract movements, the short-term spectrum is typically computed every 10–20 msec using a window of 20–30 msec. The spectrum can be represented directly in terms of the signal's Fourier coefficients or as the set of power values at the outputs from a bank of filters. The envelope of the spectrum can be represented indirectly in terms of the parameters of an all-pole model, using linear predictive coding (LPC), or in terms of the first dozen or so coefficients of the cepstrum—the inverse Fourier transform of the logarithm of the spectrum.

One reason for computing the short-term spectrum is that the cochlea of the human ear performs a quasi-frequency analysis. The analysis in the cochlea takes place on a nonlinear frequency scale (known as the Bark scale or the mel scale). This scale is approximately linear up to about 1000 Hz and is approximately logarithmic thereafter. So, in the feature extraction, it is very common to perform a frequency warping of the frequency axis after the spectral computation. Researchers have experimented with many different types of features for use in speech recognition (Rabiner & Juang, 1993). Variations on the basic spectral computation, such as the inclusion of time and frequency masking, have been shown to provide some benefit in certain cases (Aikawa, Singer, et al., 1993; Bacchiani & Aikawa, 1994; Hermansky, 1990). The use of auditory models as the basis of feature extraction has been useful in some systems (Cohen, 1989), especially in noisy environments (Hunt, Richardson, et al., 1991).

Perhaps the most popular features used for speech recognition today are what are known as mel-frequency cepstral coefficients (MFCCs) (Davis & Mermelstein, 1980). These coefficients are obtained by taking the inverse Fourier transform of the log spectrum after it is warped according to the mel scale. Additional discussion of feature extraction issues can be found in section 1.3 and section 11.2.

11.3.2   Dealing with Channel Effects

Spectral distortions due to various channels, such as a different microphone or telephone, can have enormous effects on the performance of speech recognition systems. To render recognition systems more robust to such distortions, many researchers perform some form of removal of the average spectrum. In the cepstral domain, spectral removal amounts to subtracting out the average cepstrum. Typically, the average cepstrum is estimated over a period of time equal to about one sentence (a few seconds), and that average is updated on an ongoing basis to track any changes in the channel. Other similarly simple methods of filtering the cepstral coefficients have been proposed for removing channel effects (Hermansky, Morgan, et al., 1993). All these methods have been very effective in combating recognition problems due to channel effects. Further discussion of issues related to robust speech recognition can be found in section 1.4.

11.3.3   Vector Quantization

For recognition systems that use hidden Markov models, it is important to be able to estimate probability distributions of the computed feature vectors. Because these distributions are defined over a high-dimensional space, it is often easier to start by quantizing each feature vector to one of a relatively small number of template vectors, which together comprise what is called a codebook. A typical codebook would contain about 256 or 512 template vectors. Estimating probability distributions over this finite set of templates then becomes a much simpler task. The process of quantizing a feature vector into a finite number of template vectors is known as vector quantization (Makhoul, Roucos, et al., 1985). The process takes a feature vector as input and finds the template vector in the codebook that is closest in distance. The identity of that template is then used in the recognition system.

11.3.4   Future Directions

Historically, there has been an ongoing search for features that are resistant to speaker, noise, and channel variations. In spite of the relative success of MFCCs as basic features for recognition, there is a general belief that there must be more that can be done. One challenge is to develop ways in which our knowledge of the speech signal, and of speech production and perception, can be incorporated more effectively into recognition methods. For example, the fact that speakers have different vocal tract lengths could be used to develop more compact models for improved speaker-independent recognition. Another challenge is somehow to integrate speech analysis into the training optimization process. For the near term, such integration will no doubt result in massive increases in computation that may not be affordable.

There have been recent developments in DSP that point to potential future use of new nonlinear signal processing techniques for speech recognition purposes. Artificial neural networks, which are capable of computing arbitrary nonlinear functions, have been explored extensively for purposes of speech recognition, usually as an adjunct or substitute for hidden Markov models. However, it is possible that neural networks may be best utilized for the computation of new feature vectors that would rival today's best features.

Work by Maragos, Kaiser, et al. (1992) with instantaneous energy operators, which have been shown to separate amplitude and frequency modulations, may be useful in discovering such modulations in the speech signal and, therefore, may be the source of new features for speech recognition. The more general quadratic operators proposed by Atlas and Fang (1992) offer a rich family of possible operators that can be used to compute a large number of features that exhibit new properties which should have some utility for speech processing in general and speech recognition in particular.

11.4 Parsing Techniques

Aravind Joshi

University of Pennsylvania, Philadelphia, Pennsylvania, USA

Parsing a sentence means computing the structural description (descriptions) of the sentence assigned by a grammar, assuming, of course, that the sentence is well-formed. Mathematical work on parsing consists of at least the following activities.

1. Mathematical characterization of derivations in a grammar and the associated parsing algorithms.

2. Computing the time and space complexities of these algorithms in terms of the length of the sentence and the size of the grammar, primarily.

3. Comparing different grammar formalisms and showing equivalences among them wherever possible, thereby developing uniform parsing algorithms for a class of grammars.

4. Characterizing parsing as deduction and a uniform specification of parsing algorithms for a wide class of grammars.

5. Combining grammatical and statistical information for improving the efficiency of parsers and ranking of multiple parses for a sentence.

The structural descriptions provided by a grammar depend on the grammar formalism to which the grammar belongs. For the well-known context-free grammar (CFG) the structural description is, of course, the conventional phrase structure tree (tress) associated with the sentence. The parse tree describes the structure of the sentence. It is also the record of the history of derivation of the sentence. Thus, in this case the structural description and the history of the derivation are the same objects. Later, we will comment on other grammar formalisms and the structural descriptions and histories of derivation associated with them.

11.4.1   Parsing Complexity

For CFGs we have the well-known algorithms by Cocke, Kasami, and Younger (CKY) (Kasami, 1965; Younger, 1967) and the Earley algorithm (Earley, 1970). All CFG algorithms are related to these two in one way or another. As regards the complexity of these algorithms, it is well-known that the worst case complexity is $O(n^3)$ where n is the length of the sentence. There is a multiplicative factor which depends on the size of the grammar and it is $O(G^2)$ where G is the size of the grammar (expressed appropriately in terms of the number of rules and the number of non-terminals). There are results which show improvements in the exponents of both n and G but these are not significant for our purpose. Of course, these complexity results mostly are worst case results (upper bounds) and therefore, they are not directly useful. They do however establish polynomial parsing of these grammars. There are no mathematical average case results. All average case results reported are empirical. In practice, most algorithms for CFGs run much better than the worst case and the real limiting factor in practice is the size of the grammar. For a general discussion of parsing strategies, see Leermakers (1993); Nedderhoff (1994); Sikkel (1994).

During the past decade or so a number of new grammar formalisms have been introduced for a variety of reasons, for example, eliminating transformations in a grammar, accounting linguistic structures beyond the reach of context-free grammars, integrating syntax and semantics directly, etc.. Among these new formalisms, there is one class of grammars called *mildly context-sensitive grammars* that has been mathematically investigated very actively. In particular, it has been shown that a number of grammar formalisms belonging to this class are weakly equivalent, i.e., they generate the same set of string languages. Specifically, tree-adjoining grammars (TAG), combinatory categorial grammars (CCG), linear indexed grammars (LIG), and head grammars (HG) are weakly equivalent. From the perspective of parsing, weak equivalence by itself is not very interesting because weak equivalence alone cannot guarantee that a parsing technique developed for one class of grammars can be extended to other classes, or a uniform parsing procedure can be developed for all these equivalent grammars. Fortunately, it has been shown that indeed it is possible to extend a recognition algorithm for CFGs (the CKY algorithm) for parsing linear indexed grammars (LIG). Then this parser can be adapted for parsing TAGs, HGs, as well as CCGs. This new algorithm is polynomial, the complexity being $O(n^6)$. The key mathematical notion behind the development of this general algorithm is that in all these grammars what can happen in a derivation depends only on which of the finite set of *states* the derivation is in. For CFG these states can be nonterminal symbols. This property called the *context-freeness* property is crucial because it allows one to keep only a limited amount of context during the parsing process, thus resulting in a polynomial time algorithm. For CFGs this property holds trivially. The significant result here is that this property also extends to the grammars more powerful than CFGs, mentioned above. An Earley type algorithm has also been developed for the tree-adjoining grammars and its complexity has been shown to be also $O(n^6)$. For further information on these results, see Joshi, Vijay-Shanker, et al. (1991); Schabes and Joshi (1988); Vijay-Shanker and Weir (1993).

11.4.2   Derivation Trees

Although the grammars mentioned above are weakly equivalent and uniform parsing strategies have been developed for them, it should be noted that the notions of what constitutes a parse are quite different for each one of these grammars. Thus in a TAG the real parse of a sentence is the so-called derivation tree, which is a record of how the elementary trees of a TAG are put together by the operations of substitution and adjoining in order to obtain the derived tree whose yield is the string being parsed. The nodes of the derivation tree are labeled by the names of the elementary trees and the edges are labeled by the addresses of the tree labeling the parent node in which the trees labeling the daughter nodes are either substituted or adjoined. This derivation tree is unlike the derivation tree for a CFG for which the notions of the derivation tree and the derived tree are the same. For TAG these are distinct notions. For HG which deals with headed strings and operations of concatenation and wrapping (both are string operations) there is no notion of a derived tree as such. There is only the notion of a derivation tree which is a record of how the elementary strings are put together and what operations were used in this process. The terminal nodes are labeled by elementary strings (headed strings) and the other nodes are labeled by the operations used for combining the strings labeling the daughter nodes and also by the string resulting from performing this operation. Thus, this derivation tree is quite unlike the standard phrase structure tree, especially when the combining operation labeling a node is wrapping (wrapping one string around another to the right or left of its head) as a non-standard constituent structure can be defined for the resultant tree.

For a CCG the parse of a sentence is the proof tree of the derivation. It is like the phrase structure tree in the sense that the nodes are labeled by categories in CCG. However, for each node the name of the operation used in making the reduction (for example, function application or function composition) has to be stated at the node also. Thus, in this sense they are like the derivation trees of HG. The derivation trees of LIG are like the phrase structure trees except that with each node the contents of the stack associated with that node are stated. Given this wide divergence of what constitutes a structural description, the significance of the equivalence result and the existence of a general polynomial parsing strategy can be better appreciated.

11.4.3   Unification-based Grammars

Almost all computational grammars incorporate feature structures (attribute value structures), the category label being a special attribute singled out for linguistic convenience and not for any formal reasons. These feature structures are manipulated by the operation of unification, hence the term *unification-based grammars*. CFGs or any of the grammars mentioned above can serve as the backbones for the unification-based grammars, CFGs being the most common (Shieber, 1988). As soon as feature structures and unification are added to a CFG the resulting grammars are Turing equivalent and they are no longer polynomially parsable. In practice, conditions are often placed on the possible feature structures which allow the polynomial probability to be restored. The main reason for the excessive power of the unification-based grammars is that recursion can be encoded in the feature structures. For certain grammars in the class of mildly context-sensitive grammars, in particular for TAGs, recursion is factored away from the statement of so-called long-distance dependencies. The feature structures can be without any recursion in them, thus preserving the polynomial parsability of the TAG backbone.

Some unification-based grammar formalisms, for example, the lexical-functional grammar (LFG) are very explicit in assigning both a phrase structure and a feature structure-based functional structure to the sentence being parsed. Formal properties of the interface between these two components have been studied recently. In particular, computational complexity of this interface has been studied independently of the complexity of the phrase structure component and the feature structure component. A number of properties of different interface strategies have been studied that can be exploited for computational advantage. A surprising result here is that under certain circumstances an interface strategy that does no pruning in the interface performs significantly better than one that does. For an interesting discussion of these results, see Maxwell and Kaplan (1993).

11.4.4   Parsing as Deduction

Parsing can be viewed as a deductive process as is the case in CCG mentioned above. The Lambek Calculus (LC) is a very early formulation of parsing as deduction (Lambek, 1958). The relationship between LC and CFG was an open question for over thirty years. Very recently it has been shown that LC and CFG are weakly equivalent (Pentus, 1993). However, the proof of this equivalence does not seem to suggest a construction of a polynomial parsing algorithm for LC and this is an important open question. The framework of parsing as deduction allows modular separation of the logical aspects of the grammar and the proof search procedure, thus providing a framework for investigating a wide range of parsing algorithms. Such theoretical investigations have led to the development of a program for rapid prototyping and experimentation with new parsing algorithms and have also been used in the development of algorithms for CCGs, TAGs, and lexicalized CFGs. For further details, see Shieber, Schabes, et al. (1994).

11.4.5   LR Parsing

Left-to-right, rightmost derivation (LR) parsing was introduced initially for efficient parsing of languages recognized by deterministic pushdown automata and have proven useful for compilers. For natural language parsing, LR parsers are not powerful enough. However conflicts between multiple choices are solved by pseudo-parallelism (Lang, 1974; Tomita, 1987). Johnson and Kipps independently noted that the Tomita method is not bounded by any polynomial in the length of the input string and the size of the grammar. Kipps also shows how to repair this problem. These results are presented in Tomita (1991). LR parsing has been applied to non-context-free languages also in the context of natural language parsing (Schabes & Vijayshanker, 1990).

11.4.6 Parsing by Finite-State Transducers

Finite-state devices have always played a key role in natural language processing. There is renewed interest in these devices because of their successful use in morphological analysis by representing very large dictionaries by finite-state automata (FSA) and by representing two-level rules and lexical information with finite-state transducers (FST). FSAs have been used for parsing also, as well as for approximating CFGs. A main drawback of using FSA for parsing is the difficulty of representing hierarchical structure, thus giving incomplete parses in some sense. Recently, there has been theoretical work on FSTs for their use in parsing, one of the approaches being the use of an FST and computing the parse as a fixed point of the transduction. The parsers can be very efficient and are well suited for large highly lexicalized grammars. For further details on these issues, see (Karttunen, Kaplan, et al., 1992; Pereira, Rebecca, et al., 1991; Roche, 1994).

11.4.7 Remarks

We have not discussed various related mathematical topics, for example, mathematical properties of grammars, unless they are directly relevant to parsing, and the mathematical results in the application of statistical techniques to parsing. This latter topic is the subject of another contribution in this chapter. It is worth pointing out that recent mathematical investigations on lexicalized grammars have great significance to the use of statistical techniques for parsing as these grammars allow a very direct representation of the appropriate lexical dependencies.

11.4.8 Future Directions

Some of the key research problems are (1) techniques for improving the efficiency of the parsing systems by exploiting lexical dependencies, (2) techniques for exploiting certain regularities in specific domains, e.g., particular sentence patterns tend to appear more often in specific domains, (3) systematic techniques for computing partial parses, less than complete parses in general, (4) applying finite-state technology for parsing, in particular for partial parses, (5) systematic techniques for integrating parsing with semantic interpretation and translation, (6) investigating parallel processing techniques for parsing and experimenting with large grammars.

Small workshops held in a periodic fashion where both theoretical and experimental results can be informally discussed will be the best way to exchange information in this area. Specific initiatives for parsing technology, for example for parallel processing technology for parsing are needed for rapid progress in this area.

11.5   Connectionist Techniques

Hervé Bourlard[a] & Nelson Morgan[b]

[a] Faculté Polytechnique de Mons, Mons, Belgium
[b] International Computer Science Institute, Berkeley, California, USA

There are several motivations for the use of connectionist systems in human language technology. Some of these are:

- Artificial Neural Networks (ANN) can learn in either a supervised or unsupervised way from training examples. This property is certainly not specific to ANNs, as many kinds of pattern recognition incorporate learning. In the case of ANNs, however, it sometimes is easier to eliminate some system heuristics, or to partially supplant the arbitrary or semi-informed selection of key parameters. Of course, this is not often done completely or in an entirely blind way, but usually requires the application of some task-dependent knowledge on the part of the system designer.

- When ANNs are trained for classification, they provide discriminant learning. In particular, ANN outputs can estimate posterior probabilities of output classes conditioned on the input pattern. This can be proved for the case when the network is trained for classification to minimize one of several common cost functions (e.g., least mean square error or relative entropy). It can be easily shown that a system that computes these posterior probabilities minimizes the error rate while maximizing discrimination between the correct output class and rival ones; the latter property is described by the term *discriminant*. In practice, it has been shown experimentally that real ANN-based systems could be trained to generate good estimates of these ideal probabilities, resulting in useful pattern recognizers.

- When used for classification, prediction or parsing (or any other input/output mapping), ANNs with one hidden layer and *enough* hidden nodes can approximate any continuous function.

- Because ANNs can incorporate multiple constraints and find optimal combinations of constraints, there is no need for strong assumptions about the statistical distributions of the input features or about high-order correlation of the input data. In theory, this can be discovered automatically by the ANNs during training.

- ANN architecture is flexible, accommodating contextual inputs and feedback. Also, ANNs are typically highly parallel and regular structures, permitting efficient hardware implementations.

In the following, we briefly review some of the typical functional building blocks for HLT and show how connectionist techniques could be used to improve them. In subsection 11.5.3, we discuss a particular instance that we are experienced in using. Finally, in the last subsection, we discuss some key research problems.

11.5.1 ANNs and Feature Extraction

Feature extraction consists of transforming the raw input data into a concise representation that contains the relevant information and is robust to variations. For speech, for instance, the waveform is typically translated into some kind of a function of a short-term spectrum. For handwriting recognition, pixels are sometimes complemented by dynamic information before they are translated into task-relevant features.

It would be desirable to automatically determine the parameters or features for a particular HLT task. In some limited cases, it appears to be possible to automatically derive features from raw data, given significant application-specific constraints. This is the case for the AT&T handwritten zip code recognizer (le Cun, Boser, et al., 1990), in which a simple convolutional method was used to extract important features such as lines and edges that are used for classification by an ANN.

Connectionist networks have also been used to investigate a number of other approaches to unsupervised data analysis, including linear dimension reduction [including Bourlard and Kamp (1988), in which it was shown that feedforward networks used in auto-associative mode are actually performing principal component analysis (PCA)], non-linear dimension reduction (Oja, 1991; Kambhatla & Leen, 1994), reference-point-based classifiers, such as vector quantization and topological map (Kohonen, 1988).

It is, however, often better to make use of any task-specific knowledge whenever it is possible to reduce the amount of information to be processed by the network and to make its task easier. As a consequence, we note that, while automatic feature extraction is a desirable goal, most ASR systems use neural networks to classify speech sounds using standard signal processing tools (like Fourier transform) or features that are selected by the experimenter (e.g., Cole, Fanty, et al. (1991)).

11.5.2 ANNs and Pattern Sequence Matching

Although ANNs have been shown to be quite powerful in static pattern classification, their formalism is not very well suited to address most issues in HLT. Indeed, in most of these cases, patterns are primarily sequential and dynamical.

For example, in both ASR and handwriting recognition, there is a time dimension or a sequential dimension which is highly variable and difficult to handle directly in ANNs. We note, however, that ANNs have been successfully applied to time series prediction in several task domains (Weigend & Gershenfeld, 1994). HLT presents several challenges. In fact, many HLT problems can be formulated as follows: how can an input sequence (e.g., a sequence of spectra in the case of speech and a sequence of pixel vectors in the case of handwriting recognition) be properly explained in terms of an output sequence (e.g., sequence of phonemes, words or sentences in the case of ASR or a sequence of written letters, words or phrases in the case of handwriting recognition) when the two sequences are not synchronous (since there usually are multiple inputs associated with each pronounced or written word)?

Several neural network architectures have been developed for (time) sequence classification, including:[1]

- Static networks with an input buffer to transform a temporal pattern into a spatial pattern (Bourlard & Morgan, 1993; Lippmann, 1989).

- Recurrent networks that accept input vectors sequentially and use a recurrent internal state that is a function of the current input and the previous internal state (Jordan, 1989; Kuhn, Watrous, et al., 1990; Robinson & Fallside, 1991).

- Time-delay neural networks, approximating recurrent networks by feedforward networks (Lang, Waibel, et al., 1990).

In the case of ASR, all of these models have been shown to yield good performance (sometimes better than HMMs) on short isolated speech units. By their recurrent aspect and their implicit or explicit temporal memory they can perform some kind of integration over time. This conclusion remains valid for related HLT problems. However, neural networks by themselves have not been shown to be effective for large-scale recognition of continuous speech or cursive handwriting. The next section describes a new approach that combines ANNs and HMMs for large vocabulary continuous speech recognition.

11.5.3   Hybrid HMM/ANN Approach

Most commonly, the basic technological approach for automatic speech recognition (ASR) is statistical pattern recognition using hidden Markov models (HMMs) as presented in sections 1.5 and 11.2. The HMM formalism has also been applied to other HLT problems such as handwriting recognition (Chen, Kundu, et al., 1994). [2]

---

[1]For a good earlier review of the different approaches using neural networks for speech recognition, see Lippmann (1989). For a good overview of ANNs for speech processing in general, see Morgan and Scofield (1991).

[2]Neural network equivalents of standard HMMs have been studied, but essentially are different implementations of the same formalism (Bridle, 1990; Lippmann, 1989) and are not discussed further here.

Recently, a new formalism of classifiers particularly well suited to sequential patterns (like speech and handwritten text) and which combines the respective properties of ANNs and HMMs was proposed and successfully used for difficult ASR (continuous speech recognition) tasks (Bourlard & Morgan, 1993). This system, usually referred to as the hybrid HMM/ANN combines HMM sequential modeling structure with ANN pattern classification (Bourlard & Morgan, 1993). Although this approach is quite general and recently was also used for handwriting recognition (Schenkel, Guyon, et al., 1994; Schenkel, Guyon, et al., 1995) and speaker verification (Naik & Lubensky, 1994), the following description will mainly apply to ASR problems.

As in standard HMMs, hybrid HMM/ANN systems applied to ASR use a Markov process to temporally model the speech signal. The connectionist structure is used to model the local feature vector conditioned on the Markov process. For the case of speech this feature vector is local in time, while in the case of handwritten text it is local in space. This hybrid is based on the theoretical result that ANNs satisfying certain regularity conditions can estimate class (posterior) probabilities for input patterns (Bourlard & Morgan, 1993); i.e., if each output unit of an ANN is associated with each possible HMM state, it is possible to train ANNs to generate posterior probabilities of the state conditioned on the input. This probability can then be used, after some modifications (Bourlard & Morgan, 1993), as local probabilities in HMMs.

Advantages of the HMM/ANN hybrid for speech recognition include:

- a natural structure for discriminative training,

- no strong assumptions about the statistical distribution of the acoustic space,

- parsimonious use of parameters,

- better robustness to insufficient training data,

- an ability to model acoustic correlation (using contextual inputs or recurrence).

In recent years these hybrid approaches have been compared with the best classical HMM approaches on a number of HLT tasks. In cases where the comparison was controlled (e.g., where the same system was used in both cases except for the means of estimating emission probabilities), the hybrid approach performed better when the number of parameters were comparable, and about the same in some cases in which the classical system used many more parameters. Also, the hybrid system was quite efficient in terms of CPU and memory run-time requirements. Evidence for this can be found in a number of sources, including:

- Renals, Morgan, et al. (1994) in which results on Resource Management (a standard reference database for testing ASR systems) are presented, and

- Lubensky, Asadi, et al. (1994) in which high recognition accuracy on a connected digit recognition task is achieved using a fairly straightforward HMM/ANN hybrid (and is compared to state-of-the-art multi-Gaussian HMMs).

- More recently, such a system has been evaluated under both the North American ARPA program and the European LRE SQALE project (20,000 word vocabulary, speaker independent continuous speech recognition). In the preliminary results of the SQALE evaluation (reported in Steeneken and Van Leeuwen (1995)) the system was found to perform slightly better than any other leading European system and required an order of magnitude less CPU resources to complete the test.

More generally, though, complete systems achieve their performance through detailed design, and comparisons are not predictable on the basis of the choice of the emission probability estimation algorithm alone.

ANNs can also be incorporated in a hybrid HMM system by training the former to do nonlinear prediction (Levin, 1993), leading to a nonlinear version of what is usually referred to as autoregressive HMMs (Juang & Rabiner, 1985).

11.5.4 Language Modeling and Natural Language Processing

Connectionist approaches have also been applied to natural language processing. Like the acoustic case, NLP requires the sequential processing of symbol sequences (word sequences). For example, HMMs are a particular case of a FSM, and the techniques used to simulate or improve acoustic HMMs are also valid for language models. As a consequence, much of the work on connectionist NLP has used ANNs to simulate standard language models like FSMs.

In 1969, Minsky and Papert (1969) showed that ANNs can be used to simulate a FSM. More recently, several works showed that recurrent networks simulate or validate regular and context-free grammars. For instance, in Liu, Sun, et al. (1990), a recurrent network feeding back output activations to the previous (hidden) layer was used to validate a string of symbols generated by a regular grammar. In Sun, Chen, et al. (1990), this was extended to CFGs. Structured connectionist parsers were developed by a number of researchers, including Fanty (1985) and Jain (1992). The latter parser was incorporated in a speech-to-speech translation system (for a highly constrained conference-registration task) that was described in Waibel, Jain, et al. (1992).

Neural networks have also been used to model semantic relations. There have been many experiments of this kind over the years. For example, Elman (1988) showed that neural networks can be trained to learn pronoun reference. He used a partially recurrent network for this purpose, consisting of a feedforward MLP with feedback from the hidden layer back into the input.

The work reported so far has focused on simulating standard approaches with neural networks, and it is not yet known whether this can be helpful in the integration of different knowledge sources into a complete HLT system. Generally speaking, connectionist language modeling and NLP has thus far played a relatively small role in large or difficult HLT tasks.

11.5.5 Future Directions

There are many open problems in applying connectionist approaches to HLT, and in particular to ASR, including:

- Better modeling of nonstationarity—speech and cursive handwriting are in fact not piecewise stationary. Two promising directions for this in the case of speech are the use of articulatory or other segment-based models, and perceptually-based models that may reduce the modeling space based on what is significant to the auditory system.

- Avoiding conditional independence assumptions—to some extent the HMM/ANN hybrid approach already does this, but there are still a number of assumptions regarding temporal independence that are not justified. Perceptual approaches may also help here, as may the further development of dynamic or predictive models.

- Developing better signal representations—the above approaches may need new features in order to work well in realistic conditions.

- Better incorporation of language models and world knowledge—while we have briefly mentioned the use of connectionist language models and NLP, all of the schemes currently employed provide only a rudimentary application of knowledge about the world, word meanings, and sentence structure. These factors must ultimately be incorporated in the statistical theory, and connectionist approaches are a reasonable candidate for the underlying model.

- Learning to solve these problems through a better use of modular approaches—this consists of both the design of better solutions to subtasks, and more work on their integration.

These are all long-term research issues. Many intermediate problems will have to be solved before anything like an optimal solution can be found.

11.6 Finite State Technology

Ronald M. Kaplan
Xerox Palo Alto Research Center, Palo Alto, California, USA

A formal language is a set of strings (sometimes called sentences) made up by concatenating together symbols (characters or words) drawn from a finite alphabet or vocabulary. If a language has only a finite number of sentences, then a complete characterization of the set can be given simply by presenting a finite list of all the sentences. But if the language contains an infinite number of sentences (as all interesting languages do), then some sort of recursive or iterative description must be provided to characterize the sentences. This description is sometimes given in the form of a grammar, a set of pattern-matching rules that can be applied either to produce the sentences in the language one after another or else to recognize whether a given string belongs to the set. The description may also be provided by specifying an automaton, a mechanistic device that also operates either to produce or recognize the sentences of the language.

Languages have been categorized according to the complexity of the patterns that their sentences must satisfy, and the basic classifications are presented in all the standard textbooks on formal language theory, e.g., Hopcroft and Ullman (1979). The sentences of a *regular language*, for example, have the property that what appears at one position in a string can depend only on a bounded amount of information about the symbols at earlier positions. Consider the language over the alphabet a, b, c whose sentences end with a c and contain an a at a given position only if there is an earlier b. The strings $cccc$ and bac belong to this language but abc does not. This is a regular language since it only requires a single bit to record whether or not a b has previously appeared. On the other hand, the language whose sentences consist of some number of a's followed by exactly the same number of b's is not a regular language since there is no upper bound on the number of a's that the allowable number of b's depends on. This set of strings belongs instead to the mathematically and computationally more complex class of *context-free* languages.

A regular language can be described by grammars in various notations that are known to be equivalent in their expressive power—they each can be used to describe all and only the regular languages. The most common way of specifying a regular language is by means of a *regular expression*, a formula that indicates the order in which symbols can be concatenated, whether there are alternative possibilities at each position, and whether substrings can be arbitrarily repeated. The regular expression $\{c^*b\{a|b|c\}^*|\epsilon\}c$ denotes the regular language described above. In the notation used here, concatenation is represented by sequence in the formula, alternatives are enclosed in braces and separated by vertical bars, asterisks (often called the *Kleene closure* operator) indicate that strings satisfying the previous subexpressions can be freely repeated, and ϵ denotes the empty string, the string containing no elements.

The regular languages are also exactly those languages that can be accepted by a particular kind of automaton, a *finite-state machine*. A finite-state machine (fsm) consists of a finite number of states and a function that determines transitions from one state to another as symbols are read from an input tape. The machine starts at a distinguished initial state with the tape positioned at the first symbol of a particular string. The machine transitions from state to state as it reads the tape, eventually coming to the end of the string. At that point, if the machine is in one of a designated set of *final* states, we say that the machine has *accepted* the string or that the string belongs to the language that the machine characterizes. An fsm is often depicted in a state-transition

diagram where circles representing the states are connected by arcs that denote
the transitions. An arrow points to the initial state and final states are marked
with a double circle. The fsm, shown in Figure 11.2, accepts the language
$\{c^*b\{a|b|c\}^*|\epsilon\}c$:

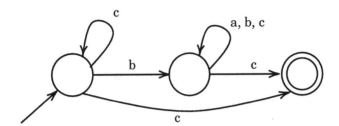

Figure 11.2: Finite-state machine diagram.

Because of their mathematical and computational simplicity, regular languages and finite-state machines have been applied in many information processing tasks. Regular expressions are often used to specify global search patterns
in word-processors and in operating-system utilities such as Unix' Grep. The
lexical analysis component of most modern programming language compilers is
defined as a finite-state machine that recognizes identifier classes, punctuation,
numbers, etc. (Aho & Ullman, 1978). But until relatively recently, finite-state
techniques have not been widely used in natural language processing. This is in
large measure the result of Chomsky's argument (Chomsky, 1957) that natural
language sentences are so rich and complicated that they cannot be accurately
characterized by means of regular or finite-state descriptions. One consequence
of this was that a generation of linguists and computational linguists came to
believe that finite-state techniques were of little or no interest.

It may well be true that complete and accurate natural language syntactic and semantic dependencies lie beyond the power of finite-state description,
but work in the last twenty years (and particularly in the last five years) has
identified a number of important problems for which very efficient and effective
finite-state solutions can be found.

One set of solutions relies on the observation that finite-state descriptions
can provide an approximation to the proper grammatical description of a language, an approximation that is often good enough for practical purposes. The
information extraction problem, for example, requires that documents and passages be identified that are likely to contain information relevant to a given user's
needs. Full-blown syntactic and semantic analyses of documents would certainly
help to solve this problem. But such analyses may provide much more information than this task actually requires. Indeed, Appelt, Hobbs, et al. (1993) have
constructed a finite-state solution that is extremely efficient compared to more
powerful but more complex extraction systems and also has very favorable recall
and precision scores. Their finite-state pattern specifications can only approximate a complete analysis of a text, but the approximation seems close enough

for this particular purpose.

There has also been growing interest in using finite-state machines for storing and accessing natural language dictionaries. Appel and Jacobson (1988) observed that the words in a large lexicon can be very compactly represented in a state-transition graph. This is because the graph can be transformed using determinization and minimization techniques that are well-known from finite-state theory, with the result that prefixes and suffixes common to many words are collapsed into a single set of transitions. Lucchesi and Kowaltowski (1993) discuss access methods for finite-state dictionary representations that permit efficient retrieval of translation and synonymy information associated with particular words.

A third set of problems require that strings be systematically transformed into other strings. For example, the negative prefix *in* in the abstract phonological representation such as *in+practical* must be realized with an assimilated nasal as in *impractical*, or the inflected form *stopping* must be mapped either to its stem *stop* (for use in information retrieval indexing) or to its morphological analysis *stop*+PresentParticiple as an initial step in further processing. One formalism for describing these kinds of string transformations are context-sensitive rewriting rules as discussed for example by Chomsky and Halle (1968). Johnson (1972) and later Kaplan and Kay (1981); Kaplan and Kay (1994) showed that for each rule of this type there is a finite-state *transducer* that maps input strings to exactly the same outputs that the rule prescribes. A transducer is a simple extension of a basic finite-state machine: as it reads its input tape and makes a transition from one state to another, it can also write a corresponding symbol on a second tape. When it reaches a final state and the end of the input, the string produced on the second tape is taken to be the output that the input string is mapped to.

Mathematically, the collection of input-output string-pairs for a given transducer (corresponding perhaps to a particular rule) constitutes a *regular relation*. Regular relations share many (but not all) of the formal properties of the regular languages (for example, closure under union and concatenation) and also enjoy certain other properties. In particular, the regular relations are closed under *composition*, and Kaplan and Kay use this fact to show that the effect of an entire collection of rewriting rules making up a phonological or morphological grammar can be implemented as a single finite-state transducer. This device is much more efficient than any scheme using the rules directly for performing the string transformations that the grammar describes. Koskenniemi (1983) proposed a different rule notation, called two-level rules, for characterizing phonological and morphological variations. These rules also denote only regular relations and can be transformed to equivalent transducers.

Future Directions

In the years since Chomsky's original criticism of finite-state techniques used for syntactic description, our understanding of their mathematical and computational properties has increased substantially. Of most importance, however, is our increased awareness of the wide range of natural language processing problems that they can fruitfully be applied to. Problems such as dictionary access and morphological analysis seem to be inherently finite-state in character, and finite-state solutions for these problems are complete as well as efficient. For applications such as information extraction, finite-state approaches appear to provide extremely useful approximate solutions. An exciting body of current research is exploiting more sophisticated finite-state techniques to improve the accuracy of approximate syntactic analyses without sacrificing their processing efficiency (e.g., Koskenniemi, 1990; Voutilainen & Tapanainen, 1993). Given these improvements, we expect to see finite-state techniques incorporated into a growing number of practical language processing systems.

11.7 Optimization and Search in Speech and Language Processing

John Bridle

Dragon Systems UK Ltd., Cheltenham, UK

An *optimal search method* is one that always finds the best solution (or *a* best solution, if there is more than one). For our purposes *best* is in terms of the value of a criterion function, which defines a score for any possible solution. *Optimization* can be defined as the process of finding a best solution, but it is also used, more loosely, meaning to find a sequence of better and better solutions.

Optimization and *search* are vital to modern speech and natural language processing systems. Although there are optimization techniques which are not normally thought of as search, and search methods which are not optimal or not defined as optimizing anything, most often we are dealing with search methods which seek to optimize a well-defined criterion, and usually we understand the search method in terms of the way it approximates to an optimal search.

Three well-known problems for which optimal search methods are important are: training a set of models for speech recognition, decoding an acoustic pattern in terms of a sequence of word models, and parsing an errorful symbol string with the least number of assumptions of errors. Speech recognition and parsing are combinatorial optimization problems: a solution is a sequence (or more complicated data structure) of symbols, which in a speech recognition system might represent words. Training the parameters of a set of models is a problem in (non-linear) continuous optimization: a solution is a vector of real numbers (e.g., probabilities and parameters of probability density functions). It is common, in speech and language processing, to reserve the term *search* for combinatorial problems, particularly speech recognition, and to use *optimization* for continuous problems such as training.

We must never forget that an optimal solution is not necessarily correct: it is only optimal given the way the problem is posed. Speech recognition based on optimal search has the important and useful property that we can usually categorize recognition errors as *model errors* (the recognition criterion was inappropriate) or *search errors* (we failed to find the mathematically optimal solution), by checking the value of the criterion for the correct answer as well as the incorrect answer. In the case of model errors we must improve the structure of the models, or the method of training or the training data itself.

A search method for ASR is usually expected to be an optimal (finds the best-scoring answer) to good (and preferably controllable) approximation. The main properties of search methods, apart from optimality, are speed and use of computing resources. Other attributes include delay (not the same as speed) and providing extra information, such as alternative answers or details like scores and positions.

For some problems the optimal solution can be computed directly, using standard numerical algorithms. A feed-forward neural network (see section 11.5) can be used as a classifier without performing a search, and matrix inversion can be used as the basis for some training methods. However, the most successful methods for dealing with timescales and sequences in speech recognition are based on searches.

The most desirable search methods are those that are provably optimal. This is the case with the standard speech recognition algorithms, which are based on dynamic programming and the Markov property. The standard training methods use an efficient re-estimation approach, which usually converges to at least a local optimum in a few iterations through the training data. The standard model structures and training criteria are chosen partly because they are compatible with such efficient search methods. Less efficient methods, such as gradient descent or optimization by simulated annealing can be used for more difficult (but possibly more appropriate) models and training criteria.

11.7.1   Dynamic Programming-based Search for Speech Recognition

The most important search techniques for combinatorial problems in speech recognition are based on dynamic programming (DP) principles (Bellman, 1957). DP is often the key to efficient searches for the optimum path through a graph structure, when paths are evaluated in terms of an accumulation of scores along a path. The Viterbi algorithm (Forney, 1973) is an application of DP, and the forward-backward algorithm (Jelinek, 1976) is very closely related. Three speech recognition problems usually solved by DP are those of *unknown timescales, unknown word sequence* and *unknown word boundary position*. Our first example is a simple whole-word speech recognizer.

Consider a simple *isolated word* discrimination system with one word model per vocabulary word. Each word model consists of a sequence of *states*, each state corresponding to a position along the word. Associated with each state is information (the *output distribution*) about the range of acoustic data (spectrum shapes, etc.) to be expected at that point in the word. Most modern speech recognition systems use word models composed of shared *sub-word models* (see section 1.5), (Poritz, 1988).

When given an unknown sound pattern (a sequence of *frames* of spectrum measurements) we shall decide which word of the vocabulary has been said by picking the word model which fits best.

Different utterances of the same word can have very different timescales: both the overall duration and the details of timing can vary greatly. The degree of fit is usually in two parts: the fit to the spectrum and the fit to the timescale. To keep our example simple, we assume that all we know (or want to use) about the timescales of words is that states are used in strict sequence, each one being used one or more times before moving on to the next one. There are many more elaborate schemes (section 1.5), most of which penalize timescale distortion. We shall also assume that best means minimum sum of individual degree-of-fit numbers, which might be distances, or strain energy, or negative log probabilities.

If we knew how to align the states of the model with the frames of the unknown pattern we could score the model (and hence the word hypothesis) by combining the spectrum fit scores. We define the model score as the result of choosing the *best* alignment. We find that score (and the alignment if we want it) using a DP algorithm, as follows: we introduce an optimal partial score, F, where $F_{i,t}$ is the score for optimally aligning the first i states of the model to the first t frames of the input pattern. We are interested in $F_{N,T}$, the score for optimally aligning all N states of the model to all T frames of the input pattern.

For our simple example F can be computed from the DP step:

$$F_{i,t} = Min[F_{i,t-1}, F_{i-1,t-1}] + d_{i,t}$$

where $d_{i,t}$ is the degree of fit of the ith state of the word model to the measured spectrum at time t. (If we are going to align state i with frame t we must align frame $t-1$ with state i or with state $i-1$.) $F_{N,T}$ can be computed by starting with $F_{1,1} = d_{i,t}$ and working through to frame T.

Simple *connected word* recognition is done by processing all the word models together, and allowing the scores to propagate from the end of one word to the start of another. In practice, we choose between words that could end at the current input frame, and propagate just the best one. A pair of arrays, indexed by frame number, can keep track of the identity of the best word ending at each input frame, and the best time for it to start (Vintsyuk, 1971). The start time for the current word is propagated with F within the words. There are several alternatives and elaborations, e.g., Ney (1984).

It is possible to operate such a connected word recognizer continuously using *partial trace-back*: when all active optimal partial paths agree about the interpretation of some past stretch of input data then nothing in the future data can change our interpretation of that stretch: we can output that result and recover the associated storage.

In a large-vocabulary system we can save a lot of storage and computation by keeping only the relatively good-scoring hypotheses. This pruning or *beam search* (Lowerre, 1976) can also reduce the delay in the partial trace-back.

The connected-word search method outlined above processes each input frame as it arrives, and considers all word endings at that time. There is another important class of methods, called stack-decoders, in which words which *start* at the same time are processed together (Paul, 1992).

We have considered tasks of finding optimal time alignments and sequences of words. It can also be very useful to find close-scoring alternative sequences (Schwartz & Austin, 1991), which can be analyzed subsequently using sources of knowledge which it is inconvenient to incorporate into the main search: for instance alternative acoustic scoring methods or application-specific systems.

Most real-time large-vocabulary systems rely for their speed on a *multi-resolution* search: an initial *fast match*, using a relatively crude set of models, eliminates many possibilities, and the fine match can then be done with much less work. Sometimes the searches are performed in alternating forward and backward directions, with a combination of scores used for pruning (Austin, Schwartz, et al., 1991). Additional discussion of search in HMM-based systems can be found in section 1.5.

11.7.2   Training/Learning as Optimization

Training is the process by which useful information in training data is incorporated into models or other forms used in recognition. The term *learning* is used for the complete system which performs the training. We normally talk about training hidden Markov models, but many artificial neural networks are defined so they include the training algorithms, so we can refer to the neural network as learning from the data.

Most early artificial intelligence research on automatic learning focussed on problems of learning structure. A classic problem is learning a grammar from example sentences. Learning structure directly is a combinatorial problem, and is very difficult. Among the techniques available are genetic algorithms (Goldberg, 1989) and optimization by simulated annealing (Kirkpatrick, Gelatt, et al., 1983). Most established learning methods used in speech recognition avoid the difficulties by replacing discrete optimization problems with continuous problems. As an example, the rules of a regular grammar can be replaced by a set of probabilities, and the probabilities define a continuous (but bounded) space within which continuous optimization methods can be used. Many types of neural networks can be seen as the result of generalizing discrete, logical systems of rules so that continuous optimization methods can be applied.

In training, we are usually trying to optimize the value of a function E of the training data and of unknown parameters θ, and E is made up of a sum over the training instances $\{x_t\}$: $E = \Sigma_t E_t$, where $E_t = F(x_t, \theta)$. Evaluation of E for a given θ needs a pass over all the training data. An example from HMMs is the probability of the model generating the training data (usually a *very* small number!)

Available methods depend on the type of response surface (form of E as a function of θ) and amount of extra information available, such as derivatives.

One of the simplest cases is when E is quadratic in θ. There are standard methods for finding the optimum θ in a number of evaluations not much more than the dimensionality of θ (Press, Flannery, et al., 1988).

When $E(\theta)$ is smooth and we can also compute the partial derivative of E with respect to the components of θ, $\frac{\partial E}{\partial \theta}$, then there are many *gradient based* methods. In the simplest case (gradient descent or ascent) we adjust θ in proportion to $\frac{\partial E}{\partial \theta}$. Variations of gradient descent, such as momentum smoothing, adaptive step size, conjugate gradients and quasi-Newton methods, are available in the literature, e.g., Press, Flannery, et al. (1988), and many have been applied for training *neural networks* of the multi-layer logistic perceptron type (Rumelhart, Hinton, et al., 1986). The motivation and application of these methods in speech recognition is discussed in section 11.5.

However, the most important methods in use in speech recognition are of the expectation-maximization (E-M) type, which are particularly applicable to maximum likelihood training of stochastic models such as HMMs. The basic idea is not difficult. As an example, consider the problem of constructing the type of word model described in section 11.7.1. Assume we have a crude version of the word model, and wish to improve it. We first align the states of the model to each of several examples of the word using the DP method outlined above, then re-estimate the output distributions associated with each state, using statistics (such as the mean) of the data frames aligned to that state. This cycle can be repeated, but usually converges well in a few iterations. In the Baum-Welch procedure the alignment is a more sophisticated, probabilistic, assignment of frames to states, computed using the forward-backward algorithm, and convergence is provable for the most common forms of model. For details see section 1.5, or e.g., Poritz (1988).

11.7.3 Future Directions

It is difficult to separate progress in search and optimization algorithms from the way that the problem is posed (usually this means the form of the models). Dynamic programming style algorithms rely on a key property of the structure of the models: the pattern of immediate dependencies between random variables must form a singly connected graph. More general (but efficient) search and optimization methods would allow the exploration of models in which, for instance, multiple parallel factors explain the data more naturally and more parsimoniously.

11.8 Chapter References

Aho, A. and Ullman, J. (1978). *Principles of compiler design.* Addison-Wesley, Reading, Massachusetts.

Aikawa, K., Singer, H., Kawahara, H., and Tohkura, Y. (1993). A dynamic cepstrum incorporating time-frequency masking and its application to continuous speech recognition. In *Proceedings of the 1993 International Conference on Acoustics, Speech, and Signal Processing*, volume 2, pages 668–671, Minneapolis, Minnesota. Institute of Electrical and Electronic Engineers.

Alshawi, H., editor (1992). *The Core Language Engine*. MIT Press, Cambridge, Massachusetts.

Alshawi, H. et al. (1994). Overview of the Bell Laboratories automatic speech translator. Bell Laboratories technical memorandum.

Appel, A. W. and Jacobson, G. J. (1988). The world's fastest scrabble program. *Communications of the ACM*, 31(5):572–578.

Appelt, D., Hobbs, J., Bear, J., Israel, D., Kameyama, M., and Tyson, M. (1993). The SRI MUC-5 JV-FASTUS information extraction system. In *Proceedings of the Fifth Message Understanding Conference*, Baltimore, Maryland. Morgan Kaufmann.

ARPA (1994). *Proceedings of the 1994 ARPA Human Language Technology Workshop*, Princeton, New Jersey. Advanced Research Projects Agency, Morgan Kaufmann.

Atal, B. S. and Hanauer, S. L. (1971). Speech analysis and synthesis by linear prediction of the speech wave. *Journal of the Acoustical Society of America*, 50(2):637–655.

Atlas, L. and Fang, J. (1992). Quadratic detectors for general nonlinear analysis of speech. In *Proceedings of the 1992 International Conference on Acoustics, Speech, and Signal Processing*, volume 2, pages 9–12, San Francisco. Institute of Electrical and Electronic Engineers.

Austin, S., Schwartz, R., and Placeway, P. (1991). The forward-backward search algorithm. In *Proceedings of the 1991 International Conference on Acoustics, Speech, and Signal Processing*, volume 1, pages 697–700, Toronto. Institute of Electrical and Electronic Engineers.

Bacchiani, M. and Aikawa, K. (1994). Optimization of time-frequency masking filters using the minimum classification error criterion. In *Proceedings of the 1994 International Conference on Acoustics, Speech, and Signal Processing*, volume 2, pages 197–200, Adelaide, Australia. Institute of Electrical and Electronic Engineers.

Baker, J. K. (1975). Stochastic modeling for automatic speech understanding. In Reddy, D. R., editor, *Speech Recognition*, pages 521–542. Academic Press, New York.

Baker, J. K. (1979). Trainable grammars for speech recognition. In Wolf, J. J. and Klatt, D. H., editors, *Speech communication papers presented at the 97th Meeting of the Acoustical Society of America*, pages 547–550. Acoustical Society of America, MIT Press.

Baum, L. E. (1972). An inequality and associated maximization technique in statistical estimation for probabilistic functions of a Markov process. *Inequalities*, 3:1–8.

Baum, L. E. and Eagon, J. A. (1967). An inequality with applications to statistical estimation for probabilistic functions of a Markov process and to a model for ecology. *Bulletin of the American Medical Society*, 73:360–363.

Baum, L. E., Petrie, T., Soules, G., and Weiss, N. (1970). A maximization technique occurring in the statistical analysis of probabilistic functions of Markov chains. *Annals of Mathematical Statistics*, 41:164–171.

Baum, L. E. and Sell, G. R. (1968). Growth transformations for functions on manifolds. *Pac. J. Math.*, 27:211–227.

Bellman, R. E. (1957). *Dynamic Programming*. Princeton University Press.

Bourlard, H. and Kamp, Y. (1988). Auto-association by multilayer perceptrons and singular value decomposition. *Biological Cybernetics*, 59:291–294.

Bourlard, H. and Morgan, N. (1993). *Connectionist Speech Recognition—A Hybrid Approach*. Kluwer Academic.

Bridle, J. (1990). Alpha-nets: A recurrent neural network architecture with a hidden Markov model interpretation. *Speech Communication*, 9:83–92.

Brown, P., Cocke, J., Pietra, S. D., Pietra, V. J. D., Jelinek, F., Lafferty, J. D., Mercer, R. L., and Roossin, P. S. (1990). A statistical approach to machine translation. *Computational Linguistics*, 16(2):79–85.

Chen, M. Y., Kundu, A., and Zhou, J. (1994). Off-line handwritten word recognition using a hidden Markov model type stochastic network. *IEEE Transactions on Pattern Analysis and Machine Intelligence*, 16(5):481–496.

Chomsky, N. (1957). *Syntactic structures*. Mouton, The Hague.

Chomsky, N. and Halle, M. (1968). *The Sound Pattern of English*. Harper and Row.

Church, K. W. and Hanks, P. (1990). Word association norms, mutual information and lexicography. *Computational Linguistics*, 16(1):22–29.

Cohen, J. R. (1989). Application of an auditory model to speech recognition. *Journal of the Acoustical Society of America*, 85(6):2623–2629.

Cole, R. A., Fanty, M., Gopalakrishnan, M., and Janssen, R. D. T. (1991). Speaker-independent name retrieval from spellings using a database of 50,000 names. In *Proceedings of the 1991 International Conference on Acoustics, Speech, and Signal Processing*, volume 1, pages 325–328, Toronto. Institute of Electrical and Electronic Engineers.

Davis, S. B. and Mermelstein, P. (1980). Comparison of parametric representations for monosyllabic word recognition in continuously spoken sentences. *IEEE Transactions on Acoustics, Speech and Signal Processing*, ASSP-28:357–366.

Duda, R. O. and Hart, P. E. (1973). *Pattern Recognition and Scene Analysis.* John Wiley, New York.

Earley, J. C. (1970). An efficient context-free parsing algorithm. *Communications of the ACM*, 13(2):94–102.

Elman, J. (1988). Finding structure in time. Technical Report CRL 8903, University of California, San Diego, Center for Research in Language, University of California, San Diego.

Fanty, M. (1985). Context free parsing in connectionist networks. Technical Report TR174, University of Rochester, Computer Science Department, University of Rochester, New York.

Forney, Jr., G. D. (1973). The viterbi algorithm. *Proceedings of the IEEE*, 61:266–278.

Fu, K. S. (1974). *Syntactic methods in pattern recognition.* Academic Press, New York.

Goldberg, D. E. (1989). *Genetic algorithms in search, optimization and machine learning.* Addison-Wesley.

Hermansky, H. (1990). Perceptual linear predictive (PLP) analysis for speech. *Journal of the Acoustical Society of America*, 87(4):1738–1752.

Hermansky, H., Morgan, N., and Hirsch, H. G. (1993). Recognition of speech in additive and convolutional noise based on RASTA spectral processing. In *Proceedings of the 1993 International Conference on Acoustics, Speech, and Signal Processing*, volume 2, pages 83–86, Minneapolis, Minnesota. Institute of Electrical and Electronic Engineers.

Hon, H.-W., Yuan, B., Chow, Y.-L., Narayan, S., and Lee, K.-F. (1994). Towards large vocabulary Mandarin Chinese speech recognition. In *Proceedings of the 1994 International Conference on Acoustics, Speech, and Signal Processing*, volume 1, pages 545–548, Adelaide, Australia. Institute of Electrical and Electronic Engineers.

Hopcroft, J. and Ullman, J. (1979). *Introduction to automata theory, languages, and computation.* Addison-Wesley.

Hunt, M. J., Richardson, S. M., Bateman, D. C., and Piau, A. (1991). An investigation of PLP and IMELDA acoustic representations and of their potential for combination. In *Proceedings of the 1991 International Conference on Acoustics, Speech, and Signal Processing*, volume 2, pages 881–884, Toronto. Institute of Electrical and Electronic Engineers.

ICASSP (1991). *Proceedings of the 1991 International Conference on Acoustics, Speech, and Signal Processing*, Toronto. Institute of Electrical and Electronic Engineers.

ICASSP (1992). *Proceedings of the 1992 International Conference on Acoustics, Speech, and Signal Processing*, San Francisco. Institute of Electrical and Electronic Engineers.

ICASSP (1993). *Proceedings of the 1993 International Conference on Acoustics, Speech, and Signal Processing*, Minneapolis, Minnesota. Institute of Electrical and Electronic Engineers.

ICASSP (1994). *Proceedings of the 1994 International Conference on Acoustics, Speech, and Signal Processing*, Adelaide, Australia. Institute of Electrical and Electronic Engineers.

ICSLP (1994). *Proceedings of the 1994 International Conference on Spoken Language Processing*, Yokohama, Japan.

IJCNN (1990). *Proceedings of the 1990 International Joint Conference on Neural Networks*, Washington, DC.

Impedovo, S., editor (1994). *Fundamentals in Handwriting Recognition*. NATO-Advanced Study Institute Series F. Springer-Verlag.

Impedovo, S., Ottaviano, L., and Occhinegro, S. (1991). Optical Character Recognition—A Survey. *International Journal on Pattern Recognition and Artificial Intelligence*, 5(1-2):1–24.

Impedovo, S. and Simon, J. C., editors (1992). *From Pixels to Features III*. Elsevier Science, Amsterdam.

Jacobs, J., v. Stechow, A., Sternefeld, W., and Vennemann, T., editors (1993). *Syntax, An International Handbook of Contemporary Research*. de Gruyter, Berlin, New York.

Jain, A. (1992). Generalization performance in PARSEC - a structured connectionist parsing architecture. In Touretzky, D. S., editor, *Advances in Neural Information Processing Systems 4*, pages 209–216. Morgan Kaufmann.

Jelinek, F. (1976). Continuous speech recognition by statistical methods. *Proceedings of the IEEE*, 64:532–556.

Jelinek, F. (1990). Computation of the probability of initial substring generation by stochastic context free grammars. Technical report, IBM T. J. Watson Research Center, Yorktown Heights, New York.

Johnson, C. D. (1972). *Formal Aspects of Phonological Description*. Mouton, The Hague.

Jordan, M. (1989). Serial order: A parallel distributed processing approach. In Elman, J. L. and Rumelhart, D. E., editors, *Advances in Connectionist Theory: Speech*. Hillsade.

Joshi, A. K., Vijay-Shanker, K., and Weir, D. J. (1991). The convergence of mildly context-sensitive grammatical formalisms. In Sells, P., Shieber, S., and Wasow, T., editors, *Foundational Issues in Natural Language Processing*. MIT Press.

Juang, B. H. (1992). Discriminative learning for minimum error classification. *IEEE Transactions on Signal Processing*, 40(12).

Juang, B. H. et al. (1987). On the use of bandpass littering in speech recognition. *IEEE Transactions on Acoustics, Speech and Signal Processing*, ASSP-35:947–954.

Juang, B. H. and Rabiner, L. R. (1985). Mixture autoregressive hidden Markov models for speech signals. *IEEE Transactions on Acoustics, Speech, and Signal Processing*, 33(6):1404–1413.

Kadambe, S. and Hieronymus, J. L. (1994). Spontaneous speech language identification with a knowledge of linguistics. In *Proceedings of the 1994 International Conference on Spoken Language Processing*, volume 4, pages 1879–1882, Yokohama, Japan.

Kambhatla, N. and Leen, T. K. (1994). Fast non-linear dimension reduction. In Cowan, J. D. et al., editors, *Advances in Neural Information Processing Systems VI*, pages 152–159. Morgan Kaufmann.

Kaplan, R. and Kay, M. (1981). Phonological rules and finite-state transducers. In *Proceedings of the Winter meeting of the Linguistic Society of America*, New York.

Kaplan, R. M. and Kay, M. (1994). Regular models of phonological rule systems. *Computational Linguistics*, 20(3):331–378. written in 1980.

Karttunen, L., Kaplan, R. M., and Zaenen, A. (1992). Two-level morphology with composition. In *Proceedings of the 14th International Conference on Computational Linguistics*, volume 1, pages 141–148, Nantes, France. ACL.

Kasami, T. (1965). An efficient recognition and syntax algorithm for context-free languages. Technical Report AF-CRL-65-758, Air Force Cambridge Research Laboratory, Bedford, MA.

Kasper, R., Kiefer, B., Netter, K., and Vijay-Shanker, K. (1995). Compilation of HPSG to TAG. In *Proceeds of the 33rd Annual Meeting of the Association for Computational Linguistics*, pages 92–99, Cambridge, Massachusetts.

Kirkpatrick, S., Gelatt, Jr., C. D., and Vecchi, M. P. (1983). Optimisation by simulated annealing. *Science*, 220(4598):671–680.

Kohonen, T. (1988). The 'neural' phonetic typewriter. *IEEE Computer*, pages 11–22.

Koskenniemi, K. (1983). *Two-Level Morphology: a General Computational Model for Word-Form Recognition and Production*. PhD thesis, University of Helsinki. Publications of the Department of General Linguistics, University of Helsinki, No. 11. Helsinki.

Koskenniemi, K. (1990). Finite-state parsing and disambiguation. In Karlgren, H., editor, *Proceedings of the 13th International Conference on Computational Linguistics*, volume 2, pages 229–232, Helsinki. ACL.

Kuhn, G., Watrous, R. L., and Ladendorf, D. (1990). Connected recognition with a recurrent network. *Speech Communication*, 9(1):41–48.

Lambek, J. (1958). The mathematics of sentence structure. *American Mathematical Monthly*, 65:154–170.

Lang, B. (1974). Deterministic techniques for efficient non-deterministic parsers. In Loeckx, J., editor, *Proceedings of the 2nd Colloquium on Automata, Languages and Programming*, pages 255–269, Saarbrücken, Germany. Springer-Verlag.

Lang, K. J., Waibel, A. H., and Hinton, G. E. (1990). A time-delay neural network architecture for isolated word recognition. *Neural Networks*, 3(1):23–43.

le Cun, Y., Boser, B., Denker, J. S., Henderson, D., Howard, R. E., Hubbard, W., and Jackel, L. D. (1990). Handwritten digit recognition with a back-propagation network. In Touretzky, D. S., editor, *Advances in Neural Information Processing Systems 2*, pages 396–404. Morgan Kaufmann.

Leermakers, R. (1993). *The Functional Treatment of Parsing*. Kluwer.

Levin, E. (1993). Hidden control neural architecture modeling of nonlinear time varying systems and its applications. *IEEE Transactions on Neural Networks*, 4(1):109–116.

Levinson, S. E. et al. (1979). Interactive clustering techniques for selecting speaker independent reference templates for isolated word recognition. *IEEE Transactions on Acoustics, Speech and Signal Processing*, ASSP-27:134–141.

Lippmann, R. P. (1989). Review of neural networks for speech recognition. *Neural Computation*, 1(1):1–38.

Liu, Y. D., Sun, G. Z., Chen, H. H., Lee, Y. C., and Giles, C. L. (1990). Grammatical inference and neural network state machines. In *Proceedings of the 1990 International Joint Conference on Neural Networks*, pages 285–288, Washington, DC.

Lloyd, S. P. (1982). Least squares quantization in PCM. *IEEE Transactions on Information Theory*, IT-28:129–136.

Lowerre, B. (1976). *The HARPY speech recognition system.* PhD thesis, Carnegie-Mellon University Dept of Computer Science.

Lubensky, D. M., Asadi, A. O., and Naik, J. M. (1994). Connected digit recognition using connectionist probability estimators and mixture-gaussian densities. In *Proceedings of the 1994 International Conference on Spoken Language Processing*, volume 1, pages 295–298, Yokohama, Japan.

Lucchesi, C. L. and Kowaltowski, T. (1993). Applications of finite automata representing large vocabularies. *Software-Practice and Experience*, 23(1):15–30.

Makhoul, J., Roucos, S., and Gish, H. (1985). Vector quantization in speech coding. *Proceedings of the IEEE*, 73(11):1551–1588.

Manning, C. D. (1993). Automatic acquisition of a large subcategorization dictionary from corpora. In *Proceedings of the 31st Annual Meeting of the Association for Computational Linguistics*, pages 235–242, Ohio State University. Association for Computational Linguistics.

Maragos, P., Kaiser, J., and Quatieri, T. (1992). On separating amplitude from frequency modulations using energy operators. In *Proceedings of the 1992 International Conference on Acoustics, Speech, and Signal Processing*, volume 2, pages 1–4, San Francisco. Institute of Electrical and Electronic Engineers.

Markov, A. A. (1913). An example of statistical investigation in the text of 'Eugene Onyegin' illustrating coupling of 'tests' in chains. *Proceedings of the Academy of Science, St. Petersburg*, 7:153–162.

Maxwell, John T., I. and Kaplan, R. M. (1993). The interface between phrasal and functional constraints. *Computational Linguistics*, 19(4):571–590.

Meisel, W. S. (1972). *Computer Oriented Approaches to Pattern Recognition.* Academic Press, New York.

Minsky, M. and Papert, S. (1969). *Perceptrons.* MIT Press, Cambridge, Massachusetts.

Morgan, D. P. and Scofield, C. L. (1991). *Neural Networks and Speech Processing.* Kluwer Academic.

Naik, J. M. and Lubensky, D. M. (1994). A hybrid HMM-MLP speaker verification algorithm for telephonespeech. In *Proceedings of the 1994 International Conference on Acoustics, Speech, and Signal Processing*, volume 1, pages 153–156, Adelaide, Australia. Institute of Electrical and Electronic Engineers.

Nedderhoff, M.-J. (1994). An optimal tabular parsing algorithm. In *Proceedings of the 32nd Annual Meeting of the Association for Computational Linguistics*, Las Cruces, New Mexico. Association for Computational Linguistics.

Ney, H. (1984). The use of a one-stage dynamic programming algorithm for connected word recognition. *IEEE Transactions on Acoustics, Speech and Signal Processing*, 32:263–271.

Nilsson, N. J. (1971). *Problem-Solving Methods in Artificial Intelligence*. McGraw-Hill, New York.

Oja, E. (1991). Data compression, feature extraction, and auto-association in feedforward neural networks. In *Artificial Neural Networks*, pages 737–745. Elsevier Science, Amsterdam.

Patrick, E. A. (1972). *Fundamentals of Pattern Recognition*. Prentice-Hall, Englewood Cliffs, New Jersey.

Paul, D. B. (1992). An efficient A* stack decoder algorithm for continuous speech recognition with a stochastic language model. In *Proceedings of the 1992 International Conference on Acoustics, Speech, and Signal Processing*, volume 1, pages 25–28, San Francisco. Institute of Electrical and Electronic Engineers.

Pavlidis, T. and Mori, S. (1992). Special issue on optical character recognition. *Proceedings of the IEEE*, 80(7).

Pentus, M. (1993). Lambek grammars are context-free. In *Proceedings of the Eighth Annual IEEE Symposium on Logic and Computation Science*, pages 429–433, Montreal, Canada. IEEE Computer Society Press.

Pereira, F., Rebecca, C. N., and Wright, N. (1991). Finite state approximation of phrase structure grammars. In *Proceedings of the 29th Annual Meeting of the Association for Computational Linguistics*, Berkeley, California. Association for Computational Linguistics.

Pereira, F., Riley, M., and Sproat, R. (1994). Weighted rational transductions and their applications to human language processing. In *Proceedings of the Human Language Technology Workshop*, Plainsboro, New Jersey. Morgan Kaufmann.

Pieraccini, R., Levin, E., and Vidal, E. (1993). Learning how to understanding language. In *Eurospeech '93, Proceedings of the Third European Conference on Speech Communication and Technology*, volume 2, pages 1407–1414, Berlin. European Speech Communication Association. Keynote address.

Poritz, A. B. (1988). Hidden Markov models: a guided tour. In *Proceedings of the 1988 International Conference on Acoustics, Speech, and Signal Processing*, volume 1, pages 7–13, New York. Institute of Electrical and Electronic Engineers.

Press, W. H., Flannery, B. P., Teukolsky, S. A., and Vetterling, W. T. (1988). *Numerical Recipes in C: the art of scientific computing*. Cambridge University Press.

Pustejovsky, J. (1992). The acquisition of lexical semantic knowledge from large corpora. In *Proceedings of the Fifth DARPA Speech and Natural Language Workshop*. Morgan Kaufmann.

Rabiner, L. R. and Juang, B.-H. (1993). *Fundamentals of Speech Recognition*. Prentice-Hall, Englewood Cliffs, New Jersey.

Rabiner, L. R. and Schafer, R. W. (1978). *Digital Processing of Speech Signals*. Signal Processing. Prentice-Hall, Englewood Cliffs, New Jersey.

Renals, S., Morgan, N., Bourlard, H., Cohen, M., and Franco, H. (1994). Connectionist probability estimators in HMM speech recognition. *IEEE Transactions on Speech and Audio Processing*, 12(1):161–174.

Robinson, T. and Fallside, F. (1991). A recurrent error propagation network speech recognition system. *Computer Speech and Language*, 5:259–274.

Roche, E. (1994). Two parsing algorithms by means of finite-state transducers. In *Proceedings of the 15th International Conference on Computational Linguistics*, Kyoto, Japan.

Rumelhart, D. E., Hinton, G. E., and Williams, R. J. (1986). Learning internal representations by error propagation. In Rumelhart, D. E. and McClelland, J. L., editors, *Parallel Distributed Processing: Explorations in the Microstucture of Cognition*. MIT Press.

Samuelsson, C. (1994). *Fast natural-language parsing using explanation-based learning*. PhD thesis, Royal Institute of Technology, Akademitryck, Edsbruk, Sweden.

Schabes, Y. and Joshi, A. K. (1988). An Earley-type parsing algorithm for tree-adjoining grammars. In *Proceedings of the 26th Annual Meeting of the Association for Computational Linguistics*, SUNY, Buffalo, New York. Association for Computational Linguistics.

Schabes, Y. and Vijayshanker, K. (1990). Deterministic left to right parsing of tree-adjoining languages. In *Proceedings of the 28th Annual Meeting of the Association for Computational Linguistics*, pages 276–283, Pittsburgh, Pennsylvania. Association for Computational Linguistics.

Schenkel, M., Guyon, I., and Henderson, D. (1994). On-line cursive script recognition using neural networks and hidden Markov models. In *Proceedings of the 1994 International Conference on Acoustics, Speech, and Signal Processing*, volume 2, pages 637–640, Adelaide, Australia. Institute of Electrical and Electronic Engineers.

Schenkel, M., Guyon, I., and Henderson, D. (1995). On-line cursive script recognition using time delay neural networks and hidden Markov models. *Machine Vision and Applications*. Special issue on Cursive Script Recognition.

Schwartz, R. and Austin, S. (1991). A comparison of several approximate algorithms for finding multiple (n-best) sentence hypotheses. In *Proceedings of the 1991 International Conference on Acoustics, Speech, and Signal Processing*, volume 1, pages 701–704, Toronto. Institute of Electrical and Electronic Engineers.

Shieber, S. M. (1988). *An Introduction to Unification-based Approaches to Grammar*. CSLI, Stanford.

Shieber, S. M., Schabes, Y., and Pereira, F. C. N. (1994). Principles and implementation of deductive parsing. *Journal of Logic Programming*. In press.

Sikkel, K. (1994). *Parsing Schemata*. Springer-Verlag.

Steeneken, J. and Van Leeuwen, D. (1995). Multi-lingual assessment of speaker independent large vocabulary speech-recognition systems: the SQALE project (speech recognition quality assessment for language engineering). In *Eurospeech '95, Proceedings of the Fourth European Conference on Speech Communication and Technology*, Madrid, Spain.

Sun, G. Z., Chen, H. H., Giles, C. L., Lee, Y. C., and Chen, D. (1990). Connectionist pushdown automata that learn context-free grammars. In *Proceedings of the 1990 International Joint Conference on Neural Networks*, pages 577–580, Washington, DC.

Tappert, C. C., Suen, C. Y., and Wakahara, T. (1990). The state of the art in on-line handwriting recognition. *IEEE Transactions on Pattern Analysis and Machine Intelligence*, 12(8):787–808.

Tomita, M. (1987). An efficient augmented context-free parsing algorithm. *Computational Linguistics*, 13(1):31–46.

Tomita, M., editor (1991). *Current Issues in Parsing Technology*. Kluwer Academic Press, Dordrecht.

Touretzky, D. S., editor (1992). *Advances in Neural Information Processing Systems 4*. Morgan Kaufmann.

Vijay-Shanker, K. and Weir, D. J. (1993). Parsing some constrained grammar formalisms. *Computational Linguistics*, 19(4):591–636.

Vintsyuk, T. K. (1971). Element-wise recognition of continuous speech consisting of words from a specified vocabulary. *Cybernetics (Kibernetica)*, pages 133–143.

Viterbi, A. J. (1967). Error bounds for convolutional codes and an asymptotically optimal decoding algorithm. *IEEE Transactions on Information Theory*, IT-13:260–269.

Voutilainen, A. and Tapanainen, P. (1993). Ambiguity resolution in a reductionist parser. In *Proceedings of the Sixth Conference of the European Chapter of the Association for Computational Linguistics*, pages 394–403, Utrecht University, The Netherlands. European Chapter of the Association for Computational Linguistics.

Waibel, A., Jain, A., McNair, A., Tebelskis, J., Osterholtz, L., Saito, H., Schmidbauer, O., Sloboda, T., and Woszczyna, M. (1992). JANUS: Speech-to-speech translation using connectionist and non-connectionist techniques. In Touretzky, D. S., editor, *Advances in Neural Information Processing Systems 4*, pages 183–190. Morgan Kaufmann.

Weigend, A. S. and Gershenfeld, N. A., editors (1994). *Time Series Prediction: Forecasting the Future and Understanding the Past.* Santa Fe. Addison-Wesley.

Wilfong, G. (1995). On-line recognition of handwritten symbols. *IEEE Transactions on Pattern Analysis and Machine Intelligence.* In press.

Wilpon, J. G. (1994). Applications of voice processing technology in telecommunications. In Roe, D. B. and Wilpon, J. G., editors, *Voice Communication between Humans and Machines*, pages 280–310. National Academy Press, Washington, DC.

Younger, D. H. (1967). Recognition and parsing of context-free languages in time n^3. *Information and Control*, 10(2):189–208.

Chapter 12

Language Resources

12.1 Overview

John J. Godfrey[a] & Antonio Zampolli[b]

[a] Texas Instruments Speech Research, Dallas, Texas, USA
[b] Istituto di Linguistica Computazionale, CNR, Pisa, Italy

The term *linguistic resources* refers to (usually large) sets of language data and descriptions in machine readable form, to be used in building, improving, or evaluating natural language (NL) and speech algorithms or systems. Examples of linguistic resources are written and spoken corpora, lexical databases, grammars, and terminologies, although the term may be extended to include basic software tools for the preparation, collection, management, or use of other resources. This chapter deals mainly with corpora, lexicons, and terminologies.

An increasing awareness of the potential economic and social impact of natural language and speech systems has attracted attention, and some support, from national and international funding authorities. Their interest, naturally, is in technology and systems that work, that make economic sense, and that deal with real language uses (whether scientifically *interesting* or not).

This interest has been reinforced by the success promised in meeting such goals, by systems based on statistical modeling techniques such as hidden Markov models (HMM) and neural networks (NN), which learn by example, typically from very large data sets organized in terms of many variables with many possible values. A key technical factor in the demand for lexicons and corpora, in fact, is the enormous appetites of these techniques for structured data. Both in speech and in natural language, the relatively common occurrence of relatively uncommon events (triphones, vocabulary items), and the disruptive effect of even minor unmodeled events (channel or microphone differences, new vocabulary items, etc.) means that, to provide enough examples for statistical methods to work, the corpora must be numerous (at the very least one per domain or application), often massive, and consequently expensive.

The fact that we still lack adequate linguistic resources for the majority of our languages can be attributed to:

- The tendency, predominant in the '70s and the first half of the '80s, to test linguistic hypotheses with small amounts of (allegedly) critical data, rather than to study extensively the variety of linguistic phenomena occurring in communicative contexts;

- The high cost of creating linguistic resources.

These high costs require broadly-based cooperative efforts of companies, research institutions and sponsors, so as to avoid duplications and to widely share the burden involved. This obviously requires that linguistic resources not be restricted to one specific system, but that they be *reused*—by many users (*shareable* or *public* resources), or for more than one purpose (*multifunctional* resources). There are many examples of the former, such as the TIMIT corpus, TI-DIGITS, Treebank, the Celex Lexical Database, the Italian machine dictionary, and a few of the latter, such as SWITCHBOARD (used for speaker identification, topic detection, speech recognition, acoustic phonetic studies), the GENELEX dictionaries and the MLCC corpus.

A controversial problem, especially with natural language materials, is whether in order to be reusable and multifunctional, linguistic resources must also be *theory-neutral*: the requirements for linguistic information of a given natural language or speech system may depend not only on the intended applications, but also on the specific linguistic theories on which the system's linguistic components are explicitly or implicitly based.

At the scientific and technical level, the solution is to attempt a consensus among different theoretical perspectives and systems design approaches. Where successful, this permits the adoption of common specifications and *de facto* standards in creating linguistic resources and ensures their harmonization at the international and multilingual level. The Text Encoding Initiative, jointly sponsored by ACH (Association for Computing in the Humanities), ALLC (Association of Literary and Linguistic Computing), and ACL (Association for Computational Linguistics), has produced a set of guidelines for encoding texts. The project LRE-EAGLES (Expert Advisory Group on Linguistic Engineering Standards), recently launched by the CEC DGXIII, is pooling together the European efforts of both academic and industrial actors towards the creation of *de facto* consensual standards for corpora, lexicons, speech data, and for evaluation and formalisms.

At the organizational level, we can recognize, with regard to the present state of the art, the need for three major action lines:

(a) to promote the reuse of existing (partial) linguistic resources. This can imply various tasks, from reformatting or converting existing linguistic resources to common standards, to augmenting them to comply with common minimal specifications, to establishing appropriate agreements for putting some resources in the public domain;

(b) to promote the development of new linguistic resources for those languages and domains where they do not exist yet, or only exist in a prototype stage, or exist but cannot be made available to the interested users; and

(c) to create cooperative infrastructure to collect, maintain, and disseminate linguistic resources on behalf of the research and development community.

The most appropriate way to organize these activities is still under discussion in various countries.

In Europe, the CEC DG-XIII LRE-RELATOR project, begun in 1995, aims at creating an experimental organization for the (c) tasks. The LE-MLAP (Language Engineering Multilingual Action Plan) has launched projects for activities of type (a) and (b) in the field of written and spoken corpora, lexicons, and terminology.

In Japan, plans for a central organization for speech and text databases have been under discussion. The EDR (Electronic Dictionary Research) Institute is, a the time of the writing of this volume, about to conclude the creation of large monolingual Japanese and English lexicons, together with bilingual links, a large *concept* dictionary and associated text corpora.

The approach taken in the U.S. was to create the Linguistic Data Consortium (LDC); although started with a government grant, it depends on membership dues and data collection contracts for its continued operations. LDC's principal mission is exactly (c) above, but in fulfilling the needs of its worldwide membership it addresses (a) and (b) as well. In its first three years it has released over 275 CD-ROMs of data for public use. Examples of its activities include:

- Publication of existing corpora previously available only to government contractors;

- Collection of speech and text data in languages of interest to members (English, Mandarin, Japanese, Spanish, French, and others);

- Creation of Common Lexical Databases for American English and other languages, with free commercial licenses for members;

- Acting as a clearinghouse for intellectual property rights to existing linguistic resources;

- Campaigning for the release of government-owned resources to researchers.

The need for ensuring international cooperation in the creation and dissemination of linguistic resources seems to us a direct consequence of their infrastructural role, precompetitive nature, and multilingual dimension. The CEC is taking a leading role for the coordination, among the EU countries and EU languages. COCOSDA (for speech) and LIRIC (for NL) are spontaneous initiatives of the R&D international community which aim at ensuring world-wide coordination. Inside the framework of EAGLES and RELATOR, the possibility of defining a common policy for cooperation between the major sponsoring agencies (CEC, NSF, ARPA, MITI) is being explored.

12.2   Written Language Corpora

Eva Ejerhed[a] & Ken Church[b]

[a] University of Umea, Sweden
[b] AT&T Bell Labs, Murray Hill, New Jersey, USA

12.2.1   Review of the State of the Art in Written Language Corpora

Written Language Corpora, collections of text in electronic form, are being collected for research and commercial applications in natural language processing (NLP). Written Language Corpora have been used to improve spelling correctors, hyphenation routines and grammar checkers, which are being integrated into commercial word-processing packages. Lexicographers have used corpora to study word use and to associate uses with meanings. Statistical methods have been used to find interesting associations among words (collocations). Language teachers are now using on-line corpora in the classroom to help learners distinguish central and typical uses of words from mannered, poetic, and erroneous uses. Terminologists are using corpora to build glossaries to assure consistent and correct translations of difficult terms such as *dialogue box*, which is translated as *finestra 'window'* in Italian and as *boite 'box'* in French. Eurolang is currently integrating glossary tools, translation memories of recurrent expressions, and more traditional machine translation systems into Microsoft's Word-for-Windows and other popular word-processing applications.

The general belief is that there is a significant commercial market for multilingual text processing software, especially in a multilingual setting such as the European Community. Researchers in Information Retrieval and Computational Linguistics are using corpora to evaluate the performance of their systems. Numerous examples can be found in the proceedings of recent conferences like the Message Understanding Conferences (DARPA, 1991b; ARPA, 1993b), and the Speech and Natural Language Workshops sponsored by the Defense Advanced Research Projects Agency (DARPA) (DARPA, 1992a; ARPA, 1993a; ARPA, 1994).

Written language corpora provide a spectrum of resources for language processing, ranging from the *raw material* of the corpora themselves to *finished components* like computational grammars and lexicons. Between these two extremes are intermediate resources like annotated corpora (also called tagged corpora in which words are tagged with part of speech tags and other information), tree banks (in which sentences are analyzed syntactically), part-of-speech taggers, partial parsers of various kinds, lexical materials such as specialized word lists and listings of the constructional properties of verbs.

The corpus-based approach has produced significant improvements in part-of-speech tagging. Francis and Kucera (1982) enabled research in the U.S. by tagging the Brown Corpus and making it available to the research community. Similar efforts were underway within the International Computer Archive of Modern English (ICAME) community in the UK and Scandinavia around the same time. A number of researchers developed and tested the statistical *n-gram* methods that ultimately became the method of choice. These methods used corpora to train parameters and evaluate performance. The results were replicated in a number of different laboratories. Advocates of alternative methods were challenged to match the improvements in performance that had been achieved by *n-gram* methods. Many did, often by using corpus-based empirical approaches to develop and test their solutions, if not to train the parameters explicitly. More and more data collection efforts were initiated as the community began to appreciate the value of the tagged Brown Corpus.

Of course, corpus analysis is not new. There has been a long empirical tradition within descriptive linguistics. Linguists have been counting words and studying concordances for hundreds of years. There have been corpora, libraries and archives for as long as there has been written language. Text has been stored in electronic form for as long as there have been computers. Many of the analysis techniques are based on Information Theory, which predates computers.

So why so much interest, and why now? The role of computers in society has changed radically in recent years. We used to be embarrassed that we were using a million dollar computer to emulate an ordinary typewriter. Computers were so expensive that applications were supposed to target exclusive and unusual needs. Users were often expected to write their own programs. It was hard to imagine a computer without a compiler. Apple Computer Inc. was one of the first to realize that computers were becoming so cheap that users could no longer afford to customize their own special-purpose applications. Apple took a radical step and began to sell a computer without a compiler or a development environment, abandoning the traditional user-base and targeting the general public by developing user-friendly human-machine interfaces that anyone could use. The emphasis moved to so-called *killer* applications like word-processing that everyone just had to have. Many PCs now have email, fax and a modem. The emphasis on human-machine interfaces is now giving way to the information *super-highway* cliché. Computers are rapidly becoming a vehicle for communicating with other people, not very different from a telephone.

"Phones marry computers: new killer applications arrive."
—cover of *Byte* magazine, July 1994

Now that so many people are using computers to communicate with one another, vast quantities of text are becoming available in electronic form, ranging from published documents (e.g., electronic dictionaries, encyclopedias, libraries and archives for information retrieval services), to private databases (e.g., marketing information, legal records, medical histories), to personal email and faxes. Just ten years ago, the one-million word Brown Corpus (Francis & Kucera, 1982) was considered large. Today, many laboratories have hundreds of millions or even billions of words. These collections are becoming widely available, thanks to data collection efforts such as the following: Association for Computational Linguistics' Data Collection Initiative (ACL/DCI), the Linguistic Data Consortium (LDC),[†] the Consortium for Lexical Research (CLR),[†] the Japanese Electronic Dictionary Research (EDR), the European Corpus Initiative (ECI),[†] International Computer Archive of Modern English (ICAME),[†] the British National Corpus (BNC),[†] the French corpus Frantext of Institut National de la Langue Française (INaLF-CNRS),[†] the German Institut für deutsche Sprache (IDS),[†] the Dutch Instituut voor Nederlandse Lexicologie (INL),[†] the Danish Dansk Korpus (DK),[†] the Italian Istituto di Linguistica Computazionale (ILC-CNR),[†] the Spanish corpora surveyed by Instituto Cervantes,[†] the Norwegian corpora of Norsk Tekstarkiv,[†] the Swedish Stockholm-Umea Corpus (SUC)[†] and Swedish corpora at Sprakdata,[†] and Finnish corpora of the University of Helsinki[†] Language Corpus Server. This list does not claim to be an exhaustive listing of data collections or data collection efforts, but an illustration of their breadth. Data collections exist for many languages in addition to these, and new data collection efforts are being initiated. There are also standardization efforts for the encoding and exchange of corpora such as the Text Encoding Initiative (TEI).[†]

12.2.2　Identification of Significant Gaps in Knowledge and/c Limitations of Current Technology

The renaissance of interest in corpus-based statistical methods has rekindled old controversies—rationalist vs. empiricist philosophies, theory-driven vs. data-driven methodologies, symbolic vs. statistical techniques. The field will ultimately adopt an inclusive strategy that combines the strengths of as many of these positions as possible.

In the long term, the field is expected to produce significant scientific insights into language. These insights would hopefully be accompanied by corresponding accomplishments in language engineering: better parsers, information retrieval and extraction engines, word processing interfaces with robust grammar/style checking, etc. Parsing technology is currently too fragile, especially on unrestricted text. Text extraction systems ought to determine who did what to whom, but it can be difficult to simply extract names, dates, places, etc. Most information retrieval systems still treat text as merely a bag of words with little or no linguistic structure. There have been numerous attempts to make use of richer linguistic structures such as phrases, predicate argument relations, and even morphology, but, thus far, most of these attempts have not resulted in significant improvements in retrieval performance.

　　Current natural language processing systems lack lexical and grammatical

---

[†]See section 12.6.1 for contact addresses.

resources with sufficient coverage for unrestricted text. Consider the following famous pair of utterances:

Time flies like an arrow.
Fruit flies like a banana.

It would be useful for many applications to know that *fruit flies* is a phrase and *time flies* is not. Most systems currently do not have access to this kind of information. Parsers currently operate at the level of parts of speech, without looking at the words. Ultimately, parsers and other natural language applications will have to make greater use of collocational constraints and other constraints on words. The grammar/lexicon will have to be very large, at least as large as an 1800-page book (Quirk, Greenbaum, et al., 1985). The task may require a monumental effort like Murray's Oxford English Dictionary project.

Corpus-based methods may help speed up the lexical acquisition process by refining huge masses of corpus evidence into more manageable piles of high-grade ore. In Grolier's encyclopedia (Grolier, 1991), for example, there are 21 instances of *fruit fly* and *fruit flies*, and not one instance of *time fly* and *time flies*. This kind of evidence is suggestive of the desired distinction, though far from conclusive.

12.2.3 Future Directions

The long-term research challenge is to derive lexicons and grammars for broad-coverage natural language processing applications from corpus evidence.

A problem with attaining this long-term goal is that it is unclear whether the community of researchers can agree that a particular design of lexicons and grammars is appropriate, and that a large-scale effort to implement that design will converge on results of fairly general utility (Liberman, 1992).

In the short-term, progress can be achieved by improving the infrastructure, i.e. the stock of intermediate resources mentioned in section 12.1. Data collection and dissemination efforts have been extremely successful. Efforts should now be focused on principles, procedures and tools for analyzing these data. There is a need for manual, semi-automatic and automatic methods that help produce linguistically motivated analyses that make it possible to derive further facts and generalizations that are useful in improving the performance of language processors.

While there is wide agreement in the research community on these general points, there seems to be no shared vision of what exactly to do with text corpora, once you have them. A way to proceed in the short and intermediate term is for data collection efforts to achieve a consensus within the the research community by identifying a set of fruitful problems for research (e.g., word sense disambiguation, anaphoric reference, predicate argument structure) and collecting, analyzing and distributing relevant data in a timely and cost-effective manner. Funding agencies can contribute to the consensus building effort by encouraging work on common tasks and sharing of common data and common components.

12.3   Spoken Language Corpora

Lori Lamel[a] & Ronald Cole[b]

[a] LIMSI-CNRS, Orsay, France
[b] Oregon Graduate Institute of Science & Technology, Portland, Oregon, USA

Spoken language is central to human communication and has significant links to both national identity and individual existence. The structure of spoken language is shaped by many factors. It is structured by the phonological, syntactic and prosodic structure of the language being spoken, by the acoustic enviroment and context in which it is produced—e.g., people speak differently in noisy or quiet environments—and the communication channel through which it travels.

Speech is produced differently by each speaker. Each utterance is produced by a unique vocal tract which assigns its own signature to the signal. Speakers of the same language have different dialects, accents and speaking rates. Their speech patterns are influenced by the physical environment, social context, the perceived social status of the participants, and their emotional and physical state.

Large amounts of annotated speech data are needed to model the affects of these different sources of variability on linguistic units such as phonemes, words, and sequences of words. An axiom of speech research is *there are no data like more data*. Annotated speech corpora are essential for progress in all areas of spoken language technology. Current recognition techniques require large amounts of training data to perform well on a given task. Speech synthesis systems require the study of large corpora to model natural intonation. Spoken language systems require large corpora of human-machine conversations to model interactive dialog.

In response to this need, there are major efforts underway worldwide to collect, annotate and distribute speech corpora in many languages. These corpora allow scientists to study, understand, and model the different sources of variability, and to develop, evaluate and compare speech technologies on a common basis.

Spoken Language Corpora Activities

Recent advances in speech and language recognition are due in part to the availability of large public domain speech corpora, which have enabled comparative system evaluation using shared testing protocols. The use of common corpora for developing and evaluating speech recognition algorithms is a fairly recent development. One of the first corpora used for common evaluation, the TI-DIGITS corpus, recorded in 1984, has been (and still is) widely used as a test base for isolated and connected digit recognition (Leonard, 1984).

In the United States, the development of speech corpora has been funded mainly by agencies of the Department of Defense (DoD). Such DoD support produced two early corpora: Road Rally for studying word spotting, and the King Corpus for studying speaker recognition. As part of its human language technology program, the Advanced Research Projects Agency (ARPA) of the DoD has funded TIMIT (Garofolo, Lamel, et al., 1993; Fisher, Doddington, et al., 1986; Lamel, Kassel, et al., 1986), a phonetically transcribed corpus of read sentences used for modeling phonetic variabilities and for evaluation of phonetic recognition algorithms, and task related corpora such as Resource Management (RM) (Price, Fisher, et al., 1988) and Wall Street Journal (WSJ) (Paul & Baker, 1992) for research on continuous speech recognition, and ATIS (Air Travel Information Service) (Price, 1990; Hirschmann, 1992) for research on spontaneous speech and natural language understanding.[1]

Recognition of the need for shared resources led to the creation of the Linguistic Data Consortium (LDC)[†] in the U.S. in 1992 to promote and support the widespread development and sharing of resources for human language technology. The LDC supports various corpus development activities, and distributes corpora obtained from a variety of sources. Currently, LDC distributes about twenty different speech corpora including those cited above, comprising many hundreds of hours of speech. Information about the LDC as well as contact information for most of the corpora mentioned below is listed in the next subsection.

The Center for Spoken Language Understanding (CSLU)[†] at the Oregon Graduate Institute collects, annotates and distributes telephone speech corpora. The Center's activities are supported by its industrial affiliates, but the corpora are made available to universities worldwide free of charge. Overviews of speech corpora available from the Center, and current corpus development activities, can be found in: Cole, Noel, et al. (1994); Cole, Fanty, et al. (1994). CSLU's Multi-Language Corpus (also available through the LDC), is the NIST standard for evaluating language identification algorithms, and is comprised of spontaneous speech in eleven different languages (Muthusamy, Cole, et al., 1992).

Europe is by nature multilingual, with each country having their own language(s), as well as dialectal variations and lesser used languages. Corpora development in Europe is thus the result of both National efforts and efforts sponsored by the European Union (typically under the ESPRIT (European Strategic Programme for Research and Development in Information Technology), LRE (Linguistic Research and Engineering), and TIDE (Technology Initiative for Disabled and Elderly People) programs, and now for Eastern Europe under the PECO (Pays d'Europe Centrale et Orientale)/Copernicus programs).

In February 1995 the European Language Resources Association (ELRA)[†] was established to provide a basis for central coordination of corpora creation, management and distribution in Europe. ELRA is the outcome of the combined efforts of partners in the LRE Relator[†] project and the LE MLAP (Language Engineering Multilingual Action Plan) projects: SPEECHDAT,[†] PAROLE[†] and POINTER.[†] These projects are responsible, respectively, for the infrastructure for spoken resources, written resources, and terminology within Europe.

---

[1]ARPA also sponsors evaluation tests, run by NIST (National Institute for Science and Technology), described in section 13.6.

[†]See section 12.6.2 for contact addresses.

ELRA will work in close coordination with the Network of Excellence, ELSNET (European Network in Language and Speech),[†] whose Reusable Resources Task Group initiated the Relator project.

Several ESPRIT projects have attempted to create multilingual speech corpora in some or all of the official European languages. The first multilingual speech collection action in Europe was in 1989, consisting of comparable speech material recorded in five languages: Danish, Dutch, English, French, Italian. The entire corpus, now known as EUROM0 includes eight languages (Fourcin, Harland, et al., 1989). Other European projects producing corpora which may be available for distribution include: ACCOR[†] (multisensor recordings, seven languages, Marchal & Hardcastle, 1993); ARS;[†] EUROM1[†] (eleven languages); POLYGLOT[†] (seven languages LIMSI, 1994); ROARS;[†] SPELL;[†] SUNDIAL;[†] and SUNSTAR.[†]

The LRE ONOMASTICA[†] project (Trancoso, 1995) is producing large dictionaries of proper names and place names for eleven European languages. While some of these corpora are widely available, others have remained the property of the project consortium that created it. The LE SPEECHDAT project is recording comparable telephone data from 1000 speakers in eight European languages. A portion of the data will be validated and made publicly available for distribution by ELRA. ELDA, European Language resources —Distribution Agency (ELDA)[†] will handle the distribution of language resources for ELRA.

Some other well-known European corpora are: **British English**: WSJCAM0[†] (Robinson, Fransen, et al., 1995), Bramshill,[†] SCRIBE,[†] and Normal Speech Corpus;[†] **Scottish English**: HCRC Map Task (Anderson, Bader, et al., 1991; Thompson, Anderson, et al., 1993); **Dutch**: Groningen;[†] **French**: BDSONS (Carré, Descout, et al., 1984), BREF[†] (Lamel, Gauvain, et al., 1991; Gauvain, Lamel, et al., 1990; Gauvain & Lamel, 1993); **German**: PHONDAT1 and PHONDAT2,[†] ERBA[†] and VERBMOBIL;[†] **Italian**: APASCI (Angelini, Brugnara, et al., 1993; Angelini, Brugnara, et al., 1994); **Spanish**: ALBAYZIN[†] (Moreno, Poch, et al., 1993; Diaz, Rubio, et al., 1993); **Swedish**: CAR and Waxholm.[†]

Some of these corpora are readily available (see the following section for contact information on corpora mentioned in this section); and efforts are underway to obtain the availability of others.

There have also been some recent efforts to record everyday speech of typical citizens. One such effort is part of the British National Corpus in which about 1500 hours of speech representing a demographic sampling of the population and wide range of materials has been recorded ensuring coverage of four contextual categories: educational, business, public/institutional, and leisure. The entire corpus is in the process of being orthographically transcribed with annotations for non-speech events. A similar corpus for Dutch is currently under discussion in the Netherlands, and the Institute of Phonetics and Verbal Communication of the University of Munich has begun collecting of a very large database of spoken German.

The Translanguage English Database (TED) (Lamel, Schiel, et al., 1994) is a corpus of multi-dialect English and non-native English of recordings of oral presentations at Eurospeech'93 in Berlin. The corpus is subdivided into TED-speeches, TEDtexts, TEDlaryngo and TEDphone. This corpus was partially funded by the LRE project EuroCocosda,[†] and ELSNET. ¡

Other major efforts in corpora collection have been undertaken in other parts of the world. These include: Polyphone, a multilingual, multinational application-oriented telephone speech corpus, co-sponsored by the LDC, the Australian National Database of Spoken Language (ANDOSL)[†] project, sponsored by the Australian Speech Science and Technology Association Inc. and funded by a research infrastructure grant from the Australian Research Council, is a national effort to create a database of spoken language; the Chinese National Speech Corpus[†] supported by the National Science Foundation of China designed to provide speech data for the acquisition of acoustic-phonetic knowledge and for the development and evaluation of speech processing systems; and corpora from Japan such as those publicly available from ATR, ETL and JEIDA.[†]

Future Directions

Challenges in spoken language corpora are many. One basic challenge is in design methodology—how to design compact corpora that can be used in a variety of applications; how to design comparable corpora in a variety of languages; how to select (or sample) speakers so as to have a representative population with regard to many factors including accent, dialect, and speaking style; how to create generic dialogue corpora so as to minimize the need for task or application specific data; how to select statistically representative test data for system evaluation. Another major challenge centers on developing standards for transcribing speech data at different levels and across languages: establishing symbol sets, alignment conventions, defining levels of transcription (acoustic, phonetic, phonemic, word and other levels), conventions for prosody and tone, conventions for quality control (such as having independent labelers transcribe the same speech data for reliability statistics). Quality control of the speech data is also an important issue that needs to be addressed, as well as methods for dissemination. While CDROM has become the *de facto* standard for dissemination of large corpora, other potential means need to also be considered, such as very high speed fiber optic networks.

12.4   Lexicons

Ralph Grishman[a] & Nicoletta Calzolari[b]

[a] New York University, New York, USA
[b] Istituto di Linguistica Computazionale del CNR, Pisa, Italy

12.4.1   The Lexicon as a Critical Resource

Lexical knowledge—knowledge about individual words in the language—is essential for all types of natural language processing. Developers of machine translation systems, which from the beginning have involved large vocabularies, have long recognized the lexicon as a critical (and perhaps the critical) system resource. As researchers and developers in other areas of natural language processing move from toy systems to systems which process real texts over broad subject domains, larger and richer lexicons will be needed and the task of lexicon design and development will become a more central aspect of any project. See Walker, Zampolli, et al. (1995); Zampolli, Calzolari, et al. (1994) for a rich overview of theoretical and practical issues connected with the lexicon in the last decade.

An important critical step towards avoiding duplication of efforts, and consequently towards a more productive course of action for the realization of resources, is to build and make publicly available to the community large-scale lexical resources, with broad coverage and basic types of information, generic enough to be reusable in different application frameworks, e.g., with application-specific lexicons built on top of them. This need for shareable resources, possibly built in a cooperative way, brings in the issue of standardization and the necessity of agreeing on common/consensual specifications (Calzolari, 1994).

12.4.2   Types of Information

The lexicon may contain a wide range of word-specific information, depending on the structure and task of the natural language processing system. A basic lexicon will typically include information about morphology, either in a form enabling the generation of all potential word forms associated with pertinent morphosyntactic features, or as a list of word forms, or as a combination of the two. On the syntactic level, it will include in particular the complement structures of each word or word sense. A more complex lexicon may also include semantic information, such as a classification hierarchy and selectional patterns or case frames stated in terms of this hierarchy. For machine translation, the lexicon will also have to record correspondences between lexical items in the source and target language; for speech understanding and generation, it will have to include information about the pronunciation of individual words.

Strictly related to the types of information connected with each lexical entry are two other issues: (i) the overall lexicon architecture, and (ii) the representation formalism used to encode the data.

In general, a lexicon will be composed of different modules, corresponding to the different levels of linguistic descriptions, linked to each other according to the chosen overall architecture.

As for representation, we can mention at least two major formalisms. In an exchange model, Standard Generalized Markup Language (SGML) is widely accepted as a way of representing not only textual but also lexical data. The Text Encoding Initiative (TEI) has developed a model for representing machine readable dictionaries. In application systems, TFS (Typed Feature Structure) based formalisms are nowadays used in a large number of European lexical projects (Briscoe, Copestake, et al., 1993).

12.4.3 Sources of Information

Traditionally, computer lexicons have been built by hand specifically for the purpose of language analysis and generation. These lexicons, while they may have been large and expensive to build, have generally been crafted to the needs of individual systems and have not been treated as major resources to be shared among groups.

However, the needs for larger lexicons are now leading to efforts for the development of common lexical representations and co-operative lexicon development. They are leading developers to make greater use of existing resources—in particular, published commercial dictionaries—for automated language processing. And, most recently, the availability of large computer-readable text corpora has led to research on learning lexical characteristics from instances in text.

12.4.4 Major Projects

Among the first lexicons to be seen as shared resources for computational linguistics were the machine-readable versions of published dictionaries. One of the first major efforts involved a machine-readable version of selected information from Merriam-Webster's 7th Collegiate Dictionary, which was used for experiments in a number of systems. British dictionaries for English language learners have been especially rich in the information they encode—such as detailed information about complement structures—and so have proven particularly suitable for automated language processing. The Longman's Dictionary of Contemporary English, which included (in the machine-readable version) detailed syntactic and semantic codes, has been extensively used in computational linguistics systems (Boguraev & Briscoe, 1989); the Oxford Advanced Learner's Dictionary has also been widely used.

The major project having as its main objective the reuse of information extracted from Machine Readable Dictionaries (MRDs) is ESPRIT BRA (Basic Research Action) ACQUILEX. The feasibility of acquiring interesting syntactic/semantic information has been proved within ACQUILEX, using common extraction methodologies and techniques over more than ten MRDs in four languages. The objective was to build a prototype common Lexical Knowledge

Base (LKB), using a unique Type System for all the languages and dictionaries, with a shared metalanguage of attributes and values.

Over the last few years there have been a number of projects to create large lexical resources for general use (see Varile & Zampolli, 1992 for an overview of international projects). The largest of these has been the Electronic Dictionary Research (EDR) project in Japan, which has created a suite of interlinked dictionaries, including Japanese and English dictionaries, a concept dictionary, and bilingual Japanese-English and English-Japanese dictionaries. The concept dictionary includes 400,000 concepts, both classified and separately described; the word dictionaries contain both grammatical information and links to the concept hierarchy.

In the United States, the WordNet Project at Princeton has created a large network of word senses related by semantic relations such as synonymy, part-whole, and is-a relations (Miller, 1990). The Linguistic Data Consortium (LDC) is sponsoring the creation of several lexical resources, including Comlex Syntax, an English lexicon with detailed syntactic information being developed at New York University.

Semantic Taxonomies similar or mappable to WordNet already exist (e.g., for Italian) or are being planned for a number of European languages, stemming from European projects.

The topic of large shareable resources has seen in the last years in Europe the flourishing of a number of important lexical projects, among which we can mention ET-7, ACQUILEX, ESPRIT MULTILEX, EUREKA GENELEX, MLAP ET-10 on Semantics acquisition from Cobuild, and LRE DELIS on corpus based lexicon development.

This concentration of efforts towards lexicon design and development in a multilingual setting has clearly shown that the area is ripe—at least for some levels of linguistic description—for reaching, in the short term, a consensus on common lexical specifications. The CEC DGXIII recently formed LRE EAGLES (Expert Advisory Group on Linguistic Engineering Standards) for pooling together the European efforts of both academic and industrial participants towards the creation of standards, among others in the lexical area (Calzolari & McNaught, 1994). A first proposal of common specifications at the morphosyntactic level has been prepared (Monachini & Calzolari, 1994), accompanied with language-specific applications for the European languages.

12.4.5 Future Directions

Although there has been a great deal of discussion, design, and even development of lexical resources for shared use in computer analysis, there has been little practical experience with the actual use of such resources by multiple NLP projects. The sharing which has taken place has involved primarily basic syntactic information, such as parts of speech and basic subcategorization information. We have almost no experience with the sorts of semantic knowledge that could be effectively used by multiple systems. To gather such experience, we must provide ongoing support for several such lexical resources, and in particular provide support to modify them in response to users' needs.

We must also recognize the importance of the rapidly growing stock of machine-readable text as a resource for lexical research. There has been significant work on the discovery of subcategorization patterns and selectional patterns from text corpora. The major areas of potential results in the immediate future seem to lie in the combination of lexicon and corpus work. We see a growing interest from many groups in topics such as sense tagging or sense disambiguation on very large text corpora, where lexical tools and data provide a first input to the systems and are in turn enhanced with the information acquired and extracted from corpus analysis.

12.5 Terminology[2]

Christian Galinski[a] & Gerhard Budin[b]

[a] Infoterm, Vienna, Austria
[b] Univerity of Vienna, Austria

12.5.1 What is Terminology?

Whenever and wherever specialized information and knowledge are created, communicated, recorded, processed, stored, transformed or re-used, terminology is involved in one way or another. Subject-field communication has become a specific type of discourse with specialized texts differentiating between a whole array of text types. When we define terminology as a structured set of concepts and their designations in a particular subject field, it can be considered the infrastructure of specialized knowledge. Technical writing and technical documentation are thus impossible without properly using terminological resources. Since the production of technical texts increasingly involves several languages, high-quality multilingual terminologies have become scarce and much desired commodities on the burgeoning markets of language and knowledge industries.

12.5.2 Interdisciplinary Research

The research field we talk about is referred to as terminology science, its practical field of application is in terminology management, which includes the creation of subject-field specific terminologies and the terminographic recording of such information in the form of terminology databases, dictionaries, lexicons, specialized encyclopedias, etc. (For overviews and recent textbooks see, for English: Felber, 1984; Picht & Draskau, 1985; Sager, 1990; for German: Felber & Budin, 1989; Arntz & Picht, 1989; for Spanish: Cabré, 1994; for French: Gouadec, 1992.)

Concepts are considered the smallest units (*atoms*) of specialized knowledge. They never occur in isolation, but rather in complex conceptual networks that are multidimensional, due to a wide range of conceptual relationships among

---

[2]This section has been compiled on the basis of current discussions in terminology science and experience in a multitude of terminological activities world-wide.

concepts. Given the limitations of natural language with regard to the representation of these concepts in specialized discourse (limited number of term elements in every language), concepts are increasingly represented by non-linguistic designations, like graphical symbols (Galinski & Picht, 1995). In addition we may distinguish between:

- symbolic representations

  - terms (including abbreviations, alphanumeric codes, etc.)
  - graphical symbols, audiovisual symbols, etc.
  - combinations of both

- descriptive representations

  - definitions, explanations, etc. as linguistic descriptions of concepts
  - pictures, charts, graphics, etc. as graphical/pictorial descriptions of concepts
  - combinations of both

Theories of terminology as they have developed over at least six decades, consider concepts as:

- **units of thought**, focusing on the psychological aspect of recognizing objects as part of reality;

- **units of knowledge**, focusing on the epistemological aspect of information gathered (today we say constructed) on the object in question;

- **units of communication**, stressing the fact that concepts are the prerequisite for knowledge transfer in specialized discourse (Galinski, 1990).

The development of terminologies as a crucial part of special-purpose languages reflects scientific, technical and economic progress in the subject fields concerned. Due to different speeds in this dynamic co-evolution of knowledge in the individual domains, specialized discourse continues to differentiate between more and more sectorized special languages and terminologies. But these communication tools become increasingly ambiguous, due to the sheer number of concepts to be designated and the limited linguistic resources of every natural language: terms are taken over from one domain (or language) into another, usually with varying meanings in the (productive) form of metaphors or analogies; new homonyms, polysemes and synonyms arise, motivating or even forcing subject specialists to standardize their terminology and harmonize them on the multilingual level in order to reduce and manage the constantly rising communicative complexity that faces their discourse communities.

But terminology research is not limited to comparative semiotic and linguistic studies of term formation and the epistemological dimension of the evolution of scientific knowledge. The agenda of terminology science also includes socio-terminological studies of the acceptance of neologisms proposed by terminology and language planners (Gaudin, 1994), case studies on terminology development by standardization and harmonization efforts, research and development concerning the establishment and use of terminology databases for various user groups and purposes (e.g., translation, technical writing, information management) and concerning controlled vocabularies for documentation and information retrieval purposes (thesauri, classification systems, etc.).

12.5.3 Terminology Management

Terminology management is primarily concerned with manipulating terminological resources for specific purposes, e.g., establishing repertories of terminological resources for publishing dictionaries, maintaining terminology databases, or *ad hoc* problem solving in finding multilingual equivalences in translation work or creating new terms in technical writing. (For terminology management see Wright & Budin, 1995.)

Terminology databases are increasingly available by on-line query or on CD-ROM (e.g., TERMIUM, EURODICAUTOM), on diskette in the form of electronic dictionaries or as private databases established and maintained by engineers, computer specialists, chemists, etc. (working as terminologists, translators, technical writers) for various purposes:

1. computer-assisted human translation;

2. computer-assisted technical and scientific writing;

3. materials information systems (spare parts administration, etc.);

4. terminology research in linguistics, information science, philosophy of science, sociology of technology, etc.

For such purposes, special computer programs have been developed (terminology database management programs), either commercially available on the international terminology market or developed as prototypes in academic research projects.

Due to the surprisingly high diversity of terminological resources that is potentially relevant to applications, terminology databases may look quite different from each other. One principle, however, seems to be the common denominator of all of them: the concepts under consideration are always the point of departure for database modeling; entries in terminology databases deal with one specific concept at a time. A terminological entry may contain not only term equivalents in other languages, synonyms, abbreviations, regional variants, definitions, contexts, even graphics or pictures, but also indications of relationships to other concepts (referencing to related entries) and subject-field indications by including thesaurus descriptors, class names from a classification system, etc., in order to easily retrieve terminological entries covering a certain topic.

12.5.4 Future Directions

Theoretical Issues: The last few years have seen a considerable increase in epistemological studies in the framework of philosophy of science concerning the way in which scientific knowledge is constantly created, communicated and changed and the pivotal role scientific terminologies play in this respect. In the light of post-modernism, complexity, fractal and chaos theories, synergetics and other new paradigms that completely change our scientific view of the world and of ourselves, it is necessary to re-examine the correspondence between *objects* we perceive or conceive and the concepts we construct in the process of thinking (cognition, and re-cognition of objects) (De Beaugrande, 1988; Budin, 1994).

The concept-oriented approach in terminology management mentioned above seems to be the key to solve a whole range of methodological problems in the management of multilingualism and information management in large international institutions as a number of innovative projects on the European level could prove (Galinski, 1994). The performance of machine translation systems could also be improved by integrating advanced terminology processing modules that are based on the conceptual approach to language engineering.

European research projects such as Translator's Workbench (ESPRIT Program) or similar projects in Canada (e.g., Translation Workstation), show a clear tendency towards systems integration: terminology products are no longer isolated and difficult to use, but fully integrated in complex work environments. Automatic term extraction from text corpora is one of the buzzwords in this type of practice-oriented research (Ahmad, Davies, et al., 1994). A terminological analysis of text corpora also includes fuzzy matching in order to recognize larger segments of texts (complex multi-word terms, fixed collocations, but also semi-fixed sentence patterns).

Within the framework of the Text Encoding Initiative a working group (i.e., TEI A&I-7) has specifically been devoted to terminological resources and their management by SGML. Chapter 13 of the P 2 Guidelines of TEI on the application of SGML in text processing is dealing with the representation of terminological resources in SGML and the creation of an interchange format. This terminology interchange format (TIF) is now in the process of being standardized by ISO (ISO 12200, Melby, Budin, et al., 1993). The exchange of terminological resources has become one of the most discussed topics in the international terminology community. In addition to the introduction of the TIF standard, many methodological and legal problems (copyright, intellectual property rights, etc.) have to be solved.

Terminologists have also joined the international bandwagon of quality assurance and total quality management by starting research projects on how appropriate terminology management may improve the performance of quality managers, and *vice versa*, how to improve reliability of terminological resources by systematic quality management in terminology standardization in particular and terminology management in general.

The interdisciplinary nature of terminology science also becomes clear in its links to research in knowledge engineering and Artificial Intelligence Research (Ahmad, 1995; Schmitz, 1993). But terminological knowledge engineering (TKE) is more than just a series of projects and some new tools—it has also become a new method of modeling and representing knowledge in hypermedia knowledge bases serving as research tools for scientists (and completely changing research methods, e.g., by terminology visualization modules), as a knowledge popularization tool in museums, and as a teaching tool or as a *hyperterminology* database (IITF, 1994).

12.6 Addresses for Language Resources

12.6.1 Written Language Corpora

Contact information for the corpora mentioned in section 12.2 is provided here in alphabetical order.

British National Corpus (BNC): http://info.ox.ac.uk/bnc

Consortium for Lexical Research (CLR): lexical@nmsu.edu

Dansk Korpus (DK): Ole Norling-Christensen olenc@coco.ihi.ku.dk

European Corpus Initiative (ECI): (in Europe): eucorp@cogsci.edinburgh.ac.uk

European Corpus Initiative (ECI): (in U.S.) LDC (see address below)

Frantext of Institut National de la Langue Française (INaLF-CNRS): Lafon@ens-fcl.fr (Pierre Lafon), dendien@ciril.fr (Jaques Dendien)

Institut für deutsche Sprache (IDS): juettner@ids-mannheim.de (Irmtraud Juettner)

Instituut voor Nederlandse Lexicologie (INL): kruyt@rulxho.leidenuniv.nl (Truus Kruyt)

International Computer Archive of Modern English (ICAME): Stig Johansson stigj@hedda.uio.no

Istituto di Linguistica Computazionale (ILC-CNR): Antonio Zampolli glottolo@vm.cnuce.cnr.it

Linguistic Data Consortium (LDC): ldc@unagi1k.cis.upenn.edu (LDC Office). The WWW page is http://www.cis.upenn.edu/~ldc. Information about the LDC and its activities can also be obtained via anonymous FTP ftp.cis.upenn.edu under pub/ldc. Most of the data are compressed using the tool Shorten by T. Robinson which is available via ftp svr-ftp.eng.cam.ac.uk

Norsk Tekstarkiv: per.vestbostad@hd.uib.no (Per Vestbostad)

Instituto Cervantes: joaquim.llisterri@cervantes.es (Joaquim Llisterri)

Sprakdata: gellerstam@svenska.gu.se (Martin Gellerstam)

Stockholm-Umea Corpus (SUC): ejerhed@ling.umu.se (Eva Ejerhed), gunnel@ling.su.se (Gunnel Kallgren)

Text Encoding Initiative (TEI): http://www-tei.uic.edu/orgs/tei

University of Helsinki: Fred Karlsson fkarlsso@ling.helsinki.fi

12.6.2   Spoken Language Corpora

Contact information for the corpora mentioned in section 12.3 is provided here in alphabetical order.

ACCOR: Project contact: Prof. W. Hardcastle, sphard@queen-margaret-college.main.ac.uk; Prof. A. Marchal, phonetic@fraix11.bitnet (The British English portion of the ACCOR corpus is being produced on CD-ROM with partial financing from ELSNET)

ALBAYZIN: Corpus contact: Professor Climent Nadeu, Department of Speech Signal Theory and Communications, Universitat Politecnica de Catalunya, ETSET, Apartat 30002, 08071 Barcelona, Spain, nadeu@tsc.upc.es

ARS: CSELT (coordinator), Mr. G. Babini, Via G. Beis Romoli 274, I-101488, Torino, Italy

ATR, ETL & JEIDA: Contact person: K. Kataoka, AI and Fuzzy Promotion Center, Japan Information Processing Development Center (JIPDEC), 3-5-8 Shibakoen, Minatoku, Tokyo 105, Japan, Tel +81 3 3432 9390, Fax +81 3 3431 4324

Australian National Database of Spoken Language (ANDOSL): Corpus contact: Bruce Millar, Computer Sciences Laboratory, Research School of Information Sciences and Engineering, Australian National University, Canberra, ACT 0200, Australia, email: bruce@cslab.anu.edu.au

Bavarian Archive for Speech Signals (BAS): Collection of more than 20 GB of German speech corpora including PHONDAT1, PHONDAT2, SI100, SI1000, SPICOS, ERBA, SC1, SPINA and the Verbmobil corpus so far published. See http://www.phonetik.uni-muenchen.de/Bas/BasHomeeng.html; email: bas@phonetik.uni-muenchen.de; phone: +49-89-2180-2807

BREF: Corpus contact: send email to bref@limsi.fr

Bramshill: LDC (as above)

CAR & Waxholm: Corpus contact: Bjorn Granstrom bjorn@speech.kth.se

Center for Spoken Language Understanding (CSLU): Information on the collection and availability of CSLU corpora can be obtained on the World Wide Web, http://www.cse.ogi.edu/CSLU/corpora.html

Chinese National Speech Corpus: Contact person: Prof. Jialu Zhang, Academia Sinica, Institute of Acoustics, 17 Shongguanjun St, Beijing PO Box 2712, 100080 Beijing, Peoples Republic of China

ERBA: Distributed by BAS. See BAS above.

ETL: see ATR above.

EUROM1: Project contact for Multilingual speech database: A. Fourcin (UCL)
adrian@phonetics.ucl.ac.uk; or the following for individual languages:
D: D. Gibbon (Uni. Bielefeld) gibbon@asl.uni-bielefeld.de
DK: B. Lindberg (IES) bli@stc.auc.dk
F: J.F. Serignat (ICP) serignat@icp.grenet.fr
I: G. Castagneri (CSELT) castagneri@cselt.stet.it
N: T. Svendsen (SINTEF-DELAB) torbjorn@telesun.tele.unit.no
NL: J. Hendriks or L. Boves (PTT Research) boves@lett.kun.nl
SW: G. Hult (Televerket) or B. Granstrom (KTH) bjorn@speech.kth.se
UK: A. Fourcin (UCL) adrian@phonetics.ucl.ac.uk
Contact for SAM-A EUROM1:
E: A. Moreno (UPC) amoreno@tsc.upc.es
G: J. Mourjopoulos (UPatras) mourjop@grpafvx1.earn
P: I. Trancoso (INESC) imt@inesc.pt

EuroCocosda: Corpus contact: A Fourcin, email:
adrian@phonetics.ucl.ac.uk

European Language resources - Distribution Agency (ELDA):
http://www.icp.grenet.fr/ELRA/elda.html

European Language Resources Association (ELRA):
http://www.icp.grenet.fr/ELRA/home.html

European Network in Language and Speech (ELSNET):
OTS, Utrecht University, Trans 10, 3512 JK, Utrecht, The Netherlands,
Email: elsnet@let.ruu.nl

Groningen: Corpus contact: Els den Os, Speech Processing Expertise Centre,
P.O.Box 421, 2260 AK Leidschendam, The Netherlands, els@spex.nl
(CDs available via ELSNET)

JEIDA: see ATR above.

LRE ONOMASTICA: Project contact: M. Jack, CCIR, University of Edinburgh, mervyn.jack@ed.ac.uk

Linguistic Data Consortium (LDC): see LDC above.

Normal Speech Corpus: Corpus Contact: Steve Crowdy, Longman UK, Burnt
Mill, Harlow, CM20 2JE, UK

Oregon Graduate Institute (OGI): see CSLU above.

PAROLE: Project contact: Mr. T. Schneider, Sietec Systemtechnik GmbH,
Nonnendammallee 101, D-13629 Berlin

PHONDAT2: Available through BAS. See BAS above.

POINTER: Project contact: Mr. Corentin Roulin , BJL Consult, Boulevard du Souverain 207/12, B-1160 Bruxelles

POLYGLOT: Contact person: Antonio Cantatore, Syntax Sistemi Software, Via G. Fanelli 206/16, I- 70125 Bari, Italy

Relator: Project contact: A. Zampolli, Istituto di Linguistica Computazionale, CNR, Pisa, I, E-mail: `giulia@icnucevm.cnuce.cnr.it`; Information as well as a list of resources is available on the World Wide Web, `http://www.XX.relator.research.ec.org`

ROARS: Contact person: Pierre Alinat, Thomson-CSF/Sintra-ASM, 525 Route des Dolines, Parc de Sophia Antipolis, BP 138, F-06561 Valbonne, France

SCRIBE: Corpus contact: Mike Tomlinson, Speech Research Unit, DRA, Malvern, Worc WR14 3PS, England

SPEECHDAT: Project contact: Mr. Harald Hoege, Siemens AG, Otto Hahn Ring 6, D-81739 Munich

SPELL: Contact person: Jean-Paul Lefevre, Agora Conseil, 185, Hameau de Chateau, F-38360 Sassenage, France

SUNDIAL: Contact person: Jeremy Peckham, Vocalis Ltd., Chaston House, Mill Court, Great Shelford, Cambs CB2 5LD UK, email: `jeremy@vocalis.demon.co.uk`

SUNSTAR: Joachin Irion, EG Electrocom GmbH, Max-Stromeyerstr. 160, D- 7750 Konstanz, Germany

VERBMOBIL: The available VM corpora are distributed by BAS (see BAS above) and ELDA (see ELDA above). For questions about the production contact A. Kipp, University of Munich, *cdrom@phonetik.uni-muenchen.de*

Wall Street Journal, Cambridge, zero (WSJCAM0):
Corpus contact: Linguistic Data Consortium (LDC), Univ. of Pennsylvania, 441 Williams Hall, Philadelphia, PA, USA 19104-6305, (215) 898-0464

Waxholm: see CAR above.

12.6.3   Character Recognition

Contact information for the corpora mentioned in section 13.10 is provided here in alphabetical order.

Electrotechnical Laboratory (ETL) Character Database:
Distributor: Image Understanding Section, Electrotechnical Laboratory, 1-1-4, Umezono, Tsukuba, Ibaraki, 305, Japan.

National Institute of Standards and Technology (NIST): Distributor: Standard Reference Data, National Institute of Standards and Technology, 221/A323, Gaithersburg, MD 20899, USA.

U.S. Postal Service: Distributor: CEDAR, SUNY at Buffalo, Dept. of Computer Science, 226 Bell Hall, Buffalo, NY 14260, USA.

University of Washington: Distributor: Intelligent Systems Laboratory, Dept. of Electrical Engineering, FT-10, University of Washington, Seattle, WA 98195, USA

12.7 Chapter References

Ahmad, K. (1995). The analysis of text corpora for the creation of advanced terminology databases. In Wright, S. E. and Budin, G., editors, *The Handbook of Terminology Management*. John Benjamins, Amsterdam/Philadelphia.

Ahmad, K., Davies, A., Fulford, H., Holmes-Higgin, P., and Rogers, M. (1994). Creating terminology resources. In Kugler, M., Ahmad, K., and Thurmair, G., editors, *Research Reports ESPRIT: Translator's Workbench—Tools and Terminology and Text Processing, Project 2315 TWB*, volume 1, pages 59–71. Springer, Heidelberg, Berlin, New York.

Anderson, A. H., Bader, M., Bard, E. G., Boyle, E. H., Doherty, G. M., Garrod, S. C., Isard, S. D., Kowtko, J. C., McAllister, J. M., Miller, J., Sotillo, C. F., Thompson, H. S., and Weinert, R. (1991). The HCRC map task corpus. *Language and Speech*, 34(4).

Angelini, B., Brugnara, F., Falavigna, D., Giuliani, D., Gretter, R., and Omologo, M. (1993). A baseline of a speaker independent continuous speech recognizer of Italian. In *Eurospeech '93, Proceedings of the Third European Conference on Speech Communication and Technology*, volume 2, pages 847–850, Berlin. European Speech Communication Association.

Angelini, B., Brugnara, F., Falavigna, D., Giuliani, D., Gretter, R., and Omologo, M. (1994). Speaker independent continuous speech recognition using an acoustic-phonetic Italian corpus. In *Proceedings of the 1994 International Conference on Spoken Language Processing*, volume 3, pages 1391–1394, Yokohama, Japan.

Arntz, R. and Picht, H. (1989). *Einführung in die übersetzungsbezogene terminologiearbeit*. Hildesheim, Zürich, New York.

ARPA (1993a). *Proceedings of the 1993 ARPA Human Language Technology Workshop*, Princeton, New Jersey. Advanced Research Projects Agency, Morgan Kaufmann.

ARPA (1993b). *Proceedings of the Fifth Message Understanding Conference*, Baltimore, Maryland. Morgan Kaufmann.

ARPA (1994). *Proceedings of the 1994 ARPA Human Language Technology Workshop*, Princeton, New Jersey. Advanced Research Projects Agency, Morgan Kaufmann.

Boguraev, B. and Briscoe, T., editors (1989). *Computational Lexicography for Natural Language Processing*. Longman.

Briscoe, T., Copestake, A., and de Pavia, V., editors (1993). *Inheritance, defaults and the lexicon*. Cambridge University Press.

Budin, G. (1994). Organisation und evolution von fachwissen und fachsprachen am beispiel der rechtswissenschaft [organization and evolution of specialized knowledge and specialized languages in the case of the law]. In Wilske, D., editor, *Erikoiskielet ja Käännösteoria [LSP and Theory of Translation]*. *VAKKI-symposiumi XIV [14th VAKKI Symposium]*, pages 9–21.

Cabré, T. (1994). *La terminologia*. Barcelona.

Calzolari, N. (1994). European efforts towards standardizing language resources. In Steffens, P., editor, *Machine Translation and the Lexicon*. Springer-Verlag.

Calzolari, N. and McNaught, J. (1994). EAGLES editors' introduction. Technical report, EAGLES Draft Editorial Board Report, EAGLES Secretariat, Istituto di Linguistica Computazionale, Via della Faggiola 32, Pisa, Italy 56126, Fax: +39 50 589055, E-mail: ceditor@tnos.ilc.pi.cnr.it.

Carré, R., Descout, R., Eskénazi, M., Mariani, J., and Rossi, M. (1984). The French language database: defining, planning, and recording a large database. In *Proceedings of the 1984 International Conference on Acoustics, Speech, and Signal Processing*. Institute of Electrical and Electronic Engineers.

Cole, R. A., Fanty, M., Noel, M., and Lander, T. (1994). Telephone speech corpus development at cslu. In *Proceedings of the 1994 International Conference on Spoken Language Processing*, volume 4, pages 1815–1818, Yokohama, Japan.

Cole, R. A., Noel, M., Burnett, D. C., Fanty, M., Lander, T., Oshika, B., and Sutton, S. (1994). Corpus development activities at the center for spoken language understanding. In *Proceedings of the 1994 ARPA Human Language Technology Workshop*, Princeton, New Jersey. Advanced Research Projects Agency, Morgan Kaufmann.

DARPA (1986). *Proceedings of the DARPA Speech Recognition Workshop*. Defense Advanced Research Projects Agency. SAIC-86/1546.

DARPA (1991). *Proceedings of the Third Message Understanding Conference*, San Diego, California. Morgan Kaufmann.

DARPA (1992). *Proceedings of the Fifth DARPA Speech and Natural Language Workshop*. Defense Advanced Research Projects Agency, Morgan Kaufmann.

De Beaugrande, R. (1988). Systemic versus contextual aspects of terminology. In *Terminology and Knowledge Engineering, Supplement*, pages 7–24. Indeks, Frankfurt.

Diaz, J., Rubio, A., Peinado, A., Segarra, E., Prieto, N., and Casacuberta, F. (1993). Development of task-oriented Spanish speech corpora. The paper was distributed at the conference and does not appear in the proceedings.

Eurospeech (1993). *Eurospeech '93, Proceedings of the Third European Conference on Speech Communication and Technology*, Berlin. European Speech Communication Association.

Felber, H. (1984). *Terminology Manual*. UNESCO, Paris.

Felber, H. and Budin, G. (1989). *Terminology Manual*. UNESCO, Paris, second edition.

Fisher, W., Doddington, G., and Goudie-Marshall, K. (1986). The DARPA speech recognition research database: Specifications and status. In *Proceedings of the DARPA Speech Recognition Workshop*, pages 93–99. Defense Advanced Research Projects Agency. SAIC-86/1546.

Fourcin, A. J., Harland, G., Barry, W., and Hazan, V. (1989). *Speech input and output assessment; multilingual methods and standards*. Ellis Horwood.

Francis, W. and Kucera, H. (1982). *Frequency Analysis of English Usage*. Houghton Mifflin, Boston.

Galinski, C. (1990). Terminology 1990. *TermNet News*, 1994(24):14–15.

Galinski, C. (1994). Terminologisches informationsmanagement in harmonisierungsprojekten der EU. Unpublished.

Galinski, C. and Picht, H. (1995). Graphic and other semiotic forms of knowledge representation in terminology work. In Wright, S. E. and Budin, G., editors, *Handbook of Terminology Management*. John Benjamins, Amsterdam/Philadelphia. winter 1995.

Garofolo, J. S., Lamel, L. F., Fisher, W. M., Fiscus, J. G., Pallett, D. S., and Dahlgren, N. L. (1993). The DARPA TIMIT acoustic-phonetic continuous speech corpus. CDROM: NTIS order number PB91-100354.

Gaudin (1994). Socioterminologie.

Gauvain, J.-L. and Lamel, L. F. (1993). Sous-corpus BREF 80, disques bref 80-1 et bref 80-2 (CDROM).

Gauvain, J.-L., Lamel, L. F., and Eskénazi, M. (1990). Design considerations & text selection for BREF, a large French read-speech corpus. In *Proceedings of the 1990 International Conference on Spoken Language Processing*, volume 2, pages 1097–1100, Kobe, Japan.

Gouadec, D. (1992). *La terminologie*. Afnor, Paris.

Grolier (1991). *New Grolier's Electronic Encyclopedia*. Grolier.

Hirschmann, L. (1992). Multi-site data collection for a spoken language corpus. In *Proceedings of the Fifth DARPA Speech and Natural Language Workshop*. Defense Advanced Research Projects Agency, Morgan Kaufmann.

ICASSP (1984). *Proceedings of the 1984 International Conference on Acoustics, Speech, and Signal Processing*. Institute of Electrical and Electronic Engineers.

ICSLP (1994). *Proceedings of the 1994 International Conference on Spoken Language Processing*, Yokohama, Japan.

IITF (1994). Final report. Multimedia knowledge database for social anthropology.

Lamel, L. F., Gauvain, J.-L., and Eskénazi, M. (1991). BREF, a large vocabulary spoken corpus for French. In *Eurospeech '91, Proceedings of the Second European Conference on Speech Communication and Technology*, Genova, Italy. European Speech Communication Association.

Lamel, L. F., Kassel, R. H., and Seneff, S. (1986). Speech database development: Design and analysis of the acoustic-phonetic corpus. In *Proceedings of the DARPA Speech Recognition Workshop*, pages 100–109. Defense Advanced Research Projects Agency. SAIC-86/1546.

Lamel, L. F., Schiel, F., Fourcin, A., Mariani, J., and Tillmann, H. G. (1994). The translanguage English database (TED). In *Proceedings of the 1994 International Conference on Spoken Language Processing*, volume 4, pages 1795–1798, Yokohama, Japan.

Leonard, R. G. (1984). A database for speaker-independent digit recognition. In *Proceedings of the 1984 International Conference on Acoustics, Speech, and Signal Processing*, volume 3, pages 42.11–14. Institute of Electrical and Electronic Engineers.

Liberman, M. (1992). Core NL lexicons and grammars. In *Proceedings of the Fifth DARPA Speech and Natural Language Workshop*, page 351 (session 10b). Defense Advanced Research Projects Agency, Morgan Kaufmann.

LIMSI (1994). Sous-corpus BREF polyglot (CDROM).

Marchal, A. and Hardcastle, W. J. (1993). ACCOR: Instrumentation and database for the cross-language study of coarticulation. *Language and Speech*, 36:137–153.

Melby, A., Budin, G., and Wright, S. E. (1993). The terminology interchange format (TIF)—a tutorial. *TermNet News*, 1993(40):9–65.

Miller, G. (1990). Wordnet: An on-line lexical database. *International journal of Lexicography*, 3(4):235–312.

Monachini, M. and Calzolari, N. (1994). Synopsis and comparison of morphosyntactic phenomena encoded in lexicons and corpora and applications to european languages. Technical report, EAGLES ILC Pisa, EAGLES Secretariat, Istituto di Linguistica Computazionale, Via della Faggiola 32, Pisa, Italy 56126, Fax: +39 50 589055, E-mail: ceditor@tnos.ilc.pi.cnr.it. Also available via ftp to nicolet.ilc.pi.cnr.it (131.114.41.11), Username: eagles, Password: eagles.

Moreno, A., Poch, D., Bonafonte, A., Lleida, E., Llisterri, J. R., Marino, J. B., and Nadeu, C. (1993). ALBAYZIN speech database: design of the phonetic corpus. In *Eurospeech '93, Proceedings of the Third European Conference on Speech Communication and Technology*, volume 1, pages 175–178, Berlin. European Speech Communication Association.

Muthusamy, Y. K., Cole, R. A., and Oshika, B. T. (1992). The OGI multi-language telephone speech corpus. In *Proceedings of the 1992 International Conference on Spoken Language Processing*, volume 2, pages 895–898, Banff, Alberta, Canada. University of Alberta.

Paul, D. and Baker, J. (1992). The design for the Wall Street Journal-based CSR corpus. In *Proceedings of the Fifth DARPA Speech and Natural Language Workshop*. Defense Advanced Research Projects Agency, Morgan Kaufmann.

Picht, H. and Draskau, J. (1985). *Terminology, An Introduction*. The Copenhagen School of Economics, Copenhagen.

Price, P. (1990). Evaluation of spoken language systems: The ATIS domain. In *Proceedings of the Third DARPA Speech and Natural Language Workshop*, Hidden Valley, Pennsylvania. Defense Advanced Research Projects Agency, Morgan Kaufmann.

Price, P., Fisher, W. M., Bernstein, J., and Pallett, D. S. (1988). The DARPA 1000-word resource management database for continuous speech recognition. In *Proceedings of the 1988 International Conference on Acoustics, Speech, and Signal Processing*, pages 651–654, New York. Institute of Electrical and Electronic Engineers.

Quirk, R., Greenbaum, S., Leech, G., and Svartvik, J. (1985). *A Comprehensive Grammar of the English Language*. Longman.

Robinson, T., Fransen, J., Pye, D., Foote, J., and Renals, S. (1995). WSJ-CAM0: A british english speech corpus for large vocabulary continuous speech recognition. In *Proceedings of the 1995 International Conference on Acoustics, Speech, and Signal Processing*, volume 1, pages 81–84, Detroit. Institute of Electrical and Electronic Engineers.

Sager, J. C. (1990). *A practical course in terminology processing*. John Benjamins, Amsterdam/Philadelphia.

Schmitz, K.-D. (1993). TKE 93. terminology and knowledge engineering. In Schmitz, K.-D., editor, *Proceedings of the 3rd International Congress*, Cologne, Germany. Frankfurt a.m.: INDEKS Verlag.

Thompson, H. S., Anderson, A., Bard, E. G., Boyle, E. H., Doherty-Sneddon, G., Newlands, A., and Sotillo, C. (1993). the HCRC map task corpus: Natural dialog for speech recognition. In *Proceedings of the 1993 ARPA Human Language Technology Workshop*, Princeton, New Jersey. Advanced Research Projects Agency, Morgan Kaufmann.

Trancoso, I. (1995). The onomastica inter-language pronunciation lexicon. In *Eurospeech '95, Proceedings of the Fourth European Conference on Speech Communication and Technology*, Madrid, Spain. European Speech Communication Association. In press.

Varile, N. and Zampolli, A., editors (1992). *COLING92 International Project Day*. Giardini Editori, Pisa.

Walker, D., Zampolli, A., and Calzolari, N., editors (1995). *Automating the Lexicon: Research and Practice in a Multilingual Environment*. Oxford University Press.

Wright, S. E. and Budin, G., editors (1995). *Handbook of Terminology Management*. John Benjamins, Amsterdam/Philadelphia. winter 1995.

Zampolli, A., Calzolari, N., and Palmer, M., editors (1994). *Current Issues in Computational Linguistics: In Honour of Don Walker*. Giardini Editori, Pisa and Kluwer, Dordrecht.

Chapter 13

Evaluation

13.1 Overview of Evaluation in Speech and Natural Language Processing

Lynette Hirschman[a] **& Henry S. Thompson**[b]

[a] MITRE Corporation, Bedford, Massachusetts, USA
[b] University of Edinburgh, Scotland

Evaluation plays a crucial role in speech and natural language processing, both for system developers and for technology users. In this section we will introduce the terminology of evaluation for speech and natural language processing and provide a brief survey of areas where it has proved particularly useful, before passing on to more detailed case studies in the subsequent sections.

13.1.1 Introduction to Evaluation Terminology and Use

We can broadly distinguish three kinds of evaluation, appropriate to three different goals.

1. **Adequacy Evaluation**
   This is determination of the fitness of a system for a purpose—will it do what is required, how well, at what cost, etc. Typically for a prospective user, it may be comparative or not, and may require considerable work to identify a user's needs. One model is consumer organizations which publish the results of tests on, e.g., cars or appliances, and identify *best buys* for certain price-performance targets. This also goes by the names *evaluation* and *evaluation proper*.

2. **Diagnostic Evaluation**
   This is production of a system performance profile with respect to some taxonimization of the space of possible inputs. It is typically used by

system developers, but sometimes offered to end-users as well. It usually requires the construction of a large and hopefully representative *test suite*. It also goes by the name *diagnosis*, or by the software engineering term *regression testing* when used to compare two generations of the same system.

3. **Performance Evaluation**
   This is measurement of system performance in one or more specific areas. It is typically used to compare like with like, whether two alternative implementations of a technology, or successive generations of the same implementation. It is typically created for system developers and/or R&D program managers. When considering methodology for measurement in a given area, a distinction is often made between *criterion, measure* and *method* (see below). It also goes by the names *assessment, progress evaluation, summative evaluation* or *technology evaluation*.

When systems have a number of identifiable components associated with stages in the processing they perform, it is important to be clear as to whether we approach the system as a whole, or try to evaluate each component independently. When considering individual components, a further distinction between *intrinsic* and *extrinsic* evaluation must be respected—do we look at how a particular component works in its own terms (intrinsic) or how it contributes to the overall performance of the system (extrinsic). At the whole system level, this distinction approximates to the performance evaluation/adequacy evaluation one, where intrinsic is to extrinsic as performance evaluation is to adequacy evaluation.

A distinction is often drawn between so-called *glass box* and *black box* evaluation, which sometimes appears to differentiate between component-wise versus whole-system evaluation, and sometimes to a less clear-cut difference between a qualitative/descriptive approach (*How* does it do what it does) and a quantitative/analytic approach (How *well* does it do what it does).

Adequacy Evaluation

As speech and natural language processing systems move out of the laboratory and into the market, it is becoming increasingly important to address the legitimate needs of potential users in determining whether any of the products on offer in a given application domain are adequate for their particular task, and if so, whether any of them are obviously more suited than the others. If we reflect on the way similar tasks are approached in other fields, we observe what we can call the Consumer Reports paradigm, which does not necessarily aim at actually *identifying* the *best* system, but rather at providing comparative information which allows the user to make an informed choice. Techniques from both diagnostic and performance evaluation may be called on to achieve this aim, but are unlikely to be sufficient in themselves—for example, assessing cultivability may be of fundamental importance in determining adequacy to a particular user's needs, but is unlikely to be addressed by existing diagnostic or performance evaluation methodologies.

The term *formative evaluation* is used in the field of human-computer interaction to refer to a collection of evaluation methodologies more closely related to both adequacy evaluation and to diagnostic evaluation in our terms. The goal of formative evaluation is to provide diagnostic information about where a given system succeeds or needs improvement, relative to its intended users and use. The role of formative evaluation is to influence and guide system design, as opposed to performance evaluation or summative evaluation, which rates systems relative to each other, or relative to some *gold standard* such as human performance. During system development, user trials of system prototypes or alternative assessments of user interface functionality are conducted, in which more or less formal measurements of usability are recorded (e.g., via study and measurement of user actions performing some representative set of tasks, possibly coupled with interviews). We see considerable potential for importing some of these techniques into adequacy evaluation of speech and natural language processing applications.

Diagnostic Evaluation

In speech and natural language processing application areas where coverage is important, for example in machine translation or language understanding systems with explicit grammars, a common development methodology employs a large *test suite* of exemplary input, whose goal is to enumerate all the elementary linguistic phenomena in the input domain, and their most likely and/or important combinations. A large, mature test suite will be structured into a number of dimensions of elementary phenomena and contexts, and may include invalid as well as valid inputs, tagged as such. Nerbonne, Netter, et al. (1993) describes a recent state-of-the-art example of this.

Test suites are particularly valuable to system developers and maintainers, allowing automated regression testing to ensure that system changes have the intended effect *and no others*, but raw profiles of system coverage *vis a vis* some test suite are unlikely to be of use as such in either adequacy or performance evaluation, both because such test suites may not reflect the distribution of linguistic phenomena in actual application domains, and because the *value* of good coverage at one point versus bad coverage at another is not in itself indicative of fitness to a user's purpose.

Performance Evaluation

There is a long tradition of quantitative performance evaluation in information retrieval, and many of its concepts have been usefully imported into the development of evaluation methodologies for speech and natural language processing. In particular, in considering any attempt at performance evaluation, we can usefully distinguish between three levels of specificity:

- **Criterion:** What it is we're interested in evaluating, in the abstract: Precision, Speed, Error rate.

- **Measure:** Which specific property of system performance we report in an attempt to get at the chosen criterion: Ratio of hits to hits plus misses, seconds to process, percent incorrect.

- **Method:** How we determine the appropriate value for a given measure and a given system: Typically some form of concurrent or post-analytic measurement of system behavior over some benchmark task.

For example, in information retrieval itself, a classic criterion is precision, the extent to which the set of documents retrieved by a formal query satisfy the need which provoked the query. One measure for this is the percentage of documents retrieved which are in fact relevant. One method for computing this, which applies *only* if the extensions of some set of needs over some test collection are *known* in advance, is to simply average over some number of test queries the ratio achieved by the system under test.

For speech recognition, where the criterion is recognition accuracy, one measure is word error rate, and the method used in the current ARPA speech recognition evaluation involves comparing system transcription of the input speech to the *truth* (i.e., transcription by a human expert), using a mutually agreed upon dynamic programing algorithm to score agreement at the word level.

It should be clear from this that the distinction between criterion, measure and method is not hard and fast, and that in any given case the three are interdependent—see Sparck Jones (1994) for a more detailed discussion of these issues.

13.1.2   The Successes and Limitations of Evaluation

As the previous discussion illustrates, evaluation plays an important role for system developers (to tell if their system is improving), for system integrators (to determine which approaches should be used where) and for consumers (to identify which system will best meet a specific set of needs). Beyond this, evaluation plays a critical role in guiding and focusing research.

Periodic performance evaluations have been used successfully in the U.S. to focus attention on specific hard problems: robust information extraction from text, large vocabulary continuous speech recognition, spoken language interfaces, large scale information retrieval, machine translation. These *common evaluations* have motivated researchers both to compete in building advanced systems, and to share information to solve these hard problems. This paradigm has contributed to increased visibility for these areas, rapid technical progress, and increased communication among researchers working on these common evaluations as a result of the *community of effort* which arises from working on a common task using common data.

A major side-effect of performance evaluation has been to increase support for infrastructure. Performance evaluation itself requires significant investment to create annotated corpora and test sets, to create well-documented test procedures and programs, to implement and debug these procedures, and to distribute these to the appropriate parties.

Of course, the focus on performance evaluation comes at a price: periodic evaluations divert effort from research on the underlying technologies, the evaluations may emphasize some aspects of development at the expense of other aspects (e.g., increased accuracy at the expense of real-time interaction), and performance evaluation across systems can be misleading, depending on level of effort in developing the systems under comparison, use of innovative *vs.* proven technologies, and so on.

The *common evaluations* referred to above have all relied on performance evaluation, in part because some of them have received funding through ARPA, which focused on *technology* rather than on *applications*. Increasing emphasis on adequacy evaluation may become appropriate if, as seems likely on both sides of the Atlantic, users and their needs come more to the forefront of funding priorities. There is a difficulty in Europe, however, in that the basic performance evaluation technologies for languages other than English are developed only to a limited extent, with considerable variation across languages.

Successes of Evaluation

As noted above, evaluation has contributed some major successes to the development of speech and natural language processing technology; among these we can count:

- Development of test corpora for speech, spoken language, written language, information retrieval and machine translation, and corresponding performance evaluation methods for aspects of these technologies. In addition, there are other shared resources, described in chapter 12.

- Creation of at least four performance evaluation conferences or workshops that have attracted increasing numbers of researchers, industry and government participants: the Message Understanding Conferences (MUCs), the Text Retrieval Conferences (TRECs), the Machine Translation Evaluation Workshops, and the Spoken Language Technology Workshops.

- Rapid technical progress: evaluation allows progress to be tracked over time; for example, the word error rate for speech recognition has decreased by a factor of two every two years, over the last six years. Also, availability of performance evaluation methods make it possible to explore new paradigms based on automated learning algorithms, as in the use of parse evaluation techniques to build parsers (Brill, 1992).

Limitations of Current Evaluation Methods

As noted above, current evaluation technology also has some significant shortcomings and gaps:

- There has been little focus on how the user interacts with a system. Specifically, there is no performance evaluation methodology for interactive systems, and the methodologies for adequacy evaluation (and for formative evaluation) are difficult to apply and not widely accepted.

- Many of the performance evaluation methods are application-specific—that is, they require that everyone build the same application in order to evaluate their system (or their system components). We have yet to develop good methods of evaluating *understanding* independent of *doing the right thing* in the context of a specific application.

- There is no evaluation methodology for assessing how portable systems are to new application domains. The current high cost of porting language-based systems to new applications hinders transition of this technology to the commercial marketplace.

- Evaluation is labor-intensive and and competes in time and resources with other activities, specifically with the development of new technical approaches. It is critical to find the right balance between technology development and technology assessment.

- Excessive focus on performance evaluation may lead to risk-avoidance strategies, where getting a good score becomes more important than doing good research. Evaluation must be counter-balanced by rewarding risk-taking, if research is to retain its vitality.

- Insufficient attention has been paid to evaluation in multilingual settings. In machine translation, there has been work on evaluation of different language pairs (English-French *vs.* English-Spanish *vs.* English-Japanese). There has also been work in text extraction for multiple languages (Japanese, Spanish). However, there is still a disproportionate emphasis on English, which presents a serious impediment to the widespread applicability of performance evaluation in Europe.

13.1.3   Future Directions

It is clear from both the successes and the shortcomings that evaluation methodologies will continue to evolve and to improve. Evaluation has become so central to progress in the speech and natural language area that it should become a research area in its own right, so that we can correct the problems that have become increasingly evident, while continuing to reap the benefits that evaluation provides.

13.2   Task-Oriented Text Analysis Evaluation

Beth Sundheim

Naval Command, Control and Ocean Surveillance Center RDT&E Division (NC-COSC/NRaD), San Diego, California, USA

The type of text analysis evaluation to be discussed in this section uses complete, naturally-occurring texts as test data and examines text analysis technology from the outside; that is, it examines technology in the context of an application system and treats the system as a black box. This type of evaluation is in contrast with ones that probe the internal workings of a system, such as ones that use constructed test suites of sentences to determine the coverage of a system's grammar. Two types of task-oriented text processing system evaluations have been designed and carried out on a large scale over the last several years:

1. Text retrieval has been evaluated in the context of:

    -   a document routing task, where the system is tuned to match a statement of a user's persistent information need against previously unseen documents;

    -   an *ad hoc* retrieval task, where the system is expected to match a user's one-time query against a more or less static (previously seen) text database.

2. Text understanding has been evaluated in the context of an information extraction task, where the system is tailored to look for certain kinds of facts in texts and to represent the output of its analysis as a set of simulated database records that capture the facts and their interrelationships. More recently, evaluations have been designed that are less domain-dependent and more focused on particular aspects of text understanding.

The forums for reporting the results of these evaluations have been the series of Text REtrieval Conferences (TREC) (Harman, 1993; Harman, 1994) and Message Understanding Conferences (MUC), particularly the more recent ones (DARPA, 1991b; DARPA, 1992b; ARPA, 1993b). The TRECs and MUCs are currently sponsored by the U.S. Advanced Research Projects Agency (ARPA) and have enjoyed the participation of non-U.S. as well as U.S. organizations.

The methodology associated with evaluating system performance on information extraction tasks has developed only in recent years, primarily through the MUC evaluations, and is just starting to mature with respect to the selection and exact formulation of metrics and the definition of readily evaluable tasks. In contrast, text retrieval evaluation methodology is now quite mature, having enjoyed over thirty years of development especially in the U.K. and U.S., and has been further developed via the TRECs, which have made substantial contributions to the text retrieval corpus development methodology and to the definition of evaluation metrics. With a fairly stable task definition and set of metrics, the TRECs have been able to measure performance improvements from one evaluation to the next with more precision than has so far been possible with the MUCs.

There are many similarities between TREC and MUC, including the following:

- Inclusion of both ARPA-sponsored research systems and other systems in the evaluations. Participation has included sites from North America, Europe, Asia and Australia.

- Use of large, naturally-occurring text corpora.

- Objective of end-to-end (*black box*) performance assessment.

- Evaluation metrics that are notionally similar, though different in formulation, reflecting the differences in the nature of the tasks.

The most enduring metrics of performance that have been applied to text retrieval and information extraction are termed *recall* and *precision*. These may be viewed as judging effectiveness from the application user's perspective, since they measure the extent to which the system produced all the appropriate output (recall) and only the appropriate output (precision). In the case of text retrieval, a correct output is a relevant document; in information extraction, a correct output is a relevant fact.

```
Recall = #relevant-returned/#relevant
Precision = #relevant-returned/#returned
```

In the above formulas, *relevant* refers to relevant documents in retrieval and to relevant facts in extraction; *returned* refers to retrieved documents in text retrieval and to extracted facts in information extraction. As will be explained below, text retrieval and information extraction represent fundamentally different tasks; therefore, the implementation of the recall and precision formulas also differs. In particular, the formulation of the precision metric for information extraction includes a term in the denominator for the number of *spurious* facts extracted, as well as the number of correct and incorrect facts extracted.

Typically, text retrieval systems are capable of producing ranked results, with the documents that the system judges more likely relevant ranked at the top of the list. Evaluation of the ranked output results in a recall-precision curve, with points plotted that represent precision at various recall percentages. Such a curve is likely to show very high precision at 10% recall, perhaps 50% precision at 50% recall (for a challenging retrieval task), and a long tail-out toward 100% recall.

A simple information extraction task design might involve a fixed number of data elements (attributes) and a fixed set of alternative values for each attribute. If the system was expected always to produce a fixed number of simulated database records (sets of attributes), and a fixed number of facts per attribute from a fixed set of possible facts, it would be performing a kind of classification task, which is similar to the document routing task. In the document routing task performed by text retrieval systems, the routing queries represent categories, and the task is to determine which, if any, category is matched by a given text. However, an information extraction task typically places no upper bound on the number of facts that can be extracted from a text—the number of facts could conceivably even exceed the number of words in the text. In addition, a given fact to be extracted is not necessarily drawn from a predetermined list of possibilities (categories) but may instead be a text string, such as the name of a victim of a kidnapping event.

Thus, since texts offer differing amounts of relevant information to be extracted and the *right answers* often do not come from a closed set, it is probably impossible for an information extraction system to achieve 100% recall except on the most trivial tasks, and its false alarms are likely to include large amounts of spurious data (as well as simply erroneous data) if it is programmed to behave aggressively, in an effort to enable it to miss as little relevant information as possible. Current information extraction systems are not typically based on statistical algorithms, although there are exceptions. Therefore, evaluation typically does not produce a recall-precision curve for a system, but rather a single measure of performance.

One of the major contributions of both the TREC and the MUC evaluations has been the use of test corpora that are large enough to yield statistically valid performance figures and to support corpus-based system development experiments. The TREC-1 collection contained two-hundred times the number of documents found in a prior standard test collection (Harman, 1993). The MUCs have gradually brought about a similar revolution in the area of information extraction, which started in 1987 with a combined training and test corpus numbering just a few hundred, very short texts, and now uses several thousand longer texts; the number of test articles has increased from tens to hundreds.

To judge the correctness of the retrieval and extraction system outputs, the outputs must be compared with *ground truth*. Ground truth is determined by humans. In text retrieval, where the system may be evaluated using corpora consisting of tens of thousands of documents, it would be almost literally impossible to judge the relevance of all documents with respect to all queries used in the evaluation. Instead, one effective method in a multisystem evaluation on a corpus of that size is to pool the highest-ranked documents returned by each system and to judge the relevance of just those documents. For TREC-3, the 200 highest-ranked documents were pooled. It has been shown that different systems produce significantly different sets of top-ranking documents, and the pooling method can be fairly certain to result in a reasonably complete list of relevant documents (perhaps over 80% complete, on average across queries).

Information extraction systems have been evaluated using relatively small corpora (perhaps 100-300 documents) and just one or two extraction tasks. Ground truth is created by manually generating the appropriate database records for each document in the test set. Ground truth is not perfect truth in either retrieval or extraction, due not only to human factors but also to incomplete evaluation task explanations provided by the evaluators and to the inherent vagueness and ambiguity of text.

Widely varying system architectures, processing techniques, and tools have been tried, tested, and refined in the context of the MUC and TREC evaluations, accelerating progress in the robust processing of naturally-occurring text. There have been exciting innovations in technologies, including hybrid statistical/symbolic techniques and refined pattern-matching techniques. The infrastructure provided by the conferences and evaluations—shared corpora, evaluation metrics, etc.—encourage the interchange of ideas and software resources and help participants understand which techniques work.

The need to isolate system strengths and weaknesses is one of the motivations underlying recent TREC and MUC efforts. These efforts have resulted in a greater range of evaluation options for participants. For example, the range of MUC evaluations has broadened from a single, complex, domain-dependent information extraction task to include also a simple, domain-independent task, and other tasks have been developed to test component-level technologies, such as identification of coreference relations and recognition of special lexical patterns such as person and company names. Various corporate and government organizations in Europe and the U.S. have sponsored similar component-technology, multisite evaluation efforts. These have focused especially on grammars and morphological processors as, for example, did the 1993 Morpholympics evaluation, coordinated by the Gesellschaft für Linguistische Datenverarbeitung (Hausser, 1994).

13.3   Evaluation of Machine Translation and Translation Tools

John Hutchins

University of East Anglia, Norfolk, UK

While there is general agreement about the basic features of machine translation (MT) evaluation (as reflected in general introductory texts Lehrberger & Bourbeau, 1988; Hutchins & Somers, 1992; Arnold et al., 1994), there are no universally accepted and reliable methods and measures, and evaluation methodology has been the subject of much discussion in recent years (e.g., Arnold et al., 1993; Falkedal, 1994; AMTA, 1992).

As in other areas of NLP, three types of evaluation are recognised: adequacy evaluation to determine the fitness of MT systems within a specified operational context; diagnostic evaluation to identify limitations, errors and deficiencies, which may be corrected or improved (by the research team or by the developers); and performance evaluation to assess stages of system development or different technical implementations. Adequacy evaluation is typically performed by potential users and/or purchasers of systems (individuals, companies, or agencies); diagnostic evaluation is the concern mainly of researchers and developers; and performance evaluation may be undertaken by either researchers/developers or by potential users. In the case of production systems, there are also assessments of marketability undertaken by or for MT system vendors.

MT evaluations typically include features not present in evaluations of other NLP systems: the quality of the *raw* (unedited) translations, e.g., intelligibility, accuracy, fidelity, appropriateness of style/register; the usability of facilities for creating and updating dictionaries, for post-editing texts, for controlling input language, for customization of documents, etc.; the extendibility to new language pairs and/or new subject domains; and cost-benefit comparisons with human translation performance. Adequacy evaluations by potential purchasers usually include the testing of systems with sets of *typical* documents. But these are necessarily restricted to specific domains, and for diagnostic and performance evaluation there is a need for more generally applicable and objective *test suites*; these are now under development (King & Falkedal, 1990; Balkan et al., 1994).

Initially, MT evaluation was seen primarily in terms of comparisons of unedited MT output quality and human translations, e.g., the ALPAC evaluations (Council, 1966) and those of the original Logos system (Sinaiko & Klare, 1972; Sinaiko & Klare, 1973). Later, systems were assessed for quality of output and usefulness in operational contexts, e.g., the influential evaluations of Systran by the European Commission (Van Slype, 1982). Subsequently, many potential purchasers have conducted their own comparative evaluations of systems, often unpublished, and often without the benefit of previous evaluations. Valuable contributions to MT evaluation methodology have been made by Rinsche (1993) in her study for the European Commission, and by the JEIDA committee (Nomura & Isahara, 1992), which proposed evaluation tools for both system developers and potential users—described in more detail in section 13.5. The evaluation exercise by ARPA (White et al., 1994) compared the unedited output of the three ARPA-supported experimental systems (Pangloss, Candide, Lingstat) with the output from 13 production systems from Globalink, PC-Translator, Microtac, Pivot, PAHO, Metal, Socatra XLT, Systran, and Winger. The initial intention to measure the *productivity* of systems for potential users was abandoned because it introduced too many variables. Evaluation, therefore, has concentrated on the performance of the *core MT engines* of systems, in comparison with human translations, using measures of adequacy (how well a text *fragment* conveys the information of the source), fluency (whether the output reads like good English, irrespective of accuracy), and comprehension or informativeness (using SAT-like multiple choice tests covering the whole text).

Future Directions

With the rapid growth in sales of MT software and the increasing availability of MT services over networks there is an urgent need for MT researchers, developers and vendors to agree and implement objective, reliable and publicly acceptable benchmarks, standards and evaluation metrics.

13.4   Evaluation of Broad-Coverage Natural-Lang Parsers

Ezra Black

Interpreting Telecommunications Laboratories, ATR, Kyoto, Japan

13.4.1   State of the Art

A *parser* for some natural language (English, Portugese, etc.) is a program that *diagrams* sentences of that language—that supplies for a given sentence a correct grammatical analysis, demarcating its parts (called *constituents*), labeling each, identifying the part of speech of every word used in the sentence, and usually offering additional information, such as the *semantic class* (e.g., Person, Physical Object) of each word and the *functional class* (e.g., Subject, Direct Object) of each constituent of the sentence. A *broad-coverage parser* diagrams *any* sentence of some natural language, or at least agrees to attempt to do so.

Currently, the field of broad-coverage natural-language parsing is in transition. Rigorous, objective and verifiable evaluation procedures have not yet become established practice, although a beginning has been made. Until recently, objective evaluation essentially was not practiced at all, so that even the author of a parsing system had no real idea how accurate, and hence how useful, the system was. In 1991 the Parseval system for *syntactically* evaluating broad-coverage English-language parsers was introduced (Black, Abney, et al., 1991; Harrison, Abney, et al., 1991), and the next year seven creators of such parsers applied Parseval to their systems, all using the same test data (Black, Garside, et al., 1993).

However, the Parseval evaluation routine is an extremely coarse-grained tool. For one thing, most of the information provided by a parse is not taken into account. But more important, the level of agreement on the particulars of linguistic description is fairly superficial among the creators of Parseval, and *a fortiori* among parsing-system authors who could or would not be included in the Parseval planning sessions. Consequently, parsers are evaluated by Parseval at a high remove from the actual parses being judged, and in terms rather foreign to their own vocabulary of linguistic description.

Currently there are plans to extend Parseval into the *semantic* realm, via Semeval, an approach to evaluation modeled on Parseval (see Moore, 1994). But there is *more, not less* disagreement among professionals regarding the proper set of semantic categories for text, the various word senses of any given word, and related semantic issues, than there is about constituent boundaries. So Semeval can be expected to turn out even rougher-grained than Parseval.

13.4.2   Improving the State of the Art

The methodology of objective, rigorous, and verifiable measurement of performance of individual parsing systems is known, albeit by only a minority of practitioners. Key features of this methodology are the use of:

1. *separate* training and test sets;

2. test data from *new* documents only;

3. *large* test sets;

4. responsible *public access* to the test process;

5. *objective* criteria of evaluation;

6. the statement, in advance, of *all* acceptable analyses for a test item;

7. test runs on a *variety* of test materials to match the sort of claims being made for the system; and

8. at least a *twice-yearly* run of a full range of public tests.

A slow transition is now taking place within the field towards the recognition of the value, and even the necessity, of rigor of the above sort within evaluation. This kind of testing is necessary anyway for effective parsing-system development, as opposed to the onerous activities associated with testing via *compromise-based* tools such as Parseval, Semeval, or others. It may never be possible to compare *all* broad-coverage parsers of a given language in terms of a *common coin* of linguistic analysis. Instead, practitioners will probably want to opt for highly accurate and rigorous performance statistics on their own systems alone, rather than extremely coarse-grained scores obtained from comparing their systems with others on the basis of laborious and even dubious technical compromise.

Another progressive development has been the appearance since 1992 of parsing systems which parse previously-unseen text without referring to a set of grammar rules, by processing, statistically or logistically, a *treebank* or set of sentences parsed correctly by hand by competent humans (Black, 1993). These systems are in theory directly comparable, and can employ more rigorous correctness criteria—e.g., exact match of the treebank parse—than can Parseval.

13.4.3 Future Directions

The remainder of the 1990s will probably see two major trends in this area. First should be a move toward the sort of rigor discussed above, when individual systems are evaluated either just to let the system developer himself or herself know the rate at and the manner in which the system is improving over time, or else for the purpose of cross-system comparisons on a given document, where this is possible (see above). Second should be a move away from evaluating parsing systems in linguistic terms at all, i.e., away from judging the parses output by a system simply on their merits as parses. This move would be *toward* evaluating a parser on the basis of the *value added* to a variety of *client systems*. These would be bona fide, fully-developed AI systems of one sort or another, with a need for a parsing component, as opposed to tasks conceived artificially, simply for the purposes of providing a *task* to support evaluation. Examples might be pre-existing systems for speech synthesis, speech recognition, handwriting recognition, optical character recognition, and machine translation. In this case the evaluation of a broad-coverage parsing system would come to be based on its performance over a *gamut* of such applications.

13.5   Human Factors and User Acceptability

Margaret King

University of Geneva, Switzerland

It is quite astonishing how little attention is paid to users in the published literature on evaluation. To some extent, this can be explained by looking at who does evaluation and is prepared to talk about it. Essentially, we find three classes:

- Researchers or manufacturers concerned with system development: The researchers do not have the resources to carry out any systematic enquiry into what a group of users might actually want. The developers mainly come into contact with users through their customer support services. In both cases, when a user is taken into account, it is an abstract, ideal user, whose needs correspond to those the researcher or system developer thinks he would have.

- Funding agencies, especially, in this context, ARPA: since what they are primarily interested in is the development of a core technology, evaluation is seen as an assessment of a system's ability to perform a pre-determined task taken to reflect the barriers the core technology should be attacking. In this perspective, thinking of an ultimate user is premature and irrelevant.

- Potential purchasers of commercially available systems: here, of course, the user is directly present, but concerned only with his own needs.

13.5.1   State of the Art

One exception to the above comes from the area of machine translation. The Japan Electronic Industry Development Association's Machine Translation System Research Committee has a sub-committee, the Machine Translation Market and Technology Study Committee, which has recently published a report on evaluation criteria for machine translation systems. (A summary account can be found in: Nomura & Isahara, 1992.)

The committee concentrated on three aspects:

- **User Evaluation of Economic Factors:** The aim is to support making decisions about what kind of system is suitable in those cases where introducing a machine translation system in the near future is being considered. Economic factors only are taken into consideration.

- **Technical Evaluation by Users:** The aim is to compare the users' needs with what is offered by a particular system, rather than to offer any abstract evaluation of the system per se.

- **Technical Evaluation by Developers:** The aim here is to support in-house evaluation of the technical level the system has achieved and of whether the system suits the purpose for which it was developed.

In what follows we shall concentrate on the first two aspects:

User evaluation of economic factors is essentially accomplished by analyzing the replies to two questionnaires, the first concerning the user's present situation, the second his perceived needs. The answers are evaluated in the light of a set of parameters relating the answers to what advantages a machine translation system could offer. The results of are presented graphically in the form of a *radar chart*, which provides a profile of the user.

In parallel, a similar exercise is carried out to produce profiles of typical users of types of machine translation systems. Seven types of systems are distinguished in all, which cover in fact the whole range of translators' aids. The committee members define a typical user for each type of system, and a profile for that user is constructed on the basis of the answers he would be expected to give to the questionnaire. This profile then becomes the profile of the system-type. Types of system can then be paired with types of users by comparing the radar chart profiles for user and for system and finding the closest match.

The validity of the procedure is confirmed by taking, for each system type, a further group of four (assumed) users, filling out the questionnaires on their behalf, and checking that the closest match is what it is expected to be.

Two points are worth making about this procedure. The first is that what is being considered is not really systems but what Galliers and Sparck Jones (1993) call *setups*, that is, a system embedded in a context of use. This is important: from a real user's point of view, there is usually very little point in evaluating a system in isolation. The ISO 9000 series on quality assessment of software makes the same point, although from a rather different viewpoint:

> "The importance of each quality characteristic varies depending on the class of software. For example, reliability is most important for a mission critical system software, efficiency is most important for a time critical real time system software, and usability is most important for an interactive end user software."—ISO (1991)

The second point shades rather to the negative; the users considered in constructing the radar charts of the system type are not real users. It is important to be aware of the dangers involved in deciding on behalf of some third party what it is he really wants or needs.

This potential weakness is partially at least counterbalanced by the second type of evaluation, called in the committee's reports "technical evaluation by users." Here, an attempt is made to determine the user's real needs and to compare them with what can be offered by specific products in order to evaluate how satisfied the client is likely to be with what is offered.

Attempts to take user needs into consideration were also made within the Esprit Translators' Workbench projects (ESPRIT project 2315, TWB I and 6005, TWB II). Catalogues were developed for describing user requirements, term banks, translation memories, machine translation, machine assisted terminology work and for checkers. The catalogues were intended to serve a double purpose, first as a way of setting up requirements specifications, and secondly as a way of evaluating to what extent a particular tool corresponds to a given user's needs. In general terms, each catalogue comprises facts relevant to the software and related to a certain quality characteristic, such as task adequacy, error tolerance, execution efficiency, ease of use, ease of learning, etc. Users can tick items which are relevant to them, give items an individual priority and rate each priority by specifying its relative importance compared to other items of the same type (Höge, Hohmann, et al., 1992; Höge, Hohmann, et al., 1993).

13.5.2   Current Work

In this section, we look at the efforts of the EAGLES Evaluation Group to build on these and other efforts in order to define an evaluation methodology where the users' views and needs are systematically taken into account.

The overall aim of the Evaluation Group is to define a common general framework within which specific evaluations can be designed. In this work it has also been influenced by the discussions reported in Thompson (1992), by the work of Galliers and Sparck Jones (1993) and by the work on evaluation within the ARPA community.

The group distinguishes three types of evaluation: progress evaluation, where the aim is to assess the progress of a system towards some other ideal state of the same system, diagnostic evaluation, where the aim is to find out where things go wrong and why, and adequacy evaluation, where the aim is to assess the adequacy of the system to fulfill a specified set of needs.

User-centered evaluation is clearly adequacy evaluation. The first problem becomes evident at this point. Adequacy evaluation involves finding out whether a product satisfies the user's needs. But users are very numerous, and have widely differing needs. It would be out of the question to work in terms of individuals. However, on the basis of surveying what a sufficiently large number of individual users say, it should be possible to identify classes of users and to construct profiles of each one of these classes. These profiles can then be used as the basis for determining what attributes of particular classes of products are of interest to particular classes of users. Then, for each such attribute, a procedure can be specified for discovering its value in the case of any particular product.

The appropriate analogy is with the kind of reports published by consumer associations, where different products of the same general class are compared along a number of different dimensions. Consumer reports typically are concerned with products based on a relatively stable technology. Transferring the paradigm to the more sophisticated products of the language industry can require a great deal of work, and sometimes a considerable degree of ingenuity. In the interest of producing concrete results in the short term, while at the same time checking the validity of the general framework, the EAGLES group, together with an associated LRE project, TEMAA, is concentrating on designing evaluation packages for market or near-market products in two areas, authoring aids and translation aids. These areas are of particular interest partly because the market is large, and therefore the results are likely to be of interest to a large number of potential users, partly because at least some of the products in these areas are based on a fairly stable technology.

If it proves possible to produce evaluation packages for a range of language industry products, they can be expected to constitute a *de facto* standard for such products. Working on how this can be done for the more modest products of the language industry lays the foundation for extending the enterprise to more sophisticated products.

13.6 Speech Input: Assessment and Evaluation

David S. Pallett[a] & Adrian Fourcin[b]

[a] National Institute of Standards and Technology, Gaithersburg, Maryland, USA
[b] University College of London, London, UK

Assessment and evaluation[1] are concerned with the global quantification and detailed measurement of system performance. Disciplined procedures of this type are at the heart of progress in any field of engineering. They not only make it possible to monitor change over time in a given system and meaningfully compare one approach with another; they also usefully extend basic knowledge.

Within the past several years, there has been widespread and growing international interest in a number of issues involved in speech input system performance assessment. In Europe, the SAM Projects (ESPRIT Projects 2589 and 6819) addressed "Multi-Lingual Speech Input/Output Assessment, Methodology and Standardization" (Fourcin et al., 1992). In the United States, the ARPA Spoken Language Program has made extensive use of periodic *benchmark tests* to gauge progress and to serve as a focal point for discussions at a number of ARPA-sponsored workshops (DARPA, 1989; DARPA, 1990; DARPA, 1991a; DARPA, 1992a; ARPA, 1993a; ARPA, 1994).

There have also been a number of international workshops, such as those held in conjunction with the Eurospeech Conferences and the International Conferences on Spoken Language Processing (Jones & Mariani, 1992). The present

---

[1]See the appendix at the end of this section for a definition of *assessment* and *evaluation* within SAM.

contribution focuses on three sub-areas: speech recognition, speech understanding, and speaker recognition.

13.6.1   Speech Recognition (Input) Assessment

To a first approximation, the task of *speech recognition* may be regarded as being to produce an hypothesized orthographic transcription from a spoken language input. The most commonly cited output is in the form of *words* in ASCII characters, although other units (e.g., syllables or phonemes) are sometimes found.

Assessment methods developed for speech recognition involve a complementary combination of system-based approaches with performance-based techniques. System-based approaches either deal with the recognition system as a whole (*black box methods*) or provide access to individual modules within the complete recognizer (*glass box methods*). For each of these approaches, quantitative appraisals of performance may range from the use of applications related (non-diagnostic) training and test data to highly diagnostic techniques, specifically oriented toward detailed evaluations involving the use of test data going from, for example, phonetically controlled speech to language independent data derived from artificial speech generation. These extremes of performance measurement fit into a continuum into which methods of global benchmarking assessment and detailed evaluation may be categorized into the following groups:

(a) application-oriented techniques based on the use of general databases, collected under what might be regarded as representative conditions

(b) the use of specific calibrated databases, which are designed to represent a broad spectrum of operational and environmental conditions which affect recognizer performance

(c) the use of reference methods in order to achieve cross-site standardization, based on the use of a reference recognizer, or referring to human recognition

(d) diagnostic methods, based on the use of specific vocabularies or specially designed sequences

(e) techniques using artificial test signals to achieve precision of control of the experimental design and/or language independence

(f) benchmarking which is based on predictive methods using system parameters and/or speech knowledge

The most frequently used methods (e.g., those used within the ARPA program) belong to group (a). Much of the data used for speech recognizer performance assessment consists of *read* speech, not spontaneous, goal-directed speech. Some of the data used for large-scale performance assessment efforts is openly available (see section 12.6).

Automatic scoring methods are used in most cases, with reliance on dynamic programing methods to align reference and system hypothesis output strings. Results are typically reported in terms of the word or sentence error percentages, where errors are categorized as substitutions, insertions, or deletions.

The statistical validity of assessment tests for recognizers has been studied (Chollet, Capman, et al., 1991), and a number of well-known statistical measures are in use, using both parametric and non-parametric techniques.

13.6.2 Speech (Spoken Language) Understanding Assessment

In *speech understanding* some semantic analysis or interpretation of the speech recognizer's output is implicitly or explicitly required—for example, where the process of automatic speech recognition is intended as input to a command/control application.

Performance assessment for speech, or more generally *spoken language*, understanding systems is substantially more complex and problematic than for speech recognition systems. Procedures for performance assessment of natural language processing systems, in general, are not yet well established, but many relevant issues have been identified and addressed in increasing detail at workshops in Pennsylvania in 1988, Berkeley in 1991, Edinburgh and Trento in 1992, as well as at the ARPA Human Language Technology Workshops.

For spoken language understanding systems, the use of reference speech databases as system input is not so clearly appropriate, because issues involving human behavior and human-computer interactivity become complicating factors. "It is particularly difficult to engage in speech evaluation where the entire system design assumes a high degree of interaction between user and system, and makes explicit allowance for [dialogue] clarification and recovery, as in the VODIS telephone train inquiry case" (Galliers & Sparck Jones, 1993).

Nonetheless, this procedure has, for example, extensively been implemented within the ARPA Spoken Language Program in the U.S., in the Air Travel Information Service (ATIS) domain, a spoken natural language (air travel information) database query task. "The evaluation methodology is *black box* and implemented using an automatic evaluation system. It is performance related; only the content of an answer retrieved from the database is evaluated" (Galliers & Sparck Jones, 1993).

A variety of procedures have been suggested for accommodating interactive systems with dialogue management and/or clarification. So-called *end-to-end* assessment methods—in which measures of system-user efficiency in task completion and/or subjective measures of satisfaction are derived—are frequently complicated by large subject-to-subject or task-to-task variabilities, and their attendant statistical considerations. It is clear that these complications will be relevant to the assessment and benchmarking of commercial technology for real applications, as well as to their detailed evaluation and future development.

13.6.3   Speaker Recognition Assessment

Speaker recognition technology is conventionally discussed in terms of two different areas: speaker identification and speaker verification (see section 1.7). Speaker identification can often be thought of as a *closed set* problem, where the system's task is to identify an unidentified voice as coming from one of a set of N reference speakers. In practical applications, *open set* speaker identification permits a rejection response corresponding to the possibility that the unidentified voice does not belong to any of the reference speakers. The task of a speaker verification system is to decide whether the unlabeled voice belongs to a specific *genuine* speaker who has previously claimed his identity to the system, or an *imposter*.

A state of the art in the evaluation of speaker identification and verification systems can be found in the Proceedings of the Automatic Speaker Recognition, Identification and Verification ETRW Workshop (Chollet, Bimbot, et al., 1994), as a summary of the initial efforts of ESPRIT Project 6819, Speech Technology Assessment Methodology in Multilingual Applications (SAM-A) (Bimbot et al., 1994).

13.6.4   Future Directions

In the shorter term, provision should be made for more accurate speech recognition scoring procedures making use of time-marked reference transcriptions and system outputs. Such procedures may prove essential when conducting multilingual performance assessment, to facilitate cross comparison and, for example, because of increased ambiguity concerning word boundaries for some languages. The adequate provision of these facilities will involve quite new approaches to the large-scale accurate labeling of speech databases.

The increasingly wide area of applications of speech recognition technology introduces new needs and new problems. The need to support fluent dialogue interaction with a range of speakers, accents, dialects and conditions of health increases the complexity of assessment and evaluation for developer and user alike. For truly spontaneous speech input collected in operational environments, the presence of disfluencies (e.g., pause-fillers, word fragments, false starts and restarts) and noise artifacts provide additional complicating factors.

The associated need for systems to be able to be trained so as to work with a range of language inputs similarly imposes a much greater burden on the organization and collection of appropriate spoken language corpora. This in turn should lead to the gradual use of more analytic and language independent techniques (glass box techniques) and an increasingly close association between work in speech input with speech output/synthesis and natural language processing.

Appendix: Assessment and Evaluation Defined

The increasing complexity of processing associated with the development and application of spoken language processing systems is necessarily tied in with an increasing need for precision, both in the methods employed for the appraisal of performance and in our use of the description of these methods.

Assessment is the process of system appraisal which leads to global, overall, quantification of performance. Assessment is related conceptually to black box methods in which the detailed mechanisms of processing are not considered. (The word itself has its origin in the latin *assidere*—to sit by—and relates to the levying of tax on the gross production of an enterprise.)

Evaluation involves the analytic description of system performance in terms of defined factors; it is concerned with detailed measurement. Evaluation is conceptually related to the *glass box* approach, in which the objective is, for example, to gain a greater understanding of system performance from the use of precision diagnostic techniques based on special purpose phonetic databases. (The word itself has its origins in the French word *evaluer*—to calculate from a mathematical expression or to express in terms of something already known.)

13.7 Speech Synthesis Evaluation

Louis C. W. Pols

University of Amsterdam, The Netherlands

The possibility of generating any existing text, any to-be-worked-out concept, or any piece of database information as intelligible and natural sounding (synthetic) speech is an important component in many speech technology applications (Sorin, 1994). System developers, product buyers, and end users are all interested in having appropriate scores to specify system performance in absolute (e.g., percentage correct phoneme or word intelligibility scores) and in relative terms (e.g., this module sounds more natural for that specific application in that language than another module) (Jekosch, 1993).

Since synthetic speech is generally derived from text input (see also chapter 5), not just a properly functioning acoustic generator is required, but also proper text interpretation and preprocessing, grapheme-to-phoneme conversion, phrasing and stress assignment, as well as prosody, and speaker and style characteristics have to be adequate. On all these, and several other, levels one might like to be able to specify the performance, unless one really only wants to know whether a specific task can properly be performed in a given amount of time.

13.7.1 Modular Diagnostic Evaluation

At this diagnostic level a suite of tests is already available, although there is little standardization so far, nor are there proper benchmarks. Also, comparability of test design and interpretability of results over languages is a major point of concern (Logan, Greene, et al., 1989; Pols, 1991). The type of tests we have in mind here are methods to evaluate system performance at the level of text pre-processing, grapheme-to-phoneme conversion, phrasing, accentuation (focus), phoneme intelligibility, word and (proper) name intelligibility (Spiegel,

1993), performance with ambiguous sentences, comprehension tests, and psycholinguistic tests such as lexical decision and word recall. There is a genuine lack
of proper tests concerning prosody, and speaker, style and emotion characteristics, but this is partly so because rule-synthesizers themselves are not yet very
advanced concerning these aspects either (Pols, 1994b). However, concatenative synthesis with units taken from large databases plus imitation of prosodic
characteristics, is one way to overcome this problem of insufficient knowledge
concerning detailed rules. The result is high-quality synthesis for specific applications with one voice and one style only.

13.7.2   Global Overall Performance

In this global category fall the overall quality judgments, such as the mean
opinion score (MOS), as commonly used in telecommunication applications.
Such tests have little diagnostic value, but can clearly indicate whether the
speech quality is acceptable for a specific application by the general public. One
can think of telecommunication applications such as a spoken weather forecast,
or access to e-mail via a spoken output. Prototypes of reading machines for
the visually-impaired, allowing them to listen to a spoken newspaper, are also
evaluated this way. In field tests, not just the speech quality but also the
functionality of the application should be evaluated.

13.7.3   ·Towards International Standards

Although presently there is little standardization and there is a lack of proper
multilingual benchmarks for speech synthesis various organizations are working
on it. Via the Spoken Language Working Group in Eagles, a state-of-the-art
report with recommendations on the assessment of speech output systems has
been compiled (Eagles, 1995), largely based on earlier work within the Esprit-
SAM project (Pols & SAM-partners, 1992). The Speech Output Group within
the world-wide organization COCOSDA has taken various initiatives with respect to synthesis assessment and the use of databases (Pols & Jekosch, 1994).
One recent intriguing proposal is to arrange real-time access to any operational
text-to-speech system via the World Wide Web. The ITU-TS recently produced
a recommendation about the subjective performance assessment of synthetic
speech over the telephone (ITU, 1993; Klaus, Klix, et al., 1993).

13.7.4   Future Directions

In the future, we will probably see more and more integrated text and speech
technology in an interactive dialogue system where text-to-speech output is just
one of several output options (Pols, 1994a). The inherent quality of the speech
synthesizer should then also be compared against other output devices such
as canned natural (manipulated) speech, coded speech, and visual and tactile
displays. Also the integration of these various elements then becomes more
important, and their performance should be evaluated accordingly.

13.8   Usability and Interface Design

Sharon Oviatt

Oregon Graduate Institute of Science & Technology, Portland, Oregon, USA

To date, the development of spoken language systems primarily has been a technology-driven phenomenon. As speech recognition has improved, progress has traditionally been documented in the reduction of word error rates (Pallett, Fiscus, et al., 1994). However, reporting word error rate fails to express the frustration typically experienced by users who cannot complete a task with current speech technology (Rhyne & Wolf, 1993). Although the successful design of interfaces is essential to supporting usable spoken language systems, research on human-computer spoken interaction currently represents a gap in our scientific knowledge. Moreover, this gap is widely recognized as having generated a bottleneck in our ability to deploy robust speech technology in actual field settings.

Among other challenges, interfaces will be needed that can guide users' spontaneous speech to coincide with system capabilities, since spontaneous speech is known to be particularly variable along a number of linguistic dimensions (Cole, Hirschman, et al., 1995). Interface techniques for successfully constraining spoken input have been studied most extensively by the telecommunications industry as it strives to automate operator services (Karis & Dobroth, 1991; Spitz, 1991). Such work has emphasized the need for realistic and *situated* user testing, often in field settings, and has shown that dramatic variation can occur in the successful elicitation of target speech depending on the type of system prompt.

Other research has demonstrated that the principle of linguistic convergence, or the tendency of people's speech patterns to gravitate toward those of their interactive partner, can be employed to guide wordiness, lexical choice, and grammatical structure during human-computer spoken interactions, and without imposing any explicit constraints on user behavior (Zoltan-Ford, 1991). In addition, research has shown that difficult sources of variability in human speech (e.g., disfluencies, syntactic ambiguity) can be reduced by a factor of 2-to-8 fold through alteration of interface parameters (Oviatt, 1995; Oviatt, Cohen, et al., 1994). Such work demonstrates the potential impact that interface design can have on managing spoken input, although interface techniques have been underexploited for this purpose. In all of these areas, research typically has involved *proactive* performance assessment using simulation techniques, which is the preferred method of conducting evaluations of systems in the planning stages.

Future Directions

Many basic issues need to be addressed before technology can leverage fully from the natural advantages of speech—including the speed, ease, spontaneity, and expressive power that people experience when using it during human-human communication. For example, research is needed to evaluate different types of natural spoken dialogue, spontaneous speech characteristics and their management, and dimensions of human-computer interactivity that influence spoken communication. With respect to the latter, research is especially needed on optimal delivery of system confirmation feedback, error patterns and their resolution, flexible regulation of conversational control, and management of users' inflated expectations of the *interactional* coverage of spoken language systems. In addition, the functional role that ultimately is most suitable for speech technology needs to be evaluated further. Finally, assessment is needed of the potential usability advantages of multimodal systems incorporating speech over unimodal speech systems, with respect to breadth of utility, ease of error handling, learnability, flexibility, and overall robustness (Cohen & Oviatt, 1994; Cole, Hirschman, et al., 1995). To support all of these research agendas, tools will be needed for building and adapting high quality, semiautomatic simulations. Such an infrastructure can be used to evaluate the critical performance trade-offs that designers will encounter as they strive to design more usable spoken language systems.

13.9   Speech Communication Quality

Herman J. M. Steeneken

TNO Human Factors Research Institute, Soesterberg, The Netherlands

Speech is considered to be the major means of communication between people. In many situations, however, the speech signal we are listening to is degraded, and only a limited transfer of information is obtained. The purpose of assessment is to quantify these limitations and to identify the limitations responsible for the loss in intelligibility. For assessment of speech communication systems three major evaluation methods are mainly used:

1. subjective intelligibility based on scores for correct recall of sentences, words or phonemes;

2. quality ratings based on a subjective impression; and

3. objective measures based on physical properties of the speech transmission system.

A comprehensive overview is given by Steeneken (1992).

13.9.1   Subjective Intelligibility Tests

These are based on various types of speech material evaluated in speaker-listener communication. All these tests have their specific advantages and limitations, mostly related to the speech elements tested. Speech elements frequently used for testing are phonemes, words (digits, alphabet, meaningful words, or nonsense CVC-words (Consonant-Vowel-Consonant), sentences, and sometimes a free conversation. The percentage of correctly recalled items of the set presented gives the score. The recall procedure can be based on a given limited set of responses or on an open response design in which all possible alternatives are allowed as a response. A limited response set is used with the so-called rhyme tests. These type of tests are easy to administer and do not require extensive training by the listeners in order to arrive at stable scores. Rhyme tests may, depending on the design, disregard specific phoneme confusions (House, Williams, et al., 1965). Open response tests, especially those which make use of nonsense words, require extensive training of the listeners. However, additionally to the word and phoneme scores, possible confusion between phonemes are obtained. This allows for diagnostic analysis. Redundant speech material (sentences, rhyme tests) suffers from ceiling effects (100% score at poor-to-fair conditions) while tests based on nonsense words may discriminate between good and excellent conditions.

13.9.2 Quality Rating or Mean Opinion Scoring (MOS)

As noted in sections 10.2.2 and 10.2.3, MOS is a more global method used to evaluate the user's acceptance of a transmission channel or speech output system. It reflects the total auditory impression of speech by a listener. For quality ratings, normal test sentences or a free conversation are used to obtain the listener's impression. The listener is asked to rate his impression on subjective scales such as: intelligibility, quality, acceptability, naturalness, etc. The MOS gives a wide variation among listener scores and does not give an absolute measure, since the scales used by the listeners are not calibrated.

13.9.3 Objective Measures

Objective measures based on physical aspects quantify the effect on the speech signal and the related loss of intelligibility due to deteriorations as: a limited frequency transfer, masking noises with various spectra, reverberation and echoes, and a nonlinear transfer resulting from peak clipping, quantization, or interruptions. Frequently used methods are the Articulation Index (AI) (Kryter, 1962) and the Speech Transmission Index (STI), (Steeneken & Houtgast, 1980). The STI makes use of artificial test signals, which are passed through the system under test and analyzed at the output-side. Such a measurement can be performed typically in 15 seconds (Steeneken, Verhave, et al., 1993), while subjective measurements require at least one hour.

In figure 13.1, the relation between some intelligibility measures and the STI is given. These results are based on cumulated results obtained over the years. A subjective qualification, based on an international comparison (Houtgast & Steeneken, 1984), is also given. The graph also demonstrates the ceiling effect of intelligibility tests making use of redundant speech material.

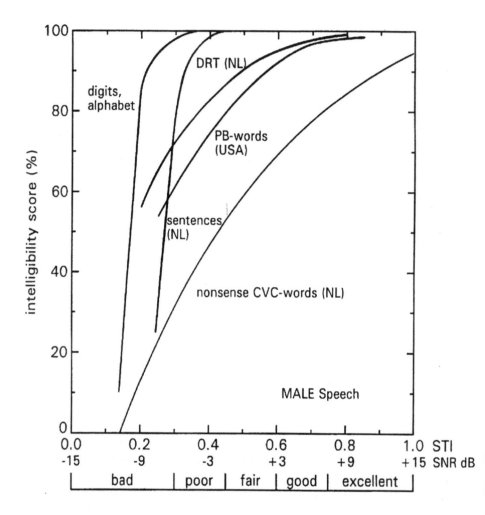

Figure 13.1: Relation between and qualification of some subjective intelligibility measures and the objective STI.

		Recognized as			Reject	Error
		a b c d				
	a	9		1			1
True ID	b		8			2	0
	c	2		6	1	1	3
	d	1			9		1
		3	0	0	2	3	5

Figure 13.2: Confusion matrix

13.10   Character Recognition

Junichi Kanai

University of Nevada, Las Vegas, Nevada, USA

The variables that affect the performance of an optical character recognition (OCR) system include variations in the clarity of printed documents, as well as their layout style. These factors contribute to the number of needed performance metrics, to the need for large quantities of test data, and the necessity of automating the evaluation task.

Traditionally, the performance of OCR algorithms and systems is based on the recognition of isolated characters. When a system classifies an individual character, its output is typically a character label or a reject marker that corresponds to an unrecognized character. By comparing output labels with the correct labels, the number of correct recognitions, substitution errors (misrecognized characters), and rejects (unrecognized characters) are determined. The standard display of the results of classifying individual characters is the confusion matrix, such as Figure 13.2.

The character accuracy is:

Recognized-Characters / Input-Characters

The cost of correcting residual errors in output is:

$W_1 \times$ Substitution-Errors $+ W_2 \times$ Rejects

where W_1 and W_2 are costs associated with correcting a substitution error and a reject, respectively.

Many OCR systems use morphological (n-gram) and lexical techniques to correct recognition errors. To evaluate the performance of such systems, word, sentence, or paragraph images are needed. Since linguistic characteristics, such as n-gram statistics and word frequency, depend on document class (or domain), standard lexicons or corpora for training and testing extracted from a variety of document classes are needed. As OCR systems employ other natural language processing techniques to improve accuracy, appropriate training and test databases must be developed.

OCR and document analysis systems recognize not only text but also other features of documents, such as extraction of articles from a page and recognition of the logical structure of an article. New metrics and appropriate resources, such as document-based test data, must be made available.

Since the notion of *accuracy* depends upon the specific application involved, application-specific metrics are also important. Such metrics can also help end users to determine the feasibility of OCR in their tasks. Consider text retrieval applications. Users of text retrieval systems are interested in words and their correct reading order and almost never in individual characters. Thus, *word accuracy* is a more appropriate metric. Moreover, for these applications, discriminating between *stopwords* and *non-stopwords* is important. Stopwords are common words, such as *the*, *but*, and *which*, that are normally not indexed because they have essentially no retrieval value. Therefore, correct recognition of words that are not stopwords is an even more important metric for these applications (Rice, Kanai, et al., 1993).

Machine translation, document filtering, and other applications require a different measure of accuracy. Many new application-specific metrics are needed to objectively assess progress made in OCR research. Examples of metrics and needed metrics are described in Rice, Kanai, et al. (1994); Kanai, Rice, et al. (1993).

Since a variety of factors affects the performance of OCR systems, a large amount of input test data must be used in the evaluation processes. Consider testing recognition of text printed in a variety of fonts. Over 3,000 combinations of typefaces and type styles are available for laser printers. If ten type sizes are used, over 30,000 test samples are required just to examine one instance of output for each input. Thus, automating both the measurement tasks and the analysis of data are essential. Aside from eliminating human error, automated experiments have the following benefits:

- Experiments are reproducible.

- The inherent consistency of automated systems tends to avoid bias toward algorithms by *excusing* certain types of errors.

- Large (statistically-significant) experiments can be conducted with little additional effort.

However, setting up automated testing systems (and metrics) is both costly and technically challenging. An example of an automated testing environment is described in Rice (1993).

There are different ways to prepare test data. Example sets of real-world document images with the associated *truth* representation are an ideal form of input test data. The *truth* representation and attributes of the input images must be manually prepared. Our experience shows that it takes an average of 2 man-hours to prepare basic page-based data from a page, including the almost 100% accurate *truth* representation. Therefore, such data are extremely expensive.

It is also possible to generate simulated data. It is customary to perturb ideal images or sample hand-written characters by adding noise. Examples of distortion models are given in Ishii (1983); Baird (1992); Kanungo, Haralick, et al. (1993). This approach eliminates expensive *truth* preparation and allows researchers to control individual noise variables.

In spite of the appeal of generating large test databases this way, their value in predicting the behavior of OCR systems under field conditions has not been established. The evaluation and comparison of real-world distortion (example sets) and simulated distortion are important new research tasks. Validation methods have been proposed by Nagy (1994); Li, Lopresti, et al. (1994).

Currently, most of the available databases are character-based. The ETL Character Database[†] mainly contains hand-printed segmented Japanese characters. The U.S. Postal Service[†] released a database containing hand-written characters extracted from envelope address blocks. The National Institute of Standards and Technology (NIST)[†] distributes a large number of hand-written segmented characters and hand-printed segmented characters.

The University of Washington[†] has released a database (UW-I) that contains 1,147 page images from scientific and technical journals with the corresponding *truth* representation. It also includes image degradation models and performance evaluation tools. The UW-II data set contains 43 complete articles in English and other data.

To objectively measure progress in character recognition technology and to identify research problems, two kinds of evaluation are needed: internal evaluation and independent evaluation. In internal evaluation, researchers' own test data sets or standard (public) test databases are used to measure and compare their progress. The creation and distribution of a variety of standard test databases is an important task in the OCR research community.

Since character recognition systems can be customized or trained to accurately recognize a given set of data, independent evaluation is also required for objective final assessment. In independent evaluation, test databases are hidden from the development process.

In 1991, the Chinese government evaluated Chinese OCR systems developed under the State Plan 863 (CCW, 1991). Tests were strictly conducted using standardized data sets. The best machine-printed character recognition rates with and without context were 97.84% and 97.80%, respectively. The best hand-written character recognition rate without adapting to a particular user was 80%.

In 1992, the U.S. Census Bureau and NIST determined the state of the art in recognition of hand-written segmented characters (Wilkinson, Geist, et al.,

---

[†]See section 12.6.3 for contact addresses.

1992). Twenty-six organizations from North America and Europe participated in this test program. About half of the systems correctly recognized over 95% of the digits, over 90% of the upper-case letters, and over 80% of the lower-case letters in the tests.

In 1992, the Institute for Posts and Telecommunications Policy in Japan evaluated OCR technology for recognizing postal codes (Matsui, Noumi, et al., 1993). Hand-written segmented character images were used to test systems. Five universities and eight OCR vendors submitted their systems. The highest recognition rate was 96.22% with the substitution error rate 0.37%.

Since 1992, the Information Science Research Institute at the University of Nevada, Las Vegas, has been conducting evaluation of OCR technology for recognition of machine-printed documents. In the 1994 study, six pre-release systems developed by commercial OCR vendors were tested using two sets of page images (Rice, Kanai, et al., 1994). These systems correctly recognized over 99% of the characters in good quality pages. However, there is a significant reduction in accuracy on poor quality pages. This study also includes other metrics, such as word accuracy, non-stopword accuracy, and automatic page segmentation.

Future Directions

In this rapidly evolving information age, the need for automated data entry systems is essential. To expedite progress in this field, there is a need for large quantities of both test and training data. This situation is likely to continue until the resources needed to provide such data are made available.

13.11   Chapter References

AMTA (1992). *MT evaluation: basis for future directions*, Washington, D.C. Association for Machine Translation in the Americas.

Arnold, D. et al. (1994). *Machine translation: an introductory guide.* NCC/Blackwell, Manchester, Oxford.

Arnold, E. et al. (1993). Special issue on evaluation of MT systems. *Machine Translation*, 8(1-2):1–126.

ARPA (1993a). *Proceedings of the 1993 ARPA Human Language Technology Workshop*, Princeton, New Jersey. Advanced Research Projects Agency, Morgan Kaufmann.

ARPA (1993b). *Proceedings of the Fifth Message Understanding Conference*, Baltimore, Maryland. Morgan Kaufmann.

ARPA (1994). *Proceedings of the 1994 ARPA Human Language Technology Workshop*, Princeton, New Jersey. Advanced Research Projects Agency, Morgan Kaufmann.

Baird, H. S. (1992). Document image defect models. In Baird, H. S., Bunke, H., and Yamamoto, K., editors, *Structured Document Analysis*, pages 1–16. Springer-Verlag.

Balkan, L. et al. (1994). Test suites for natural language processing. *Translating and the Computer*, 16:51–58. papers presented at a conference.

Bimbot, F. et al. (1994). Assessment methodology for speaker identification and verification systems: an overview. Technical Report SAM-A Project 6819, Task 2500, SAM-A, Martigny, Switzerland.

Black, E. (1993). Parsing english by computer: The state of the art. In *Proceedings of the 1993 International Symposium on Spoken Dialogue*, Waseda University, Tokyo.

Black, E., Abney, S., Flickenger, D., Gdaniec, C., Grishman, R., Harrison, P., Hindle, D., Ingria, R., Jelinek, F., Klavans, J., Liberman, M., Marcus, M., Roukos, S., Santorini, B., and Strzalkowski, T. (1991). A procedure for quantitatively comparing the syntactic coverage of English grammars. In *Proceedings of the Fourth DARPA Speech and Natural Language Workshop*, Pacific Grove, California. Defense Advanced Research Projects Agency, Morgan Kaufmann.

Black, E., Garside, R., and Leech, G., editors (1993). *Statistically-Driven Computer Grammars of English: The IBM/Lancaster Approach*. Rodopi, Amsterdam, Atlanta.

Brill, E. (1992). A simple rule-based part of speech tagger. In *Proceedings of the Third Conference on Applied Natural Language Processing*, Trento, Italy.

CCW (1991). Research achievements on Chinese character and voice recognition. *China Computer World*, 349. Written in Chinese.

Chollet, G., Bimbot, F., and Paoloni, A., editors (1994). *Proceedings of the ESCA Workshop on Automatic Speaker Recognition, Identification and Verification*, Martigny, Switzerland. ESCA.

Chollet, G., Capman, F., and Daoud, J. F. A. (1991). On the evaluation of recognizers—statistical validity of the tests. Technical Report SAM-ENST-02, SAM.

Cohen, P. R. and Oviatt, S. L. (1994). The role of voice in human-machine communication. In Roe, D. B. and Wilpon, J., editors, *Voice Communication Between Humans and Machines*, pages 34–75. National Academy of Sciences Press, Washington, DC.

Cole, R. A., Hirschman, L., Atlas, L., Beckman, M., Bierman, A., Bush, M., Cohen, J., Garcia, O., Hanson, B., Hermansky, H., Levinson, S., McKeown, K., Morgan, N., Novick, D., Ostendorf, M., Oviatt, S., Price, P., Silverman, H., Spitz, J., Waibel, A., Weinstein, C., Zahorian, S., and Zue, V.

(1995). The challenge of spoken language systems: Research directions for the nineties. *IEEE Transactions on Speech and Audio Processing*, 3(1):1–21.

Council, N. R. (1966). Appendices 9–15. In *Languages and Machines: Computers in Translation and Linguistics*. National Academy of Sciences, Washington, DC.

DARPA (1989). *Proceedings of the Second DARPA Speech and Natural Language Workshop*, Cape Cod, Massachusetts. Defense Advanced Research Projects Agency.

DARPA (1990). *Proceedings of the Third DARPA Speech and Natural Language Workshop*, Hidden Valley, Pennsylvania. Defense Advanced Research Projects Agency, Morgan Kaufmann.

DARPA (1991a). *Proceedings of the Fourth DARPA Speech and Natural Language Workshop*, Pacific Grove, California. Defense Advanced Research Projects Agency, Morgan Kaufmann.

DARPA (1991b). *Proceedings of the Third Message Understanding Conference*, San Diego, California. Morgan Kaufmann.

DARPA (1992a). *Proceedings of the Fifth DARPA Speech and Natural Language Workshop*. Defense Advanced Research Projects Agency, Morgan Kaufmann.

DARPA (1992b). *Proceedings of the Fourth Message Understanding Conference*, McLean, Virginia. Morgan Kaufmann.

Eagles (1995). Report of the spoken language systems working group 5. Technical report, EAGLES, EAGLES Secretariat, Istituto di Linguistica Computazionale, Via della Faggiola 32, Pisa, Italy 56126, Fax: +39 50 589055, E-mail: ceditor@tnos.ilc.pi.cnr.it. In press.

Eurospeech (1993). *Eurospeech '93, Proceedings of the Third European Conference on Speech Communication and Technology*, Berlin. European Speech Communication Association.

Falkedal, K., editor (1994). *Proceedings of the of the Evaluators' Forum, 1991*, Les Rasses, Vaud, Switzerland. ISSCO, Geneva.

Fourcin, A. et al. (1992). ESPRIT project 2589 (SAM) multi-lingual speech input/output assessment, methodology and standardization. Technical Report SAM-UCL-G004, SAM.

Galliers, J. R. and Sparck Jones, K. (1993). Evaluating natural language processing systems. Technical Report 291, University of Cambridge Computer Laboratory. To appear in *Springer Lecture Notes in Artificial Intelligence*.

Harman, D., editor (1993). *National Institute of Standards and Technology Special Publication No. 500-207 on the The First Text REtrieval Conference (TREC-1)*, Washington, DC. National Institute of Standards and Technology, U.S. Department of Commerce, U.S. Government Printing Office.

Harman, D. (1993). Overview of the first Text REtrieval Conference (TREC-1). In Harman, D., editor, *National Institute of Standards and Technology Special Publication No. 500-207 on the The First Text REtrieval Conference (TREC-1)*, pages 1–20, Washington, DC. National Institute of Standards and Technology, U.S. Department of Commerce, U.S. Government Printing Office.

Harman, D., editor (1994). *National Institute of Standards and Technology Special Publication No. 500-215 on the The Second Text REtrieval Conference (TREC-2)*, Washington, DC. National Institute of Standards and Technology, U.S. Department of Commerce, U.S. Government Printing Office.

Harrison, P., Abney, S., Black, E., Flickenger, D., Gdaniec, C., Grishman, R., Hindle, D., Ingria, R., Marcus, M., Santorini, B., and Strzalkowski, T. (1991). Evaluating syntax performance of parser/grammars of English. In *Proceedings of the Workshop On Evaluating Natural Language Processing Systems*. Association For Computational Linguistics.

Hausser, R. (1994). The coordinator's final report on the first Morpholympics. *LDV-Forum*, 11(1):54–64.

Höge, M., Hohmann, A., and Mayer, R. (1992). Evaluations of TWB: Operationalization and test results. Final Report of the ESPRIT I Project 2315 Translators' Workbench (TWB).

Höge, M., Hohmann, A., van der Horst, K., Evans, S., and Caeyers, H. (1993). User participation in the TWB II project: The first test cycle. Report of the Esprit II Project 6005 Translators' Workbench II (TWB II).

House, A. S., Williams, C. E., Hecker, M. H. L., and Kryter, K. D. (1965). Articulation testing methods: Consonantal differentiation with a closed-response set. *Journal of the Acoustical Society of America*, 37:158–166.

Houtgast, T. and Steeneken, H. J. M. (1984). A multi-lingual evaluation of the Rasti-method for estimating speech intelligibility in auditoria. *Acustica*, 54:185–199.

Hutchins, W. J. and Somers, H. L. (1992). An introduction to machine translation. In *An introduction to Machine Translation*. Academic Press, London.

ICDAR (1993). *Proceedings of the Second International Conference on Document Analysis and Recognition*, Tsukuba Science City, Japan. AIPR-IEEE, IAPR.

Ishii, K. (1983). Generation of distored charaters and its applications. *System, Computer, Controls*, 14(6):1270–1277.

ISO (1991). Information technology—software product evaluation, quality characteristics and guidelines for their use. Technical Report 9126, International Organization for Standardization.

ITU (1993). ITU-TTS draft recommendation p.8s: Subjective performance assessment of the quality of speech voice output devices. Technical Report COM 12-6-E, International Telecommunication Union.

Jekosch, U. (1993). Speech quality assessment and evaluation. In *Eurospeech '93, Proceedings of the Third European Conference on Speech Communication and Technology*, volume 2, pages 1387–1394, Berlin. European Speech Communication Association. Keynote address.

Jones, K. and Mariani, J., editors (1992). *Proceedings of the 1992 Workshop of the International Committee on Speech Databases and I/O Systems Assessment*. COCOSDA.

Kanai, J., Rice, S. V., Nartker, T. A., and Nagy, G. (1993). Performance metrics for document understanding systems. In *Proceedings of the Second International Conference on Document Analysis and Recognition*, pages 424–427, Tsukuba Science City, Japan. AIPR-IEEE, IAPR.

Kanungo, T., Haralick, R. M., and Phillips, I. (1993). Global and local document degradation models. In *Proceedings of the Second International Conference on Document Analysis and Recognition*, pages 730–736, Tsukuba Science City, Japan. AIPR-IEEE, IAPR.

Karis, D. and Dobroth, K. M. (1991). Automating services with speech recognition over the public switched telephone network: Human factors considerations. *IEEE Journal of Selected Areas in Communications*, 9(4):574–585.

King, M. and Falkedal, K. (1990). Using test suites in evaluation of MT systems. In *Proceedings of the 28th Annual Meeting of the Association for Computational Linguistics*, volume 2, pages 211–216, Pittsburgh, Pennsylvania. Association for Computational Linguistics.

Klaus, H., Klix, H., Sotscheck, J., and Fellbaumn, K. (1993). An evaluation system for ascertaining the quality of synthetic speech based on subjective category rating tests. In *Eurospeech '93, Proceedings of the Third European Conference on Speech Communication and Technology*, volume 3, pages 1679–1682, Berlin. European Speech Communication Association.

Kryter, K. D. (1962). Methods for the calculation and use of the articulation index. *J. of the Acoustical Society of America*, 34:1689–1697.

Lehrberger, J. and Bourbeau, L. (1988). *Machine translation: linguistic characteristics of MT systems and general methodology of evaluation.* John Benjamins, Amsterdam, Philadelphia.

Li, Y., Lopresti, D., and Tomkins, A. (1994). Validation of document image defect models for optical character recognition. In *Proceedings of the 3rd Annual Symposium on Document Analysis and Information Retrieval*, pages 137–150, University of Nevada, Las Vegas.

Logan, J. S., Greene, B. G., and Pisoni, D. B. (1989). Segmental intelligibility of synthetic speech produced by rule. *Journal of the Acoustical Society of America*, 86(2):566–581.

Matsui, T., Noumi, T., Yamashita, I., Watanabe, T., and Yoshimuro, M. (1993). State of the art of handwritten numeral recognition in Japan—the results of the first IPTP character recognition competition. In *Proceedings of the Second International Conference on Document Analysis and Recognition*, pages 391–396, Tsukuba Science City, Japan. AIPR-IEEE, IAPR.

Moore, R. C. (1994). Semantic evaluation for spoken-language systems. In *Proceedings of the 1994 ARPA Human Language Technology Workshop*, Princeton, New Jersey. Advanced Research Projects Agency, Morgan Kaufmann.

Nagy, G. (1994). Validation of simulated OCR data sets. In *Proceedings of the 3rd Annual Symposium on Document Analysis and Information Retrieval*, pages 127–135, University of Nevada, Las Vegas.

Nerbonne, J., Netter, K., Diagne, A. K., Klein, J., and Dickmann, L. (1993). A diagnostic tool for German syntax. *Machine Translation*, 8:85–107.

Nomura, H. and Isahara, H. (1992). JEIDA's criteria on machine translation evaluation. In *Proceedings of the International Symposium on Natural Language Understanding and AI*, Kyushu Institute of Technology, Iizuka, Japan. part of the International Symposia on Information Sciences.

Oviatt, S. L. (1995). Predicting spoken disfluencies during human-computer interaction. *Computer Speech and Language*, 9:19–35.

Oviatt, S. L., Cohen, P. R., and Wang, M. Q. (1994). Toward interface design for human language technology: Modality and structure as determinants of linguistic complexity. *Speech Communication*, 15(3–4):283–300.

Pallett, D., Fiscus, J., Fisher, W., Garofolo, J., Lund, B., and Prysbocki, M. (1994). 1993 benchmark tests for the ARPA spoken language program. In *Proceedings of the 1994 ARPA Human Language Technology Workshop*, pages 49–74, Princeton, New Jersey. Advanced Research Projects Agency, Morgan Kaufmann.

Pols, L. C. W. (1991). Quality assessment of text-to-speech synthesis-by-rule. In Furui, S. and Sondhi, M. M., editors, *Advances in speech signal processing*, chapter 13, pages 387–416. Marcel Dekker, New York.

Pols, L. C. W. (1994a). Speech technology systems: Performance and evaluation. In Asher, R. E., editor, *The Encyclopedia of Language and Linguistics*, volume 8, pages 4289–4296. Pergamon Press, Oxford.

Pols, L. C. W. (1994b). Voice quality of synthetic speech: Representation and evaluation. In *Proceedings of the 1994 International Conference on Spoken Language Processing*, volume 3, pages 1443–1446, Yokohama, Japan.

Pols, L. C. W. and Jekosch, U. (1994). A structured way of looking at the performance of text-to-speech systems. In *Proceedings, ESCA/IEEE Synthesis Workshop*, pages 203–206, New Paltz, New York.

Pols, L. C. W. and SAM-partners (1992). Multi-lingual synthesis evaluation methods. In *Proceedings of the 1992 International Conference on Spoken Language Processing*, volume 1, pages 181–184, Banff, Alberta, Canada. University of Alberta.

Rhyne, J. R. and Wolf, C. G. (1993). Recognition-based user interfaces. In Hartson, H. R. and Hix, D., editors, *Advances in Human-Computer Interaction*, volume 4, chapter 7, pages 191–250. Ablex Publishing Corp, Norwood, New Jersey.

Rice, S. V. (1993). The OCR experimental environment, version 3. Technical Report ISRI TR-93-04, University of Nevada, Las Vegas, Nevada.

Rice, S. V., Kanai, J., and Nartker, T. A. (1993). An evaluation of OCR accuracy. Technical Report ISRI TR-93-01, University of Nevada, Las Vegas, Nevada.

Rice, S. V., Kanai, J., and Nartker, T. A. (1994). The third annual test of OCR accuracy. Technical Report ISRI TR-94-03, University of Nevada, Las Vegas, Nevada.

Rinsche, A. (1993). Evaluationsverfahren für maschinelle übersetzunngssysteme: zur methodik und experimentellen praxis. Technical report, Kommission der Europaeischen Gemeinschaften, Bericht EUR 14766 DE.

Sinaiko, H. W. and Klare, G. R. (1972). Further experiments in language translation: readability of computer translations. *ITL*, 15:1–29.

Sinaiko, H. W. and Klare, G. R. (1973). Further experiments in language translation: a second evaluation of the readability of computer translations. *ITL*, 19:29–52.

Sorin, C. (1994). Towards high-quality multilingual text-to-speech. In *Proceedings of the CRIM/FORWISS Workshop on Progress and Prospects of Speech Research and Technology*, pages 53–62, Münich.

Sparck Jones, K. (1994). Towards better NLP system evaluation. In *Proceedings of the 1994 ARPA Human Language Technology Workshop*, Princeton, New Jersey. Advanced Research Projects Agency, Morgan Kaufmann.

Spiegel, M. F. (1993). Using the ORATOR synthesizer for a public reverse-directory service: Design, lessons, and recommendations. In *Eurospeech '93, Proceedings of the Third European Conference on Speech Communication and Technology*, volume 3, pages 1897–1900, Berlin. European Speech Communication Association.

Spitz, J. (1991). Collection and analysis of data from real users: Implications for speech recognition/understanding systems. In *Proceedings of the Fourth DARPA Speech and Natural Language Workshop*, Pacific Grove, California. Defense Advanced Research Projects Agency, Morgan Kaufmann.

Steeneken, H. J. M. (1992). Quality evaluation of speech processing systems. In Ince, N., editor, *Digital Speech Coding: Speech coding, Synthesis and Recognition*, chapter 5, pages 127–160. Kluwer Norwell, USA.

Steeneken, H. J. M. and Houtgast, T. (1980). A physical method for measuring speech-transmission quality. *J. Acoustical Society of America*, 67:318–326.

Steeneken, H. J. M., Verhave, J., and Houtgast, T. (1993). Objective assessment of speech communication systems; introduction of a software based procedure. In *Eurospeech '93, Proceedings of the Third European Conference on Speech Communication and Technology*, volume 1, pages 203–206, Berlin. European Speech Communication Association.

Thompson, H., editor (1992). *The Strategic Role of Evaluation in Natural Language Processing and Speech Technology*. Human Communication Research Centre, University of Edinburgh.

Van Slype, G. (1982). Conception d'une méthodologie générale d'évaluation de la traduction automatique. *Multilingua*, 1(4):221–237.

White, J. S. et al. (1994). The ARPA MT evaluation methodologies: evolution, lessons, and future approaches. In *Technology partnerships for crossing the language barrier: Proceedings of the 1st Conference of the Association for Machine Translation in the Americas*, pages 193–205, Washington, DC. Association for Machine Translation in the Americas.

Wilkinson, R. A., Geist, J., Janet, S., Grother, P. J., Burges, C. J. C., Creecy, R., Hammond, B., Hull, J. J., Larsen, N. J., Vogl, T. P., and Wilson, C. L. (1992). The first census optical character recognition systems conference. Technical Report NISTIR-4912, National Institute of Standards and Technology, U.S. Department of Commerce.

Zoltan-Ford, E. (1991). How to get people to say and type what computers can understand. *International Journal of Man-Machine Studies*, 34:527–547.

Glossary

ACCOR: a language corpus
ACH: Association for Computing in the Humanities
ACL: Association for Computational Linguistics
ACL/DCI: Association for Computational Linguistics' Data Collection Initiative
ADPCM: adaptive differential pulse-code modulation (PCM)
AI: Artificial Intelligence; also Articulation Index
ALBAYZIN: a language corpus
ALLC: Association for Literary and Linguistic Computing
AM: acoustic model
ANDOSL: Australian National Database of Spoken Language
ANN: artificial neural network, also NN
AR: autoregressive (model)
ARPA: Advanced Research Projects Agency (U.S.), predecessor of DARPA
ARS: a language corpus
ASCII: American Standard Code for Information Interchange
ASR: automatic speech recognition
ASR: automatic speech recognition
ATIS: Air Travel Information Service (task)
ATLAS II: Japanese-English translation system by Fujitsu
ATM: asynchronous transfer mode
ATR: a language corpus

BMFT: Bundesministerium für Forschung und Technik, German Federal Ministry for Research and Technology
BNC: British National Corpus
bps: bits per second
BRA: Basic Research Actions
BRAMSHILL: a language corpus
BREF: a language corpus

C_0: first cepstral coefficient
CAD: Computer-Assisted (or -Aided) Design
CADCAM: Computer-Assisted Design / Computer-Assisted Manufacture
CAR: a language corpus
CART: Classification and Regression Tree
CCG: combinatory categorial grammar
CD-ROM: compact disk—read-only memory
CELP: code-excited linear prediction
CFE: Caterpillar Fundamental English
CFG: context-free grammar
CKY: Cocke, Kasami, and Younger (algorithm)
CL: controlled language
CLAWS: Constituent-Likelihood Automatic Word-Tagging System
CLE: core language engine
CLR: Consortium for Lexical Research
CMN: cepstral mean normalization
CMU: Carnegie Mellon University
CPU: central processing unit (of a computer)
CSC: character shape code
CSLU: Center for Spoken Language Understanding
CSR: continuous speech recognition
C-STAR: Consortium for Speech TrAnslation Research
CUG: categorial unification grammar
CV: consonant-vowel phoneme sequence
CVC: consonant-vowel-consonant phoneme sequence

DARPA: Defense Advanced Research Projects Agency (U.S.), successor to ARPA
dB: deciBel
DBMS: data base management system
DBMT: dialogue-based machine translation (MT)
DK: Dansk Korpus
DP: dynamic programming
DPCM: differential pulse-code modulation (PCM)
dpi: dots per inch (resolution quality)
DRT: discourse representation theory
DSP: digital signal processing
DTW: dynamic time warping
DoD: Department of Defense (U.S.)

EAGLES: Expert Advisory Group on Linguistic Engineering Standards
EBMT: example-based machine translation (MT)
ECI: European Corpus Initiative

EDI: electronic data interchange
EDR: electronic dictionary research
ELRA: European Language Resources Association
ELSNET: European Network In Language And Speech
EM: expectation maximization algorithm, also estimate-maximize
EMIR: European Multilingual Information Retrieval
ESCA: European Speech Communication Association
ESPRIT: European Strategic Programme for Research and Development in Information Technology
ETL: Electrotechnical Laboratory (Japan)

F_0: Fundamental Frequency
FIR: finite impulse response filter
FOPC: first order predicate calculus
FSA: finite state automaton
FSM: finite state machine
FST: finite state transducer
FUF: functional unification grammar framework
FUG: functional unification grammar

GIST: Generating InStructional Text
GPD: generalized probabilistic descent
GPSG: generalized phrase structure grammar

HAMT: human-aided machine translation (MT)
HCI: human-computer interaction
HG: head grammar
HLT: human language technology
HMM: hidden Markov model
HPSG: head-driven phrase-structure grammar
Hz: Hertz (cycles per second)

ICAME: International Computer Archive of Modern English
ICASSP: International Conference on Acoustics, Speech, and Signal Processing
ICR: intelligent character recognition
ICSLP: International Conference on Spoken Language Processing
IDS: Institut für deutsche Sprache
IIR: infinite impulse response filter
ILC-CNR: Istituto di Linguistica Computazionale
ILSAM: International Language for Serving and Maintenance

INaLF-CNRS: Frantext of Institut National de la Langue Francaise
INL: Instituut voor Nederlandse Lexicologie
Interlingua: language independent semantic representation
IR: information retrieval
ISDN: integrated services digital network
ISO: International Standards Organization

JEIDA: Japan Electronic Industry Development Association
J-RASTA: Relative Spectra PLP with Jah smoothing

LC: Lambek Calculus
LCD: liquid crystal display
LDA: linear discriminant analysis
LDC: Linguistic Data Consortium
LD-CELP: low-delay code-excited linear prediction (CELP)
LE: Language Engineering
LE-MLAP: Language Engineering Multilingual Action Plan
LFG: lexical-Functional grammar
LIG: linear indexed grammar
LKB: lexical knowledge base
LM: language model
LPC: linear predictive coding
LR: Left-to-right scanning, rightmost derivation parsing
LRE: Linguistic Research and Engineering
LV-CSR: large vocabulary continuous speech recognition

MAHT: Machine-Aided Human Translation, see also HAMT
MAP: maximum a-posteriori probability
MAR: multivariate auto-regression (AR)
MAT: machine-assisted translation
METEO: Canadian meteorological bulletin translator
MFCC: mel-frequency cepstral coefficient
MIT: Massachusetts Institute of Technology
MITalk: Dennis Klatt's MIT speech synthesizer
MLDB: multilingual lexical data base
MLP: multi-layer perceptron (ANN)
MMSE: minimum mean square error
MMSEE: minimum mean square error estimator
MOS: mean opinion score/scoring
MRD: machine-readable dictionary
MSR: multiple split regression
MT: machine translation

MTDB: multilingual terminological data base
MUC: Message Understanding Conference

NIST: National Institute of Standards and Technology (U.S.)

OGI: Oregon Graduate Institute of Science & Technology
OGI_TS: OGI Multilanguage Telephone Speech Corpus

PACE: Perkins Approved Clear English
PAHO: Pan American Health Organization
PCA: principal components analysis
PCFG: probabilistic context-free grammar
PCM: pulse-code modulation
PDA: personal digital assistant
PDL: page description language
PECO: Pays d'Europe Centrale et Orientale
PEP: Plain English Program
PLP: perceptual linear prediction

RASTA: relative spectra perceptual linear prediction (PLP)
RELATOR: a language corpus
RM: Resource Management task
RPS: root power sum
RST: rhetorical structure theory

SAM: Speech Technology Assessment Methodology
SAM-A: Speech Technology Assessment Methodology in Multilingual Applications
SGML: Standard Generalized Markup Language
SLS: spoken language system
SLU: spoken language understanding
SNR: signal-to-noise ratio
SR: speech recognition, also ASR
SRI: Stanford Research Institute
SSC: speech synthesis from concept
STI: speech transmission index
SUC: Stockholm-Umea Corpus
SUNDIAL: a language corpus
SUNSTAR: a language corpus
SYSTRAN: SYSTRAN language translation system

TAG: tree adjunction grammar
TED: Translanguage English Database
TEI: Text Encoding Initiative
TES: Telephone Enquiry System
TFS: typed feature structure
TI: Texas Instruments
TIDE: Telematics Initiative for Disabled and Elderly people, sponsored by the European Commission
TIF: terminology interchange format
TIMIT: Texas Instruments—MIT speech corpus
TKE: terminological knowledge engineering
TREC: Text Retrieval Evaluation Conference
TtS: Text-to-Speech

UKA: University of Karslruhe
USPS: U.S. Postal Service
UW: University of Washington (Seattle)

VC: vowel-consonant phoneme sequence
VERBMOBIL: a european language translation project
VLSI: very large scale integration (microchip technology)
VQ: vector quantization

WOZ: Wizard of Oz (data collection method)
WSJ: Wall Street Journal corpus
WSJCAM0: Wall Street Journal, Cambridge, language corpus zero
WST: word shape token
WWB: Writer's Workbench
WWW: World Wide Web

XUNET: Xperimental University NETwork

ZIP: Zone Improvement Code (U.S. Postal Service)

Citation Index

Index

Von Canon Library

103743

P 98 .S93 / Survey of the state of the art in human language tech